AN EDUCATIONAL HISTORY OF
THE AMERICAN PEOPLE

FOUNDATIONS IN EDUCATION
HAROLD BENJAMIN, *Consulting Editor*

AN EDUCATIONAL HISTORY OF THE AMERICAN PEOPLE
second edition

ADOLPHE E. MEYER, Ph.D.

*Visiting Professor of History of Education
University of Illinois,
Emeritus Professor of Educational History
New York University,
Member of the Authors League of America*

McGRAW-HILL BOOK COMPANY
*New York   St. Louis   San Francisco
Toronto   London   Sydney*

AN EDUCATIONAL HISTORY OF THE AMERICAN PEOPLE

to **JERRIE**

PREFACE

Fifteen years ago or so, when I laid the first plans for this book, I aspired to do two things. For one, I wanted to explore and scrutinize the great vista of American educational history as it stretches from our faraway colonial yesterdays to our more or less recent past. Next, I wanted to relate my observation as adroitly and agreeably as candor and courtesy allow, and in an English which in any case would be free from the curse of professional jibberish. This purpose I see no reason to abandon, and so in the second edition it remains unaltered.

The assumptions which underlie the present volume are the same which upheld its ancestor, namely, that educational history is at bottom a form of social history, and that at all times there reigns a discernible relationship between education and society—that the former, so to speak, reflects the latter. Do these assumptions hold water, then an understanding of educational history obviously presumes an understanding of the society which gave it being. For this reason I have been at pains to interweave my accounting of the educational past with its cultural context. In the earlier pages, which deal with the republic's remote and shadowy past, the reader may well be innocent of some of the republic's history. Hence I have ventured a considerable rehearsal here. Later on, however, when the reader enters the century we now enjoy and extol and he is more likely to be at home in its salient historic events, the going should be a great deal easier. Here, therefore, I have been sparing with historic detail and have resorted to the cultural context only where it is plainly an important cause.

Though my objectives and assumptions remain unchanged, this is by no means saying that putting the *People* into its new garb has been simply an exercise in bringing it materially up to date. There have been a number of alterations both in substance and in form. Every chapter has been repaired and overhauled, new and relevant matter brought in and old and worn out stuff elbowed out. The truth is that not only has every chapter been given revision, but often enough it has been granted the boon of an entirely fresh composition. In one instance, namely the Yankeefication of the Puritan, the process of putting the business on paper took on such a huge proportion that a wholly new chapter resulted.

In its first bow to the public, the *People* entertained a considerable adornment of footnotes, useful, I believed, and academically always in good fashion. But from spies stationed throughout the land, and including a battalion of psychologists and physiologists, I presently learned that oftentimes such notes are more a hindrance than a help, and that they may even be a bane to easy and effective reading. The upshot is that in its new attire the *People* has been divested of its footnotes—but not utterly nor completely. Where their essence was explanatory and pertinent to the text I have rerouted them, in the guise of exposition, into the body of the text itself, and where it was simply documentary, I have escorted them into the bibliography. As a result the bibliography has grown like a tapeworm—it has become, indeed, something of an essay. Like its forerunner in the first edition, it is not content to display itself as a mere booklist, but seeks rather to serve as an instructive commentary, giving aid and counsel to the reader who wants more knowledge and light on some of the topics discussed more generally in the text.

Though, as I have hinted, I support the educational historian's cultural-reflectionist assumptions, it is only fair to state that I have some qualifying ifs and buts. Educational history, I believe with its experts, is social history. Yet it is also the history of school organization and law, of teaching methods and psychology, and of the arts and sciences. It is not merely the history of the commoner. It is also, and significantly, the history of the great man, the odd man, the dreamer—even, indeed, the seer. The educational history of the American people, so conceived and so executed, is thus far more than a historic scrutiny of case work. It is in truth the history of all the people, and it is from this standpoint that I have tried to write it.

In my quest for information and my effort to hold down slips in dates and names, I have depended, often enough, on the aid and advice of uncountable readers, both lay and professional. To list them all is, of course, beyond possibility, and though here they must be nameless, my gratitude to them is nonetheless deep and sincere. But to some on whose kindness and patience I have leaned not a little, my debt is even greater. There is, for one, my associate Prof. Joe Burnett, and colleague in many a gay venture; Prof. H. K. Hutton, of the venerable Pennsylvania State University, a friend of the court whose sage counsel, though not always heeded, has been imponderably valuable; and several eager and energetic graduate assistants in the Department of History and Philosophy at the University of Illinois, especially Roy Daniels, Erwin Johanningmeier, and Terry Lindenberg. Finally, I owe thanks to Thomas Edward Radcliffe, Jr., librarian in charge of the incomparable reference room of the University of Illinois and associate reference librarian Dorothy Miller Black. They have in their hands not only one of the largest reference morgues in this land, but they also know where to find the tiniest shred of information ever heard of. Without their help the gaps and blanks that ornament this work would be vastly more numerous.

ADOLPHE E. MEYER

CONTENTS

AN EDUCATIONAL HISTORY OF
THE AMERICAN PEOPLE

ARVARD

BROWN

WM + MARY

1
ANTECEDENTS

All sorts of desires lured the first colonists to the New World. Some itched
for adventure, some hungered for riches, some longed to Christianize the
Indian. Many braved the sea to escape the despairs of Europe—its hard
and trying ways, especially its religious tyrannies, and the burning and
bleeding of its witless wars. Not uncommonly the colonists were part of a
patriotic enterprise, cogs, as it were, in the machinery of their national
economy, with its restless hunt for raw materials, new trade routes, and
greater and grander markets. Nearly all sought advantages of one kind or
another, for themselves, for their monetary backers, for crown and flag,
and very often for all of them rolled up in one. But whatever motives
brought the colonists to America, they came to the New World carrying
bags packed with their Old World culture. At bottom, hence, their settlements began as European outposts, the furthermost frontier of an old and
vaunted civilization.

Speaking broadly, that civilization rested on the relic of the Greco-
Roman legacy and more immediately on the historical foundation of medieval Christendom—a foundation which had been shaken if not shattered
by the high voltage of the Renaissance and Reformation. To these two
forces Western man owes much of his fundamental makeup. By the seventeenth century, moreover, when the settlement of the original colonies got
under way, the European was already showing a tangible trace of what
one day would become the hallmark of the modern age.

Three elements were worked into its design—the individual, the middle
or merchant class, and the national state. Economically, it showed a capitalistic tinge. The chartered trading company, the forebear of today's
huge corporate endeavor, was already in active business, and in the making
of early America, two of them, the London Company and the Plymouth
Company, were destined to be in the forefront. In varying manner and
proportion these elements formed the basis of colonial civilization. One
catches a glimpse of them in the settlers' mode of living, in their social
ideas and practice, and in their economic, political, and religious institutions. And one sees them, of course, in their educational views and
practices.

2   As the curtain rose on fourteenth-century Europe, the beckoning
new age was beginning to bubble with the intellectual and cultural effer-
vescence of what has since drifted into chronicles as the Renaissance.
Europe was no stranger to such bubblings, though since the fall of Rome
they had been pitifully few. Yet even without spectacles one is able to
spot them in Italy as early as the sixth century, when Benedict, an abbot
then but now a saint, labored to rouse his colleague monks from their

stupor of ignorance. They appear again some two centuries later, when Charlemagne undertook to inspirit his palace associates with at least a dash of rudimentary knowledge. A few centuries more, and intellectual stirrings were announcing themselves anew, livelier now and more insistent, in an awakening interest in the writings and jurisprudence of the Romans, in the infiltration of Moslem learning, and in the rise of great cathedral schools and the first universities. Some of the world's most supple minds engaged in such endeavor, shiny intellects like those of Albertus Magnus, Roger Bacon, and, the most incandescent of them all, Thomas Aquinas. But upon all such cerebral industry Mother Church fixed her watchful eye, stern, piercing, inescapable, and at pains at all times to halter the inquiring mind with her Christian theological assumptions. Consequently, though the stock of learning increased, its progress remained placid and reserved, confined always within the safe preserve of orthodoxy.

The Renaissance burst the walls of intellectual conformity. In hustling towns like Florence and Venice, where life throbbed with the concerns of every day, thinking men, stuffed for generations with the warmed-up speculations of academicians shuttered in their world of learning, sought the ease of day in the classics of ancient Greece and Rome, In them they uncovered a world vastly different from their own, a world full of charming surprises, sometimes even gay and reprobate—in short, a world of infinite delight, but one of challenge and instruction as well. Soon the interest in classical antiquity was winging over the Alps into the rest of Europe. The to-do over the old-time Greeks and Romans bred an ever-growing desire for their writings. So limited was the supply and so great the passion to obtain them that to hear of grown-up men sniffing in old and moldy houses in hopes of retrieving some errant manuscript presently ceased to be a novelty. Meanwhile, as the fifteenth century unrolled, the printing press, but recently invented, was beginning to reproduce the available classical writings on a scale hitherto undreamed of. Moreover, because so many of the prized thoughts of antiquity happened to be embalmed in Greek, and since knowledge of that tongue had fallen on lean days, instruction in it became desirable. This need, too, was met. And so, as the Renaissance unfolded in full florescence, intellectual Europe was bathed in the brilliance of a great classical revival.

The Renaissance was more than the discovery of a luminous past. A tonic of self-expression, it stimulated artistic activity, letting loose its genius in unforgettable pieces of art, sculpture, and architecture. Nor was there any loitering among men of science and philosophy, though their activity, it must be said, was less full and vigorous. The Renaissance soared from the culture of the moneyed burgher class, and it flourished most freely among the patricians of trade in thriving towns of wealth from Paris to Basel to Florence. Although it was never a movement of the majority commoner, its spirit was never negligible—in fact, its salient worthies, its da Vincis and Michelangelos, its Erasmuses and Thomas Mores, bequeathed posterity a magnificent and, one may hope, imperishable heritage. Unlike its predecessor, the many-centuried Age of Faith, the Renaissance drew its strength from the earth rather than from the sky. Its interest, hence, centered in man and what his hands and brains produced here and now, rather than in his postmortem reward, whether heavenly or infernal. From the new era's rediscovery of the classical legacy, it flowed irresistibly into the wide sea of human affairs—into commerce, politics, and diplomacy and even into military science and what passes currently as the science of society.

It also left its mark, of course, on education. The bookish pedantry of medieval learning was cast aside for the classical ideal of a liberal education. Stuffing the memory with facts and definitions was rejected for understanding and clear and honest thinking. Needless to say the classics were extolled: Greek and Latin and, in time, Hebrew. What was sought, an ideal to be sure, was the cultivation of a harmonious alliance of body, mind, and spirit—in brief, a civilized man, of an assured and easy presence, of urbane habit and utterance. Reserved for the elite, whether intellectual or merely moneyed, this teaching was entrusted to hired tutors. Subsequently, after the knell of its faded youth had stilled, the movement, once so full of life and hope, stiffened into the classic tradition of European education, a tradition which was institutionalized in the Latin grammar school of England, the *collège* of France, and the *Gymnasium* of Teutonic lands and which in one form or other made its way over the Atlantic.

3 The wine of the Renaissance proved a somewhat heady drink. Not only did it caress the tongue, but it emboldened the spirit as well. "My own age always repelled me," lamented Petrarch, a leader in the Renaissance vanguard—so much, he went on, that he would have preferred to have been born in any other period but his own. There was something in the air that made such discontent contagious, for the more Renaissance thinkers exulted in the civilization of Greece and Rome, the more some of them inclined to berate their own. They made assault on the restraints of their age, the sterility of its schoolmen, the follies of its people. Nothing escaped their gunplay. Indeed, in the end it became the historic lot of the Renaissance not only to give its countenance and support to Europe's rising individualism and secularism, but also to begin the work of sapping the prestige of the medieval church.

Dissent and disturbance were nothing new to Holy Church. Heretics and schismatics had snarled at her more than once before. Yet always she had been able to bring her delinquent children to their senses or, failing that, to make an end of them in the flame and fire at the stake. But now the forces harassing her were many—and they were prodigious. Not only religious, they leaped up at every turn—from sovereigns of states who were feeling their national growing pains and whose interests clashed with those of Rome; from merchants lathering to rid their enterprise of ecclesiastic controls; from land-starved peasants drooling for a morsel of the church's rich and juicy holdings; and from people everywhere cursing the Roman tithe-taker. The manifestation of a secular temper (modern in not a little of its mood), materialistic, and often hoggish in their motives, these forces combined with others of a religious and moral nature to converge on medievalism's last great stronghold.

The campaign against the church got under way in 1517. It began without fanfare—one might even say it began innocently—when a German friar and theological professor, Martin Luther, dismayed by certain tactics of ecclesiastic fund raising, formulated his displeasure in his *Ninety-five Theses*, which he nailed to the door of his church at Wittenberg. Composed in the scholar's Latin, they addressed themselves, as per medieval university custom, to men of learning, challenging them to hold formal debate with Luther on any or all of his propositions. But the *Ninety-five* soon hopped over the academic fence. Translated into the vernacular and printed, they spread like a flash, and pretty soon they were being read and talked about all over Europe. Presently, what Luther had intended to be a staid and scholarly colloquy had flamed into a furious and far-flung controversy. As it gathered more and more heat, it blazed into open insurrection, engulfing not only the professional ranks of God but all Christian Europe as well, and splitting the once hard and solid rock of Peter into Protestant and Catholic segments.

Luther took his main stand on Holy Writ. Neither Pope nor council, but the Bible, he insisted, was the authority, sole and infallible, for Christian belief and conscience. Are the children of Adam incurable sinners, incapable of enduring virtue and decency? Then priests and good works serve them to no purpose. Let them put their trust instead in heavenly grace, for by their faith alone can they hope to rise post-mortem to eternal bliss. It was Luther's contention that the baptized Christian acquired a sort of priestly quality and that, with the aid and counsel of the Holy Ghost, he would be able to interpret the Word Divine and penetrate its truth. But as this principle was put to work, the fact soon became apparent that one man's truth was another's falsehood, and that for all the guidance of the Holy Spirit, there could be as many interpretations as there were interpreters—indeed, soon it became plain that Protestants could spawn Biblical interpretations with all the fecundity of the shad. There thus ensued an amazing propagation of sects, a process which still goes on. As year took after year, the Protestant register displayed not only Lutherans, as is to be expected, but also Huguenots, Dutch Reformed, Puritans, Presbyterians, Anglicans, Dunkards, Quakers, and

Shakers, to be followed shortly by Methodists, Baptists, Episcopalians, Mennonites, Muggletonians, Witnesses, Latter-day Saints, Holy Rollers, and shoals of many more.

For all their inspiration in the Sacred Word, oftentimes Protestant creeds were at vitriolic odds. Against the ogre in the Vatican they could enjoy a common rage, but when it came to resolving the differences among themselves, they fell apart. Although Luther had made a point for a man's liberty of conscience, the reformer had no intention of extending such freedom wholesale, and certainly not to jackasses so beclouded as to cherish dogmas which differed radically from his own. As such doodles showed themselves more and more, Luther, gnawed by doubts, did violence to his former confidence. Reason, he now came to suspect, is the subversion of salvation—it is, he wrote in the twilight hours of his threescore years, the "Devil's harlot." Luther's sentiment befitted the age, a sullen, stormy age, bigoted and fanatical, overridden by theological absolutism, whether Protestant or pontifical, and hence hostile to an unencumbered and rational explanation of the cosmos.

If the times were antagonistic to the free journeying of the mind, this is not saying that culturally they were listless. On the contrary, there was industry aplenty. The first massive movement in which the battle for the minds of men was waged with the weaponry of printed words, the Reformation bestormed the literary front with broadsides, satires, and caricatures. Most of them, as one might suspect, were of a flaming temper and were fiercely partisan, and save for the charming irony they afford historians of human progress, they have long since lapsed into the realm of things worth forgetting. But there were some sober and substantial achievements too, at times even bordering on the sublime. It was Luther who stirred his followers with his rousing hymn "A Mighty Fortress Is Our God," and it was Luther who rejoiced and edified them with their first satisfactory Bible, with help, it is true, from Melanchthon (born Schwarzerd), an expert in Greek, and Aurogallus (born Goldhahn), a master of Hebrew. The first important book to robe its utterance in modern German, it set an unforgettable linguistic standard. What Luther accomplished for German letters, Calvin, with his *Institutes for the Christian Religion,* achieved for French, and Tyndale, with his *New Testament,* achieved for English.

For the vast human throng to whom the written word was a mystery, such glories, unhappily, were sealed in the vault of ignorance—hence the Protestant insistence on the necessity for teaching their believers how to read. Not only did Protestant leaders lay plans for enabling their faithful to come to the holy truth in Bible and catechism, but as time wore on, some of them put upon their rulers to establish schools for this very purpose. The years saw these hopes bear fruit. It is to Protestantism that we credit the rise of the vernacular school, a school offering instruction to every child, free to the poor, with required attendance at its sessions when parents neglect their duties to their children and Almighty God. Putting their principal stress on reading, religion, morality, and—whenever music was not under denominational taboo—hymnody, Protestantism's first elementary schools, even when they enjoyed the friendship of civil support, were sectarian and thus utterly different from their innumerable flock of current descendants.

Although Protestant commanders recognized the need for instructing the huge mass of plain folk, in the Reformation's early stages they were even more concerned with preparing recruits for the sacred calling. To this end they resorted to the secondary school with its conventional stress on ancient languages (including Hebrew), some exercise in the tonal art, physical culture, rudimentary mathematics, and the safer propositions of elementary science, to reveal, as Luther succinctly put it, the "wonders of divine goodness and the omnipotence of God." For those aiming at places of the greatest preferment, there remained the universities, the bastions of theology and the training stations for the higher service in church and state. For the gentle sex, needless to state, any learning beyond the lowest was out of reach. Not only could they never shepherd a flock as lady pastors, but as the Biblical injunction plainly said, their task in life was to tend the hearth, to feed and comfort their husbands, and to gladden them over the years with copious progeny. Such was the general theory, and so it stayed for centuries—until, in fact, the French Revolution, when it began to be blistered by the critical blowtorch.

4 Of the thirteen colonies which became the republic, all except Georgia were founded in the seventeenth century. Though their inhabitants issued from many lands, the civilization which eventually took root was preeminently Anglo-Saxon. More numerous than any of the other nationalities, the English made themselves master of the Colonies. Wherever Englishmen hung up their hats for any length of time, their language made itself at home, and so did their customs and traditions and their ideas of society, religion, and education. Riveted to the English mode of living were the same powerful forces which had directed the course of civilization on the Continent. But though they had been wrought by the same forces, the Englishman who stepped into the seventeenth century differed in many particulars from the Continental across the Channel. And since these peculiarities played an important part in the making of America and in the education which arose there, a closer look at them becomes necessary.

As the 1500s moved into the 1600s, English society, like that of the mainland, was arranged into a number of clearly differentiated classes. But the barriers which separated one estate from another were not quite so hard and fast as those entertained by the rest of Europe, nor were they insurmountable. Yet they had entrenched themselves in England's way of life, and they were generally regarded as desirable for the commonweal— even, for that matter, by Omnipotence ordained.

At the top of England's social ladder sat the aristocracy, or titled peerage. Blue of blood as well as red, and nearly always the possessors of a well-filled pocketbook, the nobility, together with the higher clergy, monopolized the seats in the House of Lords, then far more puissant, of course, than its present enfeebled heir. Conservative, even reactionary, the peers could generally be counted on to give their support to causes cherished by the Crown and the Established Church.

A rung below the high and mighty lords stood the landed gentry, who, though lacking the plumes and spangles of their betters, comported themselves altitudinously nonetheless. They were not so numerous, but not uncommonly they were rich, and some of them occupied high political posts. From their cream came the larger part of the House of Commons.

Challenging their sway was the surging middle class of merchants, traders, and manufacturers. The most virile, the most ambitious, and probably the most able group in England at this time, they had gained impressively in wealth and strength during the nation's great expansion during the reign of the first Elizabeth.

The next group was something of a mixture. Most important among its varied elements were the yeomen, the small and independent farm owners, praised by fabulists again and again as the backbone of the nation. Their political influence, though contained, was nevertheless important. Not only could most of them vote, but among rural voters they also counted for the greatest number.

Below the yeomanry ranged the mass of tenant farmers, artisans, and petty tradesmen. They lacked the suffrage; even so, now and then one of them managed to lift himself into a minor political job and thus proceeded to groom himself and his posterity for the better things of life.

Still lower down huddled the farmhands, journeymen, and servants. Their number, as usual, was overflowing; their income, light; their rights, negligible; and their lot, grim and dismal.

Finally there were society's inescapable dregs—the sediment of habitual paupers, vagabonds, beggars, thugs, thieves, drunks, harlots, and other servants of the Devil, ciphers all in the cold arithmetic of life.

In its essence the motherland's social system was duplicated in the American colonies. By the end of the seventeenth century all its representatives, high and low—forgetting for the moment the blooded peers— had settled here. Yet the aristocracy, though in conspicuous absence, made itself felt, and some of its higher illuminati, such as Baron Baltimore, Lord Carteret, and the Duke of York, destined someday to warm the royal throne, exercised no little influence in the shaping of colonial events.

5   The bonfire which Luther had unwittingly kindled in 1517 did not spread its rages to England until more than a decade later. When at length the Reformation caught the English in its flames, its immediate causes were personal and dynastic rather than religious and moral. Though he was—and in the secret dungeons of his soul remained—a Catholic, Henry VIII broke with Mother Church when she refused to nullify his marriage to the Spanish Catherine, who had been unable to bless the royal union with a prince. By the Act of Supremacy (1534) Parliament established an English church, free of the Roman tether, while Henry, once lauded by the Pope as the Defender of the Faith—he had written a tract against the upstart Luther—now undertook to head and protect the ecclesiastic newcomer, the Church of England. However, it was not until Henry's son, the young and delicate Edward VI, made this thronal ascension that Protestantism became England's legal and official faith. Then the *Book of Common Prayer* and a confession of faith were adopted, and to forestall any backsliding, under cover or above, every man, woman, and child was made to accept them.

In the train of Edward's short reign Catholicism was reinstalled, but its sojourn, agonized and blood-drenched, was only transient, and when the hapless Mary Tudor was succeeded by her younger sister Elizabeth, the English were hauled back to Protestantism. By the Acts of Supremacy and Uniformity—both dated 1559—the Anglican Church became the state church with the sovereign as its exalted head. Upheld by levies on the public pocket, the new church became the official and established church of the land, and the only one enjoying legal rights. All others were "dissenters."

These enactments brought peace. But it was a peace that dangled precariously. Devout Catholics refused to knuckle under. Suffering all things, they worked and prayed, planning, scheming, and bleeding to restore their church to her former power and grandeur. As for the Protestants, the passing of papal authority by no means sufficed them all. Some, like the Puritans, clamored for a more thorough and devastating reform. It was all very well, they growled, to renounce the Pope and to make Protestantism the established form of worship, but what was needed even more was a chaste Protestantism, a Protestantism decontaminated of the last vestige of Romish pollution. Another group, the Separatists, hurled out altogether the notion of an established church and insisted on the right of every congregation to worship the Lord according to His directions.

6   The uproar over ecclesiastic doctrine and practice was not merely a haggling over faith and doctrine. Eavesdrop behind the outer turmoil, and you will sense a far more complicated struggle. It was, in truth, a phase of the national coming of age, the involved and mysterious process by which the country was growing to modern statehood. As England had cast off more and more of her feudal trappings, new social classes had come into being, and as they made their bid for standing and the power to promote it, religious and political issues were given new meaning and purpose.

Three major groups locked in the struggle. There was, for one, the Established Church. Braced by the support of the blooded peers and of men of wealth and position, the Anglican Church was fittingly conservative, the advocate of divine right, and the defender of things as they were, an upholder of a state wherein the supreme powers were invested in the crosier and the scepter. In the marriage of church and state, whose authority, Anglicans contended, came down from God on high, England's ruling conservatives felt they had the surest and most effective combination.

Confronting them stood a second group, the Puritans. Composed principally of the lesser country gentry and of the higher middle class and driven by a fanatical belief in a mission they thought divine, the Puritans snarled at a social order which thwarted them in their aspirations. At first they regarded themselves as Anglicans, seeking to cleanse the Established Church of the lingering Catholic corruptions. But the swift whirlpool of events soon sucked them into the controversy over the nature of state and church authority. Rejecting the principle of divine right, they upheld that of representation; against the power of bishops, they pitted that of the synod; and against that of the sovereign, they confided their trust in parliament. But let no one embrace the delusion that the Puritans were connoisseurs of democracy. Did they, nonetheless, prefer synod and parliament? Then they did because in them, rather in the absolute will of bishop and king, they discerned the most effective instrument for hoisting themselves into the political saddle. What the Puritans wanted was not a mere sweeping out of Roman leftovers—charming as such a prospect must have seemed to them—but the control of the Established Church itself, the very body politic of which the church was the spiritual arm.

More radical than even the exigent Puritans were the Separatists. Overshadowed socially and economically by the Anglicans and the Puritans, they had the support of small farmers, artisans, and workingmen. Like the Puritans, they sneered at the Anglicans and their Established Church which they found "full of filthy traditions"; but unlike their fellow critics, they would have no truck with such indecency, and they stalked out of the Anglican stall. It was the Separatists' belief, as it had been Luther's in the springtime of the Reformation, that a man had an innate right to worship his Maker by the light of his conscience and that in man's search for the truth of God, no one might trespass—neither king nor bishop nor anyone else. Each congregation, the Separatists insisted, should manage and run its own affairs. Known as *congregationalism*, this form of church government—though, unhappily, not the illumination behind it—was to become the fashion in early New England.

7   Although religious and moral questions dominated the stage, the sixteenth century was witness also to prodigious, far-stretching economic developments. The gold and silver bullion fetched from America had given the Old World a much-needed shot in the arm. Minted into coin, the precious metals speeded the metabolism of trade and commerce, thereby enhancing the chance for an imaginative and not too squeamish man to pile up a fortune. As the century proceeded to its end, farming was still the Englishman's primary occupation, but raising sheep, not only for their succulent legs and chops but also for their wool, which was converted into human vestments, was on the rise and was even promising to become a first-class national enterprise. At about the same time, Providence contrived to introduce the English to the idea of the joint stock company—an idea which appealed immensely to their acute sense for moneymaking and which they lost no time in putting to work. Not only did the new organization enable men of moderate means to join their betters in grand economic ventures, but because more and more of the nation's wealth was being pumped into England's emerging colonialism, the stock company was also presently to play a lively part in forwarding the motherland's colonial policy.

Sad to say, all this economic dazzle had its tawdry side. The gold and silver which poured so profusely into the Old World had not bestowed its benefits on all alike. The prodigies of finance and commerce managed to make off with the lion's share, while laborers and men of meaner rank had to scratch for what was left—a not unusual spectacle in human annals if one may put any confidence in the Marxian syllogisms. As the supply of gold and silver augmented, the price of staying alive also increased, and, as usual, wages could not match the fierce inflationary pace. The consequence of this economic hurly-burly bore heavily on the wage earners. A further aggravation of their woe was the landowners' novel practice of putting their farmlands into pastures, stocking them with sheep, and, to keep them from touring to faraway spots, fencing them in. Tending and policing a flock of grazing sheep, as everyone knows, requires the attention of only a man and a dog. As a result, as more and more acres were turned into sheepfolds, more and more farmhands lost their jobs. In the older days, before Henry VIII had broken up the monasteries, the down-and-out had recourse to the charity of the monks. But now the king's almoners were gone and their successors showed no inclination to a kindly heart. And so, as the sixteenth century dropped toward its sunset, hordes of Englishmen, willing and able to work but out of luck, were suffering in want and hunger with little more than a pallid hope to sustain them.

This wishful glimmer, as it turned out, was no mere rushlight. It so happened that England had reached the point in her economy where either she expanded colonially, or she would slide down the chute into national mediocrity. Her store of raw materials, despoiled and almost exhausted by centuries of reckless use, had reached the moment when their scarcity threatened the nation's economy. Take, for example, the case of lumber. The equivalent of oil and iron in the modern age, timber was the industrial heartbeat. Indeed, in certain industries—for example, shipbuilding—to be without it meant ruin. To a sea-encircled people like the English, a large and effective fleet, whether for the spoils of war or for peace, had long since been a national necessity. But now that trade had entered the oceanic era, when the rivalry of nations reached over the sea as well as the land, any threat to the existence of a robust and energetic fleet was a cause for alarm. The hope that a new continent might somehow revitalize England's sickened industry had buoyed up her statesmen and economists—even her metaphysicians—long before the first planting of colonial Virginia. Even the Puritan settlement in New England, though ventured by men and women of a predominantly godly bent, was nonetheless given its start by the London Company whose purpose, there is no gainsaying, was more economic than saintly. There were, of course, other reasons for England's coming to America—her resolution, for example, to arrest the gathering power of Spain, her hope to locate a direct waterway to the Orient, and even a yearning to make the Indian a decent and decorous Christian. Outweighing any of these goals, however, was the overriding reality of economic necessity.

8   Like the rest of his cultural baggage, the colonist's outlook on education flaunted European labels. Resembling in its main aspects that which obtained overseas, early colonial education discloses traces of the Renaissance, but even more of the Reformation. In it also are class and economic discrepancies of the first order. For at the end of the sixteenth century, man had not yet devised such a thing as free, universal, tax-supported education. The notion that every child had a natural right to education just as he had a right to breathe was not yet afoot; neither was the doctrine that education was the responsibility of the secular arm. Regarded everywhere as a privilege that went with blood and money and as the concern of the church rather than the state, education, beyond the filmiest rudiments, was the preserve of a small minority, most of whom hoped someday to ascend in the affairs of state or church, to run the family estate, or to carry on in trade or commerce. As has already been remarked, it was not until after the Reformation that the masses provoked a measure of serious educational concern. Then, because of Luther's discovery that the passage through the pearly gates would be, if not guaranteed, then at least greatly facilitated by a knowledge of

Holy Writ, instruction in reading became desirable. As the years ticked on, elementary schools appeared in a number of Protestant lands. They made headway especially where Calvinists were at the wheel, as in Scotland and in Holland and Geneva. But they made progress too among other believers, particularly in some of the German states. Although they imparted instruction in reading, and now and then in writing, their excuse for being was religious—hence their stress on piety and rectitude, on the Bible and the catechism, and sometimes on psalmody.

Such schools were usually administered by the parish, as in the Netherlands and in Scotland, and in some of the German realm they got help from the secular pocket. Even so, the schools generally charged a small fee, with the proviso, however, that the poor were to have their learning free. Since girls as well as boys were credited with the possession of souls which needed to be salvaged, primary schools were open to both sexes. But in everyday practice this was not always the rule. Nor was school attendance mandatory. As for instruction, what could be expected from an age which insisted that the nature of man, and especially in its juvenile edition, was wicked and depraved? True to the spirit of the day, the schoolmaster was prized less for his brain than his brawn. That the commoner's child seldom transcended the primary school and that, in truth, only a handful of children ever mastered its barest essentials is surely no cause for wonder.

In the case of the middle classes, the merchants and traders, the men of means and position, the situation was naturally quite different. Already in the Middle Ages fathers with a favorable cash balance were employing private masters or dispatching their sons to special burgher schools or, sometimes, guild schools. As is to be expected, the cultural standards of the successful man of commerce were inspirited by profane and utilitarian aspirations. Hence the learning they sought for their young was of the sort which would speed their way to the golden calf. Putting its stress on what Franklin called the "useful learning" rather than the "ornamental learning," it concerned itself with such subjects as reading and writing, the arithmetic of the counting room, certain modern languages, a jigger of commercial Latin, and once in awhile a dash of business jurisprudence.

The more altitudinous learning, the kind which scrubbed and waxed the intellect, was reserved for the secondary school and the university. The daughter of the classical Renaissance, secondary schooling, as reference has been made, had started in Europe as a refined and liberal creature, eager to cultivate the individual and especially to set him free from the ball and chain of scholastic pedantry. But the liberal idea soon grew arid, and in the end it withered away. What had started as an adventure descended into the cant of words and definitions, of grammar and syntax, of rote memory and intellectual surrender. With the advent of the Reformation and its subsequent immersion in the subtleties of theology, the secondary schools—Catholic as well as Protestant—devoted themselves more and more to molding tomorrow's man of God. To this end the ancient tongues were given a preponderant stress, not only for the edge they presumably put upon the mental faculties, but also in anticipation of their professional employment.

The repository of the highest learning, then as now, was the university. Calculated, like the secondary school, to put a shine on the mind, the university opened the way to the professions. From its medieval inception, it had specialized in law and medicine and in philosophy and theology. In the sixteenth century, with its strong interest in the sacred and ghostly sciences, the theological faculty was naturally a thriving concern, and since national and class ambitions were already on the march, the demand for men who could make their way through the tortuous lanes of the law was understandably on the increase.

9   Like Continental learning, that of England reflected religious motives and social disparities. The sons of the nobility and the prosperous gentry obtained a classical education, sometimes from a hired mentor, but more often in the public schools, such as Eton or Rugby and the like, which, for all their name, were not public but private and which, by the standards of their day, were expensive. As for the sons of the fairly well-heeled middle class, most of them gave their custom to the parish schools, where they were put upon getting the hang of the elementary Rs, religion, and Latin. The doors of these seminaries were not shut to the poor, though usually it was hard to pry them open and the passage past them was extremely narrow. Like the universities, most grammar schools offered help to the bright and ambitious boy of the lower classes, but such subsidy was not abundant—nor, for that matter, were such boys.

For the lower orders, indeed, the chance to snare a measure of decent schooling was next door to nothing. As pretty nearly everywhere on the Continent, the state kept itself aloof, preferring to consign the business of education to the keeping of the church. True, here and there one comes upon private vernacular schools which owed their existence to communal effort and which were the beneficiaries of some public support. Mostly, however, the schooling available for the masses was proffered more in the vein of almsgiving than in that of intellectual zeal. Hanging over it not uncommonly was a spirit of haughtiness which viewed the ruling classes as superior creatures, specially dowered and hence the plain favorites of Omnipotence. In consequence, it was only meet and right that those charged with teaching the inhabitants of society's cellar should seek to enlighten their wards not only in the simple elements, including piety and virtue, but even more in a proper respect for their betters.

A boost for education—slight to be sure, but far-reaching, nevertheless—came from an unexpected quarter. The calamitous depression which had bowled so many of the lower ranks during the sixteenth century had swollen the army of dependent poor and, by the same token, the bands of roving beggars. To provide some succor and also to bring them to heel, Parliament had enacted a number of measures culminating in 1601 in the Poor Law. Laying taxes on all men of property within a given parish for the care of its paupers, the law ordained that poor and dependent children were to be bound out as apprentices and given acquaintance with some useful trade. This practice, engendered in economic and social ferment, established itself in permanence, and when, in later years, the English set themselves up in the New World they brought it with them.

10   Although the colonists were minted from a common European civilization, they were marked by deep and obvious differences. Not only were they diverse nationally, but they varied also in their social standing, political experience, cultural interests, and religion. The settlement of some, like the New Englanders, in compact agricultural villages proved a spur to communal enterprise. Consider, on the other hand, the Virginians. Dwelling on comparatively large acreages and diffused over an enormous surface of earth and water, they found communal action far more elusive.

The American environment, with its motley climate and geography, soon hatched other differences. It is no wonder, for example, that the Massachusetts settlers did not farm on any ambitious scale for profit; for their soil, stony and shalelike, granted its harvest grudgingly. Still, there were compensations. Certainly it was less onerous to put the ax on the ever-present forest. Out of the tall, stately pines the settlers fashioned the world's finest masts. And soon the ring of the woodsman's ax was being matched by the beat of the shipwright's hammer. Nor did it take the New Englanders very long to sniff the possibility of stout profits from marketing the cod and herring, then cavorting in their coastal waters. The Puritans made full use of nature's bounty, and with the aid of their sheltered bays and excellent harbors, their diligence presently built a spry and gainful commerce.

The broader plains of the Middle Colonies were better suited to husbandry. Blessed with fertility and a cordial climate, most of the midlands could be persuaded to yield a pleasant reward. Here the rivers, which often flowed deep and broad, could be navigated far upstream. That in time's passage they should become the traveled lanes of trade and commerce was only natural.

The South, too, had been kissed by a benevolent nature. The necessities of life grew with ease, timber was plentiful, and the waterways and harbors were excellent. At the same time, the competition from the Northern neighbors was scarcely light. Fortunately for the Southerners, they soon found out that tobacco could be grown with a fine profit, and so it was not long before the weed took over as a Southern staple. Sought almost everywhere, it became the magic passkey to wealth, and for years to come it was to be the undisputed kingpin of Southern economy.

In religion the colonists were as variegated as their land and climate. Apart from Roman Catholics in Maryland, the great bulk of settlers were Protestant. Throughout the South the Anglican rite prevailed, although inland toward the mountains one ran into Scotch and Scotch-Irish Presbyterians, while on the Carolina shorelands there were small clusterings of French Huguenots. New England was in the hands of English Calvinists, while New Netherland was run by the Dutch variety. After the colony succumbed to the English, the number of its Anglicans rose. But there was a fair sampling of several other creeds—in fact, there were even some Puritans who, fed up by the harsh certainties of their theocratic overlords, sought to disencumber themselves of their burden in freer and more congenial parts. In Pennsylvania, because of the great tolerance of its founder, there were more sects than in any other colony—more, it is likely, than in any other land in Christendom. Most numerous, especially in Philadelphia and its nearby vicinage, were the Quakers. But there were also Presbyterians, besides Anglicans, Baptists and Methodists, Lutherans, Dunkards, Mennonites, Moravians, and several others.

The civilization of the colonial settlers, conditioned as it had been by their European experience as well as by the compulsions of their American environs, accounted in no small degree for their attitude toward education. Into it merged the broad principles of the Reformation, the fiats of Luther, Calvin, Knox, and Zwingli, and also the special contentions of creed and sect, and, in particular, the inexorable pressures of economics, class, geography, and climate.

There was, for one, the type of education peculiar to most of New England. In Massachusetts, with its Calvinism, its religious solidarity, and its effective alliance of church and state, it was simple for the Bible Commonwealth to assume an educational role, to fashion policy, and by law to seek to give it execution. Nor should one overlook the significance of the agricultural village. The cornerstone of Puritan New England, it facilitated communal enterprise. The combination of state, church, and compact community made the creation of the town school all but inevitable.

The religious unity so typical of Massachusetts was lacking in the Middle Colonies. Here, instead of one dominant, engulfing faith, there was a vast aggregation of denominations whose Christian interpretations were not only divergent, but often in sharp and scandalous contention. Instead of a town school, such as adorned New England, the midlanders had recourse to the parish or parochial school. True, for a spell New Netherland, with its established Reformed Dutch Church, operated a number of town schools which received support from the civil purse. But after the coming of the English this agreeable tie was broken, and thenceforth every denomination had to fend educationally for itself.

In the South, where the populace dwelt on wide-flung plantations, a town school was obviously out of the question. But there were yet other obstacles. Like their countrymen on the ocean's other side, the Southerners looked upon education as a private endeavor, the affair of the individual and not of the government. Like their high-toned brothers in the motherland, the Southern governing classes entertained a preference for private schooling, usually of a tutorial cut. Sometimes, under favorable circumstances, they shipped their sons abroad to acquire knowledge and gentility in one of England's ivied shrines. The offspring of the lower classes, needless to say, were not asked to brave such hazards. For them education was mainly vocational, heavily suffused, as one might suspect, with Anglican right-thinking, and it was vouchsafed largely through a system of apprenticeship or through out-and-out charity.

While the colonial culture was thus unfolding, flags of alien cultures were rippling beyond its confines, to the north, the west, and the south. There, too, efforts were being made to bring a measure of light into the bleak and savage wilderness, chiefly by the French and Spanish, and in particular by their holy men seeking to propagate and fortify Catholicism. True, the mark they left on American education is today only dimly discernible, but nevertheless it is a mark. One may see it, if one takes the trouble, in a whole tier of states from Florida to Louisiana to Texas, New Mexico, Colorado, Arizona, and California.

2
THE BIBLE
COMMONWEALTH

The hope nursed so long by Puritans that they might reform the Church of England, to rid it, as they said, of "its petty anti-Christs and paltry popes," came to a disappointing end in the reign of James I (1603–1625). Not only did "God's silly vassal" explode their dream, but, what portended even worse, he vowed to make them conform or "harry them out of the land or else do worse." Some, taking him at his dreaded word, actually departed for more hospitable Holland, whence, in 1620, a small detachment set sail for America.

For Protestantism the next few years were dark and difficult. On the Continent, indeed, it even appeared doomed. Locked in combat with the Catholic legions—a struggle which bled and burned Europe for thirty years—Protestant forces were reeling under the might of Generals Tilly and Wallenstein. In France the troops of Cardinal Richelieu had obliterated the Huguenots. And in England, Charles I (1625–1649) was showing himself even more antagonistic toward dissenters than his paternal predecessor, the first James.

It was in such murky times that Puritan leaders conceived the idea of migrating to America to found a Bible commonwealth in accordance, they were sure, with specifications that the Lord God had confided especially and singularly unto them. The fact that southeastern England, a Puritan enclave and the seat of the cloth-weaving industry, was then suffering a ravening depression may have been another celestial visitation. So, at all events, it was commonly regarded. But whatever its origin, real or imaginary, its baleful effect lay heavy on the land, and doubtless it gave recruitment for the colonial venture an added boost. Even John Winthrop, a landed gentleman from Suffolk and destined to be the colony's first governor, let out word that not only was he of a barren pocket, but save for possible pickings in the New World, he saw no relief in the years ahead.

In the year 1630, the beginning of the so-called "Great Migration," about one thousand colonists caught their first glimpse of the wooded shoreland of Massachusetts. The following year the colony was well under way, and although stupendous difficulties hampered it on every side, its growth was nonetheless rapid. In another five years the colony had spread along the vast coastal reach from Maine to Narragansett Bay, while within its borders it could count more than fifteen thousand Anglo-Saxons. Meanwhile, on the Massachusetts flank, in the rivered grassland between Hartford and Springfield, the colony of Connecticut was taking on its early form and substance.

Although most of the new settlements were of a small proportion, they were soon being caressed by an agreeable prosperity, growing grain, raising livestock, and catching an endless run of fish, all of which the colonists were able to dispose of profitably to new arrivals in the Lord's Garden, where, they were in hopes, God would "save them from the general calamity." Their overwhelming bulk comprised the yeomen, or, in present phraseology, the small landowning farmers; but there were also artisans of a variety of skills, besides a scattering of gentry and, of course, the colonists' leaders, their indispensable ambassadors of God.

2   The Puritanism brought to New England sprang from the thinking of John Calvin, its leading metaphysician and its foremost theologian. Put forth in 1536 in his main work, *The Institutes of the Christian Religion*, its propositions filled some eight hundred pages in a French so lucid that ever since the book's appearance, connoisseurs of Gallic prose have admired it for its clarity, if not its charm. Like Luther, his fellow reformer in Germany, Calvin acknowledged the Bible as "God's eternal decree," Christendom's sole and infallible authority, the basis of its laws and bylaws and, accordingly, of all Christian conduct, whether sacred or secular, overt or otherwise. Again, like Luther, Calvin declared for a Heaven where life was a never-ending round of bliss and a Hell that was deep and hot, full of fume and fire. But where the German held out the hope that by faith and Christian rectitude a man might someday enjoy eternity among the angels, the Frenchman rejected such a notion out of hand. "God," he let it be known, "not only foresaw the fall of the first man and the ruin of his posterity in him, but arranged all by the determination of His will." Chosen by God in the womb of time, a lucky few, whatever their mundane record—whether they had practiced as throat slitters or child stealers or as men of the utmost decency and kindliness, and whether they were babes or grizzly gaffers—unfailingly would land in Heaven; but the vast and overwhelming rest, just as unfailingly, God had reserved for eternal blistering. Those headed for the pearly gates had been picked, Calvin asserted, "because of His gratuitous mercy, totally irrespective of human merit." The others He had translated to their doom because of His divine judgment, which was "just and irreprehensible." God's action, humanly speaking, was thus wholly capricious and irrational, and nothing one might do would alter one's postmortem predestination.

At the heart of Puritan dogma was the absolute and unconditional will of God, which, Calvin insisted, was the source of all things. From this assumption Puritanism worked up the view that every aspect of life —every act, thought, and feeling, whether in the open or behind the blind —bore moral significance and hence lay under ecclesiastic jurisdiction, and everyone within its reach was subject to its control.

3   The Puritan state, following its Calvinistic model at Geneva, was a theocracy, a partnership of state and church, with the latter leading the former. Its pastors set about interpreting God's holy ordinances as laid down in Holy Writ, and its constabulary put them into execution. Under the theocracy's constant vigil the Puritan's conduct became a public spectacle. His neighbors made it their business to know all about him, from what he ate and fed his beasts and birds to the smell of his breath and the sick friend with whom he told his wife he had sat up the night before. Inasmuch as a man was at all times accountable to his theocratic overlords for his acts and thoughts, citizens were under bounden duty, for their own sake as well as his, to keep him straight and righteous and never to hold secret their knowledge of his vagrant dallying. So close was the theocratic tie that crimes and misdemeanors against the public peace were, in truth, malpractices against God. "He that shall be treacherous and false to the civil government," warned the Rev. Urian Oakes, a Harvard president and, hence, a man who ought to know, "is guilty of high treason against the Lord Jesus."

The unit of local government was the township. Organized to give the settlement its essential solidarity, the town was designed to fortify the faith by discouraging the dispersal of the godly. The town's focal point was the village. Here, strung out on either side of a long main street, huddled the freeholders' cottages, adorned with their tiny gardens and berry patches and their infant fruit trees. Here stood the tannery, the smithy, and the workshops of the artisans and craftsmen, and there rumbled and creaked the gristmill and the sawmill. Sometimes, as the years moved on, there might be a schoolhouse. Scattered about lay gaudy little plantings of wheat, rye, barley, and Indian corn. Through the landscape there usually curled a little stream from which arose the tranquil slopes of the common pasture.

Within walking reach of everyone was the church. It was not the magnificent mansion of God the Puritans had known on the Atlantic's other side. In fact, it was not even a house of God—not even, for that matter, a church—for the fathers, finding no such usage in the Good Book, shied away from it in their utterance. Nor, by the same token, did they invest their house of worship with a churchly air. Gone, for one, was the holy cross, gone the reaching spire, gone the stained-glass windows. No smiling cherubs beamed from the walls, no benign Madonnas, no Joseph and his colleague ass—not even a rainspout with a roguish, outlandish head. Such beguilements, the fathers knew very well, gilded the Roman harlot, and they would not have them. Were their sacred houses plain and primitive, untouched by the lure of charm and beauty? Then they were also the embodiment of a faith, dour and demanding, and the perfect expression of the alliance between church and state. The church was the place set aside not only for the official religious exercise but also for the transactions of public affairs, for the maintaining of roads and bridges to the fixing of the pay and perquisites of the town pastor, its schoolmaster, and its dog whipper. It was, in short, a meetinghouse for theocrats.

4   Like their compatriots overseas, the Puritans put their trust in a society erected on the groundwork of class distinctions. To a select handful —the ministers, the magistrates, and, as time wore away, the successful merchants and men of affairs—went nearly all the power and influence, and the glory. Only those perched on the airiest social crags were honored as "mister" or "gentleman." A first-class artisan had to content himself as a "goodman," while his spouse had to struggle along as "goodwife." Servants, hired hands, and unskilled laborers, useful in their place and even necessary, were nevertheless devoid of social hemoglobin, and hence were addressed by their given names. To the class-ridden Puritan it was a matter of simple sense that the whereabouts of his church pew should depend on whether God had put him on earth as mister, goodman, or just plain Sam—in fact, at New Haven for a spell anyone of a lesser rank than goodman was assigned no seat at all. And to make an end, as late as the eighteenth century enrollments at Harvard and Yale were arranged not by alphabetical convenience, but in accordance with the social standing of the student's parents. Only those atop the social heap were allowed to show themselves in lace and fancy ruffs, embroidered caps, gold and silver buttons, and similar sartorial splendor. When, for all that, the wives of successful glaziers, carpenters, and other goodmen of consequence succumbed to Satan's cozening and proceeded to bedeck and bedizen themselves in finery and frizzled hair, they were subject to penalty. Even the scales of justice were rigged to favor those of high degree. It was generally accepted that under no circumstances should a gentleman ever be publicly humiliated by the application of the lash. Did the juridic bench, for example, hold a certain Mr. Josias Plaistowe guilty of having pilfered corn from the Indians? And did the court fine this knave and order in addition that henceforth he "should be called by the name of Josias and not Mr. as formerly"? Then his servants who had been aides and associates in his thievery enjoyed no such luck. For them the court ordered a public whipping.

Not unlike their fellow humans then in the Lord's menagerie, the Puritans suffered neither toleration nor democracy—indeed, toward such gratifications they actually harbored a deep aversion. " 'Tis Satan's policy," wrote Thomas Shepard, a specialist in divine science and therefore qualified to speak, "to plead for an indefinite and boundless toleration." False thinkers like Roger Williams who bore this hellish tag were, of course, chased out. When the dreadful Quakers appeared to preach their hostile creed, they were flogged and jailed for their pains, and when such measures failed to cool their missionary fever, they were hanged. True to their half-feudal origin, the founders of the Bible State accepted most of their motherland's aristocratic practice, with its small portion of privileged high and mighty, admired and adulated by the multitude as the heirs of Solomon and Pericles. Contrary to the Thanksgiving Day editorials which annually instruct and uplift the people of our great republic, the Puritans voiced their time's disrelish for democracy. Not only did they put no stock in its axioms, currently cherished, but as a people ordering their lives by God's sacred blueprint, they were at pains to bolster their dislike by the Bible. The Rev. John Cotton, after long days and nights of prayer and search, could trace no democracy in Holy Writ. "I do not conceive," he announced after plumbing it deeply from cover to cover, "that ever God did ordain [it] as a fit government for either church or commonwealth." "The Holy Ghost," the *Puritan Platform of Church Discipline* went on in full accord, "frequently, yea always where it mention church government, ascribeth it to elders, whereas the work and duty of the people is expressed in obeying elders."

And just as God had shed His preordained grace on His chosen few, so none but the most godly were clasped to the bosom of church membership. Those attaining this benison were denominated *Saints,* while the rest, the overwhelming majority, were known as *Strangers.* But whether Saints or Strangers, there was no getting out of church attendance, which in all cases was mandatory. Yet the Saints at least possessed Heaven's required passport, with all the possible visas, though not the assurance, of course, that they would ever make the celestial trip. But while on earth they alone enjoyed the felicity of being eligible to vote and hold office. "No man," affirmed a statute of 1631, "shall be admitted to the freedom of this body politic, but such as are members of some of the churches."

Such was the Puritan Zion. Over it, like an awesome cloud, hung the absolute and unsparing will of God, the frowning shadow of Calvin, and the ever-imminent verge of damnation. A Bible state, it was conceived in Holy Scripture. A theocracy, it was ruled by the stern hand of ecclesiastics. It has been likened to a form of Oriental despotism, though this doubtless is a stretching of the facts. Without question, however, it was an oligarchy wherein a handful of the sanctified, though enormously outnumbered by the damned, were nonetheless the colony's appointed and rightful leaders. Yet, for all their cocksure certainty, the overlords, as men and as theologians, were of a superior cast. Their theology may have been harsh, and their outlook warped and forbidding, but no one can say that they were ignorant. The heirs of the Renaissance and, more particularly, of the Reformation, not a few of them were college men, and all of them were for their time superbly educated.

5   Thus, there were good reasons why those in charge of the Bay Colony should have recognized the importance of education. Having themselves received a first-rate schooling, they naturally inclined to sympathize with its worth. As inheritors, moreover, of the Protestant tradition, they were convinced that reading the Bible was the Christian's sacred duty

and that knowing how to read was therefore of capital importance. Like all
Protestant sects, the Puritans fretted over the problem of perpetuating
their faith. How to implant God's transcendental truth in the young?
How to assure the colony a corps of learned men of God when the
present ones had transferred their operations to their eternal predestination? Such were the questions which wracked the minds of the colony's
ruling Saints and on whose wise solution so much depended. The fact
that Massachusetts was a theocracy and that its populace was securely
wrapped in religious solidarity was an enormous advantage when it came
to formulating and executing its educational policy. Not only was the
usual chasm between state and church nonexistent, but the common sectarian brawls which everywhere tore Protestants apart were also absent.
Thus, whereas Protestants outside New England were commonly obliged
to rely on the individual efforts of their parishes to promote their educational programs, the Puritans could always expect, and get, support from
the church's ready and willing partner, the state.

Soon after settling themselves in their new Zion, the Puritans turned
their thoughts to the schooling of their young. True to their European
and semifeudal provenance, they regarded education as a tool to advance
class interests and to nail down the prevalent social order. The view, then
common, that education was a church function naturally received their
hearty acquiescence. If, as happened, the colony's lawgivers occasionally
ventured into educational spheres, this was not because of any secular
bent, but rather because as godly men they were putting into law the
considered judgment of their reverend clergy.

In the mid-thirties, after the Great Migration was well under way,
a number of towns began to dally with learning. Early in 1635, for
example, Boston's town fathers recommended that "Brother Philemon
Pormort shall be entreated to become schoolmaster for the teaching and
nurturing of children among us." Whether he acceded is hard to say, the
records on the subject being somewhat disheveled. We do know for a
certainty that in the following year a number of well-fixed Bostonians
dipped into their privy purse to "maintain a free schoolmaster for the
youth with us." There is ground to believe that a school was actually
propagated and that it may even have been the celebrated Boston Latin
School, the first colonial secondary school of which we have any news
and one which is still in active practice. But it was not until some years
later—in 1644—that Boston undertook to search the town till to extract
the sum of £8 to help cover the cost of keeping a school the year preceding. Meanwhile, at least two rival towns had beaten Boston for the
honor of being the first to give a hand to some form of public schooling.
To historic Charlestown, in illustration, goes the distinction of adorning
itself with the first town-supported school—probably a Latin grammar

school—with its appointment in 1636 of a publicly paid master, while Dorchester is credited, three years after, with being the first to make provision for a permanent town school, again of the grammatical variety.

Though these details are of interest mainly to historical taxidermists, they are not entirely devoid of meaning. They make it clear, for one thing, that in the beginning there was no general state action in the realm of learning. Whatever schooling was envisioned or actually provided, its essential nature was local. Because of this localism, the schooling which came into being was inevitably diverse, and what held for one town did not necessarily hold for another. Even in the matter of support there was no uniformity, schools being kept sometimes by endowment, sometimes by sundry license fees, sometimes out of the communal pocket, and sometimes by a combination of the three. One thing, however, these records do reveal is an obvious concern for the schooling of the young.

6   The gnawing dread that someday their store of trained and learned leaders, whether cleric or civilian, would run out caused the Puritan fathers to put their first stress on the secondary and higher learning. To such effect a thorough grounding in Latin and at least a grammatical acquaintance with Greek became indispensable, and to make such knowledge available the colonists resorted to the so-called "grammar schools." Old familiars to the English, such seminaries of learning trace their line back to the Middle Ages, when their forebears, the monastic and cathedral schools, were performing their various labors of instruction. Time saw these schools rise and sometimes even shine, only, as the Middle Ages ran aground, to falter and decline.

Such, up to a point, was the story of St. Paul's at London. Once a flourishing shrine of light, the school had fallen into decrepitude, until, by the end of the fifteenth century, it lay on the verge of extinction awaiting only, as it seemed, its last breath and a decent burial. Instead, a number of Humanists, with aid and counsel from Erasmus, took the school in charge, doctoring and tending it and, even better, restoring it to a fresh and vigorous life with hearty dosing from the classical bottle. Other schools presently had recourse to similar swigs, and by and by the Humanists' dream of molding a polished and cultivated person, amiably skeptical and illuminated by a liberal classical education, was enjoying a gentle prospering.

So things continued, more or less, until the mid-sixteenth century, when the Renaissance cascaded into the Reformation, and matters of faith and morals assumed a commanding importance. The fortune of the grammar schools rose and subsided wih the flux and flow of the religious tide, but in any case the Humanists' ardor, which had fed their lambent flame, was considerably dampened. What was left was the substance but not the spirit, namely, Latin, classical to be sure, but confined and constrained by denominational assumptions.

Such, at bottom, was the grammar school to which the New England fathers gave their approval and support. Bred from the Renaissance, it still aspired, as its partisans let it be known, to instruct youth "both in humane learning and good literature." But impinged upon as it was by the Reformation, the Humanistic ideal became subordinate to the demands of creed, so that instead of seeking to transmute a youth into a civilized and urbane man, functioning freely and harmoniously on all his cylinders —mental, physical, and emotional—the grammar school undertook to rear not only a man who was well filled with the classical learning but also one who at the same time would always keep himself within the safe bounds of an impeccable orthodoxy.

Our knowledge of the first New England grammar schools is blanketed with uncertainty. During the seventeenth century at least eleven hung out their shingle, and of these, four—Boston, Cambridge, Dorchester, and Roxbury—have been in continuous practice ever since. The most famous, by long odds, is the Boston Latin School. It is the patriarch of the clan, having come into being as the Free Grammar School of Boston as long ago as 1636—although, suffering the immemorial compulsion of historic institutions to make themselves out as hoary as possible, it claims to have ornamented this earth at least a year earlier.

Apart from the Puritan overtone, the New England grammar schools were pretty much like their cousins across the ocean. Students attended their sessions usually for seven years, starting out when they were seven or eight, when they were expected to be able to read a simple English sentence and when they were strong enough, presumably, to withstand the batterings of Latin grammar. Once safely through its ordeal and peril, the boys took on the Latin heavyweights from Ovid and Cicero to Caesar, Virgil, Horace, and Livy, besides engaging in sparring bouts with Corderius, Erasmus, and several others. After six years of such battling, when a lad had reached the point where he was expected to hold his own with such formidable fellows, he was put in addition upon Greek grammar, a noble tongue but for learners no less booby-trapped, whereupon, if he happened to attend the Boston Latin School, he made acquaintance with Isocrates, Homer, Hesiod, and the New Testament, all, of course, in the original. If one may rely on the testimony of the Rev. Cotton Mather, who finished his grammar schooling as a mere kiddie not yet twelve, in cases of budding genius such as his own, boys of special promise were sometimes introduced to Hebrew. The general idea behind all this linguistic and literary exercising was to teach boys to read, write, and hold converse in Latin, besides laying the foundation for Greek—or, in a nutshell, to enable them to confront their questioners at Harvard successfully should they ever be seized by a craving to secure admission to college.

Grammar schools varied a great deal from place to place, but aside from Boston, probably none entertained its learners with such a sumptuous classical spread. Not uncommonly, in fact, the grammar school was not a school at all, but someone on intimate terms with Latin, say, a holy clerk or, more rarely, a master in the primary school, who imparted his knowledge to those who volunteered for it. Often enough there were such men, but, rather sadly, no mad scramble ensued to receive their knowledge. In any case, however, whether the instruction was delivered in school or by a person outside, nearly always it was rendered gratis. Not even the lofty Boston Latin School levied a tuition fee, except on those who happened to be so unfortunate as to be non-Bostonians.

The Boston Latin School, as was remarked a page or so ago, is the most celebrated of New England grammar schools. From its classic chambers trafficked a host of boys destined for a front bench in the college of American immortals, as witness Benjamin Franklin, Samuel Adams, John Hancock, Josiah Quincy, and Robert Treat Payne, all signers of the Declaration. The list is long, and in another era when the Stars and Stripes rippled over the ancient school, it becomes longer still with Ralph Waldo Emerson, Charles Francis Adams, Henry Ward Beecher, and more recently, Charles William Eliot, George Santayana, and Leonard Bernstein.

Not only does the school sparkle with the names of its illustrious sons, but it is also the workplace of meritorious teachers. The most distinguished in colonial times was Ezekiel Cheever, who taught and rattaned his protégés for almost forty years, until at ninety-two, with a beard as profuse and amazing as his life, he died greatly regretted. One encounters Cheever not only in educational chronicles but also in the corridors of American letters. Hawthorne thrust him into the pages of *Grandfather's Chair*; President Stiles of Yale took note of him in his diary; and Cotton Mather, a very grave and learned man and in his childhood one of Cheever's prodigies, soared to the higher ecstasies when in a jingle, he warbled the praises of his master's virtues.

Though the New England grammar school was under the civil arm, in a theocracy, needless to say, the church spoke with authority. When, for example, in 1654 President Dunster of Harvard was openly carrying on with heresy, the colony undertook to warn its town fathers "not to admit or suffer any such to be continued in the office or place of teaching . . . that have manifested themselves unsound in the faith or scandalous in their lives." Years later, in 1701, when the power of the theocrats had emaciated into a pale phantom of its former self, the colony, for all that, ordained that all candidates for grammar schoolmastering must bear the approval not only of the town's parson but of his brethren in the frock in two adjacent towns as well. Nor was the importance of religion overlooked. True, its hallowed axioms and postulates were not imparted systematically in a series of courses ranging from elementary to advanced. Even so, in one form or another religion was inescapable. The boys greeted their day's work in a hopeful prayer, and when their labors were done, they signaled their thanks to God in words of solemn grace. Their catechism, marked and dog-eared by years of hard use, continued to instruct them, and so, of course, did the psalmbook and the Holy Scriptures. Headed by their master, they filed to church to give attention to the weekday sermon. Of a Saturday afternoon they made preparation for the coming Sabbath, and on the Monday following they were examined and cross-examined on the parson's sermon.

7 Several years after the advent of the Puritans in Boston Harbor, their lawgivers in the General Court appropriated £400 "towards a school or college." Unfortunately, the hoped-for promotion of knowledge had to wait for awhile, first to enable the settlers to combat the Pequots, an Indian people of a very unfriendly disposition, and next to allow the pastors to extinguish the heretical bonfires set by Anne Hutchinson, an advanced thinker even more menacing to orthodoxy than the red men. By 1636 both perils were apparently in sufficient check to permit the project to get under way. Accordingly a board of overseers was appointed, and a house was bought at Newtowne—later to become Cambridge. Its back to the Charles River, the building was set in about an acre of ground, which, if not distinguished for its cathedral-windowed elms, at least served mankind usefully as a parking lot for its cattle. When, a few years later, John Harvard died, bequeathing half of his estate and all his books—some £800 and three hundred volumes—to the institution, the college was promptly named for its benefactor, a practice which has since become a common and honored one in the American higher learning, as witness such prodigious intellectual plants as Duke, Leland Stanford, and John B. Stetson—to mention only three. The purpose of the college, its "Rules and Precepts" presently announced, was "to know God and Jesus Christ which is eternal life. Therefore to lay Christ in the bottome is the only foundation of all sound knowledge and harmony."

Harvard's first chief executive—and faculty—was Nathaniel Eaton. A man of great learning—"a rare scholar" Cotton Mather pronounced him—Eaton had frequented the great groves of England and the Netherlands, and in his Latin dissertation he had offered the world his counsel on the important subject of the Sabbath. He took upon himself the cares of office, administrative and pedagogic, in 1638, when he heard his first recitations. Yet underneath his fine show of learning the man was actually a rogue—a saint, as it were, in a grimy shirt. Not only did he club his students and assistant "with a stick big enough to have killed a horse," but he is reputed also to have victualed them with worn-out meat and uncleaned fish, and worse yet, for a chaser he served them senile and degenerate beer. When, after a year, the Puritan fathers found out how grossly fortune had played her japes, they promptly turned the fellow loose. But when Eaton departed, he could afford a complaisant smile, for with him eloped a substantial part of the college cashbox.

Needless to say, Eaton's chicanery gave the fathers a bit of a turn, and for a year they shut the college down. When, in 1640, its sessions reconvened, Henry Dunster, an English farmer's boy with a Cambridge degree, sat in the presidential chair. No one can say that he was an intellectual dazzler. True, his revision of the *Bay Psalm Book,* a rather grim and graceless work, gave that production some literary improvement, but it was far from enough. Dunster's gifts leaned more toward administration, organization, building, and gathering in goodwill and money—all highly prized these latter days in a college president, and lucratively rewarded. Unhappily, fate placed Dunster on this earth much too early, and his remuneration for a long time was scarcely more than modest; in truth, not even his fringe benefits included much—not even, as the college voted to a later president, "the contents of the south privy . . . to be at the President's Disposal." During Dunster's regime the college was incorporated, its staff augmented by a couple of tutors, and the process of its endless expansion begun with the erection of a new building—a "fair and comely one," which cost at least £1,000. At the same time, with the excommunication of all horned tenants from the campus, Harvard's intellectual air was rendered fresh and wholesome.

Yet, despite his meritorious accomplishments, in the end President Dunster was found wanting. The bald truth is that in his Biblical searching he had found no warrant for the Puritan's insistence on infant baptism. Instead, he declared for adult baptism, and not by a mere sprinkling of water, but by total immersion. The president's false thinking was not only painful but also heretical and against the law. It must be said, in equity, that the authorities did their utmost to salvage him and even dropped to their knees to pray for him, but to no avail. His error had insinuated itself too deeply in the sanctum of his soul, and rather than recant, in 1654 Dunster resigned. He betook himself and his apostasy to Plymouth, where five years later death arrested him.

Designed to service the young male for high Puritan places, whether sacred or secular, the college received only those who could translate Cicero and similar literati on sight and who could "make and speak Latin in verse and prose," besides making sense of Greek nouns and verbs. Once over these hurdles, the prospect copied the college laws, paid his fees, and submitted a bond to ensure his adherence to such practice in the future, whereupon he was admitted to the college and lodged in its quarters. He was now booked for a prescribed course in grammar, rhetoric, logic, arithmetic, geometry, astronomy, ethics, ancient history, Greek, and Hebrew, the typical bill of fare in those days at an English college. Those with a hopeful eye on holy orders immersed themselves thoroughly in Sacred Writ—in the original tongues—besides introducing themselves to Wolleb's *Abridgement of Christian Divinity* or Ames's *Medulla Theologicae*, then two favorite handbooks in divine science, but long since resident in oblivion. Students who overcame this formidable material—usually it required four years—took their bachelor of arts some time in July at a festival enriched by the presence of the colony's foremost *eminenti*, lay and ecclesiastical, and celebrated not only with prayer and speechmaking, but also with the consumption of expansive roasts of beef and liquids far more powerful than water. Preparation for the master's degree exacted another three years of special grappling with moral and theological science, after which the young man emerged a proud and learned man, itching to confound the enemies of Calvin, and also, of course, to serve his fellow citizens in some post worthy of his new and hard-won merit.

Harvard began life patterned upon the English model, which is to say, as a college, the lineal descendant of what Robert of Sorbon had humbly begun in thirteenth-century Paris as a hostel to furnish free food and lodging to a small number of empty-pocketed theologues. Four hundred years later the college had transformed into a community of students, living under the same roof with their masters, who, besides instructing and policing the collegians, assisted at their meals and prayers. It was, observed the ever-ready Cotton Mather, "the college way of living."

To Harvard goes the glory of having been the first college in colonial America—though not the first in the New World. A Jesuit college had preceded it in Quebec, and long before Harvard was even a twinkle in the founder's eyes, the Spaniards were conjuring up universities in Latin America. Their first grove was planted, in all likelihood, as early as 1551 at Lima, Peru. Another followed two years later in Mexico. A third appeared in the Argentine in 1613, and a fourth in Bolivia eleven years later. Until 1693, when Virginians founded their College of William and Mary, Harvard was the only center for advanced learning in the original colonies. In New England it was to remain without a rival—not to say a peer—until 1701, when a group of Congregational pastors, all Harvard graduates, appalled and alarmed by the way their alma mater was succumbing to the blandishments of the advancing enlightenment, created the Collegiate School of Connecticut, now known as Yale University.

The first college in the Colonies was not a popular institution. Economically, its inclination was toward exclusiveness, since the cost of studying there, which ran as high as £75, was beyond the reach of the vast majority of New Englanders. Even intellectually, the college reserved its tutoring and training for the few, a small and select number of the colony's youth who, in the not too faraway future, when the fathers had shed their mortal clay, would be called upon to serve the Bible State as its ministers of God, its lawmakers, magistrates, and diplomats or maybe even its governors.

But maintaining a college in the wilderness—or even a small number of Latin schools—was no easy task. Strife with the Indian simmered constantly, and sometimes it blew up in long and bloody warfare. There was forever an insufficiency of money—for lingering years, in fact, students paid their tuition bills not with coin of the realm but with an amazing array of commodities from delicatessen and dairy products to boots and shoes, hardware, lumber, and even livestock. The generation which saw Dunster's elevation to office also was witness to the gigantic struggle between Charles I and the Parliament. As fortune turned more and more against the monarch, his adversaries naturally had good reason to stay in England. And as their migrations gradually oozed to a trickle, New England inevitably felt the effects. In fact, for a time the number of departures from the commonwealth exceeded the number of arrivals. The upshot was not only a falling off in the population but, as the years wearied on, also an economic slump of a fearful sort.

Black days now descended upon the college. Empty chairs and dwindling enrollment consumed it, while its means, always underweight, grew gaunt and ribby. It was a situation worthy of Dunster's talents. He scrimped and squeezed; he passed around the hat, and he proceeded —indifferent, it almost seems, to harsh reality—to build a college. Such spectacles show themselves on the stage of history every now and again, and all too often they end in sorrow. But when, in 1654, Dunster made his exit, arm in arm, it will be remembered, with the Baptist Jezebel, he could nevertheless look back on a fair success. By donations, whether of cash or worldly goods or labor, and by taxes, the college capital had taken on a healthy countenance, so fair and glowing that the president's annual wages had increased to a comfortable £100. Meanwhile, the down-sliding enrollment had stemmed and turned about to bulge the college walls with more than fifty students. They came from all over, from New England, of course, but also from New Amsterdam and Virginia and even Bermuda and the motherland. Finally, so well was the quality of Harvard's work regarded, that in England both Oxford and Cambridge accorded its degrees a rank and dignity equal to their own. That this should be, in spite of all the hardship, harassment, and discouragement, is testimony not only to a dogged spirit but also to a high devotion, to say nothing of an almost unbelievable effort and sacrifice, and not, of course, on the part of Dunster alone, but of numerous others, many of them plain and humble folk and long since sealed in the vast vault of historical anonymity.

8   On education's lower plane, unhappily, the colony's accomplishments were not so lustrous. Suffused with class and religious elements, the schooling of the common child put its main weight on faith and morals and, of course, on reading. At first the imparting of these blessings fell to parental or private hands, the older generation fulfilling its responsibility as best it could, with occasional proddings—one may be sure—from the ever-watchful parson. Nor was it uncommon, as the years ran on, for some enterprising goodwife to receive some of her neighbors' children at her fireside, where, besides dispatching her household tasks, she led these fledglings to their letters. In addition—though where she found the time historical science has not yet figured out—she sometimes taught the girls how to knit and sew and even how to stitch a sampler. Occasionally she granted some moments to spelling and counting, although for the common folk such instruction was then still something of a rarity. As a true Puritan, she was, of course, under orders to impress the official faith and virtue upon her charges at all times and everywhere. That her efforts should be compensated, if not always with the merry music of money then at least in some other agreeable manner, was surely no more than right and seemly. In her official capacity such a lady pedagogue was known as a *school dame,* while the court over which she presided was a *dame school.* Such seminaries of knowledge were common enough on the other side; in fact, in the old country they continued to flourish, more or less, until the nineteenth century was in its early seventies, when England at last got round to accommodating its people with free, tax-supported, public elementary schools.

Another importation was the writing school. Sometimes this was simply a touring scrivener who gave lessons in his specialty whenever he could find a customer. True to its name, the writing school concentrated on the second R, for which it supplied itself specially with paper, pens, and ink—luxuries then not always found in the run of lower schools. Occasionally the writing school also dealt with numbers and, to suit individual need and taste, with reading. But until late in the century the demand for such schools was slight, and hence their number remained comparatively small.

With the motherland and the other colonies, the Bible State shared a high confidence in the importance of training its young to become self-supporting workers, thereby not only fulfilling the duties imposed upon it by Calvin's God but also replenishing the land with fresh and qualified hands and by the same touch, reducing the number of jobless poor. To such ends the Puritans employed the systems of apprenticeship, a favorite in Europe since the Middle Ages, but refined and improved as the world grew older and somewhat wiser. Under the apprentice scheme a child —unless fortune had presented him with a wise and well-fixed father— was bound out for seven years or so to a master, who for a fee undertook to teach him the knacks and secrets of his trade or craft. Much more than an instructor, the master draped himself in the paternal toga, feeding and housing his ward besides keeping him in decent and sanitary raiment. For his part, the apprentice was expected to grant his master a filial obedience, applying himself diligently not only to learning but also to rendering his superior whatever reasonable services he commanded. Should the youngster ever fall short of his part of the bargain, the master had the right—nay, the duty—not only to reprimand him but also to lay on the corrective rod. Needless to say, in a theocracy where an understanding of the faith and its correlative morals besides a grasp of reading counted for so much, masters, like fathers, were put upon to ply their apprentices with the essential instruction. It is no more than right to note that in an age when the fair sex was universally discriminated against, in the domain of apprenticeship this was not the case. Like their brothers, girls were subject to apprenticeship, but unlike the lordly male, they usually served a shorter time, not in any case beyond their eighteenth birthday, when, presumably, they were old enough and smart enough to snare a good provider.

9   As the years ambled on, it began to be noticed that some masters were prehensile men, more eager to squeeze their underlings than to instruct them. In sad truth, even some fathers, it appeared, were growing lax in schooling their children. Finally, in 1642, to make an end of such untowardness the commonwealth ordered the town's selectmen to conduct regular inspections, either in the home or in the workshop, to ascertain whether the younger generation was effectively versed in reading, the tenets of Puritanism, and the principal laws of the colony. Whenever such a roundup revealed a child's attainments to be under par or when parents and masters refused to submit to such investigations, they could be fined. Moreover, with the magistrate's assent, the selectmen could put out as apprentices the children of such persons—whether fathers or masters—as were deemed "not to be able and fit to employ or bring them up," which is to say, those incorrigible stiffnecks who refused to bow to the majesty of the law.

Enacted to deal with the "great neglect of many persons in training up their children in learning and labor which may be profitable to the commonwealth," the law of 1642 was a plain echo of the English Poor Law of 1601 and its forerunner of 1562, the Statute of Artificers. These, as has been said before, sought to ease the growing economic distress and, among other things, had put pauper children under apprenticeship. But, at bottom, the Massachusetts law was angling for bigger fish. Instead of aiming primarily at economic sanitation and establishing a form of child maintenance, the statute represented the Bible State's first stalwart effort to ensure the perpetuation of the faith through the education and

training of its young. In effect till 1648, when it was given some amendment, the law fathered similar measures in the rest of New England.
Connecticut, in fact, thought so well of it that it adopted it entirely, word
for word. Only Rhode Island, where state and church were separate, paid
it no heed.

Without plainly saying so, the law of 1642 laid down the principle
of compulsory education. But it did not establish schools, nor did it
require compulsory attendance at the learner's bench. Here and there,
as has been hinted, the performance of the school dame sufficed to meet
the law's requirement; elsewhere the town itself sometimes made provision
for some sort of schooling. Even so, there must have been some temporizing, for in 1647 the General Court took a more forceful stand by ordering
every town of fifty households to offer instruction in reading and writing,
it being, as the law gave warning, the "one chief project of the old deluder
Satan to keep men from a knowledge of the Scriptures." The measure
went on to require towns of 100 households (and booming towns they
were) to furnish instruction in Latin grammar so that youth might be
"fitted for the university." Although the act did not go so far as to summon forth a school, its net effect was pretty much the same. What the
law did call for was the appointment of "one . . . to teach . . . all such
children as shall resort to him." Lest there be some misunderstanding
or haggling over who was to square the bill, the law specifically stated
that the teacher's wages were to be paid either "by the parents or masters
or by the inhabitants in general." With some modification the ordinance
was kept in force for the rest of the century, and like its predecessor of
1642, it became the model for similar lawmaking elsewhere in New England, except, once more, in easygoing Rhode Island.

The "Old Deluder Satan Act," as the measure came to be called,
stirred up no tempest of applause. To the poorer settlers the law not only
seemed harsh, but also actually imposed a burden. In a frontier land
where labor was scarce, fathers needed their sons to lend a hand with
plow and ax, to build hen coops and cow barns, and for dozens of other
things. And what went for the male went also for the female, for like
their brothers, girls had to pitch in around the house, making beds, scour-
ing pots and pans, replacing wayward buttons, and so on and on without
ever an end. Subduing the ABCs and their academic comrades, most fathers
agreed was fair enough in principle, particularly if its end was to placate
the Lord; but in the common man's working world this meant that parents had to do double and even triple work, a prospect which set none
of them to howling with laughter. Where, for one reason or another,
a town was without a schoolmaster and parents had to bear the extra
burden of illuminating their own children, the law must have seemed mean
and cruel indeed. For all the theocracy's power to deal stiffly with those
who might flout its edicts, violations apparently were not uncommon. Not

only did magistrates have to dress down recalcitrant fathers and masters, but sometimes they had to deal out punishment to the towns themselves. But even when they raised their fines to heights never ventured before, and even though they turned on the full horsepower of their authority, the efforts of the theocrats ended in fatuity. To sidestep the law, townsmen resorted to all sorts of tricks and subterfuges—indeed, some of them, already suffused with Yankee shrewdness, were not long in figuring out that frequently it was cheaper to pay the fine, however high, than to hire a schoolmaster at what was then regarded as a fair and decent wage.

The law of 1647 has obtained diverse explanations and appraisements. Some have saluted it as testimony to the Puritan's ardor for learning. Others, taking a different tack, have contended that it was only a pious hope and that at best it was granted an imperfect obedience. Some have scented in the act something of almost apocalyptic importance—nothing less, in truth, than the "cornerstone of our American state school system" —while yet others view the whole business as an "effort to . . . impose the Puritan creed upon the first generation of native New Englanders." But in the case at bar direct evidence is, of course, as imponderable as it is scarce. For the moment, hence, the controversy might better be left to rhetoricians and metaphysicians and similar addicts of speculative science than to objective historians. The fact, however, that in the 1640s the commonwealth was a theocracy, unsparing in its moral and religious purpose and prodigious in its power, would scarcely make the Old Deluder Satan Law a fitting "cornerstone" for the American state school systems which came upon the scene in the nineteenth century under conditions vastly different from those which obtained in Calvin's sacerdotal Massachusetts. Unlike the Puritan church-state, the states which subsequently made up our republic dissociated themselves from ecclesiastic entanglement—indeed, not to have done so would have made them subject to challenge on constitutional grounds. Laic rather than religious, they conceived of primary education not as a stick to make Satan leap and tremble but rather as a means to snare ends which were usefully and sometimes even gratifyingly earthly.

Nevertheless, for all the meanings put upon it, the law was the first of its kind in the land. And for all the disapproval and artful dodging it produced, it was widely aped; in fact, in 1671 all New England, except infidel Rhode Island, possessed some form of compulsory education.

Was the law of 1647 dissimilarly executed from one town to another? Then it was also dissimilarly interpreted. Take, in illustration, the matter of girls. Some Main Street Blackstones argued that the word "children," as embedded in the law, could not, even by the widest stretch of juridic imagination, be made to include the female. Contrariwise, there were town fathers who brooked no such sophistry, and they issued unequivocal orders for their schoolmaster to deal out his knowledge to girls and boys alike.

But between this idealism and the general practice there yawned a wide gulf. And if the fair ones found it hard to storm the primary school, then the Latin grammar school was impregnable. Designed for future masters of a world wherein the male was clearly God's appointed cock of the walk, the grammar school reserved its boons solely for the short-pants elite. However, while towns were barring girls from the public schools, this is not saying that a young miss, worthy of her kinship to Mother Eve, was allowed to enjoy the bliss of ignorance. Through the efforts of her parents and sundry relatives and the aid of a sympathetic pastor here and a school dame there, many a lass was rescued from the dark and deep abyss of illiteracy to become, as the years traipsed by, an educated and virtuous Puritan. Yet, as everywhere else, it was not until the nineteenth of the centuries, when the world had advanced somewhat in its enlightenment, that girls were put on a fairly even footing with boys.

10   Did Calvin hold a grisly view of the life in store for nearly all of us after death? Then his view of man on earth was no less shuddering. From his introduction to this planet man has been a sinner, and though the baptismal sprinkling had washed away the stain left on him by Adam's original sin, at best he remained an incurable reprobate, doomed $9\frac{1}{2}$ times out of 10 to roast and sizzle in the stoves of Hell. And what held for the grown-up held also for the child. That the years of childhood possess a nature all their own, though hinted at by an occasional sage, was a view which if, thought of at all, was dismissed as an utter and palpable absurdity. To the Calvinist, as indeed to everyone else on this spinning ball, the child was but a vest-pocket edition of his elders, which is to say that he was eligible for Hell. But with Calvin the cards were heavily stacked, and the young child's chances for wings and a halo were almost zero. Though the gurgling tot, wriggling in his crib, might appear innocent enough to most of us, to God's singularly perfect eye the babe, stripped of his camouflage, appeared for what he was, namely, depraved, unregenerate, and damned. To Him, so the Puritan clergy labored to explain, the infant is as hateful as a viper, a rattlesnake, or at least an alligator. By their very nature, warned the erudite Cotton Mather, an expert in divine pathology, children are "of Death, of Hell, of Wrath."

With juvenile depravity of such epidemic proportions, there was obvious work to be done. Though Puritans loved their progeny no less than the Lutherans and Anglicans—and maybe even Catholics—loved their own, still, to raise infants from their subhuman order it was necessary not only to protect them always and everywhere with salvos of thou-shalts and thou-shalt-nots but also to drum their sterns with frequency. Early in his life—the earlier the better—the child was given acquaintance with

Holy Writ, with its charms and promises, but more especially with its caveats and taboos. Once he had mastered the trick of reading, he was under orders to head through the Holy Book, and not merely once and at random, but from start to finish, over and over again until the day when he himself came to his end.

At first the Biblical message issued to him from the lips of his parents and, of course, his parson. Then, when he was of sufficient age and prowess, he was made privy to his letters. Commonly he encountered them for the first time in the so-called "hornbook." An old acquaintance to the English, it had come to use during the fifteenth century, but it was not until the Reformation in the century following that its employment became more or less the rule, not only in England but also in the lands across the Channel.

For all its name, the hornbook was not a book at all, but a board shaped somewhat like the paddle used in certain tribal rites celebrated by the Greek-lettered lodges which continue to enrich American life on the college campus. As is common enough with other things, people of wealth and tone sometimes employed hornbooks which let the world know of their ability to enjoy the smart things of life, backing them with leather, handsomely tooled, and sometimes even spangled with jewels. But whether a hornbook was, so to say, a Rolls-Royce or a Ford, its essence was in every case the same. On the board was a paper sheet whereon were printed the ABCs in small and capital letters and a short syllabic procession from ab, eb, ib to di, do, du, whereupon, fitttingly enough, came the benediction. On the more pious boards this was reinforced with the Lord's Prayer. Sometimes, however, as a sort of disturbing afterclap, the Our Father was supplemented with some of the numbers which in ancient times had badgered and baffled the Roman schoolboy. To safeguard the precious paper from youth's sullied paws, our ancestors hit upon the idea of covering the printed sheet with a thin strip of pellucid horn, as transparent as our present-day plastic; hence the name "hornbook."

In the schoolroom, as in the home, the Bible naturally took precedence over every other work, whether sacred or profane. But other writings soon rose up to buttress the inspired word. One of the first was John Cotton's *Spiritual Milk for Babes Drawn out of the Breasts of Both Testaments*, published in London in 1646 and reprinted in America some years later under the title *Spiritual Milk for American Babes*. But milk or no milk, and whether for Americans or aliens, for babes it must have been a powerful brew, compounded as it was with discourses on the Trinity, original sin, God's wrath, the Last Judgment, and the ministry of the law.

The most popular schoolbook, by enormous odds, was the *New England Primer*, a literary peewee of less than ninety pages, incarcerated between paper covers some 3 inches wide and 4 inches long. First heard of in 1690, it continued to rumble from the presses to reach its apogee in the eighteenth century, though Bostonians were still resorting to its light and learning as late as 1806. It was required reading in church and school, and no Puritan home, however scrimped, was long without it. America's first best-seller—not counting the Good Book, of course—it spawned some three million copies before it was finally laid to rest.

Though the *Primer* was naturally most appreciated in New England, where the faithful spoke of it reverently as the Little Bible of New England, embodied in such incarnations as the *New York Primer*, the *Columbian Primer*, and even the *American Primer*, it drove a lively trade in other latitudes, even in such Gomorrahs as New York and Philadelphia. Like similar books abroad, the *Primer* merchanted reading and religion, in prose and poesy. Good children, it counseled, should

> *Fear God all Day,*
> *Parents obey,*
> *No false Thing say,*
> *By no Sin stray,*
> *Love Christ alway,*
> *In Secret pray,*
> *Mind little Play,*
> *Make no Delay*
> *In doing Good.*

Here is another of its apologues:

> *I in the Burying Place may see*
> *Graves shorter there than I;*
> *From Death's Arrest no Age is free,*
> *   Young Children too may die;*
> *My God, may such an awful sight*
> *Awakening be to me!*
> *Oh! that by early Grace I might*
> *For Death prepared be.*

As the years dallied by, the Primer's contents underwent some overhauling and retouching. But from first to last it featured the alphabet from A to Z. It taught that

> *In Adam's fall*
> *We sinned all*

and that

> *Young Obadias*
> *David, Josias*
> *All were pious*

And finally,

> *Zaccheus he*
> *Did climb the tree*
> *His Lord to see.*

The first *New England Primer* bedecked its pages with pictures of Adam and Eve, without even a blush to clothe them, standing alongside the most costly tree in human annals, in addition to shots of various delegates from the zoological world, from cocks, cuckoos, and crocodiles to "the butterfly in gaudy dress," all of them pictorial banquets for famished childish eyes, the first time, indeed, that there had been pictures in schoolbooks since 1658, when the Czech Comenius (born Komensky) employed them in his Latin text. As was only meet, the first *Primer* displayed a full-page etching of Britain's reigning sovereign. But as the Revolution loomed, and kings and their commissars became suspect, the picture of General Washington elbowed out the likeness of the royal George. Such political reflections, however, were of a minor key. Towering over everything else was the effort to implant the true religion.

Second alone to the *Primer* was *The Day of Doom, or a Poetical Description of the Great and Last Judgment. With a Short Discourse about Eternity,* published in 1662. Its author was Michael Wigglesworth, at twenty a Harvard alumnus and the first native Dante to step from its groves, but for most of his earthly span a practicing preacher at Malden. Cast into 224 eight-line stanzas, *The Day of Doom* reports on what goes on in Heaven on that fateful Last Day. From its opening close-ups of the celestial scene, with the trumpet blasts summoning sinners before the Judge to hear His Honor's pronouncement of sentence on the eternally damned, Wigglesworth's lay is representative of the official theology of his time and place, as dirge-breathing and as ghastly. Although its employment in the schoolroom was probably extracurricular—collateral reading, as it were—its hair-raising strophes were highly endorsed on all sides, and especially by the ordained divines and pedagogues. For all its 1,700 lines, children were commonly urged to learn it by heart. Lest the little ones entertain some happy doubts about their own depravity, the Rev. Mr. Wigglesworth hastened to remind them that to the Lord Jehovah,

> *You sinners are, and such a share*
> *as sinners may expect;*
> *Such you shall have, for I do save*
> *none but mine own Elect.*

In consequence, they are condemned to an eternity of writhing in the brimstone bowl, but because of their youth they are put upon to suffer on one of its more quiet fronts.

Under the spell of the theocrats who had given it its start, education in Massachusetts flourished as nowhere else in early colonial America. It is true that the Bible Commonwealth enjoyed a set of advantages not given the other colonies, as, for example, one people, one language, one religion, and a small community, tightly wrought, within easy access of church, meetinghouse, and school. Under the circumstances communal action and control confronted no great problem. At the same time, let it not be forgotten that life in the wilderness was under the shadow of ever-present danger and that for all the dedication and devotion of the settlers, their battle for survival, not only of the flesh but of the faith as well, required an almost unbelievable will and courage and integrity. Despite its staggering difficulties, the colony saw the advent of the first English college in America, the first secondary school, and, very likely, the first publicly supported elementary school. The idea of compulsory education, though no longer a novelty in the seventeenth century, Massachusetts put into law. Literacy, as a consequence, was high in New England—higher, there is good reason to believe, than anywhere else in the Colonies. People of means, as usual, fared better in their education than the poor, but the poor of Massachusetts fared better than the poor in other parts, for they were at least required to know their letters. The fact is, however, that despite the great stress on education—nay, because of it—the people remained Puritans. All ideas hostile to the official theology, whether they fell from the pen or from the lips, were under prohibition, and persons who persisted in giving them utterance were banished, and sometimes they were treated even worse. It is a fact that book reading flourished and that certain book vendors made a good deal of money. But it is also a fact that what the people read and what occupied their serious thoughts was almost entirely religious and theological. Their men of God were of a quick and eager mind, and their salient ones must have been extraordinarily dowered. But their first and consuming concern was Puritanism, a stark and forbidding Calvinism, and for most of its believers a damnation that was inevitable and irreparable. Under the iron clerical hand, the free journeying of the mind was hazardous—indeed, it was impossible.

For all that, the Puritan prophets of perdition nurtured a love of books. The ideas residing therein may appear to many of us to have been futile, even preposterous—not to say barbaric. Even so, they were ideas. Thus the love of learning took hold, and though, as the colony succumbed to the lure and challenge of the world which bubbled all about, the interest in books wilted and even appeared dead, yet it was only dormant. Before another century it was to burst into the literary splendor of the Golden Age, with Hawthorne, Lowell, Thoreau, and Emily Dickinson to give it vigor and color. Another half century, and it blossomed anew in the Educational Revival, with James Gordon Carter, Horace Mann, and Henry Barnard to give it zest and meaning.

3
FROM PURITAN
TO YANKEE

Almost from the start the Bible State fell prey to forces which its leaders, strive as they would, could not curb. Stealthy at first, and insinuating, they became steadily more insistent until, as the seventeenth century edged toward its end, it was easy to see that for all the vigilance, resolution, and whipcracking of its theocrats, the commonwealth was not the well-kept garden of the Lord its makers had so prayerfully projected.

The high religious ardor which heated the colony's first settlers had cooled in the succeeding generations, and as it subsided, the stress on training for orthodoxy began to lose some of its fire. Also, wooed by the possibilities of a more sumptuous earthly life, more and more New Englanders began to give some earnest thought to the betterment of their material estate and condition. Not a few, contemplating the shabby and uncertain rewards they wrested from a recalcitrant soil, turned their backs to their plows and dung forks and resorted instead to some other occupation. They were for the most part small practitioners. But as men go, they were of a colossal industry, and some of them were also of a very resourceful kidney. True to Calvin's dictum that thrift and enterprise were somehow pleasing to the Heavenly Father, they worked hard and saved their money, and a few of them were presently in possession of a very handsome capital.

Thus arose the merchant-capitalist. He was, in full feather, a man of endless venture. His brigs and barks headed in all directions—northward to the Newfoundland banks to pack their dark and smelly holds with cod and herring and then across the long and hazardous ocean lane to the southern ports of Europe and to the island planters strung along the Caribbean. New England's excess products, especially its timber, its meat and livestock, and its grain, the merchant disposed of in the Indies, where, because of an overbearing sun, such things grew indifferently.

Yankee merchants drove a brisk business, trading their wares for sugar and molasses and other West Indian specialties or, not uncommonly, for bills of exchange, which served them as cash when they bargained for goods in the markets of the motherland. Their English purchases they hawked on the home front, or when their well-trained noses happened to sniff the seductive scent of profit, they did business with their fellow colonists to the south.

Though someday their children's children would revile slavery and labor powerfully to destroy it, New England's business nabobs of the eighteenth century suffered no such decency of the heart—as, indeed, no true lover of ducats then did anywhere else. Not even the reverend clergy showed an inclination to cry the practice down—in fact, a few of them owned a slave or so themselves. Year after year, slavers freighted their vessels with rum and set sail out of Boston Harbor or Newport or Salem for coastal Africa, where they exchanged their liquid gold for slaves, for which planters in the Indies and the colonial South were willing to part with a good deal of money. This in turn the slaver invested in more molasses, which by and by he would transform into rum, which in its turn would be made to fetch more slaves. In fairness, however, it should be said that the number of men engaged in such nefarious commerce was not large; even so, it included some of the colony's most elevated moral and social notables, as witness, for one, the liberty-loving Peter Faneuil.

For all their capacity for moneymaking, without ships New England's masters of commerce would have been badly crippled, like a man, so to say, without legs. As early as the colony's swaddling days the need for sturdy oceangoing craft, whether for catching fish or for hauling passengers or cargo, was obvious; in no time at all, hence, New Englanders were transforming the grand old monarchs of their ancient forests into the finest vessels then afloat. By the middle years of the eighteenth century the building of ships had matured into a robust and thriving concern. So well regarded were ships fashioned by New England hands that even in the mother country they entertained a high demand—in truth, on the eve of the Revolution, of every three of England's merchant vessels at least one had been launched and baptized in American waters. It was a fact which filled English shipwrights with dark fears and the Yankee countinghouse, in contrast, with a lush and gratifying revenue.

The vital sap of trade was rum. Rationed, not infrequently, to workers on land and sea, it constituted part of their wages, a tonic to their health and welfare. Wherever the trader put down his feet, on the Guinea coast or in Newfoundland, in the Indies or in the sister colonies, rum was nearly always a satisfactory medium of exchange. Rum paid for the fisherman's catch; rum bought the slave; and for rum the Indian yielded his pelts of fur. Though Satan himself urged its hearty use and his disciples were said to consume it rather heavily, even so, New Englanders were far from renouncing it. Not only did they employ rum in the marketplace, but they also resorted to it for friendly inspiration. The people's drink, especially among the large run of folk who had no purse for the finer wines and liquors, rum graced their great occasions. It launched newlyweds on their connubial course; it solaced mourners at the bier of the departed; and it celebrated even the ordination of a reverend man of God. Because of its vast and useful service, rum enjoyed a steady custom—so steady, indeed, that producing it in sufficient supply presently became a booming industry. In consequence, as year drifted after year, distilleries became a common sight. By the mid-eighteenth century there were at least a score in Newport and as many, doubtless, in Boston, but rum plants prospered also in the smaller towns, especially along the ocean front. In them men with an eye for quick and easy gain invested their extra cash; and from them rum flowed, even in hard times, like oil from a well.

2   Although trade and commerce continued to increase and expand, and even bade someday to become New England's reigning concern, this is not to say that farming was done for. On the contrary, for a long time it was to be the colonist's principal occupation. But the farmer's calling, forever troubled, found itself increasingly harassed—particularly when, as so often happened, his practice was small. Land, which once he could have had for a song, was getting hard to come by. Not only were the older settlements more densely populated, but all too often when ground therein was available, it was played out and unsuitable for gainful husbandry; or if it could still be coaxed to bring forth a decent harvest, then its price was usually out of the common reach. Willy-nilly, hence, seekers of land were forced to put down their stakes farther inland, where, as more and more installed themselves, they proceeded to propagate new settlements. Unhappily for them, their migration had been foreseen by speculators who, making ready to render them their service, had rounded up large tracts of land, buying it cheaply and holding it for ransom on some tomorrow, to the substantial benefit, needless to say, of their bank accounts.

Did the merchant-capitalist, specializing as a realtor, work his sorceries upon the common farmer? Then, turned moneylender, he also made his jump through hoops. Of an undernourished and stunted pocket, the hard-pressed farmer borrowed money to buy his land, to erect his house and sheds, and to people his domain with livestock. When seedtime came, he negotiated a loan, or he bought his supplies on credit. Such indebtedness weighed heavily upon him in foul weather or in fair. The one brought him crops too scrawny to pay for his cost and labor; the other buried him and his colleague farmers under a yield so flush that prices avalanched to the lower depths. Toil as he would, at year's end the farmer thus beset saw the bulk of his earnings drain off to his creditors. Thus shorn—and at times even stripped of his house and holdings— he came to regard the moneyed gentry somewhat suspiciously. Sometimes he even disliked them violently.

3   As the merchant increased his wealth, he also climbed in power and position. Palpably a somebody, he gratified his soul with all the glamor and glitter of his caste. His dwellings and their furnishings were the finest art and money could obtain, and so were his garments, and his food and drink. Royal governors and their courtly placemen may at times have snubbed him, but if they did, this neither dashed nor daunted him. Hardheaded, self-reliant, and individualistic—often cantankerously—he absorbed himself in the vigorous pursuit of his practical interests, and to such a purpose he was ready to adopt any workable device. Democracy for the most part left him cold, and he put no more stock in it than the Saints, whose dominies had long since convinced them that the Almighty himself was against it. But in order to get what he wanted, the merchant needed a say in making the laws which governed him—a right the Bible Commonwealth had conferred exclusively upon its church members, who, even at their very peak, never counted for more than a small minority. The passing years, it is true, had seen a slight relaxing of their stranglehold, but it was not until 1691—when the colony, bowing to the will of the Crown, put its governance under a new charter—that the oligarchy of Saints slipped away forever.

Under its new writ Massachusetts became a royal colony with a government something like that of the province of Virginia. Although the suffrage now ceased to be a monopoly of the sanctified, this is not saying that it was without strings. Only freeholders with a yearly income of no less than £40 or men having property worth at least £100 could vote for their agents and advocates in the colonial legislature.

Fortified with the suffrage, the merchant assigned his talents to politicking—an art, it soon turned out, wherein he was no less adept than in that of making money. In any case, when measures were needed to forward and safeguard his interests, he exerted his influence on his lawgivers without restraint, with the result that in important matters he was able nearly always to work his will. So his fortune rose higher and higher, and as it soared, trade and commerce took on the air of an august and flourishing institution.

Meanwhile the common people, though gagged when it came to voting for their colonial lawmakers, showed no willingness to let things stay as they were. They too felt the tug of worldly urges, and in their various sessions in their town halls or in their taverns, or even in their casual meetings about town, they were full of stir. Not only did they fume and spout over local issues, but they also voted thereon, and sometimes some of them snared a minor public office.

4   When Puritans dwelt in tiny villages, fenced off from the world at large, it was easy for them to believe that God had settled them in the wilderness to protect them from the contagions of a sinister and sinful world. So at all events their leaders let it be known, and so the first comers were persuaded. But as the years ticked on and Yankee vessels fanned out over the immeasurable sea, the colonists' early isolation, despite its heavenly inception, disintegrated and disappeared. Drumming up trade with his widespread clients, and dealing with them, whether from afar or face-to-face, the New England merchant got to know many of them familiarly. With some he even struck up a pleasant relationship, and when on occasion one of them chanced a journey to the trader's habitat, the man of affairs entertained him in a refined and becoming manner. Did certain Puritan divines lament such hobnobbing and warn against its risks? Then it did not take the merchant long to convince himself that such alarms were false and that his customers, taking one with another, were mostly men of merit who bought his goods, paid their bills, and made his heart leap with yet more orders. There followed an understandable tempering of his prejudices—even, indeed, an alteration of his religious premises. In 1654, to illustrate, Boston merchants, in the clutch of their new enlightenment, made public appeal for an end of the law against Anabaptists, which is to say those who were antagonistic to infant baptism. At the same time, some men of commerce showed a disposition toward loosening the vise which clamped state and church together and which provided the theocracy its surety and power. Time, in fact, saw some of them even amend their belief in Hell.

But it would be a mistake to assume that such thinking constituted the only rift in the Puritan Zion. There was as well the subtle yet irrepressible prod of Europe's eighteenth-century intellectual revolution, the so-called "Enlightment," with its deep and vital concern in worldly matters, its jaunty skepticism, its rationalism, and above all its insistence on a scientific examination of the natural and physical worlds. There was in addition the commonwealth's political unfoldment, not only in questions fevering the province and the towns, but in the larger issues involving the colony and the royal government—issues which grew more and more intense and which in one way or another drew in all the people, whether of high degree or low. Finally, there was the decline of the agricultural village, and with it the movement of men and women beyond the old frontier. All these forces, whether solitary or in congress, worked upon the colony's culture, turning it as time drove on from one which was solidly and implacably Puritan into one which was not only different but, in some respects, even its antithesis. "Truly," sorrowed Samuel Torrey, a consecrated man, "the very heart of New England is changed, and exceedingly corrupted with the sins of the times."

5   As the theocrats lost their political grip, the sway of religion and theology over the colony's thought and discourse weakened. The learned pastors, it is true, continued to immerse the land with outpourings about sin and perdition, but their melancholy manifestoes were given a lesser ear. More and more, men were turning their minds to laic writings, especially such as savored of the pungency of the world in which they lived, works seasoned with the problems of government, politics, and economics and with trade and commerce. To keep them apprised and up to date, John Campbell, who presided over the Boston post office besides a modest bookshop, presented his fellow townsmen with their first newspaper, the *News-Letter*, the second journal to be ventured on this side of the Atlantic. Launched in 1704, it steered a restrained and

wary course, confining its reporting to happenings overseas, customs clearings, death notices, and similar safe and sedate matters. As a result, it suffered no collision with the censor and was able to dispense its tidings until Bunker Hill and Lexington made its inspiration obsolete.

Less discreet than the *News-Letter* was the *New England Courant,* started in 1721 by James Franklin and his brother Benjamin, an apprentice then and only sixteen, but already full of journalistic juices. At odds with the high-flown conservatives then in eminence in church and state, James undertook to lambaste them, frothing his columns in their behalf with satire and lampoonery. The paper's lustiness and its added tang of forbidden fruit proved unfailingly tempting, and its issues, hence, were in high demand. Unluckily, sometimes its editor allowed himself an utterance too free and saucy, whereupon the outraged targets of his derring-do had him silenced or even stored in jail. On such painful occasions the younger Benjamin tended shop, getting out the *Courant* much in the vein of the furloughed James, but with an infinitely greater talent for abstaining from trouble.

For their more substantial brain food, readers relied, of course, not on the press but on books. Far on in the seventeenth century, Boston counted at least a score of booksellers. Most of them carried on an energetic commerce—in fact, by 1724 their number had augmented so much that they decided to join hands in support of their mutual interests in a sort of merchants' guild. As a sideline to their daily endeavor of book selling, some of the more enterprising dealers also rented out their most requested stock—for a modest fee, of course—thereby not only enriching themselves but spreading knowledge and culture as well. Boston soon became the hub of the colonial book business, with the result that some of its citizens were thoroughly well read. Such a votary of the printed word was Samuel Adams. An inveterate devourer of ideas, he made his way through the works of such masterminds as Hobbes and Hume and Locke besides Rousseau and Montesquieu—and so, more or less, did the other Adams, his cousin, the illustrious John.

Nor were books on science marking time. Their patronage, to be sure, was on a lesser scale, but they were being read just the same. Let your eyes amble over some of the book lists of the day, and you will behold the flower of Europe's scientific revelation, from the cerebrations of Copernicus and Kepler to those of Newton, Boyle, Gilbert, Descartes, and several others. Such erudite studies, needless to add, were for the few, and then as now their presence in a bookcase may at times have been more for show than use. Nevertheless, they had their readers—indeed, even gentlemen of the sacred cloth, innocent of the irreparable damage such works someday would wreak upon their confidence in an invisible world, populated by witches and werewolves, had recourse to the more important scientific treatises. Ordained servants of the Lord not only pondered the new arcana but, on occasion, also made reference to them in their sermons for the light they shed on inscrutable Omnipotence. "I give thanks to thee," Cotton Mather confided to God, "for the benefits and improvements of the sciences, granted by thee unto these our later ages." Meanwhile, however, he labored full blast to keep the demons of the unseen world from executing their malicious shenanigans in Massachusetts.

6   The early Puritans, as has already been mentioned, put a great store in the power of education. Through its magic workings they aspired not only to implant their Calvinism in the young but also to give it firm and solid lodgment until the arrival of that awful day when the Lord Jehovah would assign them to their predestinate quarters in the post-mortem state. To such effect the Bible State ordered instruction in reading and writing and in the laws and postulates of religion and morality. For those of a mind to lay the foundation for service in church or state, there were the Latin grammar schools. For that handful, finally, with the cash and desire for yet more light, there was the college. So things stood during the Puritan heyday, or at all events as long as the common-wealth's leaders, civil and divine, were able to work their will. But once the secular tide began to wash over the old theocracy, and in time even sweep it away forever, the education which had served the fathers lost much of the reason for its being, and presently it began to undergo some modification. It is to these changes that we shall now direct our attention.

Massachusetts had scarcely been put under its new governance when, in 1692, its lawgivers in one vast juridic thrust sought to put into effect all the laws which had been in operation just before the colony's charter rattled its last. The Bostonian Justinians might as well have spared their pains, for His Majesty's Privy Council, which now had the last word in such matters, had no taste for the measure and dumped it forthwith onto the junk pile. From that day on compulsory education in the colony led a hard and onerous life. Done, for one, was the act of just fifty years preceding, the law of 1642, and its various revampings thereafter, which had declared not only for compulsory education but also for the mandatory apprenticing of youngsters whose parents persisted in letting them waste in ignorance. Henceforth, the only compulsory apprenticing which town fathers might enjoy was to confine itself to the progeny of the poor. As has already been said, children thus bound out were to be rehearsed in some trade or craft, besides the official piety and virtue, and, if they happened to be so lucky as to be boys, in literacy.

The plague which overran education in the commonwealth soon spread into the rest of New England. True, in 1690 Connecticut's General Court put its foot down on the inability of some of its striplings "to read

the holy word of God and the good laws of the Colony," when it directed
parents and masters "to cause their respective children and servants . . .
to be taught to read distinctly the English tongue." To make it clear
they were not fooling, the jurists provided severe penalties for indivi-
dualists who might take it into their heads to disregard the law. Sad to
say, the measure rang no rafters with applause, either from parents and
masters or from the intended beneficiaries of its boon and protection. As
more and more years went by, Connecticut's statesmen, discommoded
by the high density of the public's displeasure, proceeded to ease the
law's exactions. Unluckily, they thereby bored so many loopholes into the
measure that pretty soon being illiterate in Connecticut ceased in any
real sense to be a tort. What held so dismally for Connecticut held also
for New Hampshire, once a part of the Bible State, but since 1679 a colony
in its own right and glory.

There remains Rhode Island, a mere grain of earth as colonies go,
but inhabited by a free-spirited and highly nonconformist folk. In 1647,
for example, while Massachusetts was making history by seeking to slip
a bridle on that old deluder Satan, Rhode Island for its part gained
immortality when, the first among English-speaking people, it inscribed a
bill for freedom of worship into its ordinance. Not given to the theocratic
revelation, Rhode Island kept state and church in separate corners. In
consequence, in an age when religion was education's main reason for
being, Rhole Islanders were content to leave the matter to their various
congregations and localities, and the colony never adopted a general
statute for compulsory instruction.

7   Although for the rest of its colonial course Massachusetts abandoned its policy of compulsory education, this does not mean that its
leaders had suffered a change of mind or that their interest had flagged.
The Old Deluder Satan Law, its allusion to the Devil's racket deleted,
was reenacted in 1692. Like its earlier incarnation, the statute required
towns of fifty families to support instruction in reading and writing and,
additionally, in Latin in those up-and-coming civic centers of at least one
hundred households. Connecticut, as was then to be expected, conceived a
somewhat similar measure, and so did New Hampshire.

But, as everyone knows, what a law says is one thing, and the way
it is observed and carried out is another. True today, this was true even
in devout and disciplined New England. Did Massachusetts in 1692 direct
its towns to dispense light and knowledge to their young? And did the
colony arm its law with stringent penalties for the disobedient? Then,
no matter how you look at it, the measure was resisted, and from first
to last it was only defectively obeyed—some towns, in truth, paid it as
little heed as possible. To make an end of such nourishment of "ignorance

and irreligion," the commonwealth, in 1701, amended and stiffened its edict, but to no great effect. Dissidents persisted—in fact, so free and open was their challenge that in 1718 the legislature, its patience run out, raised its fines on scofflaw towns to heights never heard of before. Even so, the flouting and finagling failed to stop, and by one devious device or another town fathers managed to weasel out of the law's requirements. All in all, as the eighteenth century approached the Revolution, probably not more than half the towns were fulfilling their statutory obligation.

In New Hampshire and Connecticut the tale is pretty much the same. Both provinces ordered towns of a certain population to provide instruction, the smaller ones in the ABCs, and the larger ones in Latin as well. Both equipped their regulation with punitive teeth. And both, to their great sorrow and regret, saw their juridic effort diverted from its purpose.

8   The causes of New England's educational tailspin are not far to seek. Pull aside the drape, and you will see some of them at work even in an earlier day, when Calvin's commandos still swung a lusty stick. Neither the law of 1642 nor the reinforcement given it five years later, it may be remembered, had happy sailing. Grunts greeted the Old Deluder Satan Act from the start, and despite the relentless efforts of the colony's lawful superiors, various towns continued to exercise their ingenuity in sidestepping their public duty.

If the theocrats found it difficult to put down opposition to compulsory education, then their eighteenth-century successors labored under an even heavier burden. Not only was the era more worldly in its tone, but it was also more liberal and a shade more tolerant. In any case, the Baptists and Episcopalians and other fosterers of faith at large in the once solidly Calvinistic stronghold, the prospect of perpetuating an undefiled and triumphant Puritanism descended into a hapless futility. With its passing, the spark which had enlivened the Puritan's zeal to teach the young began to waver, and here and there it even threatened to go out completely. Needless to say, in such a baleful world getting townsmen to part with their money to support instruction in even the barest elementals became harder and harder.

When the colony was still young, it could always count on its preachers to rally a lagging cause. Not a few of the reverend fathers were lettered men from Oxford and Cambridge; some were also of an astute and nimble mind; and all worked fervently to cultivate literacy and piety in the rising generation. Alas, time eroded their ranks, and as the eighteenth century unfolded, the stock of high-grade pastors, able and eager to carry on for education to arrest its menacing decay, had dropped into short supply—so short that it was altogether insufficient for the business.

What did the town school even more hurt, and what finally laid it low, was something far more pressing. New England's first villages, as has been said, were minute and compact, their houses not far apart, strung along a single street, in the sight of church and meetinghouse and in the course of time, a school. With nearly everything, so to say, within doorstep range, walking was the rule, and everyone with feet engaged therein. Consequently, when it came to ordering their children to make tracks for school, fathers suffered no qualms. But to this simple setting the years brought change. A populace which originally had banded around its church and meetinghouse was now, by dint of various circumstances, beginning to spread out. As a result, keeping up the town school fell on troubled times. In the older days, when the school was within easy reach of everybody, there was no problem; but for children who now dwelt on the far side of distance, the journey became long and rigorous —in the wintertime, in truth, when the land lay stiff beneath ice and snow, it even occasioned something of a danger. Fathers, hence, had good reason to keep their children home—a judgment which for once reaped a unanimous filial support.

From such corrosive conditions emerged the so-called "moving school." In essence, this was simply a schoolmaster who, instead of displaying himself to his clients in the town school, would migrate from village to village, holding sessions several months in one, then proceeding to the next, thence to yet another, and so on, until he had exercised his solemn rite in the entire township. It was a beat which, before its course was done, might occupy him as long as three or four years. Need it be added that in a land whose folk regarded thrift as a virtue ordained in Heaven and who therefore were inclined to think twice before parting with a single farthing, the time such a touring maestro served in a community was in exact ratio to the amount of cash that community had paid into the township's treasury?

The moving school was bred from expediency and compromise. Resorted to with unhappy doubts, it soon fell foul of complaint, some of it very tart. Some knowledge, of course, it did bestow, but its offerings at best were skimpy, and their distribution was unfailingly unequal. By its operation the moving school favored the largest community, which because of its size deposited the largest levy in the town's tax chest and thereby obtained the schoolmaster's longest sojourn in service. On the other hand, the smallest community, which paid the smallest tax, had to get along with a mere leftover.

The hoots and howls which whirled up against the moving school, pumped up also, no doubt, by feelings of civic pride and honor, presently caused villages to demand the right to establish a school of their own. Thus was born the district school. By this scheme a township arranged itself into districts, each with its own school, taught and patrolled by its own master, and each kept going by the disbursement the district made to the town treasurer. Granted lawful status in Massachusetts after York-town, the district system quickly entrenched itself not only in the late theocracy and the adjacent states but also in latitudes extending far to its south, and even in some of the settlements sprouting in the trans-Allegheny plain.

It has become etiquette to festoon the district school as a democratic institution, a practice which may well be more sentimental than judicious. In the sense that the district school was summoned upon the scene by the voice of the people and that through the communal enterprise it afforded a measure of schooling to every child—in this sense it doubtless deserves a kindly applause. That it lasted so long, however, was due not so much to any democratic idealism as it was to its cheeseparing financing. The plain fact is the cost of keeping the district school was paltry, and even though the knowledge it expounded as a rule was spindly, what counted above all with the taxpayer was not its shabbiness but its cheapness. Later, in the nineteenth century's middle age, when Horace Mann and Henry Barnard grabbed their tomahawks to do battle for decent schools, it was the district school, now senile and hopelessly inadequate to its task, which received the full force of their assault.

9   Could the Rev. John Cotton have peered through some spectral spyglass into an early eighteenth-century schoolhouse, there would have been very little to startle his postmortem eye. What it caught, in fact, would have been pretty much what it caught a century or so earlier, when Parson Cotton was serving his time on earth. The school's repertoire still leaned heavily on learning's first two Rs. Here and there, to be sure, some arithmetic was also being ventured, but no genius had yet risen to mystify and alarm the young with history, geography, and the ABCs of science. For all the siren come-hither of a rising worldliness, the school was still, first and foremost, the workshop of the Lord. The *New England Primer*, come unto this vale in the late 1600s, was still spreading its gloom and wisdom, and though to the astral Cotton this booklet was a stranger, he would certainly have granted it approval—especially if, after leafing through it, he had come upon the "Spiritual Milk for American Babes," which had been siphoned directly from a theological concoction of his own.

Once the possibilities of the *Primer* had been exhausted, the pupil introduced himself to the Psalter and, of course, the Bible, which, like his elders before him, he was expected to read again and again from its first inspired syllable to its last. Such in the main was the range of the child's bookwork until the dying years of the seventeenth century, when spelling books arose to bring reinforcement in the struggle to inject knowledge into the young. No great shakes any of them, these books have long since passed into *limbus infantium* in the afterworld of literature. The first speller of any consequence, and the first serious challenge to the *Primer's* long-held monopoly, was *A New Guide to the English Tongue,* issued in 1740 from an English press. The work of Thomas Dilworth, an Englishman and a pedagogue of some repute, the *Guide* addressed itself not only to spelling but to all the linguistic flora and fauna, from accent, syllabification, and pronunciation to grammar and reading. Though composed in a laic key, the book was not averse to touching up its language lessons with moral counsel—even with "prayers for different occasions." It was a loyalty to Omnipotence not readily overlooked, and when the work went into print, it carried the approval of "several clergymen and eminent schoolmasters"—all veiled in anonymity. The book reaped Dilworth a fine gratification. Statesmen saluted him; poets lauded him; and, best of all, schoolmen, whether in the motherland or in her colonies, or even in Ireland, employed his *Guide* in their everyday practice. As a result, it proceeded through edition after edition, some forty in slightly more than forty years.

If Dilworth's days were sweetened by success, then the writers on arithmetic enjoyed no such felicity. They had been at the business in England as far back as 1542, when Recorde put together his *Arithmetic: or the Grounde Art.* The next century saw the coming of a few more such treatises, all engagingly titled, as witness Wingate's *Arithmetique Made Easie,* Ward's *Young Mathematician's Guide,* and Mather's *Young Man's Companion.* But despite such allure, none excited any wonder, and except for the fact that they were breaking ground in a hard and stony field and that some of them were destined to be pirated by American printshops, they scarcely deserve the right to clutter our memory.

The first schoolbook on numerical science which received more than a cursory nod in the Colonies was *The Schoolmaster's Assistant,* written in 1773 by the industrious Dilworth. Prefixed by "An Essay on the Education of Youth," which the author threw in "humbly . . . for the consideration of parents," the *Assistant* included everything then known to arithmeticians, from "whole numbers" and "vulgar fractions" to "duodecimals." In addition it sprinkled its pages with helpful problems of which not a few dealt with wines and a variety of spiritus frumenti. Dilworth's *Assistant* failed to generate the aurora borealis set off by his older study of the English tongue, but still it was a success, and until the early nineteenth century it remained the undisputed champion of the breed.

But there was teaching in the world before there were schoolbooks in it, and such for long years was the case of the third R. When the call for instruction in arithmetic scarcely existed, there was no great need for a text, and neither master nor pupil was pained by its absence. Even when a father insisted that his heir become acquainted with the ways of numbers, for all practical purposes the master's knowledge usually sufficed. Not uncommonly he had hoarded it in his notes—such is the craft's eternal way. Given form and a teachable coherence, their essence was set before Junior for him to copy and ponder and absorb. By this route he not only mastered reckoning's basic canon and operations but, in the process, also compiled a notebook of his own. It was to render him service longer than he knew—in fact, long after he had left the bench and his memory had dimmed and was in need of a quick and effective pick-me-up.

10 The grammar school held itself steadfast to its venerable way. The curious new world, with its boom of commerce and its beckon of science, had not ruffled it, and the path it trod had witnessed the fall of its classical footsteps for centuries in the mother country and over here, redisposed a bit from time to time, perhaps, but still the same procession. What the grammar school prized it had always sought: to instruct and edify youth "in humane letters and literature," which is an older way of saying "in the humanities and the ancient classics." The spotlight the school threw out continued, as in its nonage, to be Latin—seven years running it beamed on every boy until at length alma mater disgorged him, honorably, let us hope, and a diploma in his clutch.

But by the eighteenth century the confidence in its wisdom was running out, and its best years lay in its wake. Apart from a few salient exemplars, as at Boston, Cambridge, Dorchester, Roxbury, and a small handful of others, the grammar school as a general thing had sicklied. In fact, in some places the hearse had already carted it away. The new sovereigns of the marketplace granted the grammar school only a curt respect. Concededly, it was all right enough in its place, and for youths eyeing a career in law or divinity its instruction, doubtless, was necessary, and maybe even valuable. But for a young live wire going upgrade in the world of commerce, Latin and Greek and all other ancient cargo of the grammar school were mainly meaningless. What such a lad needed was a head packed with useful and practical knowledge—the kind which would enable him to cast accounts, to compose clear and powerful letters, and to be on easy terms with alien lands and waters (even if only in an atlas)—besides a current foreign language or two and maybe the rudiments of business law. For the reigning proponents of the grammar school, such learning was not learning at all, but a fraudful imitation thereof, and so they excoriated it fore and aft. But the odds were against them, and for all their indignant lament and dissent, the grammar school continued bit by bit to decline, to become, as time strode on, an unsceptered monarch among barbarians.

11 Meanwhile, a flourishing private schooling had leaped into flame. Nearly all its practitioners were strangers in the academic world, though a few had frequented the higher grove—indeed, in their midst there were even three who had carried the torch at Harvard but who, because of a sad weakness of character or because of crimes they had committed against the Holy Ghost, had tumbled from their high position. Leaning heavily on the doctrine of personal success, the private teachers stood ready to give instruction in whatever their clients wanted and were willing to pay for—to help them, as one of their masters put it, "to make an amiable figure in the world." The advertisements they ran in the Bostonian journals were gorged with their numerous offerings, from elemental numbers to the highest mathematical branches, and from physics to astronomy. There were offerings in surveying, fortification, and gunnery. For prospective captains of the ocean sea not a single thing necessary to their success was missing, from navigation to marine law—even "drawing as far as it is useful for a compleat Sea-Artist." For landlubbers of discriminating taste there were French and music and painting—in fact, there was even dancing, which only yesterday the theocrats had condemned as carnal, especially if it was executed to the tune of lascivious music and, even worse, by male and female together. Finally, let it be noted that even in those remote days there were Johnnys who stumbled over reading. For such poor wights Joseph Ward, of the English Grammar School at Boston, recommended his own secret wonder drug by which their deficiencies promised "to be perfected in a short Time. . . ."

Taking one with another, the private schools put themselves to a good deal of trouble to accommodate their trade. Not only did they supply instruction in what it wanted, but they also rendered their prodigious service day and night in winter's cold and summer's heat, twelve months around the yearly clock. Some of them lodged their students, bedding and boarding them besides training them to become successes. In the main the private establishments reserved their attractions for the strong sex, the weaker one then not being expected to know anything beyond the kitchen and the parlor and, of course, the Good Book. A few bold adventurers, it is true, admitted girls as well as boys to their sessions, but such practice was a rarity, and the public sense of right and decency worked powerfully against it. But the fair ones, as is their immemorial wont, took delight in having the last word. If the male sages were bent on banning girls from the presence of boys in the pursuit of self-improvement, then their sisters could be just as uppish by opening private seminaries of their own. Here, haloed in their gleaming tresses, they applied themselves to the usual academic subjects, besides perfecting themselves in the arts of dance and tone, needlecraft, and painting. And if their girlish daintiness denied them access to navigation, or even gunnery, fortification, and similar warlike enterprise, then they more than made up for it by exploring the peaceful possibilities of millinery and hairdressing.

All in all the colonial private school did Americans a good service.

To be sure, to be eligible for all its boons and perquisites, whether real or fancied, its beneficiaries had to put down their cash on the barrelhead, so many shekels per course or lesson as the case required—a practice which, though considerably damaged by the inroads of public education, is nevertheless still going strong. Time saw the stress on the pursuit of knowledge which was helpful to one's everyday living gather power and momentum, to become the substance of the so-called "academy." The first secondary school to respond to the American's pragmatic appetite, the academy, as we shall see in later pages, was in essence a private shrine directing its attention to the offspring of the well-placed *bourgeoisie*. But until the early nineteenth century, when democracy, with its free and public high school, unhorsed it, the academy prevailed.

12   Except possibly for the addition of arithmetic, what the common boy living in the eighteenth century was put upon to learn was pretty much what his father's grandfather had had to grapple with the century before. Not only had novelty eluded the primary school's larder of learning, but the fashion in which its stock was dispensed had remained unchanged, and so had the scene of the academic performance. There was, of course, no palace of learning in those faulty times, no gorgeous network of corridors and chambers, no labs and gyms, or any of the other appointments that constitute a high-class modern school. Instead, a solitary room sufficed, a stark assemblage of board, drab and drafty, its physical equipment neither pleasant to the spirit nor much in anybody's way, stripped, it almost seems, to war footing. The learners varied in years as they did in height and heft, and they ranged from tender debutants to hardened veterans in their nascent teens. They sat uncomfortably on roughhewn benches, long slabs of quadrupedal oak or maple, worn and patinaed by countless bottoms, and carved and whorled by generations of nameless da Vincis. Before them loomed the master, walled in behind his desk, high and pulpitlike, with a well of ink, a quill or two to give it tone, and a switch, frowning and ever ready, to testify to his authority.

It was not an atmosphere in which minds burgeoned with agreeable reflections. Nor was it meant to be. For as the world then understood the learning process, it was believed to function best when it was belabored with difficulties—even antagonisms. Those whose sad fate it was to be impounded in the schoolroom—some forty, more or less—were under orders to keep quiet and do their work. Not fused into a working entity, they never performed in concert; instead, each settled down to his own appointed task, this one to the ABCs, that one to spelling, another to the catechism, and yet another to something else. The class recitation, so highly favored in the century following, had not yet been vouchsafed to pedagogical science. In its absence, the master operated on his charges one by one. When the teacher issued his call, the pupil two-stepped slowly toward the presence, and after disposing dutifully of a nod—"making one's manners" it was called—he submitted to a gush of questioning. If what he had learned hung well in the memory, he was set upon his next task. But if he fell into error or silence, he was not only roasted but also fanned. And though his psyche suffered and his backside smarted, he was expected to accept his mauling graciously and never again allow his scholarship to lapse.

For such uncomplicated practice the professional requirements, needless to say, were simple. Generally a birchman's head was not weighted heavily with knowledge—much more useful to the effective execution of his craft was a muscle of steel and a voice of brass. At all times, of course, he was to be free of taint, which is to say a man of virtue who eschewed all heretical thought and conduct. To make sure their man filled their bill, the guardians of the public weal—the town's practicing parson, that is, and the selectmen—delved closely into his mind and habit. If he passed muster, he was given approval and a certificate signed and delivered by the pastoral hand. There remained the matter of his duties and other usufructs which might drop his way. Not regulated by law, his pay became subject to the process of hand-to-hand bargaining between the teacher and his hirers, a contest wherein the former was generally bested, so that the rewards of his office were rarely more than modest. Tenure was then unheard of, the science of social justice not having reached its current state of perfection. Still, if the master steered clear of all seduction, his job was reasonably secure. Usually his appointment ran for six months or so, whereupon he put away his books and birches to devote his surcease from intellectual cares to earning his keep in some less exigent calling, say, as a cow tender or plowman, or even a keg washer. Later, when school reopened, the business of bargaining resumed, if not in the same locale, then somewhere else; or, as often as not, the master, having found an occupation less menacing to his blood pressure, liberated himself from teaching for good.

Masters in the grammar school were usually men of a better cut. They were at least the familiars of Latin, and some of them knew their way in Greek. Some had burned the lamp at Yale or Harvard, and not a few had taken holy orders. As a class they were well esteemed, and their life was generally sweeter and happier than that of their brothers puffing and chugging in the primary school. Though some had wandered into pedagogy merely to tide them over until a pulpit came their way, once in the teaching craft, many of them inclined to stay. Some not only stayed but, year after year, performed their feats in the same school. Samuel Savil, for example, was a twenty-year man at Braintree, while John Rogers and Silas Tupper each piled up twenty-five years at Sandwich. But the longest service of all—the longest, indeed, known in colonial annals—

must be credited to Ezekiel Cheever. All in all his practice stretched over seventy years, beginning at New Haven, proceeding to Ipswitch, thence to Charlestown, and hauling up at the Boston Latin School, where Cheever, forgetting time, played Socrates for thirty-eight years until he was ninety-two, when death stopped him.

13   If, under the stress of the lively hopes and aspirations of an emerging merchant world, the ancient grammar school fell from favor, then on the other hand the college, rolling with the secular current, presently found itself surging in new directions. The troubles which had plagued Harvard in the late 1600s had almost ceased, and though other bogeys threatened, the promise of brighter tomorrows was plainly discernible. The Treaty of Utrecht, signed in 1713, made an end of Europe's War of the Spanish Succession, an eleven-year hemorrhage which on this side of the water worked its calamity under the name of Queen Anne's War. The outbreak of peace—even if only for a pitiful moment—engendered a new prosperity, and under its spell Harvard boomed with a zest and vigor it had not enjoyed before.

By 1718 the number of its students, which not so long ago had thinned to a measly handful, had swollen into a horde of more than 120. To be inscribed in Harvard's roster, a student, like generations of his predecessors, had to demonstrate a ready competence in Latin, both oral and written, and at least a working knowledge of Greek. Harvard's recruits issued from many and various backgrounds. Some were blessed with wealth and comfort, and a few knew the bitter taste of poverty. The sons of merchants, bankers, clerics, lawyers, and now and then a farmer, they flocked to Cambridge not only from New England but from several other colonies as well, and even from the Indies and the motherland. Though their main enterprise presumably was study and they still engaged, as had their forebears, in a good deal of required daily praying, they were not averse to having fun. But young blood, as everyone knows, has a way of bubbling over, and sometimes student friskiness went too far, whereupon masters were obliged to mete out a restraining penalty. For venial indecencies, such as cutting the Sabbath worship, playing cards, making unseemly noises, or even harboring a pistol, there were fines; but for such outrages as blasphemy, robbery, and fornication the performer faced expulsion.

Though in her choice of presidents Harvard had occasionally boggled, fortune usually ran with her. So it had been when the college was still in its springtime, and so it continued in the years after the theocracy. In that era of mounting secularism two men stand out, John Leverett and Edward Holyoke. The one, a merchant's son, was trained in law; the other, staunch in his Calvinism, was, for all that, a liberal of dauntless resolution—"Guts" his students admiringly dubbed him. Both were honest and honorable men, and both, of course, were sons of Harvard. To Leverett, who manned the bridge from 1708 to 1724, goes the honor of putting Harvard's disorderly finances under rule and order. He procured the college's first endowed chair, the Hollis professorship of divinity. He had a hand in getting the college a bigger and better telescope, a magnificent instrument three times the length of its predecessor, which measured only 8 feet. Finally—and in the long run doubtless much more important—by refusing to knuckle under to powerful obscurantists, whether sacred or profane, Leverett planted the Harvard liberal tradition.

Holyoke, who labored in his high office from 1737 to 1769, had the good sense to nurse and strengthen this tradition. Despite the animosity of conservative pastors and other crepe-hanging critics, Holyoke managed to bring reform to Harvard's courses of study, which, scarcely altered after more than a century of use, had subsided into sterility. Under the president's progressive reign, antiquated texts, many of them of a hoary Aristotelian tinge, were ousted by works of newer sages, as, for example, Locke and Newton, to cite only two. Not content with heaving out a ruck of dubious and tired-to-death knowledge, Holyoke applied his corrective hand to Harvard's system of teaching, whereby an instructor taught every subject in the curriculum—a system which was old even before Harvard was born. Save only in English, which every faculty brother was expected to teach and comprehend, instructors now became specialists, this one trading in Latin, that one in Greek, another in philosophy, and still another in a variety of science. In its essence, it is, of course, an arrangement which for all the wear and tear of time still obtains in the higher learning.

Nowhere was the secular drift more strikingly on display than in the subjects students dwelt upon in their master's theses. Not a few, to be sure, still groped through spooky metaphysical fogs to tell us whether angels have matter and form, whether there is a hierarchy of rank among demons, or whether Adam, like the rest of us, sported an umbilical cord. But the passing years saw such pious quiddity fall from fashion to make room for such earthly and pressing questions as to whether civil government is absolutely necessary, whether blood actually circulates, or whether it is wrong to smuggle goods in order to withhold revenue from a king.

Did eighteenth-century Harvard shake the dust of Aristotle from its feet? Then at the same time it gave aid and encouragement to the more advanced and skeptical searchings of his challengers, the rising men of science. The college braved the plunge as early as 1712, when it engaged Thomas Robie to spread the light in mathematics and the natural sciences. This he did as well as he could for almost a dozen years, cluttering his chamber with mystifying machines besides teaching his students and busying himself between times with the study of alcalious salts, spider bites, and solar and lunar eclipses and other heavenly phenomena. In 1725, in recognition of Robie's sterling qualities, the Royal Society immortalized him as one of its brethren.

Robie's successor was his student, the talented Isaac Greenwood. He had sipped his learning at the Harvard spring, but when the source ran low, he shipped for London to perfect himself in the Newtonian science. Historians pay tribute to him as the first native American to succeed in assembling an arithmetic book, *Arithmetic: Vulgar and Decimal,* published at Boston in 1739, but aside from the singularity of its origin the work was of minor consequence. More important was Greenwood's elevation to the professorial purple, when, in 1728, the college planted him in its second endowed chair, the Hollis professorship of mathematics and natural philosophy.

There is no gainsaying Greenwood's hard industry—at all events in the early years of his academic portfolio. He applied his full diligence to fathoming the mystery of mine-damp and the aurora borealis. He proposed a study of the winds and the weather, especially as they bore on the variable temper of the sea. And like his illustrious teacher, he occupied himself with the sun, the moon, and the stars, and again like Robie, he embalmed his favorite observations in print, some of them even in the august *Philosophical Transactions* of the Royal Society. Unhappily, he found it necessary to stimulate his mind with the bottle, to the damage of his equations and the shame and scandal of the college. When his colleagues took him to task for his "dishonor to God," Greenwood was in tears to repent. Henceforth, he promised in an apology before faculty and students, in solemn inquest gathered, that given another chance, he would be impervious to the jug. Six months the college allowed him to expiate his sin. Alas, the poor man slipped again, and this time the Hollis chair in mathematics and natural philosophy announced a vacancy.

The man who took Greenwood's place was John Winthrop, the fourth John of that eminent family. Just three years over twenty when, in 1738, he was invited to install himself in the Hollis chair, Winthrop was a merchant's son, born and bred in the commonwealth, and educated at Harvard. For four decades he was to grace the Harvard faculty, a dowered and imaginative scholar and a salient scientist in the American grove. Honorary *legum doctor* by the University of Edinburgh, he was elected to the Royal Society, the first American teacher in actual practice to be thus celebrated. Twice he was offered the college presidency, which he did twice refuse. Annex to this the fact that Winthrop was also a teacher of surpassing excellence, and you have, in truth, an extraordinary man.

In an age when our scientific knowledge was still girdled by small frontiers, it was easy for a man to traverse the whole scientific domain. Thus Winthrop roved and explored. He was, some say, the first American to master Newton's *Principia* and to impart its substance to his students.

But it was the star-sprinkled infinity up yonder which took his fancy, and hence astronomy became his specialty. He put his glass on Mercury to observe its transit across the sun; he headed a posse of scientists to Nova Scotia to track the transit of Venus; and to him we credit the distinction of being the first in America to make scientific inspection of the spots on the sun. The familiar of electricity, he lectured to his learners on its mystery, and as the years wore on, he penetrated it far more deeply than Franklin, his friend and admirer. When, in 1755, on All Saints' Day the earth quaked at Lisbon at the very moment when its cathedrals thronged with the faithful, massacring them in shoals, Winthrop offered two lectures to explain earthquakes as natural phenomena rather than as the manifestations of an indignant Heavenly Father. He was rewarded for his effort with not a little abuse from the reverend clergy. Even so, he stuck manfully to his guns, and his feat has since been recorded in the scrolls as a victory for academic freedom in at least one dominion of knowledge.

But it was in the laboratory—his "apparatus chamber" he called it—where he was at home. Here, amidst a forest of ingenious and awesome paraphernalia, John Winthrop urged his apprentices to "question and prove," not only introducing them to knowledge but—more important—also investing at least a few of them with the principles of the scientific method which, disdaining knowledge by hearsay, accepted only that which plausible and impartial evidence had established.

4
SOUTHERN
LAISSEZ FAIRE

Save for Roman Catholics who migrated to Baron Baltimore's Maryland, the people who left England to settle along the seafront of the great Chesapeake Bay and the lands to its south were generally in agreement with their country's way of doing things. They were not, like the Puritans, a dissident and disgruntled minority, bent on establishing a holy land of Saints and Strangers. Nor were they, like the Quakers, seeking to bring forth a Heaven on earth, where all God's children, the lions and the lambs, might dwell together in peace and brotherly love. As a general thing, the Southerners were of a conservative cast, and in the main they gave their confidence and support to the English system, with its outlook on law and government, its social arrangements and public works, and especially its official Anglican Church. Their coming to America, hence, was not dominated by an itch for religious and moral uplift but rather by the more elemental and mercenary desire to better their personal condition.

Like the colonization of New England, that of the South was an act in the drama of national expansion. Here Britain conceived the idea of planting her flag as a counterweight to the Spaniard, entrenched in his Florida fastness since 1565 and rubbing his hands in anticipation of helping himself someday to the rest of North America. In the New World the motherland, like any other self-respecting land with an eye to power and greatness, sought the raw materials so desperately essential to her industrial well-being. Here she aspired to fill the nation's depleted economic bin with timber and its by-products of pitch and tar and resin, all indispensable to the continued prospering of her fleet, whether for the endeavors of war or peace. Here also she dreamed pleasantly of unearthing a vast store of iron and copper and, even more pleasantly, of discovering a still vaster store of silver and gold. Finally, in tune with the era's reigning economic fashion, in America the mother country wanted to settle colonies which would bring her a steady and comfortable revenue, promoting her interests at all times and devoting themselves dutifully to her continuous advancement.

The effort to realize this Eden was a substantial one. Directed by the London Company, and fueled and powered by the money of its stockholders, it propagated the first English colony in America when, in 1607, about a hundred men and boys put up their rough little huts at Jamestown. They had come in the midst of spring, when Virginia was aburst in all its greenery, fresh and fragrant, the air full of song and murmur, and springs so clear and trees so lush and large that they defied credulity. The land was rich with game and fowl, and the rivers crowded with fish, while on the watery bottom crabs and oysters jostled for *Lebensraum*. Yet behind this limitless expanse of grandeur there crouched dangers of an imposing and deadly sort. There were the Indians, for one, to whom the land belonged and who entertained no desire to give it away. There was a climate which, though of a seeming friendliness, to Anglo-Saxons could be treacherous. There were the ever-present vermin, the lice and fleas and ticks, and the most insidious troublemaker of them all, the malarial mosquito. Finally, there was the weakness of human character, the lust for power and gain, which, pitting man against man, brought discord and disunity to the settlement. Singly and together they worked their havoc upon the colony as the plagues of Yaweh did before the antibiotic millennium we now enjoy.

Yet for all the staggering handicaps, the colony was scarcely on its legs when pitch and tar and turpentine began to flow. As early as 1608 the first glass factory in colonial America made its debut, and soon after there followed an iron smeltery. But all this striving, dogged and painful though it was, was doomed. The truth is that the masterminds who, in the plush remoteness of their London offices, undertook to chart the economic path for the South knew very little about that region and even less about what it might profitably produce. Neither they nor all the gold of the London Company, nor even the redoubtable British will, could stand up to the South's climate and geography. It was these which in their inexorable way set the course for its economy and hence for its culture and also its education.

2   The die which settled Virginia's economic fate, rather curiously, was a weed, the Indian herb called tobacco, or in the botanist's Latin, *herba nicotianna*. No stranger to the English, it had been introduced to them as far back as the 1560s by Sir John Hawkins, that curious coalition of antithesis, a slave runner and a buccaneer, but also a patriot and in no small measure the father of the fleet which routed the Spanish Armada. Though at the time the government had put the weed under embargo, nonetheless, for a reasonable consideration French and Flemish seamen saw to it that the Englishman's needs were taken care of, and of an evening when the day's work was done, it was not uncommon to witness men and women—and even small children—smoking. They smoked their tobacco in long clay pipes, snuff not being vouchsafed to humanity until the more civilized days of Anne, and cigars some time later. They smoked not only for the pleasure and gratification the practice brought them but also because certain advanced medical thinkers recommended it as "excellent for rheums and other diseases of the lungs," as well as for its efficacy in purging "raw humors, obstructions, and other crudities out of the system."

In tobacco annals the year 1612 must be circled in a blazing red, for that was the year when John Rolfe, who subsequently made sure of his place in history by becoming the spouse of the beauteous Pocahontas, developed a new method of processing the herb. The result was a leaf far better than its Indian grandfather, more amiable to the paleface nose and throat and infinitely more delectable to his palate. So remarkable was its appeal that pretty soon smoking became the European rage. True, James I, a Scotsman and hence something of a moral scientist, denounced the practice as wicked and unchristian, "a filthy novelty whereby men's breaths are corrupted by a stinking smoke." Nevertheless, doctors continued to offer their testimonials in its behalf, and people puffed their pipes more avidly than ever—in fact, in some of England's shrines of genteel learning, schoolmasters were reported teaching their scholars "the fashionable way of bringing smoke through their nostrils."

The upshot was that the demand for tobacco soared to stratospheric heights. Presently, indeed, the plant was being grown in Virginia to the exclusion of almost everything else, and the cultivation of tobacco was well on its way to becoming the colony's primary occupation. In fact, starting out pianissimo in 1618 with an export crop of some 20,000 pounds, within a decade Virginia was disposing of a round ½ million pounds. By and by the fever crossed the Potomac into Maryland, and by the 1680s the two provinces were exporting an average 28 million pounds annually. As good as money—and as inconstant in its power to buy—tobacco became Virginia's cash equivalent.

As might be guessed, growing the weed on such a lavish scale gave rise to a number of unforseen developments. Despite the motherland's calculations, her Southern children comported themselves in a most unfilial manner. Instead of playing the part, as had been expected of them, of the kingdom's industrial steward and provisioning England with an ever-enlarging supply of raw materials, the Southerners, enchanted by the possibility of converting tobacco into handsome bank balances of their own, declared for an agrarian career. Some Southern parts put their time and effort into the cultivation of rice and indigo, and the years saw them blessed with a fine prosperity; but by and large it was tobacco which made the planter's blood dance in his veins. Not only did it give his purse an agreeable bulge, and hence that of the entire province, but by the same token the unparalleled scale of its production ricocheted economically and socially, bringing forth a culture which was unexpected and at utter variance with the plans so carefully laid at London.

A cousin to the common garden petunia, the nicotine plant grows with the same devil-may-care abandon of its kinsman—in Virginia, it poked up its head even in the streets. But the plant is also a gross and voracious feeder, and to grow it successfully year in and year out, one has to fortify the earth on which it lives with copious servings of nutritious manure or, in lieu of this, when the land becomes too starved and weary to support a profitable crop, to abandon it and plant afresh in virgin ground. The land's abundance naturally leaned the grower to the latter course, so that even the meanest planter found it advantageous to have at his disposal at least a few hundred acres. At the start the great plantations contained themselves within modest limits, and only a part of them was put under plow and harrow. But they were dispersed over a far-flung space, so that until on in the eighteenth century, with the blossoming of Charleston, Williamsburg, and Annapolis, a flourishing town life, such as existed in New England, was out of the question.

3   Tobacco growing and its attendant hunger for land was kept in check at first by the scarcity of help, for though the plant, true to its vulgar denomination, grows like a weed, to keep it in health and contentment required the hard and persistent industry of numerous hands. The hope had flickered for a time that those out of pocket and out of work, then swarming in England, might be dispatched to the Colonies. But the hazards of herding such a huge cargo over the treacherous sea and, even more, the forbidding cost of such a venture worked heavily against it. Hence, to fetch labor to the New World, a system of indenture was resorted to. It was a sort of "travel now pay later" scheme by which a colonist or one of his agents, say, a moneylender or a ship captain, would lay out the cash for the immigrant's passage, while the latter contracted to pay off his indebtedness not in so-and-so many easy installments but by his toil and sweat.

The bulk of such servants were laborers, but there were representatives from pretty nearly every craft then favored in Christendom, from cobblers, carpenters, and coopers to butchers, clothiers, millwrights, blacksmiths, and even staymakers—indeed, even schoolmasters. They entered practice wherever duty summoned them, not only in the Southern Colonies but in the others as well. Once his obligation had been discharged—usually the term of indenture ran about four years—the worker was scot free, and in a land of high wages and cheap land his road to fortune was wide open. From Virginia some of the liberated workers betook themselves to other regions, northward to Maryland and Pennsylvania, or they trekked farther inland toward the mountains. Some set themselves up as artisans, and some became tenant farmers. But not a few of them stuck to their moorings, where presently they advanced themselves into small landowners, a feat which, had it been effected in the old country, would almost certainly have suggested the handiwork of the dark and unspeakable powers.

The fact that such a miracle was actually possible gave an added zest to the lure of America. As a result, the number of people turning their heels to the Old World to start life over in the New climbed higher and higher. In 1671, to cite some figures, Virginia's Governor Berkeley estimated that there were some forty thousand head in his domain, of whom six thousand were indentured servants, and two thousand Negro slaves. Another dozen years, and Governor Culpepper took pride in letting it be known that the number of white servants, male and female, had doubled.

But even this steady stream could not quench the gigantic thirst for labor. As happens only too often where money is at stake, the American labor shortage presently began to spawn some sordid and degraded practices, such as bagging recruits for the Colonies by kidnapping the helpless and unwary, stealing children and selling them into bondage, and exporting some of England's foremost undesirables, its bankrupts, for example, its thugs, felons, harlots, and other fugitives from virtue. There was temptation and excuse aplenty for the latter course, though it did not solve the problem, for, as was soon found out, such folk were not the best of all possible workers—not a few of them, in fact, showed a powerful aversion to hard work. Though incoming ships kept on replenishing the labor supply, pestilence and death kept on hacking it down, and finally, of course, there was always the inevitable day when the bonded worker's servitude came to its appointed end and his master would have to look for a replacement.

The scarcity of cheap labor prompted a few planters to look longingly toward Negro slavery. But by the economic ground rules of that time, the black traffic happened to be a lawful monopoly of the Dutch, the Spanish, and the Portuguese, and save for the help of privateers and smugglers, obtaining Negro slaves in British America was next to impossible. Early in the eighteenth century, however, the outlander's grip was broken, and thenceforward the field for the slave trade was wide open.

The Negro's cheap labor favored the advent of the large plantation. Thus, where by the seventeenth century's middle years a farm's average size ranged from 400 to 500 acres, a generation later it had doubled, and during the century's last few years plantations running several thousand acres had ceased to be a novelty. Needless to say, on such an imperial space tobacco could be raised on a scale hitherto not even imaginable and, more important, with a very large profit. On the other hand, the small and free-lance planter soon found himself neck-deep in trouble, for the tobacco he had to grow and harvest and cure with his own backbreaking labor he also had to sell in competition with the product raised by slaves. Plainly, in such a contest the cards were marked, and as the years limped on, many a small farmer threw up his hands and gave up the struggle. Reduced to ruin, some of them hunted greener pastures to the north; others moved to the Carolinas where slavery was not so common; while others yet headed for the frontier. Meanwhile the rich grew richer.

Although the increase in slavery failed to liquidate the small planter, nevertheless, it bore heavily upon his social and economic position. By the eighteenth century the class structure had hardened considerably, and though it never became encrusted with caste upon caste, still, its fortunes lay under the powerful hand of a relatively small group of wealthy landowners.

4   As the South swept into a flourishing agrarianism, it hatched a society with marks that were distinctively its own. Hovering over it in the faraway distance were the titled but absentee landlords, great and glittering dignitaries like the Duke of Albermarle, the Earl of Clarendon, and Baron Baltimore. True to their ivied past, they had expected more or less to run their massive holdings on feudal lines. But such luminaries were a mere handful, and in a country glutted with land and starved for labor, they were soon obliged to adopt less antiquated aspirations.

More realistic were the merchants. Some were disposed to put their capital in the various colonial undertakings, letting it work its silent magic, while they disported themselves in the comparative ease and comfort of Mother England. Others, in hopes of a bigger and better achievement, not only put up their ducats, but even braved the ocean to settle here. Unlike their colleague merchants in New England, their sub-Potomac facsimiles took no pleasure in the boom and bustle of the marts of business. Instead, as soon as they were able many of them esconced themselves on elegant estates where, aping the English high and mighty, they assumed the airs and prerogatives of the landed gentry. Socially, they had a good opinion of themselves, and they inclined to take a lofty tone toward their lesser brethren, the smaller landowners and the artisans. Time saw some of these lordly gentlemen assume the name and manner of "cavaliers," while generation after generation of their descendants gloried in their legacy of blood and tradition, bogus though these were. In fact, it was not until the present iconoclastic century, when put under the searching glass of Thomas Jefferson Wertenbaker, at the time a Princeton don, that the cavalier myth was finally blown up.

Less pretentious than these altitudinous fellows, but eager and pushful, were the yeomen and artisans. Landed in America as free men, they practiced their various callings. By working hard and pinching their pennies, not a few of them managed to obtain a small piece of land, and until the competition of the wealthy slaveowner brought them hard times, they were making a successful thing of it.

Still lower on the human ladder were the indentured servants. A great many of them, as has been said, had been lured to America by its promise of its richer milk and sweeter honey, and once their servitude came to an end, they proceeded in one way or another to take advantage of their many chances. But to innumerable others fortune brought no such hope and happiness. Ignorant and poor, they continued to wear themselves out in a life of promiseless plodding until death released them from their wretchedness.

Finally, there were the slaves.

All in all, there was a great gulf socially between the wealthy planters and the masses, and, again, between the small farmers and the Negroes.

5   Like the Colonies to the north, the five Southern provinces were overwhelmingly Protestant—apart, of course, from Maryland in its younger Catholic days. By the eighteenth century all of them had established the Anglican Church. Yet this was due not to any absence of other sects, but to the fact that the reins of government lay in Anglican hands. So it was, for example, in South Carolina in 1704, the year that colony sanctioned the establishment of the Church of England. During the seventeenth century Virginia was the sole colony, not only in the South, but in the whole New World, where the overwhelming proportion of settlers worshipped according to the lights of the Anglican teaching.

Taking one with another, the Southern Anglicans did not, like the Puritans, absorb themselves to any extent in discussions of moral and divine science. Not given to Calvin's killjoy grimness, they relished larking and merrymaking for the pure delight of it, dancing and drinking, and carrying on far more openly than their compatriots in the Bible fastness. Even so, let the fact not be forgotten that they were no more tolerant of dissent than the Northerners, and like them, though less strenuously, they were at pains to make men good by force and law. With the Puritans they shared the vast credulity of their day, and they kept a keen lookout for the dark and malevolent powers that ride through the air. Their lives too were deranged and disturbed by witches, and now and again they found it necessary to put their sorceries under a hard brake. But whenever they took such a step, they were careful to try their witches in accordance with the settled principles of English law; and if they found the defendants guilty, as oftentimes they did, nearly always they were content to flog them or banish them rather than to butcher them.

Though it enjoyed support from the public purse and protection from the secular arm, the transplanted church never attained a hearty vigor. Once again implacable geography exacted its toll. In a land so sparsely settled, with its inhabitants scattered about like buckshot, the odds against a flourishing village church were astronomical. The pastors who manned the Southern parishes were saddled with a highly taxing office. Did they seek to preach the word, to baptize and give communion, to unite lovers, and to speed the soul departed? Or did they strive to teach the young, to catechize them, and to probe their knowledge of sin and rectitude? Then they could not, as per primordial custom, confine their essential efforts to church and parish house. Nor could they, like their sacredotal colleagues in New England, contain their flock within eye range of their constant vigil. To minister to all their spread-out faithful demanded a hard and endless effort and long journeying in the saddle through bog and thicket, with the added dangers of hostile beasts and snakes and insects, besides potshots from the lurking Indians—and all this for a paltry pay, and with only the barest prospects of advancement. Under the circumstances the Anglican cleric, on grounds both personal and professional, preferred to remain tucked in the comparative safety of the homeland, while the South continued for years to suffer a shortage of meritorious and competent divines. In fact, lamented Sir William Berkeley, of ministers, as of "all other commodities, the worst are sent us." They were, Governor Nicholson chimed in, "a pack of scandalous fellows."

Almost from the beginning the imported church developed traits which set it apart from the mother church. Differences crept into its organization and governance—in truth, they stole even into its liturgy. Save for Christmas and Good Friday, holy days were ignored. The short supply of professional men of God generated a herd of lay readers who recited sermons in the reverend pastor's stead. To the horror of Anglicans on the ocean's other side, Southern Anglicans frequently administered Holy Communion to unconfirmed Anglicans, which is to say half-Anglicans or worse, and they even went so far as to perform the matrimonial rite not at the holy altar of God but within the profane setting of a private home. Not even the dead were safe from malpractice, for distance and the region's infernal heat often made a man's last ride to the parish graveyard quite unthinkable; and so, for all the caveats of Anglican bishops abroad, frequently the departed was laid to rest in the unsanctified earth he had once helped to farm. Only the church's basic doctrine remained immaculate, and so did the venerable view that education, like the Twelve Apostles and the Holy Trinity, was the concern not of the state but of the church.

6   In education, again, one is at once reminded of the mother country. Thus, as the Englishman's outlook of life permeated his country's educational ideas and practices, so too it bore upon those of the South. Here, as over there, education was regarded as the business not of the state but of the person. It was, indeed, not the natural and unquestioned right of every child, but a privilege which marched with wealth and blood. Here, as over there, the cleavage between the favored classes and the human slag which constituted the lower ranks of life was recognized as the will of the Heavenly Father, and hence it was incontestable and even desirable. Here, as over there, the education of the well-heeled was entrusted to the care and custody of tutors and private schools, while that which fell to the multitude was left to kind hearts and charity. And, finally, since the state shied away from taking an active hand in the schooling of its children, a proportionately larger part was accepted by the church, though never in the bold and forceful manner of the Massachusetts Calvinists.

Although Southern education was styled along English lines, pretty soon the pressure of American conditions necessitated some alteration. True, in the American South, where the populace was swallowed up in a sea of space, a town school, or even a parish school, could have been little more than a mirage. Yet in a land where the servant and laboring classes counted for more than half the population, and where the meaner classes were increasing the number of their young so copiously as to alarm their betters, the government could ill afford to sit idly by. Hence as year chased after year, one colony after another engaged to provide some sort of apprentice training for the children of the servant class, the dependent poor, the orphaned and illegitimate, and the mulatto issue of white mothers.

The first step in this direction was taken in 1642, when Virginians instructed the colony's guardians and overseers of orphans to illuminate their wards "according to their best endeavors in the rudiments of learning. . . ." Twenty years later Marylanders followed suit, and on their heels came the Carolinians, and in their wake the Georgians. More in the tone of the English Poor Laws and the Statute of Artificers was Virginia's law of 1646, which declared "for the better educating of youth in honest and profitable trades and manufacturers as also to avoid sloth and idleness," a virtue with which, it seems, children of those imperfect times were "easily corrupted." Directed especially to the relief of "parents whose poverty extends not to give them [the children, that is] breeding," such endeavor was to "forward no less their own good and their parents' comfort," as it was to "improve the honor and the reputation of the country." In keeping, moreover, with the "laudable custom in the kingdom of England," the measure went on to order the establishment of a workhouse school at James City to which each county was to commit two children "of the age of seven at least, either male or female . . . to be in the public flaxhouses under such master and mistress as shall be there appointed, in carding, knitting, and spinning, etc." To facilitate the erection of such edifices the legislature voted the governor five tons of tobacco "to be paid him the next crop. . . ."

In the ensuing years this act was revised and amplified several times, and in various incarnations it showed itself not only in Virginia but in the other colonies as well. In 1668, to come to cases, Virginia's lawgivers put upon counties and parishes to establish workhouse schools like the one at James City, and for the same reasons. Somewhat in the vein of the Massachusetts law of 1642, it sanctioned taking "poor children from indigent parents to place them to work in those houses." In 1705 the Virginia lawmakers required the colony's boy apprentices to be given acquaintance with reading and writing. Not quite a half century later, in 1751, the same boon was granted to girls.

7   The Southerner's first venture into learning is dated a dozen years after the founding of Jamestown, when, in 1619, the Virginia Company reserved several thousand acres of land and the sum of £1,500 to found a university at Henrico, with a missionary branch for the "conversion of the infidels," which is saying the Indians. Shortly after, an altruist, whom chroniclers have been able to identify only as "Dust and Ashes," proffered £550 in order to bring light to the Indian in "the Christian religion and good manners." Not insensitive to the needs of his fellow whites, Dust and Ashes offered an additional £450 to make possible the schooling in England of "some of the male children of the Virginians." About the same time the philanthropic spirit invaded Patrick Copeland, a holy clerk in service aboard the "Royal James," when he undertook to gather funds from his marine parishioners to launch a free school in Virginia to the end of instructing and improving the young in the "principles of religion, civility, and humane learning."

Yet in spite of this idealism—or maybe because of it—nobody succeeded in translating it into actuality. As a matter of unhappy truth, at Henrico the Indians not only had no taste for Christianity and its good manners but even cherished an active dislike for Christians, and instead of allowing themselves to be made righteous and refined, in 1620 they exterminated almost the entire population of Henrico City. Some years later, when the Virginia Company sought to revive its plan for adorning Henrico with a higher intellectual seat, it suffered another shock when its money ran out and it lost its charter. But, as moral history tells us, time has a way of righting wrong, and subsequently Henrico won distinction far and about, not, it is true, for its bubbling fountains of learning, but for the virtuosity of its racehorses and the surpassing merit of its track.

All the while, however, the philanthropic idea persisted, and in 1634 it bore its first fruit. In that year a planter, Benjamin Syms (also known as Symes, and sometimes as Symms) bequeathed 200 acres of land and, better yet, the milk and offspring of eight able and industrious cows for the purpose of endowing a school which was to be free of access to children resident in the adjoining parishes of Kiquotan and Elizabeth City. Another generation, however, had to pass before Syms's constructive idealism could be matched. Then, in 1659, in the very same Elizabeth City, a similar school was brought upon the scene, this time by the legacy of Dr. Thomas Eaton, a man of tender heart but also of a full and flowing purse. Outgiving Syms by several hundred acres, the doctor further aided the cause of learning with a number of buildings, a couple of Negroes, a score of hogs, and a herd of two bulls and a dozen cows. Unluckily, the historical archives say almost nothing about these ventures, but there is reason to believe that they spread their benefits mainly before the sons of the favored orders, in whom they labored to plant a knowledge of the fundamental Rs, some Latin, and, of course, the principles and practices of the official faith and virtue. Though our knowledge of these schools is swathed in uncertainty, their progress seems to have been fair enough. At any rate, in 1649 the news went out that the Syms School was the possessor of a "fine house." Just how many scholars the school served and instructed at the time has eluded historical searchers, but its enrollment of horned cattle, we know, ran to no less than forty, mostly female. In 1805, fittingly enough, the two schools merged to become Hampton Academy. Another century or so, in 1902, and a portion of their endowment was transfused into the Syms-Eaton Academy, which, in turn, was later converted into the Syms-Eaton High School.

Needless to remark, Virginia had no corner on gentlemen of vision and goodwill. Nor were their gifts confined to real estate, which, even when it was of a princely heft, was scarcely cause for amazement in a country where land was seemingly boundless. Let the fact not be overlooked that South Carolinians were as easygoing with their cash as they were with land. Nor was their largess a patrician monopoly—indeed, more often than not the rich man's gift would be fattened by numerous donations from lesser folk. In those times as in these, there was no lack of organized public spirit, as witness the Bethesda Orphan House, near Savannah, Georgia, the oldest shelter for parentless young in the republic, the South Carolina Society, and the Winyaw Indigo Society. All these brotherhoods, and several others like them, directed some of their charitable traffic toward education though this is not saying that their members were unaware of the rewards to be obtained through their own self-improvement. Take, for example, the Winyaw brethren. At Georgetown, not only did they found a school which kept its flag on the pole till 1861, but they also convened once a month, on fair days, to hold parley on the successful growth of the indigo plant, besides bringing the glow of gladness to the gathered comrades with frequent ladlings from an ever-present and ever-refillable punch bowl.

The biggest and most widespread organization for educational good works was the Society for the Propagation of the Gospel in Foreign Parts, or, for the person who wastes no words, the SPG. Chartered in England in 1701, the society dispatched its missionaries overseas to bring, as it announced, "the surrounding heathen to the truth," or in plain translation, to instruct the Indian and the Negro "in the tenets and worship of the Church. . . ." To attain this goal its specialists introduced their scholars to the catechism and Psalter, their most useful prayers, besides the secular ABCs. The century saw these men work their skill and zeal

not only in the Colonies but wherever Anglicans were in number, in latitudes reaching as far north as Canada and as far south as the Caribbean.
In some places—notably in sin-ridden New York—they reaped a high
and even astounding success, but in the vast and forlorn stretches of the
wilderness South, they ran into difficulties that would have daunted even
the angels. Not only were they haltered and hampered by the unholy
alliance of the natural elements, but they also confronted obstacles imposed by man himself. In a region where the Established Church was
transparently weak and its clergymen often second-rate, realizing the
ambitions of the SPG was not easy. Not only did the gospel propagators
in North Carolina run into the heathenry of Indians and Africans, but
they had to contend also with Quakers and Presbyterians and similar
heretical folk. Headstrong and unregenerate, these people not only shut
their ears to the Anglican truth but went out of their way to make
converts for their own. It was, asseverated John Urmstone, one of the
SPG's evangelical professors, a "hell of a hole." Almost as bad was South
Carolina, whose juridic sages in 1740 outlawed the teaching of writing
to slaves. All in all, the society's industry in the South was comparatively
small—in fact, in Virginia it was almost zero. Yet for all that its achievement was not altogether negligible. True, the society's first concern was
to immunize the young against sin and error and thereby make them
understand their place in God's established order; nevertheless, the fact
remains that in so doing the SPG was able to snatch at least a few
from the clutch of total illiteracy.

8   Although communal life scarcely existed, common endeavor in
education was not lacking. Here and there planters would join one another
to nail together a one-room schoolhouse. Its site, very often, lay in a
field which only yesterday was bursting with tobacco but which now,
exhausted and abandoned, had gone to waste—hence the name *old field*
school. If, as sometimes came to pass, the teaching role befell a reverend
clerk, he exercised it usually at his fireside, in which case his seminary
was spoken of as the *parson's school.* To such retreats of learning children
traveled the long miles over rough and unsure country lanes, through
field and brush and woodland, past the reeded marshland, some afoot,
some on horse, and some by boat. They came, one may be sure, not
without reluctance to be stored for the best and fairest part of day in
a drab and dingy cubicle to bend over their catechism and ABCs. Now
and then some odd and gifted lad managed to get past these historic
rudiments, and occasionally he learned to wade in the shallow depths of
beginner's Latin. When parents had sufficient means, they sometimes
engaged a full-time and, if possible, competent master, but such Elysium,
of course, was not the rule. Generally instruction fell to unskilled hands,
and usually they labored for a meager reward, a pittance rendered them

in victuals or tobacco—sometimes, we are told, a teacher sweat and
suffered for no wages at all. The years, it is true, brought some betterment to his lot, but also a measure of regulation. Thus, just before the
end of the seventeenth century a birchmaster in regular practice was
expected to furnish some sort of proof of his fitness for office, whereupon, after paying the governor's clerk his accustomed honorarium of a
couple of pounds of tobacco, he was issued a license. But this requirement
was never rigorously carried out, and the quality of teaching, even when
gently judged, remained in large part of a lowly order.

Even so, the existence of such instruction, together with the better
sort found in some of the endowed schools, is not to be lightly dismissed.
Spare though it certainly was, it represented at least a brave attempt
at education, which, though mean and shabby under the glare of our
present-day standards, was still a brave attempt. And if Southern whites
grew to man's estate less innocent of the written word than was once
believed to have been the case, then their attainment, such as it was,
was due in no small degree to just such striving.

9   As in New England—indeed, as everywhere else and at all times—
the child of the wealthy was better serviced. But in the South, where
government ventured into education as little as possible, the disparity
between the schooling of those in the upper reaches of society and the
schooling of those in its lower stratum was far vaster than in Calvinistic
Massachusetts, where the warfare against Old Hornie and his cloven-
hoofed, flesh-forked minions ordained a knowledge of reading for every
child, regardless of where it had pleased God to station him in life.

For the Southerner of good fortune there were tutors, and as the
years edged away, he could avail himself of some pretty fair private
schools. Now and then a father might even dust off his old and battered
Latin grammar and summon his recollection of law and letters to impart
them to his heir. The distractions which assail us on every side today
—the seductions of radio, television, and the movies, the beguilement of
the press, whether grave or merely comic—were unknown to our less
civilized ancestors, as were the many other marvels by which progess
has enabled us to while away our mortal hours. For the Southern planter
there was little chance for leisure during most of the year, but when
it came, as it did during the winter's long siege, it swarmed upon him
like the Biblical locusts. Under the circumstances, it was not uncommon
for a grower to fill the caverns of his idle hours by supplementing his
knowledge of life and living with the wisdom of books. For a father to
play mentor to his son was thus not simply the discharge of paternal
love and duty. Often enough, one guesses, he did it to break the fetters
of his monotony.

As the years advanced, the family tutor became a household figure.

At first, of course, a hired pedagogue was a scarcity, and for a planter to lodge one beneath his roof was cause for no little envy. As the Colonies made their way through the eighteenth century, the demand for young men versed in the classical lore was fed not only by the groves of England but more and more by the adolescent colleges to the north. If their r's were not too burry and their provincialisms not too numerous, Scotsmen were in high favor, not only for their well-packed heads but also for their stern propriety. On occasion a tutor was of the holy calling, a newcomer in the sacred ranks or in the Colonies, who had entered into teaching only transiently while he awaited his summons from a pulpit. Sometimes, when no tutor was to be had—or, at all events, when none deemed worthy of such an important post could be found—the pastor took upon himself the tutorial burden. Not infrequently the tutor was mustered from the indentured servant ranks. However, because he was prized, especially when he happened to be an able and upright fellow, his life was generally agreeable. Oftentimes, in truth, he was granted privileges and immunities not usually allowed to practitioners of his humble art, such as being suffered to sit with his betters at their meals, assisting at their prayers and domestic councils, and joining the family to charm an occasional guest. Sometimes he even charmed a planter's daughter and walked her to the altar.

Now and then a planter's neighbors, or possibly his kinfolk, would consign their children to the tutor's charge. In such instances the young came to share the grower's home. When such a flock threatened to increase beyond house capacity, a special schoolhouse was sometimes erected to contain them. It was by such a route that the small private boarding school took shape.

As more and more years wore out, the number of private schools gradually augmented—in fact, by the eighteenth century about half of Virginia's parishes could boast of at least one or more. By the eighteenth century's middle age they had become profuse enough, apparently, to have to hustle for customers. In consequence, like their counterparts in New England, not a few of them let loose their fancy in public advertisements. Tailored, on the whole, after the English Rugbys and Etons, the best of them strove to emulate their venerable and sniffish manner. The young Southerner they introduced to the three Rs, the no less indispensable catechism and prayer book, and, needless to say, a polite and stately conduct. But the high goal, as ever, was the ancient classics, from Cicero to Virgil, and from Ovid to Xenophon.

In the South, as in the North, however, the challenge of the newer disciplines—the living languages, mathematics, and the sciences—was putting its pressure on the hoary Greek and Roman standbys. In Charleston, to cite an instance, the house of Mrs. Delaweare announced its readiness to teach not only every sort of mathematics, from low to high, but also such arcane subjects as dialing, astronomy, gauging, and—for good measure—fortification. At Chesterton, Maryland, Charles Peale, whose main claim to fame today is that he fathered the artist Charles Wilson Peale, offered the same curricular stock as la Delaweare, besides Latin and Greek and the art and science of fencing. In Williamsburg an early Johnnie Walker, less well known, doubtless, than his current alcoholic namesake, gave public notice of his willingness to bring young gentlemen to terms with reading, writing, and arithmetic, as well as the "most material branches of classical learning, and ancient and modern geography and history." As an added inducement, he promised parents that he would exert himself at all times to improve his clients' morals. Meanwhile, Master Walker's wife and helpmeet stood ready to teach young ladies all kinds of plain and fancy needlework, or if called on by some choosy patroness of art, she herself would be glad to assemble a very fetching piece of millinery. It did not take long for other lady entrepreneurs to grasp the importance of catering to the special cultural requirements of young and high-class ladies. For them, indeed, there was no want of opportunity to cultivate themselves, not only in needlecraft, but also in waxwork, watercolors, the art of tone and dance, and, as one schooldame let it be known, "several other embellishments necessary for the amusement of persons of fortune who have taste."

The tradition of such salons, as everyone knows, has lingered, not only in the sub-Potomac belt but throughout our incomparable democracy. Its current exemplars, the high-toned and decorous prep school and the finishing school for the fashionable fair ones, surrounded and overwhelmed though they are by the public school of the American masses, still rustle their proud but far from universal way.

A few of the wealthier gentlefolk, intent on the cream of the cultural cream, sent their sons—and in rare and extraordinary cases their daughters—to England. But such practice was far from general. Certainly a father's belief and trust in English culture must have been almost overmastering for him to have been willing to expose his offspring to the graveyard of the Atlantic. Once the child found himself safe on his legs in England, his parents' anxiety still smoldered, for in an era when child mortality lurked around every corner, the fear that he might succumb to some untamed pestilence, especially smallpox and diphtheria, cast a constant shadow on every home.

When it came to the higher learning, the situation was somewhat different. Not that the perils were considerably fewer, but a collegiate stripling, having begun to sprout hair upon his lip, constituted a somewhat lesser risk. The case was altered too by the absence—until the shank of the seventeenth century—of a college in the South. Even so, not many Southerners went to their books at Oxford or Cambridge, or to be converted into jurists at the Inner Temple or Inns of Court, both in London, or—if they chanced to be from the Roman side of the fence in Maryland—to take instruction in the Jesuit colleges in France.

10   The huge spread of land which cut off one planter from another put a severe burden on communal diversion, and especially on any lively interparlance of ideas. Not counting the stray occasions when they savored the pleasure of entertaining a houseguest or when they themselves adventured into the limitless world beyond their doorsill, growers were left pretty much to their own devices. Some amused and edified their spirit by planting beautiful gardens; others bred horses or raised gamecocks, or they puttered with bricks and mortar. Not a few prowled the fields and woodlands slaughtering unwary birds and animals. Those of a more reflective habit of mind resorted to reading. To this end they encircled themselves with books—their libraries, indeed, were sometimes superbly stocked, and a few of them even took on a substantial size, as witness those of Robert Carter, with a hoard of over a thousand volumes; John Mercer, with some fifteen hundred; and the younger William Byrd, with four thousand, from folios and quartos to duodecimos, all tastefully bound and worth a prodigious heap of tobacco in the public market.

In the early years of the seventeenth century works of piety dominated the shelves, with the ancient classics running next. As the years strung along and the appetite for sacred letters lost some of its edge, treatises of a higher practical value, especially in law, farming, or even medicine, revealed themselves more and more. But the century had long since ebbed before Southern taste began to cultivate some of the English literary masters. Once sampled, however, their writings worked themselves into acceptance, and by the middle of the eighteenth century the demand for them was steady—steady enough, at any rate, to prompt the opening of a couple of bookshops, one at Williamsburg and the other at Annapolis. Dig through their notices in the gazettes of their day, and you will unearth offerings of the newest arrivals from overseas, from the works of Smollett, Swift, and Shakespeare to *The Prince of Abyssinia, The Turkish Spy, Peregrine Pickle,*—and if you grub hard enough—*Tom Jones,* then as now considered by the pure as a gross and wanton work.

The advancement of knowledge is seldom easy; nevertheless, even in the Southern wilderness the obstacles were not insurmountable. Much of such enterprise, true enough, was mere pastime and of no ponderable value. But some of it was the work of men gifted with the essential qualities, and it was often carried on with fierce and unflagging industry. Such a man, in some degree, was John Tennent, a medical practitioner in eighteenth-century Virgina. He appears to have been very alert for new ways to advance his science. Did the Senecas, for example, make an adept use of rattlesnake root as a cure for snakebite? Then Tennent undertook to test its mysterious powers, not only against the viper's venom, but also against pleurisy, pneumonia, gout, malaria, and various other aches and ills man has been heir to ever since the fall of Adam. From his data Tennent put together *An Essay on the Pleurisy*, which appeared in print in 1736, the first contribution to materia medica to come out of Virginia. Two years afterward he delivered himself of an *Epistle to Dr. Richard Mead concerning the Epidemical Diseases of Virginia*, wherein he essayed to explain the "surprising efficacy of the Seneca rattlesnake root." To pursue his studies under full draft its author found it necessary to steal time from his regular practice—so much, unluckily, that presently it fell apart, and he ran into heavy debt. Though medical science has long since dismissed Tennent's boons to the human race as trash, in his own time his claims were gravely attended to. At all events, for informing the world about the wonders of the Seneca rattlesnake root, the General Assembly awarded Tennent £100, a handsome bonus, surely, for an essayist, and sufficient for awhile to rescue him from his creditors. Not to be overshadowed, at London the Royal Society emblazoned its membership roll with Tennent's name.

Far less given to chasing moonbeams, and infinitely more scholarly, was another Virginian, John Clayton, for fifty years an assiduous and respected clerk in Gloucester County. If posterity still holds him in honor, however, it is not for his endurance as a public servant, but for his talents as a botanist. So powerful was this man's passion for the world of plants, that from time to time he found it necessary to play hooky from his clerical cares in order to rove and inspect the countryside, braving pugnacious insects and perilous snakes and other desperadoes of the animal world to round up information on the Virginia flora. His trail during the many years traversed one county after another, from the rivered flatlands of his native Tidewater to the eastern rim of the Blue Ridge Mountains. Meanwhile, he kept in diligent touch with the world's foremost botanists, both foreign and domestic, sending them specimens of his findings, inquiring about the progress of their studies, and soliciting them hopefully for criticism of his own.

Time saw his research culminate in print between covers of *Flora Virginica*. Issued in its first edition at Leyden in 1739 from the pen of his Dutch admirer and fellow savant, John Frederick Gronovius, and with the helping hand of the celebrated Linnaeus, the study was a thoroughly excellent piece of work. Not only did it bring Clayton a prompt and pleasant acclaim, but it also fetched him an election to the Royal Academy of Sciences of Stockholm. In 1773, when the Virginian Society for the Promotion of Useful Knowledge came into being, its members bestowed its presidency upon Clayton, then in his eighty-first year, and only a few months before he was gathered to his fathers.

Among Virginia's early men of science, the name of John Mitchell stands out above the rest. His birth was achieved in Scotland—though there are those who bespeak this place of honor for Virginia—and he was educated for medical practice at the Universities of Edinburgh and Leyden. Nature deluged him with many gifts: he was intelligent and imaginative, and his eagerness to forward knowledge knew no bounds. A first-rate medico, he was heavily called upon for his professional service; yet somehow between his grapplings with chills and fevers and all the other human ailments then prospering in Virginia, he found occasion to undertake scientific studies of one sort or another. We hear of him first as a botanist with his publication of a monograph, dated 1738, and embalmed in Latin. There followed several others, of which some brought him a very favorable notice—in fact, of such high worth was his work regarded that in England the Royal Society eagerly received him as a member.

But botany was only one of Mitchell's scientific concerns. Observe this man as the years crept over him, and you will see him engaging the American possum to figure out the cycle of its life and the use to which it put its pouch. A little while longer, and you will notice him taking an active interest in the "causes of the different colours of people in different climates." And so on and on, from the "preparation and uses of potash" to "earth salts," "electrical cohesion," and "water which turns iron to copper." His last work, which death denied him the pleasure of witnessing in type, concerned itself with the nature and causes of yellow fever. Betweentimes he managed to fill three books on America, all of a political tinge, besides putting together the first satisfactory map of the British and French domains in North America. Put out in 1755, it passed through one edition after another—it was, in fact, still making the rounds even after the coming of the American Republic.

11 After the collapse of the Virginia Company's plan to open a college at Henrico, the idea of enriching the land with a shrine for the higher learning suffered a prolonged eclipse. Then, in 1661, it reappeared when a project was set afoot to found a college, but this too ended in nothingness. Thirty years later, in 1691, the notion stirred anew when the colony bespoke Britain's Lords of the Treasury to give their support to the establishment of a colonial college. To add conviction to their appeal, the colonists laid up a fund of £2,000 and dispatched their foremost ecclesiastic, a Scotsman of the Anglican rite, the Rev. James Blair, to London. The man pleaded with the tongue of angels, but his task bristled with difficulties, and two years wearied by before his prayer obtained an agreeable answer. When he returned to Virginia, he had bagged not only the assent of the sovereigns William and Mary, but an order for £2,000 and a plan for a building from the board, it is thought, of the celebrated Christopher Wren. In addition Blair had separated several hundred extra pounds from divers connoisseurs of learning, besides obtaining the greater part of the estate of Robert Boyle, the scientist, then but lately deceased. In fact, the masterful Blair had even cast his incantation on some pirates who, snagged in the toils of the law, eagerly added to his collection in exchange for a few kind words from him in high places.

The building began to rear itself in 1695 at Middle Plantation, now Williamsburg. One of the most sumptuous mansions in Virginia, it towered 3½ stories high, and its walls of brick stood 3 feet thick. As was only meet and right, the college bore the names of its royal sponsors, and just as meet and right, the honor and burden of its presidency fell to the Rev. Mr. Blair. He was destined to remain in practice for half a century, until he was ninety, when his time came to die.

The College of William and Mary—the second center of higher knowledge in the Colonies—began life uninspiringly. Scarcely more than a grammar school, it was operated by a master and an assistant. Its main building was not finished till 1700, and six years later—and twice again thereafter—it went up in smoke and flames. Meanwhile the tobacco gentry, rolling up their wealth faster than ever, turned up their noses at the native learning and sent their sons to the more fashionable institutions across the sea. Nonetheless, the college stayed on its legs. Gradually its faculty increased, and by 1729 it was in the hands of half a dozen professors, besides aides, adjuncts, and miscellaneous handymen.

Launched as a cradle for Anglican divines, the school nevertheless offered some of its illumination in the secular arts and sciences. It was at William and Mary, to give an example, that the eminent George Wythe in 1779 ascended the first professorial chair of law in America, and the second one in the English-speaking world. A signer of the Declaration and a member of the Constitutional Convention, he was the mentor of Thomas Jefferson, John Marshall, James Monroe, Henry Clay, and several others of high mark. It was Wythe who organized the land's first school of public affairs, and long before such things were even dreamed of, he made his apprentice jurists put their book learning into practice in moot courts and a student legislature, where, under his eye and counsel, they hammered the airwaves with argument as they repaired existing laws and proposed new and, if possible, better ones.

William and Mary's annals shine with many other academic innovations. As early as 1776 it founded Phi Beta Kappa, the first intercollegiate fraternal order in America. It was the first college to spangle its high-standing scholars with medals of gold; the first to entertain the elective and honor systems; the first colonial college to elevate itself into a university; the first to bear the torch in political economy; the first to cultivate the modern languages; and the first with a school of modern history.

Finally, it was at William and Mary and not at Harvard, however fair, where the social graces were given their first encouragement by the American higher learning. They came in, it is true, somewhat sneakily when, in 1716, the college allowed one William Levingstone to make use of one of its chambers "for teaching the scholars and others to dance while his own dancing school in Williamsburg be finished." Nor was it long before the Rev. Hugh Jones was advising the college authorities that music, dancing, and fencing might be taught "by such as the president and masters shall appoint at such certain times as they shall fix for these purposes."

To be admitted to the college a youth had to have an easy command of Latin and Greek. Lest there be any doubt on this score, he was examined and appraised by the president, with aid and inspiration from the faculty and a small squad of clergymen privy to the more delicate points of the ancient languages. If he held himself well, he was granted the rank and dignity of "student," and to give visual proof of his new significance in life he displayed himself to the world in academic robes, the regalia, so to say, of his occupation. Four years were usually necessary for him to snare the bachelor of arts, while for the master's seven were required. Two philosophical schools stood ready to instruct him. In one, the School of Natural Philosophy and Mathematics, be made acquaintance with physics, metaphysics, and mathematics; in the other, the School of Moral Philosophy, he came to terms with rhetoric, logic, and ethics, and then went on to confront natural and civil law. The grind of lecture and study, as tedious then, no doubt, as ever, was given an occasional sprucing up with debates, declamations, and other confections of eloquence and erudition. Sometimes such occasions were turned into a public ceremonial in which, however, the chief rhetoricians were seldom the students, but rather their elders, the parsons and politicos and some of the colony's higher illuminati.

For those aspiring to the holy cloth there were two courses in divinity, one concentrating on Hebrew and Holy Writ, and the other on the "commonplaces of divinity and the controversies with heretics." During the college's younger years the number of its theologues remained small. In part this may have been due to the difficulty of obtaining the prerequisite foundation, but an even greater deterrent must have been the dreary and disheartening future facing an ambassador of God as he pastored through the South's vast and uncertain reaches. But eventually, as the prospects for a sacerdotal life began to brighten, more and more young men stepped up for courses leading to holy orders, took their degrees, shipped for England for ordination, and returned to pound a Southern pulpit. In fact, by the Revolution's outbreak a rather high proportion of Virginia's reverend clergy is said to have been of native stock. Even so, as the murmurings of dissent with the mother country grew more sullen, the interest in divinity fell more and more to the pressure of public affairs. More memorable, in consequence, than the college's alumni in sacred frock are some of its secular saints, in illustration, Thomas Jefferson, John Marshall, James Monroe, Edmund Randolph, and several other of almost equal incandescence.

The skepticism which fed the mundane spirit bore an extraordinary harvest. For students it yielded a measure of freedom, which in the academic grove was then still embryonic. Even their masters inclined to relax their old decorum—in fact, some of them, bedazzled and bemused by the turn of circumstance, broke through the bounds of elementary prudence, disporting themselves in pothouse revelry until the morning's early watches, when they lumbered home, uncertain and heavily laden. Such extracurricular activities not only undermined virtue but also alienated parental confidence. For skepticism, as was common knowledge even in those innocent times, was the bedfellow of atheism, and since the run of Virginians still harbored the hope of becoming angels when they died, they were at pains to safeguard their sons from the hazards and incitements of the higher learning. The disgrace and scandal, needless to say, saddened the college fathers, and they made no little pother about it. In fact, in 1779, thy swept the old school clean, purging it of its pollution and, while they were about it, establishing chairs in medicine, mathematics and physics, moral philosophy, law, and economics, all graced by men of great learning and the highest rectitude.

The advantages which allowed education to thrive very early in Massachusetts were missing in the South. The Virginians did not, like the New Englanders, lodge themselves in compact little settlements, but lived instead on scattered plantations, forming more or less individualized and self-sufficient domestic centers. Under the circumstances, communal life, which flourished so vigorously in the New England town, was a stranger to the South, and so, per consequence, was the town school. The houses of learning which did in fact appear usually identified themselves—if they bore a name at all—not with the places they adorned but with the benefactors whose gifts had made them possible. Immured in virtual isolation, the Southern planter had little chance to indulge in the play of mind on mind, so familiar, and even necessary, to New England people. Hence his culture, wanting the sturdy blood of interparlance, tended to be inbred and conservative.

The partnership of state and church, which worked so admirably in theocratic Massachusetts, was of course absent in the Southern Colonies. There, not only did the Established Anglican Church lack the fine passion for learning which marked the New England ministry, but, save for a few superior men, its ordained representatives, often enough, were far from being well educated themselves. As for the state, the general attitude toward education was that of the motherland, which is to say that it regarded the schooling of the young, like the food we swallow and the clothes we flaunt, as a strictly personal matter, and so it preferred to abstain from it as completely as possible. Hence, unlike the situation in Massachusetts, in the South neither the state nor the church exerted itself with any force to advance the public enlightenment.

The education which prevailed in the South reflected the great social and economic cleft which separated those of high and low degree. The rich planters accommodated their children with private tutors, and on occasion they sent them to private schools, either here or abroad. Near the end of the 1600s they finally succeeded, after several false starts, in gracing their land with the higher learning. The College of William and Mary, the second to appear in the Colonies, was for a long time little more than a pale and puny grammar school. But when it came into its own at last, it gave sustenance to not a few of the Founding Fathers. For the commonality there was a small number of schools and other forms of academic endeavor, succored and supported at times by benevolence, at times by tuition, and at times by both—but not in any event by government. Only the lower ranks of life, the children of the servant and menial class, the orphans and the illegitimate, and similar castaways from fortune, were provided for by the state. For them there were workhouse schools and compulsory apprentice training.

5
MIDDLE COLONY PAROCHIALISM

New Netherland   Sandwiched between New England and Maryland were the Middle Colonies, a stretch of earth and water which today embraces New York, New Jersey, Delaware, and Pennsylvania. In the early seventeenth century both the British and the Dutch flung hungry looks at this spacious region, the one by virtue of the explorations of John Cabot (born Giovanni Caboto), a Venetian navigator in English hire, and the other because of similar geographic searchings by Henry Hudson, an English shipmaster in the pay of the Dutch. But the Hollanders got here first, and they were the first to press their claim. Dutch traders arrived as early as 1610, a year or so after Hudson is credited, perhaps mistakenly, with being the first white man to lay eyes on Manhattan and then to sail up the river which—together with a great oceanic bay; several cities, towns, and hamlets; numerous streets and a boulevard; and a host of worthwhile articles from paper towels to fur coats—now helps to immortalize his name.

But a decade labored by before the Dutch attempted to organize their New Netherland venture. Then, in 1621, the Dutch West India Company was chartered. Like its senior sister, the Dutch East India Company, the newcomer was a trading corporation, dedicated to the convenience and private profit of its stockholders. A state, so to say, within a state, it enjoyed enormous powers, such as maintaining a private army and navy, negotiating treaties, and establishing and governing colonies. True, this authority was held in some check by the supervisory control exercised by the States General in Holland. But their reins, stretched over the broad and difficult sea, were never taut or exacting. This state of affairs, and the fact also that the colonists had no voice in the laws they were forced to obey, in effect gave the governor the powers and prerogatives of an autocrat.

At first the Dutch made no serious effort to colonize their new domain. Indeed, one might well ask, why should they? For the motives which sent so many shiploads of Europeans to the New World were for the most part absent in the Dutch republic. Here was a stalwart people, substantial and prosperous, with jobs aplenty and good pay, with a measure of burgher freedom, and with a religious toleration which, if not without limits, was nevertheless extraordinary for its time. In consequence, during the infant years of their American venture, the Dutch inclined to regard their transatlantic holdings not as a place to deliver themselves up to a fuller and happier life, but rather as an outpost in their vast and scattered commercial realm, full of aching trouble, but also, for money-minded folk, a land of superlative possibilities. Look at it how you will, the influx of settlers never more than trickled. By 1664, when the province lowered its flags to the English and when Massachusetts could count some twenty-five thousand inhabitants, and Virginia some five thousand more, New Netherland could barely scratch together a rough nine thousand.

In Dutch America the West India Company—like the Virginia Company in the South—sought the forest products needed to keep industry pulsing in the home country. For a spell the settlers devoted their efforts to producing tar and potash and felling trees to saw and cut into staves and lumber. But the business proved too costly, and instead of netting an agreeable profit, the stockholders found themselves balancing their accounts in red. What was needed, obviously, was a product more readily to be had, singular, if possible, and noncompetitive—a staple, say like the tobacco plant in the country of the Chesapeake or sugar in the Indies. The Dutch found their answer in the valley land of the Hudson and the Mohawk, where presently they were engaging in a lucrative trade with the Indians, swapping anything the natives craved, from knives and firearms to blankets and booze, for their precious skins of beaver, fox, and mink. Time saw their stock of exports grow in variety as well as bulk. Dutch vessels still carried tar and potash and lumber, but they also packed their holds with whatever they could gainfully turn over, from flax and hemp and grain to pork and salt, and even tobacco. But in the end, when the balance sheets were cast and a man of commerce surveyed and appraised his transactions in the marketplace, more often than not it was fur which gladdened his capitalistic heart and brought radiance to his jowls. Like their hustling neighbors to the north, the New Netherlanders steered their ships to every compass point, not only across the ocean to homeland harbors, but through inland creeks and rivers and up and down the long Atlantic shoreline from New England waters to the massive Chesapeake.

2   What catches the eye at once in Dutch America is its stupendous diversity. Its first residents—forgetting the Indians—were not Dutch at all, but Walloons, some thirty families of them, translated to these shores in 1623 from what is now a part of Belgium. Others shortly followed, the Dutch of course, but there were also representatives from Ireland, Scotland, and England, and not a few from Germany, Scandinavia, and France. There was even a light sprinkling of Italians, Portuguese, and Spaniards, mostly sailors shoring up for a transient respite from the rigors of the sea or fugitives for one cause or another from their native soil. In the realm of faith and conscience the show was no less fantastic. The official and recommended way to bliss eternal was laid out by the Dutch Reformed Church, to whose support everyone was made to contribute a modest subsidy. But beyond that a man was free to make ready for the afterworld, whether in its upper or lower house, as he saw fit. As a result the land harbored not only communicants of the Dutch established church, but also Huguenots, Baptists, Quakers, Lutherans, Presbyterians—even Puritans and a handful of Jews and Catholics. When the non-Dutch grew numerous enough to arouse political misgivings, the rulers made them pledge allegiance to the Dutch republic, but even then they were not made to accept the Dutchman's official faith. To some of its ordained dominies, such freedom not only offered an intolerable affront to the true religion but also boded no good. And so, with the support of Governor Stuyvesant, they put their heads together to contrive a program of religous repression. But the outcry against such un-Dutch folly brought a prompt rebuke from Amsterdam, and the new order was quickly quashed. Save for such passing frenzy, religious worship in New Netherland enjoyed a rare and exultant liberty.

Notwithstanding the national and religious crazy quilt within its midst, New Netherland remained overwhelmingly Dutch. Though the ear might be assaulted by a babel of tongues, it was the Hollander's rough guttural which bruised the air most often. Though the Lord might be cherished and venerated in a score of ways, it was the *kerk* of Holland, the Reformed Dutch, which alone was His official and established temple. The Dutchman's mark was everywhere. One discerned it in his quaint and gabled houses, not a few of them several-storied and of brick, a handsome splash of pinks and purples and glittering reds and yellows. The Dutchman's hand was visible in the narrow, twisting streets, in the canals and windmills, and in his trim and tiny gardens, specks of fresh and haunting beauty in the ever-imminent wilderness. It announced its presence in his shops and storehouses, in the humming wharves and shipyards, and in the rush and rumble of a busy folk, but a folk full of sense and not too busy to enjoy the pleasures inspired by conviviality and civilized food and drink, either at home or at some not too far-off taproom. Finally, as in the sea-environed motherland, there was the sense of the ever-present world of water, of creeks and rivers and coves and bays, and of the limitless outstretched ocean, without which life to these people, whether in the old country or the new, would have been unthinkable.

3   The nature of the colony, so variegated in its elements and yet so predominantly Dutch in its culture, was reflected, as usual, in education. But its start was slow, and it never got up much steam. The great sparseness of the population and the scarcity of towns inveighed against the progress of learning, and so, of course, did the interminable variety of creed and language. Add to these detriments the absence of any real representative government, and you make communal action, such as in New England, all but impossible. Luckily, there were also a number of insistent countercurrents. The most powerful one, as might be expected, was the pressure of the Protestant tradition, with its stress on Bible reading. That the colony's official church was of a Calvinistic strain was also an advantage, for wherever Calvinists manned the governmental quarterdeck, they made it their business to ally state and church in a war of literacy against the Prince of Darkness. In fact, in Holland it was an established practice of the civil and ecclesiastic authorities to make joint provision for schools and school attendance. They examined and licensed the schoolmaster, dickered with him over his wages, and issued him his orders. The great ecclesiastic synods formulated the broad educational plans, but it was up to the secular arm to put them into execution—an obligation which, in sad truth, it sometimes forgot to honor.

In Dutch America, as in the Low Countries, the bond between school and church was close. Over here, as over there, the paramount educational influence was religion. In the colony, as in the parent land, the state committed itself to the furtherance of the church established. But in New Netherland this responsibility was lodged in the West India Company, which, all things considered, did not seek to deprive itself of its obligation. In fact, as early as 1629, the company asked the settlers to devise some means whereby they would be able to support a schoolmaster. But the company's duties went much further than mere requesting; it was also expected to furnish and maintain schools and, more important, to keep them in funds. Inspired, however, by business rather than pedagogic ideals, the directors permitted themselves no spending spree. On the contrary, they were at pains to keep an eye on every penny. Not only did they dole out ink and paper with a restrained and cautious hand, but to avoid their waste or loss, they also kept a diligent record of their consumption. Under the righteous Stuyvesant, moreover, a code for the master's conduct was drawn up. Some time later, as was no more than fair, his pupils were treated to a similar favor.

Usually, though, such important matters were left to trained specialists in moral theology, namely, the Classis of Amsterdam, which was the directing arm of the Dutch Reformed Church. Although distance tended to weaken its muscle in the colony, in education the power of the Classis remained primary. Thus, the reverend brethren, sitting in Amsterdam, peered into a prospective teacher's head, and if its store of knowledge was sufficient and his orthodoxy beyond reproach, they stamped and labeled him approvingly. Whenever the colony issued a call for a schoolmaster, the Classis singled him out, gave him its official endorsement, and with hope and prayer sent him on his way. His duties did not await his arrival in the New World, but began the moment he set his foot on ship, where, barring seasickness or some other act of God, he conducted classes in the three Rs and the proper form and substance of prayer, besides giving heed to his pupils' manners. which he was bidden "to bring . . . to modesty and propriety."

4   Nine villages were chartered in New Netherland, and probably each, at one time or another, kept a school. But the scholastic amenities were meager. Sometimes there was a schoolhouse; more often pupils gathered their knowledge in the master's home. Once, for a timeless moment of history, a school held its sessions in the village tavern, the scene of so many other instructive events. As an aspect of village governance, the school was financed out of the civil purse. Nevertheless, as then was custom, instruction was not free, and save for the poor, all children were made to pay a fee. Such proceeds were a rightful part of the master's wages, and to ensure their payment he had authority to collect and pocket them before he gave a single lesson. Though the school was financed out of the secular till, it was nevertheless in the service of the church, its liegeman, as it were, charged with teaching the one true faith and straining to advance its influence everywhere and at all times. To this end it relied on Protestantism's tried and trusted standbys, reading and religion, with concessions now and then to writing and arithmetic. Twice a week at least the master drilled his little learners in the common prayers and the questions and answers of their catechism to prepare them for their dress parade at the Sabbath service, where they were expected to flaunt their knowledge with correctness and alacrity. As was only right and prudent, prayer started off every schoolday, and when dusk brought its labors to a halt, glories to God ascended heavenward. Beyond these haggard offerings there was nothing, except at a parent's rare request, and for such special accommodation, if it could be rendered, the schoolmaster was allowed to command a modest honorarium.

In the spheres of secondary and higher learning, Dutch America, unlike the alert and resolute theocracy to the north, threw forth no light. It was an indignity which brought mournful vapors from the faithful, and in the Great Remonstrance they addressed to the home government in 1649 they spared no words in saying so. But ten years limped by before their woe was given notice, and when at last the colony was rejoiced by the coming of a Latin master, he came too late, for the grammar school which now took shape was barely under way when the colony fell to the frown of English cannon.

Collegiately, the tale is even sadder. True, some of the colony's forward-lookers dreamed picturesquely of the day when New Netherland would enjoy the honor of entertaining a Harvard all its own, the nursery of its future men of God, and hence a glory to the Kingdom. But they dreamed in vain. Not till 1766, more than a century since New Netherland had become no more than a geographic expression, did the Dutch obtain a college. Known then as Queen's, but now as Rutgers, it was scarcely the shrine of divine science which had warmed their forebears' fancy, for the world those men had celebrated and adorned had vanished beyond recall. Although Queen's promised to serve the needs and interests of the Reformed Dutch Church, it was already animated by a newer and more worldly spirit. It was their endeavor, declared the college fathers, "to promote learning for the benefit of the community and the advancement of all denominations."

5 The close affiliation between state and church displayed itself in what the colonists expected from their schoolmaster. Commissioned not only to instruct and ameliorate his pupils, he was also put upon to give assistance to the reverend pastor. During Sunday's devotions he engaged in various pious exercises. He recited passages from Holy Writ, supplementing them for good measure with the Ten Commandments and the Twelve Articles of Faith. He intoned hymns and led the flock in sacred singing. Now and then, when the preacher was borne down by the ills and griefs which life deals to us all, the master stepped into the pulpit and volunteered a sermon. In addition he performed the common functions of a sexton, dusting and sweeping the church, polishing its brass and woodwork, pealing its bell, and on snowy days shoveling a lane to its doorway. When parents added an infant to their circle and presently undertook to purge him of the stain left by Adam's shameful sin, the teacher assisted at the baptismal ceremony, spreading tidings to the faithful of its imminence and providing the parson with his necessary instrument of a basin full of water. For the proper celebration of the Lord's Supper, the teacher supplied the minister with bread and wine. Finally, when death came to one of the faithful, it was the schoolmaster who dug his grave and helped to bury him in a correct and decorous manner. A folk of honor as well as piety, the Netherlanders were far from expecting their schoolmaster to contribute all these extra labors out of the simple kindness of a Christian heart. On the contrary, for each and every service he performed beyond the call of classroom duty the master was entitled to collect a fee—a right which no false pride prevented him from asserting.

Yet despite his exalted office, the Dutch schoolmaster was seldom of a laudable professional mark. In fact, the colony's very first birchman, Adam Roelantsen, like Harvard's first executive-in-chief, was something of a rogue. Given to a blustering and bawdy utterance, he found himself in one suit for slander after another. Even worse, the man cherished a strong affinity for schnapps, and an even stronger one for the fair sex. As was predicted by New Amsterdam's moral element, this wolf in teacher's clothing came to a disgraceful end. Found guilty of attempted adultery, he was sentenced to be flogged and exiled. But such a fate, especially with winter's arrival not far off, Roelantsen pleaded, would lay a heavy burden on his four innocent kiddies, and so, tempering justice with prudence, the court ordered the execution of the sentence stayed—permanently, as things turned out. The hard truth is that, try as it would, the Classis of Amsterdam found it almost impossible to entice first-rate men to a province which was raw, with only the rudest comforts, and whose directors, for all their ethereal sermonizing, were bent on wringing the last penny from their investment.

6   When, in 1664, New Netherland rang down its flag to the English, the new proprietors inclined to leave the Dutch schools pretty much as they were. Circumstances altered somewhat some ten years later, when, after a brief rebellious outburst, the Dutch political sun in America went down forever. Deprived of its former right to broach the public purse, the Dutch school, now dependent entirely on the church for its revenue, became a parochial institution. In outlying country enclaves, however, Dutch education continued more or less as of old. There, while the Dutch hung on desperately to their culture for another generation, the school lingered in the old tradition. But as more and more years departed and the number of English unsparingly increased, the Dutch grew acutely sensitive to the engulfing Anglo-Saxon. Though their school continued, at bottom, to serve as the nursery for their Calvinism, it was now assigned the extra burden of safeguarding the Dutchman's way of life. But events were against it, and the striving was doomed, in spite of all the prayers and labors of the preachers and teachers and the fidelity so valiantly displayed by the older Dutch. Bullheaded though the Hollanders were, the pressure of the English and the compulsions of the unfolding civilization were too much for them. And so, as the older generation of Dutch increased in years, it became their melancholy fortune to see their children taking on more and more of the Englishman's manner—even, in fact, speaking his outlandish tongue, and in the process disdaining and forgetting their own.

Today they are all in their graves, young and old, and less remains to remind us of their presence in New York than of the presence of the ancient Romans in their vanished empire. Except for the Dutch, however, New York would have no Brooklyn on which to exercise its humor and no Bowery to stimulate its savants of society. Harlem is a name of Netherlandish origin, and so are Nassau and Cortlandt and Yonkers—even Barnegat and Spuyten Duyvel. Underneath Manhattan's pavements traces of Dutch canals are still vaguely perceptible. Dutch is the "scow" which rides New York's rivers, and Dutch the "boss" who gives his orders—even the cruller and the cookie are Dutch in origin, and so are coleslaw and the waffle. Had the Dutch not started it, there might be no New Year's reception, and Santa Claus would never have been heard of. Less intangible than such relics of a vaporous past is the actual presence of the Reformed Dutch Church. Not only has it eluded mortality, but here and there some of its ancient sacred houses, though weathered and worn, remain in active service. In truth, across the river from Manhattan's toe, on Staten Island, there still rises one of the church's familiar handmaids, an old Dutch schoolhouse, trim and tidy as the Dutch would want it, the oldest colonial schoolhouse, it is believed, which currently stands in this republic.

New York   In 1664, as reference has been made, New Netherland surrendered to the English, then under the second Charles. Soon to be known as New York, the colony became a proprietory province, the possession of James, Duke of New York and Albany and the sovereign's brother. The duke never honored America with his presence. Instead, he preferred to rule his province from a cautious distance, entrusting its fortunes to a governor and a council. Some of James's surrogates were excellent, wielding their authority with a benign and competent hand. To a people roweled by deep antagonisms and fevered by a fierce local pride, they made concessions which, if they accomplished nothing else, at least lessened dissent and disorder. Even so, the caste of wealthy merchants and landowners remained a power as before, and as they were to be for years on end, dominating the colony's political and social life. The gulf that separated this handful of high and mighty from the large generality of the populace disclosed itself time and again throughout the eighteenth century in the colony's social and economic friction, the feuds of politics, the brawls of national groups, and, of course, the disparities in educational opportunity.

In its educational policy New York's government followed in the footsteps of the motherland, which is saying that, sustained by an easy indifference toward the education of its people, it did almost nothing. Apart from insisting on the right to license its practicing schoolmasters and to oversee the training of apprentices, the colonial government—just as in the sister colonies below the Potomac—left education to the care and responsibility of others. The Dutch schools, as has been remarked, were allowed to carry on, but since they no longer enjoyed official favor, they now functioned parochially, as did the schools of other sects.

2   If the official attitude toward education was somewhat less than lukewarm, then on the other hand it was certainly not hostile. The Society for the Propagation of the Gospel in Foreign Parts—the same band of evangelical pedagogues who trooped the vast and sparsely peopled stretches of the South—was given the governor's approval. The spearhead of the Established Church's missionary work, the gospel propagators, it will be recalled, pined to bring the Word to the Indian and the Negro and to any other non-Anglicans who would give them an ear. In New York, with so many of its inhabitants living in sin and error, they came on a vineyard which was precisely to their taste. Entering practice in 1703, a bare two years after the society's inception, its representatives, though rudely denounced and opposed in sectarian quarters, nevertheless succeeded in lavishing their industry upon an ever-widening audience. In fact, as the years rolled on, the brethren were able to extend their sphere of influence up and down the entire colony, operating not quite a dozen schools until the Revolution, when their royalism made them repugnant to American patriotic sensibility.

The SPG designed its schools for the service and salvation of the poor, and hence they were of a more or less charitable inclination. But in tune with the spirit of those nongiveaway times, its altruism was carefully measured, and whenever any of its beneficiaries could afford the modest tuition levy, he was expected to lay it on the counter. Needless to say, for those traveling in the better circles such schools were much too wretched to be attractive. Yet they were backed by no less a worthy than the governor, who, as the society's chief secular potentate, reserved the right to grant its masters his official sanction before turning them upon the young. At all times, moreover, they were under official eye, with frequent descents upon their classroom seances by the governor's appointed inspectors. Taking it all around, though, the SPG enjoyed a favor which, if not actually official, was the next best thing to it.

As for the quality of the SPG's work, it was less than fair, though it was probably no lower than that of most of the schooling then dispensed to life's lowest ranks. As always in such cases, the main stress fell on the truths and mandates of the Church of England. Children, thus, were set upon memorizing their common prayers and the questions and answers of the authorized catechism. Meanwhile, they were broken in in reading, and when they could make sense of that art and mystery, they introduced themselves to the Good Book. In addition, they dabbled in writing and arithmetic—lightly, to be sure—seldom more, as one of the SPG professors let it be known, than "to relieve the common occasions of the vulgar people," which, he went on, "is the most the people aspire to." If the young managed to get off gently in their tussles with the three simple Rs, then in the promotion of their virtue they relished no such ease. Not only did their masters dose them stiffly with moral admonition, but all the books they suffered through, whether pious or profane, were powerfully rigged for righteousness. The virtues which were impressed upon them were not merely the elemental ones that Christendom esteems and recommends, such as honesty, sobriety, courtesy, cleanliness, and the like. Imbued with the social values of the upper classes, the masters were to teach the lowly once and for all that in the life which God for them ordained it was their fortune to be followers, which, translated, means that they were to make their peace with things as they were and hence never to be lax in the respect and duties they owed their betters.

3   It is no more than fair to note that in its concern for education the government of New York was thoroughly impartial: it paid no more mind to secondary schooling than to the elementary kind. The Latin school, begotten by the Dutch shortly before the intrusion of the English, ailed on for a time—just how long no one precisely knows. Almost forty years trickled by before the new rulers came forth with a proposal, in 1702, to instruct New York boyhood in "languages and other learning." But the school which came into being was anemic from the first, and after only a few months it hobbled, unlamented, to an end. Three decades passed before the General Assembly persuaded itslf to try once more to encourage—thus it said—the teaching of Latin, Greek, and mathematics to the up-and-coming New York male. Fortifying this grizzly triumvirate, however, were such rakish newcomers as bookkeeping, geography, and navigation, all dear, of course, to New York's business heart. In accord with the motherland's tradition and that of her intellectual emulator, the Southern aristocracy, the school was designated a *public school*. Yet this is not to say that it was tax-supported and free to all on equal terms, but rather that like Eton, St. Paul's, Harrow, and similar genteel and ivied shrines, it was to educate a small proportion of its attendants with the compliments of the house. The city's second venture into higher schooling fared somewhat better than the first, though it was scarcely more commendable. This time, at all events, the school at least prevailed for a number of years. But from the start it was sickly, and in 1738, at the age of six, it shut its eyes forever. Meanwhile in the North, but three years preceding, the Boston Latin School had become a centenarian.

4   As wherever Anglo-Saxon fashion set the tone, New York invested itself with a private schooling of a robust and protean sort. A good part of it, ministering to the heirs of wealth and standing, offered to perfect them in the delicate points of good taste and deportment and in such nice things of life as dancing, music, and painting. But New York being New York, it did not take the local Platos long to mix the ornamental with the practical and to proffer their counsel in anything for which they could dun a fee. Did Manhattan's budding man of affairs, for example, hope someday to traffic in commerce overseas? Then let him learn to hold palaver in French or Spanish, or even in Italian or Portuguese, by the "best method . . . for twenty shillings per quarter." Or maybe he envisioned himself as a man of practical action? Then let him master the mariner's art, or maybe surveying or bookkeeping. Or could it be that he was of a scholarly cast of mind? Then let him betake himself to Thomas Reynolds "at the house . . . Opposite the Three Pigeons . . . in William Street" to drink in Latin and Greek. For those on whom fate had forced the necessity of earning their keep by day, the school of John Walton, once a frequenter of Yale, announced nocturnal instruction in anything the heart and mind desired, from the three Rs to the "same things which are commonly taught in colleges."

Nor were girls overlooked. Sometimes the sweet ones were taught in the rude company of the male. More often, though, in deference to public feeling, such intermingling of the sexes was discountenanced and they had to suffer in separate chambers. The feminine share of learning included the usual three Rs. For those of a vigorous mind there was Latin. Not a few nibbled at the fine arts, from needlework to music, both vocal and instrumental. Now and then the ambition seized some of them to seek perfection in the art and science of cookery.

5   Although instruction in plain and fancy knowledge was apparently plentiful, for a young New Yorker yearning to ornament his calling card with an A.B. in the wake of his name, the chances were nil. Under the circumstances, either he resorted to fraud or resigned himself to self-denial or, if he was really in earnest, he betook himself to some foreign grove, say, Harvard or Yale or William and Mary, or one yet more foreign on the Atlantic's other shore. The Dutch had lamented this dreary lack, but their tears availed them nothing—in fact, the colonial era was almost out before New York could pride itself with a house of higher learning. A project to establish a college was set afoot in 1747 with a public lottery, a common device in those days to raise cash for the furtherance of worthy causes, such as those of libraries, colleges, and churches—even, indeed, the winning of the American Revolution. Exhorted "to be adventurous," New York's burghers were quick to show their civic mettle, and presently—in exactly five years—they had amassed over £3,400 for the fund. Two years later, in 1754, King's College—now Columbia University—was ready to commence its work. If, as we are sometimes told, such things can happen, then Harvard's founding fathers must surely have raised a ghostly eyebrow. For the new college, though certainly pious, made no overt reference to any intention of educating its students for the pulpit. Ostensibly King's was nondenominational with a board of trustees composed of eminent lay figures, besides divines from various Protestant groups—Lutheran, Huguenot, Dutch Reformed, Presbyterian, and Anglican, all presumably civilized men and all appreciatively admired. For all its avowed nonsectarianism, however, the college entrusted its presidency to none save Anglicans.

The college's religious liberalism reached even into the student body.

No person, declared the college charter, was to be turned back on grounds of religious belief. Nor was there any desire "to impose upon the scholars the peculiar tenets of any particular sect"; instead, the college undertook "to inculcate upon their tender minds the great principles of Christianity and morality, in which true Christians of each denomination are generally agreed." But tender-minded or not, very few of the vast horde who currently jam Columbia's corridors—in truth, not many even of its learned faculty—could have gained entry into the original college. To be received into its novitiate, the aspiring bachelors of arts were expected to wrestle successfully with all the important speeches of Cicero, besides the first books of *The Aeneid,* and, as an apostolic afterpiece, with several chapters in Greek from the Gospel of St. John. In addition, they were to be "versed in the first five rules of arithmetic, i.e., as far as division and reduction." Once safely past these barricades, they still faced the possibility of rejection—unless, that is, they had the knack of writing "a good legible hand." If so they had, then the honor of becoming freshmen fell upon them.

Perhaps even more disturbing to right-thinkers than the college's nonsectarianism were some of the laic animadversions of its first president, the Rev. Dr. Samuel Johnson. Groomed intellectually at Yale, he had shed its simple Congregationalism for the more ravishing Anglicanism, making himself a master of its sacred theology and, in the passing years, a member of its holy priesthood. He was doubtless highly dowered, a man who knew his Latin like a Roman and his Greek well enough to make speeches in it. The friend and mutual admirer of Benjamin Franklin, and like him the familiar of the Enlightenment and its active partisan in America, Johnson shared some of the doctor's intellectual boldness. True, in his Christian piety the president gave ground to nobody. The college's first aim, he was quick to make clear, was "to teach its children to know God in Jesus Christ, and to love and serve him in sobriety, godliness and righteousness of life. . . ." But beyond these essential virtues, there beckoned a "further design." To attain it Johnson declared for a curriculum stocked not only with the conventional religious and classic nostrums but also with offerings in commerce, geography, history, government, and navigation. The knowledge of all nature "in the heavens above us, and in the air, water, and earth around us, and the various kinds of meteors, stones, mines and minerals, plants and animals, and everything useful for the comfort, convenience, and elegance of life, in the chief manufacturers relating to these things"—such was the president's summary of what a first-class college should teach.

It was a vista, as we shall see in later pages, of Jeffersonian sweep, and one not generally to the taste of inveterate academicians, and certainly not to the taste of the doctor's board of trustees. And thus, instead of treading a trail toward a new intellectual frontier, the first president of King's had to content himself with escorting his students over the familiar classical highroad, ancient and heavily rutted, but for all that, safe from the filibustering sciences. The college faculty and its president tied up all in one, Johnson imparted instruction in all the subjects. Except for retreats to safety when smallpox was rampaging in the city, he performed his duties year in and year out until 1763, when he put aside his books and retired. In spite of Johnson's zeal for secular learning, it became his fortune to be remembered not for any particular accomplishments therein, but as a metaphysician, the foremost expert in the America of his era on the idealistic propositions of the immortal Bishop Berkeley.

New Jersey   The territory separating the Hudson and the Delaware, known today as New Jersey, was the Duke of York's gift, in 1664, to his friends John Lord Berkeley and Sir John Carteret, both of whom were already well-heeled with real estate in the Carolinas. The two men divided their prize, the one taking title to its western portion, or West Jersey, and the other to its eastern part, or East Jersey. The land was no stranger to the white man's presence, though it was only sparsely settled with huddlings here and there of Finns and Dutchmen besides Englishmen and Swedes. By 1665 the new owners were ready to exploit their realm. In order to people it more amply they offered land at low and pleasant rates, and as a special inducement to settlers they even went so far as to assure them liberty of conscience as well as a voice in the making of their laws and the laying of taxes. In return the colonists were put upon to pledge allegiance to the reigning sovereign and, needless to say, the Lords Proprietor Berekeley and Carteret.

From its beginnings New Jersey frothed with conflict and contention. Stuart that he was, James had bestowed his gift somewhat in the vein of an Indian giver, and when the owners undertook to rule their province, they soon learned that whatever ruling was to be done would be done by the ducal James himself. Not until 1680 was the dispute put to sleep. Meanwhile Berkeley, sickened of the whole business, sought to cure himself by selling his holding to a couple of Quakers for the sum of £1,000, a mere bagatelle today, of course, but a fantastic figure in its time. But the purchasers, anesthetic to their ideal of brotherly love, began to act most unseemly, and presently they were bellowing with unspeakable ferocity. Save for the deft mediation of William Penn and their plunge into bankruptcy, their eternal shades might still be haggling. Put under the authority and control of a triumvirate of Quakers, West Jersey now became powerfully attractive to their fellow worshippers, hounded and bedeviled abroad, as so many of them were, for their beliefs, religious and otherwise. But doubts and uncertainties over land titles and the rights of owners continued to torment the colonists, so that for years they found themselves snarled in one lawsuit after another. Not until 1702, when James at last lay quiet in his coffin, were the two Jerseys united, in form if not in amity, as a single royal province under the jurisdiction of the Governor of New York. Finally, in 1738, Jerseyites were accorded the pleasure of giving obedience to a governor all their own.

2   With so much trouble frazzling the colony, its rulers had neither time nor inclination to concern themselves with education. Except for an act of 1693 empowering towns to open schools when "meet and convenient," the government kept itself aloof. Even this meager measure made little headway, and two years later the lawgivers, true, more or less, to English usage of their time, washed their hands of all responsibility by the simple device of passing it to someone else, in this instance the towns. All that was asked of them was that they pick three representatives annually "to appoint and agree with the schoolmaster." But in a land swarming with so many Christian sects and factions, this could be little more than a wistful hope. In the end almost the only appointing and agreeing which was feasible was consummated not by the towns, but by the churches. Consequently, the education which came to pass in New Jersey could be little else than parochial and private. It became, in sum, not unlike what prevailed across the river in New York.

If New Jersey's achievement on learning's lower level was somewhat pallid, then in its higher reaches it glinted a bit more brightly. As reference has already been made, the eighteenth century had witnessed a slackening of the old-time religious fervor and, per contra, a mounting interest in worldly matters. The secular spirit drew its strength not only from a small band of intellectuals but also from the hardy skepticism of sailors along the coast, from profit-minded merchants and artisans in the growing towns, and from frontiersmen pushing toward the West. The challenging ideas of the Enlightenment blowing in from intellectual Europe gave it reinforcement, and presently, as we have seen, they were even putting their grip on some of the holy men of God, in illustration, the learned president of King's, Dr. Samuel Johnson.

But venerable ways die hard, and early in the thirties of the eighteenth century the old theology let loose a stupendous counterattack. Its first blast shook Northampton, Massachusetts, when the elder Jonathan Edwards, an unrelenting Calvinist, full of moral purpose and one of the greatest mastodons of theological science the New World has yet produced, began a series of sermons in support of Puritanism, excoriating those who had ceased to take its mandates gravely and promising them an everlasting bath in a sea of blazing brimstone unless they gave up sin. From Edwards's hair-raising rhetoric emerged America's first revival, the so-called "Great Awakening." Soon it reached into every hamlet of New England, and thence it poured over the rest of the land. Less excruciating, perhaps, than the Hell-haunted Edwards, but no less cocksure and infinitely more hypnotic in the voluptuousness of his eloquence, was George Whitfield, a follower of John Wesley, the authorized father, among historical genealogists, of Methodism.

There is no gainsaying the success of these divines, evanescent and incomplete though it was, as the abolition of sin in this imperfect world must ever be. To square their accounts with God, sinners everywhere rushed to confess and repent, and empty pews began to fill, while dwindling congregations began to burgeon. At the same time not a few men of earnest piety, appalled by the revival's uproar, its stampede of frenzied confessions and conversions, and the evangelistic go-getting of some of its managers, turned their back on the faith of their fathers for the suaver and sedater amenities of the Anglicans. As more and more penitents crowded back to God, the need for an educated ministry took on a new insistence. For, like the Puritans of a younger Massachusetts, the newly anointed dreaded the coming of a day when there might be a lack of trained and learned pastors. From their fears and from their hopes rose four colleges, all nurseries of divinity, Brown and Dartmouth in New England, and Rutgers and Princeton in New Jersey.

3   Princeton, which made its bow in 1746 as the College of New Jersey, was the creation of Scotch-Irish Presbyterians. It came upon the world with little more than a noble motive to uphold it. Long years lumbered by before it possessed even a plant of its own, its students gathering for instruction in scattered hamlets, usually in the home of the president or some benevolent divine. After a decade of such uncertain wandering, the college finally anchored itself at Princeton, for which it was named and which it has adorned and enlivened ever since. Concerned like Harvard—already a matron in her second century—to prepare young men for the sacred shroud, Princeton, for all its early travail, managed to climb the long and slippery hill to become the mecca of Scotch-Irish America, casting its spell far and wide beyond the Jersey border. Its first presidents—Jonathan Dickinson, Jonathan Edwards, Aaron Burr (not the third Vice President and duelist, but his father)—were all New Englanders and all of the holy faculty, but its students issued from all over the land, from the North and from the upland South. On leaving alma mater, prepared and elevated in divinity, they made for the far-flung Presbyterian marches, from Pennsylvania to Virginia, and beyond the vales and ridges of Kentucky and Tennessee, where they devoted themselves to teaching and preaching the Holy Word until at length God's mercy retired them from their earthly labors.

The college was scarcely thirteen years old when its fourth president, the Rev. Samuel Davies, came into office. Considering his times and the restrictions imposed upon his calling, he was an astoundingly liberal man. Like King's Samuel Johnson and others of that advanced company, he had fallen prey to the shifting culture. To the chagrin of conservatives, the new president not only gave his support to the secular subjects but even stocked the library shelves with the newest works in mathematics and the Newtonian physics. He favored English prose over the ancient Latin poesy; worse yet, he introduced psalmody and organ music into the chapel service—an indecency President Stiles of Yale predicted would surely be of "ill consequence." Finally, and most dismaying of all, Davies gave his approval to stage plays. When he bade his students his last farewell, he delivered himself of his entire academic outlook in a single sentence, as wise as it was terse: "Be the servants of the church," he urged them, "the servants of the country, the servants of all."

Pennsylvania   The colony of Pennsylvania was founded in 1681. The largest proprietory province in America—as large as England and Wales together—this gigantic plot was given to William Penn to settle a debt the Crown owed to his father, the late Admiral Sir William Penn. Under the terms of the grant Penn became almost absolute sovereign of the colony. In return he pledged fealty to the Crown and the payment every year of a couple of beaver pelts.

The man who got this regal realm has come down to us as an outstanding yet strangely enigmatic figure. The son of a professional seafighter, Penn was, for all that, a declared pacifist. Though a believer in the gospel of brotherly love, throughout his life he was embroiled in hubbub and dispute. He believed firmly that in God's eyes all men are equal; yet he also believed that the rich are the Lord's appointed stewards of the lesser folk. The champion of liberty, he found himself caged behind bars again and again. He hobnobbed with men as diverse as the ermined James of England and the crepe-robed Quaker Fox. Forsaking all personal advantage, Penn quit the gayest court in Europe to work and serve among Christ's humblest followers.

2   What predestination was for the Calvinist, the Light Within was for the Quaker. Something of God, he believed, resided in every one of us. To him the Divine Presence was a confider and consoler, a conscience and a guide. With the Heavenly Father manifesting himself intimately to each of His faithful, the Child of Light had no need of the customary ecclesiastical baggage. He was neither baptized nor confirmed. His pious assemblies were stripped of every formal ceremony. No serenading of Heaven graced them, no Holy Communion, not even a paid, consecrated servant of the Lord. Liturgy and sermon the Quaker found not only gratuitous but distasteful. Twice a week, he and the brethren betook themselves to their meetinghouse, where, seated in silent meditation, their eyes glazed in a kind of solemn ecstasy, they attended the visitation of the Light. In their everyday living Quakers sought simplicity. Their dress, like their speech and manner, was of the plainest. In a class-saturated world they recoiled from class distinction. They took their hats off to no mortal man—or woman. The highest and the lowest they addressed with "thee" and "thou"—a form of speech then reserved for creatures of the meanest rank. With the bullheadedness which reaped them scorn and sorrow, and even jail and death, they put down their collective foot against war, capital punishment, the tithe gatherers of England's Church Established, and oaths of any kind, whether with hand on Book or plain profanity.

Pennsylvania was to be run as a Holy Experiment, a godly utopia where people were to live side by side in goodness and brotherly love. "You shall be governed by laws of your own making," declared Penn, "to be a free, and if you will, a sober and industrious people." By the Frames of Government of 1682 and 1683, the proprietor became the colony's governor. But with its dedication to equality and fraternity, the Holy Experiment could ill afford to close its ears to the voice of the people. To some degree this voice made itself heard in the governor's council, which was elected by the freeholders, but it made much more stir in the assembly. In fact, by the century's end it was sticking its nose into lawmaking and into amending and overriding the proposals of the governor and the council. As a result, the run of Pennsylvanians enjoyed a measure of personal freedom not given to the other colonists.

But the true ruler of the Quaker commonwealth at bottom was the collective Light Within. The source of its spiritual strength, this also governed its moral direction. Not only were gaming, guzzling, and cursing deemed untoward, and the practitioners thereof severely dealt with, but for years the lid was firmly clamped on dancing, music, stage spectacles, and books of a sinful or other unseemly nature. But beside the more substantial monument of Quaker social justice, in hindsight such taboos appear trivial. Under William Penn, the Quakers treated the Indians in a refined and amicable manner, freighting their chiefs with gifts of goodwill, assisting at their powwows, making treaties with them, and, best of all, holding implacably to their given word. Quakers abolished jailing for debt, and in an era which made pilfering a 5-cent handkerchief a high and deadly crime, they conferred the death penalty only upon assassins. Pennsylvanians were singularly free to cross their governor, a right they relished and exercised to the utmost. Most illustrious, though, in the Quaker catalog of good works was their practice of complete religious freedom. No one—so commanded the law—was to suffer for his "religious practice in matters of faith and worship."

3   Open without strings to all creeds, Pennsylvania, as might be expected, attracted all creeds. At first Quakers predominated. But pretty soon others were on the scene—Anglicans, Lutherans, Presbyterians, and Pietists, besides Mennonites and Moravians and coveys of several more. In fact, were you to name a sect at random, somewhere in Pennsylvania almost surely you would run across it. The powerful suction of the colony's hospitality was magnified yet more by the abundance of cheap and fertile land. To its rich and expansive acres the province drew people not only from Britain but also from across the Channel, from Germany especially, and from its neighbors—even, indeed, from the faraway reaches of Russia. As the years ran on, more non-English settled in Penn's land of hope than in any of the other original colonies.

Among the thousands and thousands who set foot in Pennsylvania the Germans and Scotch-Irish played an effective part in the making of its civilization. Most of the Germans came from the lovely and productive Rhineland, especially from the Palatinate, which in their better days they had farmed with a fine and dexterous skill. Some of them were Lutherans, and some were German Calvinists. But a great many more held to some form of Pietism, whose cardinal principles, like those of Quakerism, stressed the inner spirituality and renounced most of the formal religious practice. In their homeland the bulk of these people had borne the weight of the recurrent religious wars. When, in 1648, the Peace of Westphalia put an end to the last and most agonizing of them, the Thirty Years' War, peace was still a fragile thing. Not only was the land in shambles, its economy shattered, and starvation rife, but before long there was yet more bleeding and dying, for crown now instead of church. Thus forever badgered and beset, the common, hardworking multitudes, the farmers, the tradesmen, and the artisans, found the heart-taking wonder of Penn's Paradise too enchanting to resist, and as one year followed another, more and more of them set forth for the commonwealth where the world seemed about to begin anew—in fact, in 1738, a little more than fifty years after the colony's start, some nine thousand newcomers from the upper Rhine went ashore at Philadelphia to make their way for the rich farmlands toward the hinterland west.

To their new haunts the Germans brought diligence, skill, and frugality. They became the colony's foremost craftsmen, its finest tanners, weavers, potters, carpenters, and cabinetmakers. They were its first ironsmiths; they pioneered in typefounding; and they made paper and wool. In farming they stood second to none, and save when the weather was on the Devil's side, their granaries choked with barley, wheat, and rye, while in their meat houses juicy hams and bacons ogled spacious slabs of beef and pork. Though the Germans ate plainly, they had no aversion to compounding their hard-earned harvest into a plentitude of tasty dishes, to which their brewmasters, the most expert this side of Germany, brought the mellowing touch of an endless flow of sudsy bliss. So effective was the German's husbandry that he was able to feed not only his own, but others in the colony as well; indeed, it was not long before he was disposing of some of his products beyond its frontiers, up and down the length of America—even, rather curiously, across the billowing Atlantic. But for all their great success in field and workshop, the Germans were politically sterile—indifferent if not incompetent. Settling in isolated little clusters, living a clannish and almost patriarchal existence, they remained apart from non-Germans, clinging with all the obstinacy of the provincial Teuton to their ancient folkways, their Protestantism, and their guttural vernacular, of which a strange barbarism still lingers in the speech of the Pennsylvania Dutch, the oldest immigrant dialect to remain in daily use in America.

The Scotch-Irish were descendants of Scotsmen who in the seventeenth century had crossed to Ireland to live on lands confiscated from the natives. But the Scotch gained neither prosperity nor peace of mind. Fanatically Presbyterian, they loathed the Irish for their Romanism no less than they did their English landlords for their Established Church, which they were made to sustain with tithes. Nor did they waste any love on the godly Quakers, whose teachings they could not fathom and which they never ceased to revile.

Of a restless, footloose nature, the Scotch-Irish trundled inland, not only settling in Pennsylvania, but roving into western Maryland, the Virginia valley, and the Carolina frontier lands. A salty folk, desperately poor, hardheaded, individualistic, and yet reared in the rough democracy of their Scottish church, they read their Bibles with their shotguns cocked as they struggled through the wilderness. They were relentless in their faith, adhering to its dour propositions with a high and bristling surety and sublimating it at times to suit their advantage. The doctrine of predestination, which promised ultimately to store nearly every one of them in a hot and flaming Hell, they accepted as they did the day and night. But while they were on earth—at least in the American sector—they took upon themselves the mission of striking down Jehovah's enemies, especially the infidel red man, whose lands and goods they seized and whom they elected for extermination. To the Quakers, whose tolerance and pacifism they abhorred, they were a source of endless irritation. Contentious and self-assertive, as frontiersmen generally are, they flouted government when it countered what they deemed to be their natural rights and interests.

However, in their faults lay an intrinsic strength. Forged in struggle, they took shape on the anvil of America to become the hammerhead of the later Jacksonian democracy.

4   Unlike the Puritans, the Quakers were not noted as lovers of learning. To have told a Quaker that a little learning could be a dangerous thing would have prompted his rejoinder that much learning could be infinitely worse. Not dependent upon an educated clergy, Quakers could rejoice, as did their governor, that they were immune to the "useless and sophistical science" of the higher learning. Though he himself had leafed through many books and had attended Oxford—and had even been elected to membership in the Royal Society—Penn, nevertheless, was wary of an "inordinate pursuit of knowledge." Not only had it brought about Adam's sad sin, but it had also despoiled the universities into dens of evil—"signal places," Penn let it be known, "for idleness, profaneness, and gross ignorance." The learning he recommended concerned itself with "setting up the Kingdom of God in the hearts of men." To such a simple, if somewhat nebulous, end, all the young Quaker needed was a handful of "sensible and practical truths." Let him learn to read and write a legible hand. Scrawny though this curriculum is in afterlight, in its day it was sumptuous, and what is more, it had to be mastered by every child, rich or poor, male or female. The commonwealth had scarcely got up steam when this principle was written into its law. For a Quaker, hence, to maintain himself illiterate was something of a feat.

If Penn looked askance at learning, he was ready enough to make suggestions for its improvement. His pedagogy was actually of an advanced order. Sometimes, in truth, it could have rolled straight out of Locke or even Comenius, the superpedagogue of the century and for a long time to come. Like Locke, Penn called for more stress on the useful and for less on the memory. "Reading many books," he insisted, "is but taking the mind from meditation." We are at pains, he lamented, to make children scholars, "to talk rather than to know, which is true canting." What he preferred for his own children was "fair writing and the most useful parts of mathematics; and some business when young —whatever else they are taught." Like Comenius, Penn stood up for knowledge of nature, wherein he discerned an "excellent book, easy, useful, and profitable." "Its rules," he went on, "are few, plain, and reasonable," and "it should be more studied." Instead of gorging the young with "words and rules to know grammar and rhetoric and a strange language or two," let them cultivate their "genius to mechanical and physical or natural knowledge. . . ." True enough, when languages serve a useful purpose (as they must have in Penn's own case, for he was familiar with Latin, Greek, French, and Dutch), they ought not to be "despised or neglected"—nevertheless, Penn insisted, "things are still to be preferred." For it had come to his notice that children would "rather be making of tools and instruments of play, shaping, drawing, framing and building, etc., than getting some rules . . . by heart." Again, like Comenius—indeed, like present-day partisans of UNESCO—Penn beheld in education the overriding alternative to war. "It would," he assures us, "give men an understanding of themselves, of the world they are born into, how to be useful to themselves and others, and how to save and help, not to injure or destroy." Like the moderns, once more, Penn grounded his pedagogy on an understanding of the child. "Cross not the genius of the child," he warned, "but match their talents well"—a chord which was to be struck again and again in the palpitant prose of Rousseau. The notion, then given almost unanimous approval, that a child learns best when his caboose is given a frequent whacking got nowhere with Friend Penn. Instead, he wanted learning to be made "easy and cheerful without much fierceness or beating." Did the child nevertheless disport himself like a budding Nero? It made no matter—let the wrongdoer be persuaded "to amendment by smiles and favor." So overborne with this principle was the Pennsylvania governor that he put it to work on his own son, William, Jr., which may—or may not—account for the lad's subsequent sad collapse from moral rectitude.

5   Although its cultural diversity obliged the province to steer an astutely neutral course, Quaker leaders were plainly aware of the government's educational role. "If we would preserve our government," Penn remarked in his *Address to Protestants,* "we must endear it to the people. To do this . . . we must secure the youth"—an axiom as old at least as Greek antiquity. By 1682 this principle had been transcribed into the Great Law by calling upon the governor and the council not only to establish and organize schools but also "to encourage and reward the authors of useful sciences and laudable inventions. . . ." In addition, all twelve-year-olds were to be introduced to some "useful trade or skill, to the end that none may be idle, but the poor may work to live and the rich, if they became poor, may not want." The year following, in 1683, parents or guardians, or the trustees of orphans, were ordered to provide instruction for their fledglings in reading and writing.

But the government was by no means content to confine its educational interest to the mere confection of laws. In fact, as early as 1683, Penn and the council dickered successfully with one Enoch Flower, a schoolmaster of twenty years' trial in England, to teach reading, writing, and account keeping to rising Philadelphians. Despite its public sanction, Flower's instruction was free only to the poor. All others had to lay down their cash at the bursar's wicket, and if anybody chanced to be so flush as to be able to spend £10 a year, Flower not only instructed him but also lodged and victualed him, besides tending to his dirty laundry. Taking one thing with another, Master Enoch fared remarkably well. In fact, after only three years of practice, he had feathered his pedagogic cap far beyond the Quaker commonwealth and was fetching pupils even from distant Barbados.

By the end of the century a number of schools in Pennsylvania were enjoying a flourishing trade, but the Friends' Public School outflourished them all. Starting in 1689, the school was to be run at the "cost and charges of the people of God, called Quakers," but it was to be open to any seeker of knowledge, no matter what his faith. In spite of its name, the school extracted fees from its clients, though it took pains to give this practice some mellowing by receiving the rich "at reasonable rates and the poor . . . for nothing." The Friends' Public School began its daily sessions under the direction of George Keith, a man of somewhat volatile habit, who, launched as a Presbyterian, changed himself into a Quaker, only to unfold later into an Anglican. The mercurial Keith endured the discomforts of his office for just a year, whereupon he was replaced by Thomas Makin, a solidly grounded Latinist, who taught his charges for almost twoscore years, until 1733 to be exact, when his luck ran out and he stumbled from a wharf and drowned. Despite such sad blows from fate, the Friends' Public School prospered—in fact, like its elder sister, the Boston Latin School, it is still carrying on, though its present designation is the William Penn Charter School, to memorialize the receipt of its original writ from Penn's own hand. Pitched on a sumptuous 20-acre plot in Germantown, it now dispenses its instruction and recreation as a country day school.

Between Quaker educational theory and its application in practice yawned a vast and unbridgeable divide. Not only were Pennsylvanians at too great odds among themselves to permit the Quakers to enforce even their mildest requirements, but some of then openly snorted at the whole business and would have no part of it. As the years drew on, moreover, the relationship between Penn and the colonists steadily deteriorated. Forced to make for England to defend his right and title to his province, Penn presently found himself snagged in the coils of litigation, and what he had expected to be only a short sojourn dragged out for long and wearisome years. Meanwhile, in the commonwealth the rulers and the people got into one another's hair. The blunt truth is that Penn, whose capacity for being fooled sometimes bordered on the miraculous, had entrusted the reins of government to inept and prehensile hands. Under the circumstances the possibility of any general educational progress soon fell apart. What aggravated matters still more was the presence of some many divergent sects, each making clamor for itself and each beating the drum for a free hand in the schooling of its children. Some of them, like the

Anglicans and the Presbyterians, despised the Quakers, and they were always ready to tamper with the Friends' good intentions and, if possible, to scuttle them. In the end the hard-pressed Quakers, pocketing their disappointment, abandoned what they once had written so hopefully into their ordinance. Thus, where but a few years back they had made the state the trustee for its youth and ordained the establishment of schools and the instruction of all its children, in 1701 they vouchsafed the right to all "religious societies or assemblies and congregations of Protestants . . . to purchase any land or tenements for . . . houses of religious worship, schools, and hospitals." The way for parochial schooling was thus legally open.

6 Free to work out their educational ideas to their own taste, Pennsylvanians now evolved somewhat in the manner of their neighbors in New York and New Jersey. Besides schools for Quakers one finds a medley of sectarian effort, as witness the charitable evangelical enterprise of the Society for the Propagation of the Gospel in Foreign Parts, besides a number of private endeavors, mainly in Philadelphia. As might be expected, the interest in education varied from sect to sect, even in truth, from one parish to another. Save for the Moravians, to give an example, the generality of Germans did little to forward learning. Where they were not altogether indifferent to its charms and benefits, they confined themselves largely to the teaching of the stark essentials, which is to say reading, some writing now and then, and, of course, their religion and its attendant virtues. Their appalling lack of cultural get-up-and-go can doubtless be attributed to their peasant background, but in a measure also to the fact that, like the Friends, not a few of them regarded the cultivation of the intellect rather dimly, and even apprehensively.

From the German, nonetheless, came two of the colony's most memorable schoolmen, Francis Daniel Pastorius and Christopher Dock. The former, a Pietist but also a very practical-minded man, had herded the first flocks of Germans to the commonwealth. Trained in law, he was, nevertheless, a man of broad intellectual interests, thoroughly acquainted with science and theology and well schooled in the ancient classics. When his duties as immigration agent reached their end, Pastorius was still not prepared to suffer the burdens of retirement. Instead, he turned his talents upon pedagogy, schoolmastering for a spell at Germantown and later in the renowned Friends' Public School. Though he subscribed wholeheartedly to the Pietists' pacifism, and was even a proclaimed lover of children, in the classroom Pastorius was strictly a no-nonsense man. In consequence, he became known far and wide not only for his fantastic stock of knowledge but even more for the corrective surgery of his ever-ready stick.

Less learned and less given to ferocity was Christopher Dock, who seeded and tended the pedagogical field for more than twoscore years. He has come down the shadowy avenue of time a devout and amiable man, one who apparently loved his humble calling. His views on education, though belabored with attacks of Mennonite piety, disclose him, even so, as one who clearly understood that the pedagogical art and mystery consist of something more than ramming knowledge into the heads of fear-ridden schoolchildren. His educational essay, *Schul-Ordnung,* which he committed to paper in the middle seventeen hundreds, did not get into type until 1770, when the celebrated Christopher Saur printed and published it. Let loose, as Saur permitted himself to advertise, "out of love for the human race," Dock's *Schul-Ordnung* was the first work to light the pedagogic wick in the colonies, and is thus the granddaddy of a line of uncountable descendants, which, as we all know, are currently multiplying with amazing fecundity.

Among Pennsylvania Germans it was, by all odds, the Moravians who toiled most bravely for education. But these people were never many, and by the Revolution they numbered barely twenty-five hundred souls. They had taken their pedagogy from the teachings of the illustrious Comenius, a leader in their church and a giant in the world of learning. On earth during the Thirty Years' War, Comenius had suffered not a little from its sorrow—in fact, for long years his great work lay on the edge of oblivion. But time became his sweet avenger, and as the years passed on, his countrymen gave him an honored niche in the national heart. The schools the Moravians erected at Bethlehem and Nazareth and elsewhere naturally made their own sectarian requirements their first concern. Even so, the Moravians stand out for a number of high achievements. In the American Colonies they were probably the first to conduct an infant school. In an era when all too often girls were nobodies, the Moravians opened a boarding school for them at Lititz and another, more advanced, for their older sisters. They labored without letup to bring light to the Indian, and sometimes they succeeded. Nor let it be forgotten that these people were head over heels in love with music—indeed, as long ago as 1742, in their *Singakademie,* their tonal artists were rejoicing the timbered hills of Bethlehem with the hosannas of Johann Sebastian Bach. So enamored of music were these simple folk that, despite the hand-wringing of grumbling Quakers, they persisted in revealing its magic to their young at school.

But it was the Scotch-Irish who struck the sturdiest blows for learning. Although they lived a rough and primitive life, these Presbyterians, like their theological cousins in New England, were bent on being literate. Not only did they breed and train their offspring in the company of the ABCs, but they also took steps to keep their supply of ministers plentifully sufficient. The first deliberate move in this direction, as far as anyone can tell, was ventured by the Rev. William Tennent, an intimate of the mysterious ways and byways of sacred science, and as familiar with the learned languages as with English. He entrenched himself and his erudition at Neshaminy, where, in 1726, he entered pedagogical service. His seminary, known as the Log College, was open to any youth of understanding mind, whether he had his eye on a prospective parsonage or not. Though Log College slipped into nothingness in less than twenty years, in its days of pristine vigor the school knew neither peer nor rival. It became the germ cell of Princeton, and prior to the founding of that college, it was without doubt the colony's most industrious drill house for aspiring Presbyterian preachers.

To satisfy the appetite for the classical discipline, and also, of course, to lay the intellectual roadbed for their future men of God, Scotch Presbyterians relied on a number of Latin schools, among which the Presbyterian Grammar School, located at New London, stands out. With the Rev. Francis Allison in command, it began its business of instruction in 1743, and before long it was enjoying patronage not only from rank-and-file Presbyterians but even from the Philadelphia high and mighty. Its stress, as usual in those days, fell almost entirely on the ancient languages, in particular their grammar and rhetoric, not only for the sagacity inherent in the venerable masters of such arcane subjects, but even more for their presumable power to strengthen the human mind. Intellectually, the Scotch-Irish easily outdistanced the stodgy Friends, and as they matured in years and experience, the former had no trouble in displacing the latter from their seat of political dominance.

As in New York, so in Pennsylvania the Society for the Propagation of the Gospel in Foreign Parts stood ready to proffer its blend of primary schooling and Anglican piety to those of low estate. But in Penn's polyglot land, with its chaos of loyalties to flags and creeds, the SPG ran into difficulties and frustrations. For the gospel drummers to dispense their educational charity was all very fine—maybe even noble—but underneath the sugar of their good works lurked the inescapable pill of Anglicanism. Not a few sectarians, especially those disdaining the common formalities of religion, viewed the whole business as a ruse—nay, a conspiracy—to seduce their children from the true religion of their fathers. Some saw the SPG as a sort of Trojan horse, loaded with rich and knavish Englishmen who were ready to pour out when the time was ripe to make themselves the colony's political overlords. Besides such sinister dreads, some folk, especially those in whose veins ran the blood of Germans, entertained suspicions that the society was laying plots against their precious faith, and even against their German tongue, no less beloved. All in all, the Propagators found Pennsylvania a reluctant vineyard. They had planned to establish a least a score of schools, but they probably never had more than a dozen. By 1763, after a decade of brave striving and blighted hopes, the organization threw up its weary hands and assigned the re-calcitrant Pennsylvanians to their all-but-inescapable damnation.

7   Although much of Pennsylvania's schooling carried denomina-tional labels, there was no lack of laic enterprise. As up North, in the colonies of Massachusetts and New York, the rising secular pressures were bearing on the holy land, particularly in Philadelphia, which in the fleeing years had turned into a booming business metropolis. In fact, by the century's middle years Penn's "green country town" had evolved into one of the largest municipalities in Christendom—the biggest in the New World and surpassed in the motherland only by London and Bristol. However sadly Quakers viewed the chase for material pleasures, money-making was clearly not on their list of vices. "What do they believe in?" sightseers in Philadelphia once asked Benjamin Franklin. "They believe," was his arched reply, "in 6 per cent compound interest." Few Yankees had a keener nose for profit than the Children of Light. The counting-house, no less than the meetinghouse, was their natural element, and some of them not only subdued its elusive secrets but in the end were destined to die rich. Not all Quakers, of course, let themselves be hoodwinked by the golden calf—many of them, it is only fair to point out, continued to cling to their plain and somber ways, and when their influence showed signs of waning, they sought, as per immemorial custom, to bolster pub-lic morality with a broadside of drastic laws. But, in the main, even the moneymakers inclined to remain in the faith, Quakers in name, if not in the free delight they took in their forbidden hedonism. In their expanding worldliness they were joined by others, in illustration, the thriving Scotch and English merchants who had descended upon the city to make their fortune. Never loath to relish their riches, Philadelphia's commercial nabobs released their libido in building sumptuous homes and gardens and sweetening their every day with the many comforts and gratifications of life. It was they who championed the arts and sciences, who patronized the concert and the stage, and who above all others in-stalled their sons in private schools.

Whenever education becomes a vendible commodity, there is, of course, no sane reason why it, any more than anything else for sale—from garters and hair curlers to stocks and bonds—should escape the pressures of supply and demand. Hence, as private schools increased in number, one observes their owners scrambling for pupils, wooing them with an alluring stock of subjects, and promising them sure and quick results with an "easy method" or even the "best and simplest method." As in other towns of business bustle, in Philadelphia instruction was to be had in almost anything, from the commonplace Latin, besides Greek, Hebrew, and Arabic, to the modern tongues. But it was the useful subjects which

were the favorites, especially mathematics, surveying, bookkeeping, navigation, and what has since graduated into natural science. Among the many
private virtuosos the name of Andrew Lamb sticks out significantly, not
only for the man's long and diligent service in the schoolmaster's frock,
but even more for the singularity of his background. A seafarer of no
mean experience, Lamb had collided with English law, and was able to
save himself from the noose only by consenting to let himself be deported
—a judgment he concurred in with admirable alacrity. In Philadelphia,
which he was to bedizen and enlighten for many a year, Lamb made a
specialty of training young men to navigate the sea. Not only did he
attend to their needs in person in his chambers, but, when requested,
he also administered instruction in their homes, and he taught them
everything marine science then required, from trigonometry and spherical
geometry to gauging, dialing, coasting, plain sailing, parallel sailing,
coastal sailing, and even great-circle sailing. Like most experts who have
mastered their craft at firsthand, Lamb was derisive of mere academicians.
"Sailors," he gave public notice, "be not cheated by landmen who pretend
to navigation, for they know nothing of a sea journal . . . and the use
of sea charts," whereas, he went on, his scholars were "qualified to go
mates the first voyage."

It would be a mistake to infer that private education reserved its
solicitude only for the carriage trade. The well-off were its choicest custom
to be sure, but what then passed for low society was certainly not overlooked. In fact, for the special benefit of artisans and other workingmen,
a private night school was opened in Philadelphia as early as 1731.
Founded by James Lloyd, it was hailed as a place "where writing, arithmetic, vulgar and decimal, and some parts of mathematics, are taught."
Three years later one Theophilus Grew, an emigrant from Maryland and
an almanac maker by trade, announced nocturnal instruction in navigation, surveying, and mathematics. The number of such lamplight groves
was, of course, small, and their increase for a long time was slow; even
so, as the sixties came into view, such schools had become common enough
to be the rule.

For the gentle sex, as usual, the chances for schooling were more
restrained; nevertheless, the fact remains that there were opportunities,
and no young lady whose parents were of any consequence needed to
grow up to be a cultural cipher. One sights the possibility of such enlightenment as far back as 1722, when a Mrs. Rhodes let it be known that
she was prepared "to teach young ladies or gentlewomen to read and
write French to perfection," besides showing them how to "flourish on
muslin after the most expeditious way and at very reasonable prices."
As the century moved on, such temples of girlish opportunity augmented,
and so did their repertoire of culture. Not only could the fair ones seek
perfection in Latin and its offspring, French, Spanish, Italian, and Portu-

guese, but they could also carry on with grammar and bookkeeping and exhilarate their psyches with music, singing, dancing, or painting. Needless to say, competition for the female academic trade was brisk, and to attract patrons the professors of young ladies went to great lengths, recommending not only their specialties but their own talents as well. One, for example, found French "so necessary and polite," while another paid tribute to his capacity for teaching his consumers to speak and write it in a grammatical and elegant manner. In music one tonal master concentrated on giving lessons in the art of playing the spinet, while a rival broadcast his eagerness to teach the "violin, hautboy, German flute, common flute, and dulcimer." Still another volunteered his services in guitar playing. Everything considered, it was French and music which exerted the greatest demand. Franklin, indeed, regarded them as indispensable to the cultivation of feminine propriety and refinement.

8   Nor was the zeal for learning confined to paid professionals. In fact, as often before in the history of man's quest for knowledge, some of its most talented seekers were amateurs, outsiders to the academic community. Philadelphia had not yet gone into its fifties when Benjamin Franklin and a few friends organized themselves into the Junto, a mutual improvement club whose members pledged, hand on breast, "to love truth for truth's sake," as well as "mankind in general." To such an end every three months each member was put upon to harangue his fellows with an essay on some instructive and edifying theme, such as, "Is it justifiable to put private men to death for the sake of public safety and tranquility, who have committed no crime?" or "If the sovereign power attempts to deprive a subject of his right . . . is it justifiable for him to resist, if he is able?" or "Whence comes the dew that stands on the outside of a tankard that has cold water in it in the summer time?" Once a week of a Friday evening they sat at a member's fireside or, if the mood befell them, in a tavern, where between forkloads of food and goblets of foaming beer, they enjoyed colloquies on the nature of sound, vapors, the perils of fiat money, or even the possibility of attaining perfection while they were still at large on earth.

The lively interest Franklin took in forwarding knowledge led him presently to lay plans for a more ambitious undertaking, one less gregarious, perhaps, than the Junto, and more mature and sophisticated in its enterprise and output. The upshot of Franklin's cerebration was the American Philosophical Society, the first guild in the hemisphere devoted to the advancement of science and, historically, still one of the national glories.

Headed by Franklin, the organization began life—the year was 1743—as a candid copy of the celebrated Royal Society of England. Its rules, its minutes announced, "were adopted from the rules of that illustrious body, the Royal Society of London, whose example the American Philosophical Society think it their honor to follow in their endeavors of enlarging the sphere of knowledge and the useful arts." It promised to aid and support the "useful subjects, either in physics, medicine, astronomy, mathematics, etc.," by encouraging studies and experiments and by acclaiming those who made them with the society's public eulogy. But its founders also entertained a friendly disposition toward the studies and improvement of America, in particular its natural resources, from its farmlands to its mines and forests. Time saw its members explore every imaginable department of knowledge, practical and otherwise. They pondered electricity, pneumatics, and hydraulics; they creased their brows over manufacturing, steam power, and canals. From time to time the society offered prizes for the best suggestions concerning the construction of stoves and fireplaces, better ship pumps, the improvement of lamps, or the preservation of peach trees. Soon after Yorktown it even offered a premium of $100 for the best proposal of a plan which would present a meet and effective system of national education for the schooling of young America.

Famous names emblazon the society's roster. There is, of course, Franklin, its cofounder and first president, and in office until 1790, when he died. His successor was Thomas Jefferson, who, as much almost as Franklin, devoted himself unstintingly to the advancement of science, both theoretical and applied. He dallied with weights and pulleys and with polygraphs and chronometers of diverse sorts. He wrote an essay on Anglo-Saxon, a memoir on "certain bones of a quadruped of a clawed kind" found in western Virginia, a paper on a proposed agricultural society, and another on a molding board for plows. He invented a dumb-waiter and a folding chair, and he was an architect of surpassing talent. Then there is John Bartram. A "plain country man," he was a Quaker until one fateful day a message from the Inner Light, a little bit too cryptic, misled him, and he rejected the divinity of Jesus, for which mistake he was read out of the meeting. For all his Quaker conditioning, Bartram succumbed to a powerful intellectual thirst to make himself one of the country's foremost botanists. There is also the laureled David Rittenhouse, self-taught astronomer and mathematician, and perfector of a miniature planetarium, the wonder of its time and still an object to startle the imagination as it reposes in its spot of immortality at Princeton University. Finally, there is John James Audubon, naturalist and ornithologist, remembered not only for his science but also for the wizardry of his artist's brush, and commemorated not so long ago on a postage stamp of the United States.

There is no need to belabor—the roll of members *elegantiarum* runs on and on. Their fame sparkled in all directions, not simply all over

America, but in the motherland and the rest of Europe, where Franklin's society, as popular parlance insisted on calling it, engendered not a little curiosity and even astonishment and admiration. Its industry was part, indeed, of the energetic traffic in ideas and other cultural enterprise between the Old World and the New, a traffic which was by no means a one-way movement but which flowed from the east as well as the west. To England's parishes, for example, America exported some of its most eminent clerics. Painters, like Copley and Trumbull, rejoiced art lovers in London, while Stuart enjoyed royal patronage even in the dark days of the Revolution. And—to make an end—the *New England Primer*, though intended to teach the Calvinistic young of Massachusetts, was printed and extensively read in England.

With so much eagerness for knowledge manifesting itself all about, the need for first-rate books became insistent. Once again the resourceful Franklin found a solution with his creation, in 1742, of the Library Company of Philadelphia. This body, which may have been the first subscription library in New World history, attained a swift celebrity, and as usual in the case of a marked success, it was soon being aped by a host of imitators. In consequence, it may well deserve credit, as Franklin assures us in his autobiography, for having mothered "all the North American subscription libraries. . . ." Not only was it the arch-propagator of a prodigious number of offspring, but by virtue of its maternal role it also contributed not a little to ameliorating the American mind and manner. Its descendants, Franklin made so bold as to assert, "have improved the general conversation of Americans, made the common tradesmen and farmers as intelligent as most gentlemen from other countries, and perhaps have contributed in some degree to the stand so generally made throughout the colonies in defence of their privileges."

Less familiar to the run of contemporary Americans than Franklin, but quite as meritorious for his intellectual accomplishments, is James Logan, an Irishman born in Scotland, a moneyed merchant Quaker, and a power in Pennsylvania politics. But his light was manifold, and in the realm of learning it shone white, sharp, and brilliant. Botanist, astronomer, physicist, Logan harbored one of the most puissant minds in the Colonies. The first one in America to import a copy of Newton's epoch-making *Principia Mathematica*, this self-tutored mathematician not only comprehended its recondite revelation but by and by was even tendering it some amendment. The gift of tongues was his no less than that of science—he could shake Greek, Latin, Hebrew, and Arabic out of his Quaker sleeves almost as readily as his mother tongue. In botany he was the first to give experimental proof that plants, like Homo sapiens, engage in the activity of sex. Nor was he backward as a writer. He translated Cicero's *Cato Major*, and Cato's *Moral Distichs*, as he said, he "Englished in couplets." When death made an end of him in 1751, he was at work on

A Defense of Aristotle and the Ancient Philosophers—an undertaking which has never suffered from a want of volunteers. But it is only when we glance at the man over our shoulder and observe him in the long ago, settled in his den, seeking to throw off his earthly cares amid his beloved volumes, that we behold him in his natural setting. His library was one of the largest in the land, and its titles in science had no equal. A book lover, he was also a book lender. To studious young men he opened his shelves with an overflowing generosity, and when at length the angels took him aloft to his just reward, he bequeathed his treasures, so affectionately hoarded and studied over a lifetime, and housed, most fittingly, in a mansion all their own, to his fellow Philadelphians.

9   While Franklin was busy hatching the Philosophical Society, he was also talking up a new kind of school—an "academy" he called it— designed to ease the Philadelphian's mounting thirst for useful knowledge. But the years have a way of edging on, and it was not until 1749, with the issuance of his *Proposals Relating to the Education of Youth in Philadelphia,* that Franklin took up the cudgels in its behalf. What he had in mind was a school which "would teach those things that are likely to be most useful and most ornamental; regard being had for the several professions in which they are intended." From this and similar pronouncements there ultimately came the Philadelphia Academy. Opened in 1751, the school was to be nonsectarian, but its trustees were nearly all devotees of the Anglican rite. Had Franklin been able to follow his own inclination, his nursery of learning would, no doubt, have laid its chief stress on the modern and practical subjects, and especially the mother tongue in all its elements, from spelling, grammar, and composition to rhetoric, letter writing, and the art and science of "speaking properly and gracefully." But the school's trustees, academically far more staid than the audacious Benjamin, were reluctant to follow him in such a mad caper. Consequently, when the academy tolled out its summons to its first clients, they could cross swords with Latin and Greek, as generation upon generation of learners had done before them. But if they hungered to savor something fresh and zesty, then the academy's bill of fare offered no end of palatable goodies. Indeed, what set the academy apart from the reigning grammar schools, whether foreign or domestic, was its commitment to render instruction in the modern tongues besides, as it let out the tidings in Franklin's *Pennsylvania Gazette,* in "History, Geography, Chronology, Logic, and Rhetoric; also Writing, Arithmetic, Merchants Accounts, Geometry, Algebra, Surveying, Gauging, Navigation, Astronomy, Drawing in Perspective, and other mathematical Sciences; with natural and mechanical Philosophy, etc. . . ." In addition the academy was ready to dabble in teacher training.

What the academy put before its pupils was scarcely novel. In both North and South, free-lance masters, as has already been narrated, were hawking instruction in more or less the same substance. The demand for enlightenment in practical as well as fancy knowledge had climbed as the interests of the age had grown more earthbound, especially in the cities, and in this regard Philadelphia was no exception. Soon, in fact, the academy was gasping with such throngs of students that in 1755, when it was, so to speak, still at nurse, it had to be changed and rechartered as the College, Academy, and Charitable School of Phiadelphia. Henceforth tuition in the classical and philosophical disciplines was to be the concern of the college. The sixth center of the higher learning to rise in the Colonies, the College of Philadelphia later became the University of Pennsylvania, which, as everyone knows, is still at work, somewhat gray to be sure, and balding, but as intrepid and exuberant as ever. For young Pennsylvanians of earnest academic aspiration, the new college was a true boon, for in an era when travel was a burden and even a menace to limb and life, they were no longer obliged to make for far-off ports, say, Oxford or Cambridge, or even Harvard, which, though less remote, was too repulsively Puritan for the comfort of the urbane Philadelphian, and especially Franklin, who relished an intense aversion to the ancient school.

To get the College of Philadelphia off to a good start, Franklin recommended as its first provost the Rev. William Smith, an Anglican, but born and raised in the chill-swept moors of Scotland. No stranger to the teaching craft, Smith had performed its operations upon his countrymen and on the sons of well-fixed New Yorkers. More important, he had composed a book, the *A General Idea of a College of Mirania,* a cultural mansion, which, though no more real than Adam in white tie and tails, addressed itself to the serious business of educating youth to become useful and dutiful citizens in a great Christian state. To such attainment the author turned aside from the common curriculum of his time, a curriculum which in the Middle Ages had flourished as the Seven Liberal Arts and which, though patched and threadbare, continued for all its hoariness to be admired by academicians everywhere. In opposition, Smith stood up for a practical and useful schooling, suitable to the conditions of America, with stress on religion, history, and agriculture—an innovation which warmed not only Franklin but also several other promoters of the higher learning in Philadelphia.

Despite his Anglican ambitions—it was bruited about that he aspired to an Anglican episcopate in America and a "pair of lawn sleeves for himself"—Provost Smith was, nevertheless, an active friend and advocate of the natural sciences, and in spite of the many burdens his executive office forced upon him, he found time to teach a course in natural philosophy, or, as the word is today, physics. It was Smith too who put forth a friendly plea for David Rittenhouse to persuade the college powers to illuminate that unlettered man of science with a master of arts, "in recognition of his felicity and natural genius in mechanics, mathematics, astronomy, and other liberal arts and sciences." At bottom, though, William Smith continued to serve God assiduously, and even when he permitted himself to be an encourager of the natural scientists, his advocacy was always marked with faith and piety—in truth, it was the Rev. Mr. Smith's conviction that the "interests of Christianity will be advanced by promoting the interests of science."

During Smith's stay in office, however, the college turned its back to Franklin's "useful learning" and bestowed its favors instead on the Greeks and Romans. But Franklin's ghost continued to steal through its corridors, and in the passing years, as worldiness grew more fashionable, Franklin's stress began to be felt anew. When this happened, somehow past frustrations were overcome, and eventually the lot fell to the college to establish the first chair in botany in colonial America, and even to usher in the first systematic instruction in medicine.

10   As for the Quakers, for many years they maintained their abnegation from the higher arts and sciences. A few of them, it is true, lifted themselves above the common plane, as, in exhibit, Bartram, the botanist; Godfrey, the deviser of the quadrant; Dickinson, the author of the *Farmer's Letters;* and—not to forget—the extraordinary James Logan. Aside from this handful, however, and two or three more, the Children of Light persisted in sifting their learning through the fine meshes of their distrust. Not until 1827, when schism threatened to rent their seamless gown of orthodoxy, did the old guard of Quakers confess that their continued neglect of the higher learning might well endanger the purity of the faith. The world being what it is, they now reversed their historic stand. Declaring for an "education equal in all respects to that which can be obtained at college," they opened the Friends' Central School. But it was not until 1856—more than two centuries after the birth of Harvard—that the Quakers at last ventured to cross the Rubicon to transform their school into Haverford College, which is still in active and wholesome practice, and justly renowned. On its heels other colleges quickly followed. There was Guilford in North Carolina, Earlham in Indiana, Swarthmore in Pennslyvania, Whittier in California, William Penn in Iowa, Wilmington in Ohio, George Fox in Oregon, and several more. Bryn Mawr, heeled and upheld with the wealth of Quaker Joseph Fox, was inaugurated near the end of the century, in 1885, as the feminine counterpart of Haverford. It is easy to forget that Quaker altruism did not limit itself to Quaker colleges. It was a Quaker, Ezra Cornell, who supplied the funds to found Cornell, and it was Johns Hopkins, another Quaker, who endowed Johns Hopkins at Baltimore. In fact, it was a Quaker who immortalized himself in the history of good works as the man who helped start Brown University on the long run to its present eminence.

To sum up the main points of the many pages preceding, let the following be rehearsed. A vast cultural difference overlay the Middle Colonies. Their people were not, as they were in the sister colonies, almost wholly Anglo-Saxons. For awhile, in fact, the flag of Holland fluttered over one of them. In the realm of faith and conscience, differences were even greater. No religious solidarity threaded together the folk of the Middle Country, as it did in Massachusetts, and no church was supreme and politically over-mastering. As a result, the Middle Colonies enjoyed a toleration unknown—nay, suspected and rejected—in the Bible State. Needless to say, there were social divisions too, but their range was the usual and familiar one, and it was the kind then in general approval.

The Dutch founded New Netherland—or more properly, New Amster-dam—in 1623, and for forty-one years they were its master. In the main they were of a commercial bent, and had it not been for the demands put upon them by their Calvinism, their educational achievement might well have been negligible. As it was, until the English intruded, the Dutch gave their countenance to the town school, and they granted it their support—not with alacrity to be sure—out of the public pocket. As a result, the Dutch were generally literate; in fact, they produced some first-rate theologians and physicians and even a few fair poets.

The coming of the English altered matters, and presently the colony, known as New York, succumbed to the educational policy of the mother-land, which is saying that in the schooling of the young, barring the desti-tute poor, the government scarcely lifted a finger. Under the circumstances, those in funds had recourse to private schools, while the plodding multitude depended on apprenticeship, the mercies of God, or charity. New Yorkers gathered no fame, as did New Englanders, for their devotion to learning. Nor was there any deep and all-embracing principle to rouse them. The first secondary school came late, and its life was short, and so was that of its successor. The first college, designated as King's but known to the world today as Columbia University, did not break upon the scene until 1754—almost a century after the coming of the English and eighteen years more than a century following the advent of Harvard.

Of the Middle Colonies, the most advanced and the most urbane, and hence the most interesting, was the commonwealth of Pennsylvania. Settled in 1682 by the Quakers, the colony stood out for its tolerance and its gen-eral culture. The Quakers—at least in their common run—shied away from intellectuality; yet they were also insistent that the young should master the elementals. Pennsylvania accommodated more sects and nationalities than any other colony—more, for that matter, than any other land on God's footstool. A unified educational program, binding all these disparate and oftentimes discordant elements into a single fabric, was thus out of the question. Consequently, parochial and private schooling was resorted to, and in time it established itself as the prevailing fashion.

Pennsylvania became the most civilized place in the New World, and for a spell Philadelphia supplanted Boston as the intellectual capital of America. Unquestionably, a large credit for this must be placed at Franklin's door. His intellectual appetite amazed even John Adams, whose confidence in the all-around superiority of Boston amounted almost to smugness. The educational program that Franklin sponsored in his academy and subsequently in his college—and also extramurally in his libraries, his publications, and his various brotherhoods of learning—has become justifiably famous. But let the fact not be brushed away that Franklin was only one among several fosterers of enlightenment, as the membership register of the American Philosophical Society visibly and magnificently testifies.

6
AFTER YORKTOWN

Not quite four million persons made up the republic which triumphed at Yorktown. Of these the greater number by far were farmers, for the land which is today cluttered with cities and factories was then mostly field and forest. The few cities which rose from the landscape were, by present standards, pygmies. Philadelphia, the largest, accommodated some 40,000 inhabitants; New York, its nearest rival, accounted for 30,000; while in the great stretches of the South only Charleston, with 10,000, could rightfully declare itself a city. Travel and the interchange of ideas, difficult enough in those days in the older and more advanced lands abroad, were even more onerous in the United States. In 1790, for example, what passed for the nation's postal system comprised less than a hundred offices, of which one alone sufficed to handle the mail of the entire state of New York. The mail was toted by stage, and even when working in relays and urging their horses to their fastest flurry of hoofs, couriers needed two days at least to traverse the stretch that lay between New York and Philadelphia. The country's primitiveness was reflected still further in the lag of its industry and manufacturing. Of the former only shipping and fishing were of any consequence; as for the latter, it scarcely existed.

Though it had brought the British lion to heel, the young republic staggered out of the arena badly mauled. Its land and property lay in wrack and ruin, and its trade and commerce barely breathed, while a debt of $75 million—a breathtaking sum in those days—glowered like a storm cloud over the land. Worse, and the cause of more forboding, was the almost unbelievable impotence of the central government. Stripped of any real authority, it ruled with a weak and hesitant hand, its sovereignty flouted and its mandates ignored, the butt abroad of mordant humors and the cause of the motherland's conviction that someday soon her wayward children would gladly crawl back underneath the maternal wing.

Nor did education escape the scourge of Mars. There was the usual grisly audit—schools shut down, or even put to the torch, and a lack of necessary materials and teachers, to say nothing of a shortage of money and a drooping morale. None of these things, however, counted for much. For in its general run education remained the boon of a privileged handful. When the doors to the charity schools no longer swung open, there ensued no great and widespread wailing. Feelings became more ruffled when private schools succumbed and when the secondary and higher learning crumbled. The war's effect on education was surely baleful; yet sad as it was, it was dwarfed by more urgent matters.

2   The class distinctions which had tainted the American air in 1776 did not drift away with the end of the fighting. For all that, the Revolution wrought a number of changes. England's high and shiny—the royal governors, their trains of functionaries, the jurists, the military and naval brass, the ecclesiastics, and an array of royalist civilians—this aspect of England, of course, had packed and gone. The effect of its departure was not an unmitigated blessing. On the one hand it removed a truculent and sniffish folk; but on the other it lost for America some of its most exemplary people and not a little of its most competent manpower.

All in all, however, when in 1789 the Constitution was adopted, the American social pattern remained pretty much what it had been before the Revolution. Wealth and property—and to some degree blood—were still the insignia of men of quality, and since property alone could unbolt the door to major political office, the rich and well born were in actual fact the ruling classes. As one might expect, the property requirement varied with the office, and it varied also from one place to another. Did a man, for example, propose to serve his fellow men as a giver of their laws? Then, if he lived in South Carolina, before he could make a stand for his office he had to offer ocular proof that he was a freeholder worth no less than $10,000. But if the fates had set him instead in the New Hampshire hills, all he needed to be eligible was a measly $500 in his pocket. Did a man, however, simply want to vote? Then in Massachusetts the suffrage was his, provided he had a freehold yielding no less than $300 a year. But across the line in New Hampshire all a man needed, besides a white complexion and a proper legal age, was a receipt from his tax gatherer that he had paid a modest head tax. With so many strings attached to the franchise the bulk of Americans had little say in the making of their laws—indeed, for every man who enjoyed the right to vote there were half a dozen who did not.

Although the years following Yorktown had witnessed no great transformation in the social order, forces of amassing power were assailing it on every side. The main drive came from the plain people—farmers, sailors, artisans, shopkeepers, and frontiersmen. It was they who fumed against the property prerequisites which barred them from the vote and important public office. And it was they who made a stir for religious liberty, genuine and unfettered, with an end to established churchdom and, per corollary, of submitting to the indignity of paying taxes to give it support. But what many hollered for most of all was a chance to lay their hands on the rich and spacious lands long since preempted and controlled by the rich, by speculators, and for a time even by the Crown.

Even before the gunshots at Lexington there had been a number of reforms in this direction. The Virginia House of Burgesses, led by the iconoclastic Jefferson, had put the ax on entail in 1776 and on primogeniture a few years following. Elsewhere events took almost the same turn, and with the advent of the Union, both these medieval modes of land tenure, which had served the Old World so effectively to hold family domains intact, had all but ceased to exist. With their exit, the chance for the establishment of a landed aristocracy blew up in smoke.

As for the divorce of church and state, this too came to pass. As has been made evident in ground traversed before, the passing years had seen a modest but steady increase in worldliness. The dark and supernatural powers of the air, once so formidable and frightening, had lost not a little of their former potency. By the same token there had been a gentle groundswell in toleration and here and there a relaxing of the bonds of state and church. Even so, on the eve of Bunker Hill all but four states—Rhode Island, Pennsylvania, Delaware and New Jersey—entertained and supported an established church. In New England it was Congregational, while in part of New York it was Anglican. The outbreak of hostilities intensified the movement toward disestablishment. The fact that the Tories worshipped at the rail of the Anglican altar and that their prayers went up for the King and his redcoats did heavy damage to the cause of established Anglicanism. Early in the war the Carolinas, Georgia, and New York uprooted it, and while they were about it, they fenced state from church once and for all. In Virginia the tempest over "religious bondage" broke loose as early as 1776, but the commonwealth was ten years older before its statesmen let Jefferson persuade them to adopt his proposal for religious liberty. The New England Congregationalists proved even tougher. Unsullied by Tory loyalties and fortified by the power of a venerable tradition, they enjoyed a high public favor, so that it was not until the next century that they were brought into line. Massachusetts, the fortress of the former theocracy, held out in one way or another until 1833, when at length it too capitulated.

The liberal spirit flamed also on several secular fronts. It was manifest, for one, in the slow beginnings of prison reform, in the slightly greater friendliness of its penology, and in the guarantees of freedom of speech and of the press inscribed in certain state constitutions. The one great aspiration which continued to sidestep fulfillment was the liberalizing of the franchise and the chance for a man to expand in public office. Three states—New Jersey and the Carolinas—required their lawmakers to be Protestants. Four others—Massachusetts, Pennsylvania, Delaware, and Maryland—exacted some religious reassurance from their public jobholders. As for the right to vote, every one of the thirteen states—or at least their lawful rulers—was convinced that this was too precious to entrust to the mob, that, indeed, it was safe only in the hands of men of place and substance, the possessors, that is, of land and property.

Progress in education was negligible. Not only was it of a minor immediate importance, but farmers, who made up the bulk of the populace, put little stock in book learning which to their closed and peasantlike minds seemed useless to their work. If a few sages in their midst occasionally showed a disposition to grant learning some slight value, almost unanimously they hackled at declaring it a public responsibility and keeping it on its legs with taxes. Let it not be forgotten, however, that no lips were sealed and no press was locked, and so it was at least possible to ring out alarms. But the appeals for reform cried up by a handful of the nation's liberals fell mostly on deaf ears. Not until the spirit of the times had become more hospitable and—more important—until the restrictions on voting and on eligibility for public office had ceased to be a monopoly of the well-fixed, could forward-lookers hope to carry on their campaign against ignorance in the hope of snaring an ultimate triumph.

3   The idea that education was a function of the national state obtained in only one major Western country—the kingdom of Prussia. There, from the century's nonage, it had been favored by the Hohenzollerns, until in the reign of the great Frederick (1740–1786), it was riveted into Prussian *Staatspolitik*. In America, meanwhile, education continued generally to be regarded as a private or semiprivate enterprise, a responsibility left by the government to the church and parent. In this respect some savants are disposed to rule Puritan New England an exception; but if an exception it was, then so was the Puritan state itself, which, as has been observed, was not a lay state but an ecclesiastic one.

The view that the education of the American people was out of place in Federal hands found its way into the making of the Constitution. Therein, like the deity, the subject was given neither notice nor specification. But this should be no cause for astonishment, since the Fathers, broken to the popular assumptions of their time, and in particular to those of the propertied order to which they belonged, did not see fit to deal with education. They were grappling, moreover, with vaster and far more pressing problems. But even had the state of the Union been less tenuous and more tranquil, it is unlikely that the Fathers would have been prone to go very far toward furthering public, tax-supported, universal education. The simple fact is that, save for a lonely few, in education they sported a conservative style and hardly any of them warmed to the notion of extending it freely to just anybody.

However silent the Constitution may have held itself on the subject of the nation's schooling, in the years ahead several of its provisions were to exert a potent influence on fixing the fashion of American education. The assurance, for example, of religious freedom as laid down in the First Amendment has become the bedrock of the nonsectarian public school. At the same time it has stood sentinel for the religious, denominational school, underwriting its right to exist and carry on, besides safeguarding the parent's right to place his child within its hands. The constitutional taboo on the establishment of a state church has carried the principle of church and state separation into the public school, and at bottom has made it secular. By relinquishing to the states the powers not specifically assigned to Federal authority, the Constitution's Tenth Amendment made the state the nation's surrogate in educational matters. Education hence has become a state rather than a national function. As a consequence, American education has evolved diversely over a network of numerous lines, but never, as in some lands—and notably in France—in an all-embracing system of national centralization.

4   Although the Federal Constitution is silent on the subject of education, some of the first state constitutions were not so reticent. In fact, as the eighteenth century faded to its end, of the sixteen states then under the flag, seven had granted space to the subject in their constitutions. North Carolina and Pennsylvania seized the chance as early as 1776. Georgia and Vermont followed a year after. Then came Massachusetts in 1780, New Hampshire in 1784, and Delaware in 1792. Most of these early statements, it is true, swathed themselves in pleasant generalities; even so, their purpose seems plain enough. To take account of a few, North Carolina declared for the establishment of a "school or schools"; Massachusetts, less vague, called for a "school in every town"; and Georgia and Pennsylvania for "one in every county." New Hampshire, for its part, counseled its lawmakers to "cherish" public schools, while Delaware recommended their establishment "as soon as possible."

The grandest and most fluid utterance emanated from Massachusetts. The work mostly of John Adams, it held that popular rights and liberties depend on "spreading the opportunities and advantages of education in the various parts of the country and among the different orders of the people." To this end it directed the "legislatures and magistrates, in all future periods of the commonwealth, to cherish the interests of literature and the sciences, and all the seminaries of them."

As democratic ideas grew more insistent, it was only natural that they should sound an echo in education. Thus, by 1820 a number of state constitutions were making reference to a system of educational democracy. The palm must go to Indiana, which invited its legislators to devise an educational system from the town school to the university "free and open to all." Candor, however, compels one to note that the state was careful to halter its benignity with restraint and to warn its Justinians to stay such benevolence "until circumstances permit."

It can be argued that these early educational statements represented little more than a dreamful wish and that, in truth, a vast breach yawned between word and deed. Still, the fact remains that such fresh visions were showing themselves and, more important, that they were being given the dignity of recognition in the states' fundamental ordinances. Not only did these early constitutions look forward to the establishment of schools, but they also laid the juridic foundation whereon brick by brick Americans erected their edifice of free, tax-supported public education.

5 Before their adoption of the Constitution, the states laying claim to that enormous terrestrial empire beyond the Alleghenies—after some rough-and-ready haggling—had renounced all their claims thereto to the national government. Even before peace put a stop to the bloodletting of the Revolution, the traffic toward the National Domain, as this land came to be known, was picking up, and as settler followed settler to the West, the Continental Congress ordered the area to be measured and mapped. Presently from the drawing board there emerged a diagram depicting townships, each six miles on a side, neatly numbered and arranged into thirty-six squares of which the sixteenth was marked off for the support of education. Two years following, when, in its Ordinance of 1787, Congress created the works to govern its dominion to the Ohio's north, it again lauded education, letting it be known that since religion, morality, and knowledge were "necessary to good government and the happiness of mankind, schools should be forever encouraged." To such purpose the new ordinance made supplement to the original grant of the sixteenth lot by setting aside the twenty-ninth for the forwarding of piety and virtue and by bespeaking two whole townships "perpetually for the purpose of education."

The first state to issue from the National Domain was Ohio, and when, in 1803, it was granted fellowship in the Union, it was duly ceded the sixteenth section of every township to support the schools. In meet tit for tat, the new state agreed to abstain from laying levies on any national grounds within its confines. This unheard-of act became something of a precedent, followed, as the years ran on, by all the states coming into the republic save only three—Texas, Maine, and West Virginia. The practice, moreover, of tapping land for school revenue was presently adopted by several of the original and more elderly states, and today, of course, like baby-sitters and lady officers in the Army, Navy, and Marines, the practice is etched in the American way.

There is good reason to believe that these early measures were responsive to pressures put upon the congressmen by organized land speculators. But there is even better reason to believe that the ordinances were the expression of a sincere desire to people the land. Nor is it improbable that they represented an earnest wish on the part of the government to promote "schools and the means of education." Whatever the motive, whether bright or shady, there is no doubt that at a time when governmental participation in education was almost unanimously dismissed as utopian, the nation's lawmakers undertook to extend a helping hand to education. Since then it has been done again and again. Upon the principle of national aid rest the Morrill land-grant laws of 1862 and 1890, the Smith-Hughes Act of 1917, the GI Bill of Rights of 1945, and various other congressional measures in educational aid, culminating only recently in the Johnsonian millennium in the greatest outpouring of educational manna the world has ever seen.

6   Although government failed to give more than a sliver of support to education, the idea of a wider diffusion of at least a rudimentary knowledge had no lack of partisans. However, where once such advocacy had been fostered almost entirely by the reverend clergy, and had flourished chiefly for religious ends, it was now intoned in lyrics whose key was seductively secular. In the infancy of the eighteenth century, as has been noted, America's heavy thinking, sniffing the pungent air of Europe's Enlightenment, had begun to turn from its preoccupation with moral and divine science to the natural and political sciences. Several generations later, as the century approached its last quarter, the darkening relationship between the Colonies and the mother country, as was to be expected, generated a tremendous boom in the general interest in politics. In evidence everywhere, it had a cerebral as well as an emotional clang. It inspirited the bulk of plain folk, and it found expression in the writings of Jefferson, Adams, Franklin, Madison, and many more.

Meanwhile the kingdom of France was being battered by the headwinds of its own oncoming revolution, and there too the country's advanced thinkers were pondering the problems of man and fellow man. Under their prying glass came a long procession of political, economic, and social phenomena. Proclaiming a faith in the inherent goodness of the human race —somewhat prematurely it would appear, looking backward—they offered to all men, but especially to those of middling and low estate, the hope of limitless self-improvement. It remained for Jean-Marie Antoine Nicolas de Condorcet to become the doctrine's most eloquent spokesman. A mathematician of parts, a dallier in metaphysics, and a gentleman in the simplest and most obvious sense that he was a gentle man, Condorcet had the hard fortune to have the blue corpuscles of aristocracy in his blood, a distinction which in the wild torment of the French Revolution put a price on his noble head. While fleeing from the Terror to which he later fell a victim, Condorcet wrote his *Sketch of the Progress of the Human Mind,* with its final chapter hymning the future triumphs of reason and man's ascension toward perfection. Such was the doctrine of progress without end, or, in the scholar's phrase, man's infinite perfectibility.

To a world whose ruling classes had been cold to the underdog, who insisted that he was congenitally stupid and impossible of any betterment and that his degredation, in fact, was ordained by higher powers—to this world the possibility of man's unlimited improvement appeared as a monumental joke. But comical or not, the idea, for all its superoptimism—or maybe because of it—was to become the seedbed for nineteenth-century humanitarianism, far-flung social reforms and public universal education.

Its first shoots sprouted in France. There after the collapse of the monarchy and the Old Regime, in an avalanche of reforms, appeared a number of proposals for education. Though they varied in this detail and in that one, in their essence they were attuned more or less to the same general theme. Nature, they insisted, bestows her gifts without special favor, whether we are cradled in wealth or poverty, in a mansion or a manger. All of us, even the poor and lowly, have a right to develop our natural capacity. To make this possible, government must somehow equalize opportunities for the schooling of its children. Only thus may the state expect the full reward of their good citizenship. "Education," avowed Condorcet, "is for the government an obligation of justice."

These golden dreams were not to be realized—not at all events for a long and melancholy interval. The bloodbath of the Terror snuffed them out. For a time even the ideas from which they were bred vanished in darkness, though they were too enchanting to be obscured forever. When they ventured forth again, they were greeted like a long-lost friend, somewhat forgotten perhaps, but happily not gone, not only in France, but in other lands, including our own republic.

Somewhat in the vein of the gallant French, a number of Americans favored a national system of education, and in 1795, when the American Philosophical Society promised an award for the best plan of education "adapted to the genius of the Government of the United States," there was a quick and hearty response. Several glittering names, in fact, gloss the competitors' list—as witness the schoolmaster and lexicographer Noah Webster, the *émigré* French statesman Pierre Samuel Du Pont de Nemours, and the Hippocrates of Philadelphia, Benjamin Rush. The prize, however, fell to none of these worthy men, but was divided instead between the Messrs. Samuel Knox and Samuel H. Smith.

There is no need here to delve into the details of the various plans, for though their makers were at pains to advance their own pet ideas, they also entertained quite a number of ideas in common, or, in the current vulgate, they produced a consensus. Education, they agreed, lies at the root of progress. Without schooling, the citizen's well-being suffers, and so does that of the nation. Education, they went on, is not only a prerequisite of the general welfare but also a child's natural and inalienable right. To ensure the possibility of its attainment, the republic needs to invest itself with a new education, one which will not only forward universal enlightenment and progress, but also stimulate leadership. To such purpose education must be publicly and nationally supported. So paramount is the importance of education to the national welfare that its course may not be left to chance, the caprice of parent, the content of pocket, or the quicksand uncertainties of local government. Education is in truth an obligation of the national state.

Such engrossment in the national learning, however, was not of the common run, and it fetched very little popular support. The tradition that education belongs in local hands hoofed and bucked it heavily, and so did various private interests, especially when they were spiced with sectarianism. Hence, it was not till some generations later, when the social climate had grown a shade more temperate, that the question began at least in some of its aspects to stir again.

Meanwhile, some of the republic's foremost statesmen were not impervious to baring their sentiments on the subject. Most of them, it is true, cloaked their thoughts in a dulcet delicacy. John Jay, in illustration, felt that "knowledge is the soul of the republic." It was, he observed, the "means to enlighten the weak and the wicked." Everything, he added, should be done to "educate all ranks of the people." James Madison, too, threw down his glove in challenge of ignorance. "The best service that can be rendered to a country," he remarked, "next to giving it liberty, is in diffusing the mental improvement equally essential to the preservation and enjoyment of that liberty." Rather interestingly, Madison also declared for subsidizing education with a general tax levy, a view so rare in those days as to occasion some snickering.

General Washington also went on record in favor of promoting the national learning. In his first message to Congress, to instance an example, he applauded the furtherance of letters and science. "Knowledge," he declared, "is in every country the surest basis for happiness." Later, in his *Farewell Address*, he tackled the subject again, exhorting his countrymen "to promote institutions for the general diffusion of knowledge."

Very dear to the President's heart was the creation of a national university. Where and how the idea of such a venture was hatched no one precisely knows. Some incline to honor Samuel Blodget as its father. In fact, in his *Economica*, a book he disgorged in 1806, Blodget discloses how in late 1775 he had revealed his vision to Washington, then stationed with his troops at Harvard. But Blodget's assertion must have escaped the General's memory, for he left no corroborative record. The first word we have on the subject of a national grove of higher learning issued from the versatile quill of Benjamin Rush, who set down its general features in an essay, *A Plan for a Federal University*, which he put forth in 1788. Such an institution, he urged, would serve to uplift and dignify the country's learning. At the same time, in a land rioting in diversity and provincialism, a national university could be counted on to forward a common national spirit. Finally, its existence would spare young America from having to make the long and arduous journey over the ocean in its quest for the highest knowledge.

Not only did Washington say "amen" to all these arguments, but at various intervals he besought the men of Congress and others to give their active aid to bring the proposed enterprise to being. In fact, the President went so far as to scout around for a fitting site, and he even made a tentative choice. What is more, in his will he left several thousand dollars' worth of securities to help the proposed university on its feet. But Congress would have no part of it. Some of the lawgivers were sure that the project would cost too much—a rather unseemly reason to be given voice in the national legislative chambers. Others had misgivings that it might encourage the formation of a national bureaucracy. Some regarded it as a threat and peril to the existing private colleges, and some contended that the Federal government had no right to stick its nose into education. Whatever the objections, real or imaginary, Washington's dream remained a dream, and his bequest has long since vanished in the deep, dark pit of oblivion. The idea of a national seat of learning, though still fluttering in the realm of fancy, continues off and on to seek its way into the world of actuality—in fact, even in our own time it still attracts admirers.

7   Like Washington and the others, Jefferson put a high trust in the power of learning, but his great "cherishment of the people" impelled him to stride further and more boldly than any of them. Of the Fathers he alone came close to the ideal of public, state-supported schooling. "Preach, my dear Sir," he wrote to his friend and law teacher, George Wythe, "a crusade against ignorance. Let our countrymen know that the people alone can protect us against these evils, and that the tax which will be paid for this purpose is not more than a thousandth part of what will be paid to kings, priests, and nobles who will rise up among us if we leave the people in ignorance. . . ."

As a member of the Virginia House of Burgesses, Jefferson sponsored three important bills: one for religious freedom, which finally enjoyed enactment in 1785; another for the creation of free public libraries; and a third for the establishment of free public schools. Put forth in 1779, Jefferson's plan for education divided every Virginia county into school districts, each some five or six miles square. Every district was put upon to maintain a school where every girl and boy was to be introduced to the three Rs at public expense for three years "and much longer at private expense as parents, guardians, or friends, shall think proper." After the three years were up, the district's most promising lad—his parents, however, had to be poor in worldly assets—was to be appointed for further free instruction in one of twenty grammar schools, where he was to improve his mind in Latin and Greek, the grammar of the mother tongue, some geography, and the "higher part of numerical arithmetic." After ruminating for a year or two in these subjects, twenty of the best geniuses "were to be raked from the rubbish" to continue their study in the grammar school, at public expense, for another four years. Of these, finally, the brightest youths were to be transmitted to the College of William and Mary, there to be "educated, boarded, and clothed," once more with the compliments of the taxpayers.

Jefferson's plan, like Jefferson himself, has been the cause of considerable contention. That its underlying ideas are not original, but probably French, is not unlikely—but it is also beside the point. That it accepts the doctrine of an intellectual elite, that it approaches the problem of educating the poor in the spirit of charity, that it fails to make school attendance compulsory, that it would have naught to do with the useful and practical subjects so necessary for the economic well-being of the masses—all this can easily be supported. Yet it is also true that Jefferson's proposal embodies the first thoughtful specific summons in America for the general diffusion of knowledge at public expense. And if Jefferson inclined toward an elite—something which in our current democracy has acquired a connotation of contempt—then let it not be forgotten that he did not assume, as did nearly all the others of his era, that the common people have no business within this cultivated circle. For them the door was left ajar— narrowly to be sure—but nevertheless ajar.

Jefferson's bill was not enacted. It was spurned, however, not for its faults but for what currently are its virtues. It was all very well to plead for an equalization of opportunity, to urge the necessity of schooling all the children of all the commonwealth—in fact, so long as these pleas confined themselves to the safe domain of rhetoric they even gained some countenance and support. But once they ventured over the line into the realm of practical action, the support sloshed down the drain. In 1817 Jefferson drew up another bill to establish public schools, but it fared no better than its forerunner. Only one of Jefferson's educational ideas was ever realized—the University of Virginia. He planned and designed the buildings, he devised its general organization, and he assembled its men of learning. Opened in 1825, a year before his death, the University of Virginia was truly "Mr. Jefferson's University."

8   In the dominion of state educational jurisprudence, as during the colonial period, an immense diversity prevailed. For all the uptide of national consciousness—the flow of new social, political, and economic currents —and despite the trickle here and there of political and social liberalism and the pleading of a small group of sagacious citizens, the states' approach to the education of their people continued in the hackneyed tradition. By the end of the eighteenth century less than half the states had actually taken steps toward establishing a system of free, tax-maintained public education.

In New England, where as long ago as the mid-seventeenth century the tax-supported school had hung out its first shingle, all the states had made provision for education in one way or other by 1800. The first general school laws to be framed appeared in New Hampshire and Massachusetts in 1789—and what went for the Bay State also went for Maine, which until 1820 was girdled to the commonwealth. In their basic elements the two statutes were pretty much the same. Both states, for example, ordered their smaller towns to support a primary school, and their larger ones a grammar school. Both also exacted a modest licensing requirement from their schoolmasters. In addition Massachusetts gave its juridic approval to the district system, already on in years and creaking in its bones—a step New Hampshire kept away from for another half dozen years.

In Connecticut—not counting minor variations—the course of development proceeded in the same general direction. But in the arrangements it made for state aid, the Nutmeg State raced ahead of the pack. It had essayed a gentle start in 1750, when it created a permanent school fund. Forty-five years following, when it hauled in a bonanza of $1.2 million from the sale of its western lands, it put the whole thumping sum into the fund. Finally, as the century turned, Connecticut began the pleasant practice of handing out the interest to the various localities.

New England's line of action, pianissimo though it was, was not followed for the most part by Rhode Island. Born in dissent, this speck of sovereign space had always shown an inclination to walk alone. When the rest of New England made state and church hand-in-hand coworkers, Rhode Island was at pains to keep them apart; and when Massachusetts ordained the tax-supported town school and the rest of New England followed suit, once again Rhode Island played an independent hand. At the century's end all the New England states had taken their first frail steps toward the formation of a system of public schools—and for once Rhode Island was among them. Its law of 1800 not only ordered instruction in the three Rs but also proffered some slight state aid. But many Rhode Islanders sneered at the statute, which they denounced as being against ethics and justice—not to say their personal freedom—whereupon in 1803 the legislature extinguished the statute. For a generation Rhode Island lawmakers laid no hand on education. When in 1828, they ventured to resume activity, they were as wary as they were hesitant, the ordinance enacted in that year being merely permissive and not mandatory.

Aside from New York, the middle states assumed little direct educational responsibility. Most of them, in fact, continued to look upon free schooling as if it were, so to say, a bone flipped to those down on their heels, and in most of them the parochial school continued to be agreeably regarded. By the close of the century only Delaware and New York had enacted school laws. In 1796 the former had launched a school fund contrived from the proceeds of its fees from marriage and tavern licenses, of which, then as now, there fortunately was no lack. Unluckily, twenty-one years came and went before any of this hoard was put to its designated use.

As for the commonwealth of Pennsylvania, back in 1776 its constitution called upon the state's givers of law to put a school in every county for the instruction of the young "at low prices." Some years afterward, however, when the state adorned itself with a new constitution, it was content merely to direct its Solons to provide schools for the poor. Out of this stipulation came the law of 1802, which undertook to establish a school for the poor in every county.

In New Jersey nothing happened until 1816, when a school fund was put under way. Four years more, and localities were granted the right to lay a school tax upon themselves if so they willed. Save in a few up-and-doing places, however, Jerseyites suffered the law as a necessary evil, and the first fruit it produced was slight. Not till 1829 did the legislature deliver itself of a general school law. Greeted with boos before its enactment, the law continued to arouse antagonism—so much so that presently it was wiped from the books, and New Jersey, following in the track of its Pennsylvania neighbor, gave countenance to the pauper school.

The strivings of New York were somewhat more resolute, and under the proddings of Governors Clinton, George, and De Witt, the state moved ponderably forward. It made a beginning in 1795, when it broached the public cashbox and extracted $100,000 therefrom to be disbursed annually among its counties "for the encouragement of schools." For all its promised benefits, the measure elicited only faint cheers, and after five years of wheezing along, it was renounced. It remained without an heir or successor until 1805, when the proceeds of the sale of some of the state's public domain were set aside for a common school fund. Under its provision, each county was to match the state's contribution dollar for dollar—a practice which since has become common enough. Taking one thing with another, the new approach attained a creditable response. In truth, within three years after the law's enactment, sixteen counties were availing themselves of its advantages, and some thirteen hundred schools operating on sixty thousand boys and girls were reported in existence. An earlier legislative creation, and one which is still on the scene, was the University of the State of New York. Founded in 1784, this body, through its board of regents, was given custody of the state's secondary and higher schooling. As is common knowledge, the University of the State of New York is not a university at all—at least not in the ordinary meaning of the term. Like the University of France, which made its debut at about the same time and to which the New York body bears some resemblance, it is preeminently an administrative mechanism. Its true nature at present is that of a state board of education.

In the South the approach to education was also marked by a protean variation. Of the original colonies, four—Maryland, Virginia, South Carolina, and Georgia—performed more or less in the middle-state style. The Virginians, as has already been set down, shut their ears to Jefferson's libertarian murmurs. Yet, in 1796, partly in response to his persistence, they braved a measure to establish public schools. It opened the way toward the levying of a tax to bring such schools into being and also to engage teachers to man them. But the law evaded the indignity of being mandatory, and so its net effect was nil. In 1810, when the Old Dominion sponsored a common school fund, it labored somewhat more effectively. The Literary Fund—such was its official name—presently was enjoying a fine prospering, so much so that in 1831 certain forward-looking Virginians proposed to tap some of the fund's accumulating interest to establish free schools. But the ruling classes still cherished a powerful aversion to such governmental altruism, and in their legislative mills the proposal was promptly ground to death. Instead, the jurists gave their approval to a system of charity schools. Meanwhile, however, the lawmakers made no objection to permitting forays on the Literary Fund to subsidize private academies and colleges.

In the rest of what used to be the colonial South, the same general gropings were in evidence. South Carolina stepped into the controverted ring of free education in 1811, when it laid the legal groundwork for a system of free public schools. Their doors were to be open to all white children, male and female, whether of high degree or low. But the rich had no inclination to expose their progeny to the risks of commingling with the offspring of the mob, and so what had started as a high and benign idea was forgotten, and the seminaries of knowledge which appeared were made to confine their services almost wholly to the poor and orphaned. After twenty-odd years of such melancholy meandering, the measure was given teeth when penalties were ordained for those who persisted in subverting it. Disdained by its well-heeled adversaries, the law continued to be scoffed, and it was not until the century attained middle age that a workable system of free schooling was ushered in.

Georgia dealt its first blows for public learning in 1817, when, like some of its sister states, it started a fund to support its schools. The initial deposit ran to one-quarter of a million dollars, an astronomic figure in those times. But the revenue it begot was not to be dispensed equally and freely to all; instead, it was to be reserved for the schooling of the very poor. All others were expected to scratch for themselves, and out of their own pocket. Like the South Carolinians, the Georgians made no real headway toward a system of public schooling until after Appomattox.

Above the Potomac, Maryland, whose ways inclined now to those of the North and now to those of the South, introduced its citizens to a school fund with a tax on its banks. Pretty soon an even greater boldness descended on its law house, when, in order to increase the revenue to help school the poor, the legislature, in 1826, resorted to a general school law. Among Baltimoreans its gleanings were negligible. Actually the Civil War was history when the Free State began in earnest to lay the foundation for its present system of public education.

If the Southern advance toward the public schooling of its masses moved somewhat sluggishly, in the realm of secondary and higher learning it frisked about in a more lively fashion. Virginia, as mention has already been made, opened its university in 1825. The commonwealth, however, was not the first in the field. The practice, for example, of extending a slight financial hand to the struggling private academies was not unusual and was to be found in several states, both beyond the left bank of the Potomac and beyond the right. As for the higher learning, in its constitution North Carolina had paved the way for a university as far back as 1776. Chartered in 1789, it was ready to instruct its first clients some six years later. Even earlier the desire for a center of higher thought had attacked patrician Georgians, and in 1784 they were able to persuade their lawmakers to charter a state university, but seven years lagged by before it actually opened. Four years later, in 1805, South Carolina followed suit.

Needless to say, these early institutions differed immensely from their current successors. All were small, and all were run on a starvation budget. The regular financing they now enjoy from taxes, and the numerous windfalls from foundations and Uncle Sam, were then unheard of. Hence they found themselves dependent on the mercy of good hearts, both in the legislature and among the laity. Their main stress academically fell on the liberal arts—a remote cry from their vast and varied offerings of today. For all their academic concentration, the first state universities were suspect to conservatives, educators and otherwise, and particularly to some of the reverend clergy who discerned in the state university a friend and promoter of the nascent secularism and an enemy, therefore, of the Kingdom of God. The warfare over the control of the new citadels of learning raged wherever they ran up their flags, and the casualties they sustained were sometimes heavy. During the century's first half, in fact, some of them came pretty close to the grave. What helped to save several of them was a congressional transfusion, the celebrated Morrill Act of 1862, which, as detailed later in these pages, for the first time made national aid to education available on a scale that was truly grand.

On toward the end of the eighteenth century three new states—Vermont, Kentucky, and Tennessee—came into the Union. Vermont, admitted in 1791, formulated its first school law the year following. By it the state gave legal sanction to the district system, and should any locality be seized by a passion to levy school taxes on itself, the state authorized it to do so.

Where voters so inclined—which, in sad truth, was not often—their communities were granted some slight subvention from the state. By 1810, however, this easygoing way was put under challenge, and as a result the town school tax was made compulsory. But as everywhere else in those fine old days, in one way or another recalcitrant localities managed to evade the law's requirement—hence another measure, dated 1821, which essayed to bring such antisocial-minded places to terms by closing all escape hatches. Five years later the Vermonters launched a common school fund. Unhappily, it yielded only slight succor to the schools, and a few years after its appearance it was sidetracked and directed toward paying off the state debt.

Both Kentucky and Tennessee had started out as havens for poor and discontented whites who, seeking richer pickings, had wandered in from neighboring states. For long years neither state was blessed with opulence, nor with what might be properly describable as an educational tradition. To be sure, as early as 1816 the Governor of Kentucky declared for the founding of public schools, but the legislators lent him no ear. Five years later a literary fund was started, but as in Yankee Vermont, its revenue presently was diverted to other ends. The lawmakers, true to their immemorial fashion, talked, delayed, and shilly-shallied until at length, in 1830, they agreed to tender aid to the common school—alas, so low had the general interest in education fallen that the law went for naught and nothing of moment occurred. Meanwhile, like so many others, Kentucky's high and mighty were satisfying their desire for learning by giving a helpful boost to secondary and higher schools. Academies, in illustration, were awarded juicy strips of land, so generously, in fact, that by 1820 almost fifty such schools had risen in the Bluegrass State. The colleges, as usual, started out more gingerly. Nevertheless, by 1829 at least half a dozen were proud possessors of charters.

In Tennessee the pattern of unfoldment was pretty much a carbon duplicate. The poor were accommodated with schools in 1823, and four years later a school fund was conceived. But it was another seven years before the lawmakers were ready to agree that a general school law was necessary. The act they now adopted authorized the district school, and, as if to make amends for their long delay, the lawmakers made education accessible to all. Such in the main was still the situation when Sumter fell.

9   As the nineteenth century got under way, the lure of the West began to be felt in earnest. Indeed, the guns of the Revolution had scarcely cooled when this was becoming evident, but it was not until after the second war with England, with the republic apparently safe on its shaky legs, that the movement toward the West began to gain in juice and momentum. The details of the rush are familiar enough, and they need not detain us here. Suffice it to observe that under its steady impetus, thousands of Americans made their way over the mountains and down the rivers into the Western valleys and on to the Great Plains beyond. By 1825 their settlements were strung along the wide Mississippi Basin, from the Great Lakes in the North to the Gulf of Mexico in the South.

The men and women who braved the terrors of the wilderness had little time for anything save the dogged struggle for survival. Hence, the impromptu civilization which they managed to establish was crude, devoid of life's simplest amenities, and all too often without its meanest necessities. In such surroundings, needless to say, schools were few. But as the years augmented and the settlements grew, the communal confidence became enhanced, and with it aspirations blossomed for a fuller and more satisfactory life. This is by no means saying that such longings were universal and that they had no opposition. The frontiersman, stone-headed, practical, and defiantly individualistic, was often suspicious, and even derisive of the things which gave life its charm and illumination—and among these not uncommonly he listed learning.

Between the end of the eighteenth century and the twenties of its successor, eight new states came to grace the Union. The first was Ohio in 1803, whereupon followed Louisiana in 1812, Indiana four years after, Mississippi in 1817, Illinois a year later, Alabama in 1819, Maine the next year, and Missouri the year after that. It was 1836 before the next state—Arkansas—was admitted. Except for Maine, all came out of the proliferating West, and eventually all began to devote some of their time and industry to the schooling of their people.

Speaking generally, the road to education was a rough and painful one. Nor were its obstacles always surmounted with equal vigor and effectiveness. In those regions, for instance, where the New Englanders happened to be of sufficient number and influence—as, say, in Ohio—the New England viewpoint gradually worked its way into the general practice. By the same token, where Southerners happened to be dominant—as, for example, in Alabama and Mississippi—the conservative outlook of the older South prevailed. In a handful of states—as witness Indiana and Illinois—where the North and South converged on each other, the approach to education was now that of the one, now that of the other, and sometimes a blend of both.

It is easy to forget that besides these developments, frail though they often were, there was a palpable whispering here and there of other civilizations. Sometimes it spoke in French, sometimes in Spanish, and nearly always its chief devotion was to Holy Church and to the propagation of her faith. It is to a Jesuit mission that we credit the founding of the first school in Illinois, as long ago as 1721. It was a Catholic man of God, a Father Raphael, who four years later opened the first school in New Orleans. And it was the third Charles of Spain, who, having drunk from the spring of French philosophy, set about organizing education in the Louisiana colony in 1771, a domain the Spaniards had acquired from the French. But under their new lords, the old settlers grew disgruntled, and it is not unlikely that Charles's zeal to forward education among his new subjects may have been less powerful than his desire to woo them from their Gallic inclination. Even so, the fact remains that under the benevolent Charles, schools appeared in Texas and California. Because of him another opened in New Orleans. It maintained its useful practice even after the Spaniards cleared out—even, indeed, after 1805, when the Americans came into possession of the province.

There is not much to be gained from exploring the details of educational developments state by state, save only as they throw light on the general picture. Let it be noted that progress—even when the winds were favorable—was slow. In Ohio, where they were often fair, the pauper school was outlawed from the start. As early as 1809, six years after its beginning, the state which has been called the "mother of colleges" acquired its first higher grove, when at Athens it chartered the University of Ohio. Betweentimes it adopted measures to lay the foundation for a system of public schooling, a task which by 1825 it had more or less accomplished.

Elsewhere the intellectual fires flared more dimly. Indiana, it is true, had built Vincennes University as far back as 1806—a whole ten years before its entrance into the Union. Moreover, as reference has already been made, its constitution was the first to recommend provision for the free education of its people, from the lowest school to the highest. Though for long years this was to be no more than a fine illusion, by 1824, nevertheless, Indiana had made steps toward the establishment of a system of rural schools and county seminaries, besides a state University. Illinois, taken into the Union in 1818, enacted the first school law seven years later, but in 1827 these good intentions died while still in infancy when the payment of school taxes was made an object of free choice. Louisiana opened a few primary schools, mostly for those out of pocket, and in 1819 it even put them under a modest supervision. In Alabama and Mississippi the pauper school prevailed, and it was not until on in the century's second quarter that a more satisfactory arrangement was undertaken.

All in all, the young republic's notable deeds were political and economic rather than educational. This was almost inescapable. To get the nation solidly on its feet, to forge its wrangling factions into the union of a single people, to give it strength and substance—such was the main and overwhelming task. All else was secondary.

Yet if circumstances elbowed educational enterprise into an anteroom, that enterprise, however frail and tender, was certainly not without significance. Though the national government had shied away from playing a forceful part in the education of the people, the thought that such endeavor was proper, and even desirable, had ceased to be a novelty. Many first-rate men endorsed the proposition, and some even essayed to bring it into being. Under the Articles of Confederation it was translated into the national ordinance as the government's policy for the National Domain. As such, it set the groundwork for Federal assistance to education, and it gave a powerful stimulus to the development of public schooling in those states which in succeeding years arose from the public lands.

The Constitution's failure to make reference to education, to signal it clearly and resolutely as the business and responsibility of the national government, was taken to mean that sovereignty over education had been delegated to the state. Thus the way was opened in the years to come for the state system of education, still in currency and still highly cherished. But even before this sanction several states had made educational provisions of one kind or another in their constitutions, in special laws, or in both.

But these were mere straws in the wind, pale portents of things to come. As the nineteenth century got under way only a few states could claim a relatively fair degree of public schooling. The venture was not easy, and the odds against it were monumental. A few liberals had battled for a more extensive diffusion of public education, free, tax-supported, and available without strings, whether economic or social, to every boy and girl. But the ruling classes stood against them almost to a man, and until their grip on the reins of government slackened, there was little that could be done. Although the states had come more and more to look upon education as their sovereign right and responsibility, and had even begun to exercise a cautious exercise thereof, they were not averse to having the business done, as traditionally, by the churches or by private vendors or, as in New England, by local effort, or even by various dispensaries of educational charity. The paramount obstacle, of course, was the revolting fact that general public education meant more and higher taxes.

7
EARLY PRACTICES

At the beginning of the nineteenth century, American education was note-worthy, if not for its distinction, then at least for its differentiation. In part a colonial heirloom and in part the offspring of conditions besetting a young and virile people, American schools were sometimes public, but more commonly they were private or semiprivate. Sometimes they were a civil responsibility; sometimes they rested in ecclesiastic hands. Some, kept in funds by private endowment, reserved their service for an audience of rank and consequence. Some, on the other hand, were the work of people of gentle heart, seeking to diffuse their benefits among the lesser folk. And sometimes the school was simply a schoolmaster anxious to make a living.

Town schools still existed of course. But in New England, where they enjoyed their greatest flowering, the district school had all but run them out. When, in 1789, Massachusetts granted legal sanction to the district school, it did the town school grave and irreparable damage. From then on the district school gained in public approval, not only in what had been Calvin's holy stronghold, but in many other parts of the republic as well. Unhappily, the district school set off no fireworks. Coming into practice at a time of educational stagnation, it suffered chronically from financial mal-nutrition, so that all too often its instruction and accommodation were of the lowest order. Nevertheless, for all its shortcomings, it met no serious challenge for almost half a century. And even when it was raked by the fire of such ingenious and relentless men as Horace Mann and Henry Barnard, it was not easily put to rout.

As for the support of schools, here again diversity riots—in fact, prob-ably the only common and recurrent note to strike the ether was man's universal distaste for paying taxes, an affliction of the human race since taxes were invented. Today's citizen may grumble at the thought of handing over his hard-gotten gains in support of the public learning, but in the end he has no choice but to do so; his colonial ancestors, however, not only recoiled from such a horror but also managed overwhelmingly to stave off its execution in practice. Instead of laying a general school tax, funds were obtained from other sources, in illustration, dog and tavern licenses; levies on billiard halls, dramshops, and similar seminaries of sin; and permits to engage in the slave trade or to enter connubial bliss. An ever-ready source of school money was the lottery, which in those days moral jurisprudence held in a far more flattering light than today.

To sustain their schools, some states, as has been noted, created perma-nent school or literary funds, but these were seldom flush, and so nearly always they fell short of their purpose. A favorite method to put spirit into a listless school fund was the so-called "rate bill." True to the timeworn canon that the cost of keeping a child in school should be shouldered by his father, the rate bill was simply a tuition bill, rendered him to cover the cost of instructing his young at school. If papa chanced to be in pocket, there was, of course, no problem—not only could he square his account with ease, but in all likelihood he also honored his children with an out-and-out private schooling. But if, more commonly, his private exchequer happened to be low, financing the family schooling could have serious limitations. A poor man—even when he longed to have his children taught—found it necessary to ease the burden of the rate bill by keeping some of them, especially if they had the hard fortune to be girls, out of school. It was precisely because of such blatant inequity that the rate bill was finally done in.

2   The subjects taught in the primary school were the common, elemental ones with the usual dosings in morality. When the church happened to be the dispenser of knowledge, as it was in the parochial school, religion naturally became a paramount objective. To today's teacher these early offerings must seem skimpy indeed. Yet their sparseness was then certainly no greater in America than anywhere else. Moreover, when they are set beside what used to be offered to the early colonial child, they seem not niggardly, but almost luxuriant.

The expanding interest in newer fields of knowledge, together with the surge in mundane outlook and national feeling, was not without effect on the nation's schooling. Noah Webster's *American Spelling Book* came out in 1783. A year later Jedidiah Morse, the father of American geography and also of Samuel, the inventor of the telegraph, issued the *American Universal Geography*. Eleven years afterward came his *Elements of Geography*, a terser treatise, directed especially at novices applying themselves to the subject for the first time at school. Another Morse creation was *Geography Made Easy*, which, befittingly, the author dedicated to his customers, the "young Masters and Misses throughout the United States." A pioneer in his specialty, Morse suffered the usual handicaps. Even so, some of his knowledge he acquired firsthand from his travels as secretary of the Society for Propagating the Gospel among Indians and Others, and also as an investigator for the national government to study conditions among the red men. A nationalist of very high voltage, Morse refused to confine his observations to the usual geographic scene, and as his work progressed through its numerous editions, it began to take aboard a substantial historical cargo. In fact, by 1789, when Yale, where Morse exercised his talents, adopted the *American Universal Geography*, about a third of it was devoted to the national past, some of it real and some merely mythical.

The first schoolbook consecrated entirely to the republic's vanished yesterdays appeared in 1787, the year the Fathers gathered in convention at Philadelphia to frame the Constitution. Compiled by John McCulloch, a printer, but not even by the farthest reach of imagination a historian, his

book has gone in the record as *An Introduction to American History.*
Rather curiously, what its author lacked in historical knowledge and understanding proved no handicap—in any event, in the book he compounded he
easily surmounted his deficiency by burgling freely from the readers of
Noah Webster.

Arithmetic was given its first American schoolbook in 1729, when
Isaac Greenwood, an addict of the subject and professor thereof at Harvard,
issued his *Arithmetic, Vulgar and Decimal.* But the volume was small and
rudimentary, and from the connoisseurs of numbers it got no radiant reception. Weightier and more potent was Nicholaus Pike's analysis of the
subject, *A New and Complete System of Arithmetic,* a vast superflux of
numerical lore of more than five hundred pages. Put out in 1788, it was
announced by its diligent maker as a "new and complete arithmetic for
the citizens of the United States." With a rule for nearly every one of its
pages, Pike's book grappled with such matters as conjoined proportion,
alligation, a perpetual almanac, tare and tret, and the rule of three. Tables
and statistics glare from its pages, often at gruesome length, but occasionally helpful as well as instructive, as witness its tips on figuring the proportion and tonnage of Noah's ark and, of even higher practical value, its
calculation of the precise number of cubic inches a man has a right to
expect in an honest pint of beer. The work carried the accolade of several
eminent and high-placed men, as, for example, President Stiles of Yale,
Governor James Bodowin of Massachusetts, and even George Washington.
But sad to say even these testimonials went for very little, for the book was
beyond the understanding of America's smaller citizens and, for that
matter, of most of its larger ones too. It was not till 1821, when Warren
Colburn entered the lists with his *First Lessons in Arithmetic on the Plan
of Pestalozzi,* that the lower schoolboy acquired a usable text. Its unearthly
title notwithstanding, Colburn's work introduced a measure of simplicity
into a hitherto bewildering subject, reducing it to the level of the American
small fry and greatly facilitating its presentation by the master. Not only
did Colburn strip page after page of forbidding pedantry, but in seeking
to put arithmetical instruction on an intimate basis, he also put it into
greater consonance with the mathematics of every day. All in all Colburn's
First Lessons did not a little to fortify the position of the third R in the
primary school.

One of the most successful books ever written is the *American Spelling
Book.* Composed by Noah Webster, a New York schoolmaster, this blue-
backed booklet appeared in 1783, and in no time at all it was knocking its
rivals off the board—even such old and well-regarded favorites as the *New
England Primer* and the various concoctions of the English Thomas Dilworth. It was not long before the speller was making its way all over the
land, in the knapsacks of itinerant teachers and in Conestoga wagons,
from the Eastern shorelands, over the Alleghenies, and into the prairie

country and far beyond. Oftentimes Mr. Webster's work was the schoolboy's only book, his library in fact, as essential to his success in life as his lunch and his beanshooter. For his labor Webster received a royalty of 1 cent a copy, but pennies then were powerful, and such a mountain of them did this man amass that presently he was able to buy his freedom from schoolmastering to devote himself entirely to the composition of his dictionary. Older than the republic itself, the *American Spelling Book* is still in print, rumbling on like a never-ending freight train and numbering by the latest count roughly one hundred million copies, pawed and pondered, it is estimated, by more than a billion readers—a record surpassed in this country only by that of the Bible.

Thomas Jefferson thought very waspishly of the laborious Noah. "I view Webster," he wrote in 1801, "as a mere pedagogue, of a very limited understanding"—an appraisal which is based no doubt more on Webster's federalist predilections than on his orthographic bolshevism. At all events it falls short of being accurate. Though Webster was possessed at all times with the pedagogue's passion to instruct and expound, and was cocksure into the bargain, his intellectual interests were of an astounding breadth. He wrote a paper on epidemic and pestilential diseases; he edited John Wingate's historical journal; single-handed, he revised Holy Writ; he discoursed on banking and insurance; he delivered himself of a monograph entitled *Experiments respecting Dew,* which among lovers of dew still holds some favor; and finally, he picked up languages as a country dog collects fleas, mastering twenty-six of them, including Sanskrit. His *American Dictionary of the English Language,* which he published in 1828 in two large octavo volumes, he continued to revise and expand until he was eighty-five, when death made an end of him. The ancestor of all the Websters of today, it incarcerated some seventy thousand words, some of which are altogether of American origin, as witness "caucus," "electioneer," and "presidential." He gave his sanction to "plantation," "hickory," and "pecan," and but for him the American skunk might still be a mere polecat. Yale adopted the dictionary forthwith—Noah was a Yale man—but not until far on in the century could Harvard bring itself to follow suit. Meanwhile, for at least a century the work continued to lead the field. There is no gainsaying that Noah Webster, Junior, Esq.—so he preferred to be addressed—was an immense success—his success, indeed, was exceeded only by his egotism.

Webster's views on pedagogy, which are as intensely patriotic as his most fevered execrations of the motherland, called for the Americanization of the native schooling. Purge the school of its British pollution, stress America, sound the drum and bugle for its history and geography, its ideals and aspirations, and infuse them in the child "as soon as he is able to lisp the praise of liberty"—such were his recommendations. In this vein he wrote his readers and histories, and even his grammars. One bumps into it even in his *American Spelling Book,* wherein he set himself the task of giving the American people a spelling which matched their pronunciation, which was then somewhat free and easy. To this end he not only brought American spelling under rule but also emancipated it from the older English usage. If today's Americans, unlike the English, write "color" instead of "colour" and "center" instead of "centre" and other words ending similarly, then their spelling must be credited to Webster.

A combination primer, reader, and speller, the *American Spelling Book* spanned literary creation from linguistic gnats like *pra, pre,* and *pri* to whales like "eleemosynary," "parachronism," "mucilaginous," and ichthyologic," and from "the barber shaves his patron with a razor" to a discourse on "Precepts concerning the social relationships." Not only did Webster set the style for American spelling, but he also made it the liveliest subject in the classroom. Indeed, because of his magical persuasion, spelling games became as common in the American parlor as bridge and canasta in the present era of enlightened progress.

3   The practice of larding the education of the poor with philanthropy, a highly approved custom in colonial America, endured well into the nineteenth century. The Society for the Propagation of the Gospel in Foreign Parts was, of course, not countenanced in the young republic, and with the outbreak of the Revolution, it shut its doors and stole away. But other bodies, more in keeping with the republican cast of mind, soon filled the void. In the larger cities, where the supply of poor people was never short, men of public spirit sometimes combined forces to raise money for the schooling of those whom fortune had left behind. Organized in the main as subscription societies, such orders began to take shape even before the passing of the eighteenth century. Their names, which usually left little doubt of their noble purpose, were as fancy, often enough, as they were specific, as witness the Philadelphia Society for the Free Instruction of Indigent Boys, the Benevolent Society of the City of Baltimore for the Education of the Female Poor, and so on.

The most prominent of such fellowships, by all accounts, was the Free School Society of the City of New York. Chartered in 1805 by the eminent De Witt Clinton, then the city's mayor, the society undertook to collect money to teach such children as "might be objects of gratuitous education." From the start it was caressed by the gods, sharing in the state's school fund and receiving grants even from the municipal fathers. From these golden eggs it busily hatched schoolhouses and a general program of free, nonsectarian schooling. In 1826, when the Free School Society was chartered anew, it was renamed the Public School Society, and it was allowed to extract a small fee from those parents who could afford to pay for its services. Of a sudden, however, school attendance swooshed down the chute, and after a short interlude a chastened Public School Society abandoned the

practice. In 1828 the state again came to the public schoolers' side by sanc-
tioning a tax to enable them to carry on.

For all the obvious merit, the Public School Society provoked no little
antagonism. The fact that it drew money from the public cashbox stirred
up a natural envy in sacerdotal bosoms, but whenever ecclesiastics besought
the authorities to let them have a share of the state fund, there seemed to
be no one to second their motion—a state of affairs which did not cause
them to blow kisses at the Public School Society. Even more disquieting
was the question of religious neutrality. Although the society had agreed to
confine its operations to a nonsectarian plane, time and again it found itself
challenged by bristling and consecrated men who charged it with having
broken its solemn pledge. The din kept up for years and penetrated even
into the juridic halls at Albany. It was largely to make an end of such
ceaseless clamor that the legislature, in 1842, gave the city of New York
its own board of education with authority to organize and maintain a
system of nonsectarian free schools. The Public School Society continued
its mission for yet another decade. When, in 1853, it drew its blinds for
the last time, it could at least seek solace in the gratification of knowing
that during its life of almost half a century, it had given light to more than
half a million children, who, but for the grace of its beneficence, would
have been doomed to ignorance.

Another boost for the poor man's learning was the Sunday school,
which had its beginning in England in the middle age of the eighteenth century. A frail creature in its youth, for years it teetered on the edge of extinction until 1780, when Robert Raikes, a printer in Gloucester and the editor
of its *Journal*, rescued it for the cause of moral and social progress. Raikes,
who was doubtless a man of open and boundless heart, had been powerfully
moved by the condition of the city's poor, and especially by the cynical
neglect of their swarming offspring. He had watched them rolling in the
muck of their wretched warrens, grimy and ragged, "given up," as he said,
"to follow their own inclination without restraint." On Sundays, when the
mills were still and parents sought forgetfulness in booze and venery, the situation was even more pitiful, for then the young had no brakes put upon
them at all. Bent on lifting these "little heathen" from their squalor, Raikes
hired a woman for a shilling a sitting to take a small posse of them every
Sunday and introduce them to their catechism and their ABCs. It was not
long before Raikes's original crew was showing a substantial increase. By
1785, in fact, his enterprise was bathing in so much favorable public notice
that it found adherents almost everywhere, and of such a number as to call
for an organization—the Society for Promoting Sunday Schools throughout
the British Dominion.

Shortly afterward the idea of the Sunday school took wing for America
—precisely when is not certain. We do know, however, that a Sunday
school modeled on Raikesian lines was opened in 1786 in Hanover County,

Virginia, and another in the year following in Charleston, South Carolina. Though the Sunday school's advance at first was languid, nevertheless it was persistent, and by the 1820s such schools were no longer strangers to America.

Unlike the current heirs to its name, the first Sunday school was no handmaid of the church. Known as a Sunday school simply because its sessions were held of a Sunday, it specialized in the homely goods of the everyday primary school. It was not long, however, before various churchmen discerned great possibilities in the Sunday school for planting the seeds of creed and Christian rectitude. Hence as the years rode on, the American Sunday school shed its nondenominational regalia, evolving in the process into the modern Sunday school, which, as everybody knows, is an annex of the church and no longer specializes in the laic arts and sciences.

Despite its serious limitations, the early Sunday school served admirably, though, it must be said, without much glory. In an age when the educational opportunity of the common people swung like a pendulum between very little and none at all, the Sunday school was clearly the poor man's oyster. Just how many boys and girls beat a path to its doors is hard to say, but their number must have been considerable—sufficient in any case to cast strong doubt on the assertion, then generally noised about, that the poor were unappreciative of education and would do little or nothing to seek its wonders for their young.

But there is seldom light, as the prophet spoke, without some shadow. Although the Sunday school was a boon for the working people, at the same time the principle of almsgiving on which it was grounded could be directed to selfish ends, as, in truth, it often actually was. To a man of property a charity which was of his own choice, and which he could ladle out as sparingly as he wished, was clearly a lesser evil than a tax which was compulsory and which could be quite high. Consequently, for many years—far too many—philanthropy was a favorite stratagem of a puissant, self-interested minority in their effort to stay the establishment of the tax-supported school.

From England was imported yet another kind of uplift—the so-called "infant school," whose best-known partisans were Robert Owen and Samuel Wilderspin. It was Owen who mothered the idea and who tended it during its precarious childhood. A successful industrialist, Owen was a rare amalgam of capitalist and utopian seer, a part owner of a productive cotton mill in New Lanark, Scotland, the accredited inventor of English socialism, and the guiding angel of a socialist heaven at New Harmony, in Indiana. Like his famed contemporary, the Swiss educational reformer Pestalozzi, Owen was convinced that most of our social acnes and malarias could be eased and even cured by education. To attain this millennium the essential thing to do was to begin the child's education while he was still in his pristine innocence. Confident that education could shape the man, Owen was even certain that "infants of one class may easily be formed into men of another class"—a dogma which marks him as an environmentalist and which bears some resemblance to the current one of psychological conditioning. By this means Owen hoped on some tomorrow to blow up the usage common to his time by which orphanages and foundling houses, and even parents, farmed out their young as apprentices to manufacturers. Not only did such unfortunates wear themselves out from twelve to thirteen hours every day for a term of nine years, but when their servitude was done, all too often what they had learned amounted to almost nothing, which is to say that as they grew to man's estate they could look forward to nothing better than poverty, degradation, and an early grave.

In 1800 Owen assumed the codirection of his plant, and during the years that followed he laid plans to put his social therapy into practice. What he dreamed of was an organization calculated to be an inspiration and mentor, not only to the children of his millhands, but even to the millhands themselves. He began, gently enough, in 1809 with a school for girls and boys ranging in years from six to twelve, introducing them to the three Rs besides perfecting the girls in the use of needle and thread. Owen's ambition to instruct and elevate the very young did not fructify until 1816, when he founded an infant school. Ministering to toddlers—its freshmen were usually of an age of three—it was to be a seminary where no one was to be "annoyed by books." Instead children were to make acquaintance with neatness, cleanliness, politeness, obedience, punctuality, and all the other kinds of virtues that teachers prize. And if books were under official frown, then so was the rattan. On the other hand, all Owen's scholars, whether kiddies or the more elderly young, were to let off steam in play and music and in the dance—even in military drill, which, mindful of the Napoleonic scourge, Owen fancied would surely help "in the country's defence."

Time saw Owen burst into an ardent student of the teaching art. In fact, to advance and improve himself in its involved and complicated lore he even made for Switzerland to observe the everyday performance of Pestalozzi and von Fellenberg, the surpassing pedagogic masters of the time. Never a man to hide his light under a bushel, especially when it came to showing off his favorite dogmas, Owen was at great pains to disclose them in public, extolling them repeatedly both in print and on the platform. As a result, his notion of teaching children while they were still of a young and tender green gradually gained a following, and in 1818 an infant school in charge of one of his own masters was opened at Westminster.

Meanwhile, Samuel Wilderspin had been attracted to the movement. Of a tougher fiber than Owen, less the star-sprinkled visionary and hence less likely to be fooled, Wilderspin derided the idea of human goodness, clinging instead to that of man's natural depravity. Under the spell of a psychology far more beclouded than that of the optimistic Owen, Wilderspin taught his infantry how to read and figure, stuffing their heads besides with a stupendous store of facts from geography to the natural sciences and, for extra measure, the New Testament. Although he accepted some of Owen's benigner postulates, Wilderspin was also infected with school-mastering's primordial occupational disease—a proclivity for formalism, words, and rote. His schools, hence, were little more than intellectual pack-inghouses. Like Owen, Wilderspin was an assiduous propagandist. To push his views—and himself—he talked and wrote with boundless industry and with great assurance. In 1824 he founded the Infant School Society, and with it at his flank, he was able to advance his version of the infant school to an accepted place in English education.

The years brought both the Owen and the Wilderspin schools to Amer-ica, but the former made scarcely any headway, while the latter darted rapidly to the fore. In the United States, especially in some of the Eastern cities, where a child was not tolerated in any of a few available free schools before he could read, the new infant school seemed to be a gift from Heaven. In it both softhearted reformers and hard-skulled citizens beheld a cheap and simple means to feed the child his first spoonfuls of literacy. The first city to embrace it, and to invest money in it, was Boston, which, in 1818, appropriated $5,000 to make the infant school a part of the city school system. Now to be known as *primary schools*, they received the ascendant Bostonian when he had safely celebrated his fourth birthday. Their task was to render him fit for the regular lower school, which now became known as the *grammar school*, or, more exactly, the English gram-mar school, to differentiate it from its venerable predecessor, the Latin grammar school. In its new array the former infant school, save for holi-days of patriotic or Christian moment, was to carry on the whole year round from January to December, and it was to be manned, as far as possible, by ladies. At first the primary and grammar schools, though they were undoubtedly relations, were not cognizant of their kinship and were, indeed, careful to maintain themselves at arm's length. Not until the middle of the century were they brought together under a common roof. Boston's recourse to the infant, or rather to the primary school, was soon followed elsewhere. Within a decade of Boston's first appropriation similar endeavors had sprouted in New York, Philadelphia, and Providence, and after five more years primary schools generally were enjoying salubrious health and vigor.

4 In 1797 the Rev. Dr. Andrew Bell published a monograph wherein he proposed a method—he had come upon its essence in India—of employing boys or "monitors" as teachers. A year or so later Joseph Lancaster, a schoolmaster who served God as a Quaker, opened a school in London where he actually ran classes in the manner suggested by the Rev. Dr. Bell.

Both men presently attracted legions of supporters, and though today it is unfailingly clear that each had devised the method single-handed, their adherents did not always think so. In fact, for long years they engaged in vehement contention, not only over who had thought up the idea in the first place, but also over the merits and demerits of the propositions put forth, respectively, by Messrs. Bell and Lancaster. The fact that these gentlemen differed in their Biblical interpretations—that the one followed his country's established rite and was even one of its ordained ambassadors of God, while the other was a dissenter and, worse yet, a Quaker—inevitably bore on the strife, converting it into a combat of sects as well as pedagogues. Both camps emitted clouds of propaganda, which, though to current eyes seems mainly nonsense, had the effect nevertheless, of giving the method itself a considerable amount of advertising.

The monitorial system was so designated because of its use of monitors. Under it a master would teach a number of older and, when his horoscope was favorable, smarter boys, each of whom would thereupon seek to lodge his knowledge in a small squad of subordinates. Monitors were articled not only as junior birchmen but as academic chore boys whose duties were of fantastic variety. There was a monitor to run the roll, another to rule the paper, another in custody of inkpots, and yet another to safeguard books and slates. There was a monitor to keep a sharp lookout on the wardrobe and a monitor to query and promote the pupils. There was even an abbot of the order, a monitor in charge of monitors. Because of the monitorial necromancy, a solitary schoolmaster could undertake the instruction of hundreds of pupils—even a thousand or so, it has been reported. Conducted thus on a gigantic chain-store scale, the monitorial method was also cheap, a feature which did not detract a whit from its glitter.

From the vantage point of today's higher pedagogical thinking, the system was, of course, of the meanest sort. Cast on a vast impersonal scale of mass production, it was obliged, for good or ill, to resort to a thoroughgoing and often consuming standardization. Its pupils stepped to class like so many marionettes, and they departed in the same click-clack manner. Singly and together they rose on command, and they sat down on command. They looked, listened, and spoke on order; they held up their slates and removed their caps on order—one might well fancy the poor devils blew their noses on order. Repetition, drill, memorization—such was the order of the monitorial day. Compared with the Pestalozzian revelation then soaring to its apogee in Switzerland, the monitorial system was clearly inferior, a piece of hocus-pocus whereby teaching and learning were reduced to an empty rite.

But within it there lurked some good things too. Coming to terms with their amazingly numerous throng, the monitorians, whether Bellmen or Lancastrians, were constrained, willy-nilly, to give some realistic heed to their theater of operation—the classroom, its appurtenances and appointments. Lighting, ventilation, noise elimination, sanitation, and similar concerns, which—but for a rare and illuminating lapse as, say, the counsel of a Comenius—had hitherto gone unnoticed now became objects of close and sober scrutiny. The monitorians gave the school world new and better equipment, such as slates, blackboards, and writing desks. They brought subject matter under rule and order, and they sorted their pupils into graded classes—a practice which was not to work itself into common use for several generations. Their recourse to the organized recitation, though overladen with commands and controls and no more spontaneous than a tired dishrag, was, even so, a technical inprovement over the older, more laborious method whereby a teacher operated on his pupils one by one, while the rest sat by, each huddled over his own particular lesson and making ready for his turn to be heard. Finally, in its search for monitors competent to discharge their duties with efficacy and dispatch, the monitorians found it necessary to subject them to special training. They thus brought to public notice some of the advantages to be had from preparing teachers for a more effective execution of their art and science.

The monitorial system enjoyed a rousing success. From Britain it swept over the Continent, from the lands that skirt the Mediterranean to the Scandinavian north, the lowlands of Holland and Belgium, and various parts of Germany. When it settled in France, not only was it vouchsafed support from the royal treasury, but presently its glory was celebrated even in dithyrambs, to become in 1818 the French Academy's prizewinning masterpiece of the year.

Nowhere was the monitorial system given a more thunderous reception than in the United States. Introduced in New York in 1806 in the well-filled chambers of the Free School Society, the system, which happened to be that of Lancaster, spread like fire in the brushwood, and within a generation it had overrun several of the larger cities from Massachusetts to Indiana to Georgia. In 1818, Lancaster, then near the pinnacle of his fame, paid a visit to the republic. Received in the grand manner, like a sprigged and spangled hero home from the wars, he devoted himself amid the huzzahs of his admiring fellows to the promotion of his system, writing and declaiming about its wonders, helping to install it now here and now there, and even, upon invitation, haranguing the people's agents in Congress assembled, little dreaming that he was marked to finish his days a poor and disenchanted man. His end came in 1838 in the streets of New York, when a horse and wagon ran him over.

One of the high charms of the monitorial scheme was its cheapness. Lancaster put the annual cost of teaching a pupil in his armories of knowledge at $1.06, and Bell, not to be undersold, subsequently pared this slim figure to an even dollar. The upshot was that of a sudden education came within reach of almost everyone. Enterprises in educational philanthropy were the system's natural beneficiaries, since by the miracle of its low cost, they were able to magnify their restricted capital. Later, when the idea of state appropriations for education began to turn from theory into fact, the lure of savings offered by the monitorial arrangement became far more pressing, and presently politicians were joining moralists to hymn its praises. De Witt Clinton, then in the governor's chair, had happy words for Lancaster, hailing him as a "benefactor of the human race," which doubtless he was, and saluting his system as a "blessing sent down from Heaven," a judgment for which the evidence so far remains inconclusive. Nevertheless, without Lancaster, or even without Bell, the cause of public education in the republic would certainly have been worse off. Lancaster and his monitors, for all their faults, provoked discussion of the whole question of public education. By gradually getting the American people accustomed to the idea, however repugnant, of defraying at least a small part of the cost involved in the enterprise of free, public education, the monitorial movement gave the nascent public schools a tremendous and essential boost.

5   But despite all effort, philanthropic or otherwise, the schooling of the masses limped. Such as it was, interest in education was directed to the more exclusive higher schools. The Latin grammar school, the acknowledged fashioner of the intellect and the training camp wherein a young man was made ready for admission to college, continued its age-beladen duties. It had prospered especially in New England, where it had originated and where some of the larger towns came to its aid with a measure of public support. But its palmy days had long since gone; the district system had made heavy inroads into it, and, even worse, it had suffered severely at the hands of the changing cultural values. The Puritans had prized its classical offerings, but the new generation, especially the business-minded Yankees, put little store in its reputed discipline. When the grammar school failed to rise to their call for an education more responsive to their everyday requirements, they befriended the academy. As the prestige of the grammar school steadily ebbed, that of the academy rose, and by the end of the eighteenth century the new school was to be found from one end of the nation to the other.

Academies were of several kinds. Launched through private effort, they never completely lost some of their original characteristics. As demand for instruction mounted, however, they were often the recipient of governmental favors. Generally, to instance one or two examples, they were given surcease from the calls of the tax gatherer. Their right, furthermore, to solicit funds and to accept gifts to bolster their endowment was commonly sanctioned in law. Occasionally their strongboxes were enraptured by the tinkle of coin taken from various civil offices or from the sale of confiscated lands. In some states—notably in New York, Pennsylvania, and Maryland—academies at times were even allowed outright aid from the public purse. It is only fair to add that some academies turned their backs to such benevolence, preferring to remain strictly private and thereby, if possible, to safeguard their autonomy. But whether private or only half private, at all times they were tuition schools, exacting their toll from all their clients, save of course those lucky enough to be invested with scholarships.

At first the academy had been a boarding school for boys only. In the passing years, however, anxious to afford girls as well as boys a chance to become civilized and cultured people, some academies bedecked themselves with a "female department," which not only purveyed the common academic stock but also dispensed instruction in such delicate and exquisite elegancies as needlecraft, embroidery, watercoloring, wax modeling, and the art of tone, both vocal and instrumental. But in those wary days the nerve of public opinion reacted sharply against such integration of the sexes, and the practice soon released a wealth of pungent talk—hence the advent of the "female academy," which, true to its name, cut itself off entirely from the rough and perilous male to light its beacon exclusively for young and gentle ladies.

Although the academy had arisen to challenge the shopworn staples of the Latin grammar school, it was neither unprepared nor unwilling to do some of its work. Usually it displayed the full repertoire of academic subjects, and like its ancient predecessor, it essayed to fit a boy for college if he—or more likely God and his father—so willed. Loyal to its reason for being, however, the academy (à la Franklin's Philadelphia recipe) leaned heavily on the practical, the languages and the sciences—"the great end of the real business of living," as Phillips Academy of Andover, Massachusetts, so crisply summed it up in 1778, when it started its sessions in its belfried, barnlike edifice, amidst furrowed land and meditating cattle.

Unfettered to an ivied past, the academy was free to sally forth in new directions—the very heart of its being was, in fact, its promise of something fresh. As the years receded and the integument of its primitiveness peeled off, the academy not only brought its curriculum up to date but, in the process, introduced such an extravagant assortment of subjects that even after all these years they still put a strain on the imagination. By 1837, for example, a roundup of the subjects taught by New York's academies disclosed not only an unparalleled number, including all the old and weathered ones from algebra to zoology, but also such jaunty newcomers to the secondary grove as the elements of criticism, marine astronomy, cartography, dialing, extemporaneous speaking, civil engineering, and at least a dozen more.

The first academies, whether for boys or girls, sprang nearly always from denominational aspirations, but as the years took off and the secular note became more strident, not a few of them divested themselves of their trappings to offer their benefits to any one of goodwill—and, of course, the perquisite pocket. To young people the academy availed a secondary schooling regardless of whether they pined on the morrow to storm the higher learning. The admission of girls, though weak and hesitant, was nonetheless an improvement over the almost monastic rigor of the Latin grammar school. The academy which gave courses in pedagogy was not the rule but the exception, but because of the imposing nature of some of its courses, it was in a position to present the lower schools with some of their best-educated masters. Its response to newer forces was at bottom the response to the voice of a new America, still in nascency to be sure, but nevertheless of a singular power and not easily to be ignored. More realistic than its Latin ancestor, broader in its appeal, and less exclusive in the makeup of its student body, the academy arose principally from the hopes and aspirations of the ambitious middle class.

6   On the colleges the Revolution fell like a blight. Most of them had suffered materially, losing precious records, books, and even buildings, so costly and hard-won. For awhile some colleges had even ceased to be, and all of them had watched their enrollment, lean enough in happier days, dwindle into a sad and tattered fragment.

When peace broke out at last, the higher learning concentrated on its recovery, but strive as it would, tiring years hobbled by before the sores were healed. Their material damage the colleges slowly repaired and offset, but the lure of learning had diminished, and for years the groves of Athena remained but sparsely peopled. Gradually students returned to the bench, but their morale was low and their behavior unruly—wicked and ungodly, some of their professors observed—and for the next generation the star of learning barely twinkled. Nevertheless, the colleges persisted, and in time their number even grew. By the end of the century the nine colonial colleges had been augmented by fifteen new ones, while the next score of years brought forth almost as many more.

Nor was the higher learning isolated from the shifting cultural stream. The currents which had overrun the Latin grammar school and swept the academy into prominence were now lapping at the college. There, as in the lower learning, though not so strongly or so engulfingly, they converged on the imperial classics. For the time being, Latin and Greek were able to hold their own, but the study of Hebrew was losing its old authority. Under the siren pressure of public opinion, the study of divinity, once first in rank among the higher studies, began to lose favor, and in 1779, under the prod of the relentless Jefferson, the College of William and Mary abandoned it. At the same time, however, the college suffered a professorship of "history . . . civil and ecclesiastical." In addition, it called for the appointment from time to time of a "missionary . . . to the several tribes of Indians," who, besides introducing them to the Father, the Son, and the Holy Ghost, was under orders "to investigate their customs, religions, traditions, and . . . their languages."

As the old favorites receded and retired, newer ones pushed forward. Even before the Revolution the modern languages had been making eyes at college faculties; now they began to flirt in shameless earnest, and so did history and politics, rhetoric and oratory, mathematics and the sciences. Not that the younger disciplines were able to usurp the place of the older ones, or that all of them were even present on every campus, for then as now the college had its guardians of academic respectability who could always be counted on to stand up for tradition and hold its challengers at bay.

But change there was nevertheless. Between the offerings of colleges of the earlier post-Revolutionary years and those of the University of Virginia there bulks an immense and striking difference. Thus while the older colleges continued to disport themselves in the sedate and somber robes of long ago, and were only timorously trying on the new intellectual finery, Virginia boldly—some thought brazenly—strutted forth in the full glamor of the modern style. Side by side with the ancient tongues, this daughter of Jefferson flaunted the living tongues of French, German, Spanish, and Italian, besides English in its Anglo-Saxon form. Just as dazzling was the array of science, which, headed by mathematics, included astronomy, chemistry, physics, mineralogy, biology, zoology, and anatomy, besides the arcane specialties reserved for prospective physicians. In addition one glimpses offerings in government, municipal law, ethics, and rhetoric.

The dismantling of William and Mary's chair of divinity in 1779 was no isolated spectacle. Intended originally to promote the cause of the Established Anglican Church—a cause which in revolutionary America had fallen into odium—the sacred chair was now regarded as "incompatible with freedom in a Republic." Interwoven, however, with the strands of republicanism was also a waning of ecclesiastic influence. The greater part of the colonial college's industry had gone into the preparation of young men for the holy calling, and during the college's first century, three of every four of its graduates were translated into the ministry. Following the Revolution, fewer and fewer youths came to fit themselves for the sacred cloth. Faced thus, on the one side, with an ever-increasing pressure from the laic disciplines and, on the other side, with an eroding demand for instruction in divine science, the college attuned itself to the spirit of the times by scratching divinity from its traditional offerings, thus opening the way for the theological school proper. Princeton, born and bred in Presbyterianism, established a theological seminary in 1812, without, however, dissolving itself from the faith of its founding fathers. Harvard took similiar steps seven years later with the creation of a separate theological faculty, while Yale followed on its heels in 1822.

For young men longing to frock themselves someday as jurists or medicos the chances for higher professional illumination were pretty slim. Ordinarily the would-be advocate of the eighteenth century trained himself for the long robe in a private school, or, like Jefferson, he attached himself somewhat in the manner of an apprentice, to a practicing attorney, clerking in his office, studying his law books, and betweentimes receiving his counsel and instruction. The deteriorating relationship between Americans and their motherland quite naturally spurred an interest in the legal mystery, as did the enlarging class of merchants and manufacturers, with their incessant need for legal advice and aid. Less common but no less urgent was the need of those, particularly in the South, whose land titles, often carelessly or vaguely drawn, were jeopardized by the claims of encroaching rivals, sometimes honest and upright and sometimes mere pretenders.

To these interests the colleges gradually responded. Late in 1773 King's College erected a "fellow and Professor of Natural law," which, however, was probably ethical rather than professional jurisprudence. In any case, soon after his nomination the chap took sail for home without ever having discharged the rites and functions of his chair. The honor of creating the first professorship in law must go to William and Mary, which in 1779 appointed the eminent George Wythe to sit as its first professor of law and police, or, as we say today, politics. For about a decade the professor performed his labors diligently, whereupon he retired, as bald as a jug, to lead an honorable and fruitful life until he was eighty, when a greedy nephew, lusting for his legacy, made an end of the uncle, but not before the old man had time to change his will.

North of the Potomac the first professorial chairs in law were founded in 1790 by the College of Philadelphia, in the City of Brotherly Love, and by Brown College, in Providence. Three years later Columbia, ever eager to please New Yorkers with its service, established a chair in law—this time of the professional variety—electing as its first occupant the Hon. James Kent, a Yale man, destined to become famous as chancellor of New York. Finer than even these accomplishments was the professor's *Commentaries on American Law,* in four well-stocked volumes, which he completed in 1830. Revised and overhauled a half dozen times during its author's stay on earth, the work went through eight further reincarnations after his departure. The years saw it become a classic, earning for Kent the distinction of being memorialized in legal annals as the American Blackstone. Almost twenty years ran by before Harvard ameliorated civilization in Cambridge with its School of Law. When it fell to work in 1817, the reins of authority at Harvard Corporation had just passed from the hands of the pastors of God to His servants at the bar. Less than a generation after its advent, under the dowered and forward-looking Joseph Story, Harvard stood out as the nation's leading center of juridic science and the foremost molder of the American legal system. Yale, never given to indecent haste, opened its law school a few years after Harvard.

Even before the American higher learning began to venture its first steps toward preparing young men for the bench, there was no lack of private law schools. The first on the scene, and the most celebrated, was opened in 1749 by the Hon. Tappan Reid of Litchfield, Connecticut, where five years later, Ephraim Kirby issued his volume of *American Law Reports,* the first of what has since become a long and endless procession. From its inception to its end a half century later, Litchfield devoted its skill to training its students for careers in law and public service. Because of the renown of its instruction—but also not a little because its matriculants from other states needed only a year to fulfill its requirements—the school attracted its custom from every state in the Union. Hundreds and hundreds took its diploma, and in their midst were some who in afteryears attained immortality of one sort or another, as witness Aaron Burr, of New York; John C. Calhoun, of South Carolina; Horace Mann, of Massachusetts; and George Y. Mason, of Virginia, to mention only four.

In medicine things moved less lively, which surely is no reason for wonder. For the healing art was then on wobbly legs and scarcely resembled its present robust and respected successor. To be sure, medical men had not been immune to the blandishments of the Enlightenment, and some of the astuter minds had even made a number of startling and important discoveries. Of even greater worth—at any rate, for the progress of the Hippocratic science—was the manifestation of a stronger and bolder scientific attitude. From Europe the freshly alerted spirit spread to America, and though its forward course was slow and stumbling, by 1765 it was sufficiently sure to bring forth the country's first systematic medical instruction in the College of Philadelphia. During the century's last years, medical faculties made their way into King's, Dartmouth, and Harvard, while the infant years of the succeeding century saw the coming of still others. Even so, for several suffering generations the spreading medical lore left a great deal to be desired, as did the predicament of medicine itself.

In truth, within the memory of some of the nation's more elderly grayheads, it was at one time neither odd nor novel for an aspiring Galen to do no time at a medical college at all, but to acquaint himself with the scary secrets of his craft as an apprentice to an established practitioner, putting himself under his counsel and instruction, pondering the occult meaning of his handbooks, and giving him aid when he probed and explored his sufferers—sometimes even holding them down while his master proceeded to carve them.

7   Although government displayed little or no enthusiasm, or will, to furnish decent schooling for its herds of common children, toward those in better station it was far more considerate—in fact, sometimes it was even unctuous. Long before the tax-supported common school had ceased to be a topic for rhetoricians, a number of states were fashioning the capstone of our educational structure, the state university. Born out of republican and secular sentiment, though by no means devoid of religious undertones, it appeared embryonically in 1776, when North Carolina made constitutional provision for a state university. But the arson and hemorrhage of the Revolution had stopped and the republic was on its legs before North Carolina's hope was at length fulfilled in 1795. Six years later Georgia State unfurled its banner, and in 1805 South Carolina made it three of a kind. Meanwhile, in Virginia a campaign led by the secular-minded Jefferson to convert William and Mary into a liegeman of the state had come to naught. But the last word was to be Jefferson's—and a gleeful gloat besides. For when the University of Virginia said hello to her first seekers of wisdom in 1825, the newcomer was the most up-to-date seat of the higher learning of the time, and the nearest to our own conception of a state university than any of its predecessors.

The first state universities, as one might guess, were small—some were scarcely more than academies. Financed by spasmodic legislative allowances, by gifts of land, by tuition fees, and by occasional hauls from genial altruists, they found the road to academic grandeur very rough indeed. Even the younger states which issued from the National Domain with their special bounty in real estate—as per the Ordinances of 1795 and 1797 —for the encouragement of the muses were strangers to an overflowing coffer.

In the senior states, where the higher learning had become almost a commonplace, the need for state universities was obviously not so great. But here too the germs of secularism and republicanism were rampaging, and in a number of states the lawmakers cast covetous looks at their ivied halls. In Pennsylvania several attempts flared up to bind the College of Philadelphia more closely to the state, but in this the Pennsylvanians were no more successful than the Virginians had been in the case of William and Mary. In 1810 Massachusetts threatened to regulate the affairs of Harvard, but the old school, full of pepper and salt, put up a whopping struggle, and after a tug-of-war of more than half a century, it walked off the field in triumph as an out-and-out corporation.

It was in green-hilled New Hampshire where the sound of combat rumbled the loudest. There, in 1816, the state moved to bring Dartmouth into its fold. Founded by a group of Congregationalists, Dartmouth had taken its charter from the royal hand of George III, and when the legislature sought to alter its articles, the college pressed its resistance in the courts. The contest was at bottom of a political as well as a legal nature. A struggle between liberal and conservative philosophies of government, which is to say between Jeffersonians and Federalists, it raised national as well as local blood pressures. Defended ultimately before the nation's highest judiciary by no less a magnifico than Daniel Webster, himself a Dartmouth son, the college won its suit, when, in 1819, Chief Justice Marshall let it be understood that a college charter, for all its unsavory monarchical origin, was nevertheless a contract and hence under the Constitution inviolable.

The educational effects of this decision reached far. Confirmed in their rights and franchises they derived from the grant of government, privately endowed institutions were now free from the specter of governmental encroachment. Thus reassured, the private college faced a bright future, one in which its endeavors and numbers were to multiply almost miraculously. Most of these seminaries of the higher arts and sciences were modest undertakings, one-building and few-roomed Heidelbergs, given in most instances to the promotion of sectarian interests—Methodist, Congregational, and Presbyterian primarily, but also Episcopalian and Roman Catholic. A great many have long since gone into the memory book, but some, like Amherst, Haverford, and several dozen more, unshackled from the bonds of their strict orthodox beginnings, continue to carry on their industry to this moment, and not infrequently in a meritorious and penetrating manner.

Deprived of the right to change a college charter, the state lost the magic stick by which it had hoped to transform the private college into a state school. On the other hand, if the state really craved an intellectual palace all its own, then plainly there was no reason why it should not create one—harder though such a course might be.

Picture Completion: Men

Hank Virgona

8
THE CRADLE OF
THE COMMON SCHOOL

In 1825 the United States was a land of about eleven million people. They were nearly all native whites, save in the South, where some two million were of Negro blood. With the acquisition of Florida and the huge stretches of Louisiana, the country had begun the process of its expansion. But it had remained overwhelmingly countrified, the vast mass of its populace dwelling in towns and hamlets which were scattered to the east of the Mississippi. Few white men—probably not more than one in thirty—had ventured beyond the river, and only slightly more were resident in cities. Such as they were, cities were few and far apart. Most of them were small, and only a handful could attest to a population of 20,000 or more. New York, which was three times the size of Philadelphia, was the largest and lodged less than 200,000, a figure considerably dwarfed by the million rounded up within the city limits of ancient Rome. In the provision of their public works and in their efficiency, the cities were scarcely more than primitive, with few of the benefits, or even the necessities, which have long since become the urban trademark. Municipal provision for water and for sanitation and health was precariously small. There were no paid firemen and no professional garbage men, whether in public service or in private, and even law enforcement was left to insufficient and ineffective hands. As yet, however, the city had been spared the grosser troubles of what now passes for industrial progress.

A quarter of a century more, and the national picture had undergone an almost magic alteration. Now the country extended to the Pacific shoreland and to the southern tip of Texas and the Rio Grande, while the number of its people had more than doubled. But they were no longer almost entirely native, for the flow of immigrants, especially from Ireland and Germany, had begun to run in earnest. A mere trickle of 30,000 in the early thirties, by 1850 it had swollen into a torrent which was more than ten times as great. As year followed year, new cities had arisen, while the older ones bulked appreciably bigger. At least thirty now prided themselves with a population of 20,000, while several others splurged with many more. In Philadelphia some 340,000 men, women, and children now rubbed shoulders, but with more than half a million inhabitants New York was still out in front.

2 The farming frontier too had edged onward; now it skirted the Mississippi. In fact, in scattered farms virgin earth was being furrowed even beyond its western bank. Nor had the movement toward the West abated; on the contrary, it was showing every sign of increase. For despite the hardships and perils, caravans of settlers, joined now by Europe's onrushing throng, continued to brave the streams and the mountains—and the Indians—to seek their fortune in the boundless spaces of the West.

Most Americans still wrung their living from the soil. As yet, little that was truly scientific was known of the soil's mysterious workings—of the trillions and trillions of invisible organisms which inhabited it and which, for good or ill, had the farmer at their mercy. Farmers entertained some slight inkling of the need for better stock, but the knowledge of animal eugenics and scientific mating had not yet been brought under the rule of science, and what was actually known about such occult matters was of little worth to the common husbandman. Such progress as the farmer was able to eke out issued mostly from hard-won experience, his setbacks and his triumphs, rather than from the probings of the laboratory. Yet for all the difficulties which dogged and haunted him at every turn, as a profitable undertaking his calling was actually improving. The need for certain products was, in fact, greater than ever—bread and meat, for example, to fill the urban belly, and raw materials, especially wool and cotton, for the mills of industry. Agriculture was also immeasurably advanced by vast, relentless improvements in the means of transport, with the proliferation of roads and canals, larger and swifter seacraft, and the advent of the steam locomotive, all of which combined to reduce time and space between farm and market.

3   The nation's industrial heartbeat was also stronger. It had been making itself evident even before the end of the eighteenth century, when the first small mills began to fleck the New England riverbanks, but it was not until after the union of steam and iron that the ancestor of today's factory came into being. Protected by tariffs and invigorated by a lusty and imaginative technology, America's infant industry gained rapidly in heft and strength. Indeed, except for financial panics and depressions, which, like the flu bug, periodically assault this fair land, the American manufacturer might have contemplated a beautiful and blissful millennium.

Even so, the land's industrial growth was little short of fantastic. Less than a score of cotton mills, for example, existed at the end of the century's first decade; twenty years more, and their number had ascended to about eight hundred; and by 1840 it had shot up almost another half thousand. The industrial concentration was greatest in the Northern coastal states, in New York, and particularly in New England. There, favored by luxuriant water power, a copious supply of capital and labor, first-rate facilities for inland transporation, and an easy access to the sea, it proved irresistible. It was in New England that the bulk of the textile industry was settled, but Yankee eyes were far from overlooking the shekels lurking in the sale of other products, for instance, firearms, clocks, pots and pans, and a herd of minor hardware, most of which lent themselves readily to cheap and easy haulage. Before very long, as the age of steel and heavy industry began to loom, it was natural and inescapable that Pennsylvania, with its priceless treasure of coal and iron, should come into its industrial own.

Meanwhile, in the South the pace of industrial unfoldment was far slower. There several factors, but especially the lack of free labor, encumbered industrial progress. For its wealth the South relied not on the factory but on the cotton field and on its ships, which bore its hopes to the processing mills of the North and overseas.

Though the farmer's banner continued to catch the breezes of the West, this is not to say that the land was bereft of industry. The manufacturer's intrusion was, in fact, relentless—so persistent that by the century's middle age Cleveland, Cincinnati, Chicago, and St. Louis had become flourishing manufacturing centers. Their success was attained not so much in the arena of cloth and hardware but rather in gastronomy, St. Louis having made itself a kingpin in flour milling, while Cincinnati was admired from one end of the republic to the other for the savor of its packed pork and the incomparable bouquet of its whisky.

The factory was a gross and ravening feeder. To survive it required the hard sinew of labor; this it got from the farm and from the ever-lengthening line of aliens. It also needed the creations of inventive imagination; these it got in a steady outpouring of new and superior tools and machines and in novel, timesaving industrial techniques. And it was, of course, forever craving capital; this it culled from the new capitalism, the combination of Wall Street and the corporation, the bankers and brokers (with their arsenal of stocks and bonds and loans and credits), and the swarms of ever-hopeful investors.

No less than the farmer, the manufacturer had been the beneficiary of the country's internal developments. Along the new turnpikes he raced his goods to remote and far-flung municipalities, and thence over the numerous waterways to their rustic consumers. The National Road, later to be known as the Cumberland Road, envisioned and financially succored by Congress, was begun in 1811 and completed some forty long and back-breaking years later. Starting at Cumberland in Maryland, it cut a swath through the mountainous barricade to Wheeling on the Ohio and to points beyond. Not only did it link the inland West with the shorelined East, but it also helped to topple freight rates. Meanwhile, under the rein of Governor De Witt Clinton, New Yorkers were trenching the biggest ditch the world had even seen, the Erie Canal. Completed in 1825, the canal brought together the waters of the Hudson at Albany and those of Lake Erie at Buffalo, thereby opening a direct water route eastward for faraway places in Wisconsin, Michigan, Illinois, Indiana, and Ohio. Not to be left behind by the go-getting New Yorkers, Marylanders put their heads together to contrive plans to bring glory and prosperity to the Free State by the construction of their own Chesapeake and Ohio Canal. Even greater spurs to human progress were the steamboat and the railroad. The development of a rivercraft so powerful that it could churn its way upstream even against the stupendous Mississippi not only revolutionized the course of inland navigation but—in the long run probably more important—opened the way to new and untapped markets for the output of farm and factory.

The first trains to run on rails, puny pygmies powered by horse and sometimes even sail, soon yielded to steam. With their conversion, the few miles of track laid by the 1820s grew like a tapeworm—in fact, within a generation they had increased a thousandfold. Still, the fifties stood on the calendar before railroad builders pulled up their sleeves and got down to serious business. At the end of that intrepid decade more than thirty thousand miles of track had been hammered into place to link the Mississippi Basin and, what in all likelihood portended even more, to put the West into economic alliance with the financial nabobs of the East.

Like that of England, though not so convulsively, America's industrial revolution spawned a shoal of problems and perplexities. The coming of the machine had been gradual enough, and in its years of youth it had effected no harsh dislocations of the old fireside and village industries. However, as the machine roared into day-to-day use, the need for its domestic precursor slackened, and presently it crumbled almost altogether. With its departure, training the apprentice began to lose its principal reason for being. As his chance to make a living subsided, the country worker yielded increasingly to the suction of the city, and in the passing years, as more and more factories fumed and fouled the air, the exodus from the countryside picked up enormously in magnitude and momentum. Meanwhile, the city horde was piling up from yet another source—the swarms of heart-filled and expectant aliens, and especially the Irish. The Hibernian flood began to swamp the Atlantic ports late in the forties, when famine and starvation weighed heavily upon the Emerald Isle. Fed up with their peasant penury, the Irish turned their back on the harsh labors of the farm. Not that hard work daunted them. They swung the pick and shovel, they carried the hod, and they laid tracks and whacked down ties to extend the infant railroads. Thousands crossed the Poconos to toil in the mines. Some came just in time to join the vanguard of the first gold rushes to the West. Some enhanced urban civilization as keepers of saloons or as policemen maintaining the public peace, from which occupation some presently graduated into politics.

Although city life offered advantages, for many a newcomer, who all too often was down on his heels, the benefits were elusive. The fight for bread and jobs was fierce, and even in good times the low and middling classes were hard pressed to survive. Sweat as they would, few of them broke the shackles of their poverty. The majority huddled in the city's shabbiest quarters, the forerunnners of slums, the grim and fetid holds of despair, disease, and death. Yet, for all their dreadful lot, their chance for something better on the morrow, though slight, was not completely absent. There was, for one, the shy promise of a young democracy, with its freedom and, more important, its suffrage. To their advantage too was a newer vision of man, more benignant and humane. Of some hope also was the growing self-awareness of American labor. Diffuse and varied though these factors were, running through them, at least through their more enlightened elements, was a common belief in the magical power of education—an education which was neither a privilege of a fortunate few nor a crumb flicked to the poor and lowly, but one which was nothing less than the right of every child in the land.

4   The generation which saw the nation transform so miraculously in its appearance and mode of living was witness also to a more spacious democracy. Intellectually, the new ideas reached florescence in the eighteenth century, in the era's philosophic rationalism, and in the Humanism of the French philosophes. From these it took aboard its essence, its confidence in the rationality of the human race and its capacity for unlimited progress. To this unfettered optimism there was presently brought the contention that the world was reigned by some sort of high design, which, when fathomed, would forever still our earthly aches and pains. Providence, some discovered presently, had even appointed the republic to become the world's model of freedom, prosperity, and the general welfare and contentment of its people. It was, its chief laureates discerned, America's mission—nay, its Manifest Destiny—to carry the torch of democracy to the ends of the earth.

By the forties the white American's struggle for his right to vote, without prerequisites of caste or pocket, came to a triumphant end. Even earlier, as has been mentioned in pages preceding, the notion that the right to govern was the reserve of a cultivated and propertied gentry had been under assault. Attacked most fiercely by the settlers in the new lands beyond the Alleghenies, the philosophy of government by class began to wobble with the ebb of Federalist power, and with the elevation of Jackson to the White House, it stumbled to its inglorious exit. Though he was rich, a cotton planter and a slaveholder, he endeared himself to the multitude, the farmhands, and especially the city proletariat. Somehow they envisioned in him a man who was like unto their own hopes and dreams, an American risen from the lower ranks, who, they were convinced, would not forget them in their battle for place and security. Jackson's ascension to the Presidency marked the first national election in which nearly all the states allowed the individual citizen to vote for the Chief Executive. It was the signal as well of a ponderable increase in the public's political interest; henceforward election campaigns were to be addressed to the bulk of the American people, the vast aggregation of common men, the imminence of whose sway must have curled the lip of the ghostly Alexander Hamilton.

5   The gospel of perpetual progress fell, like the Biblical mustard seed, on fertile ground. From it rose not only a more sumptuous democracy but also a host of humanitarian causes, some trivial and preposterous, some of high and capital significance. The craze for moral uplift, which at one time or another seizes almost every American, was never greater than during the middle of the nineteenth century. From it sprang crusade after crusade: drives to keep the Sabbath chaste and sanctified; drives for women's rights and better and more civilized jails; campaigns to rid us of war, crime, vice, smut, atheism, booze, and nicotine; and, the most inflammatory and engulfing defiance of them all, abolition. Though they were propelled generally by the horsepower of their own certainties, the reformers were not so totally idealistic as to scoff at being practical in their methods. Through organizations and propaganda, and especially through the pressure they were able to exert on their ambassadors and attorneys in public office, they agitated with a fine and adept hand. They were met head on, needless to say, by forces which were equally shrewd and no less cocksure; yet, for all that, they managed not infrequently to come out on top. Such, as we shall see in later pages, were the nature and strategy behind the drive and counterdrive—for the free, tax-supported common school.

A constant source of the uplift was religion. At the beginning of the century, seeking to offset the Revolution's devastating effect on the republic's moral and religious life, the nation had burst into a powerful religious revival, the so-called "Second Great Awakening." The movement pressed over the entire land and struck at every group, high and low, from New England's intellectual cells to remote and dispersed mudholes in the trans-Appalachian wilderness. It kept going for at least a decade, and wherever man has continued to enjoy personal parleys with Beelzebub, it has been followed by others of a lesser voltage, perhaps, but no less indomitable. While it endured, it stimulated the national appetite for religion, made churchgoing more popular, enlivened the pulpit, and kindled a need for more and more parsons—a demand some churches essayed to meet by extending their facilities for training in divinity. Finally, the Awakening inspired new zeal for Bible reading. Indeed, in some quarters it gave fresh power to the contention not only that the Good Book was inspired in Heaven, but also that its words were literally and teetotally true and that, in spite of what science might teach, it was in this vein alone that it had to be read and taught —a view which, as everyone knows, still prevails in current fundamentalist circles.

As the Awakening picked up scope and strength, it entertained a rich and protean program of Christian endeavor. The revivalist camp meeting worked itself into the American way, and even today, wherever the appetite for virtue threatens to lose its edge, the evangelist's voluptuous rhetoric is still cherished and given a hopeful ear. Specialists in rectitude penetrated even into the infamous West as far as Oregon, not only to salvage the godless Indian, but also to restore the fallen pioneer, whose cascading morals, it was feared, had made him as wicked as the red man. Nor were the infidels in foreign parts overlooked—in fact, by the century's middle years American men of God were explaining the meaning and consequences of sin to people deprived of such knowledge, thereby saving souls all over the globe, in the Near East, India, Burma, and even Africa, China, and the Hawaiian Islands. The reformer's task, as is well known, is one of constant trial—such is the power of evil. Luckily, for the cause of good works, the revival bred a host of dedicated allies, all zealous to bind and heal, as witness the American Bible Society (1816), the General Union for Promoting the Observance of the Christian Sabbath (1828), the Young Men's Christian Association (1851), and several others, all equally zealous.

In their stand on humanitarian matters the churches were seldom in full accord. For example, on such a combustible question as abolition there were differences of opinion within a sect itself, often even within a congregation. Nearly all churches countenanced movements for universal peace, temperance, Sabbath observance, and similar causes. In general they stood up for prison reform and for a more humane treatment of the insane, but they had grave misgivings about the rights of labor, and nearly all of them cherished even grimmer doubts about more rights for women. They were in disagreement too over the question of the common school. Those, like the Presbyterians and the Congregationalists, whose confidence in schooling had dug itself firmly into their habit of mind through long and toilsome experience conceived little antipathy toward universal public primary schooling, provided, of course, that it was not of a hostile or godless kind. But others, like the Lutherans and the Quakers, whose denominational considerations outweighed all else, were stoutly at odds with the idea of a common school which was secular and tax-supported.

There is no gainsaying that the revival was a force of great and sweeping power and that the mark it left ran long, wide, and deep—but in the making of America the lure of the world about was no less vital. The call of the West, the crescendo of industrialism, and the rise of John Doe, with his triumphant assumption of the reins of suffrage and his pressure for economic and social advancement—all these drives and urges, mundane and selfish though they were, were deep-seated and not easily stayed. For all its strength, the Awakening could not flag them, nor could it lessen or control them. More and more the American's life was succumbing to worldly values.

6   Even before the coming of the factory, workers in a number of trades had banded together to forward their special interests and welfare. They had, in fact, even permitted themselves the luxury of an occasional strike; such an engagement, however, was confined to a local front, and it was not yet ridden by class feeling. Nor, for that matter, was there any idea of welding the diverse and wide-flung constituents into the units of a single, national organization. The first step toward such an end was not taken until 1827, when Philadelphia's bricklayers and carpenters and a few practitioners of other arts and crafts joined hands in the Mechanics Central Union of Trade Associations. By and by similar brotherhoods bobbed up in several of the major industrial centers. But none of these efforts was stalwart, and none of them was executed on a national scale. In fact, it was not until 1836, when the American cordwainers reached out on a countrywide range, that the land was honored with a trade union befitting a vibrant and maturing people.

As with pretty nearly every other group, organized labor soon found out that its fortunes, for weal or woe, were dependent on the state of the general economy. When the winds were favorable, as they were from 1835 to 1836, the workers moved forward. But when hard times fell on the land, as they did in the panic year of 1837 and in the baleful period following, they lost ground. Then, as the pall of depression lifted and the nation braced itself for another wave of prosperity, labor too made ready to snare some gains of its own. Its pace, however, was hobbled, and its advance was largely local. Indeed, when the fifties were almost done, only four trade unions of a national caliber existed.

Yet for all its seesawing, in the advancement of liberal causes—in many of which, needless to say, its motives were tinged with self-interest— labor was to play an active part. It was labor that called for an end of the age-worn practice of jugging a man for debt. It was labor that raised its collective voice against the seizure of an indebted craftman's tools and, yet more callous, his home. Labor hurled its anathemas against the corporation and urged the dissolution of all chartered monopolies. One of labor's major yearnings was a ten-hour day, and naturally it was not in the least averse to getting higher wages. And finally, it was labor, among others, that made itself articulate in its demand for the establishment of a free, tax-supported common school.

7   It was only natural that the country's gigantic progress, its liberty, wealth, and power, together with its unbounded confidence in even greater triumphs just around the corner, should have fevered a nationwide patriotic sentiment. Ideologically, there was a national devotion to the American way, its freedom, democracy, and opportunity. Politically, the surging nationalism was disposed toward a stronger and more active Federal authority, though such a view was fiercely countered by local and regional interests. National honor fevered aggressive and imperialistic phobias and, in the forties, brought the United States into war with Mexico, a conflict which in historical afterlight appears to have been anything but irrepressible. Economically, the national flame burned with white heat among the merchant and industrial gentry in their cry for protection against alien competition, and also among the laboring order in an accumulating resentment of the immigrant in their midst, and especially his lower level of living, his indecent willingness to work for lower wages, and what to every right-minded American seems to be his pigheaded resistance to Americanization.

The national spirit flared up even in religion, particularly in the forties, when the number of Catholics in the land spurted from 650,000 at the turn of the decade to a tally of more than twice as many at the decade's end. As the number of Romans grew by leaps and bounds, so also did their Holy Church, with her retinue of consecrated servants, from archbishops and bishops to parish priests. It was a spectacle to shake the angels—unless they chanced to favor the Catholic rite. No less alarming on earth, its challenge brought forth a militant American Protestantism. Asserting that the glory and grandeur of the republic lay entirely in the Protestant tradition, its spokesmen polluted their piety with intolerance—even, indeed, with anti-Catholic vendettas. As tempers welled up, fear shook the composure of high and low alike. The mob applied its talents to riots, arson, and pillage. In the pulpit the Rev. Lyman Beecher turned the thunder of his eloquent wrath against insidious Rome, while Samuel B. Morse, no less inventive in espionage than in telegraphy, conjured up bogeys of papist plots to destroy our beloved democracy by the stratagem of a massive immigrant infiltration.

The national temper was visible even in the realm of learning and letters. Suffused with the era's utilitarianism, Americans addressed themselves not so much to the advancement of scientific theory as to practical ends. Hence, the genius for whom Americans reserved their admiration was hardly a Newton or a Priestly, or even a Cavendish, but rather the deviser of something which could be put to everyday use, in illustration, laughing gas, a rotary press, a telegraph, a rubber raincoat and hat and shoes to match, a six-shooter, or even an earpick. The fountainhead of scientific theory, as a result, was not in America but in Europe.

Even as the republic was being incubated, Noah Webster envisioned the glories of a national literature. But the literary starlight was slow to shine. In the Jacksonian heyday patriotic calls for national letters went out anew. "We want a national literature," clamored the historian John Palfrey, one which, he hoped, would become a "permanent common object for patriotic attachment and pride." In 1837 the national chord was entoned again by Ralph Waldo Emerson. In a historic discourse, delivered at Harvard before an assemblage of Phi Beta Kappans and now preserved as *The American Scholar,* Emerson exhorted his countrymen "to cast out the passion for Europe." Although this sentiment was sharply challenged, the following years saw the coming of an indigenous literature. The age produced Bryant, Whittier, Longfellow, Cooper, Irving, Thoreau, and Holmes. And just as the century entered the middle years, Herman Melville's unforgettable *Moby Dick* appeared, one of the splendors of American letters, but doomed to languish in obscurity for more than half a century. The same fate befell the emotional rhythms of Walt Whitman's wild but magnificent *Leaves of Grass,* which was written in 1853.

Inevitably the bubbling national ego animated an interest in the country's past. The advent of historical societies in various parts of the land was one outcome. The first on the scene was the Massachusetts Historical Society, which was founded in 1794 "to mark the genius, delineate the manners, and trace the progress of society in the United States, and . . . to rescue the true history of this country from the ravages of time and the effects of ignorance and neglect." The organization was in its thirtieth year before it was joined by a similar-minded clan—this time in New York. The newcomer was the work of John Pintard, a somewhat showy fellow, a barker with a plume in his hat, who was never at a loss for glittering schemes, some merely to give greater substance to his pocket but some also of benefit to learning. Gnawed by a passion to conserve historical documents, Pintard organized a historical museum under the banner of what is now Tammany Hall. But the project floundered and presently it came to grief, whereupon its sponsor applied his skill of persuasion to the legislature. It was an art which rarely failed him. Not only did Pintard succeed in coaxing the lawgivers into establishing the New York Historical Society in 1804, but some eight years later he also managed to cozen them into subsidizing it with an appropriation of $12,000.

On the heels of New York other states quickly followed. Soon, indeed, the zeal to unearth the historical past and to incarcerate it in the permanence of some tangible record broke out locally, in illustration, in east Tennessee in 1833 and in western Pennsylvania a year later; in the counties of Essex and Worcester, Massachusetts, the one in 1821 and the other in 1825; and even in municipalities, as in Albany, New York, in 1821, and in Marietta, Ohio, in 1841—to set down only two. Though purportedly they were quarrying the national past, the early historical associations were disposed heavily to provincial drumbeating, and in consequence, their examinations of the bygone American experience confined themselves for the most part to memorializing the past events of the state of which a particular society happened to be a part. Not until the century's last quarter, in 1884, did the American Historical Society begin its important work of putting the American past in a truly national frame.

The first historian of any reputation to rise in the republic was Jared Sparks. He was of a slight and unassuming background, and the education he managed to pick up came the hard way. Out of Harvard, he made his way into divinity, gracing a Unitarian pulpit at Baltimore for a spell, only to return to the city on the Charles to take over the *North American Review*. His editorial talent and, even more, his capacity for recognizing literary confections that were tasty to the intellectual palate of his readers soon converted his magazine into the nation's foremost journal of criticism, and one with a national audience to boot.

While he was still of a young age, Sparks took upon himself the task of gathering the writing of George Washington, then already the head god in the national pantheon. It did not take Sparks long to decide that if he were to display Washington's literary remains in a refined and dignified manner and offer them to the public view, "a national interest and a national feeling would be excited." The result was the *Life and Writings of George Washington,* a twelve-volume production. Finished in 1837, it received an instantaneous acclamation, and for the next twenty years it was to maintain its author in fine monetary health. So well was it regarded that presently it obtained Sparks an invitation from Harvard to sit as its McLean professor of ancient and modern history, the first professorship in secular history in a university of the United States. In 1848, when Sparks completed his *Library of American Biography,* a massive concoction in twenty-five volumes, his fame leaped even higher. Put together by writers from every nook and cranny of the land, the work offered the most impressive biographic delicatessen of its time. The subjects in its gallery include all —or nearly all—the salient worthies of early America, from Captain John Smith and Patrick Henry to James Otis and James Oglethorpe. All of them, as the accountants of their days on earth make clear, were patriotic virtuosos of the highest dazzle—all, that is to say, save the fallen Benedict Arnold. The telling of his tale Sparks reserved for himself in the *Life and Treason of Benedict Arnold,* a work so tearstained and upsetting that its attraction for connoisseurs was almost irresistible.

Posterity has identified Sparks as the father of historical scholarship in America. There is no question that the man had a nose for documentary records and that he devoted many laborious hours to tracking them down and arranging them for the service of savants yet unborn. But he was also a patrioteer, a self-appointed custodian of reputations rather than a critic of their worth. "It would be an act of unpardonable injustice," he said of Washington, "to bring forth compositions, and particularly letters with no design for publication, and then commit them to the press without previously subjecting them to a careful revision." To fit his heroes into their marbled niche he took pains to revise and retouch their utterances, gilding and glossing as he went along. It was, to be sure, a pious exercise, which the ground rules of those days palliated but which, viewed in retrospect, is scarcely a dispassionate examination of the record, but rather a scholarship with, so to speak, the shirttail of propaganda peeping out.

A writer rather than a prowler in archives was George Bancroft— indeed, those packed granaries of yellowed paper offered little to prick his interest. Barely thirteen when he introduced himself to Harvard, he emerged the darling of his professors, who staked him to several years of travel and study abroad. There he augmented his wisdom at Heidelberg, Berlin, and Göttingen, and when he got the chance he visited Pestalozzi to examine his teaching method. When he returned to the United States in 1822, he had achieved command of several European tongues, besides enjoying a nodding acquaintance with Goethe, von Humboldt, Lafayette, Gallatin, Lord

Byron, and a herd of ladies and gentlemen of the blood—a distinction which set him apart from the vast run of his contemporaries, whether lettered or not. Bancroft's major work, the *History of the United States,* was begun in 1834 but was not completed until half a century later, and though it occupied a dozen obese volumes, it got no further than 1789. The study was an immediate success. The provincial-minded, it is true, offered it only sneers. For all that, it made its way into home after home, and as the work went through edition after edition, it made its author not only famous but very rich as well. Even so, he remained a Jacksonian democrat to the core, a trait which, like his histories, rewarded him handsomely with one public job after another, from Collector of the Port of Boston to Secretary of the Navy—even, indeed, Minister to Great Britain.

If Bancroft's well-fitted tomes managed to become something of a national best-seller, then it was because their maker set the country's heartstrings to humming. When he walked upon the stage with his first book, the land was still in the clutch of colliding localisms, and the meaning and surety of the nation's purpose had yet to be achieved. These deficiencies Bancroft undertook to rectify by giving the American people a work of a single piece conceived on a truly national scale. A seer rather than an impersonal recorder, an evangelist rather than a restrained and disciplined historian, Bancroft devoted his energy to preaching the message of America's destiny. He spun his thoughts into words of an unforgettable luster —suffused oftentimes, it is true, with red, white, and blue, but beguiling, nonetheless, and, more important, believed. Today in a world of altered values, they have all but lost their spell. But the snow-cloaked heights which eluded Bancroft were scaled by others, notably Parkman and Prescott. Of the twain, Francis Parkman has best withstood time's ravages. His first book, *The Oregon Trail,* which was issued in 1847, has even attained the stature of a classic.

As for the other learning, it too pulsed with nationalism, though perhaps to a lesser degree. Calls still went forth from time to time for the establishment of a national seat of the higher learning. Such demands, however, were growing scarcer, and their tone was more pianissimo. Vanished altogether were the partisans of a national school system, such as had been active when the republic was struggling to get on its feet. But, as the common school began to beckon, it was given the approval of patriots who saw the purpose of such an institution as fundamentally civic. Not only was it expected to transmute the young into true and effective Americans, but as more and more outlanders settled in the United States, it was to Americanize them as well.

Such was the second quarter of the century in America. It was in many ways an extraordinary epoch. Within its span the country's early doubts turned to confidence. The stripling nation grew almost beyond credulity in size and population, the number of its cities increasing and its frontier receding farther and farther to the west and south. The volume of immigration grew larger and larger. There was an enormous material advance: the development of waterways and highroads, the unfoldment of the railroad, the onset of steam and the machine. Commerce and professional farming expanded. But there was also the swift and foreboding rise of industry, with its underlying capitalism, its factories, and its workers—the starting point for social, political, and economic complexities affecting generations yet unborn. Beside this scene of swift, engulfing change, the South was comparatively static, remaining agrarian, slaveholding, in the grip of its moldering traditions, and bent upon their preservation.

The transformations of the era were not simply of the sort that arrest the eye. Some were less perceptible to the common senses, but were penetrant and far-reaching in their consequences. The supreme social fact of the era was the advance of the common man, with his rise to political power, enriched by a growing recognition of human worth and dignity. This was an age of gaudy hopes and gusty aspirations, of dreams of better worlds and unending progress, of moral and humanitarian causes, of reform and uplift movements. It was a period of national awakening, of exhilarating stir, and of the kindling of optimism and self-confidence, and even of braggadocio, which springs from freedom and from the sense of realization and achievement.

Such was the cradle of the common school.

9
THE EDUCATIONAL AWAKENING

There were few public schools in 1825, and those which were about were of low esteem and generally hard beset. Their support was still meager, and only here and there was it drawn from a local tax. A few states had worked their way toward a school fund, while some of the younger ones extracted their revenue from grants of land. But whatever their sources, few of them, whether singly or in concert, yielded a gratifying income. In consequence, public schooling languished badly, with little to commend it either to the poor, whose opinion of it oftentimes was disdainful and even cynical, or to the rich, who nearly always were against it.

The grizzly dogma that education was not the seemly business of government still persisted. Some, it is true, had ventured to attack this view. But their number was small, and their jeremiads too rarefied to make much impression on the public mind. More numerous and far more effective were their opponents, who insisted that learning, like dreams of love, was an entirely personal matter and that for a state to undertake to give free instruction to everyone at public expense was an invasion of privacy.

All this naturally gave private endeavor a ponderable advantage. For some of the young this meant having recourse to a private tutor, a grammar school, or an academy. For the generality it resulted in attendance at some private denominational school, a parochial school, or, frequently, a charity school. Though they were supposedly given to furthering the intellect, the private operators were not always able to resist the temptation of governmental favor. Indeed, some of them voiced bitter disapproval of the slight help government occasionally tendered a public school, and, what is more, they went to great lengths to have such proceeds directed to their own pockets. Their efforts were sometimes fruitful, and in a number of states —New York, Pennsylvania, Delaware, and Indiana—private academies were the recipients of a modest handout.

As the republic passed through its amazing transformation from the twenties on, the old notions of educational prerogative began to totter. It was all very well for the Founding Fathers to entertain such lofty views, for at bottom they were simply a reflection of the world which they adorned. But in the fast-changing and complicated new America, where every white male citizen could express his wishes at the polls and might even ornament some public office, such ideas were palpably running against the democratic tide. What was needed, some now began to urge, was a school which would induct all the young, whether of low or high estate, into the evolving national life. Such a school, its partisans announced, could not be confided to private hands. On the contrary, it must be free and open to all, and its support must come from the public purse. Such were the first glimmerings of the common school, or, in the vernacular of today, the public school.

2   The educational awakening which was to give us the common school derived its main strength from the city. No other stage could have been more admirably suited to the zealous reformer. Here were wealth, ambition, and power, but here also swarmed the poor, the meek, the exploited. Here stalked vice, disease, and despair—all the familiar bedevilments of civilization. The city not only posed the problem, but of all places it was best disposed to grapple with it. It alone commanded the means and resources, without which the common school could have been little more than moonshine—shimmering, perhaps, and full of wonder, but still moonshine.

The city, of course, was where the labor movement made its struggling start and where the workingman, pining to improve his condition, issued his first summons for better schools. As the twenties made way for the thirties, labor groups in a number of cities, and especially in the large ones of New York, Philadelphia, and Boston, set off a clatter for free and tax-supported schooling. Though the labor movement led a battered life, and —as has already been noted—following the panic of 1837, fell on lean days, for all that, the support it rendered the common school was of no little consequence.

Again, it was the city which saw the coming of educational charity, the instrument with which Raikes and Owens and other seers like them sought to cauterize the social wounds. But in America, as in the motherland, such educational good works proved inadequate to their purpose. Its practitioners were eager and willing enough, but the task laid upon their shoulders was far too onerous, and for every person they managed to assist there were hundreds—nay, thousands—whom they never reached.

Yet, instead of quenching the humanitarian's fire, the impotence of his charity merely made it burn more fiercely—such is the human way. Actually, the inadequacy of his dispensations reflected not so much on his ends as on his means. When charity was almost the only way to school the underdog, the humanitarian had no great choice. But the common school offered him a marvelous alternative, and it was to this that he now directed the full energy of his effort. From the poor and submerged he was seeking to deliver, he evoked little more than apathy; from the rich he proposed to tax, he reaped mostly execration and a resistance which would have turned away men of the common run. The support for the common school came from neither the low nor the high, but from the middle—from a scattering of liberals in public office, from ministers and educators, from the leaders of labor, and from a small fragment of thinking citizens. Like all militant causes, the agitation for tax-supported schools consumed huge drafts of money, time, and energy. Indeed, before it was at an end, it had sapped the health and strength of some of its staunchest messiahs.

It was in the North that the movement stormed its first ramparts, but a generation was gone before its victory was sealed and delivered. South of the Potomac the drive developed more gingerly. There the opposition proved a great deal tougher, the social and economic tradition more restraining, and the urban centers from which the movement drew its essential sustenance much fewer in number. The hopes which it continued to inflame were dampened by the catastrophe of the Civil War and its miasmic aftermath. But they were never extinguished completely, and in later years, when trouble and travail began to lose their grip and circumstances became more benign, the reformer once more moved into action.

The ideal of universal tax-supported schooling was first embraced by a small band of active partisans. Resorting to every trick then in the propagandist's satchel, they staged meetings, wrote broadsides, and buttonholed lawmakers. They aired their views by means of a wide range of organizations, exerting their declamatory pressure wherever they could. Their syllogisms were as diverse as their audiences. In the case of the civic-minded, for example, they made an appeal to conscience; to employers they offered a better-trained and better-disciplined work force, one so virtuous and constant that it would never incline, as it did in Europe, to toss bombs at capitalists; finally, for the masses they conjured up enchanting vistas of lush pastures awaiting their young once they had subdued the three Rs.

3   Among the numerous fraternities to give their support to the reformation of American education two stand out above the rest—the Western Literary Institute and College of Professional Teachers and the American Lyceum. The former, founded in 1832 by Albert Picket in Cincinnati, made rapid headway, and pretty soon its chapters were on hand in almost all the states. Through the press, but even more through its roving orators, it sought to boost the cause of the common school.

Meanwhile, in 1826, Josiah Holbrook, a Yale man and one of some historical stature, had hatched the Millbury Lyceum No. 1 Branch of the American Lyceum. Designed, like its forerunner, to instruct and edify the general folk, the lyceum essayed, among other things, to give tone to the American conversation, establish libraries and museums, direct recreation, and do its utmost to bring victory to the campaigners for public education.

From its humble start at Millbury, the American Lyceum, like the locusts of Biblical fame, swarmed into every corner of the republic, not merely into its culture-consuming cities, but into its innumerable Mudvilles as well. Everywhere it showed itself prosperity brushed its cheeks—save in the Old South, where the appetite for public enlightenment was somewhat impaired. As the lyceum went into high gear, it worked itself into the national habit, carrying its message into state after state and generating cells in a number far beyond Holbrook's wildest expectation. Within eight years, in fact, Millbury Lyceum No. 1 had multiplied three thousand times. The American Lyceum, *Harper's Magazine* informed its readers in 1858, "has now become a fixed American institution."

For its trade in knowledge, the lyceum relied principally on the lecture. Its touring Ciceros dilated on an almost endless range of themes, from the sun to the honeybee, and from Mohammed to the legal rights of women. The lyceum served the nation's country people much as the newspaper did the city dweller. The radio of yesterday, it scattered a ray of brightness, sometimes instructive and diverting, to bring cheer into the emptiness of the wintry night. Though plain folk dominated its lists, there were big names too, for instance, Daniel Webster, who was the author and president of the Boston Lyceum, besides Ralph Waldo Emerson, Oliver Wendell Holmes, Horace Greeley, and William Lloyd Garrison—and even Charles Sumner, Louis Agassiz, Lucy Stone, and Elizabeth Stanton.

The lyceums not only offered an introduction to the arts and sciences but also produced reforms in the schools themselves. Holbrook, who overflowed with pedagogic raptures, took delight in all the latest innovations, but the apple of his eye seems to have been the normal school. As the lyceum labored up the slope for the common school, it declared itself for better schoolbooks and teaching methods. In truth, risking ugly looks from the teaching rank and file, it even called for an amelioration in the birchmasters themselves. Holbrook apparently practiced what he preached, and in his classes he entertained his students with an amazing array of apparatus, illuminating slides, globes and charts, and other esoteric charms calculated to expedite the learning process. In this country old Josiah was the first to amalgamate manual training, farm work, and book learning. Unluckily, the seminary he founded for this purpose on his father's farm came to naught.

As with current bodies engaged in the propagation of learning, representatives of the far-flung lyceums assembled annually in national convention. In all, there were nine such solemnities—the first in 1832—and like their present-day successors, all made an effort to catch the public eye. Though they have long since this vale departed, what they talked about still strikes a familiar ring, in illustration, manual training, the lecture method, whether religion should be taught, who should ponder the classics, how the sciences should be divulged, whether wicked pupils should be clouted, and—in importance by no means the least—how to befriend and bemuse lawgivers for the cause of the public learning.

As American today as gas stations and pizza palaces, the convention was well regarded even in the Jacksonian era, and in their fondness for it schoolmen were no different from other up-and-coming Americans, either then or now. In nearly every state they raised their voice for educational progress, exhorting legislators to bestir themselves in its behalf. Though there was ever a gulf betwixt their pleas and the legislative response, as doubtless there always will be, the effect of their striving in the end must have been penetrating and powerful. Without it, it is more than likely, the campaign for better schools would have been considerably retarded.

4   Indispensable to the movement for the common school was the printed word. The invention of the rotary press begot the penny newspaper, whose least attraction was surely not its cheapness, a fact which was evidently appreciated by its ever-growing clientele, and also a fact which was quickly pounced upon by the reformer. Not only was editorial opinion dragooned in support of the common school, but some newspapers even filled precious space with accounts of educational progress overseas. Intellectually, however, the newspaper was a double-edged blade, editors being, like the rest of us, men of divergent tastes. Consequently, for every journalistic cry for school improvement, there was always a countercry from the opposition.

More useful, though more restricted in its lure, was the educational press itself. The offspring of an incipient professional spirit, it flung its manifestos mainly at the teacher, though no doubt it was willing enough to give its counsel to the layman. In the forefront of America's pedagogic journals was *The Academician,* published in New York by Albert and John Picket, father and son. Like many of its successors, it lived a haggard life, and it endured no more than a couple of years, from 1818 to 1820. The two decades following saw the arrival of at least a score of educational gazettes and the departure of almost as many. There were, to instance a few, the *American Journal of Education,* put out in Boston by William Russell from 1826 to 1830; the *American Annals of Education,* its heir and assign from 1831 to 1939; and the *Common School Assistant,* which was published at Albany from 1836 to 1840 by J. Orville Taylor. There was Barnard's *Connecticut School Journal,* Mann's *Common School Journal,* and Wiley's *North Carolina School Journal.* And there were yet more. But towering high above them all, and the longest-lived by far, was Barnard's *American Journal of Education,* which appeared a few years after mid-century.

Among the gazettes of pedagogy there ranged the usual differences. A few were dinosaurs, but most were amoebas. Some were well arranged, of jaunty mien, and even ably and intelligently written; but others had the reek of failure plain upon them. For all their variation, however, they also bore resemblances, particularly in what they had to report. Then, as now, they concerned themselves with the shoptalk of their craft—its heavens and its hells; the newest in everyday schoolmastering; the latest in methodology, schoolbooks, appliances, and accessories; and, far less frequently, alas, ideas. And all of them gave their countenance and support to the common school.

As for the finest in pedagogy, the journals of that day descended upon their subject in a far more comparative vein than most of their present successors. Already in *The Academician,* one sights discourses on the endeavors of foreign schoolmen—of the Swiss Pestalozzi, for example, his fellow countryman von Fellenberg, and England's monitorial rivals, Dr. Bell and Mr. Lancaster. What the Pickets set afoot in their columns, William Russell, Horace Mann, and Henry Barnard kept going in their own, and under a plentiful head of steam. For an era so strongly colored with nationalism, the schoolman's courting of alien pedagogics might appear odd—even, indeed, unpatriotic. Actually, it was nothing of the sort. Fundamentally indigenous, the common school issued from the crossing of several elements, and the climate in which it grew up was that of the Jacksonian democracy. As for pedagogic speculation, at least in its loftier reaches, this was another story. In this domain, as in that of theoretic science and medicine, the seedbed happened to be Europe—and so it was to be almost until the passing of the century. What the more enlightened advocate of the common school was after was a school firmly lodged in American ideology, but one which at the same time gave accommodation to the most up-to-date and progressive practices to be had anywhere. The one he got from America, and the other from Europe.

5　　The Old World's educational doings not only were disclosed in the press but soon became the object of close and firsthand observation. Granted, the number of Americans who headed for Europe to inspect its schools were small, but among those making the long and arduous journey were to be found the frontliners in the battle for better American schools, men like Stowe, Barnard, and Mann. What these men recommended, though it was frequently the cause of harsh and derisive words, was nevertheless in no case to be taken lightly.

Although several Americans had scrutinized European education early in the century, the first report to reach the United States which was granted more than a polite respect was the work not of a native, but of Victor Cousin, a professor of philosophy and dean, or headmaster, of France's Higher Normal School. Commissioned by the French government, then under the uneasy scepter of Louis-Philippe, to study German education, Cousin exposed its salient features in candid and meticulous detail in 1831. The following year his survey was printed, and in 1834, translated into English, it appeared in London. In America it was seized upon by pedagogic pundits and promptly found its way into the educational journals.

Cousin's dissection of Prussian education, and particularly his warm endorsement of it, was surely an extraordinary event in the history of Franco-Prussian relations. What seized this Frenchman's eye was the stupendous efficiency of Prussian schooling; the spectacle of national authority over education; its centralized secular control; its trained and expert teachers; its up-to-date methods; its planning, financing, and supervising; and finally its bold and outspoken employment of the school as an instrument for national ends.

To the American school reformer's ear much of this was noble music. Admittedly, its beat was Prussian and monarchical, but its air was nonetheless seductive. With a change here and an alteration there to bring it into consonance with the American way, he was convinced that it might be put to an effective use in the campaign for better schools. The evils of the Prussian system, observed Horace Mann, "were easily and naturally separable from the good"—and of the latter he apparently felt there was a great deal.

A few years after Cousin had placed Prussian education under the glass, Calvin Ellis Stowe set out for Europe. Stowe, who was a man of God and a professor of sacred science at the Lane Theological Institute, was also the mate of the immortal Harriet Beecher. The first purpose of his voyage was to buy books for his college library, but before he took sail, the Ohio legislature had commissioned him to take a close look at Europe's schools and to render a report thereon. His monograph, *Elementary Education in Europe,* he transmitted in 1837. Like his Gallic forerunner, Stowe soon succumbed to the Prussian Lorelei. He too was charmed by the well-oiled thoroughness, the trained and competent masters, and especially the magic power of the Pestalozzian method. So immensely impressed was Stowe that he proceeded forthwith to belabor the Ohio legislators—and those of other states—to take a cue from the wonder-working Prussians. "If it can be done in Prussia," he reminded them, "I know it can be done in Ohio." They listened gravely and even ordered 10,000 copies of his report to be printed and a plentiful supply thereof to be placed in every school in the state. But beyond this flutter of esteem their emulation of the Prussians was quietly postponed. The truth is that almost half the century was done before grammar and geography were added to Ohio's three Rs; it was past midcentury when the schools were made free; and midcentury was long since in history before the state acquired its first normal school.

Even so, the Stowe report left its mark. The years saw some of its substance reprinted in the *American Journal of Education.* As was no more than proper, the *Journal* also gave an account of Stowe's life. Though it was veiled in anonymity, the piece was actually the work of Stowe himself —a deception which apparently was far from singular among the educational *prominenti* of the day. Precisely what effect the report had on the remaking of American education no one, of course, can say. One may go along with the learned Barnard and trace "not a little of the advancement of the common school during the next twenty years to this report." Or, until the evidence becomes more conclusive, one may prefer to hold one's peace. In either case it makes no great difference. That Stowe's findings stirred up a new and gusty educational concern and that they provoked weighty words about the whole American educational enterprise—of this there is not the slightest doubt. The report itself was cordially saluted in several halls of lawmaking, in Massachusetts, Pennsylvania, Michigan, North Carolina, and Virginia, where it was commandeered for reprinting and distribution. As a blow in the war for school reform it was certainly one of the best.

There are other pilgrims, and there were other reports. Alexander Bache, the grandson of Benjamin Franklin and a West Pointer, toured not only Germany but also Great Britain and France, besides Austria, Switzerland, and Holland. His observations, which were published in 1839, ran to over six hundred pages. Somewhat earlier Dr. Johannes Julius, a Hamburger, was bidden to discourse on the theme of Prussian education before a Massachusetts legislative committee, who heard him decorously but abstained from action. In 1839 Benjamin Smith, a Virginian, expounded similarly before the Governor of his state, who passed the message on to the lawmakers but who, greatly to Smith's sorrow, paid no heed whatsoever. In any case his report leaned heavily on the others, particularly Stowe's, and said nothing that had not been said before. Finally, there was Horace Mann.

Mann visited Europe in 1843, when he was secretary to the Massachusetts Board of Education. Though his sojourn was brief, he observed a great deal. So much, in fact, did this man discern that it required reams of paper to set it all down in his annual report to the board—his famous and unforgettable Seventh. Not content merely to play the reporter's part, Mann also made himself a critic. German education, on the whole, he lauded, while that of England he found wanting. More significant, however, than his apportionment of praise and censure was the reason which lurked behind it. Did the English, for example, drag their educational feet and the German skip with theirs? Then clearly this should come as a sober warning to the people of Massachusetts, for in England government played but a minor educational role, while in Germany its impact was felt at all time and everywhere.

The Seventh Report was much more than an exercise in comparative education; it was a siege gun in Mann's warfare for school reform. It has evoked attention for the rage it roused, and it has been hailed for its forthright candor. Most important, however, is the fact that it struck the mark.

6   In 1825 the stage was being set in Massachusetts for what has since gone into the record as the Public School Revival. To it the coming years brought the generalship of Horace Mann. Meanwhile, the fates had assigned the task of getting the revival started to another, somewhat less dramatic and less monumental, but no less mulishly devoted. He was James Gordon Carter, a plowman's son, hatted and robed at Harvard, and at twenty-five a schoolmaster and the composer of a pamphlet on education —his historic letters on the free schools in New England, which saw their first publication in the *Boston Transcript*.

It was far from an exhilarating piece. Through it trudged the sad cortege of New England learning, once the Puritan's pride, but now a relic of run-down schools, inept teachers, cheeseparing economy, and inefficient administration. In 1826 Carter let go with another indictment, *Essays on Popular Education*. The second treatise, like the first, pointed the way to the commonwealth's educational resurrection. Its main stress fell on the training of teachers, and to get this under way, it proposed the establishment of normal schools. The legislators gave Carter's recommendation their sober thought and then turned their backs on it by the hairsbreadth of a single vote. A year later Carter opened his own normal school at Lancaster, the first of its kind in Massachusetts. Meanwhile, Carter's failure to convince the lawmakers reaped a small but important concession when they created a town school board to exercise a general surveillance over the district school, then in a low state and hopelessly adrift. Bitterly opposed by the districts—it was, they growled, an intrusion into their constitutional rights—the measure marked the Bay State's first step toward asserting itself in the supervision of education. Years later came the final blow when Carter, himself now a maker of law, successfully piloted toward enactment a bill establishing a state board of education. The bill carried the signature of one of its most ardent partisans, the president of the Massachusetts senate, the Hon. Horace Mann.

When Mann betook himself, as he announced, from the bar "to the higher sphere of mind and morals," he was one year over forty. Born in 1796 in the village of Franklin, Massachusetts, he came from a home which, like so many others, was consumed with the relentless struggle to make a living. Mann's parents were of moderate means, but not as the national folklore would have it, poor. They were farming people, hard working, self-sufficient, with generations of Calvinism in their veins. The harsh mandates of Calvin, especially as expounded ex cathedra from the Franklin pulpit, proved a harrowing experience, and though the passing years weaned Mann into the gentler fold of the Unitarians, the dark shadow of Calvin haunted his inner spirit even in maturity. Life was not easy for young Mann; at the same time its burdens were certainly not unbearable. True, there was little time for books—a short sojourn in a district school under instruction as dingy as its setting. Even so, this is not saying there were no other chances.

His sister Lydia, for one, mixing housewifery with pedagogy, grounded him in spelling. Then there was the uncertain tutoring of Samuel Barrett, a touring schoolmaster and a tosspot, but helpful for all that. There is evidence too that Mann put in some years in the one-room academy of Parson William Williams at Wrentham, where besides rehearsing himself in Latin he made acquaintance with mathematics.

During these formative years Mann acquired a knowledge which, as Lydia took pains to remind him, laid the foundation of his later learning, even though by current standards it was spare and certainly hard-gained. From it, too, he derived a moral earnestness which, as he ripened in years, became an overpowering force and which walked beside him to the end. The intense disrelish that he acquired for the endless and onerous exactions of husbandry generated a zeal to rise to better things, which in time brought him to college. From the struggle of his youth he acquired a sense of reality, an appreciation of the practical which was to serve as a magnificent counterpoise to his unshakable romanticism. From his early acquaintance with hard work he obtained the habit of tremendous industry. This served him for better or worse. It made him a man of indefatigable action, but it exacted its pound of flesh in the ruination of his health.

Such was Horace Mann at twenty, when he was received in the halls of Brown. Here the humanitarianism which was to animate him through all his later years began to show itself with vigor, culminating in an address he offered to his graduating fellows at commencement. Its title was "The General Advancement of the Human Species in Dignity and Happiness"—a refrain which put its author in the company of Condorcet and other apostles of man's unlimited perfectability. It was a theme he was to sound to the last.

The next few years he served alma mater as librarian and tutor, specializing in the ancient classics, but making ready to become a lawyer. In 1823—he was now twenty-seven—he was able to hang out his shingle, and like many another aspiring jurist, he was presently sucked into politics. Four years following, he won his first office, a seat in the Massachusetts legislature, where he could still be found ten years later, when his appointment to the board of education dislodged him from his lawmaking career.

To his new post Mann brought a record which stamped him as a man who believed in human betterment with a fierce and romantic devotion. In the legislature he had campaigned for religious freedom, for the humane treatment of the insane, and for jails that reformed rather than merely penalized. He had fought for temperance (he never smoked and never drank), for the prevention of pauperism, and for the right of handicapped Negro children to attend special schools on equal terms with whites. And he flung himself wholeheartedly into the struggle for better schools.

Mann's task as secretary to the board was to study the wasting school system and, if possible, to prescribe a cure—a commission which was exactly to his taste. To rouse the citizenry from its sloth he stumped up and down the commonwealth, like a postman making his appointed rounds in weather fair or foul, organizing conventions and public meetings and disgorging philippics on his favorite subject. From his tireless pen streamed the whole ghastly story of shanty schools without the slightest sanitary facilities, windowless and full of stench, often enough without even the convenience of an outdoor privy—the "slave stowage of children," Mann called them. From primordial school buildings Mann proceeded to secularism, stupid and incompetent teachers, dilapidated equipment, supervision in full collapse, and so on, to standards so low they were out of sight. His criticism brought down upon him tornadoes of howls and catcalls and not a little personal abuse. Reactionary men of God tried to make him out an atheist; politicians hinted that he was a public enemy. Some limned him as a spinner of gossamer utopias; others saw him as a crass materialist. Even after all these years there are those who seek to denigrate him, not, it is true, for his educational reform, but for his willingness to advance it within the bounds of a conservative capitalistic order—a charge which holds water but which is also beside the point.

The battle was joined in full fury in 1843 with the publication of his Seventh Report. The Bostonian schoolmasters, Mann hinted therein, were mediocre, and their supervisors he labeled sleepy. The situation is not without humor. When the Boston birchmen retaliated by issuing their "Remarks on the Seventh Report to Mr. Mann," their burly antagonist retorted with a "Reply to the Remarks." When they essayed once and for all to hush him up with "A Rejoinder," Mann let them have a full broadside with an "Answer to the Rejoinder to the Reply to the Remarks on the Seventh Report," and this time the masters cried "Enough!" The Seventh Report stirred the wind not only on the home front, but even across the sea. Translated into French and German, it was enormously read and admired, especially in France, where in later years, after the collapse of the third Napoleon and his Second Empire, Mann's republicanism and anticlericalism struck a responsive chord. Even the English government, whose abstention from playing a strong and vigorous part in the education of its multitudes Mann had criticized, honored the Seventh Report with a generous reprinting. The years saw public opinion swing more and more to Mann. His renown winged its way westward and southward and, indeed, even beyond the Rio Grande into Latin America, where, as in Massachusetts, his name became the rallying cry for crusading school reformers.

The reforms brought forth during Mann's regime swept into every province of education. Appropriations, though won, as usual, only with a struggle, were almost doubled. Two million dollars, a breathtaking sum in those times, went toward the erection of new and better buildings—superior even to the fine edifices with which status-conscious New Englanders gratified their hogs. Bigger pay envelopes overran the teacher's cup of joy, but in return he was bidden to hustle up a better service. To give him a helping hand, the state founded three public normal schools, the first of their myriad flora to bloom in this republic. Supervision, inspirited with an infusion of professional merit, was made stronger and more effective. The number of high schools was augmented, though only slightly, for the revival's principal concern was concentrated on the common school. School libraries were increased, and their stock and service expanded and improved. Meanwhile, schoolbooks, purged of any lingering Calvinistic residuum, were brought into concord with the spirit of the new America. Shaken too was the old indifference to pedagogy. Once dismissed by teachers as a dubious light, it was now heightened by the incandescence of its leading experts then at work in Europe. In sum, during Mann's dozen years in office education in his state was transformed from a sad and lowly joke into a system of the highest worth and dignity.

In 1849, his health shattered by overwork and the ceaseless hammerings from his foes, Mann retired. For a time he deliberated in Congress, a successor in office to John Quincy Adams. Later, in 1852, reentering the pedagogic ring, Mann became president of Antioch College, in Ohio, today celebrated for its bold educational liberalism, but then— except for coeducation and nonsectarian instruction, and the inquisitive hogs which occasionally invaded its lecture halls—just another center of the liberal arts. But for Mann the new position was an anticlimax. His main work was already enshrined in history. He had, as he said, labored in the cause of public education, toiling unstintingly into the late watches of the night, without a single day for recreation, and for wages which at their very crest reached no higher than some 30 cents an hour. When death made an end of him in his early sixties, he had at least the contentment of knowing that he had not worked in vain. He had, as he once had slyly hoped, avenged himself on the commonwealth for the paltry wages it doled him by returning to it infinitely more than their worth in good.

Since then posterity has sought redemption. At Boston his statue stands sentinel before the State House. In New York he honors a niche in the Hall of Fame. Schools everywhere bear his name—in fact even the Post Office Department has paid tribute to his memory by printing his likeness on one of its stamps.

7 What Mann had wrought in Massachusetts Henry Barnard accomplished in neighboring Connecticut. There are striking likenesses in the work and thought of these two men. Both studied law, both attained political office, and both forsook statecraft to devote themselves to educational reform, in which both achieved a high success. But there were also some protruding differences. Where Mann's boyhood felt the constant touch of austerity, that of Barnard was caressed with ease and plenty. Where Mann's early schooling was hard-won, that of Barnard was the finest money could buy. Both men were religious, but where Mann, repelled by the dour doctrines of Calvinism, took to a liberal Unitarianism, Barnard adopted the conservative outlook of the Episcopalian. Finally, both men dedicated themselves to humanitarian causes and as lawmakers worked assiduously in their behalf, but of the two Barnard was far more reserved—one might even say hesitant—and in later years his zeal for reform burned out in all but education.

Barnard's interest in education was born in 1835, when he called on Europe. On returning to America some two years later, he was elected to the legislature, where, in 1838, he worked successfully to give Connecticut a state board similar to that of its neighbor across the border. Like Mann, Barnard, now twenty-seven, became the board's first secretary. Like Mann, again, Barnard turned with alacrity to the work of reform, traveling through the state, launching meetings, compiling reports, and composing instructive monographs for the *Connecticut Common School Journal,* which he founded and edited. Unluckily for educational progress, a strong antagonism still worked powerfully against it, and in 1842, Connecticut's givers of law, bending before second thoughts—and an anti-free-school governor— abolished the board.

Barnard was not long finding another job. Pretty soon his services were besought by Rhode Island, which summoned him to make a study and appraisal of its schools. From his accounting there emerged a measure similar to the one assassinated in Connecticut, and in 1845 Barnard found himself installed as Rhode Island's first commissioner of education. Taken all around, his accomplishment falls into the same general categories as that of Mann, and there is thus no need to embroider its several details. Let it suffice to observe that when his labors reached their end, Barnard had succeeded in giving the Rhode Islanders a school system which was on a par with the best in the land.

Meanwhile, the tidings of Barnard's sterling virtues did not pass Connecticut by, and in 1851, after the usual posturing and speechifying, the legislature persuaded the commissioner to return to head a new normal school and to resume his duties as secretary of the board, now gloriously resurrected. The reforms Barnard had fathered in Rhode Island he now summoned forth in Connecticut. He worked, as usual, without stint or limit, driving himself unsparingly until, in 1855, almost dead from exhaustion, he was obliged to quit.

The same year Barnard walked out of his office saw him help found the American Association for the Advancement of Education. He served as its first president and, more important in the long run, tended its *American Journal of Education.* It is when we take a backward look and review his labor as the *Journal's* editor and publisher that we catch a glimpse of the man's towering stature. In its thirty spacious volumes is planted the account of every educational thought and practice to come out of the nineteenth century. Through its several thousand pages run its editor's doctrine and criticism, which, taking one thing with another, even now come close to sense and which, for diggers in the historical past, constitute a veritable gold mine. To the *Journal's* editor, finally, must be credited the adroit and tireless support of virtually every educational reform of consequence undertaken in the United States before the eighties. Into his beloved *Journal* Barnard poured not only the full measure of his learning and devotion but also the greater portion of his personal fortune.

Barnard's boundless appetite for work presently returned him to the academic community. For a time he presided over the University of Wisconsin. Thereupon he betook himself to Maryland to take charge of St. John's, which currently enjoys celebrity for its dedication to the so-called "Great Books," but which in Barnard's time was a conventional dispenser of the liberal arts. Though the new president bowed to no one in his esteem of the ancient disciplines, the cockiness and self-infatuation of their upholders ran against his progressive grain. In the college, in consequence, he embarked upon a campaign to bring them back to earth—an undertaking in which, before he was done, he was successful. In 1867—he was then approaching the frontier of sixty—Barnard left the grove of higher thinking to serve as the first United States Commissioner of Education. When he died in 1900, an advanced and luxuriantly bewhiskered octogenarian, he stood at the edge of poverty. Most of his fortune, which once had been considerable, had, like his energy and health, been lavished on the cause of American public education. "I am ambitious," he once confided to Mann, "of being remembered . . . because of some service, however small, done in the cause of humanity in my day and generation." No one could have written a truer, more fitting epitaph to the lifework of Henry Barnard.

8   Although New Englanders took the lead in making education a dominant state concern, it must be said in equity that efforts at reform presently displayed themselves in the rest of the nation. Their design was similar, though in harmony with their cultural setting they varied in detail and in the tempo of their unfoldment. In Pennsylvania, for example, the heavy skirmishing was over the pauper school, while in New York for a time the contest raged over the elimination of sectarianism. This is, of course, not saying that there were no other contentious bones to pick. The same issues and the same contestants sprang up everywhere. Now the controversy ignited over the educational powers of the state authority; now over the government's right to lay school taxes; now over its right to conscript children to learn their ABCs. Some apostles cried out for better teachers, better methods, and better books; others bawled for more and better buildings. But whatever the special stress, the ultimate end was the same. Was the general pattern similar in its essence? Then so was the labor which brought it forth, the social feeling which was its seed, the national soil wherein it sprouted, the publicity and propaganda which gave it notice, the pressure on the lawmaker, and, of course, the industry of its visionaries, so vast in scope and so tremendous in effect. The Awakening glistens with famous names. There is New England, of course, with Carter, Mann, and Barnard. But there is also Kentucky, with Robert J. Breckenridge; North Carolina, with Joseph Caldwell, Calvin Wiley, and Archibald D. Murphey; Ohio, with Calvin Stowe, Samuel Lewis, and Samuel Galloway; Michigan, with Isaac E. Crary and John D. Pierce; Indiana, with Caleb Mills; Illinois, with Ninian Wirt Edwards and Jonathan Baldwin Turner; Louisiana, with Alexander Dimitri; and California, with Jonathan Swett. And so the train passes, here soon, there late, through one state after another, from Sandy Hook to the Golden Gate. But wherever and whenever it showed itself, always leaders emerged ready and willing to direct it to its goal.

10
THE STATE SYSTEM
COMES OF AGE

When education was the possession of a favored few, the burden of maintaining it was obviously no great public problem. However, as the common school began to operate and more and more children headed toward their ABCs, financing the scholastic enterprise became ominously complex. Even the early fathers, as has already been related, had not been immune from the troubles of school support and had found it necessary on occasion to supplement their usual sources of tuition and philanthropy. The notion of laying a school tax on the general populace or, at all events, on its propertied members was not, however, acceptable to them. And so, as we have seen, they resorted to a number of special sources, from lotteries and permits to enter matrimony, to levies on bankers, slave traders, and similar men of more or less glitter. For a time, moreover, additional funds were pumped from rate-bill assessments and from the sale of public land.

In 1795 Connecticut, seeking a way to stabilize the uncertain flux and flow of its revenue, invested the money it was amassing from its land sales into a permanent school fund. The advantage to be had from such an arrangement was not long lost on the sister states. Not only did some of them follow Connecticut's example, but by the nineteenth century they had done it in such a manner that the spectacle of the permanent school fund had ceased to be a novelty. Whatever lingering doubts it may still have raised here and there were stilled, if not blown up, when in 1837, the Federal government opened its vaults and disbursed a surplus of $28 million among the twenty-six states—a feat of statecraft which so far history has not repeated. Of this vast bounty nine states put their entire proceeds into a school fund, while eight others ventured to deposit at least a portion of it.

Unhappily, the high hopes in which the funds had been conceived never came quite to their fulfillment; instead of providing what they were supposed to provide, fund after fund rotted in waste and corruption. Even in Connecticut, where the money was tended in competence and honesty, there was trouble. For as the fund took on more and more heft, the very fact of its existence was used to beguile and disarm the school tax advocates, and in 1821 such little taxation as was still in vogue was ended. This action presently strained Connecticut's fund so badly that the schools, suffering more and more from financial anemia, sank into feebleness.

2   In 1825 it was fairly plain that the time-honored kinds of school support were no longer sufficient to their task and that the sources of school revenue needed to be put on a firmer and surer footing. Once again it was the cities which brought the need into the open and gave the direct school tax its cautious start. In the beginning, however, the levy was not mandatory, but merely permissive. Adopted in a number of states, the permissive laws provided for a degree of local option whereby certain cities were enabled to organize school districts with the right to levy taxes if their voters so willed. Mild though such concessions were, on every side they were lambasted bitterly. There were the usual rages of the abhorrers of taxes of any sort, and especially new ones. Others, more plaintive in their wail, sought to cry down the tax as unethical since it put its chief burden on able and thrifty people—presumably like themselves. Finally, there were those more or less sharp-eyed folk who, not taken in by sentiment, saw in the whole business the foreshadowing of general and mandatory school taxation. Once the school tax stuck its foot in the door, then presto, they warned, it would be in the room.

Nor were the lawmakers themselves all aglow over the new device. Often, indeed, they only half countenanced it, and their support was obtained only after long and persistent pressure. Even then, the laws they made were frequently watered and ineffective. In Missouri, for instance, it was possible for a spell for districts to lay their levies, but only with the consent of two of every three voters—a likelihood against which the odds were stupendous. In Illinois one did not have to pay a school tax unless one had agreed to do so in writing beforehand. Even where school taxes were suffered as a necessary evil, all too often there were loopholes in them. The most prevalent was the belief that only the teacher's wages fell within the province of public expenditure—not the schoolhouses or the desks, benches, books, paper, ink, rattans, firewood, stove, spitoon, and other more or less familiar accessories of learning. In 1825 Ohio allowed its communities to erect their schoolhouses with the help of a public subsidy, but before they could profit from such largess, they had to give proof that the sites for the buildings had already been donated. As late as 1870 North Carolina's highest tribunal held that funds for the public schools, unlike those for its jails, were not necessary public expenses. The judicial sapience was still honored as late as 1903.

For all its bruises, the permissive system continued to hang on; indeed, as the years moved forward, it enjoyed a steady prospering, and in some quarters it even obtained a high civic acclaim. It became, in this respect, what a few soothsayers had once so direfully foretold, namely the veiled beginning of general, compulsory, and inescapable taxation. But the middle of the century had come and gone before the idea had gained anything like a general foothold—in the Free States, at any rate, if not in the slave ones. And before this came to pass, it was necessary to drum up votes not only for the principle of free, tax-supported schooling but also to dispose of such dubious educational practices as educational charity, state handouts to private schools, the rate bill, and free schools for paupers only.

3   It was in Pennsylvania that the drive against the pauper school took on its sharpest edge. There the free schooling of the poor had been asserted in principle as far back as 1790, when the state's constitution declared for the establishment of "schools in such number that the poor may be taught gratis." But almost twenty years separated the utterance of these facile words and their realization in everyday practice. When the constitutional hopes fructified at last in a law of 1809, the enactment won few friends. Men of property harbored an aversion toward it, since by it their taxes unfailingly went up, and the poor shied away because once they stepped up to accept its benefits, they found themselves advertised as lowly paupers. For, as the law exacted, a poor child could have his schooling with the compliments of the state only if his parent publicly confessed his poverty. Rather than thus affront their self-respect, the poor preferred to raise their children in the privacy of ignorance. As a result, the act of 1809 failed dismally. In fact, by the end of the twenties such schools as it had actually brought into being could assemble fewer than five thousand pupils, and through the commonwealth's entire length and breadth only half of its 400,000 children between five and fifteen were reported bending over their books.

Despite the hostility it incited, the statute was kept on the books till 1834, when the Free School Act made an end of it. Under the new deal the state was divided into not quite a thousand districts, each to be sustained out of local levies, but with additional help from the state treasury. As it turned out, the new arrangement proved no more satisfactory than its predecessor, and when the lawmakers returned to their deliberations in 1835, they were put upon at once with demands for repeal. The Senate gave its prompt assent, but in the nether house the going was much rougher. There, egged on by the powerful rhetoric of Thaddeus Stevens, a defiant minority not only managed to hold the fort but in the end even succeeded in gaining reinforcements to push through a measure which actually was more exacting than the one under attack. The new legislation put the ax on the odious pauper-school law, and at the same time it made provision for local and county taxes with supplemental aid from the state, but also also with state control and supervision. Thus Pennsylvania laid down the design for free and universal schooling. Bitter-enders could spurn the whole business—and for a time a number of them actually did. But, as usual, the sweet balm of state aid was hard to resist, and so within four short years nearly all the districts—more, indeed, than four out of five—were lined up, palms itching and outstretched, in favor of the new order.

As in Pennsylvania, so it was almost everywhere else—less dramatically perhaps, but with the same result. Throughout the republic, wherever the pauper school was rooted, the battle against it was joined. In the East it was gradually routed; in the South it held out for a time, but there too it came to grief; and in the West it had never existed.

4   The world which saw the passing of the pauper school also watched the rate bill gather up its wraps. An English heirloom, the rate bill was bottomed on the premise that none but the poor should receive their learning free. By it a parent was assessed in proportion to the number of children he kept in school. First put to use in New England, the rate bill was not long in spreading its charm to other parts, and after Yorktown its use was no longer an exception. Usually its levies were moderate, but moderate or not, they were sufficient to put a brake on learning. Where the family flock was copious or when poverty bore upon it, the rate bill was sure to cause some earnest figuring. To relax the strain on his budget, a father might send only some of his progeny to school. Or, since the rate bill's charges were calculated on a day-by-day basis, he might seek to ease his financial burden by sending them to their sessions for only part of the time, instead of every day, throughout the entire school year; or he might grant an education only to his sons, and not to their sisters. Because the rate bill was really no more than a false-face tuition bill, where parents could afford it, they could—and did—avoid its exactions and stigmata altogether by committing their children to the care and counsel of a private establishment which was hence more beneficial to their social standing.

In the absence of a general school tax, and the howls the mere idea of such a horror would set off, the rate bill, though also suspect and disdained, was accepted as a somewhat lesser evil. Still, its strength began to ebb when states started to adopt the permissive laws. Since these were enacted to impose a tax on all who qualified for such an honor, whether they were blessed with offspring or not, cities found it possible to maintain what at bottom amounted to a free school. But long years dragged by before this came to be, and when it did, its first appearance, as has been said, was in the cities. Beyond the urban borderline in the far-flung rustic pampas, where the antagonism to the tax-supported school, fortified by the prejudices of long-standing tradition, was much tougher, the rate bill continued to command a following. This was the support which conserved it in state after state, long after cities had done execution on it. New York City repudiated the rate bill in 1832, Buffalo in 1838, Brooklyn five years later, and Syracuse five years after that, but the Civil War was already history before the state as a whole was able to pronounce the rate bill formally and legally dead.

5   From its colonial inception the American school had taken its tone from the immediate environs. Sometimes it was the child of the town, and sometimes of the district. Sometimes it issued from philanthropy, and sometimes from the strivings of the sacred ministry. Whatever its origin and whatever its reason for being, in all its operations, from the subjects it tried to reveal and teach, to the masters it hired and sometimes fired, the school was a reflection of its setting. With the coming of nationhood the idea of a national school system flickered for awhile, but it was little more than a false dawn, the dream of a handful of thinking men, and it never came into actual being. Representing the general American sentiment, the Constitution, as has already been stated, said not one jot or tittle about the nation's learning and has remained mute on the subject unto this day.

When schooling was not a public requisite, the states naturally had little reason to give it concern. Some of them, it is true, framed constitutional declarations on the subject, but, taking one with another, such pronouncements were nearly always swathed in vagueness, and they carried little weight. As long as communities gave their tacit approval to the state's obscure and dexterous utterance, education was approached, like the village toper, as a problem of purely local concern.

In a rustic world, with travel and intercommunication still in puberty, educational localism possessed some indubitable merits. It was, at base, a response to local needs and urges, and thus it afforded a community the kind of education the majority of its voters wanted. In this sense it may have been, as some have maintained, of a democratic essence. But if so it was, then the blessing was not unmixed. For if public opinion was on the fence—as it often was—or if it was at the mercy of myopic backyard politicking, the progress of education obviously was severely hobbled.

Nevertheless, when the drive for the tax-supported school began, it was localism which brought its first succcesses—for what, after all, was a permissive law but a right yielded locally? It was localism, again, which enabled the more enlightened communes, especially in the cities, to erect the first tax-maintained common schools. And again, behind the principle of state aid lurked that of localism, furtive, perhaps, but real nevertheless —for what the state chose to offer, a locality might reject or accept as it pleased. No community, sober and sane, was ready, of course, to show a bearer of gifts the door, even though in the end his bounty had strings attached which might be unpleasant. In fact, looked at sharply, state aid disclosed prerequisites which, though neither harsh nor menacing, actually obliged localities to measure up to standards which, left to their own devices, they would have inclined to spurn.

As the state became financially enmeshed in the educational enterprise, the problem of regulating and safeguarding the spending of its money became more and more acute. It was all very well for the local citizenry to drop curtsies at the feet of the state, acquiescing in its demands and stipulations in order to fetch a financial grant. But after they had carted away the money, what was there to ensure the complete and unadulterated fulfillment of their promise? Had communities been less human, such misgivings might have been no more than a sophomore's exercise in ethical science. As it was, the skepticism was warranted. Some communities, though eager enough to extract the last penny of state largess, were far less anxious to submit to the state's authority. With one hand, so to say, they saluted the state's benevolence, while the other they raised in defense of their vaunted local rights. So firmly were these entrenched and so stubborn the intention not to yield them, that the century was well along its way before the state was able to exert full control over its schools.

6   The first steps in this direction were taken as long ago as 1784, when New York founded the Board of Regents of the State of New York to keep an eye on the secondary and higher learning. Eleven years following, a system of financial assistance was decreed, but in 1800 it was allowed to lapse, only to be revived some twelve years later, refurbished and ornamented by a state superintendent of common schools.

The first to honor the new office with his presence was Gideon Hawley. He came to his post in 1813—he was then twenty-seven—and he left it some eight years later. Less evangelistic than Mann and less learned than Barnard, he was nonetheless a man of fine capacity who performed the labors of his office with all the diligence of an ant. He harvested data and translated them into tables; he administered the school fund with a rare care and caution; and he directed his authority to enforce the school law into the state's remotest Main Streets. When he yielded the burdens of his office in 1821, he could afford the pleasure of a smile. Not only had the number of schools doubled during his regime, but attendance had also increased. In fact, in 1821, in all New York only one-half child in every ten failed to appear at the schoolroom for at least a part of the year—a record which in those days bordered on the miraculous. For all his good qualities, fortune played Hawley false. A Whig politically, he became the target of the Van Buren Jacksonians, and when they came to power they marked his office in their bag of spoils—but not without a fight. The act roused the legislators' ire—"a gross outrage" some said it was—and to give the spoilers their tit for tat, they proceeded to entrust the supervisory duties to the secretary of state, where they stayed more or less unaltered until 1854, when a superintendent of public instruction took over. Meanwhile, in one way or another Hawley continued to serve in the educational arena until he was eighty-four, when death made an end of him. In American educational annals, Hawley enjoys the singular distinction of having been not only the first school superintendent to grace the land but also the first of a long line to be separated from his office because of the vagaries of political fortune.

The move toward stiffer state control presently manifested itself in other states. In 1826 Maryland Free State created the office of superintendent of public instruction, but two years later it was disestablished. Meanwhile, in one manner or another, various states declared for some form of educational surveillance. Such was the case, for one, in Illinois, which in 1845, like New York, cast its secretary of state in the part of supervisor.

The same holds for Vermont and Louisiana and for Pennsylvania and Tennessee. The first state to maintain the school superintendency continuously from the very beginning to the present day was Michigan, which in 1829, while still in territorial status, presented its citizens with a superintendent of common schools. By the middle years of the century, sixteen of the thirty-one states had made provision, directly or otherwise, for such a public functionary.

Though the contemporary state superintendent is as different from his antecedent as the rocket ship is from the oxcart, he bears a historical kinship. Now, as in the beginning, his title is of an amazing and unruly diversity. In truth, the state superintendency has entertained a host of designations, which, all things considered, are not only more varied but also more elegant than most others in the public service, in illustration, commissioner of education, director of education, superintendent of public instruction, superintendent of public schools, and superintendent of public instruction and director of education. When Virginians are not in haste, they address their watchdog of the schools as superintendent of public instruction and secretary of the state board of education; West Virginians have contented themselves with superintendent of free schools; and Utahans have settled for superintendent of public instruction and director of vocational education. Again, today as yesterday, the state superintendent ascends to office sometimes through appointment, but more commonly through election. In most states he must be a man of rectitude, professional experience, and competence—and, in these days of sinister subversion, of sworn and undefiled patriotism. The superintendent still is, as he was at the start, the state's highest school official. Among his duties are some for which the office was first created, for example, the gathering and disseminating of educational information, the compiling of statistics, the granting of subsidies, and the general encouragement of education. But these historic functions have been dwarfed by a herd of newer ones. In one way or another, the superintendent puts his mark on every aspect of the educational program, its molehills and its Alps, from texts to teachers, from school finance to jurisprudence. For weal or woe, he is administrator, adviser, policy maker, and overseer—and sometimes, in times of scandal and dispute, he even dons juridic robes. In the steady proliferation of its functions and responsibilities, and in the immense multiplication of its power, the office reveals more vividly than all the miles of print on the subject how the American public learning has proceeded from primitive localism to state centralization.

7   While the state was assuring itself of a stronger and more effective role as guardian of its schools, the battle against unlimited localism was being pursued on other fronts. Specifically, the assault was aimed at the shortcomings of the district system. Born, as has been pointed out, in a rudimentary and rustic age, the district school was the natural offspring of its cow-and-chicken setting, and in the early nineteenth century it could be sighted in most parts of the land. Not only had the system attained a considerable following, but it also enjoyed the special blessing of the state itself. Never seriously challenged from on high, the power it exercised in the operation of its schools had taken on a staggering proportion.

In a simpler period all this had been very convenient, and maybe even meet and fitting. But with the rise of the city and its teeming collective requirements, the district system was plainly behind the times, and a drag besides on municipal aspiration. In its own sphere the district board was absolute, a taxing body in its own right, maintaining its own school, engaging its own birchmen—and fixing their duties, their wages, and other usufructs—and setting its own standards. Thus, in all legality, it could—and did—snicker at the city's first efforts toward a citywide coherence. Frustrated time and again by its district princelings, the city, like the state, called the obstreperous parts to order by placing all its schools under a city board and supervisor.

As early as the twenties, New Orleans had placed its primary schools under a board of regents and a director. But it remained for Buffalo, in 1837, to conceive the office of city school superintendent. And it was the city of Providence, a year later, which made the office professional as well as merely administrative. In the same year Louisville and Maysville, Kentucky, armed themselves with superintendents. In 1839 St. Louis followed their lead, with Springfield, Massachusetts, close on its heels. But getting the superintendency solidly on its feet was arduous work, and long after the fifties were in the shadows, the old-style district school was still to be reckoned with. Indeed, even the seventies had departed before the movement toward city centralization had gained sufficient juice and power to make the city superintendency a national commonplace, as familiar today in the American scheme of things as Cokes and freeways.

An extension of the state's drive may be found in its counties. Although the duties of the first state superintendents were in themselves not onerous, the geographic stretches over which they ranged were often colossal. In time, as free public schooling steadily took on heft, it became plainer and plainer that not even a draft horse like Horace Mann could singlehandedly come to effective grips with the ever-multiplying functions of the state's supreme educational seat. From this realization there slowly evolved what is now the county superintendency. Rising in a number of ways—here, say, from the office of town superintendent, and there from the county board's special function of administering land grants—the county superintendency became in the end the coordinating link between the central and local authority. In his beat the county superintendent is second in command to the state superintendent. His duties, like those of his chief, were at first principally clerical and fiscal. Sometimes he was empowered to inspect schools and occasionally to keep a watchful eye upon the goings-on of the classroom and the merits of its masters. In an age when Americans set their hearts on electing all their public jobholders, high and low—unless specifically prevented from doing so by the Constitution—the superintendent's office was usually elective. Consequently, its professional nature, such as it was, was often overladen by the self-evident truths of practical politics. First appearing in the thirties, the county superintendency made slow advance—in fact, by the middle years of the century it had settled in fewer than a dozen states. But after Appomattox its pace picked up, and by 1870 it had invaded all the senior states, while today, of course, it prevails on every side.

8   As localism stultified the progress of the tax-supported common school, so did sectarianism. Sanctioned across the centuries as education's arch-custodian, the church had invested herself with high powers and prerogatives in this particular sphere. Though the years had seen these powers whittled down, even following the Revolution, it was not unusual for church schools to receive financial succor from the state. But under a growing and assertive worldliness, the practice evaporated more and more, until, in 1833, when Massachusetts put an end to what remained of state support for its churches, it blew away completely.

In the public schools, signs of secularism had been visible even earlier. Thus, while in the colonial past it had been the minister's common responsibility to decide upon the fitness of the schoolmaster and even, as in Dutch America, to muster him into minor sacerdotal service, as the years dallied past, the power of the sacred office diminished, becoming mainly subtle and indirect. Nevertheless, the ecclesiastic dominion was still a power, and when it chose to act, as it sometimes did, it could be very effective.

For the youngsters the receding clerical sway revealed itself in a number of pleasant ways. True, the infant damners and child floggers had not died out, and their doctrines still haunted the chambers of knowledge. Even so, a new spirit was on the wing, and here and there one caught a few faint glimmerings in support of a mellower treatment of the young. However, before the sentiment of humanity illuminated the common schoolroom, whole forests of rattans were to be put to their dreaded use. Meanwhile, there could be thanks for other boons. No longer, for example, was Cotton Mather's hair-raising *Spiritual Milk for Babes* in use. Even the *New England Primer*, once as omnipresent as the Old Deluder himself, was giving ground, and in 1823, when it appeared in the Woodstock edition, though it still scared the young with Adam's fall in which "we sinned all," it also entertained them with the bear "who the forest prowls making surly sounds."

These and other wonders, however, came wearily and at long intervals. Following the familiar process by which the school adjusts itself to the shifting fashion of public taste, they stole into being almost imperceptibly, and to the general public they were often scarcely noticeable. Indeed, in 1827, when Massachusetts put an end to the practice of buying sectarian texts with the taxpayers' money, the commonwealth was merely bestowing legal recognition upon a situation which was already in actual existence.

As the state's intention in the matter of school control became clearer, the churches, alarmed by the state's steady and relentless penetration into a dominion once exclusively their own, marshaled their forces to resist. The combat, as might be expected, was fiercest where parochialism was in its fullest force. In Pennsylvania, with its horde of parish schools and its subsidized denominational schools for the poor, often cradles not only of faith and virtue but of alien tongues and cultures as well, the fight concentrated against the remodeled Free School Law of 1834. In Massachusetts the churches took the field against the establishment of the state board of education, and when for all their hopes and prayers, it came to being nonetheless, they joined forces to unhorse it. They resisted Horace Mann at every turn, denouncing him as Antichrist, and when it was ordained that in the public school the Bible was to be read without comment, they protested that such "public schools are Godless schools." That note, of course, still echoes—indeed, of recent years it has even increased in stridency. In his own day, however, Mann was more than a match for such obscurantists. Consequently, when he walked out of office for the last time, the nonsectarian pattern of Massachusetts public schooling appeared to be fixed. But Mann made his farewell just on the eve of the great surge of Catholic immigration. Subsequently, as Holy Church grew in number and influence, the nonsectarian nature of public education, which naturally caused her anguish and distress, was challenged anew. Not only did the church cry down the public school, but it also demanded state assistance to run schools of its own. The century was already half gone when the uproar came to its end at last with the adoption, in 1853, of a constitutional amendment prohibiting any religious sect from sharing the funds appropriated for education.

In New York City, where most things are likely to be on the grand scale, the battle between the legions of God and those of Caesar was fought with a becoming ferocity. It was provoked, innocently enough, in 1820, when the Bethel Baptist Church, which had opened a small nonsectarian school for the poor, was allowed by special act to share in the state's school fund. Almost at once other religious clans made a stir for similar help—a state of affairs which, understandably, brought gray hairs to the Public School Society, the city's favorite purveyor of free education. To allay the society's misgivings, the legislature introduced the practice of handing the city's share of the state's school appropriation to the city council, letting that body fret over the problem of apportioning and distributing.

For the next few years peace descended on Manhattan. But in 1831, when the council granted funds to the Roman Catholic Benevolent Society to conduct a school for orphans, and turned down a Methodist request for similar aid, the old wounds bled again, and for the few years following they festered with no cure in sight. In 1840, when the council rejected a Catholic plea for a division of the city's school fund, the rebuffed Romans repaired for Albany to seek redress from the legislature. They were given reinforcement by a Scotch Presbyterian and a Hebrew church, an ominous alliance, indeed, and one cemented in this case by a common and over-whelming itch for school money. But the lawgivers, sniffing hidden political booby traps, preferred to move gingerly, if at all. Finally, after two years of wary temporizing, they took action. For New York City they established a board of education and charged it with running the public schools. At the same time—more enduringly, doubtless, than they ever dreamed—they laid down the principle that no public funds might be employed for the furtherance of sectarian ends. Upon this laic foundation the present public school system still stands.

In other states the sectarian issue fanned similar bonfires. Everywhere there were demands and counterdemands, even libels, assaults, and street fights. Needless to say, the problem was not simply one of religion and the public purse; as it natural and inevitable in our fair democracy, it presently took on a political tone. Thus, in 1841, the Whigs of New York declared against sectarian schools. A decade later, or thereabouts, the Know-Nothing party, though applauding the use of the Good Book in the public school, frowned upon the sectarian school. Everywhere, more or less the same solution was finally arrived at. State upon state adopted constitutional measures tabooing the use of public money for sectarian purposes. Sometimes, of course, doubts have arisen to plague and baffle us as to what is sectarian and what is not. Is it sectarian or not, for example, for teachers in the public school to array themselves in religious robes, to wear the sacred collar and the cassock? Is it sectarian or not to chant the Lord's Prayer in the public house of learning? And, finally, is it sectarian or not to warble Christmas carols or to present the Christ child's story in children's playlets? All these problems, and others even knottier, have tortured the public mind. Nor have the efforts of lawmaking served to arrest them. As befits the national and inherent diversity, the answers and solutions which have been essayed vary from ocean to ocean. Thus, where one state says "yes," another says "no." Sometimes, when doubts have become disputes and disputes have raged unresolved, the help of the courts has been enlisted to bring them to an end. But, for all such disturbance of the public peace, the nonsectarian nature of American public education, though still under assault—and it seems, with a mounting firepower—has so far succeeded in holding its ground.

11
BOOKS, SUBJECTS, AND
SCHOOLS: THE NEW LOOK

The cultural upheavals which fashioned the common schools and elicited the capital and authority to make them going concerns were at the bottom of several other new developments. Once again these had their origin in the cities, and it was there that they got their first foothold. There the three Rs were overhauled and replenished with other subjects; there the hoary combination of primer and prayer book was abandoned; and there the moldering operations of schoolmastering began to be sharply and critically examined. It was in the city where group instruction was introduced and where primary and intermediate schools first showed themselves, where they fused into the full-grown elementary school, and where, in the end, they were capped and consummated by the public high school.

Bred from the Reformation, the first American schools, as we have seen, were scarcely more than nurseries for the faith. Preparing their novices for the inescapable Judgment Day, they put their main store in reading and particularly in piety and goodness, with never-ceasing threats of brimstone just around the corner. Writing was of little consequence, and arithmetic counted for even less. Usually, in fact, when the mystery of numbers was broached, it was done for a special cause and under private hands. Nevertheless, in the course of the seventeenth century, the three Rs gradually assumed the respectability of a regular offering, and for a school to be without them would have set it down as somewhat inferior.

A few generations more, however, and the schoolboy's life began to be much more harried. The menace to his peace and comfort was begun with the publication of Noah Webster's famous speller in 1783 and was reinforced a year later with his grammar, and then with his reader in 1790. Taken together, this triple threat to ignorance flaunted itself as *A Grammatical Institute to the English Language, Comprising an Easy, Concise, and Systematizing Method of Education, Designed for the Use of English Schools in America,* a literary thousand-legger which daily parlance soon reduced to Webster's *Elementarie.* On its heels appeared the geographies of Jedidiah Morse and Nathaniel Dwight, both of which came out in 1795. The subject of arithmetic, as has been observed, lagged behind. But in 1821, when Warren Colburn burst upon the world with his *First Lessons in Arithmetic on the Plan of Pestalozzi,* its lean days were done, and having been made sufferable at last to novices, the subject gained rapidly in popularity. In the same year Davenport's *History of the United States* arrived upon the scene, and so did Goodrich's work of the same title. The former, which need not long detain us, was no more than a historical question-and-answer box. A compendium of names and dates, the Declaration of Independence, and the Federal Constitution, it became the archetype of cram books, which today rise ceiling-high in student bookstores the land around.

The work of Goodrich, who in his gayer moments as Peter Parley composed tales for kiddies, was, for all its limitations, a coherent exposition. It enjoyed a fine popularity, and there was soon a brisk trade in it. In fact, in scarcely more than a decade, its first edition ran triumphantly through forty printings. The first history book to include a study of the Constitution, it has been commonly credited by *prominenti* of this specialty with having launched the study of government and public affairs in the American schoolroom.

Laic in tone, and written with an eye to the simple pedagogic niceties, the majority of these books were granted a hearty welcome. Schoolmasters generally commended them, and doubtless deservedly so. For not only did they render valuable service to teachers by unsnarling and clarifying their subjects for them, but they also simplified the business of imparting it to the learner. Their extraordinary success brought them, as usual, the flattery of flocks of imitators, Webster's book alone being but the first of dozens more or less like it, though not always with the luster of the original.

Several notches lower in renown than Webster's masterpiece, yet high in the esteem in which they were generally held, were Caleb Bingham's *American Preceptor* (1794) and *Columbia Orator* (1797) and Lindley Murray's *English Reader* (1800). All these books sold handsomely, and were their authors currently in practice, they would no doubt be riding to their studios in Cadillacs. The first of these, the *American Preceptor*, was composed on a system of gradation, which is to say its substance proceeded from the easy to the difficult. It was a system which had been urged upon schoolmen as far back as the first century by the Roman Quintilian, but which for some reason was still so rare in actual practice as to be almost unique. Like most of its competitors, the *Orator* fragranted its pages with selected prose and poesy and with nosegays gathered from the speeches of the patriots. In a day when memorizing was still the indispensable calisthenic for the growing mind, the passages were expected not only to trip freely from the lips but also to be known by heart—an affront, of course, to a schoolboy of any self-respect, but a custom which continues to commend itself to proud parenthood everywhere.

With the issuance in 1836 of the Rev. Dr. William Holmes McGuffey's *First* and *Second Readers,* juvenile reading entered a new era. If signs count for anything, their author was destined for great things in life. Born in poverty, he walked many weary miles to borrow books and read them at night by the fire's flame. Later he flung himself into schoolmastering, swinging his battle-ax betweentimes for the advancement of Ohio's common school. Time saw him mount the academic podium, first at Oxford, Ohio, where he professed the classics, and then at Cincinnati College and Ohio University, where he presided as executive-in-chief. His career came to its appointed end in a blaze of glory, when he became professor of moral philosophy at the University of Virginia.

The *First* and *Second Readers* were soon joined by others, to become a series of six—*The McGuffey Eclectic Readers*. Graded from cover to cover, they were also illustrated. The palled solemnity of so many of their forerunners McGuffey sought to lighten in his *Readers*—but not altogether, as witness the sudden death of a fractious lassie and the heart-to-heart colloquy between mother and daughter on "What Is Death?" But for such necrotic dialogue the *Readers* offered many happy chasers with gay glimpses of kiting, skating, ball playing, and hoop rolling; with likenesses of the peers and commoners of the world of birds and beasts, friendly and otherwise; and with felicitous views of papa and the family flock of an evening at the fireside. For three generations and probably even more, McGuffey dazzled young America with "George Washington and His Little Hatchet," "Woodman Spare That Tree," and such immortal lyrics as "The Old Oaken Bucket," "The One Horse Shay," and "The Boy Stood on the Burning Deck." To these time brought the enrichment of numerous others, including some of Longfellow, Whittier, Dryden, Milton, Wordsworth, Shakespeare, and similar literati of quality.

The *Readers* rocketed into an almost instantaneous fame, and soon they were finding employment in the hives of learning all over the republic —except in New England, which crooked its knee at other altars. For half a century they and the Bible, and possibly, the rags-to-riches rondos of Horatio Alger, Jr., constituted rural America's principal reading matter —not counting, of course, its library of almanacs and patent-medicine solicitations. Needless to say, rivals soon confronted the *Readers* on every side. But "Old Guff" was ready, and by and by their threats were laid. Like most high-class wars, whether gory or not, the combat was borne upon in a measure by the lure of the golden calf. In the long run, however, the *Readers* not only cleared the field but also attained the almost unbelievable sale of 125 million copies.

From all this, rather sadly, McGuffey plucked not a penny more than $1,000—somehow his Scottish canniness had failed him, and he had sold his entire rights for quick cash on the barrelhead. Perhaps his eternal shadow, flitting over Oxford, Ohio, has since seen fit to forgive this transient aberration in the knowledge that Miami University, where once he taught, has celebrated his memory with a McGuffey Museum, which accommodates not only hundreds of his famous *Readers* but also the octagonal revolving desk which served him during his earthly prime, besides many other relics. Nor is such testimony confined to the academic grove. It was Henry Ford I, the author of the apothegm that "history is the bunk," who confessed that in his secret heart Lincoln, Edison, and McGuffey reigned as honorable exceptions. It was Ford who, in 1925, commissioned the reprinting of the *Readers,* thereby causing such a demand for the originals that their price soared into outer space. And it was Ford who translated McGuffey's natal log cabin from its resting place in Pennsylvania to its present repository at Ford's museum at Greenfield, Michigan. Nor does silence sit on lesser folk, as witness the Federated McGuffey Societies of America. With chapters all over the land, the federation, like the Daughters of the American Revolution and similar sodalities of organized devotion to past American grandeur, is dedicated to keeping hallow the memory of its special hero, the—up to now—immortal William Holmes McGuffey.

During colonial days the formal study of grammar had been reserved for the pupil of alert and robust mind, and for several generations, as has already been mentioned, he relied for his grammatical exercise almost wholly on Dilworth's *New Guide to the Mother Tongue*. First printed in 1740 in London, the book made its way into New England, where soon it was reprinted. The Revolution presently dimmed its popularity, and with the appearance of Noah Webster's grammar, its light went out. But even the momentous Noah soon had rivals, notably Lindley Murray's *English Grammar* (1795) and Caleb Bingham's *Young Lady's Accidence* (1799). Of the two, Murray's volume was clearly the more impressive. So ordered and comprehensive, in fact, was its handling of the subject that its author became venerated as the father of English grammar—though that paternity is today under the challenge of specialists in family trees. Gifted though Murray was in occult participles, pronouns, and prepositions, he was not unsympathetic to youth's natural indifference to such grammatical fauna. Hence to make them more arresting, and also maybe more intelligible, he undertook to show their essential traits and tactics pictorially—a practice which is still regarded highly by current masters of the pedagogic art. Despite the repellent character of his subject—or, more likely, because of it—Murray found a large and agreeable audience among American schoolmasters and even among those in England, where he brought his earthly span to an end. In the United States his book passed through no less than fifty editions, while a capsule version of it attained a production of 120,000 copies.

The tremendous outpouring of schoolbooks was not without its shady aspects. It was no light task for a schoolmaster—even, indeed, for a pedant—to keep abreast of them all, and all too often he threw up his hands. In those times as in these, the seductions of the book drummer were powerful—sufficient at all events to cause the adoption of some shoddy writings. When teachers understood next to nothing of the advantage of employing a uniform text, the relentless piling of schoolbooks could be, and often was, overwhelming. Actually, in certain places the situation became so muddling that it was not uncommon to encounter children in a single school approaching the same subject in a labyrinth of different books. It was largely to bring some order to this tangled traffic that the call for a uniform textbook went out. But the route to such a wonderland was littered with hazards, and the movement along its way was slow and faltering. In truth, the sixties were upon us before the use of uniform texts became general and school authorities here and there began to issue lists of recommended books.

2   The new-style schoolbook, as has been said, was a response to the shifting culture. To its inexorable workings the school itself was of course responsive. Thus, on the one hand, textbooks displayed and developed new subjects, while, on the other hand, schools initiated courses wherein the new books found themselves at home.

Where the Puritan schoolboy had been taught little more than reading and writing and the inevitable axioms of his religion and morality, his nineteenth-century successor had much more to annoy him. Not only had the three Rs become permanent fixtures, but in some cities they were appearing in such novel guises as declamation, oratory, grammar, word analysis, spelling, and ciphering. Some schools were even trading regularly in geography, American history, and civics. Nor was it unusual for girls to give some heed to sewing. As the curriculum thus became more and more crowded, subjects jostled one another for their place within it. For years, for example, arithmetic contended with grammar, and geography with history. The one subject which vanished from the public school was religion. But the vacuum it left was promptly filled with a new and omnipresent stress on virtue and good works. As a consequence, every subject from reading to history—even crass arithmetic—appeared cleansed with moral detergents, and every schoolbook, from Webster to McGuffey, had its pages pomaded and powdered with the ethical postulates that make for a good and upright life.

As the years trailed off, the curriculum transformation became food even for legislative cerebration. Where, for example, the Massachusetts law of 1647 had been content to command instruction in only reading and writing, its successor in 1789 called in addition for spelling, grammar, English usage, and a correct and decorous deportment. Some forty years later the commonwealth went so far as to demand a familiarity with geography, and in 1857 it added American history to the list of its prescriptions. Similar changes overtook the rest of New England, besides some of the Western states, in particular Ohio and Michigan, in whose settlement New Englanders had played a leading hand.

3   As the curriculum dilated more and more, so also did the school. It had started out primitively as a one-room shanty, frequented by urchins varying in their years and bulk as in their hygiene and appearance, scaling academically from novice to veteran, and with a term of duty that was all too brief—often, indeed, indeterminate. It evolved into an organization whose attendants were neatly differentiated, cooped in separate chambers, each subject to its own master, with group instead of individual instruction and with more days to the school year and more years to the total operation. As a whole, though, this transition was far from swift—nor can it be said to have been general. Its fulfillment bridged the half century before

the Civil War, and it was effected mostly in the cities and in some of the
more peopled and prosperous counties. In the rural hills and dales, which
accounted for five of every six Americans, the Little Red Schoolhouse continued for generations to dispense its old and threadbare offering.

Although the pace and detail of the metamorphosis varied from place
to place, the factors which lay behind it were common to most of them.
Basically these were the pressure of a growing population and the swelling
school enrollment, with the never-ending necessity to make provision for
them. The invasion of new subjects and the proliferation of the older ones
complicated matters still more, and so, needless to say, did the climbing
flood of textbooks. To come to terms with a situation which was moving
from confusion to chaos, some communities had recourse to organization.
As far back as 1789, to cite a case, Boston founded three reading schools
and three writing schools for children between seven and fourteen. But to
gain entry to them, their clients had to be familiar with the simpler chal-
enges of spelling and reading. In the beginning such seminaries were separate, and sometimes they even lay far apart, but eventually they gravitated
together under a common roof. By the beginning of the twenties, Bostonian
small fry could discharge all their academic feats in a single two-room
schoolhouse. The mystery of writing and arithmetic they unmasked on the
ground floor, while for their explorations in reading, and its dependencies
of spelling, accentuation, grammar, and composition, the pupils ascended
to the floor above. Each chamber could store some two hundred children,
and was usually staffed by a triumvirate of masters, each, however, under
his own flag and running his recitations to suit his taste and talent.

To be granted admission into this Eden it was still necessary to have
command of the fundamental steps. To make this possible, the city conjured
up the so-called "primary school." It was, in essence, an infant school
modeled on the practical idealism of Samuel Wilderspin, already referred
to, and designed to introduce the four-year-old to the ABCs and have him
fit and ready some three years later to carry the burden of the higher reading and writing school, which now assumed the name and stature of "English grammar school." Altogether the rising Bostonian served a ten-year
stretch in the elementary school, three years of it in the primary school and
the rest in the grammar school. The differentiation of elementary schooling
into a higher and lower order was followed presently by yet another novelty
—in 1823, the reading school ventured to arrange and organize the offering
of its four classes. A quarter of a century later the city fathers outdid themselves and all their forerunners when they hit upon the idea of manning
every class in the grammar school with a master all its own. Another eight
years, however, were to come and go before the primary school was vouchsafed the same concession.

Elsewhere the pattern was more or less the same, though, of course,
it varied somewhat with the locality. Most communities, like Boston, man-

aged ably enough with an elementary school composed of two parts. Others, true to the schoolmaster's immemorial zeal to label everything neatly and precisely, carried differentiation still further. Toledo, for instance, put its young through an elementary school made up of primary, secondary, intermediate, and grammar divisions, each of a two-year run. By the same token, the age of induction varied. Thus, where Boston articled its pupils when they had turned four, elsewhere the age was five, and more commonly it was an elderly six. Where the child was fed a light curricular content, as, for example, in the district school, he needed less than six years to put down his fare. In the city, on the other hand, not unusually as many as nine years were required.

Classifying pupils in accordance with their years and their scholastic attainment and screening them into grades, each with its own master, had become familiar enough as the forties turned into the fifties. The theory of graded instruction was, in truth, no novelty. It had been recommended more than once before, notably by Jan Amos Comenius in the seventeenth century and by the Christian Brothers, who at the same time actually put it to use. But in America it remained for the monitorial brethren to tackle the idea and work it out and, by their marked success, advertise its virtues. In the more traditional house of knowledge a cautious beginning was braved when, in consideration of the swarms of pupils he was put upon to face, the master was granted reinforcement in the shape of an assistant, a sort of academic corporal or Pfc, and when in order to reduce the classroom bedlam and thereby make it possible to run recitations with a semblance of decorum, a number of side cubicles were set off from the main classroom. Unlike the graded school we currently esteem, its ancestor was a stranger to coordination. There was no principal to direct and police it, and each teacher, divorced from the doings of his colleagues, enjoyed an absolute monarchical power in his own domain.

Such a system, needless to say, was full of waste, and as the common schools showed signs of attaining permanence, they began to be taken to task for employing it. Not only did Horace Mann upbraid them for their inefficiency, but in 1843, in his Seventh Report, he was also at pains to point up the comparative superiority of the graded schools then flourishing among the Prussians—an unseemly act, of course, and not to the good conscience of 100 percent Americans, whether teachers or mere civilians. Yet among the Boston birchmen, who were almost solidly against it, one stood up for Mann, at least on the subject of the graded school. Three years after the report's appearance, John Philbrick undertook to translate his concurrence into the reorganization of the Quincy Grammar School. Another year, and the plan was embodied in a brand-new building. For its day Quincy was something of an eight-day wonder. Four stories high, this edifice of learning offered benches to almost seven hundred pupils, a personal office for the principal, a dozen classrooms, a clothes closet, and an auditorium so spacious that it could hold the entire student troop, all the teachers, the principal, and, if need be, the board of education and some guests as well. Besides festooning the urban school in a new architectural grandeur, Quincy marked the coming of the full-blown graded school. There is some reason to believe that Quincy may well have given rise to the notion, now discountenanced, that a school must at all times reserve a desk and bench for each of its juvenile horde. In its own time, however, before such assumptions succumbed to skepticism, Quincy rolled in euology, and during the next few years graded schools were popping up all over the city. Some time later, Philbrick, his constructive vision now rewarded with the city superintendency, brought the new revelation into the primary school. Meanwhile, in a variety of manners, the graded system showed itself elsewhere, and by the fifties it had become fairly common. This does not mean, however, that it had become the universal rule, for it was a reality only in the urban centers. In the rest of the nation, which is to say the bulk of the republic, sifting and sorting pupils into grades remained more or less a theory. In some country schools, indeed, it remained a stranger to practice even long after the passing of the century.

4   The forces which brought forth the American elementary school also pressed upon the secondary school. They had been at work, in some measure, in the eighteenth century, when challenging the Latin grammar school, they engendered a more popular curriculum, one which eventually became the mark of the academy. To most of its patrons, who issued largely from the middle classes, the academy gave training for the station into which fate had put them, and in which presumably most of them would live and work and die. To a small proportion, whose eyes were fixed on a higher preferment, it offered the intellectual groundwork then demanded for admission to college. All in all the academy, like the republic itself, was a patchwork of diversity, full of lively juices, some running this way and some that way, but generally in consonance with the pragmatic outlook of the American people.

The academy rose to the crest of its renown during the nineteenth century's middle years, at about the time the common school was nailing down its first solid victories. These, of course, did not impinge directly on the common school. But it was not long before its obvious class appeal made the academy a target for the partisans of demos, as did the fact that although it made a great to-do over its status as a private enterprise, at the same time it was not above trying to lay its hands on the public till. Once the common school had safely navigated past the shoals of infancy, the limited chance it offered the commoner to obtain a measure of learning beyond the free school subjected it to critical assault. Was it meet and proper to force the young to come to terms with the common Rs and to grant them access for such an end in a free, tax-supported public school? Then by the same token it was just as meet and proper to give similar assistance to those with the great yearning for yet more knowledge.

The idea, then still a fledgling in civilization, was accorded the treatment which commonly befalls novel ideas when they threaten to invade our pockets. It ran into a hostility, more rancorous even than that which once bedeviled the common school. But for all the antagonism toward it, the idea would not wilt and die. On the contrary, presently it was even granted a respectful ear, when a few common schools, bowing to parental insistence, began to offer studies beyond those required for the elementary diploma. A postgraduate projection of the lower school, it constituted the innocent beginning of what later on, much enhanced and refined, was to become America's free public high school.

The goal achieved its first success in Boston in 1821, when the English Classical School opened for business. Soon after, the city fathers deleted the "classical" stigma from its shingle, rechristening their creation as the English High School to quell any smoldering suspicion about the school's actual motives. Kept by funds from the public purse, the school was to furnish free, nonclassical secondary schooling to the sons of the "mercantile and mechanic classes." To be allowed into its sanctum, a boy had to have no fewer than twelve birthdays behind him besides a firm grasp of the three Rs. For the three years during which the boys of English High wore out their benches, they put their minds upon composition, grammar, and declamation, including—so their teachers let it be known—the "best English authors, their errors and beauties." In addition there were ponderings over theoretic mathematics, besides some of its applications to surveying and marine science. Most of the remaining time was given up to geography, history, logic, and moral and political philosophy. With no recess for letting off steam in the pursuit of noncurricular gratifications, the boys were spared at least the terror of studying foreign languages.

Late in November, 1825, Boston gave public notice in the *Columbia Sentinel* of its quest for a master to teach in a proposed high school reserved exclusively for the fair sex. He must, the ad announced, not only be ready to shine his light and reason on the three Rs in all their useful forms and adornments but also be able to match the capacity of his clients in Roman, Grecian, American, and general history, besides algebra and geometry and a dash of science, including the elements of botany, chemistry, physics, and bookkeeping—not to forget Latin and French, moral philosophy, the evidences of Christianity, and several other mysteries as well. Whether such a walking Sorbonne ever made application has escaped historical sleuthing. Certainly he was not present in 1826, when young Bostonian ladies were given a high school all their own; nor was the school anything like the well-stocked seminary suggested in the *Sentinel*. In fact when the school approached its inaugural day, its store of knowledge had been severely pruned, and it was to be conducted on lowly monitorial lines. Even so, it must have met a prodigious need. With space for only 130, it soon found itself turning away more girls than it accepted. But the clamor for its benefits continued. In fact, in two years it became so uproarious that the city fathers, utterly flabbergasted by such a vast phenomenon, abolished the school outright. By way of softening the blow, however, they proceeded to extend the range of the girls' elementary school.

The year which celebrated the opening of Boston's first public high school saw the rise of a similar shrine in Portland, Maine, followed three years after by another in Worcester, Massachusetts. In 1825, New York City, always reluctant to stand idly by in someone else's glory, opened what is commonly regarded as the first high school to arise outside the Yankee belt. Meanwhile, beyond the left bank of the river separating Manhattan from Brooklyn, a school destined to endure unto the present was approaching its fortieth anniversary. Chartered in 1787 by the University of the State of New York, it began its practice as the Erasmus Hall Academy with a roster of twenty-six boys. Some thirteen years following, the academy broke with its monastic segregation when it hazarded to admit "young ladies" to its classes. Finally, in 1896, the academy was transformed into the Erasmus Hall High School, a public enterprise under lease to Brooklyn, then not a mere borough of Greater New York, as it is today, but a free and independent city. The state's first chartered secondary school still stands, a museum now, renovated and restored, yet full of haunting memories, as it gazes in amazement upon its tree-lined, ivy-towered quadrangle, gray-stoned, lovely, and imposing, a memento to Cambridge, which inspired it, and the present learning place of some six thousand boys and girls—the largest public high school in the nation.

What gave the American high school its first real impetus, however, was not these few and scattered efforts, but a law which Massachusetts adopted in 1827. Fought for by the redoubtable James Gordon Carter, this statute, though it took pains to make no overt reference to a high school, called upon every town of 500 families to offer instruction, tax-supported and under the public hand, to teach American history, geometry, bookkeeping, and surveying, besides the common run of elementary subjects. In addition, towns of 4,000 were required to complete the wardrobe of their offerings with courses in general history, rhetoric, logic, Latin, and Greek. Like the memorable enactment of 1647, which had threatened the Old Deluder Satan, the law of 1827 made its provisions mandatory. But as in the case of the older measure, Carter's law was greeted with snorts, and within a couple of years, when compliance with its ordinance was made permissive instead of compulsory, it sank into futility. For the next generation the measure rolled, like a ship adrift, from compromise to compromise, sometimes gaining, sometimes wasting, until in 1857 it achieved a glorious resurrection. Restored to its original writ, it was now accepted, its boons and blessings ready to be received and enjoyed.

For all its vagrancy, the Massachusetts law of 1827 was of historic importance. The first state law to decree the public maintenance and support of high schools—in substance if not in actual name—it became the model for similar undertakings elsewhere, notably in Maine, Vermont, and New Hampshire. By the sixties some three hundred high schools had been sighted in various latitudes and longitudes throughout the land, as far west as San Francisco, and as far south as New Orleans.

Despite this impressive showing, it was no easy matter to bring the high school into the brotherhood of America's public learning. For years the academy's prestige told heavily against its public rival. Lined up against this upstart were the same cabalists and propagandists who had waged war on the common school. As we know, there was a yielding on the issue of public support of the lower school. But beyond that, the antagonism of tax-supported schooling continued flintlike and unbudging. The oscillations of the law of 1827, its enactment, abandonment, and restoration—all within a period of thirty years—represent, in the gross, the advance, retreat, and ultimate success of the advocates of the free public high school. Even after the sixties the controversy continued to set off public fevers. In fact, it was not until 1874 that it finally lost its heat, when the Michigan Supreme Court, upholding the city of Kalamazoo in litigation brought by one of its citizens, declared its high school a legal and proper part of the state's public school system. There had been similar cases and similar verdicts in other places before. Nevertheless, though the Kalamazoo verdict said nothing new, its words were hailed as something of a juridic masterpiece. In consequence, its overriding effect was to make it the final word on what had been a very controverted question.

In spite of its name, which is held to be of Scottish provenance, the high school is native to the United States, while the Latin grammar school, which it supersedes, was an importation from the older world. The one was in key with national and democratic aspirations; the other, born and bred in a world of caste and privilege, inclined toward exclusiveness. The high school, conceived as an extension of the lower school, completed the learner's education. The grammar school was in its essential aspect a specialist in getting its boys ready for the higher learning. The modern high school still exercises its original function, but like the Latin school before it, it now also will prepare its pupils for college accommodation, if so they desire. As an extension of the elementary school, the American high school wrought the first stage of an educational ladder, offering the child a continuous schooling from his first faltering steps toward the ABCs to the final triumphant bagging of his high school diploma. To make this possible the high school mustered its freshmen at an age of no less than twelve, or when, presumably, they had brought the primary elementals to heel. By contrast, the Latin grammar school rounded up its budding Ciceronians when they were nine or thereabouts—again an old and alien custom, and one which still obtains in many places the world around.

The coming of the educational ladder in America was fateful. It gave coherence to the native educational organization, and in the years ahead, as it was perfected and extended, it provided the opportunity—forgetting for the moment the caprice of fortune—for every youngster to ascend, rung by rung, to the loftiest educational pinnacle. In the meantime, clinging for the most part to its effete tradition, Europe had developed a dual system, with one set of schools for the commoner and another, separate and distinct, for the elite, whether intellectual or social or merely moneyed.

5   Like the lower and the middle learning, the American college struck out in new directions, but its advance, as usual, was more cautious. For the most part, it kept a decorous reserve, like its colonial arch-father apportioning its revelation among but a fragment of the public. Then, reassured by the jurisprudence which underlay the decision in the Dartmouth College case, it multiplied with astounding abandon—more than a hundred new colleges were doing business by midcentury, and close to another hundred in the ten years following. Over half of them were one-building, denominational institutions, set in rutted and undrained land, surrounded often enough by fowl and livestock, but consecrated to Christian endeavor and the classics and straining to fit the bulk of their registrants for the clerical stole. But despite their confined and strict beginnings, their roster glitters today with venerated names, as witness Amherst, Haverford, Oberlin, and dozens of others like them. Their appeal, like their scope, has of course long since undergone an enormous overhauling and no little enhancement.

If the Dartmouth verdict was a boon for the private Oxfords, then for their public relatives, the state universities, it was assuredly no calamity. Blocked from dragooning the private college into their ranks of liegemen, certain states now established universities of their own. But their advance was labored, and their increase languid—much slower, in truth, than that of the conventional colleges—and until after the middle years of the century the country was comparatively free of them.

The opposition to the state university was substantially the one which had harried the lower school. All the ancient dirges were intoned, from the sad and clichéd wail that education was no business of honest government to the equally mournful lament that its support was somehow saddening to God. There were the usual outcries from affrighted parsons who beheld in public education, and especially in its advanced and highest order, Satan's mask of secularism and even atheism. Rather oddly, even the established colleges looked darkly at the newcomer, not, however, for the intellectual upheavals it boded to bring forth, but rather for the threat it posed to their enrollments and hence the cashbox of their bursar.

Yet somehow public higher learning moved ahead. When it finally attained permanence, it formed the last and topmost rung of the American educational ladder. Its origin, for once, lay not in New England, or even amid the opulence of the big towns and cities, but in sub-Potomac lands, in Georgia and North Carolina, both of which, as was indicated some pages back, had chartered universities as early as the eighteenth century. Neither of them was a truly secular spring of learning, and a generation dawdled by before one appeared. When it came, in 1825, it was the University of Virginia, the dazzling materialization of Jefferson's imagination. For years that university was belabored by the guardians of academic rectitude, both secular and sacred, but as time wore on, it was able to surmount most of its afflictions and to swing its beacon in an ever-widening circle far beyond its campus, especially into the higher learning of the South. However, it was in the vast range of the National Domain, with its bountiful benefits of land bestowed by the Ordinances of 1785 and 1787, that the state university showed its greatest prospering. In New England and what had been the Middle Colonies, it had a harder time. The first to open its gates was Vermont, which, in 1838, rechartered its university into a state university.

As the colonial college had resigned itself to the attraction of a religious culture, so the state university submitted to the pull of the secular world. Reflecting the opinions of its parent, the state, it favored the newer intellectual wonders—the sciences, natural and political, and the modern tongues, especially French, the language then of diplomacy and politesse. But this is not to say that religion was a spent and negligible force. Sometimes, as we have seen, it was quite the opposite, in illustration, the Second Awakening, the attendant gush of moral and humanitarian causes seeking to save souls, and the power or denominationalism itself. Not only was its potency discernible in the founding of more and more houses for sectarian learning, but sometimes it bore even on secular teachings. Sometimes, for example, the stars were searched through Presbyterian telescopes, and even the writings of the Greeks and Romans were dunked and sterilized in Total Immersionist assumptions. It was not until the nineteenth century had flowed into its second half that the University of Michigan, under the resolute hand of its president, Henry P. Tappan, finally succeeded in cutting itself loose from the restrictions placed upon its men of learning. The first state university to accomplish this feat, Michigan incited a number of others to follow her lead. Needless to remind ourselves, the triumph of academic freedom has been neither full nor final. Generally, the savants of the state universities have been as free as those in the private groves to seek the truths of their specialty as they determine and see fit. But this is not to say that they have been scot free from all molesting or that they have not been dogged, and even cashiered, on grounds transparently political or economic rather than for a want of scholarly competence, or that even in our own age of light and tolerance they have attained a permanent immunity against such malignancies.

The secularism which enabled the higher learning to wrench itself free from the grip of religious domination was not confined to the state universities. It soon filtered into the older sanctuaries of learning, slowly but inexorably, crowding the ancient classics and crying up the newer disciplines of science, government, history, and the living tongues and letters.

6 In a land where the machine rumbled louder and louder, the idea of a higher technical training was sure to show itself soon or late. From the forties on, in fact, the men of Congress were besieged with demands to lend a hand in the establishment of colleges to teach agriculture, architecture, the mechanic arts, and similar specialties. One of the most persistent advocates of such a program was Jonathan Baldwin Turner, a campaigner for the common school in Illinois, a college professor, and the author of a plan for a state industrial university. For long and wearisome years Turner's plan, along with several others, was to fever the talk of the nation's lawmakers. At length, in 1859, they volunteered some action with the passage of a bill awarding 20,000 acres of public land for each state for each of its congressmen in the House and Senate to endow a college "to teach some branches of learning as are related to agriculture and the mechanic arts." But President Buchanan, ridden by doubt and misgivings, had persuaded himself that Congress had no right to give away the public land and that even if he had, the proposed law might not work. In consequence, he laid down his veto. Not daunted, the Hon. Justin Smith Morrill, senator from Vermont and the farmer's friend, tried again, and on July 2, 1862, with Lincoln in the White House, the bill, which had its germ in Turner's original proposal, was signed into law.

Save for the increase of each grant from 20,000 to 30,000 acres and the inclusion of military science and tactics—to contribute in a measure to the winning of the Civil War—the new statute was a carbon copy of its ill-starred predecessor. Known as the Morrill Act of 1862, or simply as the Land-Grant Act, the measure was a stroke of statecraft rarely encountered among lawgivers. From it came the so-called "land-grant colleges," of which some seventy are now in operation. Because of its wonder-working drug a number of worn-out and sickly state universities were saved from the surgeon's knife, and even in certain instances from the embalmer's parlor, while at the same time, several new ones were brought into being. All the states, including Alaska and Hawaii, have been its beneficiaries. All told, they have picked up almost 12 million acres of the public land. With their cultivation of the practical and liberal arts, or—in Franklin's memorable phrase—the useful and ornamental arts, their foremost representatives have long since achieved a rank and reputation which is second to none in the American higher learning.

When, in 1962, the American people took time to memorialize the first centenary of the enactment of Morrill's law, the scheme of higher learning which it had propagated had become the country's largest single contributor of its trained and educated manpower. Students have flocked to the land-grant groves, not only from every corner of the republic, but from all over the earth as well. More than half of the nation's men of science have prepared themselves in land-grant schools, and of the thirty-six Nobel prizemen then in circulation, eighteen had taken their degrees in one of their founts of learning. From the land-grant labs and research rooms has filed a long and dazzling array of discoveries, from television and talking movies to hybrid corn, streptomycin, and the cyclotron. The Morrill law certainly has rewarded the republic richly, and the senator whose name it shares merits all the monuments—if not the speechifying—created in his honor. It is easy, however, to forget that when heroes are adulated and admired, not uncommonly their annunciation has been made with help. Surely it is no denigration of the senator from Vermont to remind ourselves that in the substance of the law which he brought forth, lie the thought and yearning and labor of Jonathan Turner.

If one may count the military, then the idea of a higher technical-training school took its first practical form behind the frowning battlements of West Point, with the establishment, in 1802, of the United States Military Academy. In civilian trappings, however, it showed itself for the first time in 1824, when the Rensselaer School—later renamed Rennsselaer Polytechnic Institute—was founded at Troy, New York. Intended for the new farmer as well as the new technologist, Rensselaer became America's first agricultural college as well as its first technical one. From the start it trafficked in novelty. It was the originator of field trips, summer study, extension courses, and similar high endeavor, as settled now in the American higher learning as cheerleaders and scholarships for hurdlers and high jumpers, but once so heretical as to be frightening. Its bold adventuring brought Rensselaer a wide and deserved acclaim, and presently it was fetching students from all over the land. Even bachelors who had served their time in the older ivied halls came flocking to it to be remodeled into higher technicians and mechanicians, or even, on occasion, to be dispatched to cap-and-gowned professorships on other campuses. Its success, as usual, prompted many imitations, though with public opinion in the mood it was, these doubtless would have come in any case. In 1847 Yale launched its Sheffield Scientific School, and at about the same time Harvard its Lawrence Scientific School, and Michigan its agricultural school. And since then, of course, such seminaries have become a dime a dozen.

The ascent of science and technics into the higher intellectual reaches led to the invention of a new academic badge, the bachelor of science, or the B.S., or sometimes, the Sc.B. degree. This clearly pointed to its holder as a man who had labored in the sciences, rather than among the venerable Greeks and Romans, as was the case of the hallowed A.B. Today, as everyone knows, this historical demarcation no longer prevails, and has, indeed, all but faded away.

7   The common school, as has already been recorded, granted its instruction to girls as well as boys. But above the elementary plane, in the high school and the college, such concessions were ill—and even somewhat cynically—regarded. To be sure, there were female academies which cast their light on the fair ones, but they ministered to the paying trade, and they were never numerous. Above, in the college, we enter a monastic world. Under the circumstances, a young miss harboring desires for higher wisdom had to either file her ardors in her subconscious, along with other Freudian hair-raisers, or seek some other means. For in America, as everywhere else in this best of all possible worlds, it was then an unarguable canon of legal and ethical science that Eve's chief reason for being was domestic and biologic. As late as the forties, when the lowest common man could hope on some tomorrow to spangle himself with the sheriff's star or even the judicial ermine—and maybe even better—his sisters, whatever their native capacities, were hedged in by taboos on every side, from a denial of the suffrage to lopsided divorce laws and a double standard, both general and matrimonial.

When the republic was still in adolescence such unequalness caused no repining. But as the nation went humming into its industrial transformation toward the sweet and happy land we now inhabit, the feminine longing for a freer and fuller life burst afire, and with it the desire for a better education. Like the movement for the common school, the cause of woman's education had its special luminaries, its Catharine Beecher, for example, and its Emma Willard and Mary Lyon. Like the Manns and the Barnards and Stowes, and the other forwarders of the common school, they waged their combat all out with reinforcements, whenever possible, from other sectors. Its was supported, among others, by an occasional amicable journalist, and in particular the persuasive Sara Josepha Hale, who for a time ran the *Lady's Magazine* and ended as editor of the unforgettable *Godey's Lady's Book*. And, again as in the case of the common school, the progress of feminine schooling was helped by the ever-accelerating pace of social and economic changes. Under their fierce friction the scope of female activity took on heft and friskiness. More and more the fragile sex was embarking on its own careers, and more and more women threatened to earn their own keep. They turned not only to teaching. Some invaded the mill and shop and, here and there, even the office, and in the ensuing generations they took pride in seizing every calling known to civilized man, even those which had once been the male's exclusive oyster, from riveting to lion taming and from journeying in outer space to holding high public office. But it was slow going. Midcentury had gone into eternity before any ponderable advance was evident—in fact, the 1900s were upon us before most of the old taboos against women were at last uprooted.

On the educational front, the first to put on the battle harness was Emma Hart Willard. She was a woman of no ordinary gifts, finely dowered and morally zealous, and the author of *Rocked in the Cradle of the Deep.* She had ventured into schoolkeeping as early as 1807, when she opened a seminary for girls at Middlebury, Vermont. But it was not until 1821, when she founded the Troy Female Academy, that she attracted any notice. Such places were then not unknown, nor were they even rare, but most of them reserved their advantages for the high-toned, and the run of them were little more than genteel finishing schools. Not a few of them, it is true, put forth grave announcements of instruction in mathematics, science, history, and similar challenging endeavor, but by and large what they stressed was charm and what in that dove-tinted era passed mellifluously, if somewhat vaguely, as "femininity." Although Emma Willard did not turn her back to the frills of the older establishments, she did put down her challenge to their assumptions. A wife, she submitted, should certainly be a connubial joy, though not, she made so bold as to add, as a vassal to her mate, but rather as a free and equal companion. It was her contention that women should enjoy the same liberties and dignities as men and that hence they should have a turn at science, mathematics, geography, and even metaphysics. Yet, for all her feminist proclivity, she shared the high solicitude of the male for woman's special and most significant emprise, homemaking. But for the miss who wished someday to snare and hold a husband who venerated and admired her, and who hoped to fill her home with love and happiness, Emma Willard prescribed not courses in charm and decorum, whatever value such disciplines may have, but rather courses in scientific "housewifery."

An even sturdier battler for this view—and a more colorful one—was Catharine Beecher, the sister of Henry Ward Beecher and Harriet Beecher Stowe. For most of her conscious life she lashed out at the idea that social odium attached to household work. Like Emma Willard, she set herself to raise housework to a place of dignity and public esteem, infusing it, while she was about it, with intellectual qualities that put it on a plane with epistemology and differential calculus. Her *Treatise on Domestic Economy,* which appeared in 1842, served to put the subject in a teachable form. For years the book was a leader in its field, boosting the subject effectively and, all things considered, even helping to drum up a measure of respect for it. Besides homemaking, Miss Beecher gave her endorsement to nursing and teaching as proper spheres for the active and ambitious woman. In 1828 she opened a Female Seminary at Hartford, where she essayed to promote her views. But her notions were too apocryphal, and the spirit of the times was too dead against them, and so her efforts fell short of success.

Blocked in pedagogy, she took to writing and lecturing. She was forever stumping, beguiling pastors, educators, and lawmakers and flaying the air with a hurricane of words for the cause of woman's liberation. She hoped thereby to promote the establishment of more and better schools for women, especially in the large and moneyed cities. Thus also she aspired to transform young women into live wires, crusading like herself to rid the female of her chains. For all her effort, success shied away from her, and her immediate attainment was negligible. One seminary sprouted in Milwaukee and another in Dubuque, but today, like her own seminary at Hartford, they are all but vanished memories. But in the department of propaganda, as a lady of vision, a resolute and influential battler for the millennium which women now enjoy with men, she was stupendous.

The world in which Emma Willard and Catharine Beecher labored afforded each of them a measure of security and contentment. Their itch to unearth and suppress evils set them apart, of course, from the generality of their fellows, male and female, but their nonconformist outlook, mellowed as it was with Christian conscience, was at all times reasoned and restrained. Hence, though their dialectic was directed at woman in the mass, their schools were always private and for the few.

Mary Lyon too was pious—indeed, in her the sacred ardor burned with a white heat. But Mary Lyon was also poor, and for years she walked in want. She was more than twenty when she gained access to an academy, and even then it would have shut her out had she not been ready to work for her keep and schooling. Like Willard and Beecher, she consecrated her good works to all women, and her school, like theirs, was private. But unlike them, she struggled to hold it open to as many as possible. "My thoughts, feelings, and judgments," she confessed, "are turned to the middle classes in society."

During her years of study and teaching, Mary Lyon conceived the idea of a school for women, second to none in the land—not even Harvard. In 1837—she was then forty—she was able to put her ideas in practice and, with help, opened Mount Holyoke Female Seminary at South Hadley, Massachusetts. Over this, for $200 and board, she officiated as principal. An autonomous, endowed establishment, devoid of any sectarian frenzy but full of pious fervor, the seminary devoted itself to the advancement of women's rights. However, the feminism of Mary Lyon was centered in learning, and she rarely ventured into the regions of bold social criticism expressed so energetically by Catharine Beecher and Emma Willard. Girls who wished their schooling to be a mere dalliance—who craved "simply to please and be pleased"—such frivolous creatures found no welcome at Mount Holyoke. For all her stress on the cerebral, Mary Lyon accorded a place to the domestic subjects, but unlike Miss Beecher, she discerned no intellectual benefits in broom swinging, bed making, and the like. If she articled her girls to Holyoke's practical and domestic industry, then the reason was simply to lessen the cost of running the place and thus bring its advantages within reach of the poorer girls.

What marks the work of America's first woman pedagogues is not the high amperage of their zeal, for after all this is not singular in the history of the human female. Nor is it their pedagogy, for time has found much of it false, and some of it even ludicrous. The marbled niche posterity has reserved for them is due not a little to their insistence, so utterly heretical when it was first flung upon the human ear, that girls have brains and that if one will only let them, the best ones can climb the dizziest peaks of learning. The many prohibitions placed everywhere on woman's quest for higher knowledge, the reformers could not of course dispel. Nor could they still the criticism, whether honest or spurious, which assailed them all about. Even so, by their vision and by their versatile and resolute maneuvering in its behalf, they at least caused some wobbling in the opposition, slight to be sure, but wobbling nevertheless.

From their relentless effort came the woman's college, not right away, of course, nor in any substantial number, for the sneers and snickers it suffered continued to afflict it for a long time. By the middle of the century, however, a number of colleges for women had appeared in the South and the West. At Macon, for one, there was the Georgia Female College, which, chartered in 1836, now aspires to be acknowledged as the first college for women in this republic. But the bulk of these maiden efforts were of a debatable value, rich in fine intentions, but poor in worldly goods, and manned all too often by professors whose light at best was dull. As intellectual searchlights, hence, they set off no brilliance, and the degrees they offered were commonly dismissed as cachets of an inferior luster. For their Harvards and Yales the fair ones had to tarry a while longer—as long at least as 1861, when Vassar declared its readiness to furnish them an education second to none—not even to that of the most advanced intellectual shrines then available to the American male.

Meanwhile, in Ohio, when Oberlin opened in 1833, it admitted four young women to its sessions on equal terms with men. Twenty years later, when Horace Mann took the bridge at Antioch College, also in Ohio, coeducation was one of its featured innovations. But the country was in no mind for such a boon of grace, especially in the cautious and upright East, where such a mingling of the sexes was recognized as a hazard to virtue and an affront to the Heavenly Father. Beyond the Mississippi's farther bank, where the science of moral pathology was apparently more flexible, every state university, saving only that of Missouri, brightened and bedizened its classrooms from the start with the presence of the sweet and lovely ones.

In the East the first man's college to take such risks was Cornell. Led by its first president, the admirable Andrew Dickson White, it braved the leap in 1872, thereby entering the historic circle not only of Oberlin, but even of the faraway Plato, who, though he had never committed matrimony during all his eighty years on earth, nevertheless made room in his academy for women as well as men. Saluted as one of the most important discoveries ever made by mortal man, coeducation, when at length it came into its own, was prized not only on social and pedagogic grounds but also—what was probably a greater determinant in its first success—on economic ones.

If women found it hard to penetrate the intellectual strongholds of the male, then their effort to get into the professional learning and, in truth, the professions themselves, confronted them with an even stouter antagonism. Elizabeth Blackwell, who was probably the first woman doctor of any consequence to grace this nation, was turned away by the medical faculties of both Philadelphia and New York, before she persuaded the medical school at Geneva, New York, to grant her access to its halls, from which, to the amazement of her male professors, she proceeded to graduate at the head of her class in 1849. With her sister, a lady Galen in her own right, she was admitted to practice in England, specializing in women's diseases and lecturing on gynecology at the London School of Medicine. But in this respect, for once, America was the home of neither the free nor the brave —everywhere the sisters turned they found the professional door securely bolted. Indeed, had they not founded their own dispensary in New York, their prowess in medical science would have come to a sad conclusion.

Even more closely guarded than the citadels of the healing art were those of sacerdotal science. When, in illustration, Antoinette Brown sought to prepare herself at the theological seminary at Oberlin, the authorities, for all their confidence in the power of woman, were appalled, and they strove with all their might to save her from her folly. And when their efforts came to naught, and she was eventually graduated, they were careful to make no mention of her on the commencement roster. Perhaps their blushes were not unwarranted, or perhaps these men were merely prudent. At all events, after her elevation to the sacred smock, Miss Brown, despite her prayers and invocations, encountered not a little difficulty in obtaining a license to preach. Finally, in 1853, the Congregationalists, throwing caution to the winds, took a chance and ordained her. But later she left their fold to become a Unitarian, an evangelist now for woman's rights, and a social salvager rather than a saver of souls.

12
UP FROM
APPOMATTOX

Like the rest of the Union, the South experienced educational stirrings. Most of the familiar elements were on show—the shock force of dedicated men and women, the conventions, the sonorous phrases, and the campaigns to mobilize the public mind and to spur the lawmakers into action. The South even had its Horace Manns and Henry Barnards, less publicized perhaps than the New England originals, but no less resolute. Unhappily, in the sub-Potomac belt, the odds against educational reform were stupendous. Not only had progress to such an end overtaken that region more tardily than the North, but when it began to move, its pace was sluggish, and its gears never shifted into high. In consequence, its advance was more stumbling and more confined, and though the promise of rosy tomorrows suffused the air, on the eve of Sumter the Southerners were barely beginning to do battle with their lagging education.

Why did the South continue loftily to ignore the renovation of its schooling? Why was its educational awakening characterized, so to say, by yawns and drowsy eyes? The reasons are certainly not far to seek. As everywhere else there was the familiar outcry against imposing new taxes for the free schooling of everybody's children, and again there was the usual moral horror that universal schooling would surely cause the established order to collapse—that, indeed, the bottom folk, and especially the slaves, might entertain indecent ideas and even rise against their betters. The doctrine, moreover, that education was a personal matter, though falling apart in the North, continued to be cherished in the South, as was its ancient running mate, the belief that once government had afforded a measure of schooling, however meager, to those who were palpably unable to fend for themselves, the state's responsibility ceased.

More important, however, than these moldering beliefs was the fact that the South was stuck in the bog of a primitively rural culture, over which, to make matters worse, hung the pall of slavery. Slavery not only shackled the South to a wasteful economic system but also debased its politics and paralyzed its thinking generally. Though the South husbanded a variety of crops, its economic and political overlords were the cotton *noblesse*, small in number, it is true, but rich in their landholdings and mighty, of course, in their powers, privileges, and prerogatives. Some eight thousand head comprised the plantation peerage. At the outbreak of the war this august handful owned some four million slaves, a prime specimen of which, statistics of the day report, was worth about $2,000. Far more numerous than the plantation plutocracy, of course, was the throng of small and hard-pressed farmers who tilled their fatigued and worn-out land, not so much for profit as for bare subsistence. The industrial revolution which had been working its wonders in the North and in the Middle West had barely grazed the South. In sub-Potomac lands the general run of business spent itself in comparatively small affairs, while their nabobs of finance, banking, and industry were several cuts below those of the North. The things, moreover, which linked men, which lessened their isolation and estrangement, and which modified and expanded their outlook upon the world—the railroads, for example, and the means for swift and effective intercommunication—of these there was still a baleful lack. Cities, which were sprouting and growing in other parts of the republic, did not sprout and grow so readily in the South. Hence there was a paucity of burgherdom, of the class of pushful, enterprising, urbanite, and laboring men—the antidote, in short, to a complacent provincialism.

2   As elsewhere in the land, such educational progress as the South was actually able to muster varied from state to state. Thus, by 1860, after many weary years of struggle, North Carolina had succeeded in scaling the highest peak then known in Southern education. At the same time the great proportion of Southern states had sunk into subterranean depths. The people of North Carolina had started to do over their schools as early as 1839 —two years after Horace Mann had begun to exercise his magic in Massachusetts—when the state enacted a law enabling North Carolinians to give life and vigor to their elementary schooling with local and county funds. A decade later the state created the office of county superintendent, and in 1852 it capped this achievement with the establishment of a state superintendency. For the next fourteen years the burden of that office fell upon Calvin Henderson Wiley, a man whom posterity has accorded credit for having done more to advance the public learning in his state than any other single individual. The circumstances which greeted Wiley when he came to his post were pretty much like those which faced Mann when he took the helm in Massachusetts. The same decrepit schools lay all about, the same down-and-out equipment, the same unspeakable birchmasters. And in the background lurked the same crippling cocci of localism, sectarianism, and an almost unanimous resistance to school taxation. Annex to this the fact that North Carolina had no educational legacy to speak of, as the Bay State did, and that its civilization was immersed in rural conservatism, and you confront a task that would have made even the Apostles pause.

Like Mann, Wiley prowled widely in his dominion, gathering his murky data and forcing them without let-up to the attention of his far-flung audience. Through the agitation of his harangues and writings, and through the teachers' organizations he helped to launch and lead, he managed, as the years swept on, not only to win friends for his crusade but even to crack his whip in the mills of lawmaking. In 1860, after eight years of hard industry, Wiley was able to point to an appreciable progress. Under his ceaseless knuckle rapping, schools had been repaired and renovated, their number ponderably increased, and their furnishings and facilities improved and enlarged. Teachers were made to suffer training before they were allowed to enter practice—of no great shucks to be sure, to modern eyes, but training nevertheless. Supervision, moreover, enjoyed a degree of professional proficiency, which, taken all around, in the South was then a novelty. Finally, some five of every seven youngsters were pondering their schoolbooks, an achievement which in the Bible Belt was then singular. So impressive had been Wiley's blast of fresh air into the state's educational miasma that other states—Virginia, South Carolina, and Georgia—were presently issuing summonses for his help and counsel. Had it not been for Sumter and its sorrowing sequence, who knows what this man and others like him might have done to get the South on its educational feet?

3   The war with the North, as every schoolboy knows, brought ruin to the South. The details are familiar enough, and they need not be reembroidered here. When the carnage came to an end, the Confederacy's best blood had drenched its battlefields. Its debt was gigantic, its purse picked clean, its credit a shambles. Its handful of cities lay in waste, the haunt of the sorry ghosts of a vanished glory. Its small industry was all but gone. Its best farmlands were scorched, and the hands to remake them were no more. Some four million slaves were now free, but they were still vassals to their fear and inexperience, their insecurity, and their dreadful ignorance.

With Lincoln in the grave, and his successor in the White House unable to throttle the radical Republicans, the South soon found itself at the mercy of a rancorous Congress. Even before the Confederate collapse, die-hard Southern whites had given notice that they would never accept the Negro as a full-fledged citizen in their midst. When Congress, nonetheless, confronted them with the Civil Rights Act of 1866, granting the former slaves full rights of citizenship, the old Confederacy took the liberty of disowning it on grounds of its lack of constitutionality. Two years later, when the Fourteenth Amendment came into being, guaranteeing the Negro's new rights constitutionally, the Southern states refused to give it ratification, whereupon Congress wreaked retaliation upon them with the Reconstruction Acts of 1867. These clamped Dixie into five military districts, each under martial administration, while the ex-Confederates, supposedly taking second thought, were expected to purge themselves for a return to national grace. To this end each Southern state was to elect delegates to a constitutional convention, organize its government, and give assent to the Fourteenth Amendment. All males of legal age, black and white, were entitled to vote and hold office—save those who had been in rebellion, which is to say, of course, the overwhelming bulk of the former leadership. The cards were therefore plainly stacked not only in favor of the emancipated Negroes—or as the vulgate then put it, the freedmen—but also in favor of the Northern

Republicans, the scalawags and carpetbaggers, and similar prehensile fellows. In South Carolina, to instance a single case, of 124 delegates assembled in convention, 76 were Negroes, of whom only 49 had the honor to be natives of the state. Of the remaining fifty-odd whites, more than half were strays from beyond its borders.

The educational articles which issued from these conclaves were mostly and principally to Yankee taste and to carpetbagger specifications. Commonly they established the essential educational machinery, laid plans for school support, and in a general way set the foundation for future legislation. Alabama, in illustration, required its general assembly to "enact necessary and proper laws for the encouragement of schools and the means of education." Texas, for its part, ordained that taxes "collected from Africans, or persons of African descent, shall be exclusively appropriated for the maintenance of a system of public schools for Africans and their children. . . ." But the laws which eventually came forth were often at hopeless odds with the constitutional blucprint. And when they were not, they were beautifully vague and commonly unenforceable. The simple truth is that the South was in no condition to come to terms with its public schooling—nor, for that matter, was it in the mood. Though its pockets had been turned inside out, it was expected by the North to make provision not only for its hordes of whites but also for the millions of liberated slaves, an undertaking which, even had the tangle and terror of the times been less harrowing, would have put a strain on the most advanced and substantial states in the Union. And to make matters worse, the South was being preyed upon by the carpetbaggers from the North and by its own vermin, the scalawag anti-Southern whites, whose waste and contumacy set the South back for generations to come.

In 1877 President Hayes lifted the dismal vigil of military occupation, and the cold war of Reconstruction gave way to the cold peace of its aftermath. Politically the policy had borne a bitter fruit. For the South the experience had been grim and costly, more damaging materially and spiritually, some incline to believe, than the war itself. Beleaguered from within and without, the Southerners staggered from Reconstruction crippled by a debt more onerous than ever, their resources shriveled and their most competent citizens either reduced to political sterility or departed to more promising places in the North and the West, or even to happier lands abroad.

Needless to say, not all Yankess were lubricious sharks. Some, indeed, were disposed to treat the South in a conciliatory, and even in a cavalier, fashion. Soon after Appomattox, organizations such as the New England Freedmen's Relief Society, the Pennsylvania Relief Commission, and several others of similar title sprang up in some of the larger municipalities to grapple with the situation. As their names suggest, they sought to ease the Southerner's miserable lot, and more especially the Negro's, by keeping him in food and raiment, putting him under a roof, and training him for his new civil charms and duties. As the years followed, the more robust and effective of these welfare guilds joined forces under the flag of the American Freedmen's Union Commission.

Among these Northern undertakings in social and economic salvage was the Freedmen's Bureau, or—to give it its full and official designation— the Bureau of Refugees, Freedmen, and Abandoned Lands. Brought into being in 1865 by Congress, the Bureau was under the command of the War Department. Its first executive-in-chief, fittingly enough, was a general who aspired to bring "unity and system" to the various and disparate strivings for good works in the South. The Bureau's first objective, like that of the voluntary brethren, was to forward the work of rehabilitation, and especially to succor the Negro, to stand guard over his new-won rights, and to advance him on his way to literacy. The Bureau executed its mass attack for five years, ridding its till, while it was about it, of close to $6 million, summoning up and staffing some 2,500 schools, and introducing about 150,000 children to their first letters.

But for all this diligent and heartening endeavor, and for all the acts of Congress and the fiats of the military to back them up, the Bureau's work was haltered by its passion for Northern and Republican idealism. Its cocky eagerness to remake Southerners in the Yankee mold blinded it all too often to the culture which was rooted far down in the local and communal soil, so that in the end the Bureau brought upon itself not only the contempt and anger of the old ruling order but also the estrangement of many men of goodwill who otherwise might have inclined to give it their aid and support. The Bureau's endorsement, for example, of a proposal to instruct white and Negro children side by side in the same room outraged Southern whites and gave concern even to the anti-Southern scalawags. In fact, the idea found skeptics even among some of the Negroes. Nor did the Bureau's capacity for blundering, particularly in its choice of teachers, help matters much. Many of its masters, as is to be expected, had been rounded up in the North. Most of them, there is no doubt, were full of benign intentions; unluckily, not a few of them were also specialists in rectitude and, hence, ablaze with moral self-ascendancy. When they persisted in crying down the Southern white as the Negro's unfailing foe and, per contra, in hymning the Northern soldier as his friend and liberator, they were heading for trouble. Not only were they socially despised, but sometimes they were also stoned and scourged, their belongings destroyed, and their schools set afire.

4   The greatest and most lasting service to Southern education came from two New England millionaires, George Peabody and John F. Slater. Peabody started the ball rolling in 1867, when he established a trust fund of $2 million "for the promotion and encouragement of intellectual, moral, and industrial education among the young and more destitute of the southern and southwestern states of our Union." His altruism, needless to say, got a hearty public approbation, and he even received a special expression of congressional gratitude, besides a glittering medal to memorialize his generosity forever. Historically, the fund he started may well have been the first of our educational foundations, now almost a commonplace in the American way—at all events, it was the first of any considerable heft.

The money from the Peabody Fund was put to many uses. In town and city it gave a hand to the struggling common school, and in the vast reaches of the Southern countryside it served to raise the rural school, if not to alpine heights, then at least to a plane which was somewhat more respectable than before and, perhaps, even a portent of better things to be expected on the morrow. Through its encouragement of state normal schools, it fostered better teaching, and by underwriting higher wages for the county superintendent, it helped to raise his office in the public respect and thereby made it professionally more attractive to able men. It was the flow of Peabody dollars, more than anything else, which offered the Negro his first great chance. Not only did it bring schooling to his young, but what was more important, it made it possible to train and rehearse the competent Negro for the teaching role. The fund, moreover, was able to work its wonder without branding its beneficiaries with the ignobility of poverty. Nor did it ever so much as hint that in the schooling of the people responsibility rested with any other body than the individual state. Thus it offended nobody in authority. In consequence, its work prospered. The passing years saw it serve not only to undermine the old misgivings about free education but also to give fortification to the new belief in a public school, tax-supported and free to all.

The Peabody Fund executed its industry for almost half a century. In 1905, when most of its feats of public service were history, its trustees decided the time had come to call it quits. Of the money they still harbored they now donated $1½ million toward the founding of the George Peabody College for Teachers at Nashville, Tennessee. Still in active practice, the college stands out as a center for teacher training in the South. The $250,000 which continued to bulge the Peabody pocket, its trustees presently handed over to the guardians of the Joseph F. Slater Fund. All in all, Mr. Peabody and his gold were very useful.

Slater's fund was more modest than Peabody's, but it was scarcely less important. Started in 1882 with a store of $1 million, it was conducted more or less in the manner of its forerunner, but with a somewhat heavier stress on the Negro's industrial education. Time saw several other hoards scatter their munificence upon Southern education. In 1907, to single out a few, Anna T. Jeanes set aside $1 million for the improvement of Negro rural education. Two years later, the Phelps Stokes Fund was created to further Negro education in general, and in 1917 came the Julius Rosenwald Fund, which directed its largess to all aspects of Southern education. Since then, as everybody knows, foundation money has grown, as it were, on trees, and some of it, dispensed freely from the well-manured orchards of Ford and

Rockefeller, has made its welcome appearance not only in the South but in the rest of the republic as well.

5   With the dismantlement of the Freedmen's Bureau in 1870, Southern education was gradually weaned from national help. But Congress did not stop playing doctor at the Southern bedside entirely. As a matter of fact, during the seventies and the eighties, several prescriptions were compounded in the capital, all intended to inject vitality into the sicklied Southern public school—and should pills and capsules fail, then as a last resort some men of Congress stood ready with the needle of Federal aid. All the recommended remedies generated a pungent controversy, but only two showed signs of any promise, and of these only one came close to being made into law.

Early in 1870, Representative George Frisbe Hoar, of Massachusetts, sponsored a measure to establish a national school system. Such an idea was, of course, no novelty. It had been put forth more than once before, with variations to be sure, and most notably in 1795, when the American Philosophical Society offered to honor the best essay on the subject with a fitting premium. Yet such themes were academic, and none of them fructified in practice. But 1870 was not 1795, and although the Hon. Mr. Hoar was representative of the Bay State, his eyes doubtless were fixed upon the South. Every state, he volunteered, was sovereign over its schools and had the right to run them as it deemed fit. Still, there were certain grave limits, and if for any cause a state should allow itself to drop below what was held to be a reasonable par for the republic as a whole, then it behooved the Federal government to take over. Let the President begin by declaring such a state in delinquency, and then let him dispatch a Federal school superintendent to the scene to take the matter in hand. To give him aid, let the Department of the Interior name a corps of superintendents for every school and congressional district within the afflicted state. In addition, Hoar's bill undertook to empower the national government to erect schoolhouses and to keep a vigilant eye on all schoolbooks. All this was to be underwritten by the income from a permanent school fund built up from the sale of national land, besides a levy of the state's inhabitants at 50 cents a head.

A gross and unseemly proposal? Of course not. A sensible one? That is much harder to answer. In any case Hoar's bill was treated to a blistering barrage. A few gave it support, but the great majority thumbed it down. The educational authority assigned by Hoar to the national government was denounced as being not only against the general public sentiment but also un-American and, some were sure, against God. Hoar's proposal, announced the *Catholic World*, aimed "to suppress Catholic education, gradually extinguish Catholicity in the country, and to form one homogeneous people after the New England evangelical type." What states'-righters, whether north or south of the Mason-Dixon line, had to say was no more complimentary

—some of their remarks, indeed, still bring blushes to delicate and decent ears. There is good reason to believe that Hoar had intended his piece of statecraft to be little more than a corrective stick to shake at negligent states and thereby scare them into progress. "I do not believe," he let it be known, that "if we pass this law, it will ever be necessary to put it in force." Yet even this confidence availed him naught, for his bill died without ever coming to a vote.

But the idea behind it stayed alive, and in time the movement to give the central government an effective educational control gained some ground. In 1872, and again in 1879, bills calling for a Federal subsidy came before Congress, but neither gained success. Then in the eighties Senator Harry W. Blair, of New Hampshire, tried again—indeed, he was to try again and again, five times in all from 1882 to 1890. What the senator proposed was in its essence not unlike the measure sponsored some years ago preceding by Representative Hoar, but with its more debatable features stricken out. Blair called for an appropriation of nearly $80 million to be apportioned during the following eight years to states having trouble maintaining their schools. But in order to be eligible for such assistance, a state had to make its public schooling free to all its children, whether white or black. It was expected, furthermore, that its schools would impart instruction in the common elementals, besides some geography and history. Also it was to keep the Secretary of the Interior supplied with any information about its schools his office called for. The money from the national strongbox was to be confided to the care and discretion of state and local functionaries. And, finally, whatever the size of the grant, it had to be matched penny for penny by state and local bursars.

The contentions over Federal help were then pretty much the same as they are now, though no doubt there was less pressure on the lawmaker. Those who stood with Blair hailed his purpose as a boon to better citizenship, which would lead to a fairer and happier life for all—a benefit not only to the South but to the whole republic as well. It was, so their argument ran, the will of the American people, and it was in accord with the sagacity of the Founding Fathers. And when measured by the anticipated harvest, its cost, for all its sumptuousness, was actually a mere pittance. On the other hand, those who took the field against Blair cherished no such hopes. What the senator from New Hampshire proposed, they insisted, was actually derisive of the Constitution, and hence of democracy, for at bottom it handcuffed the state to the central government. Worse yet, despite the prerequisites and conditions it laid down—or, it is not unlikely, because of them—inescapably it would be turned into a preserve for the politician. Finally, a grant of $80 million, no matter how it was sliced and distributed and no matter what splendors it would ultimately propagate, was still a staggering pile of money—far too skyscraping, surely, for the government to disburse on education.

As has been said, Blair introduced his bills in the Senate five times, and on three occasions—in 1884, 1886, and 1888—his colleague senators gave their blessing. But in the House, where the anti-Southern feeling still ran high, the representatives quickly laid the dragon low.

6   With the exit of the Northern soldiery the Yankee interregnum receded into history. Even before that, however, its constabulary endeavor had showed signs of slackening, and by the middle of the seventies, only a little of the late Confederacy remained in radical hands. Left to resolve her own difficulties, the South reverted to the control of former Confederates, whose antipathy for the Northerner soon forged them into a solid anti-Republican bloc, the so-called "Solid South." Bent on wiping out every speck of the Northerner's doing in the South, whether for good or evil, they proceeded, among other things, to repudiate their state debts and, while they were about it, a generous portion of their Reconstruction costs. The Negro's rights, so hard-won, were promptly shorn of actuality, and though the Fourteenth and Fifteenth Amendments were there to assure him of his constitutional guarantees by various strategems and deceits these descended into a cynical fatuity.

The road to better times in Dixie has been long and tortuous—it was traversed somewhere in the present century. Meanwhile, hagridden by their misery, Southerners sighed in memory of their golden yesterdays—an absurdity, to be sure, but a familiar psychological phenomenon. However, by the eighties there were signs of a promising industrial development. Atlanta, for one, was exploiting its riches of coal and water and the cheap labor of its numerous children, and it was presently developing a textile industry which in the years to come was not only to prosper but even to become a challenge to the primacy of New England. By and by the hum of the spindle was joined by the roar of the steel mill—an industrial cacophony which, though moderate at first, was portentous and was ultimately to make Birmingham a sub-Potomac Pittsburgh. Meanwhile, North Carolina and Virginia concentrated on tobacco production, to which time added the mass planting of the soybean and the lowly peanut, while Arkansas busied itself with lumber, and Texas and Oklahoma made ready for the millennium of oil.

As for agriculture, the principal enterprise in the South before the war, troubles badgered it on every side. Not only had the old plantation system gone to wrack, but it was hard to figure out just how to replace it. For a spell hopes were placed in the operation of farms by hired Negroes, but their innocence of such a role led to inevitable failure. What emerged as the years went by were the system of crop liens and farm tenancy, both of which were sprung from a want of capital. True enough, the crop lien system enabled the hard-put farmer to borrow money on his prospective harvest, but all too often his need made him prey to the shyster money broker, so that in the end he was commonly worse off than ever.

Any way one looks at it, the pace of recovery moved with all the swift-
ness of a snail. Indeed, for all the rosy cheer of a rising industry, as the
century made for its exit, the fortunes of the South were still at a low ebb.
It was—to cite one of its own sages, the Hon. Walter Hines Page—a land
of woe and abysmal ignorance, a land suffering from ecclesiastics and politicians, an unhappy land of "forgotten men."

Under the circumstances, the free functioning of education, whether
of the lower kind or the higher, was obviously hard beset. All the well-
known scars were visible—short school terms, defective attendance, poor
and insufficient equipment, senile and decrepit libraries (or none at all),
below-zero teachers, and an illiteracy which staggers the imagination. And
over it all hung the shroud of poverty, for the funds which had been so
laboriously built up had sunk from sight. But even sadder was the darkening of the spirit. For Reconstruction had made the common school a Yankee
school, and an object hence of bilious suspicions.

The supreme and incontrovertible social fact in the situation was, of
course, the presence of the Negro. Was he to be granted access to the public
school on free and equal terms with the whites? Or was he to be set on his
bench in schools restricted to his race? Northerners in the main pressed for
the former, but Southerners opposed it almost to a man. Several Reconstruction governments, it is true, yielded on the matter, and had hazarded the
establishment of a coracial public school. But the overwhelming bulk of
whites detested and derided it, and wherever it appeared, they went to great
lengths to keep themselves and their children aloof. Such was the dominant
cast of mind, a disturbed and rancorous sentiment, and so it smoldered long
after Appomattox. In fact, by the end of the century every Southern state
had declared itself, either in its constitution or in its statutes, for the maintenance of a separate school.

Schooling the Negro was not simply a social question, or even an
ethical one; it had a pronounced psychological overtone also. For many
the question was not whether black and white should tackle their studies
together or separately, but whether the Negro actually had the capacity
for the process we call "learning." And if so he had, should he apply his
talents to the same subjects as the Caucasians? Or should his learning be
of some special sort? Today such concerns no longer flog our mind—science and democracy have disposed of them. However, when they first began
to flay us, they resulted not only in stormy feelings but also in an array
of answers which ranged from flat negatives to equally flat positives, with
an assortment of qualified yes's and no's in between.

Meanwhile, through scattered private searchings the answers to such
enigmas were being sought in the laboratory of daily practice. One of the
first to grapple with them was Samuel Chapman Armstrong, a general, but
behind his stars and spangles something of a seer and a moralist of the
first magnitude. It was Armstrong's assumption that what the Negro needed
far and above all else was not the recondite learning stored in books, but a

practical and useful training, which would arm him to cope with the problems of everyday living. To such purpose Armstrong dedicated the work of Hampton Institute, which he opened in 1868 and where, somewhat on the model of his Swiss forerunner, the eminent von Fellenberg, of Hofwyl, he put emphasis on making his students good and upright Americans, besides introducing them to farming, the manual arts and crafts, and in certain instances the art and science of teaching.

Doubtless much of Armstrong's endeavor might long since have been all but forgotten, had it not been for the achievements of his famous pupil, a Negro, Booker Tallifero Washington. As with Armstrong—as, in truth, with nearly all the great nineteenth-century educational reformers—there was in Washington much of the vague and mysterious yearning of the romantic. And, like the romantic again, his confidence in education as an instrument for social reform knew no bounds. At the same time there was in him a common sense seldom found in dreamers. The combination of the two qualities is discernible in his work and thought, and one catches glimpses of it in his writings, especially in his *Character Building*, which appeared in 1902, and his *Working with the Hands*, written two years later.

Like Armstrong, his mentor, Washington inveighed against the intellectuals who insisted that what every Negro needed was a liberal education —the "craze for Latin and Greek learning," he called it. His own preference ran rather to the practical—to rendering the Negro useful unto himself and society and thereby, he was cheerfully sure, more acceptable to Southern whites. Such was the mainspring of Washington's purpose at Tuskegee, the institute for Negroes which he founded in Alabama in 1880 and over which he presided until 1915, when death retired him. The school, like so many others swathed in high hopes and great visions, began its mission on the well-known shoestring, stressing the homely virtues and their familiar copybook formulas, from tidiness and cleanliness to self-reliance, besides giving instruction in a few of the simpler vocational knacks and mysteries. From the start the school was plagued by faultfinders, but Washington's velvet ambassadorial touch gradually calmed them, and presently money was rolling in not only from the massive philanthropic vaults of the North but even from less spacious ones in the South. When the present century was just beginning, the fame of Tuskegee had girdled the globe. Its enrollment stood at approximately fourteen hundred men and women, and its offerings represented some thirty different industries. In addition it made a feature of its special classes in cookery, a night school, and a children's house, which was reserved as a practice station for its teachers in training.

There came a time, of course, when Washington and his light began to dim and it ceased to satisfy the Negro's longing. For one thing, the industrial training which Tuskegee favored became outmoded as the machine and mass production crowded into our way of living. For another, the younger generation of Negroes—or at all events, their brighter and more eager exemplars—who pined to shine as doctors and lawyers, or even as professional men of learning or as ambassadors of God, looked askance at Washington's disparagement of intellectual training. Nor was his policy of patience and forbearance toward the Southern whites acceptable, least of all his counsel that the Negro should cast his political lot with his declared enemy, the Solid Southern Democrat, and thus, by suffering dutifully, reap the goodwill of the reigning white Democracy.

Chief among Washington's critics stood William Edward Burghardt Dubois, a young Negro with a razor-sharp mind and a Ph.D. from Harvard. His assault on the Washington strategy was let loose in 1903 in *The Souls of Black Folk*. It was Dubois's contention that playing underling to his self-appointed betters would get the Negro precisely nowhere, and that without the ballot the Negro was doomed to just another kind of servitude. It is mainly to Dubois that we owe the National Association for the Advancement of Colored People—the NAACP—which he helped to found in 1909 and which after all these years is still on the scene stronger and more active than ever.

At the nineteenth century's end it was plain that the South, which had dragged itself along after Reconstruction, was getting back on its legs. New and expanding industries, previsioned so hopefully in the eighties, had now begun to materialize. They not only agreeably enlarged the Southern pocket, but they also bred a new class of citizenry, a virile middle class, bent on blowing up the old antagonisms. In 1898, moreover, when the Northerners went off to fight the Spaniard, the Southerners, finding that they liked the Latins no more than the Yankees did, followed suit, and presently they found themselves in Cuba, bleeding and dying for a common cause side by side with their buddies from all over the Union. In education too there were traces of a changing wind, especially in the enlarging municipalities. The ancient hostility, for example, toward the support of the common learning with taxes, though certainly not done in, was at least showing signs of mellowing. Indeed, in some quarters there was even an insistence on greater and more effective levies and on laws sans loopholes to make the business stick. Of even greater consequence, perhaps, was the presence of a handful of men of civic spirit, who were willing and able to give the movement for decent public schooling the illumination and organization it so sorely needed. Besides Walter Hines Page, whose name has already been instanced, there were such men as Charles Aycock, Governor of North Carolina; Andrew Jackson Montague, Governor of Virginia; and Edwin A. Alderman, in scholar's frock at the University of North Carolina and later also the occupant of its presidential chair.

It was through such meritorious men that the Conference for Education in the South was summoned into being. Inaugurated in 1898, chiefly by the evangelical hand of the Rev. Edward Abbott, of Cambridge, Massachusetts, the venture had been given form and substance as the Conference for Christian Education in the South. As its name suggests, the organization's interests were predominantly pious, and its membership overwhelmingly ecclesiastic. But it was not long before its educational interest struck a secular note, and by 1900 the conference had issued membership cards to an appreciable number of the more prominent and influential laity. The year following—it was 1901—in order to facilitate the execution of its piling tasks, the conference established the Southern Educational Board. Specifically this body was to exert itself on behalf of "free schools for all the people." The pinnacle of all this striving was reached in 1903, when the General Education Board was formed. Incorporated by an act of Congress, the board was lavishly capitalized out of the vast wealth of John D. Rockefeller. Though it pledged itself to forward education in all parts of the land, in apportioning its golden millions the board favored the South, where its nuggets helped the advancement not only of the lower learning but also of the middle and higher varieties and of certain specialized studies in the agricultural and industrial arts and sciences.

With so much valiant encouragement Southern education presently found itself entering what connoisseurs of such matters have been pleased to designate the "Second Revival." Its principal phases are pretty much like those of similar revivals in other times and places, and so the details need not be rehearsed again. Suffice it to observe that during the first ten years or so of the century whose blessings we now enjoy, education in the South was greatly overhauled, renovated, and improved. The revenue for supporting public education was doubled, and in some states even tripled. Some of this money was translated into new buildings and facilities; some passed into bigger paychecks for teachers; some went for libraries; and some was set aside for more and better training schools for teachers. In 1915, all states, apart from Georgia and Mississippi, had laws for compulsory schooling, and even though they were still ventilated with loopholes aplenty, more boys and girls were attending their lessons. With an average school year of 130 days, moreover, the youngster found himself articled to his letters for a longer annual siege than ever before in Southern pedagogic annals.

It has been urged that all this moving ahead was pitifully slow and that, for all its promise, it still left the South behind the rest of the nation. None of this can be gainsaid; still, the fact remains that it was an advance. Since then, though clouds still hang menacingly overhead, more and more rays have broken through. The South has begun to produce some first-class literary men—even, indeed, a Nobel prizeman. Its school of sociology at Chapel Hill, in North Carolina, has long since been among the country's best. Even its journalism, though still rich in cheeselike aromas, has nonetheless shown signs of improvement, as the rising number of its prizewinners impressively attests. As in the gray gloom of Page's "forgotten man," Dixie is still belabored by its preposterous politicians, but for every such mephitic mountebank as Heflin and Bilbo, there is now at least a small posse of earnest and intelligent men, free spirits, ready to rise in challenge and give them battle.

What holds for certain aspects of the Southern culture, as is almost axiomatic in educational history, holds also for its education. The cleavage in quality between the South and the rest of the land has become perceptibly narrower. By the middle of the century, for example, nearly all the Southern states had brought the span of their academic years up to the national par, and a few had even surged beyond. Attendance also has shown signs of picking up. As prosperity has descended more voluptuously upon the South, its investment in the educational enterprise has slowly appreciated. Thus, the value of its school property has risen; teachers' wages have become more tolerable; and there are more and better-stocked libraries. The higher learning, as usual, inclined to move more slowly. Most of the private groves are still stuck in the bog of intellectual provincialism, unable, and even unwilling, to challenge regional standards and their own magnolia traditions. Even so, of late there has been some stirring, and in four seats of advanced learning—Vanderbilt, Emory, Tulane, and Duke—there have been momentous doings. All are blessed with money, and three of them have ventured to confide their fortune to presidents of Northern background and experience. To lure the finest talent to their fold, they have fattened the professorial pay check. In this respect, with 200 alien faculty members on its roster, Duke has combed the world. All these institutions have expanded and ameliorated their instruction and services, and all have raised their academic sights. "We in the South," declared Alex Heard, the Savannah-born head of Vanderbilt, "cannot duck behind the thought that if we show up in the rear ranks of national ratings, the ratings measured the wrong things."

None of this is to say that the South has routed all its problems. Integration continues to fever and palsy some of its parts, and until a cure is effected Southern education obviously must suffer. Nor has educational improvement in the South been equal in all the states, even, for that matter, within a single state. On the contrary, there are unhappy disparities, and what is true for, say, North Carolina and Florida is far from true for Alabama and Mississippi. What Southerners need, said Edgar Knight in 1950, then in academic harness at the University of North Carolina, is "to do qualitatively what it has been doing quantitatively for many years and at great odds"—an opinion which, when it was offered, could also have been applied to numerous other spots in this fair and far-flung land. What the South needs especially, Knight went on, is a far more vigorous concern for knowledge. More than any other part of the republic, the South needs to put its best brains to work in a scientific examination of its own peculiar problems. To this end it needs to give encouragement and financial support to its scholars and scientists more than ever before. If signs count for anything, this is coming to pass. Federal aid and the Age of Grants are paving the way.

13
THE DEVELOPMENT
OF EDUCATIONAL THEORY

When education was a relatively light concern, there was obviously no need for an elaborate pedagogy. The task of the colonial schoolmaster may not have been easy, but the purpose behind it was fairly simple. To curb the child's self-assertion, to rid him of the old Adam still lurking within him, to pack his memory with facts—in short, to tame the child and make him fit for man and God—such was the essence of the schoolman's burden. With no uniform text to ease his way and without graded instruction, which had not yet been revealed or invented, the master taught his underlings one by one, assigning to each his lesson, and hearing it once it had been dutifully engraved on the slabs of his recollection. Although reformers had risen time and again to bemoan the schoolman's stale and tortured ways, and particularly the stress he put upon loading the brain with facts, often occult and inutile, the teaching brethren were dead to any understanding. Through the eighteenth century, and for much of the nineteenth, rote remained the birchman's establshed rite.

Nevertheless, in the wings offstage a new voice was waiting to be heard. It came with lyrical passion in the utterance of Jean-Jacques Rousseau. At war with a civilization he deemed an artificiality and a curse to human happiness, Rousseau proposed to guide man back to nature. The picture of the natural man, the so-called "noble savage," he drew for us in 1760 in *La Nouvelle Héloïse,* a lush and palpitating tale of more than a thousand pages. The natural society and its governance he delineated two years later in *The Social Contract,* and in the same year in *Emile* he set down his views of a natural education. No other pedagogic treatise has ever caused so much rumpus, and none has ever been more controverted. The reigning literary referees lauded and denounced it. The English greeted it with cheers and twice rendered it into their language, a compliment they had never before vouchsafed a Frenchman. In Paris, meanwhile, and in Geneva, the common executioner purged *Emile* in a pillar of fire and right-thinkers everywhere called for Rousseau's arrest. No writer surely could ask for more. Drummed out of circulation, but briskly bootlegged, *Emile* fetched readers by the herd, a testimonial not always as much to a book's worth as to its bouquet of illicit fruit. Rousseau, as some insist, may have failed to be great, but if he did, then he failed with genius.

In *Emile,* as in all his serious writings, Rousseau extolled what he believed was the simplicity and goodness of nature. Education, he insisted, must listen to the voice of nature, and its heart must be the child himself. "Begin," he bade the teacher, "by studying your pupils thoroughly, for it is very certain you do not know them." Books he dismissed with a sweep of the hand. "I hate books," he growled. "They merely teach us to talk about what we do not know." Instead of books, Rousseau called for a learning by experience, for healthy bodily activity, for sense and muscle training, and for the study of things by observation. "Our first teachers," he declared, "are our feet, our hands, and our eyes. . . ."

It was Rousseau's conviction that nothing—not even religion—should be taught a child until he is able to understand it—a doctrine which, cloaked psychologically, is currently known as "readiness" and which is still of good account. The stress on rote, then next to the rattan the most indispensable instrument in the teacher's kit, Rousseau knocked off the board. Contrary to the declarations of learned theologians, whether of Romish or Protestant persuasion, Rousseau avowed that at birth the child is good; that his personality is a thing of dignity demanding deference and understanding; and that his natural proclivities, his urge, for example, to clown and cavort, to wave his arms and swing his legs, and to grate his larynx with shouts and yowls, as well as his love of play and his almost feline curiosity—in short, his native drive to function freely—all this should be put to use in education. Needless to say, Rousseau's views were too radical and too extravagant to be bearable to men of common dust. But the sough of his word music bemused men everywhere, causing some of them not only to ponder his startling evangel but sometimes even to seek to put the best of it into practice. "Though my own notions may be erroneous," confided Rousseau, "I shall not have lost my time, if I inspire better ones in others." And such precisely was his effect.

2   One of the first to catch the radiance of Rousseau, and the first to sprinkle his own sparkle over America, was a Swiss, Johann Heinrich Pestalozzi. Though he confessed that much of *Emile* is bizarre and at times even nonsensical, its central theme, nevertheless, excited his wonder. Education, he nodded approvingly, should never turn its back to nature. It should, he went on, develop all the child's native powers and capacities naturally and freely, and it should include the hands and heart as well as the mind. Children, Pestalozzi insisted, have a nature all their own, and for grown-ups to ignore and misunderstand it is folly, full of waste and even peril. The young, he seconded Rousseau, have rights and a dignity which demand respect; but unlike the advocate of nature, Pestalozzi sought to give balance to his program by insisting that education's ultimate end must be social progress. Indeed, Pestalozzi's first brush with education was as a teacher of the poor and bedraggled whom he had taken to his fireside—beggars, as he said, whom he wanted to teach to live like men.

Pestalozzi's efforts to penetrate the nature of his fledglings and to devise appropriate ways to tutor them brought him to the frontiers of modern psychology, though he lumbered over the cowpath of trial and error with nary a scientific signpost to guide him. Disdaining the universal stress on memory—"empty chattering of mere words" he called it—Pestalozzi courted his learners with an appeal to the senses. In them rather than in books he discerned the reservoir of all our knowledge. Resorting to the spoken rather than to the written word, he conceived what he called the *object lesson,* which by the use of things instead of books about things besought the child to move step by step from what was visible and touchable, and sometimes hearable and smellable, to generalizations which lay, at first encounter, impalpably beyond. Thus learning swerved from its timeworn stress on the culling and hoarding of facts for their own lifeless sake in the new direction of their actual use and, it was hoped, their understanding.

Enchanted by visions though he was, Pestalozzi soon realized that a method, whatever its surpassing quality, was no better than a teacher's ability to put it into effective use. For this reason he forged a program of teacher training, a practice which, though not novel, was then still something of an oddity. So successful was Pestalozzi in this venture that presently its marvel was being talked about by discerning men and women the world over. So dazzling, in truth, had become the repute of the humble Johann Heinrich that in 1808 the kingdom of Prussia, then in the throes of treating itself to the most up-to-date education to be found in Christendom, dispatched seventeen of its most talented teachers to Switzerland, staking them to their keep and tuition for three years so that they might perfect themselves in the new methods and, while they were about it, warm their hearts with the ideals of this extraordinary Swiss.

In America, Pestalozzian views also aroused interest, but their materialization in the schoolroom was slow. The first breezes of what in afteryears was to become the Pestalozzian movement brushed America in 1805, when William McLure composed a piece on some of the more startling features of the new pedagogy. A year later Joseph Neef, a soldier once in the service of Napoleon and later, for the better one hopes, a teacher in one of Pestalozzi's schools, translated himself to the United States. For a time Neef schoolmastered in Philadelphia and in the Middle West, with occasional flings at writing. Though his influence, on the whole, was of no consequence, his books on educational theory and practice—to wit, his *Sketch of a Plan and Method of Education,* which he offered the world in 1808, and his *Method of Instructing Children,* which he volunteered some five years later —have been honored by memorists as the first of such treatises in English to be published in America. Almost a score of years after Neef's landing in the New World the historian George Bancroft, fresh from his academic triumphs at Göttingen, opened an academy at Northampton, Massachusetts. Despite its confined objectives, the school grounded its work on Pestalozzian postulates—in fact, it even let it be gently heard that it aspired in some measure to give aid to the advancement of social progress. Meanwhile, in 1821, Pestalozzian pedagogy was given a further boost with the appearance of Warren Colburn's *First Lessons of Arithmetic on the Plan of Pestalozzi,* a text, which, as mentioned earlier, was to achieve a smashing success, both

financial and pedagogic. Still another stimulus for the newer methods derived from the campaign for the common schools and especially from the
vastly discussed writings of its leading heralds, Messrs. Stowe, Barnard, and
Mann. The commonwealth of Massachusetts, in fact, showed its appreciation
by hiring a Pestalozzian, Arnold Henry Guyot by name, a Swiss-American
by blood and a well-regarded geographer in his professional endeavor. All
in all, though, as a movement Pestalozzianism made no great splash until
after Appomattox.

When the new education at length bestrode the American stage, it attained a grand success, and it maintained itself in favor for at least twenty
years running. The man who directed it and who was responsible in no
small degree for its fine showing was Edward Austin Sheldon, at thirty the
school superintendent at Oswego, New York, and the first of a long line to
serve it. Like Pestalozzi, Sheldon had introduced himself to teaching by taking the wretched and lowly under his wing, and again, like Pestalozzi, he
believed education to be the perfect analgesic for all our social aches and
pains, the indispensable prerequisite for human progress. In 1858, while
summering in Canada, Sheldon chanced into a museum, where he caught
his first glimpse of Pestalozzian materials. Though these happened to be
of English origin, and a poor second to the genuine original, Sheldon took
to them, and he resolved then and there to introduce them in the Oswego
schools. To this end the necessary materials were imported, a training class
for teachers was inaugurated, and an expert was transported from England
to give them light and counsel. At the same time the course of study was
altered with a shift from the conventional stress on the piling up of facts
to the observation of things. In 1861 the reform received something of an
accolade when the city fathers founded a normal school to train their future
Pestalozzis.

There was of course no lack of critical growling. Sheldon, some asserted, was a mere pothunter; others, more contemptuous, set him down as
a gaseous fellow, a man given to rainbow visions who let fancy get the
upper hand. Whatever the man may have been, the fact remains that the
Oswego plan was presently being lauded by the country's outstanding educators. In 1865 the National Teachers Association—now the NEA—after
some grave searching into the matter gave object teaching its collective
benediction. In the meantime, New York State had taken an interest in the
venture, even helping to sustain it with a gratuity every year of $3,000.
Finally, in 1866, the state's interest bubbled over, and New York made Oswego its second state normal school. Pretty soon, it was joined by a half
dozen more, all up and stirring, and all dedicated to the advanced thinking
of Oswego.

For a generation or so Oswego radiated its light over American teacher
training, and with it the essence of the Pestalozzian revelation. Visitors
swarmed to Sheldon's schools from all directions, even from foreign parts,

to stare at their wonders, while students thronged to them for training and improvement. The demand for Oswego graduates was seemingly insatiable, and presently they found themselves installed behind some of the finest desks in the land as teachers, principals, superintendents, and even presidents of some of the leading seminaries of pedagogy. Coming at a time when the normal school stood on the brink of expansion, the Oswego movement started a fashion which was not to spend itself for almost a quarter of a century.

In its approach to learning and teaching, Oswego was something utterly new in America. Leaning heavily on the senses, it put its store in observation. The use of objects became its hallmark, the spoken word subordinating the textbook, while memorizing was supposedly stripped to its barest minimum. All this called for a teaching skill which at the time was almost beyond credulity, requiring as it did not only a more piercing and intimate understanding of what a teacher was trying to teach, but also a resourcefulness in planning a lesson and, through deft and illuminating direction, in guiding it safely to its hoped-for destination. All this gave extra weight to the need for better teaching.

Inevitably the new pedagogy bore on what youngsters studied. Now that Junior was expected to observe actual things, his ability to communicate what his senses had captured became of capital importance. In consequence, the stress on correct and effective utterance mounted, and out of this there eventually issued a deliberate and systematic attempt to teach the proper use of the spoken word. Not only did the confidence placed in observation result in oral language instruction, but with a hand from the perceptive William Torrey Harris, then superintending at St. Louis, it also brought about the modest beginning of the pursuit of knowledge in elementary science.

Of Pestalozzi's legionary disciples, none rose higher in his own right than Phillip Emmuanuel von Fellenberg. No less than his idol, old Johann himself, Fellenberg burned to improve the world, and especially those whom the fates had done a disservice. To this high end Fellenberg devoted much of his plentiful fortune by running a school—the Institute—on his estate, located at Hofwyl, a geographic flyspeck in the Swiss republic. It addressed itself primarily to the poor, offering them instruction in the three Rs besides a simple farm and vocational training. In the interest of what the students of society refer to as "human relations," Fellenberg also accommodated the offspring of the well-to-do. They too were made to work with shovel and hayfork, but, unlike their lesser comrades, they abstained from cart making, blacksmithing, leather training, and suchlike utilitarian endeavor. Instead they were made to suffer the hard labors of a classical education.

For all this idealism, Fellenberg was an astute administrator with a sharp head for business practice. He ran his school from 1804 to 1844, and during his regime it enjoyed a rewarding prosperity. Twenty-five years after its inception, the Institute reached over some 600 acres of billowy country, checkered trimly with luxuriant fields of grain and sprawling pastureland and set off with a judicious dash of woodland. It boasted as fine a school for tomorrow's farmers as your eyes could find, an up-to-date seminary for teachers, particularly those who planned someday to confront pupils in a country school, which is to say the bulk of them. In addition the Institute enhanced its pedagogic service with a printing plant, a tailoring studio, another to advance the art and science of blacksmithing, and yet several more.

Taking one thing with another, Fellenberg's work gathered a high and deserved respect, and pretty soon its chief promoter found himself the object of far-flung public adulation. To Hofwyl people streamed from near and far to eye its practice at close range and to report thereon when they got back to their native haunts in an ever-rising mountain of print and paper. The Institute bred the usual flattery of imitation, not only in the Old World, but in the young one over here as well. But the coming of the mill and the machine dissipated its strength in the republic, and so did the opening of the vast stretches of fertile farmland beyond the Mississippi. Later, after they had long since been taken for dead, the main ideas behind the Fellenberg movement stole from their crypt. With its hand-labor features—now as useless as the vermiform appendix—plucked out, they were at the bottom of the call for an advanced and sophisticated instruction in the agricultural and mechanic arts, which in the passing years burst into bloom in the so-called "A&M colleges," which, of course, are still in flourishing activity, and one of the prized possessions of the American people.

Pestalozzi's fame will stand, no doubt, as long as the Alps themselves. He piloted education in a new direction, and he gave it a lift it sorely needed. But his teachings were hampered by an inadequate and often fatuous psychology, and they lacked a scientific underpinning. Like many another innovator, Pestalozzi suffered at the hands of his would-be interpreters. Despite his insistence, for example, that education should at all times be attuned to the child's nature, the procedures imported from England had degenerated into a dull and hollow formalism. "What," for example, an English Pestalozzian wanted to know, "is an oyster?" "It is," the child's answer came back, "an animal, opaque, marine, natural. . . . The outside is rough, scaly or laminated, irregular. . . . The mollusk is soft, eatable, nutritious, cold, smooth, lubricious." Such cant, unluckily, Oswego had failed to eliminate. In truth, as more and more years took off, the object method became, like its forerunners, just another way of cozening children to assemble, classify, and commit to memory a massive host of facts.

Pestalozzianism reached its summit in America in the late sixties and seventies; after that it slid downhill, and by the eighties it was out of date. Its passing was brought about not by its general assumptions, many of which we still cherish and employ, but rather by its ingenuousness and exaggerations. What finally brought it to rout was the work and thought of another schoolman, a professor and a German, Johann Friedrich Herbart.

3 Herbart was not, like Pestalozzi, moved by a passion to lift the lowly. Nor did he, like Rousseau, pant for the best of all possible worlds. Instead, Herbart took God's tortured earth pretty much as it was and, in his rational way, sought to make it understandable and, if possible, somewhat more tolerable. Unlike his two predecessors, he was almost free of sentimentality—by contrast, indeed, he was hardheaded, a diligent and dutiful man of learning who confined himself for most of his threescore years to his searchings in the academic cloister. In putting education under his prying glass, he probed far more deeply and more penetratingly than Pestalozzi. While the latter arrived at his findings through hand-to-hand encounters on the actual scene of learning, the former relied a great deal more on a calculated intellectual dissection of the problems lurking therein. Where Pestalozzi wed his thinking to his wishing, Herbart stalked his quarry with the chill discrimination of the clinician. As a result, the German professor was able to put education on a surer footing than his less dowered forerunner.

Like most pedagogic thinkers before and after him, Herbart laid a great weight on the moral purpose of education. But the postulates which bottom right and wrong, he declared, emanate from the society they are supposed to keep in peace and happiness. Consequently, education's purpose is to condition the child in the morality of the social order of which he is a part. Not knowledge or even the improvement of the mind, but the molding of a good and upright man should be education's primary aim. "The term *virtue*," Herbart declared, "expresses the whole purpose of education." To apprehend what underlies good and evil, Herbart took a close look at man's interests and activities. The former, which—to no one's surprise—he found to be many and varied, had their roots in man himself, his environs, and his relations with others. The latter resulted largely from the demands forced upon him by the society in which he lived and functioned. Through the object lesson Pestalozzi had brought the child to the world of things, and through the spoken word he had endeavored to provide for the child's dealing with others. To these Herbart added a third, namely, the establishment of a fair acquaintance with the cultural legacy and especially with the subjects of literature and history. But the great purpose to be achieved thereby was not to set the learner ablazing for the loveliness of letters or the recollection of some great and irretrievable bygone event, but rather to elevate and fortify his virtue.

Herbart extended the frail and uncertain journey Pestalozzi had undertaken into the front yard of educational psychology, formulating as he went along a number of important theorems—notably his doctrines of interest and apperception—and weaving them ultimately into a larger cloth, his method of teaching, the so-called "Formal Steps."

Herbart heartily endorsed the proposition put forth from time to time by educational reformers that a child's learning is most effectively started when it is set into flame with the spark of interest. In his typically methodic manner, however, the professor put his scalpel on interest in order to figure out precisely what it is. After some careful examination, he was able to put his finger on two varieties: the spontaneous, free and easy sort, which a child generates without any external stimulation, and the fabricated sort, which is conjured up by his teacher to make him want to learn. The view, set in motion as long ago as the fall of man, that in order to be of any lasting value learning must be burdensome and even distasteful did not go very well with Herbart. Not only did he regard interest as indispensable to the launching of the learning process, but he also believed that in the event of its absence, it behooved the teacher to resort to every trick in the schoolman's repertoire—a view which is, of course, currently well regarded.

Pestalozzi, as will be recalled, made much ado about going from the known to the unknown, as did Rousseau before him, and several others before Rousseau. Herbart entertained the same conviction, but, as usual, he subjected it to a sharp critical analysis. In consequence, he overhauled and enhanced its meaning. Dressed up psychologically, it appeared in a new and more sophisticated guise under the name of *apperception*.

Interest and apperception became the groundwork whereon Herbart erected his teaching method. Denominated the Formal Steps, they made their advent as a quartet, namely, clearness, association, system, and method, but in the hands of Herbart's successors, the four became five:

Preparation Essentially an application of the doctrines of interest and apperception, this undertook, like a virtuoso of public speaking, to put the learner into an attentive and receptive cast of mind. The lesson's purpose was explained, and such previous knowledge as might help to throw light upon it was brought to bear.

Presentation The new material was presented, analyzed, and clarified.

Association The new material was compared with the old and familiar, important likenesses and differences being noted.

Generalization The facts noted in the foregoing were given formulation in a general statement, principle, or rule.

Application True to the time-honored dictum that nothing is ever learned until it can readily be put to use, the learner's grasp of the generalization was put to the test of appropriate problems and exercises.

Like Pestalozzi's object lesson, the Formal Steps came into pedagogic favor not only in their native land but beyond its frontiers as well. During the nineteenth century's last quarter, the steps were actually in high fashion, and no up-to-date master could afford to ignore them; thereafter, however, under the impact of a more advanced psychology and sociology they began to lose face.

In addition to the aforementioned theories, Herbart came forth with several more. Among educators, for instance, he was the first to come up with the thought that subjects should not be taught as insulated entities, each separate and distinct from the others, like so many independent organs detached from the body of human knowledge to which they belong and which in one way or another they keep alive. This business of association Herbart called *correlation*, which after all these years is still its name. Although the professor merely hinted at such a possibility, his followers laid heavy hands upon it. Not only did they alter its name to *concentration*, but they also tried to apply it at all times and in all directions, and in massive and overpowering doses. The effect, needless to say, was excessive, often strained, and sometimes not a little comic.

Herbart devoted most of his life to a pertinacious study of education. Relying mainly on experience and reason, his method of attack was essentially that of the philosopher. Yet it was Herbart who suggested that a science of education is possible, and it was he who made education a field for university study—a feat which, when it was consummated in Germany, was looked upon by academicians as something of a wonder, some said for good, but many more said for ill. True to the age-old professorial custom, Herbart delivered himself of a high pile of books, as heavy in their gross avoirdupois as they were in erudition. But he also ran a graduate seminar, and in connection with his pursuit of educational theory and its application in practice, he conducted a model and demonstration school where he and his associates tested and overhauled their doctrines and where they observed and criticized the teaching of their apprentices.

Herbart's vogue began in Europe in the middle sixties of the nineteenth century, a score of years or so after its author's death. Like Pestalozzianism before it, it presently came to America. It was brought in by Americans who, having caught glimpses of it abroad, came back agog for its propositions. Through their unflagging zeal, and especially through the writings of the McMurry brothers, Charles and Frank, and Charles De Garmo, its high priest at Cornell, the Herbartian gospel gained an ever-growing following, and in 1892 the National Herbart Society was formed. Founded to study the Herbartian theories, the association carried on with a fine success for about a decade, when, expanding its purpose, it cast its Herbartian label to the wind and became the National Society for the Scientific Study of Education.

Once under way the Herbartian movement progressed swiftly. Like Pestalozzianism a generation earlier, it too overran the American normal school, and where only yesterday the master pedagogues had hymned sense perception, oral language, and the object lesson, they now sang glorias to interest, apperception, and the Formal Steps. Today the Herbartian syllogisms lie in the limbo of stale and outworn ideas. But when the flush of youth caressed their cheeks, they threw fresh light on the nature of learning and teaching, and though they lacked the benefit of scientific confirmation, they were for their time the best to be had and in the advancement of pedagogy not a little useful. What undid Herbartianism was not only the fatal hand of time but also the refinement of the technique of educational research. In this sense Herbart might well be thought of as an assassin of some of his pet teachings, for after all was it not Herbart who had declared that the study of education could someday be made scientific?

There are those who contend that Herbartianism is abandoned, a relic of the past. Perhaps they are right, but the facts appear against them. Who but cynics would scoff at moral character as an end in education? Who but loons would undertake to teach the young without the powerful charm of interest? Even correlation remains, and so do the Formal Steps, if not in the original, then at least as an echo, and sometimes even as an echo of an echo. Indeed, as late as 1926, when Professor Henry Morrison of Chicago uncovered his Morrison Plan, it fell, like the Herbartian formula, into five parts, in illustration, (1) exploration, (2) presentation, (3) assimilation, (4) organization, and (5) recitation. This is not saying, even in a remote degree, that present-day promoters of the educational art and science are Herbartians. It is merely suggesting that at the bottom of Herbart's doctrine there was not a little that was of intrinsic soundness and that given refinement and modification, it has filtered into current pedagogic usage.

It is only fair to add that even when its light was white and bright, Herbartianism was not without its gray, unseemly spots. Underlying the work and thought of its partisans was the purpose of conserving the cultural heritage, a lofty motive without a doubt, but one which in Herbartian hands was overborne with a heavy intellectual stress. The noble and poignant tones which inspirit great literary art escaped them. All too often under their direction the study of literature absorbed the student in bagging and storing names and dates, recognizing rhetorical flora, and impaling them, neatly labeled, in the pages of his memory book. Did Herbartians overplay the importance of the mind? Then they underplayed the importance of the feelings and the hands. The needs and problems which nag and gnaw us throughout our days on earth eluded them completely. Though they elaborated at length on man's many-sided interests, they passed by his many-sided personality without so much as even a nod of recognition. They did not, like Pestalozzi and his magnificent disciple, von Fellenberg, exert themselves to improve the multitudes by helping them vocationally. Nor did they, like Rousseau, catch a glimpse of the inner man, of that complex web of nonrational urges which tug and shove—at times overpoweringly—within us all.

4   To direct our attention to this aspect of education became the lot of Friedrich Wilhelm August Froebel. Rebuffed and repressed as a child,

Froebel sought solace in the byways of his inner being, growing into young manhood a shy and sensitive youth. The tranquility of spirit for which he longed he found in introspection, in philosophy, and in a deeply personal religion. For years he was without vocational mooring, drifting from one job to another, never quite content and yet never knowing what he wanted. Then, in 1805, fortune's hazard put him in the German schoolmaster's long-tailed frock in a small Pestalozzian school in Frankfort on the Main, and now his search was done. For in teaching, Froebel had stumbled into his native element.

The serenity and happiness he found in teaching animated his pedagogic aspiration, and in 1808 we see him tracking to Switzerland to learn and teach under Pestalozzi. For two years Froebel drank in the master's wisdom, perfecting himself in the art of his methods, but sneaking off even then into his own pedagogic dreamland. What he discerned therein was a new school, peopled by children too young and too small for the rigors of the regular bench. There he envisioned a place where children might flourish without tears, amid the warmth of sympathy and understanding, without the drudgery of drill and homework, but enlivened with song and play. Such was the first vista of the kindergarten.

On his return to Germany, Froebel attended sessions at Göttingen and Berlin, whereupon a sardonic fate thrust this shy and gentle man into a soldier's uniform to help rid the fatherland of Napoleon. At length, in 1816, with the Corsican on an enforced and permanent sabbatical, Froebel was able to open a small school, which he proceeded to run in the Pestalozzian vein, but with play and music as added features. The school was pressed hard from the start, though somehow it managed to hold on for over a decade. It was during this period, however, that Froebel's thinking crystallized and he set down his theories in *The Education of Man*, or, in his own tongue, *Die Menschenerziehung*, the only book on education he ever wrote.

It was Froebel's conviction that "all education was as yet without a proper initial foundation" and that "until the education of the nursery was reformed nothing worthy and solid could be obtained." To help put these ideas into practice he urged the special training of "gifted and competent mothers"—a fantastic idea, as anybody can see, in an age when Germany's intellectual halls, from the lowest to the highest, were manned almost 100 percent by the strong and superior sex.

In 1837 Froebel returned to the green-robed hill of his beloved Thuringia. Here, in Blankenburg, he opened a school for the very young and gave it the flabbergasting name of *Kleinkinderbeschäftingungsanstalt;* but after some sober second thoughts, he amended this to "kindergarten," a word which is known today the world around and which bids fair to endure to the end of this whirling ball itself. The kindergarten was conceived as the child's own world. Here he was to "develop in harmony, peace and joy within himself, and with those around him." It was to be a world where he could romp and frolic in concert with his mates, a rich and gaudy wonderland of activity, of song and story, of clay and sandpile, of color, paste, and scissors. To make this dream come true Froebel and his colleagues devised special games and songs for their tads and tots besides various activities to satisfy their hunger to be up and doing. Despite all his romantic bubbling, Froebel could not avoid the academician's inclination to label and classify everything in sight. Thus, activities were not just activities, but "gifts" and "occupations." The former, Froebel went to great length to let the world know, were unchangeable in form and substance, say, cubes, spheres, and cylinders, and they entertained some symbolic meaning. The latter were materials which underwent alteration as they were used, for example, such everyday things as clay, cardboard, sand, and the like. But the center of all interest was the story. Narrated by the teacher, it permeated all activity. It made itself felt in the child's language, his song, and his play, and it found its way into the things he made. Meanwhile, Froebel let his invention take flight in the tonal art in one of his most charming creations, his *Mutter- und Koselieder*, which made its bow in 1843 and which some years following was put into English as *Mother and Play Songs*.

A man of deep religious feeling, Froebel sensed the mysterious presence of God in all growing things. Education's great purpose, hence, was not to cage the personality which lies latent in every child but to set it free. So conceived, education puts its major stress on the unfoldment of the native personality, and the kindergarten, as its name suggests, becomes the garden where it is made to grow and flourish. Such growth contended Froebel, must be self-development, not willy-nilly to be sure, but lovingly watched and tended, and yet self-development for all that. Holding the mirror up to nature, the kindergarten takes the child as he is, a creature brimming with urges to be up and doing. "To learn a thing in life by doing," declared Froebel, "is more developing, cultivating, and strengthening than through the verbal communication of ideas." Hence the kindergarten's luxuriant provision of self-activity. Here Froebel ran far beyond his precursors, and not a few of his successors, for among schoolmen he was the first to appreciate the enormous educational value of the child's own world. There is in Froebel a recurrent undertone of Rousseau, especially in his veneration of nature and the development of a free personality. At the same time, unlike the Genevan, Froebel was careful to put a brake on any untoward individualism. Man should live in peace and harmony not only within himself but also with those about him —and this, Froebel urged, should go on "in all the various circumstances of life, in the family and school, in domestic and public life." Hence, not only was the kindergarten dedicated to self-development and self-realization, but it was also a community for social interaction.

Much of Froebel's thinking took place on a plane of airy mysticism.

Consequently, his writings, and even some of his kindergarten practices, are shrouded in an inscrutable and at times far-fetched symbolism. Today Froebel's mysticism remains but a memory, and if his kindergarten has triumphed over the havoc of time, it is not because of any esoteric pipe dreams of its creator, but rather because of the soundness of its psychological and sociological foundation.

Froebel's days came to an end somewhat as they had begun, on a melancholy note. A child in life's everyday affairs, he saw his kindergarten under the constant menace of debt. Time, it is true, had brought it friends, but those who bore it malice were far more numerous. Worse yet, Froebel's free spirit had marked him for the suspicions of the Prussian bureaucracy, then in one of its black reactionary moods, and in 1851, unable and unwilling to distinguish between Froebel and an active anti-Hohenzollern nephew, the authorities banned the kindergarten on the grounds that it was socialistic and "calculated to train the youth of the country to atheism." Despite vigorous efforts to have the ban rescinded, it remained in effect for almost a decade, by which time Froebel had left the earth.

Had he been able to hang on just a few more years, Froebel would have seen kindergartens rise in fame beyond his native Thuringia. Nowhere, however, were they more hospitably received than in the United States. Brought here by Germans who turned their backs to the fatherland after the collapse of their liberal hopes in the disastrous Revolution of 1848, the kindergarten got its start in the Middle West. There, in 1855, in Watertown, Wisconsin, Mrs. Carl Schurz, a former student of Froebel, founded what may have been the first kindergarten in the United States. It was a modest, private venture, and it was run in German. Yet through it and others like it, and through Henry Barnard and other persuaders, the Froebel propositions gained support. In 1860, the first English-speaking kindergarten, a private one, was opened by Elizabeth Peabody in Boston, and some eight years following, a special training school for kindergarten ma'ams was established in the same city. Finally, in 1873, Froebel's invention made its way into the public service when St. Louis opened what has commonly been acclaimed as the first tax-supported kindergarten in America. From then on, except for transient lapses, as when patriots disowned it as a German menace during the First World War or as a waste of public money during the Great Depression, the kindergarten has captured the American heart, so that today about half the republic's five-year-olds rejoice in its numerous benefits.

As time passed and the kindergarten worked itself into the American educational way, not a few of the ideas which animated it soared into the elementary school. The belief, for example, that the human young are active animals—an indecency for Christian ears when Froebel gave it utterance— is surely no longer the singular possession of the kindergarten. So also the view that play has educational value. And so likewise with creative educa-

tion, self-expression, learning by doing, and several other advanced practices which currently enliven progressive elementary schooling, whether private or public. Time saw them break into the secondary school and even
gain steadily in favor—until, that is, of late, when because of their reputed
overstress on the nonintellectual phases of human behavior, they were indicated as deleterious to the national welfare.

The kindergarten's traffic in such constructive activities as needlecraft,
weaving, and paper folding, along with the use of clay, sand, glue, and
paint, presently inspired an interest in a more ambitious kind of hand training and led in the course of time to a development which Froebel, even in
his most delirious speculations, had not foreseen. The first people to invest
their schools with manual training were the Finns, who, in 1866, under the
counsel and direction of Uno Cygnaeus, a Froebel devotee and one of their
salient educators, managed to get courses in metalwork, wood carving, and
basket making into the schools. From the Finns the movement passed over
to the Swedes, who proceeded to make woodworking a regular part of their
public schooling.

It is not unlikely that the economic promise of such training proffered
to Sweden's little man helped to promote it in the public confidence. More
specifically, though, its advance was the work of Otto Salomon, a schoolman
of some consequence among the Swedes, and eager for the new revelation.
Some of his ideas appear sound enough even in our own day of marvels, as,
in illustration, his insistence that what pupils make should be useful as well
as ornamental and that they should do their own work from start to finish.
But like so many other workers for better worlds, Salomon was also the
author of some extravagant poppycock. It was his contention, to come to
cases, that the schoolboy's confection of hat racks, footstools, rolling pins,
and the like would not only inspirit him with a high regard for the dignity
of labor but somehow also serve to better his virtue. Salomon was convinced
not only that the fabrication of such articles would develop the specific skills
involved in the process itself but also that subsequently these would transfer
to general situations, so that the neatness and exactness and precision a pupil
exercised in making a spitoon would attend him in the general circumstances of his daily life, from, say, his maintenance of a clean and sanitary
person to his choice of surrogates in Congress. Though psychological science has long since discredited such claims, in Salomon's day, and indeed
for many a day to come, the belief in such transferred training was almost
unanimous, and—right or wrong—it helped no little to advance the teaching of the manual skills.

From Scandinavia the manual training movement made its way to
other lands. It appeared in England by midcentury, in France shortly after,
and in Russia and the United States some years after that. What gave it
powerful advertisement in America was an exhibit by the Russian government in 1876 at the Centennial Exhibition, where it showed samples of some

of the work done by its boys in the Imperial Technical School at Moscow. The handiwork caught the eye of the president of the Massachusetts Institute of Technology, John Runkle, who presently permitted himself to bathe it in a hearty encomium. Rather curiously, the presidential eye was not always alert, for at the same centennial show it completely overlooked the very excellent display of Sibley College of Cornell University, which included all sorts of amazing items, from lathes and plates to precision tools, and even a steam engine. Be that as it may, Runkle's authorative approbation of what he had discerned stirred up a lively interest in the manual training movement—so much that pretty soon steps were being taken to give it room in various municipalities throughout the country. The laurel of being first must be hung on St. Louis, where, in 1880, a manual training high school, a private one affiliated with Washington University, was opened. The first manual training high school of the public species was opened for business in the nineties at Baltimore. Presently manual training descended upon the lower learning, and by 1890, some half a hundred of its mansions, mostly along the Atlantic seaboard, were giving it accommodation in one way or another. As the movement gathered more support, it fanned out wider and wider, until at length the great day came when, here and there, girls won the right to risk their life and limbs with saws and planes besides scissors and gas stoves.

Today, whatever favor the movement still obtains, it has all but ceased. Not only have the doctors of the psyche exploded its seductive transfer claims, once its partisans' ace of trumps, but even the tools themselves have changed from the simple manual ones of only yesterday to the gigantic mechanical mastadons which now rock and rattle in every farm and factory. Still, though the pristine days of manual training have joined the endless past, the promise it bore has drafted into industrial education and into the arts and crafts, where currently it thrives abundantly.

5 ʹ While America's Pestalozzis and Herbarts were occuping themselves with revamping our educational theory and practice, in other sectors developments of consuming significance were taking shape. They were borne upon, for one, by the growing power and proliferation of the machine and the factory and, for another, by the new and startling pronouncements issuing from the labs of the natural sciences. Up and moving in England and the United States and in certain German states by the 1850s, the two movements dashed ahead prestissimo, picking up in pace and pressure as they moved along into the new century to bring forth the civilization in which we presently delight and tremble.

If, as certain experts hold, education is actually a reflection of the society of which it is a part, then obviously these forces should in some way have put their mark upon the schools. In a word, science and industry had a right to expect some earnest attention from the schoolmen. But the generality, as is common enough, were of a conservative cast, not given to frittering away their time on novelties and convinced beyond any doubt that what counted in the practice of their ancient art lay not in the subject matter under study, but in the mental discipline their pupils could extract therefrom. To the brethren of the chalky finger, the training that schoolboys obtained from their day-by-day combat with the old-time classics was not only sufficient to its end but even tried and perfect, and hence beyond mundane challenge.

To shake the masters and to rouse them to pay professional heed to the events fermenting all about became the work and pleasure of a nonpedagogue, even, indeed, an antipedagogue. Herbert Spencer by name, he was born in 1820 in Derby, England, the offspring of Methodist parents, and he died eighty-three years later, a bald and vibrissaed evolutionist and an agnostic, proud to the end that the knowledge he possessed and cherished he had acquired not because of his formal education but in spite of it. A man of such a frame of mind could hardly be expected to put much stock in the classical tradition, and in 1859 in the *Westminster Review,* in the first of four essays, he asked: "What knowledge is of most worth?" It is, he answered, science. Science it is for self-preservation; science it is for gaining a livelihood; and science it is "for the most perfect production and enjoyment of art in all its forms." For all purposes of discipline—intellectual, moral, and religious—the indispensable key, once again, is science. This, Spencer concluded, "is the verdict on all counts."

A pretentious plea? Without a doubt. But it was also fresh, and it was illuminated by a rich and lucid prose, and hence one marked for attention. Under the Spencerian blowgun the custodians of Latin and Greek for the first time found their complacency disturbed. Not only had Spencer put their incomparable classics on the defensive, but his magnificent manifesto had also brought him a vast and appreciative audience.

Briefly, the advocates of teaching science grounded their argument on two main points. It was their contention that what mattered in education was not so much method and drill, as the classicists so doggedly insisted, but the actual content of what was studied. The ancient tongues, they argued, for all their venerable service in the halls of knowledge, were hopelessly out of step with the modern beat. On the other hand, not only were the sciences in step with the gusty tempo of the current culture, but to be ignorant of them was to be ill prepared for modern living. The Spencerians' second claim centered on the subject of mental training. In brief, it disposed not of the doctrine but of the hoary assertion that in the training of the mind the classics had no rival. Are academic subjects supposed to train the mind? Then the sciences stand ready to do the job—just as well as the senile classics, and, more than likely, even better. Today that dialectic no longer holds water. For through the searchings of scientific psychology, the theory of mind training has fallen into decay, and no educator of any standing, and in his right mind, would publicly subscribe thereto.

But when Spencer proclaimed his defiance, mental training faced no such challenge, and so on that score his argument was unassailable. Though its author was as cocksure as any classicist, and at times as unpleasantly narrow, there was ardor in his words, and he knew how to press his case. What he marshaled into print was a plain and forceful statement of the views of the foremost thinkers of his era, and the discussions which rained down as a result served admirably to clear up the pedagogic clouds. Through his various emissions, the schools were vitally and permanently affected. The installation of a "modern side" in England's tradition-dripping schools is one example of his influence. The rise of science as a respectable school subject is another.

As with Herbart and Pestalozzi and other European educators, Spencer was gravely attended to over here, and the flares he lit on the Atlantic's other side had their flaming counterparts in this country. In the American world of learning, science was, of course, no newcomer. Franklin and Jefferson had been all for it, and so had President Johnson of King's College and President Smith of the College of Philadelphia. Even in colonial times various sciences were on tap in a number of academies and private schools and in a few of the brasher and more enterprising colleges. In the sixties, when the Pestalozzian wave rolled over America, through the use of objects in learning, here and there a rudimentary science had begun to seep into the lower schooling. Early in the following decade, at the urging of William Torrey Harris, science was given a cautious introduction in the St. Louis elementary schools. All in all, however, when Spencer let go his hurricane, the role of science in the cast of school subjects was minor.

The most notable, and by all odds the most articulate, partisan of the Spencer dogma, or at least the essence of it, was Charles William Eliot. A professor of chemistry at Harvard, he had risen to its presidency in 1869, and in the years that followed he proceeded to elevate the oldest of American colleges into an institution of surpassing excellence, respected and esteemed the world around. Naturally, when Eliot cast his vote for Spencer and insisted that the sciences be given a meet and fitting place in the curriculum, he spoke with authority, and though his summons aroused antagonism, as the century faded from the scene the idea had prevailed not only at Harvard Yard but on other campuses as well. Not only did the sciences attain a place of rank among collegiate offerings, but before long they were being accepted as academic currency to meet part of the requirement for college admission. True to the Spencerian spirit, moreover, Eliot sought to loosen the traditional rigidity of college study by the ejection of all required courses and their replacement by the so-called "free elective system," whereby a student studied only what he wanted to. Today, despite democracy, the right of unlimited election is no longer the campus vogue, and even at Harvard it has long since picked up its hat and stick and departed.

Not only cheers, however, fell to Spencer and his clan, but also scoffs —there were, in truth, a good many of the latter. But hosannas or anathemas, the fact remains that Spencer succeeded in putting the limelight on the great gulf which ranged between the old and wearied offerings of the school and the world booming beyond its walls with fresh and stupendous happenings. In modern educational history Spencer may well have been the first to point to what specialists in social pathology call the "cultural lag." As has been remarked, Spencer's brief for the study of science reaped richly, and in this, education—and hence mankind—was the gainer. But if the upshot of it all was for the good, some of the reasoning behind it was far from impeccable. To knock out the classicists, the Spencerians bludgeoned them with their own club. Like the one, the other contended that the mind, if exercised, can be strengthened and that the sharpness and exactitude it displays in dealing with, say, osmosis or the reduction of hyponitrous acid would in the long run transfer to life's more general situations, whether political, social, economic, moral, or religious. This doctrine is known as the *transfer of training*, and as stated a few pages ago, modern psychologists have done it in. The training, moreover, which Spencer favored was primarily cerebral. The majestic spell of art and music and literature which exalts and enraptures the human spirit left him almost unmoved. In a word, what the Spencerians urged was the replacement of a one-sided classical training by an equally one-sided scientific training.

COLLEGE COURSES
AT HOME

EARN
WHILE YOU
LEARN

MEN & WOMEN! STEP UP TO THAT BETTER JOB.

14
THE RISE OF
A NATIVE PEDAGOGY

For most of the nineteenth century, as we have seen, the best in American educational theory was of foreign provenance. Not only were the generality of American schoolmen not much given to examining the inside of things, but they were predominantly absorbed in practical action. In education the Americans' concern involved them in the making of the common school, fetching sufficient financial support from the taxpayer, devising the mechanism for its operation and control, and carrying the system of free and tax-supported benefits into the higher loft of the secondary learning. As for the nature of education, its philosophic bedrock, its aims and principles, and its sociological meaning and implications, together with the inscrutabilities of the psyche involved in the learning and teaching process—all this by comparison appeared remote and estranged from the everyday business of keeping school. When, at length, it began to be realized that a teacher, like any other craftsman worthy of his practice, could profit by training on a body of knowledge and basic skill, the Americans turned their eyes to Europe, first to the Pestalozzian concepts and then to those of the Herbartians.

Meanwhile, the republic had also been undergoing a transformation. The number of its people had gone up and up. Immigration, which had started to increase impressively by the forties, continued to grow even more, and by the eighties the number of aliens coming to the United States amounted to several million a year. The mass of them, however, now hailed from the Slavic and Latin belts rather than from northern and central Europe. Cities all over the land were growing like the fabled bean stalk, both in number and in size, while the number of farms, on the other hand, was diminishing, though their output, rather paradoxically, was actually on the rise. Since Appomattox the nation's industry had boomed prodigiously, and so had its commerce and trade, and hence also its wealth. Nor had there been any lightening of the chip on the national shoulder, with its gospel of Manifest Destiny. In fact, by the end of the century the national spirit erupted into war against the Spaniard, and as a result not only was he driven out of the hemisphere, but by the acquisition of some of his far-flung possessions the republic had festooned itself in the imperial ermine.

In this America, and especially as a result of the expanding democracy following the Civil War, free public education flourished. But soon it ran into snags. The simple fact is that as year took after year, the demand for public schooling had bounded up so swiftly that presently the number of its would-be beneficiaries was far too vast to be accommodated by the teachers and facilities which were available. To minister to its immense juvenile throng the emerging public school put its trust in a uniform and ordered routine. It arranged its stock of learning in graded and classified subjects and taught them by a clocklike schedule, special years being reserved for mastering certain facts and operations. Thus, for all the sapience of Herren Pestalozzi and Herbart, teaching was reduced to loading pupils with knowledge, dosing them stiffly with homework and examinations, and, needless to say, prodding the loafers and flogging the wicked. The learners' attainments, such as they were, were translated into marks, the best of which went not necessarily to those who steamed and chugged the hardest, or even to those who once in a blue moon showed the gleam of genius, but rather to those who from the pits of their remembrance could haul up the biggest assemblage of facts.

Such, in broad strokes, was the state of affairs in the American public learning during the late years of the dying century. Infused though it was with fine and expansive motives, it suffered from the harsh realities of a capricious fortune which made it the prey of its own promise to help and advance mankind. Confronted with colossal numbers of students, it was forced willy-nilly to resign itself, like a well-run nut-and-bolt mill, to standardizing the output of its mass production. It was, of course, education of a drab and dreary sort, but until someone came along to send it packing, it was the rule.

2   Several first-rate men arose to the challenge, but one stands out not only for the luster of his own performance but also because in some of its aspects it foreshadowed principles and practices we still honor and employ today. Francis Wayland Parker was born in New Hampshire in 1837, the descendant of a long line of Protestant parsons. Three years after his arrival—so at least it has been recorded—he introduced himself to learning in the village school. Another three years, and he found himself bound out to a farmer. Between his apprentice labors he attended sessions at the local district school, and before long he was able to work his way through the Good Book and *Pilgrim's Progress*, the substance of his boss's library.

When he was thirteen he turned his back to the cows and chickens and made off, adding to his knowledge as the years went by and, like Froebel, drifting from one job to another, until at the age of sixteen he entered teaching service at a half dollar or so a day as principal, faculty, and janitor of a one-room country school of seventy-five pupils. Again like the kindergartner, he found teaching to his liking, less romantically perhaps, yet sufficiently to keep him at it in one way or another to the end of his days. His efforts to dispense enlightenment were interrupted when he volunteered to assist the Union in the Civil War. A casualty to its carnage, he emerged a civilian in good repair, an officer now as well as a gentleman, and once more in pedagogic livery, first as a principal in his native state and then in a normal school at Dayton, Ohio. In 1872—he now could count thirty-five years besides a retreating hairline—Colonel Parker set out for Germany's founts of higher learning to perfect himself in philosophy. While he was in the Reich he made it a point to observe at firsthand the latest educational developments, many of which had their source in the pioneering of Pestalozzi, Herbart, and Froebel. Some of them apparently seduced his fancy. At all events, on his return to the states, he undertook to put them to trial, beginning in 1875 at Quincy, Massachusetts, where he superintended, and later at Chicago, where in eight years he became head of the Cook County Normal School.

The touch of New England is discernible in Parker. Fevered by an insatiable desire to advance humanity, he assuaged his yearning with Yankee horse sense; democratic to the core, he was a persistent and assertive individualist; and a liberal in religion, he renounced the stern theological dictates of his fathers for the mellower outlook of the nonconformist. Under the spell of Emerson, whom he admired, Parker dreamed resplendently of infinite human betterment and of progress without end. Like Emerson, Parker was something of a transcendentalist, delivering himself every so often of an apothegm which might have done credit to the Concord Plato himself. Yet like William James and the pragmatists of a later day, Parker had a horror of anything which was declared to be fixed or final. "O Lord," he prayed, "preserve thou me from the foregone conclusion."

In what ways did this man seek to improve America's schools? He sought, for one thing, to lift the curtain from the darkness of its spirit, to let in the light of joy, so that the child might flourish freely. In a day when schoolmasters, almost to a man, continued to freight the brain with a mass of facts, often useless and obtuse, Parker stood up, with Froebel, for the child's interest in making things. What counted above everything else, as the colonel saw it, was not the consumption of subject matter, trimly arranged like so many checkers on a board, but the child himself—a palpable echo, of course, of Rousseau. In the child's personality Parker glimpsed the seed of tomorrow's manhood; hence it behooves us to let it function freely in all his work. Does Little Willie itch to draw the sound of a bass drum? Then let him. Does he then proceed to confect a crayoned tangle meaning precisely nothing? No matter. At least it is his own creation and a thousand times more worthwhile than if he had made a copy, however flawless, of a Titian, a Raphael, or even Popeye the Sailor.

Parker, who had picked up a good deal of his own knowledge from hard and direct experience, put a wary caution in the claims made for book learning. "The best taught school in a densely populated city," he let it be known, "can never equal in educative value the life on a good farm, intelligently managed"—a manifesto which may have endeared him to the country's husbandmen but certainly not to the vendors of its books.

Nor should it be a cause for wonder that Parker, who had started to work while his legs were still short and tender, should extol the virtues of hard work. "The entire purpose of education," he announced, "consists of training the child for work, to work systematically, to love work, and to put his brains and heart into work," a pronouncement which, needless to say, has been eyed somewhat skeptically of late, not only by the American young but by their elders as well.

3   It was at Quincy that Parker attained his first celebrity. There he set off his heresies by blowing up the school's conventional formalism—"its old, stiff, and unnatural order." Forcing children to sit as still as wooden Indians, which was common enough at the time in the American cells of learning, was put under prohibition. Instead, there was to be "work with all the whispering and noise compatible with the best results." The colonel concentrated his most blazing fire on the prevalent teaching methods, replacing them, when he got the chance, with some of the practices he had run into in Europe. Geography, for instance, he made the "study of the earth as the home of man." To this end Parker followed the example of Rousseau and Pestalozzi, by which a child's grasping of his surrounding neighborhood became more important than his trying to know by heart the precise whereabouts of Anatolia, the trade balance of Coo, or the ins and outs of the Ob as it makes its move to the sea. Although Parker conceded that in the study of numbers "certain facts should be absolutely automatic," he was at pains to hold these to a minimum, putting his main stress instead on the arithmetic of everyday use. What held for figures held also for the mother tongue. Instead of spouting glibly about the various cases of nouns, the strange and sinister moods of verbs, and similar grammatical tidbits, the young were put upon the national idiom by reporting on what they had seen, heard, and felt—and maybe even smelled. At Quincy, Parker brought in the arts and crafts; he introduced nature study to the laboratory; and he bolstered and expanded it with treks in field and forest, to bogs and waterbanks, to observe nature at close range and to put down on paper with ink and paint what the senses had perceived and captured.

Behind it all beckoned the shadow of the gentle Froebel, for never before in America had the schoolchild been bathed in such warm and tender solicitude. At Quincy he flourished naturally, true to his being, busy and creative, using his head, of course, but also his arms and legs; his spirit was free to rise, and yet he learned to be mindful of the meaning of work and his responsibilities to his fellows. But let it not be forgotten that Parker made his bow to the Herbartians too, with his adoption of their principle of correlation, by which subjects were taught in terms of their interrelationship around a common core.

There were, of course, the familiar flare-ups of horror and indignation. Parker and his associates found themselves cried down as quacks and dunderheads; their methods, a public scandal, were said to be calculated to make the young even more stupid than their elders. At length, in 1879, the controversy reached its crux when right-thinkers summoned the Massachusetts Board of Education to deal with the colonel and his saboteurs by putting the Quincy pupils to the test of a special examination. But to the shock and dismay of Parker's would-be axmen, the examiners could find no tort. Not only did the Quincy young read, write, spell, and figure with alacrity and confidence, but they also handled themselves superbly in history and geography; and what is more, save in mental arithmetic, they performed in a manner which was superior to that of the rest of the Bay State pupils. Though Parker was rubbed in the muck, he was also the object of approval —a fact which the malice borne him could not efface. Like Oswego in its Pestalozzian glory, Quincy attracted folk from all around. Indeed, in the years just before and after the board put Parker's recruits under official scrutiny, some thirty thousand visitors, Americans and outlanders, made the round of Quincy's schools. "Under Colonel Parker's new system," reflected the *New York Times* (July 5, 1883), "the schools of Quincy were lifted out of the old rut and they now lead all the other schools of the state."

From Quincy, Parker migrated to Boston, and thence to Chicago, where he continued to reform education and transfix conservatives with horror. At the Cook County Normal School, which he directed for eighteen years, he assembled one of the finest corps of teachers in the land—for that matter in any land. With them he continued to make war on the flyblown practices of the conventional school. Thus, instead of pressing the child into the common mold, Parker called for "quality teaching," by which he meant the performance of men and women who exercised their industry with feeling and imagination, as artists rather than as mere technicians. Did the everyday school deal overwhelmingly in arid subject matter? Then let it look more understandingly at the child himself, his natural appetite for art and music, his urge to shout and caper, his need, in short, to function freely. Not only did Parker set tremendous store by such noncerebral interests, but in the arts and music, in manual training, and in physical culture he made it a point to hire special teachers to stimulate the development of such activities.

Although the colonel borrowed from Europe's great masters, he was no mere aper of other men's ideas. His liberal leanings, and especially his confidence in the democratic process, swept him far beyond the Continentals. When, at the beginning of his labors, his teachers were haunted by misgivings, Parker met them in a weekly conference, where they aired their fears and doubts and in concert sought to straighten out their problems. When Parker's innovations palsied parents with fright, he assembled them in a parent-teacher guild, the first in Chicago and one of the first in the land. By this means he thrashed out his views with confused and often bellicose fathers and mothers, and in the end he converted most of them into energetic supporters. But in his dealings with politicians he was less success-ful. They blocked him at every turn, strangling appropriations, damning his work, and even making a mock of his integrity. And so, when the chance offered itself in 1899 to be rid of such nefarious footlings Parker translated himself to the new and privately endowed Chicago Institute Academic and Pedagogic, an enterprise which almost immediately merged with three other institutions to become the School of Education of the University of Chicago. He headed the new school when it began in 1901, but the year following he was dead.

Meanwhile, in 1901, on Chicago's northern front the Francis W. Parker School had run up its flag. With Flora Cooke, one of Parker's former colleagues on the bridge, and a crew of sixteen men and women, nearly all of whom had trained under the colonel at Cook County Normal, the school was dedicated to carry on in the Parker spirit. So it reached out bravely for more than thirty years, endeavoring, like the man whose name it bore, to bring inspiration, understanding, and dignity to teaching in America.

4   Parker's successor was his friend and colleague John Dewey. He had come to Chicago in 1894 after a decade of teaching college students, first in Michigan, then in Minnesota, and then again in Michigan. A New Englander like Parker, Dewey was born in 1859 in Burlington, Vermont, a rising town of some ten thousand people. His passage through boyhood ran the common course, with the usual engagements in play and school and time off now and then to enjoy the aches and sniffles that descend upon us all. Occasionally young Dewey did odd jobs, and on Sundays he dutifully listened to his pastor. Intellectually, he showed no signs that destiny had appointed him for greatness. When he entered the University of Vermont, he subscribed to no special aspirations—indeed, until he was a junior his record was, like many another, one of diligent indistinction. Then, of a sudden, in a physiology course, a book by Thomas Henry Huxley set him afire. The blunt materialism of Darwin's magnificent contemporary ignited him. He had always been certain, as an earnest Christian, that man's life on earth was shaped by moral will; never, in any event, had the thought assailed him, as the iconoclastic Huxley now asserted, that life's determining forces were unalterably material.

For Dewey, the divide between these views was not only wide and deep but also disturbing to his sleep. During the year following he worked unsparingly, burning the oil far into the night to bridge the chasm. Though the answer dodged him, in the process his scholarship began to dazzle, hoisting him to the pinnacle of his class with the finest grades in philosophy ever recorded. Moreover, as the campus receded farther and farther into memory, the fact became apparent that the young man had adorned himself with the philosopher's regalia.

For a time Dewey served in crossroad schools. But philosophy kept making eyes at him, and when the opportunity came, he repaired to Baltimore to study at the Johns Hopkins University, a new kind of higher research house, and still in infancy. There he put himself under the lead and light of men whose names have since gone into the national gallery of immortals, as witness Charles Peirce and Granville Stanley Hall. But his favorite was George Sylvester Morris, less scintillating to be sure, but nevertheless a man of spacious ideas and a teacher of the first estate. Morris guided his accolyte to the philosophic idealism of Hegel, who endeavored to dispel the distinction between mind and matter by declaring matter to be illusory. The universe and everything in it, from the tadpole to the whale, is based in "spirit," and life is the never-ending upward struggle toward God's Universal Mind. It was an evangel that, for the time being, brought Dewey the reassurance he craved—at all events, the bogey of Huxley had been disposed of.

5 Dewey arrived at Chicago full of hope and Hegelian certainty. Behind him stretched ten years of academic industry. He had given instruction and advice to a herd of students. In keeping with academic fashion he had contributed his weightier intellectual treatises to the gazettes of learning. He had also put forth a book, his first, a volume on psychology, then still a satrap of philosophy. And he had not faltered in his conviction that the ultimate reality is God.

But the Hegelian haven into which Dewey had so hopefully steered a decade back had lost some of its magic power to shield and soothe. For all the tug of the Hegelian postulates, everywhere there was the inescapable countertug of the Middle West. A land brimming with the juices of life—a universe, as William James put it, that was "wide open"—it sizzled and bubbled in political, social, and economic ferment. It was a world full of astounding possibility, of no holds barred, of hoggish buccaneering, where a shrewd and not too squeamish man might grab a quick and easy fortune. But it was also a world which wreaked its implacable havoc. During Dewey's sojourn, Middle Western America skidded into hard times, and for every fat magnifico it hatched, there were legions of life's losers drifting in helplessness and despair. In such a chaos of dog-eat-dog, and especially in Chicago, where things metamorphosed before one's very nose, it is no wonder that a social-minded man like Dewey found it harder and harder to invest his confidence in the soft blue sky of the Hegelian snuggery, wherein reality was not matter, but an absolute and unalterable spirit. As a result, Dewey's intellectual concern now veered toward the social problems which raged and rioted all around. And so, as the earth spun on, his thinking began to lay more and more weight on social reconstruction, and especially on the conflicts generated when the forces of democracy, science, and industry collide.

6   Two years after coming to Chicago, Dewey, his wife, and a few
neighbors opened a small school for their children. True to Dewey's philosophic credo that ideas attain validity only when they are applied successfully in action, the school was to serve as a testing place for philosophic and
educational principles. In actuality the new venture was regarded as a laboratory of the department of philosophy. Its official designation, in fact, was
the Laboratory School, though in just recognition of its founder's meritorious service, today it is spoken of often enough simply as the Dewey school.
Launched in January, 1896, with Dewey and his helpmate as pilots, the new
school started with sixteen pupils and a couple of teachers, and though the
waters it traversed during the next few years were often rough and heavy,
nevertheless, six years later, its journey almost at an end, the Laboratory
School listed 140 girls and boys, a staff of twenty-three instructors, and a
corps of ten assistants, all budding graduate students at the university.

The idea of a school experimenting with children was no novelty in the
nineties. Pestalozzi had toyed with it, and so after him had Froebel, Herbart, and several others. Even so, the idea was still brash enough to make
right-thinkers shudder in mortal fear. The Dewey school was, in truth, quite
unlike the conventional affair, with its lines of benched and muted young
awaiting their master to quizz and drill them. The usual hand-to-hand grap-
ples with the three Rs, the drills in spelling and grammar, and the forced
marches in history and geography were nowhere to be found. Instead, small
gangs of young were busy at various things. Some might be huddled over a
book, a map, or even a stone or a bug, dead or alive and kicking. Others
might be making things with hammer and saw or with paint and brush.
Still others might be engaged in free discussions energetically carried on.
As for the teacher, instead of confronting her charges from atop her podium, she was up and about, her statuelike reserve discarded, lending a
hand here, suggesting there, and hearkening to the lavish jabber of question and comment. No death-house solemnity intruded here. Instead there
were activity and talk, the incessant, gusty chatter which emanates from
children interested in what they are about.

What Dewey sought in the Laboratory School, as he explained, was "to
carry into effect certain principles which Froebel was perhaps the first con-
sciously to set forth." To this purpose it undertook "to train children in
cooperative and mutually useful living." Like a few of his forerunners,
Dewey had observed that the roots of all educational activity reach deep
down into the instinctive and impulsive doings of the child. Outside the
cubicles of learning, he was being taught by pretty nearly everything he
tackled. And he learned not because he was put upon to do so but because
his interest goaded him. Especially was this the case when he played. Did
he need to choose up sides? Then he must needs remember the necessary
incantation. Did he yearn to fly a kite? Or sail a boat? Or maybe take a
walk on stilts? Then he gave himself tirelessly to the task of overcoming the

essential and underlying mysteries. As in life, Dewey believed, so it should be in school. What the child learned should take its cue from the hearth and the community. In a word, the school should reproduce in miniature the "typical conditions of social life."

Under the circumstances, the Herbartian prescription, with its stress on the formal imposition of subject matter "from above and from the outside," the darling then of every thoroughgoing schoolmaster, got only frosty glances from Dewey and his coworkers. He called instead for what in the argot of pedagogy currently passes as the "activity program" and which in its full florescence comprises every aspect of the child's individual and collective living, from play and recreation, construction and creation, to contacts with nature's greenery, the birds and beasts, and the man-made culture revolving all about him. All subjects—even the old and patinaed Rs—were to be derived from the child's activities rather than from a logically prearranged system of academic hand-me-downs preserved in schoolbooks. Thus transformed, said Dewey, the school is inspired afresh. Now the "child's habitat," where he learns by "directed living," it no longer halters and hobbles him with lessons "having an abstract and remote reference to some possible living to be done in the future." Education, as the schoolman's parlance presently had it, is not preparation for life; it is life itself.

Although the Chicago school urged letting children do what comes naturally, it also urged that the school is principally and essentially a social institution and that an individual's development is a social process. The function of education, as Dewey saw it, is to harmonize individual traits with social ends. The cult of self-expression, so eagerly promoted by certain progressive schools, got no support from Dewey. "Deplorable egotism, cockiness, impertinence, and disregard for others" was his blunt appraisal of the unleashed juvenile individualism.

The Dewey school is surely not singular. Did it cast its censure on an outworn pedagogy, on its veneration of words, on rote and drill and examination? Then so had Colonel Parker, and so had Pestalozzi and Froebel, and even Rousseau, Montaigne, Comenius, and several others of that company. Yet in a certain sense Dewey's school was breaking ground never turned before. The first truly philosophically oriented school to grace this land, it has in this respect remained without a peer or even a rival.

Though the school was designed as a testing station for educational principles, Dewey was actually drilling deeper. What concerned the professor was not the probing of educational theories as such, but rather certain hypotheses of culture, philosophy, and psychology then taking shape in his head. He was seeking, for example, to bring together and reconcile what to the cursory view appeared to be conflicting entities, in illustration, the child and the curriculum, school and society, interest and effort, and the like. Behind these dualities Dewey discerned intellectual and cultural cleavages which had come to the fore as the republic ran full tilt from its simple bucolic fireside economy toward the complex industrial and commercial one we now enjoy. For the school, Dewey was convinced, this cultural transformation bore an immense and inescapable significance. The new approaches to method and curriculum which he was putting under scrutiny at Chicago, he said, were "as much an effort to meet the needs of the new society that is forming as are the modes of industry and commerce."

On American education the immediate effect of Dewey's digging was next to nothing. For the general public, what the professor was up to was too much outside its tried and trusted manner to make sense. In fact, even the bulk of practicing schoolmen found that it did violence to their sacred canons, and they tried their best to let everybody know it. In consequence, Dewey received the treatment the world usually reserves for men of originality who fly in the face of established beliefs and customs, which is to say that his work was laughed at and yelled against. His methods, critics freely confided, pampered children; they failed to lodge the fundamentals within them; they made them "contemptuous of authority." Worse yet, presently whispers were being loudly dropped that at bottom the professor was seeking to undermine the honor and glory of the American way—even, in fact, the belief in the Heavenly Father. Such and similar aberrations Dewey sought to put down and correct in a little volume, *The School and Society*, which appeared in 1899. He might as well have saved his breath. Diffuse and belabored with a leaden and abstruse prose, the book was not the sort that those who read find difficult to set down. And so like the school itself, it convinced hardly anyone. However, as the years wore away and what the professor was up to came into sharper focus, the volume was granted another printing, and this time it received the attention and respect it deserved. Not only did it sell, but as time unfolded, *The School and Society* saw itself converted into one civilized tongue after another—in truth, at the moment its message even resides in glorious reincarnation between paper covers.

7   In philosophy, as reference has already been made, Dewey started under the spell of Hegel, an idealist; then he moved in with the pragmatists, with whom, in the guise of an instrumentalist or experimentalist, he remained unto his end. Philosophically, he was of the same clan as William James, the father of pragmatism, and Charles Peirce, the coiner of the word and one of the most prodigious and incisive philosophical minds to rise in America. Philosophy's first task, as Dewey saw it, was to figure out not how one knows the world, but rather what must be done to control and better it. To such an end the philosopher puts his mind upon the conflicts which perplex and bedevil our current society, especially those which issue from the clashing relationships of democracy, industry, and science. Stripped of its usual weighty words, the philosopher's problem is "to clarify men's ideas as the moral and social strife's of our own day." Thus viewed, pragmatism has scant use for the philosopher's time-honored flights into the problems that reach above and beyond the borderline of human experience. Instead of dealing with God and the vast vaporous universe that transcends the world in which we weep and laugh, as per the metaphysician's immemorial custom, Dewey made man and his earth his primary concern. "Better it is," he declared, "for philosophy to err in the active struggles of its own age and times than to maintain a monastic impeccability."

Let the philosopher unbolt the door of his academic cell and venture into the world in which we pulse and breathe. Let him, in the mood of the scientist, approach his problems with an experimental eye. And like the white-cloaked searcher in the lab, let him regard none of his findings as forever fixed or settled. For the universe itself is evanescent, and to seek to explain its mystery in trim and measured formulas about absolute and everlasting verities is a waste of time. For truth is as changeable as man himself because it evolves as he evolves. We have to live today, said William James, by what truth we can get, and be ready on the morrow to call it a falsehood. When philosophy thus sallies from its cloister, it does not mean, so Dewey asserted, the "lowering in dignity of philosophy from a lofty plane to one of gross utilitarianism." Instead, it signifies that philosophy's prime function has become that "of rationalizing the possibilities of experience, especially collective experience." It is, in a word, the harnessing of human intelligence to human improvement by means of an experimental method.

8   The Laboratory School came to its historic end in 1903, and in the next year Dewey betook himself to New York to teach philosophy at Columbia University. For the next decade he confined his sapience to philosophy, with only minor excursions into education. Then, in 1916, with the publication of *Democracy and Education*, his long furlough from pedagogy came to an end. Almost at once the book placed Dewey in the front row of American thinkers. Beladen though it is by a heavy and graceless utterance, *Democracy and Education* has been hailed as the most important work on education to be composed by an American—in fact, some reviewers, bemused doubtless by the wish that fathered their thought, made so bold as to place it several notches above *Emile* and *The Republic*. However pundits on some unsentimental tomorrow will appraise it, the fact remains that in its heyday —roughly between the two world wars—the work served as none other before it as a prime instigator in the remaking of the native educational theory, the infallible writ, as it were, of the vast majority of the nation's professional schoolmen.

In *Democracy and Education* Dewey set down his philosophic theorems and their educational corollaries. In education, he held, with Pestalozzi and Froebel, two aspects meet the eye, the psychological and the social. The burden of education is to steer the one, the child's natural and personal impulses, to the other, namely, a desirable social behavior. Morally, Dewey contended, a child is trained when he is put upon to meet the demands of living properly with his mates. It thus befalls the teacher not to fill his ears with moral sureties, but rather to create situations from which the child will derive his concepts of right and wrong as they work upon the common weal. As in his Chicago salad days, Dewey went to great lengths to stress the thought that first and foremost the school is a communal hive and that its endeavor should bear upon the everyday activities of society at large. Let it not be forgotten, he urged in addition, that what goes on in school should be gounded on the child's daily living at home and at play, for these two are the wellspring of his primary experience. But this is by no means saying that the school should maintain itself at all times within the familiar social patterns. Its task is not simply to reflect the world outside; it is also to anticipate a better world and, hence, one may hope, a happier one. Actually, insisted the professor—somewhat in the vein of Pestalozzi and Condorcet— in a free-functioning society education is the fundamental instrument of social reform and progress. Toward such an end it behooves the school to plot its course. Such, Dewey insisted, is the essence of a democratic society. By contrast, the handing down of prefabricated precepts, inflexible and unalterable—whether moral, religious, social, or political—is the sure sign of a closed, authoritarian society.

It was Dewey's belief that in education, as in life, our attitude should be scientific. Nothing, he declared, should be taken for granted as being fixed or immutable. All truths, no matter how venerable and venerated, must be subjected to a persistent probing and testing. And what we believe should at all times be based on plausible and impartial evidence. Thus undertaken, education becomes a resolute, unsparing, endless venture—a "continuous reconstruction of accumulated experience."

The whole thing can be summed up in a nutshell—a bit large, perhaps, as nutshells go, but still a summary. Education is actual living and not just getting ready for living on some distant and unpredictable tomorrow. Education is the process of growing, and as long as growth goes on, there is education. Education is a never-ending overhauling and reassembling of previous experience. Finally, at its best and fullest, education is a social process, and to make this process flourish the school must be a democratic society.

9   As might be expected, in his educational ponderings John Dewey drew on the pedagogic capital of those who had labored before him, in particular Froebel and Herbart. Like the former, Dewey contended that education at bottom is growth, but unlike the kindergartner, he put no stock in the proposition that growth is an unfoldment of latent principles. For Froebel's metaphysical theories Dewey's earthly pragmatism plainly had no use. Dewey dispelled the pale pink fog of mysticism in which Froebel had veiled his "gifts," and if in his school the child dallied with cubes and spheres, then it was simply to entertain and exercise his budding skills. Froebel, of course, had not been indifferent to life's actual occupations. He had even spoken of them, somewhat idylically, in songs by which his protégés warbled their praise of bakers, carpenters, plowmen, and similar men of calloused hand. Dewey's concern, however, applied itself more to what the child himself was about—hence the stress on social occupations of "real meaning," for instance, those which are essential to yielding our food, clothing, and shelter. A thoroughgoing idealist, Froebel, sensing God's mysterious presence in all things, was sure that all growth was ultimately toward the Infinite and Eternal. Not only did Dewey believe that such speculations were idle, but he considered any planned development toward a remote and uncertain end to be futile.

On a few issues the two men entertained a measure of agreement. Both called for "creative activity," though not of the same sort or for the same reason; both wanted the child to learn by doing; and both insisted that the school must be a living society where the child learns by his experience in the communal enterprise.

The Herbartian doctrines, taking one with another, left Dewey far more discommoded. For Dewey, the Herbartian scheme of things was too cocksure. Herbart's way of teaching, with its trim and ordered planning, Dewey found too pat and dogged. The great weight the German put on the systematic teaching and learning of subject matter ran against the Dewey grain. Yet, for all the difference in their fundamental stress, on a number of points the two men stood fairly close. Both saluted the importance of individual difference, and both submitted, with Rousseau, that in order to teach Little Willie anything, one must first be privy to the facts of his essential nature. Both also agreed that without interest, effective learning cannot prosper. However, for Herbart interest was simply the lure and stimulus to effort, and once the latter was in evidence, the former, having played its designated part, was ushered to the nearest exit. For Dewey interest and effort were not separable entitities. They might be as different as, say, husband and wife; yet they were also partners, for better or worse. Interest spurs learning, but learning flourishes only in the presence of interest.

As for methods of teaching, the two men stood as far apart as possible. Whereas Herbart put his confidence in the Formal Steps, Dewey placed his in the so-called "Act of Thought." Where the one proceeded logically, the other moved psychologically. Thus set down, the essence of Dewey's method becomes identical with that of orderly reflection. The process goes into gear when the learner is confronted by a "genuine situation of experience." From this his thinking is set in motion by a "genuine problem." To solve it, he gathers information and makes observations. Bringing these to bear on the problem, he sights plausible clues and explanations. These, said Dewey, "he shall be responsible for developing in an orderly way." Thus, well-heeled with data, he is to test his findings in application "to discover for himself their validity"—or, one might venture to murmur, their lack of validity. Sheared of explanatory details, the Dewey Act of Thought flaunts five neat tags, one for each of its elements: (1) activity, (2) problem, (3) data, (4) hypothesis, and (5) testing.

10   Critical huzzahs notwithstanding, *Democracy and Education,* like the Laboratory School in the nineties, had little immediate effect on the general practice of the American school. The truth is that Dewey's cogitations were over the heads of the common run of readers, whether in secular robes or pedagogic. What was needed was someone to translate them into intelligible parlance and, if possible, someone to siphon them into the practice of the newer and bolder schools. In time both appeared. By 1918 William Heard Kilpatrick was unraveling Dewey's thoughts before his enormous audience at Columbia's Teachers College, inspiriting them, like a wizard, with a twinkle and clarity they had not known and, while he was about it, converting hearers in brigades. Meanwhile, at Ohio State, Boyd Bode was working a similar wonder. From the learning chambers of these men, and others like them, issued an ever-lengthening train of teachers, not only versed in the Dewey lore, but also able and eager to put it into practice, especially in the American lower learning.

In the meantime the Progressives had begun to flavor their own program with some of Dewey's sauces. As will be observed later on, they too called for a new education, and especially one giving more concern to active learning, a working and amicable entente between home and school, with less dogmatism and coercion on the part of teachers toward their pupils. Unlike the professor, however, the Progressives never laid down a systematic philosophy on which to cultivate their promised land. Nor was most of their labor in any real sense experimental. Only a handful of them thought of the school as a social laboratory where the germ of social reconstruction should be planted. Even so, through the Progressives some of Dewey's ideas passed into the public learning. The road, needless to say, was rough and rocky, for those who governed the public schools continued, as has ever been their wont, to esteem themselves as upholders of things as they are, and certainly not as tinkerers in social novelty. Not until the unhappy thirties, when the country was reeling in depression, was such conservatism put to effective challenge.

Nonetheless, on American education Dewey left a mark that runs long, thick, and wide, and the land is richer for his presence. Helen Parkhurst, who sought to liquidate the old-style "lock-step" recitation with her Dalton Plan of individualized study and progress; Carleton Washburne, who overhauled the schools of Winnetka, Iillinois; William Wirt, who devised a plan of work, study, and play for the schools of Gary, Indiana; and a host of other American educational worthies—all have testified to the spell of John Dewey.

When Dewey opened his Laboratory School, the notion of experimenting with Junior was so rare as to be an oddity, and the mere thought of it was sufficient to send out an alert to the police. Today experimenting with kiddies in even the nethermost grades occurs every day, except Sundays. In the nineties the recitation was as familiar as horsecars and high starched collars; though that method still has its devotees, their number is thinning fast as it yields more and more ground to the adherents of pupil action and problem solving. As a consequence, the schoolhouse has become a combination library, laboratory, kitchen, workshop, and recreation hall. Whereas in the nineties a pupil confined himself preeminently to book learning, today his activities range almost without limit, from shop work and club gatherings, to tooting and banging out the "Stars and Stripes" in the band, to dropping in on museums, ten-story garages, the battles for everlasting peace in the UN, and, on good days, the deliberations of the people's surrogates in their marbled mills of lawmaking.

When the Dewey school was still in infancy, the principal concerns of American schooling were mental and moral; today they extend to every department of life, from the child's health, his emotional equilibrium, and his personality to his ability to get along with humankind. To come to terms with such nonacademic affairs some schools have brought guides and counselors, and similar trained and lettered wizards, into their midst. The barriers which once frowned so formidably between the child's bench in school and his life in the buzzing world outside have been steadily reduced. Today's youngster is no longer caged up with books, a pad of paper, and a well of ink. He also prepares and serves meals, sanitary, edible, and sometimes even savory, their vitamins and calories accounted for and duly recorded. He builds and ornaments ranch houses and attends patrons in the school's store, bank, or commissary. In the more enterprising and fearless schools he is even given the counsel and instruction that will someday, it is hoped, make for happy and enduring wedlock.

As for discipline, the up-to-date educator, together with Dewey—though not altogether because of him—contends that even the small fry must learn to make their decisions between right and wrong; hence the emphasis put on student self-government. Even teachers have become inoculated with democratic juices. Thus, where years ago their schools were run by orders dispatched from the superintendent's tower on high to the principal's office, and thence down to the meanest birchman in the ranks, in some schools today teachers elect their chairman—or in very up-to-date seminaries of learning, their coordinator—into office; sometimes, it has been reported, they have even been asked to render their collective advice in the selection of a school head. In schools of an enlightened and liberal cast even the faculty meeting has yielded to the newer tone. Where only yesterday (or, at any rate, the day before) the faculty was assembled to give an ear to their leader's fiats, currently, often enough, they gather in congress with him to ponder their common problems. There have even been occasions when they have been invited to give a hand in shaping policy.

11 From the First World War through the Depression and the Second World War, Dewey devoted his philosophical acumen more and more to the examination of the American social order. His confidence in the experimental approach to the problems which shame and sorrow us all remained with him to the last. It is, he said, the "sole dependable means of disclosing the realities of existence . . . the sole authentic mode of revelation." As for democracy, years ago he had concluded that if it is to succeed, its principles must extend to industrial as well as civic and political life. As president of the League for Industrial Democracy, Dewey worked with lavish energy to forward the fuller democracy. But the cord which bound his thinking to social advance was still education. "The first step," he declared, "is to make sure of an educational system that informs students about the present state of society and enables them to understand the conditions and forces at work." Once this has been attained, "students will be able to take their own active part . . . in bringing about a new social order." What is more, if American education was to develop a truly social purpose, educators had to move toward making the school itself a cooperative community. This idea, moreover, was to infuse even the administration so that "oligarchical management from above may be abolished."

Like nearly all Americans, good and true, Dewey permitted himself the gratification of sunlit visions, but he was far too realistic to be susceptible to their intrigue, the delusion, namely, that his proposals, however plausible, were immediately achievable. Approaching his earthly end at more than ninety, however, he enjoyed the satisfaction at least of knowing that much of the modification of American education during the fifty years preceding had been in harmony with his thinking. That alteration, of course, had not been of a sweeping and engulfing dimension, and most of its more radical manifestations were to be found in the lower schools. Although Dewey has been cheered and applauded near and far, it is only fair to point out that he was also subject to a torrent of ceaseless criticism, some honest and scholarly, some bilious and spurious, and emanating from men as wide apart in dignity and merit as, say, William Randolph Hearst and Robert Maynard Hutchins. Nor should it be overlooked that not a few of these changes were doubtless predestined and would have come about in one way or another regardless of Dewey's labors, for as he himself observed, they were the product of the evolving social order.

Despite the acclamation in the groves of professional teacher training, and despite its effect upon educational practice, the Dewey viewpoint continues to inspire doubts, not only among the commoners of the laity, but among the peerage of philosophy as well. Pragmatists, of course, relish it, and so in greater or lesser measure do their various offspring, the experimentalists, reconstructionists, and progressivists of one shade or another. Challenging it, on the other hand, are a variety of realists, idealists, and Catholic Scholastics and Neo-Scholastics.

12   Save for Herbart and some of his successors, realists have had only a relatively light effect on the making of American educational practice, though this is certainly not to suggest that they have been laggards in the domain of theory. In truth, they trace their historical line as far back at least as classical antiquity. Their basic notions about the nature of man, his aspirations and goals, says Harry S. Broudy, a classical realist in practice at the University of Illinois, have their roots in Plato and Aristotle.

With a lineage so long and venerable, it is only natural that realism, like idealism, should have produced a number of hybrids. Generally at odds with the pragmatist's heavy stress on flux and change, realists, from Aristotle on, have inclined to put a primary emphasis on knowing the world as it confronts us. There is, so runs their recurrent note, a certain constant "scheme of things" to which, for all our great yearning for something better, we must learn to accommodate ourselves. To live efficiently in this complex and peace-disturbing world, messianic hopes will not suffice; one must come to effective grips with reality. Hence, for survival, to be properly educated is not only a basic need but also a basic right. It is, indeed, a child's inalienable right, and to make certain that he obtains it becomes an obligation of society.

In this society, the school's primary function, declares Broudy, is to develop intellectual habits in its students—all else becomes subsidiary, a fringe benefit, as it were. To perform its labors efficaciously, the school must be in the hands not of bright and devoted amateurs but of men and women who, by dint of diligent, formal study, have mastered the tested body of knowledge and skill employed in teaching, which is to say the science of education. Such a body of professional knowledge belongs to the trained educator and is no more the possession of the layman, however gifted and discerning he may be, than that of medicine or law or divine science is. With the problem of living in this world taking on a greater and greater complexity, and with education moving more and more into mass production on every level of schooling, amateur teachers coming from "good" colleges, Broudy warns, will not suffice unto their task. They will be, he declares, "as helpful as caviar in a famine."

Does the traditionalist—say, Herbart—lean heavily on a curriculum centered in subject matter? Then Broudy turns it down on the grounds that it is defectively integrated, that it pays no heed to current social problems, and that all too often it does not contribute effectively to the retention of the information it seeks to implant. Does the pragmatist, on the other hand, pin his hopes on a curriculum centered in solving problems? Then Broudy rejects this too, for the reason that problems which are real to novices are usually so simple that they can be solved without having any formal knowledge and without using even a rudimentary scientific method. To replace the aforesaid procedures, Broudy has recommended a general education which would drastically revise our elementary and secondary course of studies by requiring (1) a systematic study of organized subjects, with special stress on reading and mathematics; (2) "problems courses" designed to help the learner to deal with problems more understandingly and, hence, more effectively; and (3) opportunities for artistic, creative expression, which, along with the gratification one derives from the pleasure of knowing and being able to think, will enhance our enjoyment of knowledge.

13   If until of late the native philosophic realists have concerned themselves but lightly with the problems of American pedagogy, then for their part the idealists have worked its garden very assiduously. Like the realists, they are of an ancient order, as old in the Western world as the Athenian height of day. Unlike pragmatism, moreover, idealism has its representatives in virtually every civilized land. In America they have been numerous, and their roster glitters with eminent stars, as witness William Torrey Harris, Josiah Royce, and Herman Harrell Horne. Of these, the latter has offered the pragmatist the hardest tussle, not only by the sheer tonnage of his output, but also by the voluptuousness of his argument. Like Dewey, but with a far more dexterous pen, Horne has put forth his view in a broadside of learned books, including *The Philosophy of Education* (1904), *Idealism and Education* (1910), *Free Will and Human Responsibility* (1912), *This New Education* (1931), and *The Democratic Philosophy of Education* (1932).

The core of Dewey's pragmatism is man; for Horne's idealism it is God. The former's philosophy is bottomed on naturalism; the latter's on theism. Does the pragmatist contend the true and the beautiful to be relative and changeable? Then the idealist holds them to be absolute and everlasting. Does the pragmatist assert that truth is but a term we use for ideas that work? Then the idealist retorts that truth is not simply a term. Ideas, he insists, are real in themselves. They are not true because they work; on the contrary, they work because they are true. Truth does not change, but as the years run off, man's understanding of it may enhance and therefore change. The purpose of philosophy, says Dewey, is to grapple with social conflicts, especially the sort which generate when the forces of industry, science, and democracy collide head on. This the idealistic Horne accepts, but extends beyond the plane of mortal man to embrace the "whole of reality," which, he says, is supernatural as well as natural. To deal with our social festerings and fevers, Dewey wields the scalpel of intelligence, and so does Horne. But for the one the operation rests in human hands; for the other, however, it has a transcendental affiliation with the Absolute, and thus it puts on a superhuman as well as a human guise. The pragmatist, like the idealist, puts an appreciable stock in the principles of growth. But where the former identifies growth with life and education, the latter makes it "man's finite way of approaching the Infinite." Longfellow, warbling the idealist's tune, sought to improve each shining hour by forever striving upward and onward—a view which caused the skeptical Morris Cohen to inquire, "Where is upward and why is onward?"

Though much of this contending seems mere word juggling, it advertises different educational stresses. Thus, where Horne sees the teacher in the capacity of an inspiring leader, Dewey, though certainly not unmindful of the importance of the personal relationship between master and learner, invests his main confidence in the value which is presently fetched when the pupil actively engages in the solving of problems. Horne, like Dewey, has a high regard for the role of interest in education, but unlike the pragmatist, the idealist puts more stock in effort and will and discipline. To serve everything on the platter of interest, he holds, is to serve pastry and no spinach. Not only is it an overstress on a beguiling decoy, but it is also false to the actuality of life itself. Like the great Frederick of Prussia, Horne can never let himself forget that although fun is fun, and even salubrious to human welfare, nevertheless duty is duty, and it must be done. The discipline in doing the disagreeable and intolerable that need to be done, Horne contends, "is worthwhile."

Nor can the idealist go along with Dewey's absorption in the concerns of everyday living. It roils him to encounter so much trafficking in the social and the practical. Not that he would fling them overboard altogether. What he wants, rather, is a fuller consideration, for example, of life's religious and spiritual aspects, a decent respect for studying for the sake of study itself, and, finally, a more adequate recognition of the esthetic experience as a joy even when pursued for no other reason than itself.

14   Dissenting from pragmatism, as well as from most of its philosophic antagonists, is the philosophy of Catholic Scholasticism. Come into being during the Middle Ages, it attained its systematic formulation in the thirteenth century, the work in the main of Thomas Aquinas, the Seraphic Doctor, now a saint and the most influential Catholic practitioner of divine science since Augustine. Three more centuries, and the Council of Trent ordered Aquinas's main work, the *Summa Theologica* to be placed on God's sacred altar side by side with the decretals and the Bible. And in 1879 the Thomist teachings were given official sanction when Pope Leo XIII issued orders that, although they were not necessarily free of error, they were to be accepted as authoritative by all Catholic theologians. Despite their old bones, they are still full of sap, and to this day they bear on all Catholic education, whether high or low. Catholic Scholasticism, as one might easily guess, is theocentric, with God, the Divine and Omniscient Absolute, as its everlasting, unchanging basis of action. Indeed, without God life is held to be meaningless, and so, of course, in such case is education.

The foundation of Catholic educational theory is embedded in the doctrine of the nature of man and his postmortem supernatural destiny. Shorn of the theologian's professional mumbo jumbo, this holds that (1) man is the Heavenly Father's personal handiwork, (2) he is a body and soul, and (3) these elemental two function as an integrated whole. Given to mortal man, moreover, is a will that is unfettered, besides a mind which, when of normal competence, is able to weigh and ponder before its owner enters upon a chosen course, whether for good or ill, a capacity which clearly differentiates Homo sapiens from his fellow creatures on land and sea and in the air. Ever since Adam savored the forbidden apple, it has been the nature of man to seek happiness, and to such an end he employs his mind and will. But inasmuch as the perfect bliss is reserved for the heavenly estate, the way to attain it is to comport oneself virtuously on earth and in accord with God's eternal laws, as they are expounded and executed by the One Holy and Apostolic Church.

The heart of the Catholic system is, of course, the supernatural. It not only underlies its theology and ethics but also runs through its whole conception of life, here and beyond, and hence inevitably it is inherent in its pedagogy. To restore the sons of Adam "to their high position as children of God," is the one, the engulfing aim of education. By the same token, the task of education is to prepare man to do everything here below "to attain the end for which he was created." But this is not to say that he must seal himself off from the world like an affrighted anchorite, abstaining teetotally from life's delights and gratifications in order to save his soul. For as Pope Pius XI assures the world in his encyclical *Divini illius magistri* (1929), "the true Christian does not stint his natural faculties, but he develops and perfects them with the supernatural," a pronouncement which the idealistic Horne, who, though while on earth worshiped as a Methodist, would surely not dispute. Thus, the pontiff goes on, man obtains "new strength in the material and temporal order no less than in the spiritual and eternal."

To this transcendental end all Catholic education, from the lowest plane to its highest snow-blown crags, must be directed. Education's every phase, from content to method to discipline, must bear on the fulfillment of man's natural destiny. And to this high goal every participant in the rearing and training of the child—from family and school to church and state—

must give full and utter heed. The bedrock of all education, needless to say, is religion and virtue; indeed, any pedagogy which is indifferent thereto, whether it follows Dewey or Marx or Nietzsche or any other such sage, is under Catholic condemnation. Not only must the young yield themselves to religious counsel and instruction at fixed and regular hours, but every subject, whether sacred or profane, must be grounded on Christian piety. Or, more specifically, in the infallible papal words of the thirteenth Leo, in his *Militantis ecclesiae* (1897), "every form of pedagogic naturalism which in any way overlooks or excludes supernatural Christian formation in the teaching of youth is false." Any method of education, Leo continued, "founded wholly or in part on the denial or forgetfulness of Original Sin and of Grace, and relying on the sole powers of the human race, is unsound."

15   The high esteem for Thomas Aquinas is not confined to the fold of Mother Church. Of late, in fact, it has drawn a ponderable following elsewhere, particularly among those who recoil from the blunt skepticism of modern science. Such New Thought has taken several forms, but far and away the most important one, pedagogically, is the so-called "Neo-Scholasticism." Its foremost rhetorician, and by all odds its liveliest one, is Robert Maynard Hutchins, once president and subsequently chancellor of the University of Chicago and, after his retirement, a high potentate in the Ford Foundation and later in the Fund for the Republic.

Hutchins's chief animadversions have been leveled largely at the American higher learning. He has flayed it again and again, particularly for its vocationalism and its gross and eager hawking of the practical, in illustration, its courses in ping-pong teaching, square dancing, cosmetology, plumbing for the fair ones, and similar confections for the trade. Not only have its shrines thereby degraded learning in America, but in aligning themselves with Mammon, they have also reduced themselves to intellectual trimmers —even, in sad fact, to anti-intellectuals. Does America wallow in a cultural bog? Does it love money more than learning? Then this is because, at bottom, its education is hollow. It is, testified Hutchins, suffering from the disease of cults—the cult of skepticism, for one, which makes reason suspect; the cult of immediacy, which absorbs itself in the present and dismisses the past which fathered it as void of meaning; and the cult of science, which professes that it alone can put the world to right and thereby save us all.

The anti-intellectualism of American education Hutchins views as a breeder of sentimentalism. From it leaps our dubious optimism, our chasing after rainbow causes, our endless efforts to uplift and save humanity. Naturally suspicious of the intellect, its connoisseurs harness their efforts to *what* one wants rather than *why* one wants it and, rarer yet, what one *ought* to want. This Hutchins deplores as a dangerous business. For such an attitude accommodates itself very readily to the view that to want a thing is to seek to get it and that in order to get it, what becomes most important is the development of the means to the desired end. Thus unlimited acquisition becomes the rule of motivation, and success the yardstick of a good education.

To end our cultural schizophrenia, and thereby put the brake on civilization's downhill slide, Hutchins and his fellow thinkers resort to the cultivation of the intellect. Not that they would ban all vocational education, or any other legitimate preparation for life's bread-and-butter scramble. But the proper province for the cultivation of the practical, they insist, lies beyond the walls of Academe. Upholding the proposition that "truth is everywhere the same," Hutchins argues that hence it must be "the same for all men" and that consequently the ends of education must be the same at all times and in all places. Virtue, asserts Mortimer Adler, the movement's dialectician-in-chief, is the same for all, whether on Main Street or on Broadway, and since the concern of education is the making of a man of rectitude, education should set the same objectives for everybody. To pragmatists and other abhorrers of absolutes, all this syllogizing is a begging of the question. Put into practice, it appears to them even somewhat nonsensical. Not only does it flout their precept that under democracy a lad should have a say in choosing what he aspires to learn, but psychologically it shuts its eyes to the differences which set one man apart from the others, especially differences in individual needs, tastes, and talents. Hutchins, however, insists that everyone between sixteen and twenty, save the palpably hollow-headed, should address himself to the same general learning, which, it goes without saying, is to be powerfully intellectual.

The Hutchins neophyte begins by exercising his brain with grammar, rhetoric, and logic. These are to serve him in the end as the tools of interparlance. Through them not only is he to develop whatever mental potency it has pleased Omnipotence to grant him while on earth, but he is also to perfect himself as an effective reader, writer, and speaker. But for the nourishment of his intellect the chief pabulum is to be theoretic mathematics, which "exemplifies reasoning in its clearest and most precise form" and which, hence, is dispensed to him in massive helpings.

The consummation of the Hutchins program is the Great Books— books which have come down the long corridor of the centuries to attain the celebrity of being classics. An approximate one hundred, they display the usual dramatis personae of letters, in instance, the *Iliad* and the *Odyssey*, *The Aeneid*, the *Bible*, and even *The Canterbury Tales*, *Faust*, and the flashings of Shakespeare. But not all are such stately worthies—indeed, some are not stately at all, as, say, Cantor's *Transfinite Numbers*, Rieman's *Hypothesis of Geometry*, Grosseteste's *On Light*, Oresme's *On the Breadths of Forms*, and several others of similar mien. But the Great Books are read not for the verbal delicacies which are spread between their covers but for the ideas which are sealed therein. These are the deathless first principles, which Hutchins contends are the same for all men in all places and at all times and which are to be mastered if the cultural confusion which befogs and befuddles current America is ever to lift.

As for the republic's highest learning, Hutchins has sounded more or less the same refrain. The university's concern for the practical and the vocational has aroused his dander again and again, and so, by the same token, has its neglect of learning for the sake of learning. The experimentalist's recourse to the laboratory procedure to illuminate the dark visions of society and morality, Hutchins has inveighed against repeatedly, insisting that the bulk of such problems are unamenable to the methods of science. Nor has he ever been able to make concessions to the view that the contemporary industrial and technical world is a thing in itself and separable from the antecedent world, that the past is, so to say, a graveyard of dead causes from which one can learn very little. Again Hutchins turns the limelight on reason. All pursuers of the higher learning would be made to grapple with the natural sciences, wherein man and nature are examined; the social sciences, which would contemplate the relationships of man to man; and metaphysics and theology, without which, Hutchins is certain, no unified university is possible. At bottom the preliminary training of every nascent doctor, lawyer, and pastor should be the same, to the effect, Hutchins has let it be known, that they would possess "ordered minds prepared for life because they have been educated in view of the purpose of life."

Neo-Scholasticism has enjoyed a generous publicity, not only in the professional reviews, but also in the journals of the laity, including such titans as *Time, Life, Harpers,* and the *Saturday Evening Post* in its more flush and florid times. Yet for all that, on the general run of American schools it has exercised no ponderable effect. The professional traders in ideas have hoofed and horned it unsparingly, though on varying grounds—realists, for its failure to deal with the world "as it actually is"; idealists, for its oversight of the "whole personality"; and pragmatists, for its doddering psychology, its intellectual snootiness, and its want of social understanding. Catholic Scholastics have on the whole been a bit more charitable. Indeed, from time to time they have showered Hutchins with rose petals. They applaud him, for example, for the "lucidity and sanity" of his theorems. And, not unnaturally, they admire his confidence in metaphysics. But beyond such brief flights of approval their cordiality fades. They can never forget that his thinking is "de-Christianized" and that "when he quotes Aquinas, he quotes an Aquinas that never existed." Worst of all in their catalog of errors is his failure to make room in his account for the supernatural destiny that awaits us all post-mortem.

As for the American public at large, its interest in the Neo-Scholastic premises has been slight at best, and its acceptance of them even slighter. To most Americans, drawn into the inescapable struggle for meat and dollars, not to say cars and television sets, the Hutchins meditations appear somewhat daft, and even a little suspect. To them the demons which Hutchins has sought to dispel are not demons at all, but angels with harps and halos, and hence essential to the continued progress of this great land.

Even at the University of Chicago, where Hutchins was in charge from 1929 to 1951, none of his primary principles fructified. Did Chicago, for example, rid itself of the devil of vocationalism? If so, then how can one explain its offerings in stocks and bonds and similar practical and utilitarian science? Did the University of Chicago come any closer to the saintly Aquinas than, say, Baylor University or John C. Smith University or Vassar or, for that matter, the numerous state universities which now bedizen and enlighten the republic everywhere? If so, then how does one account for its doctoral theses in dishwashing methodology, hosiery advertising, and the fashion cycle in women's underwear?

Plainly, at the University of Chicago the Neo-Scholastic doctrine made no great dent. The fact is that it was ill regarded by its men of learning, and time and again they dressed it down. Though Hutchins lights no candle on the altar of democracy, as is the common style today in university administrative circles, in his dealings with the faculty he bowed to their common will. But if his philosophy made no great headway at Chicago, this is by no means saying that Hutchins himself exercised no influence there. During his investiture in the presidential toga, he touched off a number of revolutions which not only helped to make his university singular in the American higher learning but also, in all likelihood, will be recalled by the recorders of the educational past for some time to come. The credit system, that pale and battered relic of American collegiate tradition, was carted out. At the same time, in keeping with William James's observation that nobody can be made to learn anything he does not want to, attendance at classroom sessions was made voluntary. The time-honored course examination was displaced by one which was comprehensive and searching and which covered a field of knowledge rather than just a small plot of it. And, even more beyond belief, and for all the fulmination of learned alumni, varsity football was abolished. But such reforms were largely on the surface, and none of them was even faintly tinged with the Neo-Scholastic metaphysic—and after Hutchins's departure to other endeavors, all of them, save only the abolition of football, went down the drain. Only in a small and confined way, in courses in the Great Books and in adult discussion, are any traces of the Neo-Scholastic doctrine discernible.

Of recent years various public libraries have featured "The Great Discussions of Basic Problems." With leaders specially trained in the Hutchins arcana, these seances address themselves to adults of "experience, maturity, and sense of purpose necessary to deal with great problems," by means of the "basic ideas found in the Great Books." To "bring to the minds and hearts of the American public the greatest works of the most original thinkers the world has known," the Encyclopaedia Britannica, in collaboration with the University of Chicago, has made available a special assemblage of the Great Books, with a two-volume "encyclopedia of ideas," the so-called "Synopticon," to help "thousands upon thousands of men and women" who hitherto have shied away from first principles "to stretch their mental horizons beyond the workaday world."

If the Hutchins doctrine has found Chicago's men of higher learning rather chilly, then at Annapolis, at Saint John's College, the same Saint John's once directed by Henry Barnard, it has been accorded a hearty welcome. Here one sees young men and women contemplating civilization for its great concepts and first principles. Here, as in the original Harvard of more than three centuries ago, all courses, from the freshman to the senior year, are mandatory. Here the young are to be "educated rather than merely trained." Hence one looks in vain for knowledge and light in Sport Skills I and II, Stage Makeup, Seafood Cookery, or even Commercial Portuguese. Instead, Saint John's students are expected to search their minds rationally, to express their thoughts in sober and sensible argument, and finally, to stand up in their effective defense in free discussion. At Saint John's, in a word, Hutchins has found the materialization of his ethereal castle. But Saint John's, for all its long and white-haired history, is merely a speck in the vast ocean of American learning—so tiny, in fact, that for the moment it is scarcely discernible.

15
THE PSYCHOLOGICAL
MOVEMENT IN EDUCATION

While Dewey and others were endeavoring to put education on a sounder philosophical footing, other searchers were addressing themselves to its scientific and psychological aspects. To civilization the study of the psyche, in one form or another, was, of course, no newcomer. The ancient Aristotle had been its familiar, and so had Locke, Descartes, Leibnitz, Kant, John Stuart Mill, and several other such intellectual titans. By the nineteenth century the subject was getting notice from some of Europe's foremost men of learning, and one of them, Dr. Herbart, even bestirred himself to give his delving a measure of mathematical exactness, while Gustav Theodor Fechner undertook to "measure" the "mysteries" of the mind with the aid of logarithmic tables, which, in case of sudden emergency, he was at pains to have handy at all times. But the first explorers in psychology were nearly all philosophers, and all too often their expeditions were carried on in the filtered moonlight of metaphysics. It remained for a German, Wilhelm Max Wundt, to project for us, with some supporting syllogisms, the picture of psychology as a true and respectable science, amenable to the rigorous requirements of the laboratory and, when thus approached, the peer—nay, the superior—of even physics. To expound his startling doctrine, Wundt composed his *Grundzüge der physiologischen Psychologie (Principles of Physiological Psychology)*, which he published in 1874 and which appeared in various editions thereafter—six in all—until the First World War diverted the students of the mind to more pressing concerns. In 1879, soon after the appearance of his book, Wundt opened the world's first university psychological laboratory. Though it was all but primitive, it was not long in making a stir. Indeed, by and by it was fetching students not only from the Reich but from all over the earth, including some very eager ones from the United States, some of whom were destined to become famous in their own right.

The first of them to receive some attention from American scholars was Granville Stanley Hall, or, as he signed himself, G. Stanley Hall. He began in 1883 by installing a psychological laboratory at the Johns Hopkins University, then just getting under wing. Four years later he put out the initial number of the *American Journal of Psychology*, the first of its sort in English and for years the cock of the walk in its specialty. Later, at Clark University, in Worcester, Massachusetts, over whose fortunes for years he watched as president—indeed, Hall *was* Clark University—he launched and edited *The Pedagogical Seminary*, an advanced journal of educational theory and practice, with learned and instructive articles from contributors the world around.

Meanwhile Hall gave aid and encouragement to the rising movement of child study. Though his methods are today severely discountenanced—he relied rather heavily on a crude questionnaire—through his vast and far-flung probing he gave a powerful stimulus to child psychology, a science then still crawling on all fours. The harvest of Hall's most diligent searching, however, is stored in his *Adolescence*, a spacious granary, filled with the subject's every aspect from psychology, biology, anthropology, and sociology to sex, crime, religion, morality, and education. The blowtorch of progress, of course, has made an end of much of its revelation. Even so, it was Hall who lifted the study of adolescence from the slough of quackery and blushful romance to a place of respect and dignity in earnest educational research.

Another to seek out Wundt was William James, a young medical student from Harvard, the same James referred to earlier as a pioneer of the pragmatic philosophy. Though James turned up his nose at German scientific meticulousness, he seems to have sniffed enough of its aroma to make him want "to work at psychology." For all his deep-seated dislike of the tedium of experimental labor, it was James nonetheless who got laboratory psychology on its legs in America. He performed this feat, innocently to be sure, as a Harvard instructor in anatomy and physiology when, sometime in the mid-seventies, he commandeered a deserted room in the old science building, stocked it with a metronome and horopter chart and similar unearthly paraphernalia, and set himself to conning the hoary and mysterious secrets of the psyche. Some time after, in 1877, he won fresh laurels when he inaugurated the first course at Harvard in what its catalog tersely announced as "psychology."

Meanwhile James had come upon the fecund genius of Charles Peirce. The son of a mathematician of some celebrity, Peirce had been reared as it were in the laboratory, and to his last day it remained his fanatical conviction that all ideas, even those of the reverend gentlemen of God, should be subject to experimental verification. "One thing," he said, "is certain, the state of facts will surely get found out . . . and no human can long arrest the triumphal car of truth." Peirce's desire for truth led him to philosophy, and in a day when the boundary between philosophy and psychology was shifting and was only vaguely staked, it is no wonder that he should have crossed it. Actually Peirce was not a working psychologist. He was, by all odds, a thinker, one of the most colossal, indeed, to come out of the republic, or, for that matter, anywhere else. A groundbreaker in American philosophy, he dug down to the bedrock of pragmatism, the very name of which he created. His theory of thought and action and of what is now spoken of as the "psychology of the act," and, even more, his theory of the "experimental method of knowing," filtered into the thinking of James and Dewey, where one can still detect it in such doctrines as "learning as an active process," "thinking as problem solving," "experience as doing and making," and several more.

In 1890 James published his *Principles of Psychology*. He had worked at it off and on for about a dozen years, and when at length it greeted him in print, it was of a truly heroic heft, a Gargantua, so to say, with close to one-half million words, over two thousand footnotes, and a welter of technical citations, all stored in two husky volumes of 1,400 pages. Yet for all its formidable learning, the work was animated with literary sparkle, a jeweled prose rarely found among professional philosophers and almost never among psychologists. Hailed as an artistic and scientific triumph of the first magnitude, *Principles* was the hornbook of budding American psychologists for at least a generation. The years, of course, have exacted their inexorable toll, and not a few of James's once-cherished pronouncements have been modified or rejected. But a few have withstood critical assaults of the most relentless sort and bid fair to abide with us for some time.

True to his pragmatism, James put his main weight on action and experience. What concerned God's noblest creature on earth was simply the "practical business of reacting to his environment." The psychologist's task, hence, was to study how man lives and grows in his environment, how he learns to grapple with it, and, if he manages to survive at all, how he mastered it. As a graduate in medicine, James quite naturally connected psychology to physiology, but unlike Wundt, he stressed not physiological structure but function. The psychological question is not how the cerebrum, the medulla, or even the nerve sciatic are built or how they look, but how they perform. In consequence, James turned his attention to man's everyday doings. For him Homo sapiens—true to his name—was undoubtedly a creature of reason, but he was also Homo sentiens, a man, that is, of feeling, and more often than not his feeling seduced his reason.

Life, as James saw it, was an ever-expanding network of habits, and man is simply a "walking bundle of habits." A man's habits, of course, bore upon his character, and every day they were shaping it for good or ill. Long before behaviorists began their bombilations about conditioning human behavior, James was proclaiming the theory of acquired reactions. "Every acquired reaction," he declared, "is as a rule either a complication, grafted on a native reaction, or a substitute for a native reaction, which the same object originally intended to provoke." Like Peirce, James was convinced that to know a thing is to know of its relations. In every response lie the felt relations of the body. "Every possible feeling," asseverated James, produces a movement, "and it is the movement of the entire organism and of each and all its parts." Or as Kilpatrick put it so neatly many years later, "The whole cat catches the mouse."

The heart of James's psychology is the "stream of conscious thought," the continuous onward-flowing current in which the self is forever involved. It turns on behavior and governs it; at times it restrains it or shuts it off altogether. The stream of thought, which is in constant flow and flux, is not only personal; it is also selective—in fact, even the organism's sense organs function to such a purpose. "Consciousness," wrote James, "does not appear chopped up in bits. Such words as 'chain' and 'train' do not describe it fitly as it presents itself in the first instance. It is nothing jointed; it flows. . . . Hereafter let us call it the stream of thought, of consciousness, or of the subjective life." And so it has been denominated ever since, not only by psychologists, but also by historians, sociologists, and anthropologists; by writers and artists; and by the more articulate gentlemen of the cloth and the teaching profession.

Though *Principles* met with a high and voluble tribute, it also ran into misgiving and dissent. Thus, while Prof. James McKeen Cattell was hymning it as "psychology's declaration of independence," Profs. Titchener and Hall were insisting that it was not systematic psychology at all, but a theory of knowledge compounded from the viewpoint of a psychologist—an unseemly view no doubt, and a harsh one, but one which in these later, unsentimental years makes sense. Even so, in the halls of higher learning *Principles* was destined for long and fruitful employment, and today not only has the work attained the elevation of a classic, but, robed in paper covers, its two volumes still make their rounds. Beyond a doubt it shifted the attention of the American psychologist from structure to function. It depicted the human organism on a canvas that was truly stupendous. And in stressing action it prepared psychology to become the study of behavior, thereby opening the way for educational psychology in all its awesome forms and phases. As the years moved on, James's psychological zealotry and the fire with which he had fed his industry began to flicker, and finally it was only ashes. But the subject the man had succored so magnificently continued to grow and expand, and today even the meanest lean-to university would redden with shame were it caught without at least a chair or two in the psychological science.

The wonders Wundt wrought in his painstaking Germanic manner James conjured up with his deft and dainty, though by no means superficial, hand. Both men helped to put psychology on a scientific groundwork; both furnished it a corps of trained and scholarly workers; and both caught a glimpse of psychology's potentialities for life's numerous and varied enterprise, and especially for learning and teaching.

Like the medicos, the psychologists have spread far beyond their ivied halls. Today their utterance is given earnest attention not only by academicians but by virtually all fosterers of human affairs. Both here and abroad the psychological clinic has become a recognized civic establishment. Psychological science may have had its germ cell in the Wundtian laboratory, but it is in America where it has thrived most sumptuously. In fact, the very word "psychology" has fixed itself into the American's everyday speech, as common as "diner," "pizza," and "pop," and it is used as readily by senators and movie actors as it is by lettered men of learning. Much of the popular belief and confidence in the psychological science is very likely of a wishful tinge, the yearning, that is, to be rich, successful, and happy, and in this respect is no different from the pumped-up faith in palmistry, numerology, astrology, and similar esoteric mysteries. For, once psychology emigrated from the academic cloister into the world outside, it attracted mountebanks and quacks in droves. But this distinction, needless to say, holds even for the more venerable sciences. Happily, besides the charlatans there have been dedicated men and women in plenty who have toiled far into the night to advance their science, and in their midst at least a ponderable number have attained a meritorious success. Long before Freud had attained European eminence he was startling listeners in America. And it was in the republic that the German gestaltists first made much impression. Many lands, of course, are aware of psychology's important role in education, and several were doing something about it long before the average American could even spell the word. But today it is in the United States that psychology and education are arm-in-arm companions, and the office of school psychologist is rapidly turning into a commonplace.

2   Like medicine, modern psychology comes richly arrayed in various guises, and like the M.D.s, its leading maestros have broken into sects, all of impeccable responsibility, but each more or less sniffish of the others. First on the scene were the structuralists, but presently they were nudged out by the functionalists, while today there are mechanists, behaviorists, gestaltists, and a miscellany of others, besides, of course, a small flock of assorted specialists.

Structuralism, fathered by Wundt, came to its prime in the later years of the nineteenth century. In the United States for over thirty years its chief advocate and expounder was Prof. Edward Bradford Titchener, of Cornell. An Englishman, born and bred, Titchener had studied his specialty under the counsel and direction of Wundt. He was, as a result, not only a confirmed structuralist but also a thoroughly disciplined man of science. Sometimes, in truth, he appeared more amazing in this respect than old Wilhelm himself. Aloof and formal, as the English often are, Titchener lectured to his students in the splendor of his academic robes, and save for his daily rendezvous with his violin, he devoted himself almost exclusively to the execution of his specialty. Not only did his scientific relentlessness know no bounds, but as the years passed, it raised awe and respect the world around. His writings found their way into more translations than those of any other English-speaking psychologist—indeed, probably into more than those of all the outstanding ones lumped together. For years one of his texts was the official schoolbook for students in both France and Japan. And when the Russians ventured to illuminate their steppes with an experimental school of psychology, they not only consulted the professor from Cornell but even heeded him.

For all his incandescence, Titchener exerted only a small influence on

American thought. Reserved, conservative, an astringent practitioner of the strictest scientific canon, Titchener spent most of his working day in the laboratory. Compared with the debonair, gladsome James, boundlessly absorbed in human doings, Titchener was an iceberg. The pursuit of scientific truth he regarded as something which was not merely dispassionate, but impersonal. Science, he held, started when men began to look upon the world "as a vast machine, working precisely as a tool or an engine works." "The concept of psychology," he insisted, "is the morphology of the mind —what is there and in what quantity, not what it [is] for." Function, in other words, is none of its business. As for the living organism, this is the biologist's domain, and into it the psychologist shall not trespass. And as for putting psychology to work on the problems of man, let the biologists and sociologists and the similarly inclined attend to such affairs. The aim of science is to establish the facts. It is no more concerned with the moral values of those facts than it is with the moral significance of the housefly or the pneumococcus. The moment science undertakes to make value judgments by separating its data into classes of good and bad it becomes wishful and ceases to be pure science.

In his method the structuralist relied mainly on introspection, or self-observation. But this was neither the fevered self-vivisection of a Rousseau nor the almost bland self-examination of James and his troop of functionalists. On the other hand, Titchener's introspection, though now generally rejected, involved a steeled, selfless, cautious, and minutely painstaking reporting of one's mental processes, with utter disregard for their worth or meaning. The psychologist's task, in short, was first to analyze, and then to synthesize mental experience.

Today structuralism is not the flourishing thing it used to be. Its fall from grandeur, rather curiously, was effected in a measure by its determination to be unsparingly scientific. Not only does the search for truth, for the sake of truth, require a rare fortitude, but it is not the way, of course, to woo and win the multitude. Peers and commoners alike pine not for truth, but for advice, and from the structuralist this was not forthcoming. His schooled aloofness gained him little support in the marketplace. Certainly, in this respect structuralism was no match for the psychology of experience and action, which not only was ready with counsel for everyday living but also gladly and eagerly accommodated itself to the advancement of service. But structuralism had its inherent weaknesses. Was it deliberately nonrational? Then it was also artificial and mechanical. Like all psychologists until the advent of the behaviorists, its adherents plumbed and probed consciousness. For years they dissected its various elements; yet at the same time they remained obdurate in their refusal to relate consciousness to personality. The study of personality, in fact, left them cold. By many modern psychologists Titchener and his clan are berated for their "atomism," which is to say their effort to understand mental life by dividing and subdividing it into its component elements and studying each one apart from the others. The belief which is given currency today holds that the behavior of every organism is interrelated and that its integrated totality cannot be fathomed by a study of the action and reaction of the organism's separate elements. Another fissure in the science of Titchener was its preponderant reliance on introspection. Though structuralists held themselves steadfast in their insistence on care and exactitude, and though they aimed at all times at the utmost objectivity, their method unhappily fell short of such a noble mark.

Despite its lacks and limits, however, structuralism, judged in afterlight, cannot be curtly cast aside. Its zeal for honest science, with no eye to the practical worth of its findings, may make no appeal to the American generality, but neither does the exact determination of π or the precise temperature of the earth's dead center. Even so, it is from the concern for such occult phenomena that civilization gropes ahead. Beginning with Wundt, the psychologist loosened the philosopher's shackles on psychology, and in time they pried themselves free completely. The findings which they made have on the whole held water, but they are mostly of a restricted sort, sometimes even microscopic, and when set against the vast backdrop of human enterprise, normal and otherwise, they seem flyspecks and insignificant.

Functionalism is of American origin. Some patriots, in fact, have saluted it as the "most characteristic American psychology." Like their structuralist forerunners, the functionalists put a considerable stock in the method of self-observation, but as in the case of a doctor, when he asks his patient where and how it hurts, their confidence was cautious, and whenever they could, they supplemented introspection with objective observation. Like the structuralist again, the functionalists ventured to explore the mystery of consciousness, but their findings, taking one with another, were scanty and of little scientific moment. But unlike the Titchenerians, when functionalists pinned their man under the glass, their research was directed not so much toward what he was, but toward what he did—hence their interest in his habits and instincts and in his feelings, sensations, and thoughts. True to their pragmatic proclivity, James and his successors did not believe that the science of human behavior must deal with facts alone. Instead, they were all for putting it to work.

Their readiness to give counsel and instruction has brought them, as it has theologians and philosophers, into the arena of human affairs. It was Dewey, a functionalist, who, in 1899, in his presidential address before the American Philosophical Association, in congress at New Haven, Connecticut, called for the application of psychology to social practice. And it was because of functionalist promptings that the huge aggregation of psychological specialists came upon the scene. The nightmare which once palsied Harvard's Prof. Hugo Münsterberg, that psychology might someday occupy itself with the civilized American's preference in cigarette holders and meerschaum pipes, holds no such terrors for today's functionalist. Such considerations are as much a part of his workaday science as the pedagogy of reading, the selection of a first-rate heliotherapist, or his scrutiny of a man's taste in malt liquor or pajamas, or even, for that matter, in professors. Luckily, Münsterberg was able in time to overcome his tremors and give appreciable assistance to furthering vocational guidance and industrial psychology, without which life in contemporary America would scarcely be the marvelous thing it is.

The willingness—nay, the eagerness—of the functionalists to emerge from the academic sanctum to examine ordinary people's problems naturally vastly increased the scope of their science. But it would be a mistake to assume that their searchings were directed merely at giving guidance; actually they advanced their psychological science a good deal. They developed a maturer methodology, they unearthed new clues to the way we learn, and they gave attention to the way motives and goals shape the course of our daily living. The functionalists were in the very forefront in sensing the significance of human behavior and dynamics, two prized and fundamental concerns of every earnest and up-to-date psychological sect. Finally, they demolished the cherished fancies about the successive steps involved in the development of our mental functions from infancy to maturity.

A kinsman of functionalism is Edward Lee Thorndike's *connectionist psychology*. For a time Thorndike gave an ear to James at Harvard, but after taking his master's degree, he made for the classrooms of James McKeen Cattell, once an apprentice to Wundt, but later a practitioner on his own at Columbia University. Thorndike's powerful mind quickly led him to the front rank of psychological science, bringing him his doctorate in animal psychology and, after a short spell, a place on the faculty of Teachers College, where he stayed until his time came to retire.

Not many have worked their field so assiduously and so tremendously. Like other pioneers of psychology, Thorndike launched himself as an observer of the behavior of animals, who, needless to say, are not given to introspective communication. From Cattell out of Wundt, Thorndike was infused with a fierce ardor for exactitude which brought him in time into the domain of educational measurement, then still uncharted. He made a comprehensive study of the nature of learning and the so-called "theory of the transfer of training," going after them with bob and yardstick and in the process exploding some of teaching's most venerable convictions. He studied and documented the nature of individual differences and mental capacities. From him came fresh and penetrating ideas on the psychological nature of skill and growth. Not only were his researches into adult learning novel and extensive, but, of greater consequence, they also put their challenge to the old and established view that only the young can learn with ease and effectiveness and that people on in age, like the proverbial old dogs, are done for. He thus helped to mount the adult education movement in this country on a firm psychological foundation. Finally, it was Thorndike who formulated the stimulus-response psychology and who in the end made S–R as familiar as the IQ to the student of education.

In educational chronicles, and especially in their references to educational psychology, the name of Thorndike must be written with capitals. During his more than twoscore years of labor at Teachers College he confronted several thousand students, baring to them the substance of his views and inspiriting not a few of them with a high devotion to the pursuit of science, though his own leaning, it must be said, was toward the quantitative and the statistical. For the majority of his students, whether they became teachers, administrators, or psychologists, Thorndike set the psychological style. Thus he put his signature upon his era. His fame and influence reached their high mark in the twenties. Since then not a few of his findings have succumbed to newer probings—such is the cruelty of progress. Indeed, even the essence of his viewpoint, the S–R psychology, has been under attack. Once almost a required article of faith in the higher pedagogical learning, its insistence that learning is a purely mechanistic process is under fire today, especially, as we shall see in later pages, by the gestaltists.

Younger than either structuralism or functionalism is behaviorism. Its founder, and for many years its reigning pontiff, was John B. Watson, though Karl Lashley, his dowered student at Johns Hopkins, did much of the early spadework and even anticipated some of its basic postulates. Like the rest of the psychological fraternity, behavorists have not always seen eye to eye, and, in consequence, they have had their schisms. Like the biologist, the behaviorist regards man as an animal, the chief among the primates, but still an animal. What distinguishes him from his comrade fauna and ranks him as their highest representative on this planet is simply the number and fineness of his laryngeal, visceral, and manual habits. So, at any rate, runs the behavorist's thesis. On this trinity he has fixed his microscopes. Only such phenomena, moreover, as are observable to the outside watcher, fortified, when possible, with the most acute precision instruments known to science, are admissible to behavoristic examination. Hence the study of consciousness, so long the indispensable staple of the psychological stockroom, was tossed out, and with it also went the method of introspection.

Behaviorism made psychological headlines with its pump-handling of the so-called "conditioned reflex." For a time, in truth, the laity was almost as aware of it as it was of the racy ruminations of Dr. Freud. The actual experimentation which begot the concept of the conditioned reflex, however, was the work not of Watson, or even a fellow American, but of an imperial Russian, the celebrated physiologist and Nobel prizeman Ivan Pavlov. Like most of us who have been to school, Pavlov knew that whenever a person consumes a savory morsel, saliva is produced in quantity, and so are the gastric juices in the stomach. Pavlov also observed that in this respect dogs behaved like men. Indeed, the glands of man's most loyal friend sprang into action even before the actual victualing began. Set a dish of seductive bones before Fido, and the mere presence of them would untap a flow of juices, as would, in fact, the mere sight of the animal's waiter. Pavlov realized, of course, that the connection between the canine salivary display and the presence of the attendant was an indirect one. This caused the Russian to wonder whether he could summon other stimuli, quite unassociated with Fido's customary dining, and make them evoke a response from the dog's salivary glands. Accordingly, while the animal was drooling over his victuals, Pavlov would stimulate him by clanging a bell or shining a light. After a number of such attempts he clanged the bell and flashed the light without, however, offering so much as a crumb, and lo and behold, Fido's mouth overflowed as usual. Such in essence was the starting point of the world's knowledge of the conditioned reflex.

The official English version of Pavlov's experiment reached these shores in 1902, and it was hardly any time before the conditioned reflex was exciting the interest of American behavioral students. By 1908, Morton Prince, for example, was venturing to demonstrate that the psychic powers of his laboratory beasts differed only slightly from those of the chief primate. Awhile later Lashley was able to show that human glands, like those of Pavlov's historic dog, could be conditioned. Watson, meanwhile, experimenting with babies, revealed that Homo sapiens is born with but three unadulterated emotions—fear, love, and rage—and that these are elicited by a limited number of stimuli. A babe, aged but a few days, fears only a loud noise or the loss of his physical support. Does he later, as an adult, flee from snakes or skunks, and does he shake and tremble before a dark and windblown graveyard? Then it is because his fears somehow have been acquired. Or, in Watsonian parlance, he has been "conditioned."

At first Watson paid slight heed to such matters. In fact, as late as 1914, he was convinced that the conditioned reflex was greatly limited in "its general range of usefulness," and that in grappling with it scientifically, there were "inherent difficulties in method." But ten years following he was of another mind. Give him a healthy and normal infant, and he could, he now asserted, condition him to become the kind of adult he wanted him to be. He could make him "doctor, lawyer, artist, merchant-chief, and yes, even beggar man and thief," regardless of his talents, penchants, abilities, vocations, and the race or nationality of his ancestors.

Behaviorism reached flood height in public esteem early in the twenties. Since then its popularity has subsided, and today it excites no more notice among the literate laity than the Rover Boys or Billy Sunday. Its fall was due in no small way to the extravagance of its pretensions. Yet Watson's cockiness notwithstanding, the psychology which he helped to nurse and put before the public eye cannot easily be brushed aside. Its claims have since been appreciably modified, but in their essence they have not been scientifically disproved. Indeed, no first-rate psychologist, sober and in his right mind, would today dispute the possibility of conditioning, nor would he be likely to cast any serious doubt on its potential value in helping to mold a child's behavior. The behaviorists undertook to conduct their operations with the calculated and rigorous procedure of the laboratory scientist, and consequently they were obliged to confine themselves to dealing with only a small part of the vast field of human behavior. At the same time, however, their painstaking methodology put new vigor into their science. It was the behavorist who put the final quietus on the introspective procedure, and it was his sharp and forthright assault on the stale practices of the older psychologies which prompted their keener and more astute practitioners to check and overhaul their professional wardrobe. Thus the behaviorist served to catalyze the development of psychology as a whole.

Gestalt psychology flung out its banner in Germany in 1912, when Max Wertheimer essayed to state some of its fundamental propositions. Not only were these of a startling novelty, but they also flaunted a decidedly heretical air and were at odds with the structural assumptions of Wundt who, though by now a grizzled and bespectacled veteran, was still a potent force among German psychologists. It was not until after Versailles, however, that gestalt psychology caught the American fancy. It made its first stir in the republic with the publication of Wolfgang Koehler's *The Mentality of the Apes* which, despite its beguiling title, was a serious work resulting from years of hobnobbing with the chimpanzees of the Canary Islands.

Skeptical over Thorndike's more or less accredited view that animals learn primarily through trial and error, Koehler put his hairy pupils into situations where their response was plainly not a random act, but one which sprang from something of a mental process. By means of a series of graded experiments he concluded that our simian cousins were, indeed, capable of such a process, and that, when confronted by a total situation, they grasped it by perceiving all its parts not as separate entities, but together as an integrated whole. Jocko apparently gave meaning to an irrelevant object by making it relevant to the situation.

"Gestalt," is German usage for "form," figure," or "shape," though in English psychological speech, the word has been generally rendered as "pattern," or by the ghastly "configuration." Whatever you name it, for its proponents it is the basic mental attribute. Every experience, they contend, has a definite and intrinsic pattern, and the various aspects of any experience reside in their sum at the moment they congeal and appear to us as a mosaic whole. Does the professor attend a session of the faculty? Then clearly his humors tag along too, his gaseous stomach, his hard-pressed spouse, a coed's perfumed note, in short, his joys and melancholies; and with them there is the effect upon him of his immediate surroundings, the hard seat he suffers in, the smoke-filled air, and his comrades *in facultate*, who please or bore him or, maybe, even sour and depress him. Whatever his reaction to the question at hand, it is borne upon by a consciousness of the environment, by its coalesced totality.

The gestaltist's basic theory may easily be followed by one of his favorite exhibits. Glimpse at the accompanying figure, and you will notice that each of its walls shows a break; yet the viewer, in his mind's eye, tends to

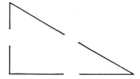

bridge the breaks and to behold the figure not as three broken parts, but as a triangle. This, the gestaltists tell us, is because we incline to react to the situation in the gross rather than to its separate and explicit details. We thus react to elements which are dominant and to others which are only partially apparent. The pattern (gestalt) of experience, however, is not necessarily fixed, nor is it at all times the same. Now one set of elements may predominate, and now they may recede and be replaced by another. Such a shift, gestaltists say, depends largely on the purpose of the moment. Holding that a rational and sensible man knows what he is about to do, and how he is going to do it, gestaltists lay great weight on the "live and dynamical context determining one state this way and that change another way." Even more, we may "experience *why* . . . a given effect should be just the one growing out of it." Thus gestaltists regard *purpose* as an integrating element of experience.

The first gestaltists did most of their work on perception. Later they turned their attention to other matters, including memory and learning, thinking and feeling, growth, development, intelligence, and personality. Learning they saw not as a matter of drilling and doing, or even stimulus and response, but as perceiving and patterning. The older theorems which related learning to stimulus and urged the necessity of use and effect to make the learning successful, the gestaltists have discarded. Much of their criticism has been aimed at the behaviorists and the Thorndike connectionists. Behavior, argued the late Kurt Lewin, a major gestaltist in his time, is not caused by neural connections; it is the release of tension which determines what we do. Imagine, for example, suggests Lewin, that you intend to mail a letter. As long as it remains unmailed, tension is resident within you, but once the message is through the slot and on its way, physical equilibrium is reestablished, and you proceed to forget about it. By the same score Lewin tried to relate psychic energies to the organism's need. The latter he portrayed as psychic forces tapping the reservoirs of energy, and as the need altered, so bodily tensions changed too. Lewin's stress on the factors behind behavior brought him to such problems as the behavior of children who find themselves in novel situations, the dynamics of their play, the relationship of tensions to fatigue and hence to effectiveness, and so on.

In his criticism of the mechanistic psychology, Lewin offered what appears to be a formidable substantiation of the wholeness of human behavior. A statistical average, no matter how vast a number of cases it is derived from, he held, can tell us very little—it is at best an uncertain light. For numbers, he argued, are delusive, and to the ever-lurking question *"Why?"* they remain forever mute. Why, in illustration, does a person in a given place act in a certain way? And why at a certain moment does a given situation have a certain structure? And why does one have precisely such-and-such a state and such-and-such a condition? The answers, Lewin felt, are to be had only from the study of human behavior in real, concrete situations, and not in any numerical figure. Only when we are familiar with the "form of definite structure in a definite environment," can we begin to comprehend the causes of behavior. To this end Lewin and his coworkers sought to build their science on what, in the phraseology of the physicist, they call *space-time concepts,* the theory being that "whenever an organism behaves psychologically, it is said to behave in a psychological field." It is known in the jargon of the trade, as the "field psychology," or even as the "organismic psychology."

Like their comrades who worship at other shrines, the gestaltists have courted the wrath of the gods whom they deny. They have been charged with making vaporish assertions, though surely in this department they have no monopoly. They have been set down as "unscientific," especially in the way they deal with mental life, since their stress on the singularity of mental phenomena precludes a repetition of cases. And finally, they have been assailed for what their critics hold to be a disproportionate emphasis on their primary principle, the "wholeness point of view."

The gestaltists, for their part, have countered blow with blow. Some of their conclusions, they have let it be known, have been substantiated by psychologists from other camps, and notably by such eminent and cautious experimenters as Coghill and Lashley. To the allegation that they are unscientific, they reply that since they hold mental life to be unique, and hence not readily amenable to investigation by any existing method, it is surely not unscientific to seek to devise a more satisfactory methodology.

For all the floggings it has taken, the Gestalt psychology shows no serious bruises. Though its claims are still the subject of fierce dispute, at least its partisans have compelled their challengers to reexamine their own ideas. In contending with Thorndike and Watson and their various issue, followers, and successors, the Gestalt brethren have formulated a pretty strong bill of particulars. At all events, their stress on the unity of an experience is of capital importance.

Another revelation from Europe, of course, is psychoanalysis. Devised by the celebrated Viennese Dr. Sigmund Freud, the psychoanalytic procedure strives to bring forth the secrets of the psyche which lie coiled in the inner grottoes of the unconscious. So far its dealings have been almost entirely with the vagaries and abnormalities of human behavior. Hence its lure has been for the medico rather than the schoolman. And by the same token, its foremost practitioners are M.D.s rather than Ph.D.s or Sc.D.s, not to mention Ed.D.s.

According to Freud, the human psyche has three separate, and yet not separate, identities. First we have the *id*, which is instinctive and unconscious; then the *ego*, which is rational and mainly conscious; and last the *superego*, which is a sort of moral conscience. In the first, the id, lurk man's primordial urges. Some of them, having been ostracized by civilized society as "wrong" or "bad," have been repressed.

Of all the primal urges which have been held at bay the foremost is sex. Erotic instinct, or *libido*, as Freudians say, grips even the babe at nurse. Indeed, his mother is said to be the infant's "first love." If his impulses are not rerouted toward other objects, they become, alas, "fixated." Integrated, they confront the world as the familiar Oedipus complex. Together with other complexes, Oedipus hides within us all, and when our guard is down as, say, in dreams, it sneaks out into the open. Dreams, Freudians assert, are the indispensable key to the mystery of human behavior.

Like all other psychological scientists, those who traffic in the unconscious have not escaped heresy and dissent. The arch-gospel of Freud, though still well regarded, has been overhauled and revamped, notably by Drs. Jung and Adler. To fathom the riddle of personality, Jung and his fellow believers rely less on sex and more on psychological types. Thus one may be "introverted" or "extroverted." If the former, then one's psyche retreats into the snug harbor of the inner self; if the latter, it advances into the world without. As an introvert you are expected to be more or less sensitive, shy, and reticent—a violet, so to say, hiding underneath the foliage. As an extrovert you are likely to be full of talk and gusto, a boomer and a booster, a joiner, and a meeting-goer to boot.

Dr. Adler's specialty was the complex, and the inferiority complex in particular. This stalks its victims when they are still in unsuspecting infancy. Its main cause, so Dr. Adler has taught, is a sense of weakness and futility, of not being wanted, or the frustrations of the effort to deal with the environment. Physical and mental deficiencies, real or fancied, may increase the complex and sometimes, unhappily, goad its harried owner over the precipice. A sense of inferiority, so Dr. Adler asserted, may cause one to become inordinately self-assertive, even seeking to lord it over one's entourage. At its worst, it results in a Hitler.

In their various appraisals of psychoanalysis the experts, once again, disagree. Some hail it as the fabulous philter for all the earthly woes. Others see it with a jaundiced eye. In Hitler's moral Reich its doctrines were forbidden as a gross obscenity, a scandal to Thor and Wotan. Its available practitioners were stored in jail, and their works heaved into the incinerator. The vast bulk of psychoanalytic findings have issued from case studies dealing with abnormal and esoteric behavior. The neurotic, the mentally sick, and the emotionally crippled have been its leading clients, and of these, to one's great sorrow, there is no shortage of supply. What bearing all this may have on the so-called "normal" is still uncertain and a matter of honest debate. No doubt, as one of several ways of prying into the bleak, labyrinthian byways of human behavior, the psychoanalytic approach has its commendable uses. And what holds for the big wide world holds also for the more confined enclave of the schoolroom. The young, like their elders, it has been established, have their measure of sad distresses and emotional gnawings.

3   As psychology came out of the cloister and applied itself more and more to explaining the phenomena of human behavior, its practical worth for education naturally augmented. Where only a few generations ago its significance to the working schoolmaster seemed vague and far away, it is today considered as essential to the schoolmaster as his chalk and board rubber. So important, indeed, has its role become that in the greater part of the republic an acquaintance with its fundamentals is currently a more or less standard requirement in the training of the prospective teacher. Applied to education, psychology lays its stress on seeking out the nature of learning—what the process is, how to start it, and how to egg it on efficiently and successfully. This, it has been found, is far from the simple elemental process it was once held to be. It involves the vast and baffling congeries of human behavior, and ranges from the ancestral roots through its conscious and unconscious forms, and it includes the study of instincts, emotions, capacities, interests, motives, and so on, almost, it seems, without end. From their expeditions into these domains, educational psychologists have returned laden with formidable and, at times, most useful data. But like the psychological practitioners in general practice, they have not always been in unanimous agreement over the actual nature of what they have unearthed or what their findings precisely signify.

Even concerning such a seemingly simple affair as, for example, the human instinct there reign different and all too often divergent views. Not only are instincts accounted for in varying manner, but in different textbooks on the subject you will find lists of instincts which are infinitely protean and diverse. Some, for example, deny that there are such things as instincts, at least of a true and undefiled kind; some will concede a couple of basic ones; and some catalog them by the score.

Thorndike, an early trail maker in the field, thrust his instincts into three classes: those revolving about food and self-preservation, those having something to do with one's response to the behavior of others, and those related to cerebral and bodily activity. Consider, on the other hand, the inventory of William McDougall, in his prime a Harvard don, but now post-mortem. As long ago as 1908 he was able to snag at least seven instincts, to wit: curiosity, revulsion, flight, pugnacity, self-abasement, self-assertion, and the parental instinct. Later he brought in laughter. Then he admitted pairing and mating and several others. In contrast to McDougall's crowded pantry, Watson's instinct list restricts its membership to fear, love, and rage.

And as with instinct, so with emotion. Once the argument ran that we inherit "patterns" of love, hatred, and fear—even of sympathy, humor, and pathos. Under the experimental eye, however, this confidence began to wobble. Watson converted many to the view that a child no older than three has but three primary emotions, namely, fear, anger, and love. These, very likely, are inborn, but the more complex and engulfing ones, such as grief and joy, are probably formed as we live, suffer, weep, and laugh. Emotions, moreover, are no mere overt manifestations. Part of the living organism, they raise and lower blood pressure, regulate the flow of glandular juices, and even alter digestion, respiration, and pulse beat. All emotions, native or acquired, intrude into our everyday living. That they bear upon the public peace and happiness should be obvious, as should the observation that they carry stupendous implications for pedagogy.

Through most of the nineteenth century, learning was commonly regarded as the acquisition of knowledge. There were, of course, numerous ways of stimulating the process, and in the hands of a lover of teaching, the business became an engrossing art. But the Pestalozzis and the Parkers were not the rule, and for every handful of their exalted order there were droves of drab and artless pendants for whom learning was nothing more than stuffing the young head with a mass of facts. That there was something hollow about such doings had been suspected time and again. Men as different and far removed as Penn and Rousseau had assailed them, and so had Erasmus, Montaigne, Rabelais, and several others of that company. However, the nineteenth century was on the calendar before the learning mystery began to be granted a more or less logical examination, when Dr. Herbart burst in with his satchel of interests and apperceptive masses. For a time, as has already been rehearsed, the Herbartian theories exerted a powerful appeal in the United States, and during the eighties, it may be recalled, their popularity was tremendous. But despite their vogue, in the subsequent years they were abandoned. What brought them down was not their un-American stress on the intellect, but rather their unsatisfactory underlying psychology.

Although the Herbartians had introduced a sounder view of learning, its foundations were almost wholly philosophic, and under scientific pressure they began to crack and crumble. This is not saying, however, that the prevalent views are solid in their mooring. At best they float in the stage of scientific theory—a notch higher, in other words, than a mere hypothesis. With the advent of a more scientific psychology, learning began to be viewed as a process somewhat akin to the forming of a habit. The learning process, some even felt, was like gravity and osmosis, a simple matter of natural law, reducible to the so-called "laws of learning." The behaviorists inclined to this persuasion, but emphasized, as one might expect, their favorite theory of conditioning. Others, of the Thorndike tribe, put their store in S–R. Given a stimulus, they chanted, there would be the inescapable response, and to attain the desired response all that was needed was a meet and proper stimulus.

In our present times these views have become somewhat suspect, and though they have not yet been read out of court, their partisans are far less sure of themselves than they were some years ago. They have been shaken, no doubt, by the charge that learning as they conceive it tends to be piecemeal and mechanical. The gestaltists, per contra, insist that learning is not simply a response to a stimulus, but something which is an integral whole. It is, they argue, an organization and reorganization of behavior in relation to a total situation. Hence, it is not just a matter of bagging and ordering facts, nor is it a matter of conditioned reflexes.

When John Locke, with some ifs, buts, and whereases, ventured to propose that the mind possessed what—for want of a better word—might be designated as "faculties," he little suspected that his carefully guarded statement would someday hatch the so-called "faculty psychology." Long after Locke's translation to eternity—more, in truth, than a century—it was the belief in high intellectual stations not only that the mind is divided into assorted faculties but that each and every one of them is something of a free principality performing its assigned task in complete independence from the others. Each of these faculties, moreover, could improve the efficiency of its performance with the aid of certain appropriate subjects. Latin and Greek, for instance, were just the thing, it was believed, to "train the mind." Geometry and algebra were the calisthenics that gave potency to the reason, and so was grammar. Simple drawing, referred to in the infancy of the present century by the Regents of the University of the State of New York as "elementary representation," fortified the power of observation. Even sewing and manual training played their part. Once, moreover, a certain power had been trained through the medium of a particular subject, it was believed to show itself in other domains as well. Did the rising carpenter, for example, obtain a measure of exactitude when he made a table? Then the exactness he displayed with hammer and saw translated itself into a general habit, and he was precise when he parted his hair or compounded a martini, or when he studied the record of his congressman or his bookie. Such at bottom was the doctrine of the transfer of training.

Before scientific psychology had come out of its teething period, the transfer theory was well regarded, and schoolmen everywhere devoted themselves assiduously to its application. But as the years proceeded certain doubts began to rise, and soon the laboratories were putting the doctrine into the test tubes. As test followed test, transfer of training got scant support. Not only was there slight scientific testimony in his behalf, but where formerly it had been a cardinal article of faith in the creed of every pedagogue, it was now roundly rejected. Even so, the psychologists continued their searching, and in time they arrived at somewhat mellower conclusions. Led by Thorndike, some of them now contended that learning is always specific and that if transfer does occur at all, it is only because of the presence of certain "identical elements." The study of, say, French would be of some help in the study of Spanish, where there is a basic similarity between the two. Trigonometry, on the other hand, would help very little, and the study of a Spanish omelet even less. It was found, moreover, that a transfer might be expected in instances where a teacher deliberately essayed to develop habits of reasoning and the making of applications therefrom. But as usual, there are other views. Thorndike's perennial opponent, Dr. Charles Judd, of Chicago, insisted that one may expect transfer only when one's experiences have been generalized in the act of learning. Still others—mostly of the Gestalt fraternity—hold learning to be something involving broad patterns. The mind, they insist, is an entity within itself and within the entire organism. Learning, hence, involves not fragmentary responses, like so much puddle hopping, but rather responses which are organized into whole patterns. Finally, there are those—confirmed and disagreeable skeptics beyond a doubt—who feel that in the actual schoolroom the whole transfer argument is mostly sound and fury.

16
THE SCIENTIFIC
MOVEMENT IN EDUCATION

While Wundt was forging psychology into the first stages of a laboratory
science, across the English Channel the eugenists Francis Galton and Karl
Pearson were introducing it to statistics. Though neither of these gentlemen
concerned himself particularly with pedagogy, the methods they employed
and the principles they upheld helped to lay the foundation of the numerical
and quantitative approach to education. From their various endeavors
evolved the sciences of anthropometry and biometry, both of which caught
the eye of James McKeen Cattell. As has already been instanced, Cattell, like
Hall, had learned the fine points of his trade from Wundt—for a spell, in
fact, he had been Papa Wilhelm's diligent assistant. At Columbia, where he
practiced as professor of his specialty, Cattell proceeded to make himself
a master of exact laboratory and statistical research and to put it to work in
his various psychological explorations. From these, in 1890, emerged his
epoch-making study, *Mental Tests and Measurement*. Of even greater moment, as we shall see, was another—Edward Lee Thorndike, a student of
Cattell, and one who was destined to outshine even his teacher and to become the accredited sire of educational statistics.

2   Although mental testing had been advocated by the American Philosophical Association, for a long time the business made scarcely any headway. Not, indeed, until America caught up with the amazing exploits of
Alfred Binet, a Parisian, who had been trained in law, did American interest in mind measuring come ablaze. Binet began his historic work in
1895, when he set himself the task of developing a more or less reliable
tool to distinguish a bright child from a doltish one. With help from his
fellow seeker, Theodore Simon, a medico, he was able to bring forth a scale
which purportedly measured what, for want of a better name, was called
"general intelligence." Far from satisfactory even to its inventors, the original Binet-Simon yardstick was given repair and revision, once in 1908, and
again in 1911. Despite its Gallic tincture, the new device won a quick interest from American students of the psyche, and in 1908 Henry Goddard
brought the tests over here to help him classify weak-minded children in his
Vineland, New Jersey, school, where he served as research director. Just
before the First World War a number of Americans were giving mental
testing some serious professional attention. But to put the Binet-Simon tests
into satisfactory use over here, it was necessary to adjust them to the American culture, a task which was completed in 1916, when Prof. Lewis Terman
published his Stanford Revision. His work spread over a dozen pages, and
its questions enabled an examiner to plumb the intelligence of anyone from
a three-year-old to what was described as a "superior adult." In addition,

the professor issued instructions for tracking down one's intelligence quotient, or IQ, though in this he was not the first, having been preceded by William Stern, an *ordentlicher Professor* at Hamburg.

Another boost for mental testing, oddly enough, was the war itself. With the aid of psychological experts, many of whom had divested themselves of their drab robes of learning for the greater sartorial elegance of the commissioned officer, the Army concocted the so-called "alpha" and "beta" intelligence tests. Employed on a gigantic scale, they threw light on the American's intelligence, revealing some amazing surprises and, what was probably more important in the long run, showing the feasibility of administering intelligence tests on a wholesale scale.

Following the war, mental testing advanced from the barracks to the classroom, and the leading students of the psyche addressed their efforts to perfecting group tests. In their quest they were immensely successful, though this is not saying that their instruments have attained perfection or that they have reached unanimous agreement on what the nature of human intelligence actually is. Be that as it may, as the years went on, large-scale testing established itself as an integral—one might even say indispensable—part of an efficiently operated school system, so much so that as the century came into its forties the schoolchild whose intelligence had not been measured at one time or another had become something of a rarity. For all their acceptance, however, ever since they were first resorted to, group intelligence tests have been the cause of doubt and dismay, and hence, as is common in our free democracy, of outspoken criticism. The fact that parents—and even teachers, who should know better—persistently misinterpret the significance of an IQ had doubtless heated the antagonism. More lately, however, as the republic's social conscience became more and more sensitive to the nation's hard-pressed nether folk, the fact that children from impoverished homes commonly do not fare so well in the scores they make has brought the group intelligence test under sharper fire than ever. In truth, largely because of the charge that such testing is unfair to such hapless youngsters, several cities, including New York, have ceased the practice of group intelligence testing.

3   Just as the nineteenth century was ebbing to its optimistic end, a new voice was raised in favor of educational research. It issued from Dr. Joseph Rice, a dabbler in public questions and the editor of the *Forum,* long since gone to its grave. What, he asked, does pedagogy need to make it an up-and-coming science? It needs, he answered, "to discover at least some truths in regard to the educational process." To show just what he had in mind, Rice set himself the forbidding task of putting an inquiring and critical eye on the spelling talents of some thirty thousand children taught in a variety of ways and dispersed over different parts of the Union.

Some of them had applied their industry to the subject for fifteen minutes daily; others had huddled over their spellers for no less than forty minutes every day. In the end Rice unearthed the finding that in achievement the two groups differed only slightly. The fifteen-minute men, it appeared, could spell as well—or as badly—as the forty-minute ones. Of greater portent than this unexpected disclosure, however, was Rice's reliance on figures rather than on the vagaries which arise from personal opinion—in truth, his insistence on quantitative testimony rather than on subjective judgment marked a novelty in American education.

Unhappily for the immediate forward march of science, Rice received the treatment which usually awaits brandishers of the revolutionary torch —he was doused with rancor and resentment. But time had seen the world make atonement for this unfriendliness, and since Rice's first venture the quantitative analysis of America's educational organism has apparently established itself in permanence. In fact, by 1915, not only had the same guild of school superintendents which a generation back had clawed Rice for his unconventionality overcome their ire to pay him a public compliment, but that year, in annual congress assembled, its members consecrated more than fifty papers to the subject of tests and measurements of educational efficiency.

Although Rice unequivocally was the first on the quantitative scene, the men who got the measurement movement under full steam were professionals, namely Drs. Judd and Thorndike. The two had gone through their intellectual boot training in the nineties as college mates at Wesleyan, where both fell victim to the charms of psychology. Subsequently, to perfect themselves in its experimental techniques, Judd shipped for the laboratory of Wundt, while Thorndike made for the chambers of James at Harvard and then for those of Cattell at Columbia. Though they were often to engage in unseemly controversy, when it came to the advancement of their common science they stood together. Judd did his main work at the University of Chicago, where he picked up Dewey's reins as head of the School of Education. But Wundt's eternal shade must have hovered about, reminding his former apprentice, as he once had in his earthly materialization, that *"a priori ist garnichts."* Meanwhile Thorndike, installed at Columbia's Teachers College, similarly inspired by Cattell, proceeded to perform his many and unforgettable feats. There, with his invention of a scale unit to measure educational achievement, he laid the groundwork for the quantitative investigation of education. At about the same time—in 1908, to be exact—one of his students, Cliff Stone, announced the first objective test for arithmetic reasoning. The year following, in the presence of the elite of the American Association for the Advancement of Science, the master revealed his own scale to measure handwriting. The year of its publication, 1910, is generally celebrated in the history of educational science as the birth year of the movement to measure the products of education mathematically.

During the next few years, within the enclosure of their mechanistic psychology, Judd and Thorndike disgorged test after test and scale after scale. Under their direction every kind of educational enterprise was put under quantitative inspection, from marks and methods to curriculum and administration. Not only did Judd and Thorndike confect their own tests and scales, but they also inspired a long line of disciples to take after them. Under Thorndike, for example, Buckingham brought forth a spelling scale, and Woody an arithmetic scale. Meanwhile at Chicago, Judd was exhorting his young men "to get the facts" and "to be exact," as they grappled with types of reading ability, handwriting movement, the role of eye–voice in reading, and similar profound matters. At the same time the movement spawned a special press, and presently a number of new periodicals, such as *The Educational Measurement Review, The Review of Educational Research, The Encyclopedia of Educational Research, The Journal of Educational Research,* and several others, appeared, their pages bristling with tables, graphs, and formulas and reports of the measurers' latest accomplishments.

From such beginnings grew the measurement movement. Its basic canon was set down by William McCall, who wrote *How to Measure in Education,* published in 1922, a pioneer in the field and for many years its most authoritative pilot. It was McCall's contention, as it was Thorndike's, that "whatever exists, exists in amount, and hence is measurable," provided, he was at pains to explain, the necessary yardstick is available.

As the twenties gave way to the thirties, measurers were conjuring up their wonders in the very center of the educational limelight. They pounced on every aspect of American learning, fixing their calipers and slide rules not only on the common educational disciplines but even on such shadowy touch-me-nots as artistic creativeness, reasoning, imagination, emotion, and personality. They sought to devise scales to reveal one's RQ, or religious quotient, or one's MQ, or moral quotient. In fact, in Wisconsin, a searcher was even able to produce a Standardization of a Badminton Knowledge Test for College Women. Needless to say, not a few of these early efforts were puerile and even nonsensical, and most of them have long since been dispatched to their well-earned oblivion. But as the years surged on and the quantitarians gained in skill and knowledge, they sharpened their gauges as well as their wits and proceeded to make their industry one of competence and deserved respect. Today the notion that in education some things can be measured is no longer a cause for jocosity. Testing and measuring have, as a matter of fact, become an essential part of the up-to-date American school, and almost no self-respecting college of education would be without a department of research or something thereto akin.

What are the things we can measure? Generally anything which is observable is measurable. It is possible to put a figure on a man's weight and altitude, the footage of his waistline, the bulge of his biceps, and other landmarks of his gross anatomy. Today every schoolboy knows there are tests for IQs, as there are for all the familiar subjects, from algebra and arithmetic to the languages and the sciences, whether natural or social. There are tests for attitudes, whether ethical or political, and whether they inhabit the province of religion, society, or race. As for aptitudes, one can measure a whole herd of them, from the simplest mechanical kind to the deep and baffling sort that constitute the phenomenon of a Dewey, a Descartes, a da Vinci, or even a navigator in outer space. Even character has become subject to metric sounding. There are tests to measure your honesty, your moral standards, and your power of will, and after you have gone through the measuring mill there is also, fortunately, a test to let you know the precise degree of your psychic tensions. All these are ponderable and possess sufficient reliability to make them almost indispensable for educational guides and diagnosticians. Even the higher learning has recourse to them—in fact, for screening college applicants such tests have become the rule. But when it comes to putting the measuring stick on the complicated act of the total organism, say, the supreme performance of a great teacher, the measurers, for all their virtuosity, have found it next to impossible to efface the personal equation. As in the case of the judges of a man's performance in letters or music or art, mathematics avails the measurers very little, and our critical dependence, for good or ill, is still a vassal to personal judgment.

Measurement has also impinged on teaching. Though the written and oral examinations which bedeviled our grandfathers still obtain, they have been supplemented by the so-called "objective tests"—or, in the student's lusty lingo, the "objectionable test." Objective tests have sprouted in several varieties, in illustration, true-false, multiple-choice, and matching, to list only a few. Another outcome of the measurement mode is the student's workbook, which has found its way into almost every subject taught in the contemporary American school. From the workbook to the so-designated "teaching machine" was only a scientific step, and though it is still in infancy, its adoption has shown no signs of abatement.

Another outcome for the national passion for fact-finding is the survey. Although its modern dress is strictly of the twentieth century, getting the facts about school conditions and reporting thereon are actually old and hallowed practices in American education. One thinks at once of Barnard and Stowe and Bache, and particularly, of course, of Horace Mann, whose celebrated encyclicals enlivened American education during the cradle days of the common school. Composed on the grand scale and written at times with dash, Mann's annual reports on the goings-on in the Massachusetts centers of knowledge—and oftentimes elsewhere—might aptly be called surveys.

Today's educational survey is of course very different from its predecessor, not only in its scope and mechanics, but even in its reason for being.

Grounded on the sociologist's searching into such matters as a family's food, its lodging, its purse, its loves and hates, and the like, the survey won favor when it became obvious that social facts bore very little significance when they were stripped from their context. What may well have been the first social survey of any scope was conducted in 1909 in Pittsburgh. Directed by Messrs. Kellogg and Devine and larded financially by the Russell Sage Foundation, it essayed a "rapid close-range investigation of wage-earners in the American steel district . . . a demonstration in social economy made graphic against the background of a single city." It hoped "to throw light on these and kindred economic forces not by theoretic discussion of them, but by spreading forth the objective facts of life and labor which should help in forming judgment as to their results. . . ."

The first actual school survey of which we have any word was inaugurated when Boise, Idaho, persuaded Calvin Kendall, a superintendent from Indianapolis, to take a look at its schools and to reveal how they might be bettered. A primitive affair, the business was transacted in a few days, and, commensurate with its simplicity, its findings and recommendations were made public in the local newspapers.

From this dulcet beginning the survey movement got under way, increasing steadily in force and substance, until by the twenties it had driven to lengths undreamed of. In time some of America's salient experts in school administration were drawn into the movement, prodigies like Ayres, Cubberley, Judd, Strayer, and others of similar caliber. It became a standard and orthodox procedure for them to enlist the services of the land's foremost educational masters and with them to run surveys in some of the larger cities. Under their surveillance came some of the country's larger enterprises of public learning, for example, those of Baltimore, Cleveland, Salt Lake City, and Portland, Oregon. In 1913 Boise treated itself to a second helping of the survey, this time on a more ambitious and generous scale. By 1914 the movement had become sufficiently important to receive special attention from the National Society for the Study of Education, which devoted Part 2 of its *Thirteenth Yearbook* to a consideration of surveys. Since then thousands of surveys have been made all over the country, and probably no year goes by without a score of important ones, besides no one knows how many lesser ones. Not only city systems, but state systems as well, have been surveyed, and there have been some national investigations, though these have usually subscribed to more limited searchings, such as, say, a study of teaching personnel or secondary education. More ambitious was the survey undertaken in 1938 during the administration of the second Roosevelt. Reinforced by nineteen supplementary staff studies, this was the first thoroughgoing and comprehensive analysis ever tackled by any nation on this planet.

As has been hinted, the first surveys were inordinately simple. Those who managed them observed and appraised the teachers. They dug into the office files, scanning records, reports, and accounts, and they evaluated the business and pedagogic ménage in general. But the judgment they expressed was personal, and inevitably it was tinged by their views and beliefs, their physics and metaphysics, and not uncommonly their prejudices. However, with the increasingly scientific mood in education, surveyors presently sought, as they said, to "objectify" their gathering of data. Instead of assaying a school system by itself, they now began to compare it with others. They were not content to rely solely on their own judgment, however, and yet in striving to be as dispassionate as was then humanly possible, their work was almost wholly that of a reporter. They were in thrall to *what was;* sometimes they even came up with *what could be;* but only seldom did they seek to reveal how unused resources might be tapped and put to useful educational service.

As measurement techniques gained more and more professional prestige, scales and tests became an indispensable tool in the surveyor's working kit. The honor of being the first standardized test to be used in a survey falls on the Courtis Arithmetic Test, which was employed as far back as 1912, when the New York City school system was put under official survey. Since then, of course, every conceivable measuring rod has been resorted to. Presently, in fact, some surveyors were compounding their own devices, as witness the Strayer-Engelhardt Score Card for Junior High School Buildings, the Bruner Criteria for Teaching and Learning Materials, the Mort-Cornell Guide for Self-Appraisal of School Systems, and yet more. To simplify matters somewhat, in the thirties the Cooperative Study of Secondary School Standards put itself to the trouble of producing a device with which it became possible for any up-and-doing school to make a rough appraisal of itself simply by comparing its accomplishment with that of schools on a list of 198, all exactly labeled and arranged according to rank.

Needless to say, today's full-scale survey can no longer be conducted by a solitary practitioner, as was the historic one at Boise. Headed by a supreme command, it is entrusted to an organized corps of experts—more or less—who emanate from life's various walks. The professors of education naturally enjoy a heavy representation. But there are also sociologists, psychologists, anthropologists, architects, doctors, engineers, and statisticians, besides management and efficiency wizards, accountants, tax specialists, and other business scientists. Under favorable conditions one may find an occasional philosopher. Like everything else in this confounded and complicated era, surveying has become the province of the specialist. In fact, agencies to conduct surveys with the requisite exactitude have been established in the foremost schools of education, as witness the Bureau of Field Studies at Columbia's Teachers College, another bureau similarly titled at the George Peabody College for Teachers in Nashville, Tennessee, and yet others.

Surveys range from the very rudimentary to the very complex. They may deal merely with departmental doings in a one-building university, they may reach out over an entire school system in city or county, or, as has been said, they may range over the length and breadth of the republic itself. Besides being resorted to for an appraisal of the teacher's everyday classroom performance and his all-around competence and efficiency, they may also address themselves to the way schools are staffed, managed, and controlled. In addition they may fix their scrutiny on the pupil's nonacademic life, his health and virtue and his general animal magnetism. Not infrequently they may study the schoolhouse itself, its facilities and amenities, such as heat and lighting, the quality of its air, the decibels in its classrooms and its corridors, the state of its hygiene, the efficacy of its sanitary watch, its janitorial and maintenance officers, and so on to the nature and condition of the provender it sets before its custom in the commons.

The school survey is as typically American as Congress and the Bill of Rights. In alien cultures it is a rarity. Several reasons, but two especially, account for the high regard accorded it. For one thing, there is the obvious urge to know the plain facts. For another, there is the factor of economics. With the relentless increase in school enrollments and the ever-ascending cost of school maintenance, school-board men, harassed by the suffering taxpayers, are quite properly seeking to placate their constituents by getting as much as possible for their dollars. All things considered, though the school survey is hampered by the limitations put upon its science, nonetheless in its public service it has been a boon. Not only has it had the great merit of uncovering flaws and wastage, but, more important, oftentimes it has pointed to better practices.

4   The scope of early American education, as has been elucidated in earlier pages, was very limited. A primary learner, in illustration, was taught the three Rs and a large amount of religion. Higher up in the secondary estate— if he scaled such heights—he took Latin, or sometimes vice versa. On occasion he made acquaintance with Greek, and always he continued the progress of his religious edification. In college the curriculum, which was classical and literary, was modeled upon the medieval Seven Liberal Arts, and since most of the collegians aspired someday to bedizen the pulpit with their presence, the sacred and moral sciences necessary to their purpose were conspicuous. In the flight of time, as the communal stress on faith and piety began to yield to secular pressures, the nation's schools presently reflected the trend. The meanest shacks of knowledge and the highest intellectual shrines alike made room for new, secular subjects, while in the public schools instruction in religion ceased. But such academic alterations came slowly—far more slowly, indeed, than those which were overtaking America as a whole.

Prior to the nineties curriculum making was left to individuals, or sometimes to small specialized groups whose industry was usually carried on locally in city and state. Sometimes, as in the case of Massachusetts, such effort led to legislation. But the century was approaching its end before the curriculum began to engage the attention of the specialist, and its study acquired a national dimension.

The new approach was undertaken in 1892, when the National Education Association appointed a Committee of Ten. Its members included some of the country's most scintillating men of learning—scholars like Charles Eliot (its chairman), James B. Angell, William T. Harris, and Henry C. King. Assigned to clarify the function of the American high school and, if possible, to furnish it a commendable standard, the committee occupied itself especially with what the high school taught. Every discipline esteemed by high school academicians of those days came under examination, from English, Latin, Greek, and the modern foreign tongues to mathematics, the natural sciences, history, and what then was generally spoken of as "civics." From its collective palavers, of which there were several and which were enlightened by the testimony of more or less eminent educators in various sectors of the land, the committee formulated a number of recommendations. For one, it made a stand for a six-year elementary school and a high school course of similar duration. Actually even in those bygone days this was scarcely a novelty, the idea being as old as the seventeenth century, when Jan Amos Comenius, that man of many parts, first offered it to the world. But in the nineteenth century the notion was still sufficiently antinomian to schoolmen to cause them to spurn it. As for the high school's supreme and all-important function, the committee delivered itself of nothing more than lofty platitudes. The high school, it gravely announced, should prepare the young for practical life. In their quest for a national standard, the committeemen were more impressive. The so-called "unit system" they concocted helped to set a national standard for the pupil's academic load at four subjects of four weekly sessions each. But the committee's most successful achievement was far more subtle and this was its benign attitude toward the elective system in the United States. By vouchsafing their blessing thereupon, its members—perhaps innocently—struck the first telling blow in the secondary school's war of liberation against the domination of college entrance requirements.

The first concentrated studies of the curriculum were conducted almost wholly by scholars sitting in the liberal arts colleges. Seen across the span of many years, this is a fact of no little significance, for at bottom they were men of intellectuality, and though their propositions often occasioned scoffs and snickers from the brethren in the lower benches, the intellectual values into which they put their trust underlay pretty nearly all their recommendations—even those which were granted support. Did the professors, for example, stand up for the practical purpose of secondary schooling? Then somehow what they saluted as practical was invariably also cerebral. Did they extol the right of election in the high school? Then they also stressed the indispensability of mathematics and the natural sciences. What they apparently expected from the high school above all was the making of a potential college academician—an expectation which very naturally caused them to favor a curriculum of intellectual discipline.

The endeavor of the Committee of Ten was soon superseded by more formidable efforts. But in the process the nature of the committees themselves underwent a change. Gradually the men of learning were shouldered out, and their places taken by the potentates of school administration, by the principals and superintendents and now and then by the more hopeful Pestalozzis of the lower schools. Then, on the heels of the First World War, examining the curriculum became more and more the business of the professors of education. At the same time the number of investigations showed a robust multiplication. In fact, on in the twenties, the NEA's department of superintendence had several committees pondering curricula throughout the country, filling several roomy volumes to present their findings. In the meantime, other organizations of enlightenment became interested, and in the twenties three of them—the Mathematical Association of America, the Classical Association of America, and the Modern Language Association of America—aided with cash from a variety of educational foundations, were running investigations of their own.

In their major premise most of these inquiries differed not a whit from those preceding them, which is to say that they put their stress on subject matter, particularly language and mathematics. But in 1926, with the issuance of a report of the curriculum committee of the National Society for the Study of Education, there was a change. Not one liberal arts professor graced the committee, and not even a school superintendent. Instead, its twelve members were all professors of education. Although they made their knee at different and even rival philosophical altars, on certain salient points they were in concord. They agreed, for example, that the curriculum should have some bearing on social need and that in their work curriculum makers should pay some heed to social change.

Some four years following, in 1930, the social aspect was stressed still more when a committee of the American Historical Association rendered its report. Headed by Dr. Counts of Columbia's Teachers College and fortified by some of America's foremost social scientists, the committee produced findings of a protean scope—in fact, it took sixteen volumes to hold them. The social keynote is discernible at once in some of the titles, to wit, *A Charter for the Social Sciences in the Schools, Geography in Relation to the Social Sciences, Social Foundations of Education, Social Ideals of American Educators, Citizens' Organizations and the Civic Training of Youth, the Nature of the Social Sciences,* and so on.

In the thirties and forties, when our civilization was under menace, first that of economic depression and then of war, momentous social changes showed themselves. It was, as we now realize in hindsight, a convulsion, a tremendous transvaluation of values. From it emerged industrial and governmental overhaulings. There were changes affecting production, management, and labor. The New Deal and the Fair Deal came into being; people dreamed of a world without political division; and a belief in the democratic mode of life was affirmed in the face of the planned utopias of totalitarian messiahs, whether from the right or from the left. The new social upheavals had their repercussions, of course, in education. But here there were also some special, though related, forces, such as the growing influence of Dewey's ideas, the bearing of the New Psychology and the New Sociology, the inventions of the educational measurers, and—to haul up—the work of the progressive educators.

In the swirl of these shifting currents curriculum study entered a new phase. The dominance of the liberal arts had of course long since run aground. Not only had the professors of education fought against it, but as the thirties headed into the forties, the appraisal of the curricula became the concern not just of the professional educationists but of experts in the curriculum itself. By the mid-thirties they were already in sufficient number to organize a guild all their own, the Society for Curriculum Study.

Many of the new curriculum masters, and especially the more important members of the new fraternity, were of a progressive inclination. Under their sway, in consequence, the approach to curriculum study was liberalized. Where formerly such studies had been reserved for a small, select class of the learned gentry, under the new management it became open to all. Curriculum revising was served now not only by professionals and specialists but also by any reflective person who might have anything of promise to offer. Every parent and teacher now had the chance to take his part, if not as a curricular surgeon, then at least as a consultant. True in crossroad hamlets, in counties, and in municipalities, it was true even in an entire commonwealth like Virginia. "The curriculum program which fails to carry editors, civic leaders, and other intelligent laymen," the NEA observed, "will encounter active opposition or lukewarm support." Thus the progress of democracy.

When such a corps goes to work on a curriculum, it may or may not hearken to the voice of science. Not uncommonly, in truth, its dicta flow from the murky well of public opinion. This has been the case especially when the school's old and trusted offerings have come under suspicion, when often enough they have been scrapped in favor of all sorts of newer wonders.

But where the stress still happens to lie on subject matter, several more or less objective approaches have come to hand. One of them, and probably the first in order of appearance, is the "analysis of the frequency of use." It rests on the assumption that civilization in this republic confronts certain unfailing needs and requirements. A first-grade citizen should know, for example, how to spell. But what words does he need to know? There was a time, if he was of normal wit and health, and in the seventh grade of Springfield, Illinois, when he had to account for "bergamot," "deutzia," "weigela," "abutilon," "erysipelas," and similar grisly dragons. In 1914, when Prof. Leonard Ayres surveyed the Springfield schools, he made on-slaught on the spelling curriculum with the following simple assumptions to give him light and direction: (1) the words taught the child in school should be in common use, and (2) the average adult confines most of his orthographic display to his correspondence. Thus armed, Ayres combed sev-eral bales of business and personal letters, assiduously counting and listing the words written therein. He found, as any man of sense might have fore-seen, that the general run of men get along very well without "deutzia," and most assuredly without "erysipelas." Instead it was their practice to phrase their meaning as baldly as possible. From these findings Ayres was able to compound a list of spelling words, the first of its kind in Christendom with a measure of objectivity to give it backbone. Since then other verbal round-ups have been made, and other lists arranged, the most extensive being that of the indefatigable Thorndike, who succeeded in collaring the 20,000 most common words in the American language and corralling them between the covers of a *Teacher's Word Book,* which presently brought forth the Thorn-dike dictionary.

As in spelling, so in the other subjects. Historic and geographic refer-ences, for instance, were determined by the frequency of their appearance in public print. In arithmetic the cue was taken, as in spelling, from com-mon use by adults. Once again it was made evident that their usage was of the starkest kind—that, indeed, the vast mass of grown-ups used the arith-metic processes most sparingly.

In the twenties another method of studying curriculum content—the so-called "job analysis"—came to the fore, especially in courses concen-trating on the vocational preparation of the young. As perfected by Pro-fessor W. W. Charters of Pittsburgh, the job analysis seeks to disclose the essential and characteristic operations of a given job, as, say, a secretary's, a bookkeeper's, or even, if called upon, a snake charmer's or a ventrilo-quist's, and thereupon to fashion the learner's course of training. Thus, instead of giving credence to the accepted notion that the pharmacist of tomorrow can be spared from failure only if he masters at least three years of high school Latin, Charters permitted himself to take a close and skepti-cal look at the Latin actually used by the practicing pharmacist. What he found, to no one's surprise, was that no medico ever made professional use of the locutions of Rome's Caesars and Ciceros. In the druggist's prescrip-tion file one found no *Gallia est divisas*, no *arma virumques*, not even a sonorous *quousque tandem*. Instead one came upon a scrawl of *nux vomi-cas, oleum ricinis, elixir aromaticums*, and similar boons for the human race. From his pharmacological gleanings Charters concluded that, for pro-fessional ends at any rate, instruction in Latin could be stripped to the shell and that the larval druggist would be better helped were he to introduce himself to the sparse and very limited Latin parlance of modern pharmacy.

Plainly, the approaches to curricular revision, like nearly all else on the American intellectual scene, has been diverse. Not only have the subjects themselves been dissected, and their content overhauled and refurbished, and some of it even pealed off, but there have also been efforts to bring subjects into closer concordance. Historically, the first allusion to such a practice was made by the erudite Professor Herbart, who recommended, with lamentable vagueness, that in education there should be "correlation." Then, early in the present century, one sights the secondary schools arranging their offerings around a "core of subjects," which are supposedly "constant" and required learning for everybody. This may well have been the ancestor of the present-day "core curriculum." A more recent curricular blueprint calls for "broad fields" of general and interrelated subjects. Even more novel is the "multiple curriculum with variables," which establishes a number of diverse but typical programs of study with required core subjects and a batch of electives on the side.

Although the curriculum has been broached over divergent paths, on a few salient principles its leading magnificoes were in accord. Generally the essence of their agreement runs thus:

1. Curricular objectives must be formulated, and all subsequent steps should be directed toward them.

2. Our objectives should be related to (*a*) the kind of world we live in, (*b*) the better world in which we should try to live, and (*c*) our philosophy of the educative process.

3. The materials of instruction must be selected, organized, and administered in accordance with the objectives.

4. The aforesaid steps should be tested, and the results appraised.

5. Since revising the curriculum is a perennial task, the foregoing steps must be continuous.

Unhappily, there is also discord. Broadly speaking, one can sight at least two contending groups. On the one side are those who put their stress on subject matter; on the other side are those who lay their primary weight on experience. In the first detachment one finds Bagley, Horne, and Judd, all now gone to rest; metaphysicians like Adler, Barr, and Hutchins; the brigades of Catholic Scholastics; and, finally, probers and analysts like Ayres, Charters, and the like. On the opposing front one finds the lamented Dewey, the bulk of pragmatic academicians and their varied philosophic progeny, and the progressives.

5   Like so many other esteemed commonplaces of modern education, the view that the nature of the child entertains a singularity all its own, and that before attempting to teach the young, one should at least understand the rudimentary facts about them, was voiced by Jean-Jacques Rousseau. But as usual, the wild weathercock from Geneva merely pointed the way and left the actual labor of exploring it to his successors. Pestalozzi made a modest start when he undertook to put his firstborn under vigil and wrote down his observations in a diary. Dr. Herbart, too, has some words to say on the subject, and so did the kindergartner Froebel. Even Darwin found time for a little searching, and in 1877 he disclosed what he had found in a "Biographical Sketch of an Infant," which he published in *Mind*. But all these and other gropings into the unknown nooks and crannies of child nature were at best crude; and so, indeed, they were to stay until science brought new and necessary insights as well as a measure of order and discipline.

Credit for fathering child study in the United States is commonly given to G. Stanley Hall. Some learned and upright men, it is true, have risen to impugn Hall's paternal claim. Even so, it matters little. For it was Hall who gave the science its first great flurry in America. As editor of *The Pedagogical Seminary,* he welcomed it to its pages, proclaiming its newest feats and encouraging monographs thereon from its foremost experts, both alien and domestic. But it was not until psychology transferred itself to the laboratory that child study began to make some scientific progress. In 1903 Thorndike published his *Notes on Child Study*. A year later William Stern, the deviser of the IQ, brought out his impressive *Psychologie der frühen Kindheit*. Put into English some time after as *The Psychology of Early Childhood,* Stern's impressive study was still enjoying use in the late twenties. Meanwhile, led by John B. Watson, the behaviorists had started their clinical work, as had the various psychoanalytic sects. Both, as we know now, suffered in their early days from overconfidence. But time has put a brake on their youthful cockiness, and today most of them are cautious, and some of them are even completely decorous. Today not only are their pronouncements attended to, but, what is more important, they carry weight. Not only did the methods they introduced serve to open the way to regions which heretofore had been inaccessible to serious research, but as their techniques became more refined, they proceeded to blow up many of our favorite myths about the human young.

Today's students of child nature cover an expansive territory. Open any of their leading texts, and you will come upon a terrain which reaches on the one hand to the infant's prehistoric days, and on the other hand to the subtle complex of his personality and the urgings to be himself. You will note a searching of his ancestral roots and of his activity and behavior even before he has honored the earth with his presence. Once he is actually here, his doings are minutely watched—from his first twitchings and reflexes to the displaying of his elemental emotions, his pains and rages and his gurglings, cooings, and yowlings. Modern child study has been much

absorbed in the factors which bear on growth—those which advance or re-
tard it and those which, unhappily, sometimes halt it altogether. Physical
examinations show up bad posture; malnutrition; poor sight or hearing;
pathological teeth, tonsils, and sinuses; and other physiologic disrepair.
With such data at hand and with the counsel and instruction of specialists,
parents and educators can help the child to cope with his handicaps, to ease
them, and maybe even to end them. As for the child's mental growth, here
his ability to learn has been under special vigilance. What is the nature of
his achievement? What prompts and spurs it on? And what holds it at bay
or even arrests it? From such observation, once again, come programs to
deal with the child's special requirements. And what holds for his body and
mind holds also for his social behavior, language, virtue, and dreams—even,
indeed, for the most inscrutable thing called "spirit."

An outgrowth of the movement for child study is the Clinic of Child
Development, which has been in operation at Yale for a number of years.
There are, of course, several others like it, but among them Yale is plainly
one of the most publicized. Under the direction of Arnold Gesell, it has
maintained a persistent watch over the child, studying him while he feeds
and talks and learns and observing him even in the watches of the night
while he slumbers and reposes. The facts which the Yale clinic has dug up
have been stored in the familiar erudite reports and dissertations and, more
important to the national happiness and welfare, in several compositions in
the homelier idiom of the laity, besides being preserved in photographs and
films and, more recently, presented on television. Dr. Gesell himself
has composed a whole shelf of more or less learned books. One of them,
written in collaboration with Dr. Frances Ilg, sketched a composite portrait
of fifty children. All were of excellent mind and came from comfortable
homes; yet when their time came, nearly all betook themselves to the public
school. Heartening though this must be for lovers of democracy, somewhat
more impressive, however, is the doctor's *Infant and Child in the Culture of
Today*. Indeed, for numerous American mothers and fathers it has become
virtually a standard reference work. An even greater attraction has been the
clinic's film, "Life with Baby," which has given instruction and amusement
to many thousands throughout the nation.

Closely linked with the child study movement is the growth of the
modern nursery school. Its beginnings again go back into time's abyss, but
until child study became the object of serious scientific attention, the nursery school was at bottom little more than a place for safe and pleasant
dalliance, an institutionalized baby-sitter, as it were. The Europeans were
the pioneers in the nursery realm, and among the English and the Soviet
Russians the movement has enjoyed a fine prospering. Among the Musco-
vites, in fact, nursery schools have become a mandatory article of the national schooling. In England, as one might guess, the movement has shown
more restraint. It began during the First World War, when mothers found
themselves enmeshed in Britain's industrial effort and in need, hence, of a

safe depository for their infant offspring. As might be expected, the nursery school grew up chiefly in the cities, and its main patrons were the working mothers. In 1920, Columbia University equipped itself with courses in the nursery field when it imported a number of England's foremost practitioners to carry on at Teachers College. Since then such work has greatly augmented, and today the nursery school may be found from one coast to the other. The chief purpose of some schools is the scientific study of the human young. Other schools, however, are more or less in the nature of service, seeking to occupy and shelter the child while mama is busy building up the family bankroll.

A new type of preschool service is Project Head Start. An integral part of the nation's assault on poverty, it is grounded on the observation that all too many children, particularly the numerous offspring of the very poor, are not ready, either physically or emotionally, to be articled at the age of six to the regular elementary school—that, in fact, under the usual conditions, the fates have marked them inescapably for academic failure. To help them surmount their harsh handicap, the Head Start centers receive their young at ages ranging from four to six, putting them under personal watch and study, feeding them, tending them, teaching and reassuring them, and thereby helping them to catch up with their luckier brethren. Launched in 1965, Project Head Start had anticipated servicing some 100,000 children in some 300 communities, of which more than half were scattered in the sub-Potomac region, at an initial cost of $17 million in Federal money. For all their high hopes, the planners found their optimism far too modest. Actually the response turned out to be six times greater.

Does the school aspire to educate every normal child? Then it also addresses itself to those whom fortune has sorely burdened, the sick and the crippled, the blind, the deaf, the mute, and those of faltering mentality. As long ago as 1760 a Frenchman was striving to teach the deaf, and scarcely a decade later another was trying to instruct the blind. From France the idea spread abroad, and presently it came to our own republic. It was a visit to a Parisian school for the blind that inspired John Fisher to found a similar seminary at Boston. Again, it was at the Royal School for Deaf Mutes where Thomas Gallaudet made acquaintance with the sign method, which in 1817 he introduced in his own school for the deaf at Hartford, Connecticut, the first such specialized school in the United States.

The work Gallaudet had begun so auspiciously at Hartford, Thomas Gridley Howe carried on and extended at Boston. More in the national spotlight than his precursor and more resplendent publicly if not more distinguished, Howe was a rope maker's son, with a B.A. from Brown and an M.D. from Harvard; he was, besides, the spouse of the immortal Julia Ward. He was a warmhearted man, civilized, solid, of good mind, and of a vitality that bordered almost on the miraculous. So overflowing was Howe's passion for action that he found it necessary every so often to escape from the captivity of everyday routine, now by traveling in the Old World, now by warring at the side of the rebellious Greeks in their revolution of 1830, now by extending a similar hand to the insurrectionist Poles. When he fell suspect to the Prussians and they made him a guest in one of their royal hoosegows, he busied himself by translating several works on the education of the blind.

Time saw him become the acknowledged master of this domain. Before his work was history, Howe had a hand in establishing the most up-to-date school for the blind in the world, stocking it with exemplary teachers and, just as important, pumping up a steady stream of money to hold it safely on its course. His success in teaching little Laura Bridgman, who could neither hear nor see him, amazed and awed the world. His relish for action made him an unsparing lobbyist for laws to accommodate and instruct the afflicted—the deaf, the blind, and even the so-called "unteachables," the mentally way down. It was an endeavor precisely to his taste, and it bore fruit not only in his native Massachusetts but also in Ohio, Kentucky, and Virginia. Long before the springtime of the present century, when Montessori appeared in Italy to salvage what were then known as "mental defectives," to make them as self-reliant as God and science permitted, Howe was intoning the very same tune.

Today, with our greater knowledge and understanding, teaching the handicapped has established itself as a going concern. Needless to say, its purpose is not to effect any cures, for these, unhappily, are usually beyond us. The end is rather to give such unlucky children a feeling of inner confidence and self-respect and to make them as self-supporting as possible in a difficult and exigent world. To such purpose many and varied forms of special education have been developed. Every year, in illustration, the national government appropriates funds for the printing of books in Braille for disposal among state schools. The states, for their part, pay for the education of their blind either in state schools or in the subsidized ones of other institutions. Most of the states and many of their larger municipalities, of course, have long since responded to the urge to do something for the handicapped. Such enterprise not only includes imparting literacy but may also involve vocational preparation. As might be expected, the colleges have not turned their backs to such needs; in fact, in more than one hundred of them young people may now follow a long line of special courses to make preparation for the day when they hope to teach the physically and mentally burdened. The year 1958 marked the beginning of a new era in Federal aid to special education, when Congress appropriated $1 million to support the preparation of teachers of mentally retarded children. Three years later the shower of mazuma pleasantly resumed when the lawgivers provided similarly for teachers of the deaf. Another bill signed into law by President Kennedy authorized yet more subvention not only for the making of teachers but for research as well. In 1965 another measure was enacted to aid in forwarding and improving educational programs for the handicapped young in every part of the republic.

Although the handicapped began to concern educators almost two centuries ago, the problems of the gifted were overlooked until the recent past. We may forgive our predecessors for a very natural oversight, for the child of extraordinary mind seemed to present no staggering problems. If, on occasion, he nevertheless did, then only too often it was because he was held to be something of a freak in need of special counsel, not in the field of pedagogy, but in that of pathology. But as the sociologists and psychologists improved their science such views were challenged, and today most of them have been put to rout. The number of studies of children of a high cerebral voltage is not very large. Nevertheless, some of them, in instance, Lewis M. Terman's *Genetic Studies of Genius*, not only have made a bonfire of some of our most prized delusions about the gifted but also have elicited fresh and even astonishing scientific comment about them. The belief, for instance, that those of exceptional brilliance range below their fellows in health and physique, Terman found to be so much humbug. In character they stand as high as is humanly bearable, which is to say that they stand as high as the best among the average, and sometimes a couple notches or so higher. Even those who shine brighter than Sirius, the Dog Star, are not wanting in social affability, but they incline to be a bit reserved. Nor do they confine their interests to the world of books. Like most of their less gifted comrades, they are not averse to letting loose their animal spirits in games, though again they may need a gentle boot in their stern to get them started. Yet for all their charms and powers, their education offered them nothing special. Save in rare cases, in sad fact, they were not even granted a faster promotion than those of average wit. Only here and there, as, for instance, in the Hunter College Elementary School, in New York City, have the gifted been given the benefit of special programs and selected teachers.

So things sat, more or less, as the century moved through its middle years, all the revelations of psychologists notwithstanding. Today, with our elaborate deference to excellence, they are transparently out of tune. To throw some light upon the matter, the National Education Association, with a grant from the Carnegie Corporation, undertook a study of the "academically talented student." From it there have come, so far, a dozen or so monographs, all concerned with providing the gifted child with an education designed and tailored to his particular requirements. Meanwhile, from one end of the nation to the other, city upon city has entered into arrangements to educate its mental wizards in a manner befitting their extraordinary gifts. In the high school the increase and spread of special classes for girls and boys with brains have been so hearty as to be almost amazing. Thus, where only a decade ago they were so rare as to be almost singular, and where only as recently as 1959 Conant found such industry to be negligible, today three of every four municipalities are engaged in it in one way or another. Nor has the lower school been cold to the needs of the gifted —in truth, more than half the nation's city elementary schools are exercising themselves in some way in their behalf.

THE NEW EDUCATION

After the passing of Colonel Parker in 1902 and the exit of John Dewey from Chicago some two years later, there was no one to try on the reformer's robes which they had worn so magnificently. This is not saying, of course, that the appetite for educational reform had dulled or that the land was now empty of school reformers. There were the usual idealistic fry of Froebels and Pestalozzis who found themselves at odds with the everyday pedagogic practice and who were burning to better it. Their ardor had been heightened in the nineties, when they ran into Herbart. Though they disavowed much of the professor's doctrine and even voiced a loud disrelish of some of it, for his theory of interest they accorded him a hearty patting on the back. Put to the test in their own rounds of schoolmastering, interest had proved itself powerfully effective, the spoonful of sugar, as it were, which not only persuaded distasteful subjects to slide pleasantly down the gullet but even helped children to fortify themselves for examinations. But such masters, needless to say, were scarce, and their names have long since drifted into anonymity. Artists rather than academicians, they were governed by their hearts rather than their heads, finding their main reward in the gratification which comes from a job well done. They worked for the most part within the enclosure of their classroom walls, and only seldom did they venture forth to hawk their views in the world at large. Whatever claims they made for the merits of their methods, such as they were, were backed by little more than their unshatterable confidence in them. Nevertheless, for all their limitations, it was they who prepared the ground for the later progressive movements.

Besides such zealotry there was also, as we have seen, the spadework of Parker and its visible influence, not only as it was expressed by the man himself, but also as his example bore upon his coworkers at the Cook County Normal School, and perhaps even more as it worked its spell on the nascent teachers who learned the essence of their art in its classrooms. Let it not be forgotten how the colonel's pedagogic liberalism lubricated the work of the school which bore his name and which, under Flora Cooke, carried on for over thirty years, a resolute and shining exemplar of the New Education.

2　　Meanwhile, two other iconoclasts hove over the horizon, one in 1904 in Missouri, and the other in 1907 in Alabama. The first was Junius Meriam, a professor in service at the state university and, like Dewey, a man full of strange and baffling heresies. The other was Marietta Johnson, a teacher of assorted experience, the founder of the School of Organic Education, and, if possible, an even greater renegade than Meriam.

Like Dewey, Meriam undertook to replace the conventional subjects by activities which arose from the child's own world. All in all, it required twenty-odd years for the Missouri professor to attain his end. When, after all his toil and sweat, he retired from the scene of active duty, he had wrought a school which in spirit was suffused with that of Froebel. Observation, play, stories, handwork—the vital organs of the kindergarten—likewise sustained the Meriam school. Not only did the professor brush out the familiar, time-tattered curriculum, but he also cut loose from the conventional school day, its cast-iron timetable, the deadening routine of its drills and exercises, its recitations and examinations. Instead of the usual run of lessons, dispatched like trains at regular ten- to thirty-minute intervals, Meriam arranged the working day into four ninety-minute seances, allowing each one plenty of elastic leeway to make it agreeable for both learner and teacher. Radical—nay, revolutionary—in its own day, Meriam's notion that learning is not a matter to be regulated by so-and-so many hours by the watch, though still not in unanimous acceptance today, is at least no longer a cause for calling out the Marines, any more than is the view that learning, when taken in leisurely stride and under pleasing circumstance, can actually flourish.

When Marietta Johnson opened her school in Fairhope, Alabama, her primary educational concern was the child. Echoing Rousseau, though with much less flamboyance, she called for an education which would take full cognizance of the natural order of human growth. Like a *Hammerklavier* sonata, or even a fine Cheddar cheese, the ripening of the intellect exacts its due time; hence, so ran the Johnsonian thesis, "there should be less teaching of facts and more time for assimilation." By this token the study of reading and writing should be held back until the mind is able to cope with them, which is, say, about the child's ninth or tenth year. On the other hand, let the youngster release himself with free and easy access to paints and clay and to hammers, saws, and chisels—even, indeed, to kilns and looms. Let him wiggle his hips, wave his arms and legs in dance, and rejoice his spirit in communal song. And let him give an eye to nature, not, however, to burden his memory with stacks of biologic data, but rather to enliven his inborn pleasure and to put an edge on his curiosity and on the powers of his observation.

When, at the age of nine or ten, the Fairhope children introduced themselves to formal learning, it was still of a moderate proportion. They addressed themselves to reading, writing, and spelling and to literature, which opened the gate not only to letters but to geography and history as well. Under ban was the recitation, with its familiar grilling of the pupil by the teacher; instead, classes were run as freely and easily as informal discussions.

Unnecessary to state, the Johnson and Meriam experimentalizing, like that of Dewey and Parker, stirred up familiar critical gales. Not only were their schools denounced on the ground of an unseemly radicalism, but their pedagogy was so utterly at variance with "sound education" as to be unspeakable. Even so, amid all the whirlpool of sound a frail note of discontent with the old way could be heard. Here and there this disaffection took concrete shape in a number of progressive schools, such as the Play School, later the City and Country School, brought into being by Caroline Pratt in New York City; the Shady Hill School, opened in Cambridge, hard by Harvard, by one of its professors, W. E. Hocking, with a helping hand from his wife; the Walden School, founded by Margaret Naumburg in New York City; the elementary school of the University of Iowa, under the guidance of Ernest Horn; and the Oak Lane Country School, which went into practice in Philadelphia under the direction of Frances Froehlicher.

In 1916, the movement for reform gathered new force and power when the General Education Board put out two monographs on the subject of an educational reformation. One was Abraham Flexner's *Modern School,* and the other was Charles Eliot's *Changes Needed in America's Secondary Education.* The two pieces enjoyed a wide circulation, and since they were the work of grave dignitaries of learning, the criticisms they volunteered made something of a splash. The year following, in 1917, the General Education Board gave educational reform another boost when, with the aid of moneyed altruists and a number of educational *prominenti,* it helped to underwrite the establishment of the Lincoln School of Teachers College, Columbia University. The new seminary of education was expected to play a double role: for one thing, it was to be a "modern school," and for another, it was to serve as a laboratory for public school experimentation.

3 The early assaults on the conventional school were followed by others, and by the end of the First World War the New Education had its agents in pretty nearly every sector of the republic. However, their rate of increase had kept itself within modest limits, and although they all glowed for the same general principles, they toiled over a wide-flung space, and with little chance to interact. Consequently, their net collective effort was disjointed and without much steam. It was mainly to end such wastage that a number of progressives, led by Stanwood Cobb, head of the Chevy Chase Country Day School, convened in the winter of 1918–1919 in the national capital, where they hatched the Progressive Education Association. With headquarters not far from the Potomac, the organization started its endeavor with a register of a few hundred cardholders. By the late thirties, however, its roster had inflated to around ten thousand, and it had become the strongest single voice for progressive education in America.

In its infancy the association was comprised mostly of parents of a progressive strain and of teachers similarly infected and in service usually in small private schools; but as year came after year, the character of membership took on more and more of a professional tone. To give its call a national reach the PEA—as people of verbal thrift presently came to designate it—gathered in annual congress, the first two sessions convening in Washington, and the later sessions in one of the Eastern cities. To project their views even further, in 1924 the brethren inaugurated a journal, *Progressive Education*, which soon ascended to dizzy heights in educational journalism. The magazine has long since folded, and its message now seems far away. Even so, its usefulness has not ended. Once a dispenser of tidings which were fresh and sprightly, it is now a rich repository of the record of progressivism's past.

In the meantime, the New Education was beginning to attract reinforcements from the higher learning. For one, there was John Dewey's reanimated interest in the study of education and the appearance in 1916 of his famed *Democracy of Education*. Out at Ohio State, Boyd Bode was busily propounding the experimentalist-progressive philosophy and psychology, while in upper Manhattan, at Columbia, William Kilpatrick occupied himself in similar maneuvers.

Gifted with a talent for clear and engaging exposition, Kilpatrick over the years lured students to his lecture halls by the many thousands, where he proceeded to acquaint them with the liberal currents of American education, a feat which presently made him talked about in the groves of higher knowledge as the "million-dollar professor." Though he won honor as the great clarifier of Dewey's clogged and clotted prose, Kilpatrick is also credited with a number of achievements which must be reckoned as coin of his own mint. Influenced by the psychology of James, Thorndike and the latter-day gestaltists, and convinced of the educational significance of a social order in rapid flux, Kilpatrick urged that the school be transformed into a "place where actual experiencing takes place."

Out of the thinking of Parker, Dewey, Meriam, and other heralds of the new pedagogy has issued the project method, whose worth Kilpatrick was one of the first to recognize. The word "project" had invaded the pedagogic vocabulary as far back as 1900, when it broke into use in the field of manual training to refer to any problem involving the making of an actual product. Time saw the term usurped by the pedagogues of agriculture and scientific housekeeping. Soon after the century turned, however, teachers were beginning to talk about projects when they had reference to any learning activities in which children had a say in choosing, planning, and directing their work under conditions which presumably resembled those of everyday living. Constructing a house for Rover, for example, was a project, and so was the production of a dress and a bonnet to match or the rearing of chickens for their eggs or for the ever-ready butcher.

With the prospering of progressive education, the project method was given a new illumination, and under Kilpatrick's deft hand it was planted in philosophic ground. In part its roots reached into Kilpatrick's reaction to the way so many teachers had done violence to Dewey's "problem solving" by converting the method into a hollow ritual for teaching the prescribed subjects of the old convention. What Kilpatrick proposed was to fuse into a single concept those elements which are indispensable to good learning. Like the Godhead, they are triune: (1) there must be a hearty participation by the learner in the learning situation, (2) there must be a full application of the known psychological principles of learning, and (3) there must be provision for the ethical element and a sense of responsibility. Weaving these strands into a single piece, Kilpatrick saw the project method as a "wholehearted, purposeful activity proceeding in a social environment," or for the reader for whom time is money, a "hearty, purposeful act."

To translate this idea into everyday practice, Kilpatrick urged that schoolwork be organized not along hoary subject-matter lines but through activities. Good projects, he was at pains to explain, would not eliminate the learning of subjects taught in the old-style school. At the same time, meritorious projects should make provision for intellectual and esthetic activities besides those involving the hands, muscles, and senses. Projects, Kilpatrick went on, can be of a creative nature, say building a boat or a rocket or composing an essay or a whodunit. Or they may simply re-create the spirit, for example, listening to a tale well told or feasting the eyes with a Rubens or the ears with a Beethoven. Some projects may be of a problematic cast, such as trying to figure out why cocks crow at the dawn of day or why a seidel of chilled beer frosts in the summertime. Finally, projects may be resorted to for implanting knowledge or developing skill, as, for instance, learning to write a neat and readable hand or even to add rapidly and correctly anytime and anywhere.

From his meditations on the project method Kilpatrick formulated his view of "simultaneous learnings." This puts its weight on the fact that you learn not just the material before you, say, the identity of the mathematical π, but also some related matters, in illustration, that the mysterious-looking π is a member in good standing in the Greek alphabet and that its decimal formulation is not simply the pat 3.1416, but, like eternity, ranges on and on forevermore. Finally, like it or not, in learning you undergo experiences which, for weal or woe, work on your attitude and ideals, and even your standards. These are the side learnings—"concomitant" Kilpatrick calls them—which he believes bear significantly on the social outcomes of learning and which, hence, every project planner must at all times keep in mind. Putting his views in a nutshell, Kilpatrick asserts:

> that we learn what we live. To live anything in a full sense is to put the self wholeheartedly into the thing and doing this in behalf of some purpose. More precisely, I learn what I live, as I accept it, to act on, and live by. . . . Thus we learn whatever we accept as true. . . . You learn not only your responses, but your way of thinking about things.

I learn in the degree that I think it feels important to me and how it fits in with what I have already learned and believed. What I thus learn I build into my character.

From its early rumblings as an insurrection against an antiqued and cobwebbed pedagogy, the mood for reform gradually shaped into a movement which, as the century unfolded, gained strength and pace. The handful of taboo breakers who had been its harbingers were followed by others, and by the twenties they and their progressive schools not only showed a hearty increase but also had turned up in every part of the Union.

As with reformers in other specialties, there are schisms among progressives. But for all their inner dissents, when they joined hands in the Progressive Education Association in 1919, they were bound by some common propositions. They contended, for example, that the young should be allowed to develop as naturally as is meet and seemly within the limits of decency and that the motives which underlie their learning should emanate from their own interests—and all this at a pace which is never under force. Like many of their predecessors, ancient or modern, progressives favor the learning which issues from active experience rather than from the building up of a vast storage of memorized facts. Progressives in the main regard education not merely as a cerebral undertaking but as the making of a well-poised person, which is to say, one who is harmoniously adjusted in every sector of his being—mental, physical, emotional, and all the rest. Nor do progressives imagine that such a high goal can be gained through the effort of the school alone, no matter how marvelous its magic. To achieve the feat, home and school must work hand in hand, and to do so with sense and understanding they need constant help and reinforcement from science.

4   The first progressives concentrated on the individual, and their program, as they liked to say, was "child-centered," an idea which was scarcely novel, whether in practice or in parlance. So things ran, more or less, through most of the twenties. But as the chill winds of depression began to howl and individualism became a national suspect, there followed a palpable shift in the progressive viewpoint. Indeed, some progressives now turned their minds to social planning. The school's function, declared Kilpatrick, was "to help youth think its way through a defensible social program." The school, suggested his colleague professor, George Counts, should "dare . . . to build a new social order," a recommendation that Prof. Harold Rugg, another colleague, emphatically seconded.

Out of the era's social and economic shambles came the John Dewey Society for the Study of Education and Culture. Come into being in 1935, it had its start in a small circle of savants from Columbia's Teachers College. In its new incarnation, however, it stretched over the whole republic, with members scattered from ocean to ocean and from border to border, several of whom, moreover, were touted very highly for the light they had flashed on social and economic problems. Consecrated to the gospel of social planning, the society embraced the proposition that "education has an important, even strategic role to play in the reconstruction of American society." Its views on this and other professional matters have been set down in a long file of yearbooks, of which several are of a high and instructive order. More mercurial was the organization's magazine, *The Social Frontier*. With economic individualism about to vanish from sight, the review set its course for the new order. In the very first issue the veteran John Dewey sounded the keynote: "Can Education Share in Social Reconstruction?" he asked, a question which, as an abbot of the order, he had been raising for over forty years, and which, to no one's surprise, he still answered affirmatively. Other articles, all orchestrated on the reconstruction theme, presently followed, in illustration, "Youth in a Confused World," "Youth versus Capitalism," "Educational Ideals and the Profit Motive," "Our Revolutionary Tradition," and "W. R. Hearst: Epitome of Capitalist Civilization." As might be readily foreseen, the magazine's appetite for social and economic change and, perhaps even more, its straining to rally America's schoolmen to its flag affrighted conservatives everywhere, and presently they let loose the inevitable counterattack. It was an opposition far too powerful for the hard-pressed *Frontier* to withstand. And so, as the country reeled from depression into world war, the magazine came to its inescapable end. The astounding fact that it had managed to hold the fort for a decade is doubtless something of a tribute to the doggedness of its supporters. In American educational journalism *The Social Frontier* was a novelty, a startling antithesis of the staid and scholarly *American Journal of Education* and an even greater antithesis of the perennial crop of its own not too brilliant contemporaries.

The attempt to make the school an effective instrument for social change unfailingly involved the social sciences. Their reason for being and the pedagogy behind them had, of course, been the subject of inquiry long before the twenties—even, indeed, before the First World War. But the schools, as usual, cherished their sweet illusions. Thus, for all the cheers which had filled the air in behalf of correlation—which, historically, had been given voice as far back as Herbart, a century or so ago—geography, history, civics, and once in a while economics were still taught in the same old style, namely, apart from one another in separate courses. Moreover, those who expounded them were expected to stick to the accepted facts, which is to say, the acceptable facts. Did the history master, for example, examine the present in the light of the past and thereby attempt to interpret it anew? If so, then he was to do it in awe and veneration, as a hymn to progress and a buttress to the established American way. By and large, discussions which braved a candid ventilation of the harsher social and economic realities were barred from the academic premises as a menace to the public weal, a calumny upon God, and, hence, a peril to the safety of the republic.

Early in the twenties the National Society for the Study of Education set some of its scientists to work on these and kindred matters. By 1923 they had produced an analysis of the "problems of American life as a basis of the curriculum," which the society inserted between the covers of its *Twenty-second Yearbook*, under the bald and glitterless title of "The Social Studies." Four years more, and they followed with *Foundations of Curriculum Making*, two staggering volumes, and the first sober and calculated attempt to tackle the subject with due consideration of the nation's social trends and problems. The society had hoped that its work would stimulate a transformation in the social studies curriculum. But in this respect—and to no one's wonder—the mills of learning continued to grind slowly.

Meanwhile, in 1921, the National Council of Social Studies had been founded. Led by the lively Harold Rugg, it sought to speed reform, taking upon itself the assignment not only of rousing the snoozing schoolmen but also of composing for them a series of social science texts and workbooks, all scored—need one guess?—in the key of correlation. Into the preparation of the Rugg books went a tremendous searching, involving hundreds of schools throughout the country, the advice and suggestions of over one thousand teachers, and the administering of more than fifty thousand tests to pupils in towns ranging in size from an anthill to a mountain. For all this stupendous industry, the books which eventually came forth were admirably presented, and as was only right their acceptance was agreeably large. The idea, moreover, of molding into a single social studies course all of the vital substance which hitherto had been treated separately and diffusely as history, civics, economics, and geography has since become an established commonplace.

It was Rugg's contention that the social studies had their reason for being in the furtherance they give to our understanding of modern life. That life, needless to observe, is not all lovey-dovey. It is, on the contrary, full of conflict and acrimony and, all too often, bedevilments infinitely worse. Such threats to the public welfare Rugg tackled with a candor seldom found in schoolbooks. As a result, they upset idealists and patriots on every side, and especially their organized guilds, such pedigreed standbys, for example, as the Daughters of the American Revolution, the American Legion, the National Association of Manufacturers, the Advertising Federation of America, and yet more. As a consequence, Rugg presently received the treatment given to Socrates—not in its entirety, luckily, for he was never made to drink the hemlock. Even so, he was charged with all sorts of crimes and misdemeanors, from corrupting the youth of America and discrediting the capitalistic scheme, to disdaining the Constitution. He was, Harold McKinnon, of San Francisco, let it be understood, a sower of the "seeds of class warfare" and the propagandist of an "earnest recommendation of Karl

Marx." One of the Daughters of Colonial Wars, somewhat more discerning, found that the trouble with the Rugg books was that they "tried to give the child an unbiased viewpoint instead of teaching him real Americanism." In the end, once again, the collective fist was overpowering: not only did the books lose much of their potential audience, but under the onslaught authors and publishers lost heart, so that many a projected and sorely needed text died in embryo.

With so many of its salient brethren panting for social reconstruction, the Progressive Education Association was obviously not the fraternity it had been in 1919, when it began its child-centered operations. Many of its fold, it is true, had no stomach for the new social revelation and continued as before to put their preponderant stress in the individual. Some, in fact, were candidly caustic. Professor Isaac L. Kandel, of Teachers College, for one, poured scorn upon the whole business. For a score of years, he pointed out in 1933, the progressive education leaders had "been vociferous advocates of individualism, the new freedom, the child-centered school, and the sanctity of the child's ego—in a word *laissez-faire* in education," but now they were bawling for "social reconstruction through the school with an emphasis on planning, cooperation, and collective will."

Even so, as the thirties unrolled, the society found itself engaged in a traffic which was distinctly different from anything premeditated by its founders. In the summertime of 1930, in illustration, at Ohio State it sponsored a workshop to extend practical advice to America's toiling schoolteacher. So much merit was there in the idea, and so much benefit, apparently, in what it propagated, that in the years ensuing it was aped and adopted by numerous other centers of higher learning.

Meanwhile the PEA articled itself for research. With committees and commissions to give it aid, it addressed itself to a vast array of problems, including rural education, community school relations, international relations, and several more of equally high importance. Its Committee on Educational Freedom (1935) bore the torch for academic freedom, while its Commission on Intercultural Education (1936) took soundings of the "tensions and misunderstandings existing . . . among various cultural groups that are parts of the American community."

By the forties, with the publication of its point of view, the society was ready to take cognizance of the way the social stream was running. Though the brethren affirmed most of their original principles, they now invested them with social significance. "Growth," the society still was sure, was the "individual's richest reward," but that boon, it was quick to add, befalls man only when he "brings good will to the shared task of creating the values for which the culture is to strive." What is the drift of all these weighty words? Translated, it was explained, they meant that when Junior bids farewell to his books and desk, his education should have given him, first, the ability and readiness to face the problems which confront and harass us all; second, a willingness to give a hand in their solution; and finally, a cultivated social conscience. In no case, however, did it mean that the association had entered into a concordat with the advocates of social planning. Indeed, on those who would begin with a social blueprint, the Progressive Education Association turned its official back.

For all its heat for social reconstruction, the association's actual efforts in that direction were decorous and reserved. True enough, for a time the PEA sponsored the rambunctious *Social Frontier,* tranquilizing it considerably, however, and changing its name to *Frontiers of Democracy.* In 1944 the association renamed even itself, becoming the American Educational Fellowship, a discernible echo of the New Education Fellowship in England, with which the progressives had off and on acted in cooperation. At the same time it made a public declaration of its dedication to a number of special purposes:

1. To give educational opportunity to every child.
2. To give higher education . . . to every youth capable of absorbing or using it.
3. To make American schools so vital . . . that they will attract and hold as teachers the most stimulating men and women of our time.
4. To establish a youth program for young people between seventeen and twenty-three to carry them over from school to active participation in the adult community.
5. To make full use of school equipment in out-of-school time for youth meetings, community activities, and education.
6. To cooperate fully with all community and school agencies working toward a truly democratic society.
7. To continue to expand educational research and experimentation.
8. To win community leaders toward making education a part of the school.

After the war, while the world was licking its wounds, the fellowship took aboard an even heavier cargo. "Inasmuch," its spokesmen explained, "as the forces that shape society are those that determine education as well, educators must understand what is taking place in the community, and must take stands as adult citizens on controversial issues of the day. It is their right and duty to participate in active political life." In addition, the fellowship pledged its support to the "reconstruction of the economic system in the direction of greater social justice and stability" and to the "establishment of a genuine world order," one "in which national sovereignty is subordinated to world authority in crucial interests affecting peace and security. . . ." Unhappily, the fellowship did not enjoy life long enough to show what it could do. In June, 1955, in its thirty-sixth year, what remained of the Progressive Education Association expired.

5   Like all new movements, progressive education, whether of the early Johnson vintage or the later grape of Rugg and Counts, has run into almost constant opposition. It has been beset and belabored by idealists like Horne, psychologists like Whipple, job analysts like Charters, and Scholastics from both Rome and Chicago. It has been under fire from such patriots as the lamented Mr. Hearst and the Hon. Senator McCarthy, the DAR, the NAM, and the American Legion. But it has also ridged the brow of lesser folk, such as parents and teachers—even professors.

The most vigorous professional antagonists of progressivism, by long odds, have been the so-called "essentialists." Though their dogmas vary no end and oftentimes, in fact, are discordant on the subject of progressive education, they have thumped down their collective foot. Come to the fore in the late thirties, essentialism holds that the school's first and capital concern must be the systematic training of the young in fundamentals, by which they mean "reading, writing, arithmetic, history, and English," besides discipline and obedience.

The chief compounder of essentialism, and for years its most charming attorney, was William Chandler Bagley. A professor at Columbia's Teachers College, and hence in progressivism's very lair, Bagley assigned himself the task of subjecting its leading precepts and practices to a salutary crying down. There were, he freely granted, some first-rate accomplishments to be credited to the New Education, such as its

> . . . functional approach to the problem of teaching and learning; the effort to build lessons of race experience upon the individual, first-hand experience of the learner; the condemnation . . . of . . . parrot-like learning; the importance to the earlier years . . . in the procedures that are reflected in such concepts as the project method and the activity program; and the effort to make school life a happy as well as profitable series of learning experiences.

But there are also a number of matters which are questionable, for instance, the lack of discipline, the condemnation of any imposition on the part of the teacher, the denial of value in the systematic mastery of lessons, and the vast understress progressives put on public effort. Although Bagley aimed his shots at the heart of the progressives, he struck at much of American education in general. Not only had it gone down the chute "of least resistance and least effort," but it had also become deplorably weak and ineffective, so much so that the standards of achievement in fundamentals in our lower and secondary schools had fallen below those of other modern and civilized lands. Worse yet, our feeble and puerile methods have contributed to "our appalling record of murder, assault, robbery, and other serious crimes."

In their various bills of dissent essentialists have assailed what they call the "debilitating" aspects of the New Education. One of their favorite targets has been the downgrade dip in academic standards. The practice prevalent in some schools, for example, of promoting every pupil regardless of whether he knows his right hand from his left foot floors the essentialists completely. "We have graduates of our schools," lamented Nicholas Murray Butler, in his palmy days as president of Columbia, "who triumphantly spell Caesar with an S, and Xenophon with a Z, who think . . . that the metric system is part of the human apparatus for digestion." Some years past searchers employed by the *New York Times* sounded similar alarms when, after a series of tests, they found American youths remarkably innocent of the republic's salient historical facts. A little more digging some years later unearthed the same ignorance in the realm of geography. And during the Second World War, Army testers disclosed a similar void in a knowledge of science and mathematics.

To end such shame and scandal the essentialists called for higher and stiffer standards, a return, they said, "to the exact and exacting studies." They would be chary in the use of projects, beguiling as some of them may seem, and the insistence on interest they would strain through the filter of common sense. The scholarship which has been sicklied by the lard of *laissez faire* they would build up and fortify with the red, juicy beef of algebra and geometry, and for good measure even Latin. What the patient needs, urged Dr. Bagley, "is a strong tincture of iron."

Not all the criticisms which have been piled upon progressives have come from enemy hands. Some of the more perceptive caveats and doubts, in fact, have been delivered by thinkers who on the whole were sympathetic to the progressive purport. Such, for one, was Boyd Henry Bode, of Ohio State. Holding, like Dewey, that the cultivation of democracy must be education's paramount concern, Bode was convinced that progressive education could become an "avowed exponent of democratic life." Unluckily, however, the progressive program appeared to be snagged in confusion and contradiction. Does it, for example, stress freedom? Then it also put an enormous weight on guidance and direction. Does it plant the individual in the very center of the stage? Then it is forever castigating the competitive nature of the current social order. Does it look upon the college as the fortress of the enemy? Then not infrequently its engagement is to prepare its young for college. Does it insist that learning occurs by doing? Then the higher its educational level, the less prevalent is its reliance on activity.

What the progressives need, observed Bode, was to stop trying, like a harried ant, to run in all directions at the same time. Let them first work out a clear and comprehensible philosophy of democracy, and having done this, let them make it the wellspring of their pedagogy. All too often, Bode went on, progressives have paid court to democracy's verbal formulas, its stale and unctuous homilies, its gaudy and meretricious whoopings. What is needed is a more intensive digging below the surface. The acceptance of the democratic principle means more than a labial exercise in its behalf: "it means the reconstruction of ingrained beliefs and habits, the reshaping of our entire way of life." What it needs is critics, not cheerleaders. To such a purpose it would be better, Bode counseled the progressives, for them to forget about the child's needs and interests and concentrate on those which bear the hallmark of the communal life.

6   Although most of the essentialists have gone to rest in the world beyond or, if not, then at least to their deserved retirement here below, their criticism nevertheless remains. A bare smudge during most of the forties, it suddenly burst into blaze when, to the national amazement, the Russians put the world's first satellite into the faraway sky. For Americans it was a day of crumbling illusions, of chagrin and wounded pride, followed by an outburst of censure of which not a little washed over education. Did Mother Russia beat Uncle Sam into outer space? Then clearly, not a few contended, the Russians could have done it only because of their sterner schooling—their emphasis on mathematics, science, and foreign languages; the rigorous and relentless demands they put upon their youth, from homework and examinations to marks and promotions; their particular attention to those of great capacity; and finally their insistence on order, discipline, obedience, and no nonsense.

There is vulnerability, of course, in this sort of reasoning; nevertheless, it served to a good end, for it was not long before the American school was being put under the sharp white light of critical examination. At Columbia's Teachers College, only yesterday the country's foremost stronghold of progressivism, President John Fisher, confessing doubts about the child-centered school, exhorted educators "to give priority to intellectual competence." On the country's Pacific seafront, as a result of a survey of the San Francisco schools, the aim of education, it was publicly agreed, is "to inform the mind and develop intelligence." In the nation's capital the Council for Basic Education, the inheritors of the essentialists though scarcely of their pedagogic illumination, turned their guns on the "softness" of the American school, its "teacher-pupil planning philosophy," its "life adjustment" courses—such as driver training, how to use the telephone, and getting and keeping a job—and, in particular, the false thinking of the professors of education.

In a softer tone, more pensive and far less garish, were the reflections of James Bryant Conant. Once American ambassador to the Bonn Republic and before that for a score of years president of Harvard, and on both counts, hence, a master of finesse, the man spoke presumably with some authority. In his report, *The American High School,* Conant rendered an account of what his eyes had seen and his ears had heard as he made tracks from school to school from one corner of the country to the other. Some he beheld approvingly, but many more he regarded unfavorably. Too many of them—some seven of every ten—were so small that their size seriously handicapped their performance. Hundreds entertained inferior programs, and equally as many a scholarship so low that to call it scholarship is to be almost facetious. And, finally, only a handful took the trouble to give any special attention to their pupils of extraordinary dowering.

As is common in our free and ingenious democracy, the new mood presently resulted in a ruck of advice and recommendations, some of it sensible and useful, but a good deal of it merely gaseous. In 1960 President Eisenhower's Commission on National Goals made public its report, and the following year the Rockefeller Brothers' Fund had its say in the *Pursuit of Excellence*. Both studies were under the direction of John W. Gardner, at the time president of the Carnegie Foundation, but at the moment in public service as Secretary of the Department of Health, Education, and Welfare. In American educational circles the name of Gardner has since acquired a connotation of a stress on quality and competence. In its full regalia, however, Gardner is at pains to explain, excellence is something more. It implies a "striving for the highest standards of life," whether political, industrial, creational, or educational. Thus we must employ the Promethean fire to prepare and equip young America for the "age-old struggle of man to realize the best that is in him," a proposition which, as we look back from the shadowy sixties, is certainly not novel in the annals of learning but which, for all that, was eagerly received.

As was to be expected, the sharp talk directed at American education has been discountenanced and disputed, but there is no gainsaying that it has generated an earnest effort at improvement. Enfeebled in the secondary school for years, and falling apart, mathematics and science rose from their sickbed, as school upon school made haste to strengthen its offerings therein —a process which the Federal government not only applauded but also aided with substantial grants of cash. The sudden deference paid to mathematics and science was not long in brewing misgiving and alarm among the votaries of the humanities. What this country needs, they insisted, is not scientists and mathematicians, but a cultivated youth, at ease in all the departments of life, which is to say, history, geography, language, and literature as well as the natural and mathematical sciences. It is, of course, an old and familiar song—even so, it was not without appeal. Indeed, so alluring was it that in 1960 the Ford Foundation gave it the kiss of approval with a grant of not quite six million dollars to render assistance to students seeking light in the nonscientific domain. Since then the statesmen on the Potomac have given heed. There is, declared the Hon. John E. Fogarty in 1962, in an address to his colleague representatives, a "pressing need for

Federal legislation that will build up a nationwide support for the arts and humanities comparable to the support that is provided in other areas, such as science and technology."

7   Although excellence in everything—including, as we are assured on television, the brewing of American beer—has become the object of national devotion, this is not saying that progressive education has stolen away and died or even that it has been completely and forever discredited. The stark fact is that the assertion commonly noised about that the children of the progressive schools give a worse account of themselves in the common learning than their fellow learners in the conventional schools is largely balderdash. One of the first to attempt a more or less scientific examination of the progressive school was Dr. J. W. Wrightstone. Did its neophytes, he wanted to know, have decent social habits? Did they put their knowledge into actual practice? Had they advanced themselves in any special art or skill? Were they on familiar terms with the three Rs? Taking one thing with another, the doctor could find no appreciable difference between the results of the old and the new type of education. The progressives had a slight edge over the others in reading, but they were behind them in arithmetic and spelling. Since Wrightstone's pioneer inquiry, several other probings, essayed in various parts of the country, have yielded closely similar results, thus, for the present at any rate, giving the doctor's findings the respectability of scientific confirmation.

The most thoroughgoing scrutiny of the older and new pedagogy that had thus far been attempted was the so-called "Eight-year Study." Fostered by the Progressive Education Association and lubricated with money from the Carnegie Corporation and the General Education Board, the investigation ran from 1930 to 1938. Its reason for being, rather curiously, was not entirely to conduct a cold and dispassionate appraisal of the facts concerning the relative merits and shortcomings of the two rival pedagogies. It was rather "to aid in the development of a progressive secondary school." But, willy-nilly, this necessitated a comparison of the older and newer approaches to learning. Carried on on a national scale, the study embraced thirty selected high schools from Massachusetts to California, all of which stocked a progressive wardrobe. Some schools were large, and some were small. Some were public enterprises, and some were private. Some not only taught but also lodged and victualed their clientele. The experimental circle was enlarged to accommodate five state universities, nine Eastern colleges for men and five for women, and half a dozen schools, coeducational and plentifully endowed. In addition, there were 1,475 pairs of "matched students," half of whom had had a conventional schooling, while the others had had a progressive kind. The actual conduct of the inquiry was entrusted to a commission of educators, male and female, from every academic level, from the valley to the mountaintop, and summoned from all parts of the land. Despite the usual difficulties, they maintained a high degree of objectivity, as high at all events as is ordinarily possible for mere mortals.

The commission's conclusions were on the whole favorable to the new pedagogy. For example, college students who had been to progressive schools were counted as somewhat superior to those from old-style high schools. Generally they displayed a greater intellectual incandescence. In dealing with novel situations they were found to be more discerning and more resourceful. Their creative talent in the arts reached several notches higher, and they may well have got more enjoyment out of the arts themselves. To their professors their scholarship was more impressive; consequently in this department they bagged more honorary gauds than their comrades. They played a more active part in college affairs. Clearly, they were collegians of parts. "If the proof of the pudding lies in these groups," the commissioners declared, "then it follows that the colleges got from these . . . experimental schools, a higher proportion of sound, effective college material than they did from the more conventional schools in similar environment." Furthermore, the commission felt, the college's traditional requirements were unwarranted.

Comments on the commission's findings were overwhelmingly friendly —the father of the wish, perhaps, but friendly no matter what. But even so, in *School and Society*, W. H. Lancelot permitted himself a skeptical doubt. "Only five schools in the entire study," he tried to make clear, "may be regarded as representative of the high schools of the nation." Furthermore, he went on, "the study has not established any superiority of the so-called progressive over conventional practices in American high schools."

The progressives' assertion that their favorite principles have penetrated the public learning is not mere self-approval. Our better public schools, taking one with another, certainly bear more likeness to their progressive rivals than to their public grandfathers of generations past. True, they still deal in bulk, and their classes, for all the enlightenment of the modern age, are still crippled by too many pupils. But their methods enjoy a new illumination. Discipline is no longer the penal affair it used to be. Not only are teachers mellower to their pupils, but their understanding of them is greater, with regard to both their visible behavior and their subconscious concealments. Like the progressives again, they teach in the most up-to-date scientific and artistic ways. And, as recorded earlier, the truly up-and-doing public school is served not merely by trained teachers but also by doctors (dental, medical, and psychiatric), nurses, sociologists, psychologists, and similar workers in human salvage. But none of this is to say, or even imply, that the progressives have been the cause of this transformation and that without them the public learning would be more or less what it was in the backward dark of the first Roosevelt, or even the first Taft. The progressives were the first to declare themselves aggressively and successfully for the new ideas, and their schools were the first to seek to nail them down into practice. Nevertheless, the New Education, whether public or private, was as much a product of the era, with its changing values, as were the transformations in business and industry.

The progressive school, when it has the advantage of being private, is not only the flouter of old ideas but also the tester of new and untried ones, and sometimes even alarming ones. The public school cannot effectively play such a part. Not only is its enterprise too large and cumbrous, but, tied as it is to the public purse strings, it must accommodate itself to the biddings of the taxpaying multitude, whose taste in schooling, in the main, is surely not experimental. Historically, the role of the progressive school seems to have been essentially that of the gadfly. Such at any rate has been the case wherever it has appeared, even during the heyday of Germany's last *Kaiserreich* or the early springtime of the Lenin and Trotsky utopia. As a consequence of its example, the best of its ideas have been adopted by the slower-moving public school. In this sense its work, though oftentimes at odds with the common beliefs of the time and often enough leading to wild claims and fancies, is nonetheless desirable—nay, it is indispensable.

18
THE HIGHER
LEARNING

At the beginning of the twentieth century the college was by present standards a modest enterprise. It prized a frankly intellectual discipline and leaned to either the liberal arts or the natural sciences. In the case of the one, its students invested heavily in Latin and Greek and in the newer humanities, and in the case of the other they immersed themselves in mathematics and science. Those devoting their energies to the ancient classics, if they held themselves well, became bearers of the venerable B.A., while the others flaunted the younger but no less appreciated B.S. On occasion, when the pursuit of knowledge and wisdom had been primarily philosophic rather than classical or scientific, the student festooned himself with a Ph.B., the bachelor of philosophy. Like their elders in the medieval world of learning, the professors continued to give their preference to the lecture as means of shedding their learning before their students. Sometimes, when the lecture was rendered to a few hundred hearers at a single sitting, it was supplemented regularly by smaller "quiz" classes, in each of which the professor or one of his assistants, like the masters in the lower schools, conducted a formal inquiry into the progress of the students' knowledge. As was only right and proper, tomorrow's Galileos and Newtons were in addition to make a face-to-face acquaintance with their science in the experimental laboratories. All students, furthermore, whether of Greco-Roman or Darwinian proclivities, were accountable to their professors for numerous essays, besides the usual tests and final examinations.

Today this simplicity, like the learning for which it labored, is pretty well forgotten. Compare the current college with its predecessor of 3 or even 2½ generations ago, and you will observe at once not only that the old intellectual stress has undergone alteration but also that the newer one of service has persistently elbowed its way onto the center of the stage. Where once the college contented itself with wooing the muses, today it teaches virtually anything for which it can gain a clientele. The B.A. and B.S., which in bygone days were clear and specific and identified their owners as graduates in either the classics or the sciences, have long since lost that sharpness of meaning. They have ceased, moreover, to be sufficient unto the present need and today find themselves in the company of such glittering letters as B.Did., B.L.S., B.F., B.N., B.P.S.M., B.S.H.E, B.S.L.A., B.N.S., B.B.S., B.C.S., A.B. in L.S., A.B. in Ed., A.B. in Soc.W., B.S. in P.A.L., B. Voc.E., B.R.Ed., B.V.A., and B.S. in H.Ec. There is, in truth, even a B.O.

2   Today's college has a much larger student body than its antecedent. Vital statistics tell us, for example, that for every youth in the groves of learning during the nineties, there were five during the Coolidge glory, and yet more on the heels of the Second World War, when the returned veterans added enormously to the number. Thereafter the tide began to ebb, but only for a fleeting moment, and as the century started its sixties, with $3\frac{1}{2}$ million collegians trudging through the college halls and with the veterans' copious offspring coming of collegiate age, the number of students once more began to run high. Though a joy, of course, to every college president's heart, the tremendous augmentation in the number of students is also a cause for his writhing stomach, his graying hair, and his sleepless nights. The simple truth is that the cost of education, like everything else, has risen, while the college income has been hard put to maintain the furious pace. Nor is its bedevilment merely economic. Some of its troubles, in truth, are academic. To what lengths, for example, should the higher learning go to keep aglow the torch of learning? And to what degree should it defer to the demands pressed upon it by its custom? Unluckily, the two are sometimes divergent. The spirit of America is surely not intellectual, nor are the concerns of the mass of college registrants. Where the college has been at pain to uphold the Muses, it has been cried down not only by the more or less literate public but also by various professors of education who inveigh against its conservatism and who, in the fashion of Dewey and the late progressives, criticize it on the grounds that it does not fit its learners "for active participation in the life of a social democracy." On the other side, where, as in the bulk of cases, the college has yielded to expedience and turned more and more to the training of its youth for moneymaking and social success, it has laid itself open to the charge of indifference—nay, hostility—to true and undefiled scholarship.

Faced with such enigmas, the colleges have naturally begun to ask themselves some questions. Sometimes, in fact, with the help of science, they have even gone so far as to turn their eyes inward. Probably the first elaborate self-examining of such matters occurred in 1914, when Wisconsin ordered a general survey of its state university to unearth, if possible, the truth about its work and thereby "to clarify some doubts in the minds of the tax-paying public of the state of Wisconsin." Although the survey movement was then still in puberty, Wisconsin proceeded in what has since become the approved and established style. Prying into the university's every crack and corner, it addressed questionnaires to its students, professors, and alumni. It called for an exposure of such matters as the professor's proficiency, the grades he issued and the manner in which he invented them, his committee work, his meeting going, and his extramural occupation, or as the word goes today, his moonlighting. From retired students the surveyors sought light on faculty advisers, secret societies, the honor system, the kinds of courses they enjoyed the most, and the teachers who stood highest on their roll of honor.

Since Wisconsin took its historic stride, scientific polling and surveying have become national everyday affairs, and from one end of the republic to the other college after college has bared its secrets to the probers. Indeed, the day will no doubt dawn when the college which does not seek to know and appraise itself may find that it is ready for the compost pile.

The idea of judging the competence and efficiency of a school brought forth not only the survey but also the practice of "accrediting" schools. The way for this was prepared early in the century, and what gave it power probably more than anything else was Abraham Flexner's historic report on the country's medical education. Its disclosure of an amazing national disparity in the standards of the nation's medical faculties and, worse, their all too prevalent lack of even an elementary norm of achievement moved the American Medical Association to seek to establish rule and order by ranking the medical schools into A, B, or C institutions. The charlatan C houses, as a result, soon fell apart; the B's held fast for a spell, but in a few years they too came tumbling down. Medical professors have clung to these early ideals with great fidelity ever since, so that currently the education of America's future Oslers and Pasteurs is on a par with the best to be found anywhere on this amazing planet.

What the medical brethren succeeded in bringing to pass within their ranks, the lawyers through the American Bar Association have sought in like manner to achieve for theirs. And as the jurists, so also the architects, the engineers, the social salvagers, and even the men in the higher estate of trade and commerce and, but lately, the teachers.

Nor have the older arts been passed by. In this domain the Association of the American Universities has been appointed official sentry. In the main it keeps its vigil over the undergraduate shrines, and more particularly their facilities for producing effective graduate students. It scrutinizes and appraises such things as classroom space, labs, and libraries, besides, of course, the quality of instruction. Colleges which meet the association's tests and standards have their names inscribed on the roll of its approval. In consequence, an alumnus of such a certified school may hope to enter any school of the higher learning, either in this country or abroad—or, when the time comes, maybe even on the moon.

3 The great growth in the number of hopefuls for a college label, especially after the First World War, when they began to gather force in earnest, compelled the colleges willy-nilly to give some thought to their requirements for admission. Across the years their demands had grown fairly standard. Commonly, by certificate or examination, the aspirant was made to give evidence that he had grappled successfully with at least fifteen units of high school knowledge, which, translated, means an acceptable performance in English, mathematics, science, history, and the languages—ancient, modern, or both. Sometimes some reassurance about his character was besought, such as a testimonial from his reverend parson, his father's banker, or, even better, some successful and virtuous alumnus.

In varying manner these practices still hold. But amplified and streamlined, the fifteen units are no longer confined, as they once were, to the purely academic subjects, and today they include the arts and crafts—even shorthand, typewriting, bookkeeping, and similar subjects of practical pretension. A greater weight is also put upon the applicant's accomplishments in high school, not only intellectual but also social, political, and sportive as well. Psychological tests, especially those which explore the candidate's intellect and emotions, are as common as the campus flagpole. Of late, with the rise of the personnel science, the interview has obtained a following, and numerous colleges now resort to it regularly. All in all, these developments have rendered a good service. When the candidates for the freshman toga are calibrated and sorted, for their judges to put on their glasses to get a better look at them obviously makes sense.

In the day when the high school's primary business was to make its striplings ready and acceptable for college work, the relationship between the higher and secondary learning was scarcely more than of an ambassadorial formality. Put bluntly, it was the simple and restrained entente of master and servant, in which the one set forth his requirements and the other undertook to meet and fulfill them. Today not only is such bossiness a tort against democracy, but it is also regarded as detrimental to the best interests of college learning. As a consequence, there has been a visible effort to bring about a better and more effective liaison. It has become a practice, for example, for colleges to ask the high school principal to appraise the qualities of his students who might be seeking admission to its freshman class. In return, some colleges engage to render the high school an accounting of the record of its graduates as college yearlings. The purpose, here, underneath the outer finesse, is to keep the recommendations of the high school within the bounds of a reasonable veracity. Aware that their judgments are under cold and careful surveillance, principals may well abstain from poetic license in their appraisals and thus make a fairly correct and dependable account of their pupils' prowess. A few colleges have taken yet another step. Not only do they undertake a thorough scanning of the high school record, but they also adjust their requirements for a degree to what a student has done in high school. One college of national distinction, for instance, grants college credit for high school work in foreign languages and mathematics when it has been meritoriously done and is in excess of the entrance requirements. But such plain sense is still a rarity.

The national confidence in education has lent itself very readily to propagating the belief that, under democracy, a college education should be within reach of every American youth. "The American people," the Truman Commission on Higher Education let it be known in 1947, "should set as their ultimate goal an educational system in which at no level—high school, college or graduate school—will a qualified individual in any part of the country encounter an insuperable economic barrier to the attainment of the kind of education suited to his aptitudes and interests." That these are not overwhelmingly cerebral or cultural—that, in fact, the mass of undergraduates are commonly anesthetic to intellectual matters and sometimes even estranged—has become plain enough. As a result, the ideal of a liberal education, once the mark of a cultivated man, has fallen under a cloud. The theory has got about that training, and especially training for job and moneymaking, success and happiness, is the higher learning's obligation and that thus any study to effect this end is laudable. The notion has prospered not only in the colleges whose announced purpose is immediately and frankly vocational—in illustration, schools of business, accounting, finance, journalism, education, and physical culture—but also in some of the older founts of liberal learning, which now offer their junior Babbitts a full range of practical edification from account casting to scenario writing, television acting, and executive assisting.

Even in less confounding times, when college offerings were held within modest and conservative bounds, it was next to impossible to disabuse students of their certainty that their education was simply a piling up of courses and that what they had gathered in, say, in histology, dialectics, and spherical geometry, has no palpable bearing on the rest of human knowledge. It may well be that their professors, as traders in their fenced-in specialties, did very little to bring their novices to any intellectual harmony. If it was difficult in the past to get students to view their learning as a fabric of a single piece, then nowadays, amid the steady and relentless proliferation of courses, it has become a thousand times harder. Some men of learning—cynics, no doubt, every one of them—have long since decided that altogether too much store is set on the passing of courses and the banking of credits, and not enough on the traffic in ideas. To rectify this miscarriage of the intellect, a number of proposals have been put forward, though none of them so far, it must be said, has yielded the hoped-for deliverance.

There has been, for one, an earnest endeavor to bring about a closer working bond between the high school and the college in the planning of courses. For another, the free election of courses, as concocted by Eliot, of Harvard, has slid down the chute into extinction. For a third, there is a movement afoot to broaden the bottom of the student's fundamental learning and to hold his specialization at bay, and even to restrict it somewhat. Finally, some colleges have had recourse to a general final examination. Known in the professional lingo sometimes as an "integration examination" and at other times as a "comprehensive examination," this covers the whole vast continent of learning and is reserved for the end of the senior year.

4   When Charles Eliot introduced Harvard to the free elective system, he was seeking, so he hinted, to lay low the notion, then in common favor, that the college student when left to his own devices would undertake little of lasting educational worth. More specifically, Eliot's iconoclasm was aimed at the massive dosings prescribed in mathematics and the classics. The free elective system blew up not only these requirements but all others as well, allowing the student a completely free hand in choosing his studies. Such was more or less the system of France and Germany, where Eliot doubtless got his inspiration. But in America the arrangement soon began to frazzle about the edges, and presently it came undone. Today, whether right or wrong, college dons agree overwhelmingly that under present American circumstances the free elective system is unworkable. It leads, as one of them announced, "to too much intellectual vagrancy."

Then why, one may ask, has it thrived so well and so long in certain European lands? The reason is surely not hard to find. For all their faults, real or imaginary, the Old World secondary schools give a tremendous exercise to the intellect. It has been argued by certain social metaphysicians that such an education is narrow and even outmoded; nevertheless the fact remains that it is an education. In the end, the students it manages to convey to the higher learning are the finest and the best-disciplined ones to be found anywhere. Thus, when, after their hard service in the secondary trenches, the students finally betake themselves to the higher field of battle, they take with them an intellectual ripeness which is seldom encountered in the run of American high school graduates. Was there a vast difference in this respect between the European and the American in Eliot's time? Then today the divide yawns even wider. And if the elective system had but a slim chance of success in that day, then in our own the odds against it are infinitely great.

Come into being under Dr. Eliot, the free elective system was substantially altered by his successor, Dr. Lowell. Where under the one the student could do his curricular shopping in the free and easy self-service fashion, under the other he was made to "concentrate" his learning in what colleges today denominate a "major." At the same time he was to "distribute" some of his studies in a variety of fields. All the same, however, he was to enjoy a sizable aggregation of options. Starting out in 1940, a freshman, for example, could choose from close to half a hundred different courses; a year later, now a sophomore, he could take his pick from thirty different fields of concentration. In the same year, however, Old Mother Harvard, still full of bounce, had a change of mind, putting a halt to the freshman's freedom of

choice and ordering him thenceforth to submit to four "courses of distribution" in three domains of knowledge—the humanities, the natural sciences,
and the social sciences.

On other campuses one runs into similar procedures, though, not unnaturally, they vary somewhat in detail. Conventionally, a certain amount
of work is exacted in English, mathematics, history, science, and language.
Once these are out of the way, the student, now risen to the rank of junior,
attacks a major in a certain specialty. In addition, he must school himself
in a couple of "minors," which again require his time and energy in a
specialty, though in smaller measure than in the case of his major. As for
the rest of his work, he is a free man, and he may cheerfully select it as he
sees fit.

5   As the colleges approached the current vocational millennium, they
began, as has been mentioned, to give a greater consideration to vocational
and practical knowledge. Most of the higher schools, even the venerated and
costly ones with Gothic edifices and esteemed traditions, have developed
such combination curricula as college-business, college-journalism, college-
teaching, and similar useful and ornamental amalgams. Their aim, on
the one side, is to slick their students with the elements of culture and, on
the other side, to prepare them, somewhat modestly, for life's labor. It is in
this vein that Vassar, some twoscore years ago, unveiled its famed department of euthenics, which strove, as it announced, to bring about the "direct
application of the sciences to the betterment of living conditions." The road
to such an end ranges from horticulture to heredity and from the family to
physiology.

The practice among many collegians of sprinkling themselves lightly
with the so-called "general culture" but, on the other hand, of dousing
themselves over and over again with their specialty has given Academe
some grave and worrisome moments. The price of the student's premature
and extravagant specializing, it is feared, may well be the neglect of "those
common spheres which as citizens and heirs of a joint culture they will
share with others." What availeth it a man, it is asked, to be on easy terms
with fickle protons and electrons, with quanta, nuclear and radar mysteries,
and similar unruly arcana, if he be a dolt and an ignoramus in the simple
sphere of the common cultural legacy? To rescue him from such a deplorable plight, an increasing number of colleges have put their confidence in
the power of a general education. The most heralded proposal to such an
end appeared in 1945. As so often before in the annals of the American
higher learning, it was conceived at Harvard, then under the hand of President Conant, and it represents the result of a year's deliberation of one of
its faculty committees. Its recommendations have been set down in a small
volume, *General Education in a Free Society,* the gist of which is that the

American high school is too vocational. What every young man needs in America, it tells us, is a basic course in English, science and mathematics, and the social sciences. At Harvard, moreover, because of the committee's revelation, the rising bachelor was made to apply himself assiduously to courses in the humanities and in the sciences, natural and otherwise, besides demonstrating, as heretofore, that he can crawl through the water for at least 50 yards. Though Harvard's president hailed the report as a "masterpiece," its contentions were no novelty. At the University of Chicago, to instance but one example, students had been made to reveal their competence in comprehensive examinations in the humanities, mathematics, and the social and physical sciences before they were admitted to any specialization at all.

Another group to look sourly on specialization as it afflicts the American learning was the Commission on Higher Education for American Democracy. Put to work by President Truman, the body reported in 1947. "The present college programs," it asserted, "are not contributing adequately to the quality of students' adult lives either as workers or as citizens." This state of affairs, it explained, has arisen "because the unity of liberal education has been splintered by overspecialization." Does the college student traffic heavily in professional and technical training? Does he attain proficiency in the art and science of chain-store management, in the commerce of stocks and bonds, or even in the methods of teaching body culture? Then all too often he falls short of "that human wholeness and civic conscience which the cooperative activities of citizenship require." To spare him from this fate the commissioners recommended a general education. Put into plain words, their program proposed to civilize the American undergraduate by (1) aiding him to develop a code of personal and social ethics; (2) getting him to take an active part in civic and communal affairs; (3) helping him to understand mankind's interdependence and its need for everlasting peace; (4) planting in him the scientific attitude which he will put to work on his problems, personal and otherwise; (5) teaching him how to communicate effectively; (6) assisting him, if possible, to adjust emotionally and socially; (7) initiating him into the mystery of achieving a happy connubial condition; (8) training him how to think critically and constructively; (9) inducing him to admire the arts and letters and to take a hand "in some form of creative activity"; and (10) guiding him to an agreeable and satisfying vocation.

6   When the college was small, it was a simple matter for a professor to enter communion with his students. Whenever a learner lagged, for whatever cause, the master could seek him out and, with effective aid and counsel or even a threatening caveat, egg him on and thereby perhaps save his head from the awaiting block. On the other hand, where his charge happened to be of wit, it was possible to grant him special attention and thus set him on the course to great and glittering achievement. But as classes began to crowd, this homely operation was sorely beset, and time saw its execution become increasingly onerous, if not impossible. The sluggish student was still able, of course, to obtain a measure of special help, but in the mass which now enveloped him, his final redemption took on a greater hazard. The dowered student, naturally, was not ridden by the witch of failure. His sterling qualities, in fact, continued as before to bring him a supply of gratifying gauds, from cash and medals to keys in honorary intellectual lodges. Apart from such tributes, however, his genius, the rarest of all plants in the pedagogic garden, received little extra care or counsel. Its full fruition, hence, was rarely attained. The college, in fact, declared President Aydelotte of Swarthmore in 1921, was guilty of intellecual wastage. "We are," he said, "educating more students up to a fair average than any other country in the world, but we are wastefully allowing the capacity of the average to prevent us from bringing the best up to the standards they could reach."

To remedy this unhappy state of affairs Aydelotte resolved to tax the student of high cerebral dowering with harder and more independent work than could "be profitably given to those whose devotion to matters of the intellect was less keen," which is to say, the bulk of the college custom. As a result, Swarthmore inaugurated a system of "honors courses," which allowed students of promise to devote themselves at the end of their second year to a special and rigorous intellectual program. As honors candidates they were made exempt from the usual hamperings of course requirements and even from the curse of course examinations. Better yet, they could sit in class or stay away, as their need and prudence whispered. But in return for such favors they were expected to apply the full horsepower of their intellect to felling a whole forest of knowledge. Near the end of their senior year they were made to confront a stiff and comprehensive grilling in a dozen or so three-hour written testings besides a vocal cross-examination. The student who made his way safely past these perilous shallows was rewarded with a B.A. of the first, second, or third class, but should his performance lack the required luster, he had to console himself with the common letters.

Today, of course, the honors plan has lost its novelty. Most first-rate colleges, and plenty of second-rate ones, have taken it on in one shape or other. By freeing the gifted from the chain gang of academic routine, it affords his powers a chance to take wing. By the same token, it gives an impressive boost to his individuality of thought and judgment. Finally, it lets him labor in his own way, under his own steam, so to say, and at his own pace. Too much stress, maybe, has been laid on the confection of essays of an endless verbal mileage and on the outcome of examination. But the complainants on this score have seldom been the bright ones, but rather

some of the professors of education. A student of stalwart IQ who knows
what he is about rarely demurs on showing the world what he can do. For
such fellows, oddly enough, even the toughest examination, once it is
viewed in afterlight, may take on an exhilarating glow.

.*7*   The philanthropy which got American education on its legs in its
years of infancy has gone on with scarcely a hiatus. In truth, right now
it is riding to a fuller height than ever. A good deal of it, as is common
knowledge, goes to the account of the higher learning, and not a little of
it is still bestowed in the simple manner of John Harvard; that is, it goes
directly into the pocket of the beneficiary. Again, as in the case of the generous John, the grateful recipients still name themselves for their benefactors, as witness Duke, Goucher, John B. Stetson, Fairleigh Dickinson,
and a host of others.

The simple relationship between learning and altruism has served us
well in the past, and at times even surpassingly, and in modest measure it
is still sufficient unto its end today. Yet with such colossal sums at stake
and with so many worthy causes panting to share them, the rich have assumed a rightful caution. Consequently, many of their fatter cats now resort
to an alter ego, the endowed foundation. There are any number of such
monetary dispensaries, and new ones are always around the corner, but a
few stand out in everyday news, as, in illustration, the Ford Foundation,
the Fund for the Republic, the Rockefeller Foundation, the John Simon
Guggenheim Memorial Foundation, the Carnegie Foundation for the Advancement of Teaching, and several more. The funds the flush Americans
thus put in perpetual storage in one stupendous hoard are usually confided
to the care and protection of a board of trustees empowered with making
up their collective mind on how it is to be disbursed. So far the foundations
have granted their bounty overwhelmingly to the private learning rather
than to its public cousin, and to the college, university, and professional
learning rather than the lower schools. It was foundation vision which supplied the essential ducats for Dr. Flexner's research on medical learning,
and it was foundation lucre which squared the bill for the Eight-year Study
—and so on and on. Every now and then such prowlings have brought dubious and unsavory matters to the fore, and where the scandal has been sufficiently grave, it has found its way into the newspapers. Such was the case
when the Carnegie Foundation put searchers to work on the nation's intercollegiate athletics. Not only did their study let loose some vile aromas, but
in the end it even helped to bring about some slight reform.

Taking one with another, the foundations have done a good job.
Granted, some of their subsidies to learning have added little to our fund
of knowledge, and some might just as well have been lavished on another
cause. Yet one magnificent blast like the survey of Dr. Flexner more than

makes up for all the dreary zeros. Nowadays, moreover, with the cost of research reaching to newer and giddier heights, and with more and more centers of the intellect finding their capital all too meager for it, the foundation money is clearly a boon—indeed without it, tracking down the rarer and more exotic truths would be impossible.

8   Besides the developments aforementioned, there have of course been several others, less widespread perhaps, but leaping and bounding all the while. There is, for one, a far bolder use of student counseling to help young men and women cope not only with problems that fever them academically but also with those which gnaw them personally. Few colleges, certainly, would hazard their work of enlightenment without the services of a dean of men and a dean of women or without at least a small force of faculty advisers. Sometimes guidance begins even before the newborn freshman has had a chance to stretch his legs in comfort under his desk. Some colleges, realizing just how green and tender the collegiate novice can actually be, set aside a whole week for such servicing. Known as "freshman week," or even "orientation week," such solemnities attempt to put the newcomer at ease by introducing him to his comrade academicians, both student and professorial, and sometimes, in places of a flourishing democracy, also custodial and athletic. In addition he is squired about the campus, noting its salient landmarks—its stately buildings and what they house; its monumented great; its library, commons, and bookstore; its fraternities and student lounges; and, more important, its hippodrome for the pursuit of sports and—in the long run perhaps even more important—the bursar's counting chamber.

    In their craft of teaching, the professors have stood resolutely conservative. While the lower and secondary learning are today all agog with pedagogic innovation, the professors have been content to rest on their laurels, and only recently have they begun to give it any notice. Walk through college corridors when classes sit in session, and you will surely hear some lecture talk. Though the method is even more ancient than the university itself, it is still, and by long odds, the favorite. It has, of course, been roundly damned, and of late especially by certain apostles of learning by doing, who consider the lecture not only unsocial and undemocratic, but a narcotic to the student as well—a view, however, which so far they have substantiated with little more than a voluptuous rhetoric.

    It is only fair to say that not all professors of the higher learning have recourse to the lecture. In fact, from the dim past on, some of the most notable worthies have favored the intellectual give-and-take of the Socratic colloquy or its offspring, the free and easy interplay of class discussion.

    The New Education, of course, has made some inroads. Not only have some of the younger colleges devoted themselves wholeheartedly to it, but some of the more effete and ancestral establishments are also increasingly dallying with projects, workshops, panels, group dynamics, and other current wonders. Like the masters in the lower seminaries of knowledge, their higher analogs now enjoy all the well-known aids to eye and ear, including radio and television and the film and sound track. Some of them, in truth, have found these to be far less burdensome and exacting than the preparation and delivery of a lecture, carefully wrought, instructive, and communicating intellectual heat.

If the colleges have evinced some reserve and even misgiving toward the newer pedagogic fashions, this does not mean that they are resolutely opposed to introducing wholesome changes. In fact, not only have some of them deviated from the old and rutted highroad, but, in several instances, the new paths which they have tracked have since been explored by others.

Take, as an instance, the University of Cincinnati. In 1906 its College of Engineering introduced what it called its "cooperative plan." Under it two students shared a regular and full-time job. While one of them studied his books, the other was at work in shop or field, disposing of his non-academic duties. After six months the couple exchanged parts, the worker now becoming a student and the student a worker. It is held by experts in such matters that under this arrangement the learner gets a better grip on the theories he has encountered in his book learning, besides, of course, putting an agreeable swelling in his privy purse.

The cooperative plan has had many imitators—in truth, one finds adaptations of it even lower down, on the high school campus. So far its chief converts have been among the scholars of technology, though it has been tried elsewhere with success. Early in the twenties, for an instance, it was embraced by Antioch College, at Yellow Springs, Ohio, then in the hands of Arthur E. Morgan, an engineer of consequence and also, rather curiously for a man of his calling, an idealist. Seeking, as it announced, to blend "a liberal college education, vocational training, and apprenticeship for life," the Antioch plan, for all that, was a venture—unlike Cincinnati—in liberal learning. Hence what the students gained from their laic labors was regarded as of only secondary consequence and of "incidental benefit." Even so, the plan won high praise, and of the various cooperative schemes to sprout in the republic, it was the most talked-about and consequently the best known both here and abroad.

Of recent years the so-called "general college" has come into our midst. It offers its instruction mainly to students who aspire to a measure of learning but who, for one reason or another, are indisposed to work for a regular degree. In this vein St. Louis University conjured up a college with neither credits nor degrees—surely something of a wonder among the many accomplishments of the American higher learning. By the same score the University of Minnesota's General College undertook to help students wishing to get some training to prepare themselves to do battle with the problems that would unfailingly sneak up to harry them in later years, especially those involving health, sex, matrimony, livelihood, and civic and social matters. At the same time, however, Minnesota's seekers of wisdom were required to make their way through a program which was a coalition of the humanities and the natural and social sciences. After two years of such grappling the student is awarded a certificate.

What has gone into the record as the "Chicago plan" came into being in the thirties, soon after the appointment in 1929 of Robert Hutchins as Chicago's fifth president. Concerned with "broad fields of human knowledge," the program set the student to taking a number of general courses in the humanities, mathematics, and the physical and social sciences. Ordinarily he devoted himself to these disciplines during his first and second years, whereupon he was made to show evidence of his proficiency therein in a series of comprehensive examinations. Once safely past these obstacles, he discarded his probationary robes and was allowed to specialize in any one of the four fields or in one of the university's professional schools. Under the Hutchins arrangement the credit system, that beloved relic of the American higher learning, was abandoned, as was the system of compulsory class attendance—and as was also, after Hutchins retired, the Chicago plan itself.

9   The changes which have come about in the college have confined themselves on the whole to the essential business of learning and teaching. At least one important development, however, has been of an organizational nature, namely, the junior college. As an idea, the junior college reaches back to the infant years of the present century, when William Rainey Harper, the first president of the University of Chicago, proposed the separation of the college's upper two years from the lower two, the former couple being designated the "academic college," and the latter the "university college." Slow to get going, the junior college movement began to show signs of acceleration during the late Depression, when a plentiful supply of cash from Washington invigorated it powerfully. It prospered especially in Missouri and Illinois, in the Middle Western belt, and in California, in the Far West, but east of the Alleghenies its forward push was a great deal slower—in fact, it was not until after Hiroshima that the junior college came into its own. As the returning veterans swarmed to the campus in an ever-swelling horde, the existing colleges, for all their strenuous efforts, soon found themselves unable to meet the demands put upon them. No one, needless to say, wanted to turn away the veterans, and so in order to give them the accommodation they craved, a number of states and municipalities began to rig themselves out with junior colleges. A fair proportion of these, we know now, were little more than emergency houses, fly-by-night Sorbonnes, which have long since dropped out of sight. But some, as has already been said, as in California, Illinois, and Missouri, where the movement was well advanced, were of the highest caliber and on a par with the best of some of the older colleges. In its present form the junior college is a two-year school, supported sometimes publicly and sometimes privately. Like some of its four-year forebears, the junior college is at times consecrated to denominational concerns. Physically, it is sometimes a part of the university anatomy; at other times it is embodied in the secondary school; and sometimes it stands by itself.

What can be said for the junior college? For one thing, where public money gives it support, it offers the advantage of two years of college training at a comparatively low price. For another thing, since the junior college is preeminently a communal undertaking, it is usually in a position to assuage the heartbreak of adjustment which often overtakes the high school senior as he unfolds into a college freshman. Finally, in slack times the junior college has been able to absorb some of the country's jobless and hard-put youth. Junior college graduates may, of course—provided they have gone to an acceptable school—install themselves as third-year students in one of the regular colleges, from which, if the fates are benign, they may eventually break forth clad in the bachelor's gown. But for the great majority, graduation from junior college marks the end of academic life. Hence, to make its students civilized as well as full of skill and knowledge, it has been urged that the junior college should serve as a finishing school rather than as a mere abbreviation of the four-year college—that it should school its students not only vocationally and semivocationally, but culturally as well.

Though the junior college is generally well esteemed, some complaints have been lodged against it, chiefly, as usual, on an economic score. Not only have the junior colleges escalated the cost of public education, which is already in the empyrean blue, but on occasion they have also snatched funds which rightfully should have helped to further the lower and secondary learning. Nor can the spectacle of the tax-supported junior college be taken by its competing private brethren with broad smiles, especially the puffing ones which even in good times have all they can do to stay alive. But just as in the latter nineteenth century the courts justified the use of the taxpayers' money to support the public high school, so the high jurists of North Carolina, in 1930, held in favor of the junior college. To make doubly sure, however, more than half the states have given sanction to such practice by the enactment of special laws.

10 Like the lower learning, as we have seen, the college suffered at the hands of the Depression. Its rosters, which during the boom years had gone up and up, now reversed direction, and as they plummeted downward so of course did the college revenue. Not only did the income from tuition wane and waste, but, even worse, the returns from endowments fell off sorely. The upshot was a widespread reduction in college budgets, in staff and services, and, unhappily, in wages.

When the republic righted itself and started to head for better times, the colleges began once more to prosper. But no sooner were they on the march than the Second World War burst upon us, and presently enrollments, thin enough during Depression days, deteriorated to bare skin and bones. In addition, many of their men of learning, forsaking the campus for the field of conflict, stored their caps and gowns in camphor, thus depleting the college's resources still further. Unhappily, far too many of this gentry, especially those versed in science and technology, never returned to don their former vestments.

As the killing and bleeding wore on, the colleges took sober second thought, and presently we see some of them overhauling their old and cherished offerings. The stress now fell on such bona fide sciences as mathematics, physics, and chemistry, besides dozens of technical arcana all important and useful, of course, to the nation's military effort. Several colleges expanded their repertoire of languages. New York University, for example, added Russian, while Hunter College, the largest college for women in the world, offered an introduction to Hindustani. Some colleges volunteered instruction in Chinese, and a few even braved the teaching of the enemy's Japanese.

The compulsions of war made an end of the usual leisurely academic composure and even curtailed the time required to invest oneself with a degree. Where, not so long before, savants had been certain that no one, not even a da Vinci, could properly ripen into a bachelor in less than four years, now the mystery was being transacted in three. In truth, in some colleges, as, notably, the University of Chicago, the feat was being performed in two years. A few groves, like Middlebury, in Vermont, speeded the process by raising the credit value of certain courses. Others, like NYU, operated at full blast day and night, twelve months a year, with a regular session, a summer session, an intersession, and a postsession, a practice which has outlasted the war and still prevails. In fact, not only does the university's School of Education subscribe to it, but it has even invented a new one, a session of January short courses, designed for its graduate scholars in physical culture.

Needless to say, the war, like the Depression, was no stimulus to the college's finances. A few of the flusher establishments were able, it is true, to surmount their afflictions. But the generality of them suffered badly, and but for the angels and the government's War Training Program, many of them would have been obliged to draw their shutters.

With the end of hostilities, as the veterans, male and female, clamored for their GI benefits, enrollments began to rise higher and higher, and soon even the lowliest horse-pond Heidelberg found itself with bulging classrooms. The sudden switch in fortune, rather ironically, brought the colleges no financial surcease. The fact is, to put it bluntly, that a student's tuition repays but a small part of what it costs to transmute him into a new and sparkling bachelor; hence in not a few houses of learning the swelling rosters were looked upon with mixed and skeptical feelings. To meet their rocketing costs, some colleges raised their tuition charges; others besought the help of scientific drive managers and fund raisers; and some turned to the moneylenders directly. Of recent years a few ingenious colleges have sought to augment their income through outside enterprise. One of them, for example, has a stake in a macaroni and noodle factory, while another is owner of a racetrack. Unluckily, the bagmen of the U. S. Department of Internal Revenue have inclined to think of such ventures, however laudable their motive, as commercial rather than educational and as subject, therefore, to tax levies. More lately, as has already been remarked, the colleges have caught the genial fragrance of foundation money, and they have been doing their utmost to make themselves worthy for at least a fair portion of it.

Even more warming to the cockles of the college president's heart has been the vast augmentation of Federal help. Beginning as long ago as 1787, when the national government set aside parcels of land in the Northwest Territory to support and prosper learning on some remote tomorrow, the makers of national law have engaged in one way or another in tendering some help to education. What began as a mere trickle in the Ordinance of 1787 was enlarged, as we have seen, by the inspiration of Senator Morrill and his land-grant writ, from which have issued our A&M colleges. But it was not until the century which our wisdom now enriches that monetary grants were offered. Actually, with WPA and other New Deal subsidies, and with Academe's lucrative war contracts and thereafter the GI Bill of Rights to people her chambers amply with students, the stream of aid has been running to the campus for some time. That stream, of course, has never suffered drought—on the contrary, it has risen steadily, so that at the moment it is overrunning its banks. It may be that the flood, like all floods, is only evanescent, that its source lies in the nation's war and defense spending, and that when peace makes an end of these dislocated times, the overflowing aid will subside. Be that as it may, for the present there is no such end in sight. Following Sputnik's ascension, Congress passed the National Defense Act, appropriating millions of dollars to underwrite instruction in mathematics, science, and foreign languages. So huge and enveloping has been the government's spending for research in engineering, medicine, and public health—in 1960 alone it ran to $12 billion—that were it, by an act of God, suddenly to cease, the impact on the higher learning might well be crippling.

Needless to remark, not all the college's problems lie in the baleful realm of debit and credit, though, as nearly always, not many will be done in without the expenditure of a substantial pile of money. Already singled out in the preceding pages, most of them are of a preponderantly academic tinge, and, given a chance, in the years ahead the colleges will doubtless give them some resolution. Not all college leaders, however, are convinced that the government's benevolence, soothing though its balm may be, is an unmitigated good. It could be, some of their more prudent and perspicacious representatives fear, that Uncle Sam may turn out to be a Greek bearer of gifts and that his benevolence might well lead to a hobbling of the college's free intellectual functioning. The real issue, some economic wizards contend, is not whether the higher learning shall be succored with Federal money or not, for this has been pretty well agreed upon, but rather how such handouts shall be dispensed. Here two views—at odds, alas,—have been advanced. One is that the money should roll straight into the college strongbox to be disbursed as the college sees meet and necessary. The other is that it should go to the students themselves, as in the case of the GI Bill of Rights, to be invested by them in whatever college they pick.

The plague of numbers still bedevils the college. At times so emaciated as to make its stay on earth precarious, the higher learning has grown to a roomy plumpness. Where, for example, in 1900 some 238,000 collegians could be counted, by 1960 registration had soared to over 3½ million, a figure which, but for the hazards of chance, bids to be some seven million by 1970. How to give such an ever-growing horde accommodation and instruction has become literally a multimillion-dollar question involving a stupendous expansion not only in adequate and up-to-date buildings and facilities but in staff as well. So voracious has the appetite for the college label grown that high school graduates, even when they stand at the pinnacle of their class, not uncommonly have found themselves rejected for admission to the college of their choice for one reason or another, but mostly because of a lack of room. It is a situation which has helped to elevate the standards of collegiate scholarship, but it is scarcely one to rejoice an earnest and capable youth.

There is yet another problem which, rooted in the depths of the American culture, does not suggest an easy cure, either physical or metaphysical, and that is the disparity in the national educational opportunity. For the lower orders, despite the soft gurgling of idealists, a college education is, like a brand-new Cadillac, sadly out of reach. A hard fate has forced the poor, whether they like it or not, to gather and accumulate in those very parts where the provisions for a decent education are lamentably below par. This, observed the Truman commission, is contributory "to the spread of a meager cultural heritage and . . . may one day tip the balance in our struggle for a better civilization."

It would be delightful to say that since those words were set in type a score of years ago or thereabouts, the problem has been liquidated and that today every able youth in our fair democracy may savor the higher learning to the limits of his taste and capacity, and regardless of his caste or condition. Unhappily, this is not the case. It is a sorrowing truth that, save for an augmentation in the number of scholarships and other forms of outside help, and for some possible derivations from the nation's so-called "war on poverty," nothing yet has happened to bring us to such an end, and the promised land is still a mere reverie.

More successful has been the war on the inequities inherent in racial discrimination. The historic verdict of the nation's highest bench, which in 1954 ruled against segregation in public schools, and the more recent civil rights jurisprudence in the Johnsonian era, give promise—at least in law—of educational equality between the Negro and the white. But the ruling, as everyone knows, has fructified but slowly, and it has put its grip only on the racial aspects of inequality.

19
ADULT AND
WORKERS' EDUCATION

Like so many other current blessings, adult education—or, as the phrase is beginning to run in America, "continued education"—is of a grizzled age. The ancient Greeks were aware of some of its charms, and some of their leading thinkers—even, indeed, such sages as Plato and Aristotle—laid down grave and erudite views on the subject. But it was not until the nineteenth century was well on its course that such learning began to acquire a modest following, and it was not until the present era was upon us that it became an established and going concern. Now prospering more than ever, it embraces at the moment around 4¼ million Americans and expects ere long to do much better.

Precisely what it is and what it ought to be is still a matter for academic disputation. As good a view as any, probably, is the following, which may be found in the *Encyclopaedia Britannica*. It is, it says, "an educational movement for men and women, young and old, who no longer are in contact with formalized education, whose primary interest lies in a vocation, but who possess a secondary interest in their own educational improvement as a sustained and continuous process. . . ."

Though this pronouncement throws no light on the size or the protean quality of the movement, it at least reveals some of its projecting features. Adult education, thus, involves a voluntary study by persons who have served their term of compulsory schooling. Unlike the regular patrons of the higher learning, these volunteers for culture devote their primary effort not to their education but to the struggle for a livelihood. All the same, their venture into education is expected to be something more than a casual dalliance; it must, in the words of one of the movement's partisans, "be planned and have continuity."

2   It was the common belief, not so long ago, that the knack of grasping new facts and ideas and of holding onto them was reserved in the main for the young and sprightly, and that their elders were at best slow in such pursuits. There were, of course, numerous venerable men who refused to give notice to such a gloomy view. And some, like Charlemagne, Peter the Great, and Frederick the Great, and such professional intellectuals as Goethe, Voltaire, Shaw, Dewey, and Russell, kept right on learning even as advanced and quivering grayheads. But they, of course, were regarded as rare and dazzling exceptions. In a way, one may suspect, the notion that people in their middle years and beyond made little headway when they came to grips with learning was a reassuring palliative to that majority whose zeal for learning had long since worn itself out.

Today, unluckily for them, such solace has been stripped away, and

no one of middle age, normal in health and mind, may settle down in comfort to exempt himself from education on the sole ground that he is no
longer in his nonage. For, after considerable searching in the matter, the
late Dr. Edward Thorndike, of Columbia University's Teachers College, revealed in the late 1920s that the "zenith of power for acquiring information, ideas, and the more subtle skills" is attained in one's early twenties.
The decade from twenty to thirty he found to be superior to any other in
this respect, while the span from thirty to forty he held to be on a par with
that from ten to twenty. Even at forty-five, it appears, "a man can hold his
own with his son at the presumably versatile and receptive age of fifteen."
Moreover, "if middle age can equal youth at youth's own intellectual specialty, adulthood may continue doggedly to claim superiority in its field of
alleged supremacy—general and practical judgment."

3   The education of the adult falls into two categories, the regular
and formally organized sort and the more or less diffuse and informal kind.
The latter is executed in a comparatively simple manner, without drumbeats
or trumpet blasts and with scarcely any deliberate organization. It relies on
such familiar standbys as museums, libraries, lyceums, forums, drama
leagues, reading circles, and women's clubs, besides the occasional help which
comes from the press, movies, and the higher ecstasies of radio and television. Now and then some of these will try arranging a systematic program
of study, but often enough their cultural operations are somewhat hap-
hazard. Even so, without their gallant industry the more formal and organized adult education would certainly find its work a great deal harder.

It is the latter, however, which dominates the field. It is served chiefly
by a variety of organizations, which range from correspondence schools and
university extension courses to special schools for adults, including university colleges and divisions of adult education. Recently they have been
joined by Rotary, Kiwanis, the Knights of Columbus, the various Y's, and
similar fraternal orders, which now and then have achieved a commendable
standard. Besides this, the labor education movement followed on the heels
of the First World War. But its special requirements tended to set it apart
from other adult learning, and soon it was operating in a domain all its
own.

4   Historically, what is now adult education can be traced back to
colonial days, when it got its start in the frail beginnings of public libraries
and an occasional discussion circle. Following the rise and swell of Jacksonian liberalism and the outpouring of national confidence which flowed with
it, a belief in the boons of culture began to be entertained, and presently
forums and lyceums were bobbing up in all parts of the country, all press-

ing for the spread of light and knowledge. Their zeal to expound and instruct not only gained them a large and eager following but also led them, as we have already seen, into the forefront of the struggle for the common school. Some of them, of course, were slight of frame and soon succumbed, but others rolled on, surviving one national crisis after another, right up to the ones we now enjoy.

One of the most celebrated was the Lowell Institute, which was founded in 1839 in Boston, then the recognized capital of the American intelligentsia, and at the height of its critical powers. The Lowell Institute, like others of its kind, concentrated on providing lectures. Unlike the generality of its followers, it adorned its platform with the mastodons of American learning, including such men as Louis Agassiz, John Fiske, James Russell Lowell, Oliver Wendell Holmes, and other eminent lay figures, all of whom were leaders in their specialty and not given to camp-meeting rhetoric. Besides its lectures the institute permitted itself a number of technical and professional courses. Boston's Golden Age, has, of course, long since faded, but Lowell continued to glisten long after its passing. In the elegance of the twenties, for example, more than twenty-five thousand persons flocked to its lecture chambers during a single season. They went to hear about "The Weather in Peace and War," "The Latin Kingdom of Jerusalem," "The History of Recent Fauna in Siberia and Central Asia," and similar sizzling topics.

The greatest institute of them all may well be the Brooklyn Institute of Arts and Sciences. Starting out in 1823, a full sixteen years before its Boston rival, the Brooklyn establishment, a century or so later, had amassed an endowment of more than two million dollars. It is the recipient, in addition, of a number of special benefits and usufructs. But the bulk of its annual revenue comes out of the pockets of its members, who in a good year number many thousands. There are several enterprises allied under the Institute's banner—to wit, the Brooklyn Botanic Garden, the Brooklyn Museum, and the Brooklyn Academy of Music. Of these the latter is the most ambitious and also the most venturesome. True to its name, it seeks to further the tonal art, but it also gives accommodation to virtually every other aspect of culture, from photography, the drama, and the dance to the sciences, natural and supernatural. Its lectures have ransacked the entire armamentarium of knowledge and have been given on occasion by some of the nation's foremost illuminati. Even more scintillating, however, have been its accomplishments in music. Its Chamber Music Associates, for example, have drawn the highest critical praise, and so have its recitals and concerts, which have been spangled by the presence of such tone masters as Kreisler, Rubinstein, and Rachmaninoff; the New York Symphony Orchestra and the Oberkirche Children's Choir; and Lily Pons, Jan Peerce, and many other illustrious warblers.

One of the oldest programs of adult education in the United States came into being in 1859, when Peter Cooper founded Cooper Union. Cooper, who proclaimed himself the "mechanic of New York," was also dowered as something of a seer, and one who was full of the pedagogic passion. "My earnest desire," he declared, "is to make this institution contribute in every way to improve each and every human being." Over the years Cooper Union has developed in several directions, and today its resources include an arts school, an engineering school, a reading and research library, a museum for the arts and decoration, and a division of social philosophy. In the main, though, it has clung to its founder's purpose, and all its offerings are with the compliments of the house to the general public. One finds among its features the usual array of lectures, besides music, opera, drama, and dance programs. In addition, it carries on in the vein of the more traditional schools, offering its clientele courses in history, politics, sociology, and psychology, both normal and pathological.

Another Manhattan project for the improvement and edification of adults is the New School for Social Research. When it came forth in 1919, its appeal was calculated to attract "persons of maturity with intellectual interests, graduates of colleges, men and women who by reading and discussion have prepared themselves for the serious study of social problems." Such on the whole has been the nature of its student body, a fair proportion of which flaunts the bachelor's degree, and sometimes even the master's. To meet the needs of such men and women, the New School has gone to great and discriminating lengths in acquiring a truly first-rate staff. The yardstick it has generally applied when making its selections requires its dons to be men of outstanding scholarly accomplishment; yet unlike their colleagues in the conventional higher learning, they must also be "able to speak the layman's language and to understand his interests"—certainly not an everyday achievement among specialists. Even so, in this department the school has enjoyed a flattering success. In truth, its professorial roster, though relatively small, has become a roll of honor, including over the years such headliners as Charles Beard, James Harvey Robinson, Roscoe Pound, Felix Frankfurter, Lewis Mumford, and yet more. In the thirties, when academic freedom in the Old World fell on sinister days, the New School availed itself of the services of some of Europe's most renowned men of learning, who, because of gross and brutal treatment, had been forced to flee their homelands.

True to its name, the New School for Social Research expounds its doctrine principally in the social sciences. Thus, there are offerings aplenty in anthropology, history, politics, labor, psychology, sociology, mental hygiene, and the rise and development of progressive penology. But philosophy, letters, and the arts have surely not been snubbed. In fact, a course in contemporaneous literature was once conducted by the sterling Henry Wadsworth Longfellow Dana.

Fortune, on the whole, has been kind to the New School. Since its beginning it has grown substantially. Today, indeed, it is not only engaged in the ordinary adult educational traffic but also confers degrees and, befittingly, has attracted world celebrity.

5   As distinctively American as baseball and banana splits is the correspondence school. Invented in the nineteenth century, it prospered steadily, growing in scope and worldly goods, until in the days of the lush twenties, with more than two million subscribers on its lists, it had become the *garde du corps* of American adult education. Since then, with depression and war upon its neck and with the rising competition of the regular adult seminaries to harry it, it has fallen from its high estate, and though it still exerts a considerable pull—especially on the backwoods masses—it is certainly not the gay and lusty thing it used to be. Save for the few correspondence divisions of the ordained higher learning, mail-order schools are frankly commercial. Hence they are not run primarily to improve and uplift civilization, but rather to hawk their goods for a profit. In consequence, a huge part of their receipts is diverted to the important business of wooing new customers. The enrollment mortality of these schools has always been high—in fact, only one of every ten of their hopefuls, so it has been figured, ever manages to complete his full fare of courses.

Like all business enterprise, whether high or low, the correspondence school has found itself belabored by rogues—often, even quacks and frauds. In the vulgate they are commonly referred to as "diploma mills." Teaching mainly the more fashionable and attractive disciplines, they specialize in short-story writing, charm and personality, cartooning, greeting-card poesy, how to be a mental wizard, psychology, astrology, and the New Thought. Most of these post-office Heidelbergs advertise themselves with sparkling frequency, and they nearly all staff themselves with supercorrespondents who are thoroughly versed in the drummer's seductive art and science. Such schools, of course, practice their fancy under the charter of the state which harbors them and are found, most often, in the sub-Potomac and trans-Mississippi belts, though now and then they steal even into such wary Gomorrahs as New York. Of recent years a few have boldly baited their offerings with an assortment of certificates, diplomas, and degrees ranging from the Pr.P (practical psychologist) to the Ms.D. (doctor of metaphysics), the U.T.D. (doctor of universal truth), and similar flashing tinsel. And to touch the Christian's pocket besides his heart, nearly all of them confer the D.D.

Naturally, the more conservative correspondence schools, for all their mercenary purport, have been at pains to keep clear of such offendings, for in truth they do them hurt. To make an end of them, if possible, they have, like the doctors and the lawyers, banded together and through their guild, the Home Study Council, have sought to bring a measure of sanitation and professional decorum to their practice.

6   During the Depression, as has been hinted, the national education suffered a national calamity. Yet, rather oddly, in the acres of adult learning hard times dropped on rich and fertile soil. Not only was there a general surge in the national demand for education, but there was also an impressive augmentation in the arrangements to cope with it. The most important single step in this direction, as might be expected, was a donation from the national purse. Thanks to this, there rose up thousands of classes for more than 1½ million grown-ups, manned by more than forty thousand unemployed teachers.

With the passing of the storm, the new interest, though born of emergency, nevertheless remained. In fact, during the ensuing years it made persistent progress, and in certain quarters it has even established itself in the regular educational program. The colleges, with their present communal ardor, are of course all for it, and some of the large ones have already affirmed their confidence in the movement by establishing divisions of adult education with an extensive stock of noncredit courses, from angling and contract bridge to the Russian novel and the contemplations of Madame Blavatsky. At the University of Chicago the Great Books have been coupled to adult education, and through branch offices in various parts of the land they are now reaching an ever-distending audience.

7   Like the church, and like business and industry, organized labor has a vast and important stake in American education. Its first manifestations, somewhat timorous to be sure, occurred over a century ago, when American workingmen lent a hand in the drive for the common school. Following Appomattox, their immediate concern was to better their wages and hours and to improve the worker's lot in general. The public elementary school still aroused their zeal, for in it they beheld not only the cradle of knowledge and civic virtue but also the necessary training ground where their young could prepare for eventual access to the skilled trades. As for the secondary and higher enclaves of learning, however, their confidence turned to doubt, and sometimes even to misgiving. For they, as has been observed, reserved themselves for those above the toilers of the land and were absorbed mainly with the more glamorous arts and sciences. In the hands, moreover, of the representatives of the middle and upper social orders, they were not only wary of the aspirations of labor but oftentimes even antagonistic to them.

Later in the century, and especially as the American Federation of

Labor assumed a tighter rein over its lieges, labor's views on education underwent modification. Thus, where formerly labor had opposed the expansion of education, it now gave it encouragement. To keep a child at his books not only was good for his enlightenment but could also palpably ward off, for a spell at least, his availability for steady employment, that is, the necessity of competing with his elders. Hence, labor now raised its clamor in favor of lengthening the term of compulsory schooling. Today, although labor still indulges in this motive, it is almost negligible—save, of course, when the plague of depression descends from Heaven upon this world below. Does modern labor, for example, call for a vast expansion of the nation's schooling? Does it hold that there should be freer access to learning on every plane, from the lowest to the highest? Then it does so not simply for the special boons this may confer upon the workingman, but rather for what it will do to advance the general welfare. By the same account it has been urging the government to accept a fuller and more resolute role and, as a corollary, to display a freer and more ample hand in the bestowal of Federal money.

On the subject of vocational and industrial education, labor has manifested a fertile resourcefulness. Across the years, the promotion of the mechanic and industrial arts showed some increase in the schools, but compared with the vigorous forward push of industry it lagged sadly behind. To remedy this deplorable state of affairs, organized labor—with cautious assistance from business and educational interests—set out to publicize the great need for Federal support of a national program of vocational education. The result, after several years of toil, was the historic Smith-Hughes Act of 1917, which made provision for national grants to trade courses in the high schools and which, in the years ahead, turned out to be the first of a long line of related acts.

The idea of initiating the wage earner in the art and mystery of trade unionism is, of course, a recent revelation. Its provenance, however, is not American but European. It first came to the fore in England, soon after Versailles, at a time when the trade unions and their political auxiliary, the Labor party, were riding the crest of public esteem. As the tidings of their maneuvers, and particularly their plans for elevating the common man, reached American liberals and progressives, it was doubtless inevitable that soon or late they should itch to let some of the new light into the republic. Some sought it one way and some in another, and among them, as so often in the American past, some turned to education. As a result, the twenties saw the coming of the Workers' Education Bureau, the Brookwood Labor College, and the Bryn Mawr Summer School for Women Workers in Industry.

But, sad to say, the liberals' hopes were dashed. True, the American Federation of Labor gave them its encouraging benediction. But lower down in the rank and file there was no great and glowing fire for the new ideas.

On the contrary, there was an abundance of rather waspish mirth over the nonsense of "grand ideas." Moreover, as Harding headed the land for Normalcy and Coolidge took it to Prosperity, the boom psychology brought contentment to the worker, and with its advent union rosters began to shrink. Like the bankers and the brokers, the workingmen were enjoying their millennium, and they were in no mood to challenge its wonders. And thus, by 1925, the president of the Workers' Education Bureau was observing ruefully that in the republic there was no pining for long-range programs of social and economic uplift, and certainly none whatsoever for workers' education.

This, of course, was before the avalanche of the stock market. Under the gray gloom of the ensuing collapse, however, the union's sickly rosters began to perk up, and presently organized labor was announcing itself improving in health and gaining in weight. The Roosevelt regime, of course, was propitious to it; in fact, under its New Deal it dispatched its gladiators into the workingmen's arena, proffering any of their unions a program of free education. For all the benignity of government, however, workers' education advanced but slowly. Nevertheless, the fact remains that it was an advance, and though it was slow, it was also steady.

8   In its American beginnings, workers' education was carried on within the ambit of general adult education. But today that relationship is a memory. Thus, where the latter reaches over a wide cultural expanse and addresses itself to every adult in the land regardless of whether he labors for his bread as a worker or not, the former addresses its mission specifically to the worker. Its endeavor, says Theodore Brameld, a professor at Boston University and one of the movement's leading metaphysicians, is "to help the worker to find his location on the scale of our socio-economic set up. . . ." It is, he goes on, "to enable him to be a better wage-earner and this means *to make him a union member* and even a *better* union member." Hence its chief concern is with the problems of the brother in the union, whether he occupies himself in the mill or sells socks at Saks Fifth Avenue. It is, says Brameld, "first and last of, by, and for the members of trade unions, whether these workers are workers in factories who wear overalls or white-collar workers." As such it is obviously something special, and thus not to be mistaken for general adult education or, if it please you, "continued learning."

Since the thirties, workers' education has appeared in various guises. Its programs have been sponsored now by government, now by unions, and now by schools. It still palpitates the hearts of liberals who, in one way or other, aspire to hitch it to their labors for a fairer and sweeter world. But their immediate influence, now as heretofore, has been slim, and since it has confined itself largely to academicians, it carries the handicap of being cerebral and thus remains somewhat suspect among workingmen. Like the rest of the American learning, moreover, the education of the American worker has been displaying itself in social, cultural, and recreational finery in hopes of attaining a closer and more amicable bond between the worker and his union. As for education in the somewhat narrower sense, it has applied itself diligently to its expert and effective presentation. To this end it has enlisted the vision and sagacity of professors of education and has even accepted a good many of their recommendations. The stock of its subjects is necessarily small, though the subjects which are taught are certainly not light. The theory it favors is confined to a consideration of the labor movement, its history, philosophy, psychology, sociology, and public works. Far more ponderable are its grapplings with the problems that belay the laboring world, for example, those involved in the relations between labor and management and the nature of their contracts, labor's political role, machine change, speedups, time-and-motion studies, and automation, down to such commonplace matters as collective bargaining, running a union meeting, and conducting a strike.

The government's chief contribution to labor education occurred, as has been said, as part of the New Deal heyday. As such, some of its main undertakings— -in illustration, the Workers' Educational Project—were ammunition in the assault on unemployment. A massive venture, it was found wherever times were hard, which is to say, almost everywhere in the land. In its prime it served some two thousand worker groups. As the pall of depression began to lift and Congress cut down its aid, the Workers' Educational Project was converted into the Workers' Service Program and was installed as a subdivision of the WPA. For all its thinned-down rations, the program continued on a spacious scale with classes, workshops, and discussion groups for workers, besides conferences, forums, radio work, motion pictures, recreation, and special exhibits. In addition it offered advice and instruction in the problems of health, housing, and employment.

9 Among unions the most impressive educational enterprise of all, so far, has been that of the International Ladies' Garment Workers' Union — the ILGWA. With a yearly drawing account of half a million dollars to uphold it, it has conducted a variety of educational endeavors both in the United States and in Canada. And with Mark Starr and others to promote and safeguard its interests, it succeeded in attaining a worthy fame. Indeed, were it not for its proletarian preoccupations and the total absence of any Christian zeal, its cultural work might readily be mistaken for that of a major YMCA. Not only does it offer a wide choice of courses, which range from such useful and informative subjects as English, citizenship, public speaking, current affairs, and parliamentary law to all the special arcana of organized labor, but it also splurges in miscellaneous gladsome doings, including excursions, dances, musicals, and plays. The accommodations for its athletes are second to very few and include practically everything associated with the recreational science, from the common gymnasium, with its familiar ropes, bags, bars, and accessory showers and massage and steam rooms, to the more advanced mysteries of bowling, soccer, baseball, basketball, and the like. Like the Harvards and the Yales, the garment workers operate their seminaries in summer, though under a somewhat lighter draft. To this end the union has on occasion made alliance with representative labor colleges, such as the late and lamented Brookwood Labor College and the Wisconsin Summer School for Workers. In accord with the newest views of the professional masters of pedagogy, the union's schoolmen hold that sound education must be fun as well as work; at bottom, however, their purpose is gravely practical. In fact, any brother yearning someday to snare a paid elective office in the ILGWU must first prove his mettle by completing a course of stringent training. And every member, whether he eyes an elective job or not, is expected to be thoroughly versed in the union's history and functions.

Somewhat similar, though less comprehensive, is the cultural exercise of several other unions. The Amalgamated Clothing Workers, for example, has a department of cultural activities, charged with promoting the schooling of its brethren. For those unable to attend its seances it has devised a series of correspondence courses. The United Automobile Workers have entrusted their educational efforts to a corps of full-time experts who not only are cognizant of the automobile workers' deep-seated hopes and longings but, for the most part, also have prepared themselves for pedagogy in some representative school of education. In Detroit, where there is the largest number of auto workers, one finds a flourishing training school. Like the clothing craftsmen, the UAW runs an exemplary correspondence school. Moreover, together with the American Federation of Hosiery Workers, it has gone into motion-picture making. Its themes, to be sure, are not the ones prized by Hollywood. Yet despite such a handicap, one of its productions, *United Action*, a documentary portrayal of one of its historic strikes, brought it, if not a downpour of Oscars, then at least a high critical acclaim.

10   Even before organized labor trod the troubled paths of pedagogy, schools consecrated to the working man had come into being. There was, for example, Avalon College, founded in 1894, in Trenton, Missouri. Breadwinner's College, created four years later, ornamented New York for a brief interval. Shortly after, and in the same incomparable city, the Rand School of the Social Sciences, with special inducements to the proletariat, was established by the Socialists. There followed by and by a college for the Finnish workers of Duluth, Minnesota, a trade union college in Boston, and a labor college in Seattle. But all these were small and primitive, full of dreary doctrine and stiff and dogmatic certainty, and in the annals of education they represented little of lasting worth.

The first of any significance was the celebrated Brookwood Labor College. Founded in 1921 at Katonah, New York, then a two-hours expedition from Grand Central Terminal, Brookwood undertook to train its interns in the essentials of labor learning. Its floodlight, as usual, fell on the social sciences and to its pioneering, very likely, the current labor school is indebted for much of its subject matter. For a spell the college bore the imprimatur of the AFL, but in 1929, sniffing some heresies in the Brookwood teachings, the federation withdrew its support. Though liberals, including John Dewey, let loose the full horsepower of their rhetoric in its defense, the school fell on baleful days. By 1937, worn out by its burden, it lowered its blinds forever. Its sixteen years had been a constant struggle for survival. Yet, for all its woes, to the cause of workers' education it rendered a historic service. Some five hundred persons roved and jabbered through its corridors—a handful to be sure. But of this number one after another rose to a high and important place in social and labor circles.

The same year which saw the coming of Brookwood saw the advent of the Bryn Mawr Summer School for Women Workers in Industry. Though its enrollment was confined to 100 selected students, they emanated from all over the states, and all of them were armed with scholarships. Save for an occasional waitress or telephone operator, they were all factory hands. Even so, the school was not truly a labor school; it was in fact committed to no particular doctrine. Its stress, such as it was, was on the liberal learning and on the development of clear and honest thinking. Hence one searches its offerings in vain for the usual union specialties on strategy, strikes, how to make and second motions, and how to be an effective sergeant at arms. Instead one encounters courses in composition, economics, and hygiene—all required—besides a choice among science, psychology, and lovely letters.

Historically, the school was the first to open its sessions to the female industrial worker, now flourishing in our midst, and its bold innovating, both social and pedagogic, brought it a deserved attention. The fact that it approached its task in the spirit of the laboratory and that it proposed no sure cures to rescue the world from its inevitable and dreadful end—this has been pretty well forgotten. Like Brookwood, it was forever hampered by a lack of ready cash. In 1939, in an effort to make ends meet, it suffered a drastic overhauling and began afresh as the Hudson Shore Labor School with new premises at West Park, New York. But the work of its life was behind it, and soon the angels took it off.

It is perhaps symptomatic of the change which has been going on in America that one of the outstanding workers' schools should have come upon the scene south of the Potomac, namely, the Highlander Folk School. Established in the Tennessee mountains in 1932, it offered knowledge and training to thousands of the working masses, whether in residence or not. Moreover, it has accepted all comers, regardless of their gods, their shade of skin, or even their place of origin. Unlike the run of schools, from the start Highlander was a cooperative effort, and though it may seem a scandal and a risk, it entrusted the management of its affairs to faculty hands. Even though the school never permitted itself to enter an affiliation with any special group or brotherhood, it has always stood as a frank pusher for the cause of organized labor. The essence of its reason for being, in fact, is—in its own words—"the strengthening of the unions through education." Its courses consequently have been tinged by the practical and realistic outlook one usually finds in the typical union school. Nevertheless, let it not be forgotten that Highlander was compounded of something more than labor metal—that from its beginning it was a communal undertaking of a very superior order. Its activity, thus, extended to every department of life, even the fine arts. In folk music, in all its aspects, it reached the highest level of accomplishment and received hearty praise. "It is," John Dewey once remarked, "one of the most important social educational projects in America."

11 Though the education of the worker has improved, its triumphs have been slowly won, and they have been obtained largely by the effort of labor itself. Outside its own sphere—save for an exception here and there—workers' education has not rooted itself in the general practice. This, naturally, has sorrowed many of its adherents, though it should scarcely have been a cause for amazement. The blunt fact is that, from their inception onward, the boards that run our schools have been controlled by the representatives not of labor, but of business and the professions, which is to say, by a class of men whose common stock of social and economic ideas is decorously conservative. Thus, in the past, when the ideas of trade unionism gained entrance in the public school, they did so not boldly, through the main gate, but shyly and discreetly, through the side door of the social sciences. Of late, though, there have been some delicate portents of a change. Not only has the labor movement itself gained tremendously in size and strength, but it has also advanced in public favor and therefore in political influence, both local and national. What the effects of this will be on the public learning the historian must leave to the science of fortune-telling. But the way the stream is flowing, it may well be that on some not too faraway tomorrow the representatives of labor will sit down side by side with the jurists, the bankers, and the successful hardware dealers and toothpaste makers who now guard the fortunes of our public schools. Here and there some hints of this transvaluation of values have been showing themselves. In Minneapolis, for example, not so very long ago, at the request of the unions, the history of the labor movement and the story of the workers' part in the advancement of the common welfare have been introduced in the junior and senior high schools.

As a matter of history, however, Wisconsin was the first state to allocate public money for workers' education, when, in 1924, it granted a small subvention to its university's School of Workers. The school began as a modest summer affair, but by and by, through arrangement with the unions, it was running a winter institute. And in 1937 it was given further importance with the inauguration of a program of extension courses and with a grant of public money to carry them on. Like most of the American establishments of public learning, however, Wisconsin has been distressed at intervals by the vagaries of politics. Keeping the project on an even keel has thus at times been immensely difficult. Soon after the beginning of the extension program—to pick out a single instance—a hostile state administration cut down appropriation for workers' education. Even so, the School for Workers, though heavily burdened, managed to survive. Continued by the university, it even succeeded in running its affairs on a self-sustaining budget.

Since Wisconsin's initial effort there have been a number of others, all freighted, however, with considerable caution. In 1938, in illustration, Virginia appropriated $1,500 to support a course in public speaking and one in labor history to be conducted by its university extension division. Some years after, Cornell—a private grove—opened its classroom to labor-management conferences, hoping thereby to let some light into their mutual problems. Goddard College, in the stilled aloofness of scenic Vermont, has declared itself for a somewhat similar venture. And only a few years past, the archmother of all our higher learning, Harvard, began an experimental course for a select group of labor leaders. Their expenses, interestingly enough, were footed jointly by the unions and the university. In addition, a number of higher schools have appeared upon the field.

Yet, were their number doubled, or even tripled or quadrupled, it would still be a mere drop in the immeasurable ocean. Though the overwhelming majority of Americans are employed as workers and though a great percentage of them carry union cards, the plain fact is that the American higher learning has done very little about workers' education. Many of its leading dignitaries, it is true, have long since voiced the great need for a full-time scientific approach to the subject, on the highest academic plane, and have even publicly gone on record as supporting it. Yet, so far at all events, no university has permitted itself to make an all-out effort to deal with workers' education in the same frank and masterful manner it employs in law, engineering, banking, salesmanship, retailing, and insurance.

INTERCULTURAL AND INTERNATIONAL EDUCATION

When the Marquis de Condorcet enunciated the doctrine of the possibility of endless human progress and, following him, Pestalozzi stood up for the idea that only through education can there be any alleviation of our social distempers and dyspepsias, the two men, as we know now, conceived much of the essential theory which underlies American public education. Risen from a democratic liberalism, the public school, for all the perennial onslaughts upon it and for all its occasional boggling, has found its way into the heart of the American people.

With the proliferation of American democracy in the latter part of the nineteenth century, the influence of the public school, as we have seen, began to spread in ever-widening circles, so that few of us today are not affected in one way or another by its transactions. Moreover, with the rise and spread of an indigenous pedagogy under the leadership first of Parker and then of Dewey, its aims and scope have been steadily altered and, in the end, greatly enriched. Today, as everyone knows, it no longer confines itself to teaching the fundamentals—whatever they happen at the moment to be—but more and more it undertakes to use its influence in easing and even ending social conflicts. As a result, not only has the work of the school acquired a greater social consequence, but as the object of its concern revealed itself more clearly, it also has engaged in tasks and missions of a social kind which in earlier days did not even tenant its dreams. There have been several such developments, but two of them—intercultural education and international education—stand somewhat above the rest and of late have gained a sizable audience.

Intercultural education, though new in its present manifestation, appeared earlier in simpler forms. Indeed, whenever pedagogy attempted to cultivate understanding and goodwill among humankind, it was trafficking, at bottom, in intercultural education. Now and then, when such efforts were woven into the coherence of some elementary organization, they generally fell under such rubrics as the "race question," "minority problems," "international understanding," and similar facile designations. From such frail beginnings intercultural education has unfolded over the years into a movement of stature and significance. Like all such developments, furthermore, it has generated a following all its own, and, like others again, it has the support of a variety of special organizations, both national and local.

2   Though the United States esteems itself as a land of tolerance and forbearance, there is, as everybody knows, a difference between the preachment and the practice. Indeed, even before the republic was out of the shell, religious and social discrimination were already stalking the land. The first Americans, as described earlier, put their confidence in a social scheme which not only differentiated the high and exalted from the low and mean but was also at unsparing pains to mark off the former as plainly superior and hence of an anointed privilege. Even the saintly Puritans, notwithstanding Thanksgiving fabulists to the contrary, turned their backs on tolerance. They chased out Roger Williams and Anne Hutchinson, and when a handful of Quakers penetrated into their Zion in the wilderness, they set upon them with clubs and dung forks, dragging them behind their oxcarts through the village streets and even putting some, who were not so lucky, to the noose. Later, as the republic grew in size and power and the tide of immigration began to rise in earnest, prejudices began to froth not only against those in a religious minority, and especially against the Catholics, but also against the several nationalities. And as the fetters of slavery were tightened upon the Negro, the spring of tolerance became further polluted with racial fears and passions. But there was then at least a saving grace—at any rate for the whites—and when discrimination weighed too heavily, the burdened could take off for the freer lands to the west. Today the frontier is only a memory, and those who find themselves hard beset have no such ready exit. Hence, practitioners in social pathology have long since convinced themselves that there is a need for grave and judicious study of the intercultural problem and for the spread of knowledge on the subject to lay our troubles and, if possible, to scotch them.

3   Currently the most ravening intercultural problems arise from the divergent cultures of the whites and blacks. The effects are felt primarily in the South, but they are present, as we well know, in other parts of the land, from New York to San Francisco. In those regions, too, Negroes are not always chivalrously treated in hotels and restaurants and other public places; not every employer willingly hires them; and certain hospitals are known to have refused them assistance of any kind. In great towns like New York, the pressure from whites has crowded the Negroes in segregated habitation, the so-called "black ghetto," which has given rise in turn to segregated Negro schools. Religious organizations have also practiced segregation.

Although not as flagrant, conflicts arising from the presence of the Jew in the community also exist and are thought by some to be on the rise. The Catholic, too, has sometimes been unwelcome, especially in the sub-Potomac region and among the lower ranks of Protestantism. In the cities and their adjacent suburbs, however, where the Catholic has installed himself in sufficient force and where his economic potency has run somewhat to his favor, he has been accepted without much trouble.

But whether it be Negro, Jew, or Catholic, the common foe behind the scene is very often the struggle for food and dollars. Before the advent of

Hitler and his ignoble epoch, except for Jews scurrying from the Czar, the large proportion of our immigrants came to better their economic standing. The unparalleled increase of their number toward the end of the nineteenth century, and the attendant competition with the native for jobs, bred doubts, suspicions, and—per never-failing corollary—rancor and hostility. Meanwhile, with the greater use of agricultural machinery and the consequent need for fewer and fewer hired hands, Southern Negroes tended to woo their chances in industry. Here, despite the fact that their access was held down, they began to reveal an unexpected industrial competence, and presently the threat of their competition was alarming rival whites. Again there were antagonisms, even riots, wrecks, and hemorrhage. To some degree the Second World War, with its colossal consumption of manpower, eased the position of the Negro and won him, in the end, advantages he might otherwise still be looking for. By the same token he has improved his place in society through the enterprise of some of the labor unions. Not only is he joining their ranks in greater number, but increasingly they are putting the force of their collective bargaining behind him.

All in all, however, such changes have come by slow stages, and fine though they are, they are insufficient to the ultimate intercultural purpose, which is nothing less than the uprooting of the hatreds and suspicions that spring from ignorance.

4   Though the need for improving intercultural relations seems clear enough, only a handful of the sovereign states have thus far done much about it, at least in their official capacity. It has been left, in the main, in local hands, to schoolmen on both the upper and lower academic planes and to organizations not engaged primarily in education, but dedicated to the protection and advancement of human rights, in illustration, the National Civil Liberties Union, the National Jewish Committee, the National Association for the Advancement of Colored People, and several other organizations devoted to the furtherance of practical idealism. In addition one finds a number of national agencies and state and local groups, supported privately and concerned in some way or other with effecting an improvement in human relations. Of late several public agencies, such as the Fair Employment Practices Commission, have been put to work, while in a number of municipalities special mayor's committees have been summoned to grapple with local problems. Finally, there is the national legislation, culminating in the Civil Rights Act of 1964 and the Voting Rights Act of 1965, both of which represent a gigantic effort to arrest discrimination.

5   Education's first venture into the intercultural realm is dated 1934, when the Service Bureau for Intercultural Education was organized.

Since then the word "service" has been stricken from the bureau's shingle, though not, of course, from its labors. The work of Rachel Davis-DuBois, the Bureau for Intercultural Education represents the consummation of her effort to introduce the young at school to the varied culture which runs through the veins of our great republic. The bureau, to instance its own words on the matter, aspired "to organize some of the schools' activities around this major social problem." Seeking to furnish "first-hand contact for teachers and pupils with fine representative personalities of America's culture groups," it relied for this purpose on its "source books, posters, and art materials," besides a "series of books on various culture groups in American life" and, finally, "courses for teachers in Education in Human Relations." Three years after its arrival the bureau joined forces with the Progressive Education Association in the Commission of Intercultural Education. Although its scope was now more fenced in, its primary concern was still the same, which is to say, to introduce the young to the "heritage of our various ethnic groups" and thereby encourage the "growth of a richer American culture." Thus it hoped "to insure the continuance of our democratic principles by developing appreciation of the unique contributions of each national and racial group to our common life" and also "to lessen individual maladjustments which are a reflection of the increasing tensions and conflicts between groups."

In 1939 the bureau enlarged the stage of its engagement, and during the next few years it maintained a consultant service with a dozen school systems on the outskirts of New York. To cast its influence over the whole republic it developed a correspondence service, it ran institutes in some of the bigger cities, and it hobnobbed with the higher learning, where off and on it gave aid and advice to workshops and professional seminars bearing on intercultural problems and where, besides, it made an effort to instigate a program of professional training for the potential leaders the movement so badly needs. Finally, it aired its views in print—in thick books by its members and in lesser monographs in its official gazette, the *Intercultural Education News*.

Ten years after its start, with a crew of experts in anthropology, psychology, and sociology to carry on, the bureau put the glare of its searchlight on the whole intercultural enterprise. What they found in the end, though vaguely surmised before they started, was that although several hundred bodies were exercising themselves in some way in intercultural affairs, the net result of their industry constituted scarcely more than a nullity. As for the effort to forward intercultural education in the nation's schools, unhappily, "even the most interested school administrators had only scattered and in some cases confused ideas as to what could be done."

To get some firsthand knowledge of such matters, especially the nature of prejudice, its pathology and therapy and its hoped-for convalescence and cure, experiments were conducted in a half dozen cities from the East to the Middle West, In one city, Philadelphia, the searchers entrenched themselves in the kindergarten and the first two grades of a handful of schools, but elsewhere their investigating covered the entire city. Such matters as tensions, the communal setting and its bearing upon the school, curricula, school organizations, and techniques and practices were put under their inquiring glass. The general idea, apparently, was "to help local personnel in finding resources in dealing with their problems."

Somewhat in the same vein as the bureau's intercultural labors are those of the National Conference of Christians and Jews, which came upon the scene in 1928. Like the bureau, the conference has put its researchers aprowl in various municipalities, where through its Intergroup Project in Cooperating Schools they have come to grips with the familiar intercultural antagonisms that roil "communities with heterogeneous racial, religious, or ethnic populations. . . ."

6   Supported out of the pocket of the National Conference and backed pedagogically by the Council on Cooperation in Teacher Education, some of the nation's foremost educational groups allied themselves in the College Study in Intergroup Relations. Conceived in 1944, it enlisted a score of selected pedagogic plants from the Atlantic to the Pacific, with the aim of improving the education of student teachers in the intercultural lore. Altogether the study concerned itself with over one hundred assorted projects, including research on ordinary adults, besides schoolchildren and college students. Some of the participating colleges concentrated on finding out better ways of teaching race relationships. Others put their main stock in the curriculum, seeking through surveys and current scientific devices to understand and appraise it and to give it an intercultural content. The college study, however, voiced its preference for "action research" over "mere fact-finding." Knowledge, it submitted, "is a way of effecting changes in behaviors." But so also, it insisted, is experience. What it commended especially was research which would lead to the "greatest insight on how to educate for the kind of life every democratic person so earnestly wants for every child."

7   Though bureaus, conferences, college studies, and similar enterprises have dominated the scene, gallant efforts of an intercultural nature have been reported in communities scattered throughout the land. They have been sighted not only in the large cities, where one would naturally expect to find them, but also in a number of smaller towns.

The first, and in its day the most talked about, was the plan adopted in 1940 by Springfield, Massachusetts. Behind this historic venture is the purpose of breaking the Springfield young to American democracy, to get them to understand "how it works and sometimes how it does not work." But this introduction was brought about not by the romantic babblings found in the common schoolbooks but through the child's daily exchanges with his fellows. Tolerance, to take just one example, was to be learned "without ever hearing the word, by accepting as a matter of course all children as comrades in work and play." By the same token, children of different ethnic groups displayed samples of their people's art, warbled their folk tunes, and pranced the ancestral dances—in short, they carried on their illuminating endeavor together in their play and in their work "without regard to the color of the skin or what church they attend."

In the high school, where the intercultural fire began to burn with greater heat, various student organizations were articled to the program. In addition, the work of the classroom itself was now directed more vigorously toward intercultural ends. In English, in the social sciences, and even in the natural ones, data, for example, were unearthed about the contribution of the alien to American civilization, the facts—real and imaginary—about the races of man and the role of public opinion, propaganda, prejudice, and so on. A gala show festooned the senior year. Denominated the "high school town meeting," it was, as its name suggests, a freewheeling palaver seeking, as its sponsors let it be known, to give boys and girls an "opportunity to practice the processes of democratic group thinking and to apply the principles of democracy to actual situations." The intercultural movement reached even into the nocturnal hours in the evening schools and the adult education program. In fact, it even made inroads into the schools' placement bureaus, which were entrusted with allaying employers' prejudices against certain races, religions, and nationalities—a colossal undertaking, but one which in this faulty world must be regarded as a rare success.

The movement for intercultural education, as has already been mentioned, is still in tender years. Whether, like so many other causes before it, it will have begun in hope only to be dashed in the end in failure or whether, like yet others, it will take a permanent place in the American school remains to be seen. Its existence, though brief, as the span of history goes, has been bathed in eulogy by an ever-growing circle of lay admirers. Yet for all the awakened interest, the experimentalizing, and the fine pedagogic zeal, the movement is still struggling to get up steam. There is, as one of its votaries lamented, a "dearth of trained leadership and there still are enormous areas needing further research." It is precisely to such purpose that New York University's School of Education dedicated its Center for Human Relations Studies in 1947.

8 Unlike the intercultural endeavors, the idea of putting education to work for the furtherance of international amity is almost threadbare with the years. One sights it at least six hundred years ago, when a certain Pierre DuBois urged upon the world the establishment of international schools, which, he was sure, might be supported from the money saved through the abolition of war—a millennium which, to our sadness, he failed to tell us how to bring about. Some centuries later the immortal Comenius put his sagacity behind a proposed Pansophic College, where the world's most luminous minds were to ruminate and sweat to bring us universal and everlasting peace. Then, in the early nineteenth century, a Frenchman, Marc-Antoine Julien, called for the creation of a body of savants to collect and disperse information about European education, not only to improve schooling everywhere, but also to foment international understanding. In the years that followed several other seers permitted themselves similar animadversions, but none ever came to fruit, and all of them have long since been forgotten.

The first American to be heard from was Fannie Fern Andrews. Though her celebrity in intellectual history has deteriorated to a minuscule footnote, in her salad days she inspired a considerable awe, and even respect. A highly talented woman, with a doctor's degree from Harvard, she was a student of international law and a connoisseur of international education. She must have been a gifted persuader as well—in any case she was sufficiently convincing to induce the State Department, in 1912, to negotiate for an international congress at The Hague. Unluckily, the fates then were in a satirical mood, and before the meeting could be called to order Mars had his foot in the citadel and the First World War was under way.

9   All the time, however, the idea persisted, and so did the indefatigable and bombproof Dr. Andrews. Following Versailles, she undertook to embody its essence in the League of Nations in the form of a permanent bureau of international education, but the peacemakers offered her no ear, and her idea got nowhere. Finally, in 1926, it found its way into the Commission of Intellectual Cooperation, the CIC. Composed of highly eminent scholars, in illustration, Madame Curie, Henri Bergson, Gilbert Murray, and similar intellectual incandescents, and hence also somewhat innocent of *Realpolitik*, the commission set itself to (1) plant and organize conferences to effect a measure of cooperation among the world's universities, libraries, museums, and other educational bodies; (2) study what schools were up to in familiarizing children with the League and its work; (3) search textbooks with the aim of deleting, or at least toning down, their too fortissimo nationalistic passages; and (4) examine the means of mass communication with the idea of giving them effective employment in advancing international cooperation. But as the twenties slipped into the thirties, such idealism obviously ran counter to the prevalent nationalism and the ambitions of its leading practitioners; hence, suspect and derided fore and aft, the CIC got exactly nowhere.

With the League sliding rapidly downhill and apparently unwilling to concern itself with international education, a group of educators, resident in Geneva, formed the International Bureau of Education. Starting out in 1925 as a modest private affair, the Bureau advanced steadily in importance and renown, so much so, in fact, that in 1929 it was translated into an intergovernmental organization controlled by its member nations and even partially financed out of their treasuries. The Bureau functioned as an international clearinghouse. It arranged international conferences, published studies in comparative education, issued a yearbook and a quarterly bulletin, and built up an international educational library. Unluckily, the Bureau's membership was neither large nor impressive. Neither the United States nor Great Britain was on its register, though each favored it occasionally with florid approval. Even so, in history the Bureau was not only the first alliance of its kind but also the first one to deliver itself of something more than glittering fatuities in the furtherance of the campaign for international education.

10 In the meantime, some of the big powers, notably the United States, Great Britain, France, and Germany, introduced a "cultural relations program." The last of these great lands to take the plunge, the United States in 1939 came up with the Division of Cultural Relations, which it made an integral organ of the State Department, gravely urging while it was about it that international cultural relations should be reciprocal, that they should serve mankind, and that they "should involve the direct participation of the people and institutions concerned." Such at least was the declared purpose; the practice, unhappily, badly missed the mark. The fact is that governments found it vastly easier to headline the marvels of their own culture than to give honest and sober consideration to the cultures of other lands. Hence, the programs which got under way, taking one with another, were commonly little more than ventures in national self-promotion —such is the human comedy.

Somewhat closer to the ideal of international cooperation were the results which issued from an inter-American understanding entered into in 1936 at Buenos Aires. Besides facilitating the exchange of students and teachers, the cultural entente between the United States and its Latin-American neighbors has brought forth a number of other things:

Assistance in translating into Spanish and Portuguese books published in the United States, and in translating those tongues into English

Translation by the State Department of suitable governmental publications and their distribution through diplomatic and consular channels

Preparation of materials for teaching inter-American subjects in thousands of schools

Facilitation of the exchange of art exhibits and the distribution of art publications

Development of a program for the exchange of music

Arrangement of exhibits of educational films, reaching an audience of over two million every month in more than forty countries

Development and distribution of radio programs to further the program of cultural interrelationships

Assistance to libraries

Assistance to schools sponsored by American citizens resident in Latin America

The maintenance by the State Department of cultural centers in various Latin-American nations

11 As nearly always happens whenever great ideas are afoot in the United States, a number of private groups were soon on hand to give their approval and support. The first, and the most significant, was the Institute of International Education. The creation largely of Stephen Duggan, now gone to the Elysian fields, the institute was established in 1919, with a subvention from the Carnegie Endowment for International Peace. In the practical work of international education, the institute remains, at least in the United States, with neither a peer nor a rival. During its long and useful career it has expedited the exchange of numerous thousands of students, professors, and lecturers; it has developed a first-rate student advisory service; and it has given its help to the Junior Year Abroad, a scheme whereby selected American collegians may spend their junior year in foreign institutions of learning. In the black gloom of fascism, with the wholesale dismissal of some of the world's most distinguished men of learning, the institute helped a number of these hapless men to establish themselves in the United States.

With so many organizations at pains to advance international education, the efforts of individual colleges in this direction might easily go unnoticed. A substantial number of them, of course, have long since been participating in programs of international student and faculty exchange, a practice which through foundation benevolence, and especially the celebrated Fulbright grants, has of late been arousing not a little interest. Supplemented and fortified by the Smith-Mundt Act, the Fulbright altruism authorizes governmental grants to qualified persons to teach or conduct research in certain selected outlands.

The student tour is yet another aspect of the international approach and is, of course, an old familiar. At first the student tour consisted of simply a professor or two squiring a small troupe of students during a summer into, say, Germany or France or some similar fountainhead of civilized enlightenment, lecturing their charges on the language and civilization and on the glories and amenities of the country (with laboratory jaunts to their *boîtes* and *brauhauses*), dosing them more or less dauntlessly with homework, examining the contents of their heads and notebooks when they were through, and, if they were found satisfactory, recommending them to their alma mater for college credit. In the late twenties the student tour developed in earnest, and with the help of the organized transportation enterprise, it was presently doing a brisk business. Its apogee was reached in The University Afloat, "a college cruising the world, offering a full-year's course of study . . . carrying an entire faculty and student body . . . a veritable floating college campus." Since the Second World War the student tour has fallen on boom days, with trips to every part of the earth, forgetting, of course, such barbed barricades as war and iron curtains. American education being diverse, some of these have been of a high caliber, while others have been little more than a pleasant scamper for easy credits.

Here and there, some of the higher learning has turned to a more or less systematic study of foreign cultures. During the summer of 1945, for example, the University of Wyoming pried into the civilization of central Eastern Europe, that region sandwiched between Germany and Russia, while the year before Cornell had undertaken a cultural dissection of the U.S.S.R. Directed by Ernest Simmons, later professing his science at Columbia, the program covered Soviet letters, art, music, history, economics, government, and society. In addition, workshops and seminars dealt with such special topics as the Russian people, medicine and health, scientific achievements, military and naval history, the theater and the cinema, and several more.

12   Closely related to the rising interest in international education has been the work of students in comparative education—indeed, without the latter the former would find itself greatly handicapped. Though, until recently, comparative education has suffered a lamentable neglect by the nation's schools of education, its roots reach into the soil of the nineteenth century, when the American common school was struggling to get on its legs and when Mann, Barnard, Stowe, Bache, and several others were scouting Europe for ideas and practices which might be put to good service over here. Their studies were necessarily rudimentary, and they were prompted not by scholarly inclinations but by utilitarian ones. Since then comparative education has come of age, and in the hands of its foremost promoters it has tended to become less and less an exercise in mere reporting. Today's experts in comparative education take themselves behind their subject's outer facade, and they emerge often enough with a far more discerning, as well as useful, revelation than their predecessors did. Given a country, they put it under scrutiny, probing, as they study it, not only the nature of its education but also the culture of which it is a part, which is to say, its man-made environment, its history and traditions, its laws (hu-

man and divine), its customs, its hopes, its public works, and so on and
on. Finally, the brethren seek to make their studies contribute to a better
international understanding and thereby "to the work and progress of the
world."

For all its silvery locks, comparative education in the United States
failed to attain any great recognition until some time after the First World
War. Then, with international cooperation sweetening the air, it began to
receive some of the attention it deserves. Giving the movement strength and
direction in the republic was a small band of specialists—lettered and honored men like Paul Monroe, Thomas Alexander, Thomas Woody, Harold
Benjamin, Robert Ulich, George Counts, and Isaac Kandel, the last but
recently departed and now more or less the patron saint of the comparative
brotherhood. Though its following, even in good days, was small, as the
years went by it gave rise to an impressive line of publications and several
organizations, all cultivating, of course, their own special ground. In the
forefront was the Institute of International Education of Teachers College,
Columbia University. Founded in 1923, it sought to extend help and counsel to the growing number of foreign students at Teachers College and,
more important, to make a full and earnest study of education in other
lands. Under its auspices a long shelf of international yearbooks were put
into print between 1923 and 1944, when the war put the damper on the
scientific pursuit of international understanding. The institute has since
gone on its way, and though here and there others aspire to emulate it,
none so far has come even remotely near it. Meanwhile, its yearbooks remain a vivid testament of its historic heyday.

13   As the Second World War wearied on, the confidence grew
steadily that somehow education might succeed in ending wars—since
everything else so far had failed—and that some international agency
working to such an end should be founded. Its chief expression, as one
might expect, was in the United States, ever a land of hope and constructive optimism. It got support here from sources of enthusiasts, even in the
highest circles, both lay and professional. Among schoolmen, the NEA educational policies commission, upholding the idea with its most sonorous
utterance, urged the establishment of a permanent international body, akin
somewhat to the vanished Commission on Intellectual Cooperation, but
with a more substantial muscle. Meanwhile, the idea was luring followers
in other lands, and in various deliberations the unofficial representatives
of most of the United Nations were giving it their approval. By 1945 the
idea was given the official countenance of the United States with its an-
nouncement of a plan for a United Nations educational agency, a plan
which was presently given the qualified endorsement of a congressional
joint resolution.

From these high-minded antecedents, time saw the rise of the United Nations Educational, Scientific and Cultural Organization, or, in alphabetical usage, UNESCO. Come upon us in London, in 1945, as a dependency of the United Nations, it comprised forty-five member lands, with Russia absent at the time, but since then enlisted in its ranks. The idea—or ideal—which illuminates and sustains it is that education can bring the nations of the world to a mutual understanding, promoting amity, justice, and welfare and thereby ensuring everlasting tranquility on earth. It is the aspiration which sugared the dreams of so many bygone seers, from DuBois to Comenius to Fannie Fern Andrews, but supported and strengthened today by a vastly greater knowledge, and certainly by a desperate urgency. Wars, UNESCO contends, are bred in the minds of men; hence "it is in the minds of men that peace must be constructed." To such purpose not only is a wide diffusion of culture a prerequisite, but at all times and everywhere the door must stand open "to the unrestricted pursuit of objective truth and the free exchange of ideas and knowledge"—a paradise which so far has eluded the highest human ingenuity but which, for all that, UNESCO is laying plans to bring about.

There is no blinking the fact that during its twenty-odd years of striving UNESCO has served us laudably, demonstrating rather than debating that, given goodwill as well as money and a little luck, things once dismissed as beyond the possibility of attainment can nonetheless be attained. UNESCO has engaged in exchanging students from one country to another on a scale hitherto unheard of. Through its reports, transmitted by the most advanced means of communication known to civilization, it has kept the world apprised of the latest educational, cultural, and scientific achievements the world around. With schools, libraries, and laboratories, it played no minor part in getting the war-torn lands back on their educational feet. Finally, it has brought the light of literacy to people, who, since time forgotten, have groped and stumbled in the night of ignorance.

Unlike its predecessors, physical and metaphysical, UNESCO enjoys the boon of monetary support from the governments which make it up. Hence, in both its dignity and its power, it is appreciably better off than its forerunner, the pale and pouchy Commission on Intellectual Cooperation. Yet despite such sterling advantages, UNESCO suffers from a number of flaws and inherent weaknesses. Its articles, for example, bar it from trafficking in matters which are "essentially within the jurisdiction" of its member nations—a taboo which at present is doubtless necessary, but one which at the same time hampers and hobbles UNESCO's free and forthright functioning. The loophole here is a chasm. For who, save Omniscience, knows precisely what lies essentially within the domestic jurisdiction? Were Gaston's anti-German fulminations, as they fevered in the schools of France before and after Versailles, a strictly Gallic affair? And were the frenzied expostulations of the Führer and his yes-men for German ears alone? Or were these, and others like them, matters that concerned us all? Even if UNESCO were to divine the answers, it is doomed by its writ to hold its tongue. The most it may do under the circumstances is to refer the business to the Security Council, at the moment not the fairest of all possible judiciaries.

The greatest barrier UNESCO will have to surmount, if its hopes are to harvest their rich fulfillment, is nationalism. Not even UNESCO's most bilious critics are likely to inveigh against the merit of its aspirations, save possibly on the score of its rarefied optimism. But between UNESCO's bold and soaring assumptions and the stark reality of national self-interest there winds a long and treacherous trail. Nationalism brought the hopeful CIC to its tomb, and unless science and the angels presently find a cure, nationalism bids to repeat its ugly ploy.

Meanwhile, UNESCO burns its lamp as best it can.

THE TEACHER
AND THE PROFESSION

The practice of training teachers goes back a long, long way. One hears of it first in 1685 at Rheims, in France. Some years following it had plodded its way to Paris, where the Abbé de la Salle had organized schools to prepare his Christian Brothers to give instruction to the progeny of the poor. It was not long before the idea crossed the Rhine to appear at Halle, where Pietist Hermann Francke ran a seminary for schoolmasters. During the eighteenth century it set its roots more firmly, especially among the Prussians. However, the nineteenth century was in session when the first state-conducted seminaries for teachers introduced themselves to this world, this time in the kingdom of Prussia. Badly mauled by Napoleon and un-frocked as a great power, Prussia took hope in its schools to help to weld a new and tougher fatherland. To this purpose the Prussians did over their educational enterprise, remodeling it from top to bottom and superimposing upon it the power and authority of the state. At the same time they made it their business to install the most up-to-date methods then known to enlightenment, which is to say, those issuing from the great reservoir of the Swiss Pestalozzi. Further, to give it effectiveness besides luminosity, the Prussians bespoke Karl August Zeller, an experienced and highly touted Pestalozzian, to settle in their land to direct the training of their school-masters. Worked out with a remorseless industry, Prussian education rushed swiftly to the fore, the cause of amazement and envy in other lands. So highly, indeed, was Zeller's work thought of that presently his seminaries were being copied all about, not only on German soil, but in Sweden and the Netherlands as well. Meanwhile, the French too had begun to shovel the dust off their moldering schools, and in the process they also emerged with a state normal school, the Ecole Normale Supérieure, which, for all the caprice of French political fortune, still proudly holds the tricolor to the staff.

In America the notion that teachers, like bookkeepers and bullfighters, might benefit themselves by training for their practice was in evidence as early as the eighteenth century. The illustrious Dr. Franklin espoused it, and with some reservations, he recommended the practice as a fitting function for his academy at Philadelphia. At about the same time—in June, 1789—some attention was given to the idea in the *Massachusetts Magazine* in a piece entitled "The Importance of Studying the English Language Grammatically."

By 1785 the notion of training prospective teachers had traversed the Potomac, and in South Carolina—to cite but one instance—Samuel McCorkle not only had the good sense to be favorably disposed toward it but even made provision for its practical application in an academy he ran at Salisbury. Unhappily, none of this fervor fixed a fashion. The bald fact is that before any movement for teacher training could become an actuality, education itself had to be set firmly on its feet. Hence, until the nineteenth century, when certain states, headed by Massachusetts, shook off their educational torpor to begin the work of creating the common school, the effective training of schoolteachers remained little more than a mirage.

In the meantime, however, among higher academicians there was no shortage of suggestions. In the forefront was Dennison Olmstead, a Yale savant, who offered "The State of Education in Connecticut." Delivered in 1816 amid the solemnity of a college commencement, Olmstead's oration has gone into history as the first call to go out in this republic for the establishment of an institution that would devote itself utterly and entirely to the business of preparing young people to become teachers. In the train of Olmstead's instructive harangue followed a couple more, one by James L. Kingsley, a colleague, and the other by William Russell, the headmaster of an academy in New Haven. The year 1825 saw the appearance of another brace of recommendations, both taking a fling in support of the idea of establishing a state normal school, one from the pen of Thomas Gallaudet, the recognized father in this country of the education of the handicapped, and the other by James Gordon Carter, instanced in previous pages as one of the instigators of the Educational Revival in the Massachusetts commonwealth.

While plans and blueprints were thus bobbing up on every side, the Lancastrians, as usual, were grappling with the problem in a calculated and practical manner. Their system, it may be remembered, was one wherein a master imparted knowledge to a small posse of handpicked monitors, some for their brains and some for their heft, each of whom was put upon to teach a squad of his lesser classmates. Because of this transfer of the master's hood, and also because of the great store the monitorians placed in the efficient running of their jampacked classrooms, they soon found it desirable to initiate their pupil pedagogues in the bewildering mazes of the monitorial rite. By the twenties, as the monitorians swung into their full stride, we see them running "model schools" for this very purpose. Their revelations presently caught the attentive eye of New York's Governor De Witt Clinton, who admired Lancaster vastly and who also was seeking to extend and broaden the educational opportunity of the multitudes. The greatest attraction of the monitorial system, however, was in the realm of money saving, and those who saw education simply as an act of ingesting facts were generally content to settle for its pittance. But those who regarded learning as something of an ineffable and creative act and who looked upon teaching as an art—that infinitesimal minority viewed the whole business as something vain and absurd.

One of the latter was Amos Eaton, the first executive-in-chief of what is now celebrated as the Rensselaer Polytechnic Institute. Come upon the scene in 1824 at Troy, New York, it was sprung from the beneficence of

Stephen Van Rensselaer, a man of ideas and imagination as well as money, and the last of the state's baronial patroons. He had cherished the hope that somehow his institute might undertake to train young men for service in the district schools to instruct children of farmers and mechanics, as he said, "in the application of experimental chemistry, philosophy, domestic economy, and manufactures," to their everyday work on the farm, in the home, and in the shop—"the diffusion," as Van Rensselaer summed it up, "of a very useful kind of knowledge, with its application to the business of living." A singular notion, no doubt, for its time—and, it could even be argued, one of extravagant fantasy—it was heartily commended, for all that, by Amos Eaton, and under his ingenious lead some of its substance was presently transformed into reality. Not only did Rensselaer Polytechnic enrich its course of study with novel methods and subjects, but its students were made to reinforce their book learning by teaching and lecturing and by demonstration experiments.

Another man of pedagogic vision—with some blind spots, as we behold him from the vantage point of the present—was Samuel Hall, an ordained pastor, who, at the behest of the Domestic Missionary Society, in 1823 opened America's first normal school, a private venture tucked amid the vernal finery of Concord, Vermont. With hopes and prayers, Hall labored for some seven years, producing up to fifty graduates annually, whereupon, in 1830, he translated himself to Phillips Academy, at Andover, where he continued to exercise his industry in the training of teachers. At Concord, Hall's pupils had to fill in the gaps in their knowledge of the elementary subjects besides trying to get the hang of a few advanced ones, especially mathematics. Eventually, those who managed to reach the third year were introduced to schoolteaching, the essence of which Pastor Hall had distilled in 1829 in his *Lectures on Schoolkeeping*. Though it was not the first treatise on the subject to appear in America, having been preceded as long ago as the mid-eighteenth century by Christopher Dock's *Schul-Ordnung*, it effect was tremendous. Not only was it to flourish in hardiness year after year, but in later days, when rivals rose to assail its primacy, nearly all of them bore a marked resemblance to their predecessor. In 1929, the centenary of its advent, it was commemorated with an exact reproduction bearing the colophon of the Dartmouth Press.

Meanwhile in New York a state program was slowly taking shape. The first step in this direction was taken when Governor De Witt Clinton lauded Lancaster and his wonderwork and urged the legislature to take a leaf from his book and provide schools for training prospective teachers. Sad to say, the lawmakers were of another view, and for all the Governor's native shrewdness and hypnotic talents, they gave him no mind. By 1827 they relaxed their stand somewhat by bestowing additional largess upon academies "to promote the education of teachers." Five years later the lawmakers named eight academies to carry out the work, gladdening their hearts at the same time with a special subvention, but taking pains to instruct the Board of Regents to keep a vigilant eye on how it was disbursed.

In Massachusetts the campaign became part of the commonwealth's educational rebirth, and the same effort which injected vitality into the drive for the common school eventually brought forth the normal school. Into its making went the more advanced experience of Europe—the revolutionary formulations of Pestalozzi and the reports of Cousin, Stowe, Mann, and similar men of distinction, and especially their eulogy of the Prussian schools of teacher training. Into them also flowed the experience of New York, which, having brushed aside the idea of special institutions to give light and guidance to its nascent masters, had turned instead to academy graduates to man the common schools. And, finally, the normal schools benefited from the strivings of James Carter, Horace Mann, and Charles Brooks (who confessed that he had fallen in love with the Prussian schools), in addition to several concerted efforts, especially those of the American Institute for Instruction.

The venture was actually broached in 1827, when Carter opened his normal school at Lancaster, a private grove and the second normal school in the United States. Like many other meritorious causes, this one was blessed more with ideals than with cash, and pretty soon it found itself heading for the rocks. When Carter's SOS to the legislature fetched no help, he had to abandon ship and watch it sink. Much less futile was Carter's career in lawmaking. To him, more likely than to anyone else, Massachusetts owes the law of 1837, which brought the commonwealth its state board of education. Two years later its first normal school, the first of the public variety in the Union, opened for business at historic Lexington with Cyrus Peirce as its head and faculty and a student corps of three, all feminine, to give his sapience challenge. With neither a title nor a name to offer it mark or distinction, Lexington passed for a "normal school," an expression which had wandered into the American language from France and which over there meant a school which set the norm or standard for the teaching practice. Finally, in 1845, after years of fulsome rhetoric which got exactly nowhere, the lawgivers put their wearied larynxes to rest and officially denominated the school and others like it "state normal schools." Late in 1839 a second normal school was opened at Barre, and the following year yet another at Bridgewater.

Despite their easy multiplication the first normal schools were scarcely more than primitive. They received girls at sixteen and boys at seventeen. Although the latter were accepted on equal terms with the former, the stronger sex apparently had no taste for pedagogy and generally abstained from its boon—in fact long after the normal school had won a measure of public acceptance, its patronage continued to come overwhelmingly from the fair ones. The new seminaries put their charges through a one-year course—occasionally a bright one might carry on for an extra year. More often, though, students found the work too onerous, scholastically and otherwise, and they abandoned the struggle before the appointed end. This is not suggesting, however, that its demands were exorbitant or even inconsiderate; on the contrary, in its infancy the normal school was little more than a puffed-up lower school. Like Parson Hall's seminar in Vermont, it rehearsed its would-be teachers in the fundamental Rs besides committing them, rather pianissimo, to some of the subjects found in the better-stocked academies, say, mathematics, physiology, the Constitution, and the history of the republic and the commonwealth. On a certain day pupils practiced on "assertive verbs"; on another they "punctuated sentences." They "copied lessons on the globe"; they put their thoughts to trade winds; they "asked the cause of the Aurora Borealis." And to hold themselves steadfast at all times against sin and temptation, they immersed themselves daily in the accepted tenets of Christian piety and morality. Finally, for those who had been lucky enough to escape failure, the great day came when they were brought into the presence of rudimentary pedagogics. Connected with the normal school was a model or practice school, a novelty at the time in American learning, but something which still has its day. Here the acolyte watched the master display in practice the principles he had suffered to learn in the classroom. And here also he was expected to try to emulate his exemplar.

For long years the life of the normal schools hung by a filament, and their increase, hence, was slow. By the mid-fifties, the commonwealth had succeeded in caressing its honor with four normal schools with a register of some three hundred students, of whom about forty prided themselves with being male. Lexington, which had started with an enrollment of three, now could count as many as thirty. For years the normal school found itself the butt of rancor and contempt, the same wave of scorn and obloquy which had weighed upon the common school in its years of youth. Not only did taxpayers make war against it, but vested interests, such as private schools and academies, which were alarmed at the financial threat it posed, also resisted it powerfully. Among some of its most furious antagonists, rather unexpectedly but not unnaturally, were the schoolmasters themselves, who because of their own want of professional training disposed of the whole idea with a lofty contempt, a slur on their competence, a dishonor which in any other land they could have challenged with sabers and pistols.

As for the nation at large, here too the idea of a state normal school set off no great stir of approval. As the century ran by its middle years, only a dozen such houses of light could be sighted in the entire land, and of these half rested in New England—four in Massachusetts and one each in Connecticut and Rhode Island. The others were scattered—in New York, New Jersey, and Pennsylvania in the East, and in Michigan, Illinois, and Minnesota in the West.

New York was the second state to favor its people with a normal school. Located at Albany, it held its first sessions in 1844 in a depot which once had served the interests of the Mohawk and Hudson Railroad but which time and circumstance had made unfit for the needs of trade and travel. Eight months after its founding, Albany State Normal discharged its first graduates, a practice which time saw expanded to four years and which under various names—now it is the State University College of Education—the school has continued to the very present.

Besides these diffuse state endeavors, a number of municipalities undertook to run their own normal schools. Boston hazarded one in 1852, and four years later New York announced the birth of its Daily Normal School for Females. By the sixties the municipal normal school had made its way from east to west. It was to be seen in Philadelphia, in Trenton, and in Baltimore. There was one on the Mississippi's right bank at St. Louis—indeed, there was even one on the faraway Pacific front in San Francisco.

But none of these early attempts radiated much heat. The truth is that among the academic rank and file, the normal school was derisively regarded. What it required from its fledglings certainly exacted no great wealth of talent—in fact, in its class it would be hard to find anything less demanding. To be eligible for admission to its sessions all one needed was a passing knowledge of the fundamentals. Ordinarily, as has been noted, the work of the normal school spanned a year—rarely more and commonly less. Even at that, less than half of its apprentices stayed at their benches for more than a few months. The greater number of them, whether in skirts or in pants, had come from the lower school, and to it most of them someday were destined to return to labor. Little more than a higher primary school, the normal school reserved the bulk of its attention for a warming over of the simple elementals. The study of pedagogics thus became subordinate, a minor character, so to say, in a cast that was far from scintillating. The chief text in use, even after more than thirty years, was still Hall's hornbook on schoolmastering, though a few others had risen to challenge it, if not to unseat it, as witness Page's *Theory and Practice of Teaching* and Abbot's *The Teacher: Or Moral Influences in the Instruction and Government of the Young.*

Though today, as we take a backward look, these seem strange, in their own time they represented the knowledge and sagacity of America's foremost teachers. For all their weighty words, they actually made little difference in the general run of schoolrooms. There was very little, indeed, to distinguish the methods then employed in the daily schoolmastering from those of colonial times. The old malignant stress on memory was ubiquitous and overmastering. And behind the ramparts there still loomed the spectral figure of the infant-damning Calvin. In all this there was to be no visible change until after Appomattox, when the humaner and somewhat more plausible gospel of the Swiss Pestalozzi infused the American practice. Until that time pedagogy in America remained a sad affair, and the training and improvement of the American teacher continued to languish.

2   The professional preparation of the teacher inaugurated during the first half of the nineteenth century in the normal school continued without any appreciable alteration until after the Civil War. In an age when special training for schoolteaching was not generally needed to qualify one for a teaching job—when, in truth, it was even considered by some to be a handicap—it made little sense for an aspiring Pestalozzi to study at a normal school. In any event, the requirement of such a seminary was meager at most. Nearly always its hopefuls came to it straight from the elementary school, and the bulk of them were from the farms. Few had surmounted the elemental subjects, and scholastically most of them were still on shaky ground. As a result, the early normal school, as we have seen, was not only a trainer in pedagogics but also a purveyor of the common branches.

As the public school gradually raised its standards, the need to man it with capable teachers became more obvious. Of this there was a glimmer as early as 1857, when Illinois established its first state normal school. After Appomattox the idea of training teachers betook itself into learning's higher sphere, when a number of colleges embarked on a program of lectures in what was then glossed as the "art of teaching." In 1879 Michigan took yet another stride when it established a full-time chair in education, the first of its kind to enrich the republic. Not long after, in 1890, New York reorganized its first normal school at Albany, changing it into the New York State Normal College and empowering it to transform its graduating students into bachelors of pedagogy. Outdoing even the Empire State Michigan in 1903 converted its normal college at Ypsilanti into a state teachers college, the first of this order of which we have any news.

A split second or so earlier, as time goes in history, New York University, then answering to the name of the University of the City of New York, followed suit with a few choice offerings which, two years anon, in 1890, were to hatch a graduate School of Pedagogy, full-feathered and on the wing. Established as an integral part of the university, it was the first of its kind in the United States. A trailblazer even then, as its successor is now, the school announced "gateway courses," one of which shed light on educational principles and values, incentives, will training, the science of thought, educational philosophy, child study, school organization, the status and tendency of manual training, and the methods of teaching subjects ranging from the three Rs to rhetoric, astronomy, and inventional and demonstrative geometry. Unsparing in its zeal for objectivity even in those days, the school set its students "to make tests of ventilation in certain accessible schools, determining by means of the anemometer the number of cubic feet of air entering the room per minute." In addition they were made to figure out the "number of cubic feet passing out."

Two years before the coming of NYU's graduate School of Pedagogy, the New York College for Teachers, under the strong arm of Nicholas Murray Butler, was founded. Five years later, in 1893, it altered its name to Teachers College, whereupon, after another five years, it was clasped to the sumptuous bosom of Columbia University, where, as everybody knows, it may still be found.

3   The notion that as members of the human race teachers are capable of infinite progress, a notion which currently is in high professional regard, is actually of an elderly age. In circulation even before the invention of the normal school, it gained in force and momentum after the normal school's advent, to become a settled principle in teacher training in America. Incarnate in the so-called "teachers' institute," the idea was first put to work in the 1840s either by Henry Barnard, then laboring in Connecticut, or by J. S. Denman, a school superintendent at Ithaca, New York —just which of the two was first, historical science has not yet ascertained. In any case, Denman was the inventor of the term if not the idea, when, in 1843, he gathered twenty-eight country schoolteachers for a two weeks' congress at Ithaca for the purpose of their pedagogic self-improvement and called the business an "institute." Meanwhile, Barnard had been trying to induce the makers of Connecticut law to put up some cash—a matter of $5,000—to forward the professional improvement "if practicable, of every teacher in the state." When the Connecticut Hammurabis turned down his plan, Barnard launched his program nonetheless, sustaining it out of his own pocket, though in fairness it must be said that he got help from some forward-looking and civic-minded burghers, both laic and pedagogic.

When, in 1844, New York established its first normal school, at least a score of institutes were standing by to give it help. All of them were voluntary undertakings, and although they enjoyed the plaudits of great and high-placed notables, and even of school superintendents, they squared their bills without any ponderable help. Their "conductors," as their leaders were called, held their sessions from the morning's nine o'clock till the evening's five, and if there was a sufficient call, they met their students nocturnally too. They spread their light in pretty nearly everything teachers needed for self-improvement, whether academic or professional, from the strange ways of spelling and grammar to the mysteries of algebra and global geography, "reading sentences in an easy and elegant manner," "the rules of mensuration of superfices and solids," and, for a sparkling chaser, "music for social enjoyment." Should learning tend to make them skeptical, as some people were sure it would, teachers could always counteract such subversion with a consideration of how to "instill virtuous and hon-

orable principles" in others. Not all the institute's industry concentrated on
the teacher's intellectual and professional yearning. Some of it, indeed, was
of a homely practicality, as witness its colloquies on how to secure peace
and order in the classroom, how to excite interest in things in which there
was no interest, how to teach reading in an easy way, how to make pupils
arrive regularly and on time, and, finally, how to arrest whispering.

Though by the fifties more than half the states could boast of having
institutes, and teachers swarmed to them likes bees to a patch of clover,
some there were, nevertheless, who failed to take advantage of their chance
for betterment. To get them to mend their ways, some boards essayed
moral suasion, but the recalcitrance persisted. Finally, some states caused
a great sensation by ordering their school boards to compensate teachers
while they sought knowledge and edification at an institute, and almost at
once the holdouts developed an insatiable thirst for self-improvement.

4   As preparation for teaching became more and more elaborate, so
also did the requirements to practice in the public schools. In fact, the people chiefly responsible for the one were also chiefly responsible for the
other—namely, the professional teachers of teachers. The drive to elevate
and dignify the standards of certification gathered force during the lean
years of Depression, when the supply of teachers, like that of the majority
of workers, not counting undertakers and gravediggers, exceeded demand.
Presently, however, the situation in teaching turned around, and with the
schools everywhere combing the market for qualified teachers, the campaign to raise requirements for eligibility began to show signs of some
relaxing. Even so, there is an appreciable difference between today's requirements for a license and those of only a generation ago. There is, of
course, the usual gap from state to state, with standards ranging from high
to low. But in at least a third of the country a college degree is prerequisite
for eligibility for a job in the lower learning, and in no less than three-
quarters of the states it is needed for a job in the secondary kind. In fact,
more and more the aspirant for pedagogic orders in the high school must
possess a master's degree or at least a suitable equivalent.

Not only has the preparation period for teaching become longer and
more exigent, but even after he is safely installed in office, the modern
teacher, like his predecessor of a century or so ago, is expected to keep on
getting better and better in the practice of his art and science. Where in
his student days, his development was said to be in the "preservice" state,
it has now advanced to the "in-service" state—so, at any rate, is the jargon.
There are a number of ways in which the progress of his professional
progress is brought to flower. One method—almost never failing—is to
make his increase in wages contingent on his continued effort to improve
himself professionally, by taking courses in summer school—or by mail,

or at night, or of a Saturday—by traveling (preferably in alien lands), or even by composing a learned and instructive book. A new favorite in the pedagogic seminary is the so-called "workshop." This differs from the conventional course in that its partakers come to it laden with problems which have arisen from their day-to-day toil and the solution of which has so far thwarted science. At his finest, the workshop conductor does not usually teach—in truth, he may not have taught for years. Instead, he eyes the various problems, dissects and weighs and considers them, and in conjunction with his audience ponders possible modes of attack. The workshop is thus recognized in the profession as a "cooperative effort to solve problems under expert guidance."

Behind the teacher's professional training lies a prodigious amount of research. Into it has gone the work and thought of scholars and specialists, particularly the professors in the colleges of education, and such leading organizations as the National Education Association, the John Dewey Society, the National Society for the Study of Education, the American Education Fellowship (now, alas, among the dead), and several others. To forward this work, as reference has already been made, national surveys have been resorted to. Sometimes they have been outfitted with foundation dollars, and sometimes they have been supported out of the public purse. Among the first were the researches conducted by Drs. W. C. Bagley and W. S. Learned under the standard of the Carnegie Foundation for the Advancement of Teaching. Among the second was the National Survey of Teacher Education. Authorized by Congress, the work stretched over three years, from 1928 to 1931. The findings, which are enclosed in a dozen thick volumes, were published in 1933 by the U.S. Office of Education. For all its scope and magnitude, however, the study was followed by another in 1938—a five-year examination of teacher education under the auspices of the American Council of Education. Nor is this the end, for as the fifties ran into the sixties, other studies, some minor and some major, were under way, and more are in progress now, as the sixties head for the seventies. And so, most likely, it will continue unto the Day of Doom.

5   The ram which battered the progressives also flung itself upon the nation's teacher training. Concentrating on its purported intellectual poverty, it made onslaught especially on its thin and deliquescent scholarship, the insufficiency of its grounding in the liberal arts, and the elaborate deference it gave to methods courses, by which technique becomes a thing in itself and superior to what is being taught. So void of intellectuality are these courses, according to their denouncers, that they are not disciplines at all. They are "puerile, repetitious, dull, and ambiguous," asseverated James D. Koerner, a potentate in the Council for Basic Education and the author of *The Miseducation of the American Teacher* (1963). They are a serious detriment to good teaching, declared Robert Hutchins, and the groves of pedagogy would do us all a service to get rid of them. Let the teachers of tomorrow concentrate instead on the liberal arts and on the tools of communication, which, in the Hutchins parlance, is to say, rhetoric, grammar, and logic.

To put more cerebral juice into their teacher training some schools —for example, Yale—returned their courses in educational history, philosophy, psychology, and sociology—the so-called "educational foundations" —to their respective parent disciplines in the college of liberal arts. Harvard, for its part, designed a program leading to an M.A.T., a master of arts in teaching, by which graduates in liberal arts concentrated upon professional courses and student teaching, besides being made to augment their knowledge and understanding of their particular specialties in the liberal arts. Under this scheme and others like it, the preparation of tomorrow's teachers has been made something of an institutional responsibility, this is, one of the academic as well as the professional faculty, an undertaking some optimists hope may in years to come make an end of the old and fevered feuding between the masters of pedagogy and the upholders of the liberal arts.

To bring some light into the highly beclouded question of teacher education in America, the Carnegie Corporation commissioned James Byrant Conant to put the business under a thoroughgoing inquest. With a staff of nine (the highest court has no more), Conant and his men made a two-year trek through twenty-two states, inspecting the work and layout of seventy-seven institutions and of sixteen state departments of education. They attended classes, made communion with teachers, and waded through textbooks, syllabi, and course outlines, and in 1963 they issued a report whose coda summed up twenty-seven recommendations. Disdaining the conventional approach to teacher certification, Conant urged that only those be licensed who bear the approval of the college as a whole; that a certificate issued in one state should be valid in all the sister states; that a state's only prerequisite for its license should be the satisfactory completion of a period of practice teaching; that a high school license should confine its validity to only one field of teaching; and, finally, that colleges so small that they can produce fewer than twenty-five elementary teachers a year should throw up their hands and abdicate from the business of teacher training.

Needless to say, Conant's twenty-seven theses made no end of the teacher-training controversy. Some, like the scrivener for the *New York Times,* regarded the Conant recommendations very highly and predicted great things for them, of which so far not one has materialized. Meanwhile, New York expressed a willingness to grant them a small but guarded tryout. But professors of education generally have cherished doubts, and sometimes even distaste and disdain. At the moment the old feud is still running.

At bottom, the national flourishing of teacher education represents a phase in the general growth of the country's educational enterprise. But in it there resides also a professional aspiration. When the New Education hove into view early in the century, the schoolman's occupation was still a low and cheerless one. Requiring the forthcoming masters to perfect themselves in the pedagogic art and science and even holding them, on occasion, to a college education thus not only gave them their chance to improve in skill and competence but, in the end, served to enhance their self-respect and, hence, to advance them both professionally and socially.

In consequence, there has followed a steady amelioration of the teacher's well-being, especially in such major concerns as pay, pensions, sick leaves, medical and hospital insurance, and, in less trying times, academic freedom. In all these matters, however, there flourish the usual discrepancies. Though some states, for example, have adopted measures to safeguard their teachers from unwarranted assaults upon their jobs, the matter of tenure is commonly in the hands of local boards. Some of the larger municipalities, treating their schoolmen as considerately as they do their policemen and firemen, hire their teachers on a permanent basis, and as long as they behave themselves, they need have no qualms. In the main, however, the large proportion of the republic's schoolteachers enjoy no such solace and assurance, and they are generally articled on an annual basis.

As for their paychecks, here too things have improved. When the century was still young, teachers in lower and secondary schools were drawing an average of $325 a year—less, in other words, than $1 a day—which, mindful of the dollar's far vaster power then than now, was still niggardly. Forty years following they had managed to multiply this figure by slightly more than 4. But as with all such observations, behind the mask of their statistics there lurks an immense variation. In New York, to illustrate, a teacher bagged an average $2,600 a year, but in Mississippi his labor netted him an average $525. Between the extremes of New York and Mississippi, some 200,000 schoolmen from one end of the country to the other were pocketing less than $100 a month, and some 25,000 were getting not a penny more than $50. Since the century's middle age, conditions have brightened somewhat. In 1963, for example, 75 of the nation's not quite 29,000 school systems were paying maximum salaries of $11,000. But of these 75 of generous heart, 49 happened to be in New York. Meanwhile, across the continent in Beverly Hills, California, teachers who are able to call themselves doctor were being cheered with an annual maximum of $14,000. For all these altitudinous figures, however, the generality of American teachers draw no more than an average of $5,700, or slightly more than factory workers.

The low wages doled our schoolteachers over the many years have been accorded a number of ready explanations. Have teachers fared worse, on the average, than, say, accountants, engineers, plumbers, and truck

drivers, and even gagmen and cartoonists? Then, for one thing, it is because until lately their number has been greater than the supply of available jobs. Moreover, the vast majority of teachers have commonly emanated from the farms and from the lower middle classes. For a large
number of them, hence, becoming a teacher, even on starvation pay, had
its charms and was esteemed as something of an elevation, a gratification,
in other words, of their status vainglory. Since teachers in America are so
often women, it has been a common contention that their wages cannot be
judged by the same yardstick put upon those in the old and more virile
callings—an imbecility, of course, in logic, but a bemusing argument just
the same. Finally, there is the fact that most teachers are paid out of the
public treasury and thus are subject to the usual parsimony of the tax-
paying interests.

Whatever the reasons, the effect of this economic cheeseparing has
had its civic repercussions. First-rate men and women have long since
turned their backs on the world of chalk and blackboard. From the time
of the Second World War, when thousands of teachers, male and female,
worked in the mills and yards of trade and industry for a lush and satisfying price, the republic has suffered a teacher scarcity. Some places, as
has been hinted, have sought to end this shortage by raising salaries and
related usufructs and amenities, and sometimes where the inducements have
been sufficiently alluring, they have been successful. However, teachers of
surpassing excellence remain in short supply, and though of late there have
been signs of some improvement, in the years ahead, when school enrollments are expected to reach higher and higher, unless the unforeseen happens and Providence leads science to find a solution, the shortage bids fair
to become graver than ever.

6   Like his comrade Americans in other callings, the teacher is a
gregarious chap and has gratified his delight in fraternity by organizing
himself professionally. He was doing it as far back as the early nineteenth
century, and he has been doing it ever since. Some of his brotherhoods are
small and provincial. Not a few, however, are national and expend their
energy in the furtherance of some special art and mystery, as witness the
American Historical Association, the American Philosophical Association,
the Modern Language Association, the Vocational Association, the Home
Economics Association, and so on and on for pretty nearly every department of the American learning.

For the more general practitioner there is the National Education Association, the NEA, which is the largest professional guild of its sort in
the republic. Founded in 1857 as the National Teachers Association, it
started out "to elevate the character and advance the interest of the teaching profession, and to promote the cause of popular education in the

United States." Despite its fine-sounding purpose, the society's founders took care not to be so rash as to proffer their benefits to women—or, for that matter, to men who exercised their teaching privily, or even in a private school. Also, with the North and South on the brink of carnage, 1857 was not a propitious moment to organize a national brotherhood.

Consequently, for many years the society's stock hung low. The tide of fortune began to turn in 1870, when the organization took its present name and made the requirements for admission to its fold less exclusive. Thenceforward the NEA's expansion never ceased, and in 1957, when it commemorated the centenary of its birth, it had rounded up some 700,000 members. The secret of its growth, if a secret it be, lies in part in its talent for amalgamation. Soon after its beginning it brought the American Normal Association and the National Superintendents Association under its flag, and in the years ensuing it added several others.

As the National Education Association increased in size, it also augmented its professional prestige. Its meetings shimmered with the names of America's educational *haut monde,* in illustration, Horace Mann, Amos Bronson Alcott, and William Holmes McGuffey, to single out but three. Among its presidents stand magnificoes like Charles William Eliot, president of Harvard, and William Torrey Harris, who, besides attracting notice as United States Commissioner of Education, managed over the years to deliver himself of no less than 175 addresses to the NEA's conventions, a record of a sort, no doubt, in the association's annals. On toward the century's end, the Committee of Ten executed its epoch-making study, and so did the Committee of Fifteen. Since then in one capacity or another the National Education Association has been similarly engaged.

Becomingly mansioned in a sparkling house of glass and metal in the nation's capital, the NEA carries on its huge and wide-flung industry by means of a variety of commissions and councils, each devoted to some specialty, for example, the Educational Policies Commission, the Legislative Commission, the National Commission for the Defense of Democracy through Education, the National Commission for Teacher Education and Professional Standards, the National Commission on Safety Education, the National Council of Education, and the National Council on Teacher Retirement. To advance its mission, the NEA pours out an annual flood of print in both its official organ, the *Journal of the National Education Association,* and its yearbook, besides a miscellany of brochures, broadsides, reports, monographs, and tracts. From 1945 to 1946, by actual count, the organization disgorged and distributed 376,519,658 pages of print, consuming nobody knows how many tons of rag and pulp and kegs of ink.

Though the American teacher has generally been contemptuous of the idea that he is a worker, and would probably have blushed to death at the mere suggestion, a few of his ancient order have ventured to join hands with organized labor. The movement was set afoot in 1916 with the founding of the American Federation of Teachers, an AFL affiliate with an enrollment of approximately three thousand. Since those primordial days organized labor, now combined as the AFL-CIO, has acquired charm and prosperity, and not a little say in national affairs. Even so, for all the union's promise to deliver the American teacher from his woes, so far, true to their immemorial timorousness, the bulk of the teaching order has kept itself aloof—in fact, where the NEA currently musters close to one million head, the AFT, though growing by leaps and bounds, at the moment enrolls some 100,000. The federation, as one might expect, busies itself not with pedagogic vaporizing but with such remorseless realities as wages, tenure, pensions, sick leaves, medical and hospital insurance, working conditions, the right to bargain collectively, and the safeguarding of academic freedom. Like the NEA, it has lobbied for what it wants, and it has worked on national and local fronts. The AFT, Charles Cogen, its president, has let it be known, cherishes no aversion to disturbing the *status quo,* as does the NEA. On the contrary, he says, it is "frankly seeking to establish a new status for teachers by means of the bargaining process." To this end, if driven into a corner, any of the AFT's close to six hundred locals may take recourse to the strike—even though the parent body has assiduously refrained from declaring itself officially for such a tactic.

As familiar to the American home as the tax gatherer and his raids on the family pocket is the PTA, the Parent-Teachers Association. Founded in 1897 in Washington, D.C., as the National Congress for Mothers, it directed its idealism to the little ones, the fireside, the school, and the community. Three years following, when they acquired a formal charter, the mothers vouchsafed membership to the fathers, and transformed their sodality into the National Congress of Parents and Teachers. Since that time the organization has grown like a tapeworm, and today it boasts of some fifty thousand locals with over twelve million members, predominantly female, and scattered to every corner of the nation. Passing its nonage during the period when the feminine drive for the suffrage burst into its triumphant climax, the PTA offered the liberated sisters a marvelous chance to let loose their libido to make and second motions, to flog the air with speeches, to vote, and to preside and bang the gavel.

In those days as in these, the main strength of the PTA lay in the silo belt, in the hundreds of suburbs and hamlets specking this widespread land. Indeed, the farther removed from the city frontier a settlement found itself, the higher usually was the communal fever for the PTA. Like radio and TV, the association served to link Main Street with Broadway, and Pipsqueak with Washington, D.C. As year took after year, and as rearing children in America raised problems grandma never even dreamed of—from the ceaseless traffic with psychologists, psychiatrists, pediatricians, and pedologists to getting Junior into college—the PTA provided a helpful source of aid and counsel, oftentimes, indeed, the only one. Today, moreover, with one household of every five on the move, membership in the PTA, omnipresent in the land's every longitude and latitude, serves, almost like a credit card, to effect liaison between the family and its new and strange environs.

Thus carried on, the PTA's labors have been all to the good. But there is a less dazzling side to the coin. Though the PTA holds itself as "non-commercial, nonsectarian, and nonpartisan," its money fetching is scarcely concerned with pennies. From its beginning the PTA has been a bourgeois stronghold, concerned overwhelmingly with middle-class interests, and hence out of key with the needs of the meaner classes at the base of the social scale, who, in truth, are the ones most in need of the PTA's helping hand. There is also the inescapable fact that despite its change of name to include fathers as well as mothers, from top to bottom the society is woman-ridden. To be sure, men have made the ascent to a local presidency, but in all the seventy-odd years of parent-teacher history, no male has ever succeeded in toiling up the slippery grade to the national presidency. Though the Parent-Teachers Association aims at high and praiseworthy purposes, all too often its monthly seances have descended into sterility. Does the PTA turn its official frown on dope, sex, and the gross brutalities displayed in comics, movies, and TV? Then it holds its official tongue on such critical issues as segregation, sex education, book censorship, merit rating for teachers, and yet several more. There have been lapses too when some local PTA, forgetting the restaints put upon it by superior powers, has stuck its nose, nonetheless, into school matters in which it clearly had no business. Finally, there have been times—all too frequent, it has been bruited—when a PTA, falling prey to fraternal sentiment, has neglected and even forgotten its real reasons for being to high-step in an endless gavotte of bridge, *Kaffeeklatsch*, teas, parties, shows, and similar social frippery. For such enterprise Admiral Rickover has bestowed upon it the order of an "infernal nuisance." It is an award, however, which, taking the good with the bad, it surely does not merit.

The efforts of doctors and lawyers to bring order and dignity to their profession are familiar enough, as are those of architects, engineers, writers, shorthand reporters, *chefs de cuisine*, and the gentry of trade and commerce. As for teachers, though their professional standing has not yet attained the windswept crags of the medicos, or even the jurists, through the efforts of the American Association of Teachers Colleges, the American Association of University Professors, and especially the National Commission on Teacher Education and Professional Standards (TEPS) and the National Council on Accreditation for Teacher Education (NCATE), they have at length taken a bold and forthright step toward improving the standards of their profession.

7   From the dawn of recorded recollection, teachers have found themselves subject to special watch. Once the lieges of priests and later the servants of the state, they have always had to toe the line of impeccability. Today, though somewhat diminished, the restraints put upon their private life still linger. In the cities, with their free and easy urbanism, teachers generally have fared better, and so long as their sinning is no more flagrant than that of the common run of burghers, they may do as they please. But in the four-corners hamlets, they may still be found shackled by decorum. In truth, save for the clergy, no other group of people—except possibly librarians—has been so subject to moralistic scrutiny. "I promise not to go out with any young man except in so far as it may be necessary to stimulate Sunday school work" are words inscribed not so long ago into a teacher's contract in the sub-Potomac belt. "I agree," conceded another, "not unnecessarily to frolic on school nights." Sometimes, like the West Point cadets, teachers have been made to pledge themselves to preserve their single blessedness—some, indeed, have even given their solemn word "not to fall in love." Contractual taboos have been placed on "immodest dress," whatever that could possibly mean in the bikini era, and on nicotine, malt liquor, card playing, and rendezvous with the opposite—dare one say it?—sex.

Graver than these interdicts have been some of a more grisly sort. Some boards have shut their doors to divorcées, and some have drawn the bolt even to married women. Some places proscribe pacifists and political leftists, and some look askance at teachers of outspoken pro-labor sentiment. Some have put their thumbs down on the hiring of Catholics, Jews, or Negroes—though such practice, at least whenever it is transparent, has been hampered heavily of late by the enactment of state and Federal antidiscrimination and civil rights measures.

Academic freedom has been subject to social pressure at all times and everywhere. The fate which overtook Socrates, and the similar one which lay in store for Aristotle, had he not taken to his heels from the smellers of un-Athenian activities, is too well known to need any further airing. The teacher's right—some say his duty—to examine a question freely and to reveal its every aspect has seldom failed to excite and affright people who disrelish any threat to their pet ideas. They have made war on it not only as metaphysicians and moralists, but as lobbyists and logrollers, and only too often they have enjoyed success. Several states have made the teaching of the evolutionary theory in the public education an untoward act and a statutory offense. Many states make their schoolmen vow fidelity to the republic, though the same states exact no such oaths from their pastors and doctors and other more or less publicly engaged practitioners. Before the Depression, when organized labor was not the force it is today, for a teacher to enter into the fraternal bonds of a labor union was a scandal, and numerous communities forbade it under penalty of dismissal. The city of Chicago, in fact, made history in 1916 when it cashiered sixty-eight of its teachers for joining a union. A superior court ordered their reinstatement, but the higher Justinians of the state supreme court overruled their lower brethren.

In the higher learning the bearers of the torch are themselves uncertain to what extent academic freedom is desirable. Ask them, for example, whether the controversies which fret the American people should be aired in the classroom, and some will say "yes," while others will say "no"—and some, it is not unlikely, will try to say both. Thus, there are those who insist that the school should reflect the communal mind and that teaching anything controversial is unseemly, indelicate, and in the end against the public interest. Others, however, contend that controverted issues need to be ventilated, though gently and impartially, and by a teacher who is bereft of any demonstrable viewpoint of his own. Others declare that to refuse the teacher the right to voice his own belief is to strip him of his official usefulness. Let all views be examined, they contend, including those of the teachers; but in the classroom let instructors keep themselves aloof from making converts.

CONSPECTUS: THE PRACTICE AND THE PROBLEMS

In the pages preceding we have tracked the historic progress of American education. Beginning in the primeval colonial setting, that education, like the colonists themselves, had its origin over the sea. Hence it bore the familiar cultural insignia of Europe, especially those which had been put upon it by the Renaissance and, even more, by the Reformation. The differences in rank and fortune which had divided the colonists in the Old World also separated them over here. As usual, the social and economic disparities manifested themselves in education. Thus, wherever schooling was to be found in the Colonies, it was cast in the European mold, which is to say that in its simplest rudiments it was attainable by the average burgher, and in special cases, as in Massachusetts and much of New England, even at public expense. In its higher and more intricate forms, however, education was not for the majority commoner. Although Protestants usually favored a measure of instruction for their children, particularly in subjects which led to an upright and godly life, such as reading, religion, and morality, they did not generally see fit to indulge their young in anything beyond this. Where ambition asserted itself somewhat more vigorously, it was accommodated with a heavy exercising in Latin, and sometimes Greek, which were directed principally toward lads who hoped someday to enter the church or at least attain a secular post of comparable worth and dignity.

But as generation succeeded generation, the marks of Europe grew thinner, and, soon or late, they wore themselves away. And what held for American civilization as a whole held also, of course, for its attendant education. And so, as the republic came of age, and especially as the outline of its democracy grew clearer, there was forged a scheme of schooling which, though at times it was of a baffling diversity, nevertheless was highly distinctive. That scheme, as has been elucidated heretofore, issued from the social ferment of the nineteenth century. The offspring in part of our democratic idealism, it is also, and perhaps in larger part, the issue of our industrial and business civilization.

Our educational system, we are sometimes reminded by men of academic discernment, is not a system at all, at least not in the ordinary sense that it is of a national uniformity and that what holds for, say, Whiskey, California, holds also for Ordinary, Virginia, and Peculiar, Missouri. The United States does not, for instance, as do several other lands, entertain a national school authority with powers to run and oversee the nation's far-flung schools. Nor is there, as among the French, a uniform national body of schools with identical courses of studies, methods, examinations, teacher training, and wage scales. Nor is there even, as in England and Wales, a minimum national standard in such a universal matter, as, for example, the age of compulsory school attendance. But if there is no national system in the purist's interpretation of the phrase, then there is at least an American system, with plain and unmistakable hallmarks, and bottomed on generally accepted postulates, most of which were arrived at after long and sometimes turbulent experience.

2   What are some of these characteristic features? And what are the principles on which they repose? For one thing, there is the divorce from national sovereignty and control, though not from Federal interest or even from Federal pecuniary assistance. For another thing, there is the so-called "educational ladder," by which our schools are joined rung by rung into a single system, from the nursery school to the graduate school. In theory there is to be equality of educational opportunity; unhappily, in actuality, the practice still plods behind the principle. For a third, American education is free, compulsory, and universal. For a fourth, though the state may compel parents to school their little Jeans and Johnnies, it may not force them to commit their young to the public school. Finally, since the Constitution ordains the separation of church and state, the public school may not teach religion, nor may the public purse be fingered for sectarian purposes, however noble and elevating they may be.

So much for the main aspects. Let us now look at some of the more salient details.

3   During the republic's younger years, some desires, it may be recalled, had been expressed for the establishment of a national system of education. But, except for a few high-minded dissertations on the subject, nothing came of these. The Founding Fathers, for their part, generally held their peace on the subject, and the beliefs they entertained in the matter they couched in an utterance which, on the whole, was beautifully vague. Even the Constitution was silent. But because of the Tenth Amendment, which reserves to the states those powers not granted by the Constitution to the national government or specifically prohibited by it to the states, authority over the schools became vested in the states. However, as was made evident earlier, it was not until on in the nineteenth century that the states assumed their full educational powers. Meanwhile, education had evolved largely as a local enterprise, subject by and large to local control and with relatively great freedom of action.

This evolution, and the compromises and adjustments which attended it, have bred the national decentralization. Instead of a national school system, Americans harbor fifty-one school systems, one for each state and one for the District of Columbia, each under its own flag and each flaunting aberrations and idiosyncrasies, but all of them more or less alike. At the same time, although the individual state reigns sovereign over its schools, it has generally wielded its scepter magnanimously, so that the republic's myriad Main Streets, through their communal school boards, enjoy comparative educational freedom.

Although no one on the Potomac may administer and police the American schools, this is not to say that the national government has no dealings with education. Indeed, to judge from an estimate put forth by the Library of Congress, it is likely that at the moment there are over three hundred distinct Federal activities in education. Governmental support, for example, is extended to such undertakings as veterans' education, school lunches, and information centers abroad. Historically, the dean of all Federal educational bodies is the U.S. Office of Education. Created a century ago, in 1867, as a department of education, with Henry Barnard as its first skipper, it was assigned to the care and jurisdiction of the Department of the Interior, only to be shifted again in 1930 and transformed into the Office of Education. In 1939, when Federal bureaus were swarming more copiously than ever, the Office succumbed to one of the prevalent reorganization schemes and was thrust into the Federal Security Agency. Not long after, when reorganization itself was being reorganized, it was incorporated in the Department of Health, Education, and Welfare, where currently it still resides.

For all its rough handling, the powers and functions of the Office remain essentially unaltered. Headed by the United States Commissioner of Education, the Office exercises supervisory powers over the schools for the Indians and the Alaskan Eskimos. Its chief traffic, however, is in the realm of rendering counsel and service. Through its experts it conducts researches and investigations; it culls the important educational facts of the day and assembles and arranges them neatly in statistical graphs and tables; and it releases a series of bulletins and other publications, of which some, like the *Biennial Survey of Education*, represent a valuable storehouse of educational information. At the bidding, moreover, of state and local governments, the Office has rendered assistance in a number of national searches and studies, including, in 1932, a survey of the country's secondary schooling.

The nature of the government's educational program has been dealt with amply in numerous special treatises on the subject, and it is not necessary to traverse the ground again here. Suffice it to mention that the endeavor is stupendous, so huge that it requires several billion dollars a year to give it support. Its most enterprising spenders at the moment, though not necessarily in the order of their fiscal magnitude, are the Veterans' Administration, the Department of Defense, the Department of Agriculture, and the Department of Health, Education, and Welfare. Of the four, the first devotes its energies to the education, training, and vocational rehabilitation of Second World War and Korean veterans, and when the time comes, it will very likely do the same for the veterans of Vietnam, and thereafter, if the earth is still turning, for any others. The Department of Defense ingests the bulk of its education money to furnish academic training to the military personnel at civilian schools and at recognized service academies, as well as to contract research and development. The Department of Agriculture, as is only right and proper, is charged with stewarding the academic breadbasket in the national school lunch program. As for the Department of Health, Education, and Welfare, its outstanding commitments in education embrace such diverse matters as support of the land-grant colleges, vocational rehabilitation, and the construction, maintenance, and operation of schools in defense plants in what are designated officially as "Federally affected areas."

The national government thus not only entertains an educational function which is palpably more than merely advisory but also executes that function in what is far from an austere and pinchpenny manner. The practice of encouraging learning materially is, of course, very elderly. It harks back to the republic's early childhood and started with grants of Federal land. As year followed year, not only were such gifts of real estate enlarged, but also the practice of digging into the public pocket made its appearance. Beginning with the first Morrill act, in 1862, and continuing to the present, various bills have been enacted to give aid and encouragement to vocational education. At the start, when the world was younger and a bit more innocent, few encumbrances were put upon such assistance, and it was not till 1911 that states yearning for Federal money were made to match the Federal stake with an equal investment of their own. All in all, the history of Federal aid discloses a gradual tightening of the reins. The first Morrill act, for instance, exacted scarcely any demands, whereas the Smith-Hughes Act, put into writ fifty-five years later, laid down a more exigent set of specifications regulating the kind of education which was to be offered by the recipients of a national grant.

Though the flow of educational aid has been sumptuous and through the years has steadily risen, the thirst for still more has not been quenched. A decade ago, for example, Congress persuaded itself to appropriate nearly $309 million for the Federal government's various educational programs apart from funds it bestowed upon veterans' education and general research and development. Up to not so long ago, national aid had been reserved chiefly for a few favored specialties, such as vocational education, scientific housewifery, military training, and the mechanical arts and sciences. Following the Second World War, the national Treasury financed the $14.5-billion GI Bill of Rights. But until 1965 the more general run of American schools were not helped and had to do as best they could with state and local capital. Unhappily, this varies substantially from state to state and from one place to another, and as it varies, so also, of course, does the quality of the schooling it is able to provide and, in consequence, the young American's educational chances. Nor did the wayward American dollar help matters. From the Depression forward its fluctuations wrought dismay and distress in the realm of public finance, and hence in public enterprise, so that at times its operation suffered correspondingly.

To obviate such hazards, the remedy of Federal aid was proposed. From the twenties on, bills to such an end appeared in Congress, but until recently they went mostly for naught. The plain fact is that, despite their high intentions, such remedies raised doubts and misgivings. Thus, even though every American state worthy of its salt would be eager enough to accept a subsidy to benefit itself, at the same time it will tolerate no one in Washington sticking an official nose into how the money is spent. The dread that Federal aid is but the first step to Federal control and that on some imminent tomorrow national commissars will come swooping down on the state to oversee its schools and teachers is a real one—so real that until the Johnsonian illumination, it has been a high and insurmountable barrier. But there were yet other bogeys. How, for example, was the national bounty to be apportioned? Were all the states to share and share alike? Or were the poorer ones to get a larger slice? In the main, the inclination was toward the latter course, the idea being that in order to guarantee a minimum educational opportunity for every American child, the wealth of the state and the number of its children should determine the figure on the check it draws from Washington. Much more hobbling has been the problem of dealing with the private and parochial schools. Shall they too obtain succor from the national pocket? Or mindful of the principle of separation of church and state, shall Federal grants be confined strictly and solitarily to the public, secular schools?

So the controversy was batted back and forth, with heat if not with light, until 1965, when at length the statesmen on the Potomac made an end of it. By their historic legislation of that year, public and some parochial schools were to fetch direct national help—some $775 million being set aside to forward various significant projects. In addition, more millions of dollars provided the means for Federal scholarships for meritorious collegians; for grants to further educational research; for the establishment of the so-called "Head Start" preschools; for the formation of a national teachers corps of roving teachers to work their special talents in the slum schools of the big cities; for a vastly enlarged cooperative work-study program to enable hard-pressed young America to stay in school while engaged in part-time work for wages the government underwrote up to 90 percent. Under the numerous clauses of the Elementary and Secondary Education Act, states and communities enjoy an almost uninhibited freedom of deciding how they will rid themselves of the national manna which gushes, at the moment, like oil from a well. Some have invested their share in special instruction, and some in music centers and planetariums; some have enriched themselves with filmstrips, projectors, copying machines, and

closed TV circuits; and some have spent their dollars to cover their unlucky have-nots with adequate and decent clothing. The only real restraint
put upon Uncle Sam's overflowing generosity is embalmed, rather oddly,
not in the aid laws, but in the Civil Rights Act of 1964. By its ordinance
the Secretary of Health, Education, and Welfare has undertaken to deny
funds for educational good works, no matter where in this republic, if they
are not made available to all without the malpractice of discrimination. Unluckily, not even this stick has been effective, racial hatred in certain places
evidently being stronger than even the love of money.

Ever since the twenties there have been hopes that the nation's education, like its foreign affairs, finance, and commerce, might be raised to the
grandeur of a governmental department with a secretary occupying a chair
in the Presidential cabinet. Such a move, its advocates believe, would ap-
propriately dignify a major national industry, one which in 1965 involved
some fifty-four million boys and girls up to the age of seventeen, attending
125,000 schools, staffed by 100,000 executives and administrators and 2
million teachers, at a cost of $42 billion a year. However, for every sup-
porter of the idea of a secretariat there are dozens who argue against it.
A central body, they insist, would be a menace to the states' historic educational sovereignty; it would impose intolerable standards and an even
more intolerable bureaucracy on the American learning. In fact, they go
on, it might even jeopardize the educational liberty of minority groups,
and especially their private and parochial schools.

The nation's educational illuminati, especially its higher representatives in the teachers colleges, are the proposal's natural partisans, and some
have even gone to great lengths in trying to get it adopted. In 1931, the
Hoover regime, in one of its multitudinous commissions, accorded the idea
some warm support, but a minority of its membership dissented very flatly.
The idea has even been carried into the halls of Congress; in fact, several
bills have been introduced, but up to now they have all been spurned.
Finally, perhaps somewhat in the spirit of compromise, the present Department of Health, Education, and Welfare was created. For the ardent
professional, alas, there is little solace in this trinity, and the drive for a
secretary of education, though, perhaps, a bit relaxed at the moment, is
surely far from spent.

4   Though the Federal role in education is certainly not slight, it is
subject to safeguards and limitations. The real authority, as has been set
forth, is not Washington, but the individual state. The largest unit of governmental authority, the state enjoys autonomy within the lines of its
frontier. Since 1784, when New York established the Board of Regents, in
one way or another all the states have followed suit. Their boards bear

different titles, and the articles which give them sanction may not have many things in common; yet in the end their activities are strikingly and overwhelmingly similiar. They are, on the one hand, the fashioners of policy and, on the other, the schools' general overseers and the state's sentinels, prefects, and directors.

The highest education office in more than half the land is the state superintendency, a position which was first devised in 1812 in New York but which did not attain prominence until some years following, in the palmy days of Horace Mann in Massachusetts. Most states elect their superintendent to his office, a system which has occasioned some misgivings, since it tends to make him a politician and, toward the end of his term of office, a supplicant for reelection and hence a mendicant for public favor. However, there is no pleasing everybody, and in states where the superintendent is appointed some people say that in the name of democracy he ought to be elected.

The responsibilities of his office are vast and manifold. His first duty, obviously, is to enforce the school laws. In part administrative, his office involves him in such duties as the certification of teachers and the apportionment of the state's school money. In part advisory, it makes him render counsel to the governor and the lawmakers, especially with regard to educational legislation, and it makes him also the adviser of the local boards, particularly in matters bearing on their rights and obligations, as they grope their way through the mazes of the law. In part juridic, the office has engrafted upon it the function of rendering judgment, particularly in cases of appeal involving the hiring or firing of a teacher. Finally, the position has also, of course, a supervisory aspect, one of its primary requirements being to pass judgment upon the work of the schools throughout the state. Taking one thing with another, if the superintendent happens to be a conscientious and diligent man, inescapably he is also a very busy one.

5   Historically, the roots of the American school, and with them the basis of its sanction, reach down into the depths of the communal soil. Starting out as a purely local endeavor, it came into being in response to the neighborhood's small and simple wants and longings. In the tremendous spread of the Southern countryside, with its scattered farms and habitations, the unit of local government was flung over an enormous space. In New England, however, where settlements were snug and compact villages, the town unit, and hence the town school, was not only natural but also preeminently practical. However, in the progress of time, as the populace edged its way to remoter communities, the town school was challenged by the district school, and in many places the former became a casualty of the latter. But town school or district school, the fact remains that the education it bestowed was still of local coloration, ministering to local needs, and run by local hands with prerogatives and powers which not only were large but also, not uncommonly, bordered on the absolute. Not till the nineteenth century, as the state became more and more active in the business of schooling its inhabitants, was the educational role of the district put under a hard brake. The process, it may be remembered, seethed for long and turbulent years, and before it was brought to a triumphant end, there had to be local inducements of one kind or another. The years, of course, have seen them bruised by time's unsparing hand, and not a few of them have passed into oblivion; yet the principle of home rule, from which they were sprung, is still as resolute as ever.

The conditions which gave rise to the small administrative unit and which in the bucolic hinterland perpetuated it for so many generations for the most part no longer exist. With the advent of the modern superhighway and buses traversing them at breakneck speed, America's Little Red Schoolhouse, with its solitary and sorely burdened teacher, is plainly an anachronism, and though several thousand one-room schools are still dispersed throughout the land, they are destined pretty soon to be among the dead. Under current conditions it has become possible for the hitherto small and separate communities to link themselves with others hard by, and thus achieve an educational standard which otherwise would have been utterly and completely out of reach. The "consolidated school," as such an enterprise is called, not only offers the taxpayer the genial caress of a lesser levy but also avails the rural young a schooling which is comparable to the best in the land.

In command over local school affairs, large and small, is the school board. Composed of the laity, it may comprise as many as forty members, or it may embrace only one. The qualifications for office vary almost without end—some, in fact, require little more than success in, say, the feed and hardware or the lime and cement business. As in the case of the state superintendency, the members attain their exalted office sometimes by appointment and sometimes by the ballot. Whatever the mode of their annunciation, they are the public's surrogate, entrusted with the care and furtherance of its educational operations. As for their duties and responsibilities, once again there is a good deal of divergence. Nearly always they are weavers of the local policy. More immediately, they engage in such affairs as the appointment of personnel, academic and otherwise; they adopt courses of study; and they invent rules for the system's effective functioning. In some places they are empowered to lay levies; in others, they must content themselves with submitting their budget to a specialized and higher authority.

The board's chief delegate and the first officer over the school is the superintendent. His position, as reference has been made, was vouchsafed in the American learning more than a century ago, but it was not until the seventies, when the pace of the nation's industrialization gathered its titantic momentum, that the superintendent became the prodigy he is now. Today the superintendency is, by all odds, the city's topmost educational post, with accompanying rewards and perquisites which by their sheer resplendence must make the common schoolman gape—indeed, save for the President of the United States, the Governor of New York State, and the Mayor of New York City, at $48,500 a year, Chicago's superintendent of schools is the highest-paid public functionary in the land. But for all its appeal, the city superintendency is a hard and forbidding office. Not only must its incumbent be an enterprising and understanding educator, but he also must be on easy terms with business, finance, and law; concerned with civic progress; and adept at making friends and influencing people, especially should they happen to be of the higher political fauna. So great is the importance of his office, and so elaborate its exactions, that special preparation for the execution of its mystery has become indispensable—a fact which, happily, has long since been grasped by every first-rate teacher-training station in the Union.

Like the state superintendent, his local analog is an extraordinarily busy man, particularly if he labors in one of the nation's teeming cities. His duties carry him in all directions and relate him now to the board, now to the teachers, and always in the end, of course, to the public. True to his name, the superintendent is the watchdog over the city's schools, concerned with their maintenance and operation, besides the instruction they offer and their extracurricular affairs. Generally, his office is charged with the appointment of personnel and, when necessary, suspension and even dismissal. In person or through subordinates, the superintendent prepares the official course of studies. And with due counsel and assistance he selects, purchases, and distributes schoolbooks and other appurtenances of modern education, from chalk and erasers to wall charts, TV sets, spiked shoes, and football suits. He gives consent to the communal use of school property, its rooms and social halls, its lawns and playing fields. He is expected to keep the board abreast of the system's ever-present needs, recommending, among other things, the construction of new buildings and the rejuvenation of old ones, the installation of up-to-date equipment, and so on. From his desk pours a constant flow of daily memos, monthly bulletins, and annual reports on the condition of education within his diocese. Sometimes, in the minor towns, he is even cast in the teaching role. There is in all this some variation, to be sure. In the big cities, where education has become a vast and flabbergasting enterprise, the superintendent's task is usually eased by a corps of lieutenants, ranging in descending rank from associate, assistant, and district superintendents to plant and business managers, subject specialists, research directors, attendance officers, lawyers, accountants, secretaries, typists, clerks, custodians, and sundry specialists in pedagogic housekeeping.

6 Of civilized lands, large and small, the United States was, in all likelihood, the first to instigate free, universal education ranging from the elementary through the secondary schools. The American educational scheme, wherein every unit from the kindergarten to the highest learning is a link in a single coordinated system, is almost beyond compare, and one would have to wander far, indeed, to encounter another quite like it. Historically, as has been observed, the idea of such an arrangement germinated in the mind of Comenius (born Komensky), a seventeenth-century Slovak and an educator of rare originality. But the Europeans disdained it, and it was in the United States, two centuries later, that the idea fructified in practice and is today cultivated with vigor and devotion.

At the beginning of the twentieth century the lower learning in the republic was spread over eight years and consisted of three primary grades, three intermediate ones, and a couple more which were known as "grammar grades." Before the war against the Kaiser and his Potsdam warlords, comparatively few Americans continued to study beyond those eight years, and a great many abandoned the struggle even earlier. The relatively small proportion who labored on found accommodation in a four-year high school—all in all, a dozen years of free schooling divided into three classifications of grades and topped with four years in the high school. The present organization still entertains primary grades, but grammar and intermediate ones are almost extinct. In fact, even the system now has a rival. Known in the professional dialect as a "6–3–3 system"—in contrast to the more elderly "8–4 system"—this installs the learner in a six-year elementary school, after which he spends three years in the junior high school with a booster thereupon of another three-year stretch in the senior high school. Some communities, having blended the junior and senior high schools into a single entity, are said to be following a "6–6 plan." More recently, when the junior college burst upon the scene, the pedagogic vulgate was further enriched with a "6–3–3–2 plan." Even more recently—in 1965—New York City shocked some of the advanced thinkers in American pedagogy by announcing its return, if not to the 8–4 scheme, then at least to a four-year high school, and with a system denominated as a "4–4–4 plan."

7 The American child as per the familiar, civilized custom, is conscripted to learning. The term of service differs from state to state, and in certain enlightened ones it may endure for as long as a dozen years. Under normal circumstances he begins to discharge his obligations at about the age of six, when he confronts his teachers in the elementary school. The arrangement has served our great republic for more than a century, and apart from the almost unanimous dissent of the small fry, it enjoys a hearty public esteem. As everyone knows, however, not all Americans are permitted to wait for the red-letter sixth birthday; in fact, almost a million are given a head start on their fellows by being consigned to a kindergarten or even a nursery school, both of which promise undoubted advantages to their alumni.

The kindergarten, it may be recalled, made its way into the republic toward the middle years of the last century, when, after numerous ups and downs, it finally took hold, somewhat precariously to be sure, in the public learning. The nursery school, however, is a more recent arrival. In fact, even as late as the twenties, our educational experts engaged in harsh debate over its values, real and imaginary. Some lauded the newcomer very loftily as a boon to the child's psyche—his health and happiness—especially as it undertook to fit him for the association with his comrades now and anon. Others, however, beheld no such glories. Instead they saw the child prematurely snatched from his hearth to be fettered with institutional shackles. During the thirties, however, as the land rolled and heaved in hard times, the nursery school became widely popular, and with the help of the New Deal's lush allowances from the Federal treasury, it made a rapid spurt. The primary reason for its being at that time was largely to create employment, not, of course, for its tots and runabouts, but for their keepers and attendants. Whatever the original motive, by 1939 the nursery schools, with some 300,000 clients, were driving a flourishing trade—a development which prompted some professors of education to call for their incorporation in the public school system as a permanent fixture.

The patrons of the nursery school range in years from two to five. As one might imagine, a great deal of their time is spent in play. They paint and draw. They sing and dance. And they make things which give pleasure and meaning to their everyday existence. Under escort, they sometimes venture on errands in the larger world about them, with sorties to parks and zoos and similar gala landmarks in the juvenile environs. Sometimes they are introduced to shops, where they barter for paper and boxes, paints and crayons, marbles and pistols, and similar extravagances of life. The more ambitious nursery schools, however, are something more than a transient harbor. Indeed, a few of them, as, for example, the Harriet Johnson Nursery School, which was established in 1919 in New York, carry on something of an experimental program.

The growth and expansion of the nursery school have been laid at the door of the republic's burgeoning industrialization. The new economy, as is well known, caused penned-up mothers to turn their backs on housekeeping for the charms and pleasures of the mill and other exhilarations in commerce; as more and more took advantage of their new chances, the problem of providing a haven for their toddlers became urgent. Today, however, this reason for the nursery school's existence is no longer regarded as paramount. True, the needs of the working mother have not been dismissed as of no account. But to educational scientists there are more important ones. Does the sociologist, for example, hail the nursery school and even urge its adoption everywhere and forthwith? Then it is because the child in school, hobnobbing with his comrades, makes his first acquaintance with the communal life, an acquaintance that will prepare and condition him to become a safe and worthy fellow citizen in later life, fit to join the ranks of the Elks or even the Moose. Psychologists too wreathe the nursery school with broad smiles. For if it is true, as their science tells us, that many of the complexes, conflicts, repressions, and regressions which groan and writhe in the hidden caves of our subconscious are stored therein during the formative years of childhood, then obviously the nursery school is an excellent place to keep watch and, should they show themselves, to lay on and put them to flight.

8   Today's public elementary school not only is secular but is also the laboratory and workplace of a budding democracy. Its primary purpose is still, as it was when it was young and full of hope, to rescue its recruits from the horror of ignorance by introducing them to the ABCs. But its methods have long since bowed to science. Thus, where grandfather began reading by the "oral method," his descendant uses the "silent method." Moreover, instead of reading a single book from cover to cover and over and over again, becoming intimate as he goes along not only with its message but also with the nature of its commas and periods, its nouns and verbs, and the like, today, for good or ill, he confines himself simply to reading. His literary range, moreover, is much wider, embracing sometimes as many as a dozen volumes. The learning of formal grammar, once indispensable in the rearing of every responsible and upstanding American, is now all but dead; it has been pushed from its Alp by a stress on acceptable linguistic habits, both in writing and in speech. Even the penman's gorgeous art is no longer a thing of honor. Where the older generation was put upon mastering a trim and lovely hand, the current one, clutching its ball-point firmly in its fist, concerns itself not with beauty but with legibility. Left-handers, once in a class with sword swallowers and bearded ladies, now wield their pen from port or starboard, whichever way Omnipotence wills. Spelling, once the classroom's pride, has lost its ancient glow. Spelling bees and the wizards they produce still flourish in scattered enclaves, but like the county fair, they are doomed to extinction. The charm of conquering the great mammoths of the dictionary has given way to the practical, with a confinement of the learner to the meager stock of everyday words. Arithmetic, too, has succumbed to the process of denaturalization. Once cried up as an exercise of the mind, it was diverted to practical and even social ends. In fact, some of newer professional educators—which does not mean, of course, the mathematicians—began to doubt the advisability of teaching formal arithmetic before the advent of the seventh grade, but Sputnik put the hard brake on such extravagant thinking, and today, instruction in arithmetic—the "new math," so called—bids once more to become red-blooded and robust.

The curriculum which started with reading and religion has long since vanished. Bit by bit it has grown and expanded. First came the full complement of the three Rs, and then music, drawing, history, geography, and literature. Could Pestalozzi tear himself away for a flitting moment from his eternity of bliss to pay us a call, his findings would surely amaze him. Not only has the old one-room school become a palace, but its offerings are almost unlimited. All the familiar old-timers are still on hand—except, of course, religion—but in addition, there are many others, as witness health, hygiene, safety, citizenship, arts and crafts, shopwork, and several more. The use of visual material for which Comenius pleaded so vigorously, but to no avail, is exemplified not only by a host of pictured schoolbooks but by several other aids as well, from drawings, charts, and posters to the crowning consummation of film and television material.

But for all the augmentation of its store, the elementary school has not been disposed to increase the time allotted for its consumption. The tendency, if anything, has been the other way. Thus, though slightly more than half the nation's lower schools still exact eight years of attendance, the rest, as has been stated before, have actually cut the period to six.

9   At the start of the century, about one-half million boys and girls were enrolled in the public secondary school. Five decades following, the number was ten times larger. In the earlier period some three of every four high school graduates went on to the college campus. Today the proportion is almost a direct reversal, and for every four now leaving the high school, three go anywhere except to the institutions of the higher knowledge. The reason for this shift is hardly mysterious. The truth is that the high school has been taken over by the plain folk. To accommodate their young and to discipline them for the rigors and amenities of everyday living was, of course, the high school's original reason for being. But in the years this purpose somehow became disrupted, and by the end of the nineteenth century the high school was addressing its main effort to transforming the bulk of its custom into college freshmen. Consequently, despite its original and historic purport, the American high school became the province of a comparatively small minority. Its benefits, declared the Committee of Ten, in its grave commentary on the matter, should be reserved for "that small proportion of children in the country . . . who show themselves able to profit by an education prolonged to the eighteenth year and whose parents are able to support them while they are in school." On intellectual grounds, there is something to be said for such a view, but on economic and social ones, it collides head on with the national belief in democracy, and so, though here and there it is still given voice, it has become highly suspect.

If the high school has thrived so phenomenally of late, then it is not merely because its conventional votaries have been overpowered by the devotees of democracy. Behind the high school's current prospering are other formidable factors, such as the increase in national wealth and, even more, the indubitable cash value a high school diploma is able to bestow upon its owner. Finally, of course, there is the fact that in a number of states the age of compulsory attendance has been pushed up to sixteen, and in some even to eighteen, which makes attendance at high school or, in any case, the junior high school, almost inescapable. At the same time, however, Mississippi and South Carolina find it possible to get along with no compulsory educational laws at all.

The high school which but a few generations back concentrated on getting its alumni into college placed its overwhelming stress on the cultivation of the intellect. Its curriculum of subjects hence was preponderantly academic, with particular attention to mathematics, the sciences, and the foreign languages. Though these still remain, the weight put upon them has lightened not a little, and whatever the reason for their presence, it is certainly not, as formerly, to exercise and strengthen the mind. Although high school teachers continue, like their scholarly predecessors, to cover the ground which is essential for admission to the boon of collegiate grace, because of the divergent needs of the large generality of its pupils, the high school, hearkening unto the communal voice, has greatly extended its repertoire. Cast your eyes on its subjects, and you will find such newer ones as automobile driving, aviation, mental and physical hygiene, human relations, home nursing, writing, acting, radio and television, and a herd of others. There is a concentration on the great callings of the human race, from husbandry and industry to business and homemaking, not forgetting the most enchanting occupation of them all, namely, leisure. Because of the enormous expansion of its functions, today's up-and-doing high school not only must have the usual array of labs and classrooms and a gym and an auditorium, but it must also bedeck itself with a kitchen, a nursery, and a sewing room, besides ateliers for the pursuit of music and art, in addition to special chambers for its aspiring hair stylists and cosmetologists, carpenters, plumbers, electricians, machinists, bookkeepers and stenographers, and similar folk of skill and toil.

Besides the coming of such newer disciplines, there have been some alterations of the older ones. Of late, for example, there has been something of a move to what the Herbartians once referred to, with a somewhat different meaning, as "correlation." Thus, where only yesterday the learner applied himself to biology for a year, which he followed, if he was successful, with a year of chemistry and another after that of physics, today he studies them all, or at any rate their rudimentary essence, in one blazing swoop in a course of "general science," and thereupon, if he is so disposed, he may tackle the others one by one. By the same score, in "social studies" he gets familiar with what was formerly broken into history, civics, geography, economics, and sociology. Similarly, in "general arithmetic," he tries to get the hang of arithmetic, algebra, geometry, and sometimes trigonometry.

The high school's steady and accelerating pursuit of practical and vocational ends is doubtless a phase of the national pragmatism. Even so, it has caused some critical comments—not many or bold—but critical nevertheless. The complainants are for the most part those of an older habit of mind, the vanishing gentry of scholars who seek to drill and dress the intellect and to safeguard the cultural legacy. It may be that in practical America the older view is doomed to become an oddity, and any support of it, hence, may become somewhat injudicious and even suspect.

It may also be, however, that a bit of the old tradition, considerably diluted, will persist. If it does, it will probably be because of some of the recommendations put forth by a few of the more enlightened colleges. The most conspicuous of such schemes, and the most publicized, so far has come out of Harvard. Specifically, this states its case in its report, *General Education in a Free Society*, which appeared in 1946. General education, as Harvard employs the phrase, has somewhat the meaning of a liberal education. It is, it goes on, "that part of the student's whole education which looks first of all to his life as a responsible human being and citizen" —and, one might add, only thereafter to his preparation for a livelihood. To attain this end, Harvard proposed that the high school hold its practical and vocational courses in abeyance while its pupils concentrate on English, science, mathematics, and the social studies, after which specialization may follow.

Actually the Harvard idea is not new in this world. In much richer form it has existed—nay, it has been put into practice—in other civilized lands. To the French, for example, it is *culture générale,* and to the Germans it is *allgemeine Bildung.* Both have taken a rather high pride in the idea and have held it dear for generations untold, and despite the sorrowful reverses these countries suffered after the Second World War, it still lies at the heart of their secondary schooling. Whenever it has been allowed to function freely, the results usually have been creditable. Thus, when young men and women in France and Germany complete their professional studies, they generally are on familiar terms not only with their special and professional mystery but also with the humanities and the higher arts. Many of them are able to follow a fugue with relish, and some can even enjoy Tolstoi or Strindberg, or even the Nichomachean Ethics.

If the American high school is no longer the intellectual seminary it used to be, then on the other hand it gives a hearty encouragement to its pupils' social and recreational advancement. Once confined to a minor place, and carried out voluntarily and after hours, the so-called "extracurricular activities" have become a major educational enterprise. Indeed, in many hives of enlightenment they have been built directly into the cur-

riculum itself with regular hours reserved for them. Where formerly they
were directed mainly by amateurs and hobbyists and similar dilletantes,
today they are the preserve of the trained expert, or at all events one who
has applied himself more particularly to giving leadership in the sphere
of student activities. As nearly always, the need for training such leaders
has been recognized in the nation's more progressive schools of education,
with offerings that extend from student activities, student counseling, and
youth leadership to graduate courses leading to M.A.s, Ed.D.s, and Ph.D.s
at NYU in methods of folk and square dancing, supervised student leadership in recreation, and camp dining-room and kitchen management problems. Though such traffic has saddened the lovers of pure learning, and
has even brought uneasy doubts to parents here and there, the fact remains
that it is a reflection of the present American culture; hence, if the proposition that the school reflects the social climate means anything at all, its
presence should be the cause for neither tears nor wonder. This is not, of
course, saying the same thing for the American culture itself.

As has been said before, the high school as it existed in the late years
of the nineteenth century usually entertained a double purpose. On the one
hand it sought to prepare a certain proportion of its learners for the higher
groves, and on the other it rendered aid and instruction to those who had
no taste for the higher meditation. The former it dosed with subjects the
colleges deemed it essential for every freshman to know, namely, English,
mathematics, the natural sciences, some history, and a foreign language or
two. The others got off a bit more easily with a touch of the academic
fundamentals and some sort of business or industrial preparation. Up to
1910 those engaging themselves in such endeavor were usually aged from
fourteen to eighteen and, in the common phrase, were referred to as "high
school students."

But, like most things, this simple usage has undergone a transformation. True, the familiar four-year high school, though it has greatly altered
and is sometimes scarcely recognizable for what it used to be, is, at least
in its essence, still among the living. At the same time, however, in the
junior high school and in the senior one, it has, if not a rival, then at
least a resolute bidder for the public favor.

The idea of overhauling the four-year secondary school, as has already
been mentioned, was in existence even before the end of the century. In
truth, in a few places—for example, Springfield, Massachusetts—it had even
been put into practice. By 1888 Dr. Eliot, of Harvard, was giving the
notion his glowing support, and in a number of his encyclicals he came
out for it very strongly. Presently, the idea was winning approval from
other stars of the national pedagogy, and by the evening hours of the century the Committee of Ten (1893) and the Committee of College Entrance
Requirements (1899) were proposing to recast the elementary and secondary learning into two periods of six years each. By 1910 such an arrangement had actually been entered into in Columbus, Ohio, and in Los

Angeles and Berkeley, California. Since then the idea has won a great following, and in some form or other it is being entertained by about half the current secondary student enlistment.

In ordinary circumstances the junior high school receives its boys and girls from a six-year elementary school, accepting them when they are a dozen years old, or thereabouts, and holding them to their books for another three years. Its purposes vary somewhat from place to place. Nearly always, though, one of its common functions has been "exploratory," which is saying that it seeks to help the young to unearth their hidden potentialities and, if possible, to relate them to a vocation. Is Junior dowered for science? Or do his talents run to the arts, fine or otherwise? Or maybe he has the makings of a first-rate mechanic, a craftsman, or a man of trade or business. Whatever his bent, the junior high school proposes to fetch it out by providing him with prevocational samplings. At twelve, as everybody knows, Junior stands at the brink of adolescence, and soon he should feel the pull of strange and powerful forces. To reassure him, the school stands ready with aid and counsel. More and more, in fact, it is relying on trained virtuosos to render the service. But the junior high school does not concern itself with only such highly personal matters. Like the four-year high school, it addresses itself to the student's natural social gropings, and for this purpose it offers him a considerable social program.

From the junior high school, the pupil with an appetite for yet more schooling passes on to the senior high school, where, if all goes well, he improves himself for another three years. Altogether, thus, his schooling runs through a dozen years—six in the elementary school, three in the junior high school, and three more in the senior high school. Though this arrangement has been widely adopted, and in progressive circles is well regarded, the traditional four-year high school is surely not on its deathbed. In fact, as has been said, about half the secondary schooling is still of the early order, and led by New York City, where once it had been all but abandoned, it is now on the eve of a glorious restoration. But if it has persisted, this is by no means to suggest that it has not changed. On the contrary, the chances are that when it is at its best, it reflects all the illumination displayed by the newer and younger organizations. In its function, curricula, and methods, and in the philosophy from which they spring, all the progress known to modern education may be found in the four-year school, including even such novelties as teaching machines, team teaching, mechanized language labs, individual study carrels, and other high-sounding devices.

10   Over the years the schools not only have enhanced their supply of subjects but also have steadily added those of a specifically vocational nature. The beginnings of the practice may be seen even in our colonial world, when various private hawkers undertook to teach whatever their clients wanted and were able and ready to pay for. The stress on the utilitarian and vocational lay behind the advance of the first academies, with their offerings in bookkeeping, law, surveying, naval science, and similar lore. From such small beginnings has come vocational education, a specialty today in its own right and, needless to say, one which is very popular. Not only has the ordinary high school committed itself more and more to providing some vocational training, but in the larger and more peopled towns there are schools fitted especially to vocational ends. Thus, one finds seminaries for future cooks, bakers, restaurateurs, garage mechanics, radiotricians, grocers, butchers, merchants, tailors, painters, musicians, and many more. Most of the colleges of vision and imagination have long since staffed themselves with departments devoted specifically to vocational disciplines and with courses that reach from leathercraft, woodcraft, and metalcraft to air navigation, shop maintenance, and occupational therapy.

Undoubtedly the prodigious surge of vocational education is due in some measure to the insistence of the surrounding culture. To meet its demands vocational educators have given their courses a depth and breadth of which they were quite innocent a few decades ago. But their endeavors would surely be less successful were it not for the magic lamp of Federal aid. The fact is that only a couple of generations ago the United States was lagging behind several other countries in the vocational preparation of the young. It was in order to remedy this deficiency that the Smith-Hughes Act of 1917 authorized the establishment of a Federal Board of Vocational Education and, more important, a subvention from the Federal Treasury to aid the advancement of the country's vocational education. Other statutes presently followed, some to promote the vocational reclamation of disabled citizens; some to assist the states in the development of special education in agriculture, trade, and industry; and some to further the training of vocational teachers. Several measures were also adopted to increase the national subsidy, as witness the George-Reed Act (1929), the George-Ellzey Act (1934), and the George-Deen Act (1936). The latter not only enlarged the bulge of the Federal grant but also widened the sphere of its development. Thus, while there were formerly but four beneficiaries—to wit, agriculture, trades and industry, home economics, and the training of teachers therein—the George-Deen Act included such activities as selling and distribution, and indirectly it gave its benediction to certain kinds of public service, as, for instance, that of the school janitor. In 1946, moreover, Congress expressed its official confidence in vocational guidance with its enactment of the George-Barden Law, which authorizes the expenditure of Federal money in its behalf.

11   The purpose of early colonial education was, first and last, religious. Hence the first American schools not only engaged in making their fledglings literate but also undertook to prepare them someday to flap their wings heavenward by introducing them to the Father's mandates, the taboos which followed therefrom, the virtues which pleased Him, and the sacred tunes He liked to hear. Under the circumstances the parish school, or its equivalent, was held in high regard, and in certain quarters it was even helped with public money. Subsequently, however, as the values of the spirit yielded more and more to those of the world which we now adorn, the school likewise gave way, and by and by it was moving along with the secular current. Even before the end of the eighteenth century, unmistakable signs of the changing fashion were visible; in fact, as early as 1792 New Hampshire put its constitutional ban upon public-supported sectarian instruction.

The American public school, now in luxuriant flower, is the inheritor of this tradition. Laic, it does not—indeed, it may not— teach religion. However, the usual difference of opinion reigns among the states, as it does among the citizenry, over what is and what is not religious teaching. Is the mere recital, for example, of a verse from Holy Scripture an act of such instruction and hence a violation of the secularized principle? Some states have said aye and have specifically forbidden it, but others have voted nay and have allowed it. Some states have purged the Good Book of certain blushful portions. And some others have even made the reading of a number of Biblical strophes a mandatory act. So the controversy over reading Holy Writ in the public school wore on from place to place until at length, in 1963, the United States Supreme Court raised its corrective voice to declare Bible reading unconstitutional.

If the question of using Holy Writ in the public school wrinkled the brow of educators, then other issues pertaining to faith and morals fret them still more. Is it, for example, in consonance with the school's secularity to permit someone to wear the sacred veil and vestment while addressing pupils in the public school? Again, some states have decided one way and some the other— some, indeed, have even given sanction to the right of the frocked brethren and sisters of religious orders to dispense instruction in the public school. Is it legal, to cite another gnawing riddle, to intone the solemn, dulcet Christmas airs in the public school or to perform playlets to celebrate the coming of the infant Jesus? Again, some places have nodded their heads up and down, while others have waved them from side to side. Finally, is the chanting of the Lord's Prayer a breach of the laic postulate and hence not legally allowable in the chambers of the public learning? Once more the answer has differed from one place to another—at all events until 1963, when the Omnipotent Nine pronounced their anathema upon the practice.

Regarding religious instruction itself, as usual the churches are not in harmonic accord. The Roman Catholic Church is, of course, 100 percent for it. As is its wont, it contends the very essence of education to be religious, and the control thereof the church's unassailable right. Among

Jews, as among Protestants, as nearly always there is no united front. Some, viewing the nation's vast and complicated congeries of religious affiliations, hold it better in the interest of the commonweal to buttress democracy by keeping state and church apart at all times and everywhere, even in the public learning. But to many Protestants such a cleavage not only is against God's revealed ordinances but also is a plain danger to the republic itself. Hence they have proposed the introduction of some form of nonsectarian religious instruction in the public school. It has shown itself mainly in states which are almost wholly Protestant, and the form it has taken is commonly the compulsory reading of a Protestant Bible—a gratuitous affront, of course, to non-Protestants, whether Christian or otherwise, and one which, as was remarked a few lines ago, is now known to be against the Constitution. More acceptable to all the faithful is the practice of liberating the young from their secular books during certain parts of the school day in order to let them introduce themselves to the theorems and axioms of their religion. Such instruction—known as "released time" — is imparted beyond the academic walls and is executed under ecclesiastic auspices.

But this practice, too, has run afoul of criticism. It is, the objectors say, a plain veto of the principle of state and church separation; it discriminates against the offspring of free thinkers, agnostics, and atheists, embarrassing them and wounding their psyche by making them witness to their comrades' escape, if only transiently, from their toil at school, while they, for their part, must sit and stew with no surcease in sight. To counter such complaints religious leaders have given their countenance to what they call "dismissed time." Under this arrangement children are simply let loose from school for an hour every week, ostensibly to report to their men of God in order to be perfected in piety and virtue, but with neither a checkup nor penalty should they stray instead to pool parlors, pizzarias, or similar dens of sin.

There have been times, sad to say, when the argument over religious instruction has become so gross that it has necessitated recourse to jurisprudence, which, in some instances, has involved the nation's highest bench. Such was the situation when Mrs. Vashti McCollum, a citizen of Champaign, Illinois, brought suit against the town board of education. Under agreement entered into by the board and the local church council, the one furnished the necessary space while the other rounded up instructors of Jewish, Catholic, or Protestant persuasion. To this Mrs. McCollum, a nonbeliever, entered a bold objection. She did not want her child tutored in divinity. Nevertheless, his abstention made him a public spectacle, subject to raillery, and thereby bringing dismay and anguish to both mother and child. In consequence, she asked the courts to stay the practice as a violation of the historic concept of separation of church and state. When the Illinois jurists ruled against her, Mrs. McCollum made appeal to the

United States Supreme Court, which, in March, 1948, by a vote eight to one, reversed the lower court. "Beyond all question," said Mr. Justice Black, who spoke for the majority, Champaign had employed tax-established and tax-supported schools "to aid religious groups to spread their faith." Hence, he went on, "it falls squarely under the ban of the First Amendment."

The decision was grounded on three main points. For one, Champaign had employed its public school buildings for religious purposes; for another, its school authorities had given support and cooperation to the program; and finally, the compulsory machinery had been put to use to help religious sects to carry out their program of religious instruction. In the Court's juridic eye any scheme of religious instruction involving any of these principles must be held in violation of the Constitution. In fact, in the mind of Mr. Justice Reed, the lone dissenter in the case, the Court's ruling "threw doubt into all forms of religious instruction connected in any way with the school systems."

But the Court's opinion, for all its weight, was not granted universal acceptance, and some communities persisted in releasing the young from their books during school hours in order to give them access to regular religious instruction at church or temple. With so many doubts freighting the matter, the issue unfailingly found its way into the chambers of justice. Unluckily, the dispute found no solution, some courts, as in St. Louis in 1948, holding against the practice, and some, as in New York in the same year, declaring for it. But four years later, when the New York case confronted the republic's highest tribunal, the New York plan of released time was upheld. Unlike its forerunner in Illinois, this did not make for a working partnership between government and religion, but merely allowed each to recognize the rights of the other. Ours, declared Mr. Justice Douglas, is "a religious people whose institutions presuppose a Supreme Being." And finally, "we cannot read into the Bill of Rights . . . a philosophy of hostility to religion."

Under prevailing conditions children whose parents want them to receive religious instruction cannot get accommodation in the public school —hence the private religious schools. Millions of the young attend them— in fact, one child of every ten. And for every one of this select group there are nine who are practicing Catholics. Such schools naturally put their main stress on faith and rectitude with courses in Holt Writ, the history and practices of the particular church, and exercisings in psalm singing, besides the usual lay subjects found in the public learning.

Although nonpublic schools operate under the eye of the state and are subject to its ordinances, their legal status and their right to carry on have been affirmed by the courts. The doctrine that somehow it is against democracy to frequent a private school or religious one and that therefore the duty befalls every parent to send his child to public school has been judicially unhorsed. For a long time it made very little headway, but in the early twenties, spurred on by idealistic Ku Kluxers, the doctrine began to lather certain patriots, and in Oregon they persuaded their lawgivers to embody it in the law. But in 1925, in *Pierce v. Society of Jesus and Mary*, the United States Supreme Court rejected the statute on the grounds that it ran counter to the constitutional provision for "due process of law" and that, in addition, it had interfered unduly "with the liberty of parents and guardians to direct the education and upbringing of children under their control. . . ." The state, the Court declared, may require all children to become educated; it may set the minimum educational standards; and in order to assure itself that its requirements are honestly and properly met, it may inspect all schools, private and parochial as well as public. But under no circumstances may it compel children "to accept instruction from public teachers only."

Another cause for enflaming the respective partisans of church and state centers is the use of public money in education. Already in the nineteenth century they were in one another's hair, but their wrangling became more vehement as the contest for universal public schooling got under way. To keep state and church apart in public education most states at the time adopted measures which outlawed or, at all events, severely crippled the use of public money for religious ends. Few churchmen, of course, have given acquiescence to such jurisprudence, and to this day a good many declare themselves strongly against it. Church and state, they submit, may be separate—but not religion and education. Since under the present dispensation the teaching of religion in the public school is under ban, the faithful must have recourse to schools of their own and are thereby incommoded by a double financial burden. For not only must they maintain their church schools, but, like everybody else, they are levied upon to support the public variety. Hence they are in effect doubly taxed.

To give themselves some easement, they have demanded a share of the public gold to help them carry on, if not their labors for God, then at least their labors for man. Interestingly enough, in a number of important tests they have emerged in triumph. Courts, for instance, have admitted them to a portion of the public money to further the health of their young on the grounds that such service is an integral and essential civic function of the school. In other instances they have been granted the right to haul their progeny to their various parochial schools in conveyances which are publicly owned and operated. But despite some yielding here and some conceding there, in its essential aspect the issue remains locked in controversy.

As in the state halls of lawmaking, so also in the Congress on the Potomac. There too the issue has rocked the House and the Senate. In truth, up to very recently almost every attempt to extend Federal aid to the states has been thus controverted. A bill drawn up by Senator Aiken of Vermont would have allowed the states to apply Federal funds to parochial schools.

As retouched by the late Senator Taft of Ohio, however, the bill allowed the exercise of such beneficence only in states whose public money was already being tapped by private and parochial schools. But even this deft strategy was insufficient, and the law died in embryo. So, more or less, the situation remained until 1965, when Congress legislated the Elementary and Secondary Education Act, under whose articles at least a part of the $1.3 billion of the national grant in aid was made available to parochial schools.

12   It is only fair to remind ourselves that not all private schools are of a religious cast. Not a few, in fact, confine their concern strictly to mundane matters, as some of them did even in colonial times, when godliness and virtue were cardinal articles for the attainment of happiness and success not only in the life to come but also in its prelude here on earth. Now, as then, a good many of them devote themselves to the cultivation of the practical as well as the ornamental arts, from bookkeeping, stenography, typing, and foreign languages to barbering, cooking, dancing, acting, and contract bridge. Nor is there any lack of the purely academic private schools. Indeed, they are enjoying a hearty prospering, particularly in some of the large municipalities where overcrowded classrooms, poor instruction, and the hazards of race relations have caused fathers and mothers to send their children to the private halls. Some of these schools are heavy with years, as witness Collegiate, founded in 1638, and Trinity, founded some seventy years later in New York City. Some—for example, Buckley, also in that sinful city—are of a rarefied exclusiveness and are harder to get into than even Harvard or MIT. Their tuition, needless to say, cruises in cerulean heights. Brearley, which caters to the fair ones, levies a tuition charge of no less than $1,650, not counting extra fees, as, for example, for instruction in how to bedizen a nag in style and decorum while galloping him through the city's Central Park.

Not a few of the country's private shrines, though they are academic, are given to the furtherance of some pet specialty which the tax-supported schools, because of their dependence on the public's goodwill as well as its cash, dare not brave. Thus, there are schools which stress the old-style phonic approach to the reading art, while others conduct their classes à la Montessori, a pedagogy which is as old almost as the century but which at the moment is enjoying a slight revival. Not satisfied to reach back only sixty years into the past, a few others put their reliance in the readers of McGuffey, which that saintly man put together over a century ago. In New York City the Lycée Français favors its learners with a curriculum which is a carbon duplicate of the one currently in use in France's halls of classical learning, while the Rudolf Steiner School, of the same city, instructs and edifies its protégés in anthroposophical principles. The Dalton School puts its seniors through their paces in anthropology and play writing, while

Hewitt prepares tomorrow's *haut monde* for their strenuous social life to come by putting its interdict on movies and parties during school nights.

Besides such specialists there are, of course, many hundreds of private schools throughout our fair republic, in country towns as well as cities, less plush, perhaps, but no less prideful, whose only purpose is to offer an education of the finest quality at a price that is commensurate with merit.

13   Besides being summoned again and again to douse the fires kindled by the disputed place of religion in the public learning, our courts have had to give their thought to the racial issue—particularly, of course, as it bears upon the rights of the Negro. The first of such legal actions of which we have any word occurred not in the heart of Dixie, but in Boston, when, in 1849, a Negro by the name of Benjamin Roberts took his troubles to the state's highest bench to seek redress from the city for its refusal to seat his five-year-old Sara in the white primary school of the district in which he was residenced. Though the jurists found for the city, its victory did not last long, for six years later Massachusetts honored itself as the first state in the Union to outlaw separate schools for Negroes.

Following the cold war of Reconstruction, the new South systematically reduced the Negro's rights, until, as the nineteenth century wore away, the best the Negro could hope for educationally was the schooling of his young at public cost, not, to his sorrow, in the company of the whites, but in houses set aside especially for his race. Although the Negro and his protectors felt this to be a transparent inequality, and even a gross fraudulence, and although they hired lawyers to help and defend them, their best arguments availed them precisely nothing. The earlier Boston verdict had taken on the power of a precedent. Not only did its doctrine penetrate into the state judiciary, but it weighed even upon the thinking of the Supreme Court. Thus, in 1896, in the case of *Plessey v. Ferguson*, involving Louisiana's mandatory segregation in its public conveyances, all save one of the jurists held such practice to be constitutional, provided the facilities, though separate, were equal. Thus the "separate but equal" theorem. Hatched in Boston, but invigorated to stupendous force by the jurisconsults in Washington, it was presently cutting a wide swath through Southern educational practice, where it gave segregation the support and countenance of the nation's highest law.

In the century in which we live the problem of race relations has been more sharply examined. It gained prominence, as one might expect, from the era's large events—its wars and depressions and its persecutions of the racial underdogs—as well as from the progress of the sociological and psychological sciences. The prodigious need for manpower in time of war brought the Negro more and more into the nation's industry and gave him a new economic and social standing. Once having savored this, he was reluctant to surrender it—indeed, he craved for more. At the same time his threatened rise tended to alarm his white competitors, whether in the North or in the South. Meanwhile, across the sea, the spectacle of the fascist pogrom made the nation hang its head, but it served also to arouse its social conscience and bring forth calls for measures against the discriminations persisting in our midst. From them emerged, in 1947, the Truman Committee on Civil Rights with proposals to the lawgivers to put them into being.

In education the combat against discrimination was inevitably carried into the citadel of segregation. There the assault was forwarded by legislation, and more particularly by the judicial verdicts compelling the admission of the Negro to certain higher public educational institutions. The first small fissure in the wall appeared in 1935, when Maryland's Court of Appeals ordered the state law school to admit a Negro to its sessions. Three years following, the University of Missouri was put upon to furnish a Negro law student an education equal to that it offered the whites. Another dozen years, and the University of Texas was ordered not simply to afford a Negro an education as good as that which is proffered the whites but also to give him access to the University of Texas Law School. And, finally, in Oklahoma, when the sages of its school of education undertook to seat a Negro apart from his colleague whites, the courts ordered the practice to cease.

Although these rulings confined their justice to individuals, they were nonetheless significant. In fact, by midcentury Negroes were making their cautious way into the groves of higher knowledge, not only in the states aforesaid, but in Arkansas, Delaware, Kentucky, and Virginia as well. Their advance, it is true, was slow and tortured, and it was hampered on every side by devious devices—but still it was an advance. But in the lower learning there was no such progress. There the drumfire of "separate but equal facilities" kept the Negro at bay, and in seventeen states and the District of Columbia segregation was mandatory, while in four others it was a matter of local option.

But in May, 1954, the Supreme Court put the stamp of unconstitutionality on such practice with its unanimous ban on racial segregation in public education. Though physical facilities and other "tangible" factors may be equal, declared Chief Justice Warren, the spokesman for the Court, "segregation of children in public schools solely on the basis of race" does have a "detrimental effect upon the colored children." "The impact," he went on, "is greater when it has the sanction of the law; for the policy of separating the races is usually interpreted as denoting the inferiority of the Negro group." Psychologically, moreover, segregation "generates a feeling of inferiority to their status in the community which may affect their hearts and minds in a way unlikely ever to be undone." Thus, the Court concluded, no matter how one looks at it, "separate educational facilities are inherently unequal." In consequence, it ordered the integration of public schools with "all deliberate speed."

The Court's decision changed no segregated heart—soon, indeed, it became clear that the end of legal segregation did not mean the end of actual segregation, that only too often the integration which was conjured up was spurious, a token at the most to keep within the law. Some states, in truth, seeking to delay, or even to thwart, integration, amended their constitutions to such an end, and some resorting to casuistry, even abolished their public schools and sent their white children to white schools maintained by cryptic private moneys. But the Federal courts' holding to the Fourteenth Amendment mowed down such legal sophistry, even though in so doing they hoofed a state's historic right to organize and run its schools as it saw fit. All in all, despite the stalling and the resisting, the deceit and chicanery, the dozen years since 1954 have seen some progress. Throughout the republic, not only in sub-Potomac regions, but in the North as well, thousands of communities have been bringing their schools into harmony with the law's requirements. Meanwhile, however, on the bull-headed segregationist front, the "deliberate speed" the Supreme Court ordered in 1954 has shown much more deliberation than speed.

14   Within the lifetime of many Americans the nation's schools have been buffeted by the gales of a capricious fortune. First they suffered in the Depression, and then during the Second World War and its melancholy aftermath. The Depression lay heaviest upon the South, but its dark shadow hung all about. Throughout the land there was a slaughter of budgets and school services. Not only were teachers' salaries slashed, but oftentimes their jobs disintegrated abruptly. Specialties like art and music, and even shopwork and kindergartens, came under the ax. Not a few places curtailed their school terms—sometimes as much as an entire month. In truth, in hundreds of small communities schools drew their blinds and locked their doors. Without cash, and with no credit in sight, building programs came to a halt, and essential repairs slowed down to a crawl. By 1933, with prosperity still hiding around that ineffable corner, the education of about ten million children was badly crippled.

Three years following, with the New Deal seeking to return the land to normalcy, the schools began to rally, and some even reported themselves as cured, though they remained somewhat shaky. Another three years, however, and the recession was upon them; now their ache and upset was worse than ever. New retrenchments came into effect, but to no great avail. Whole states, in fact, were now in the red. Georgia, for example, owed its teachers some $5 million, while Ohio, the mother of colleges and presidents, reported its school fund to be $17 million short. And so on, sadly, throughout the land.

As the thirties made their baleful exit, war was once more afflicting the human race. And when, after long and wearisome years, the carnage ended, it left the usual wrack, only greater this time, and worse and more engulfing than anything before in human history. With it there came, of course, the familiar dislocation and decline in schooling. Though the republic had been spared the material shambles caused by the actual destruction overseas, its education had suffered and showed it very plainly. With prices inflated and materials short, $5 billion, it was figured, was needed to bring us out of our tailspin. Even worse, and far less replaceable, was the depleted stock of qualified teachers. During the war, as has already been stated, they had put aside their books and rulers and, combining patriotism with economics, had taken better-paying jobs in industry, and many of them, to no one's surprise, enjoyed their new estate so well that they turned their backs to teaching forever. Sad to say, the morale of those who continued teaching, bedeviled as they were with high prices and low pay, sank below sea level.

As America made its way through the fifties, education was laboring under various handicaps. But in this great land nothing is ever hopeless, and even amid the decay and deterioration there were plans and programs directed to the creation of more and better schools to prepare more and more Americans for life in a world of freedom and plenty. For all their differences in a jot here and a tittle there, the suggestions had a more or less similar—and even familiar—ring. There should be an improvement in teachers' wages, working conditions, and fringe benefits and in the standards for licensing them for their ancient calling. Schools must be made safely democratic and their chambers accessible to all in fact as well as theory. A planned building program to reach the exploding number of young Americans should be developed. The school and the community, whether in city or country, should interact for the common good. Finally, of course, there must be more money, from both the state and the Federal till.

Though American education is at present under heavy strain, this is surely nothing new. It was sorely beset after the Revolution and after the Civil War. Things were at a low ebb in the early nineteenth century, when James Carter sounded his historic alarm in Massachusetts and when Horace Mann grabbed his war clubs to battle for school reform. In years following, toward the century's end, new demands were thrust upon the public school, which, already suffering from too large an enrollment, found its operations dreadfully burdened. Criticism, then as now, fell, like a cloudburst, from every quarter. It reflected, as usual, the ferment and vitality which are implanted in the American manner of life. This is inevitable and inescapable, and no friend of democracy would want it otherwise. Always, moreover, the American people have somehow risen to the challenge. To be sure, their present experiment in mass education is by far the greatest the world has ever known, and also we are confronted by dangers our fathers never dreamed of. Even so, to hold, as some wet blankets do, that the American people are not rising to their emergency is not only pessimism, but a grave misappraisal of their educational past.

BIBLIOGRAPHICAL NOTE

For the student of America's educational history who wants a fuller view of the nation's cultural heritage, and, maybe, a more intimate one, there are any number of useful and instructive, and even agreeably written, books. The problem, indeed, is not a shortage of stock but an overpowering abundance. For a start, the student can serve himself no better than to look into George Bancroft's *History of the United States from the Discovery of the American Continent* (10 vols., 1834–1875) and Francis Parkman's *France and England in North America* (9 vols., 1865–1892). Both works, to be sure, are old-timers, and some of their views are today in disrepute; even so, the panorama their searchlight swept has never been surpassed. A junior, so to say, by comparison, but already entertaining its first arthritic pains, is Charles and Mary Beard's *Rise of American Civilization* (4 vols., 1927–1942). Written under the rubric of economic determinism, which is to say that money rules the world, an assumption which in some spots is today under assault, in its youth the work relished the distinction of being a best seller with all the riches and usufructs that attend such a caprice of fortune.

The important part played in the making of the nation by the Americans' trek beyond the Alleghenies toward the Pacific and the consequences it has brought upon us are recounted in Frederick Jackson Turner's classic *The Frontier in American History* (1920). Although its premises no longer excite the hearty clap-clapping they once did, in the main they are still amiably regarded. In a class by itself, and for years unrivaled, is Vernon Louis Parrington's *Main Currents in American Thought* (3 vols., 1927). A Pulitzer magnifico, Parrington gave special notice to "what the fathers thought and why they wrote as they did," but in his reactions to large themes he sometimes fumbled badly. Merle Eugene Curti's *Growth of American Thought* (1943; 3d ed., 1964) tackles the subject from the "broad cultural viewpoint." Though it too speared a Pulitzer, its prose is heavily starched—nevertheless, for the serious worker the book is at the moment the leader in its class. Ralph Henry Gabriel's *Growth of American Democratic Thought* (1940) records our intellectual annals from 1815 on. Its title suggests its particular leaning. Harvey Wish's *Society and Thought in America* (2 vols., 1950) and Nelson Manfred Blake's *History of American Life and Thought* (2d ed., 1963) scout more or less the same territory. Both are workmanlike jobs, and either one should give the student a pretty good understanding of the course of American life and thought. There remains Samuel Eliot Morison's coda to a lifetime of study and writing, the *Oxford History of the American People* (1965). Sumptuous and scholarly, it is for all that full of bounce, with a felicity of prose vouchsafed more often to the savants of France than to those of America.

The literature of American educational history is also formidable, and it would take no little fortitude to attempt to bag it all. Fortunately, there are a number of breviaries, glosses, and summas to take the student by the hand, and the one that leaps to mind at once is Paul Monroe's *Cyclopedia of Education* (ed., 5 vols., 1911–1913). Though it was assembled over a half century ago, it carries its years charmingly, and its expositions, historically speaking, still offer useful service. Confined to the more recent past are the ruminations of the *Encyclopedia of Modern Education* by Harry Rivlin and Herbert

Schueler (eds., 1943). Bracing and supplementing these works is the *Encyclopedia of Social Science* (15 vols., 1933). It is currently undergoing renovation and enlargement.

Nearly all the standard repositories of knowledge make some mention of the educational past and especially of the outstanding thinkers and toilers in the vineyard. The *Encyclopaedia Britannica* (24 vols., rev., 1963) gives the subject a fairly generous exposure, and the student would do himself a favor to comb its index. Finally, for the man who needs to fortify his knowledge with figures, graphs, tables, charts, and similar statistical effluvia, there is the *Biennial Survey of Education in the United States*, published by the U.S. Office of Education from 1919 on.

For a bibliography of educational history, the fullest archive at present is William Wolfgang Brickman's *Guide to Research in Educational History* (1941). Its store of information is diligently cataloged with all the relentlessness of a German *Oberlehrer*, and it includes references to materials not only in English but in the major European tongues, besides Hebrew and Yiddish. Although its author occasionally loses himself in the contemplation of academic flyspecks, for beginners his counsel is certainly of help.

On the history of American education there are a number of general works, written mostly of late with an eye on the college textbook market. The oldest of which we have any knowledge is John Cleaves Henderson's *Our National System of Education* (1877). Henderson was also the author of *Thomas Jefferson's Views on Public Education* (1890), a pioneer study of almost four hundred pages but now almost forgotten. In Henderson's train followed Richard Gause Boone with *Education in the United States: Its History from the Earliest Settlements* (1890) and Edwin Grant Dexter with *History of Education in the United States* (1904). For the general student these works are too far gone in years to be of much worth, but for anyone who might be curious about the history of educational history, they are in their way indispensable.

The first book of any importance in the field was Ellwood Patterson Cubberley's *Public Education in the United States* (1910; rev., 1934). For years Cubberley's book was the cock of the walk, and though rivals appeared after death bore him away, the book has never ceased to retain a modest custom. Belabored in spots, however, with a piling up of detail, Cubberley reads at times like a stockjobber's report, and although the man reveled in work and play in the paradise of California, he was not a little overawed by the New England tradition. It was largely to give the record a corrective balance, especially regarding the part played in our educational past by the South, that Edgar Wallace Knight, himself from below the Potomac, brought out his *Education in the United States* (1929). Spruced up decennially thereafter with a fresh chapter, but otherwise neither rectified nor amended, it showed itself in its last earthly shape in 1951. The volumes of both Knight and Cubberley offer elementary bibliographic counsel, and for those who admire such confections, they have conjured up some "questions for discussion." For light on Cubberley, in his capacity not only as an educational historian, but as a writer, verse maker, editor, teacher, administrator, school surveyor, humanitarian, and philanthropist—in sum as a salient contributor to the progress of twentieth-century American education—the student should refer to Jesse Brundage Sears and Adin D. Henderson, *Cubberley of Stanford* (1957).

More restricted in scope than either Knight or Cubberley, but richer in detail as far as it goes, is Paul Monroe's *Founding of the American Public School System* (1940). The ancestor of America's educational historians—their Adam as it were—Monroe professed his subject for numerous years at Teachers College, Columbia University, where he inspired embryonic Ph.D.s to produce a cupboardful of graduate studies, some of them very recondite and meritorious.

Of recent years, as the social stress impinged more insistently upon our deliberations over education, a number of educational histories, attuned to the newer key, have come upon the scene. Listed in order of appearance, they go thus: *The School and the American Social Order* (1947; rev., 1963) by Newton Edwards and Herman Glenn Richey; *A History of Education in American Culture* (1953) by Robert Freeman Butts and Lawrence Arthur Cremin; *The American School in Transition* (1955) by William Earl Drake; *A History of American Education* (1956) by Harry Gehman Good; *Formative Ideas in American Education* (1964) by Vivian Trow Thayer. To the aforesaid, several more could easily be added, but the ones cited are sufficient for most purposes. More specialized, as their titles hint, are Isaac Leon Kandel's *Twenty-five Years of American Education* (1929); Adolphe Erich Meyer's *Development of Education in the Twentieth Century* (1939; rev., 1949); and Lawrence Arthur Cremin's *Transformation of the School: Progressivism in American Education* (1961).

Historians, as everyone knows, are given to nosing in primary sources, and in this respect their educational specialists constitute no exception. Of source anthologies, in fact, they have put together a fair amount. A modest start was made by Burke Aaron Hinsdale in his *Documents Illustrative of American Educational History* (1895). Better known and still in the running is Ellwood Cubberley's *Readings in Public Education in the United States* (1934), which, as its name serves notice, gives supplementation to its author's text, already described. Heftier and heavier is Edgar Knight and Clifton Hall's *Readings in American Educational History* (1951). Until recently, these two works held a monopoly in the field, but in 1964 they were challenged by Carl Gross and Charles Chandler's *History of American Education through Readings*. Steering clear of the track laid out by their forerunners, Gross and Chandler turn instead to less frequented side trails to look at writings on education not only from the hand of professional pedagogues, but also from that of such literati as John Greenleaf Whittier and Washington Irving, besides a number of contributions from other branches of the laity. Of a somewhat similar leaning, but more sociological in its overtone, is Rena L. Vassar's *Social History of American Education* (2 vols., 1965). More circumscribed in their purport and content, but effective all the same, are Robert Francis Seybolt's *Source Studies in American Colonial Education: The Private School* (1925) and Paul Monroe's *Readings in the Founding of the American Public School System* (microfilmed, 1941).

Rather oddly, there are not many digests setting forth the verbatim gist of the educational views of prominent Americans. The ones we have are mostly short, and nearly all are in the McGraw-Hill Educational Classics Series, which is now out of print. They are Charles Flint Arrowood's *Thomas Jefferson and Education in a Republic* (1930); John Seiler Brubacher's *Henry Barnard on Education* (1931); and Thomas Woody's *Educational Views of Benjamin Franklin*. Roy John Honeywell's *Educational Work of Thomas Jefferson* (1930), though up to its armpits in doctoral erudition, nonetheless contains many of Jefferson's most charming thoughts on education. Covering the same ground is Gordon Canfield Lee's *Crusade against Ignorance* (ed., 1961), a paperback in the Classics in Education Series, Teachers College, Columbia University. There remains Merle Curti's *Social Ideas of American Educators* (1935; rev., 1965). Though, strictly speaking, this is not a source book, still its passages are frequently alimented with direct quotations.

The relics which historians hold dear are scarce in the domain of education—save, of course, where they still remain in active daily use. Here and there, however, some of the moldier ones are beginning to catch the taxidermist's eye, and as the republic's educational youth recedes more and more into the abysm of the past, the effort to hold on to some of its mementos will doubtlessly increase. The McGuffey Museum, situated at Oxford, Ohio, was conceived for such a purpose. In historic Cooperstown, New York, in connection with the Farmers' Museum, one may view a carbon duplicate of an old schoolhouse, together with the decor and appointments said to have been favored in those parts in the early nineteenth century. At Monroe, New York, there is a replica of the town's first schoolhouse, erected in stone and in public service more than a century ago. What is believed to be the oldest colonial schoolhouse still standing, and in an excellent state, the Voorleser House, may be sighted on smog-free days on Staten Island, settled in New York's harbor.

To keep abreast of current literature in educational history, the student should ponder the *History of Education Quarterly*, which not only carries essays on the subject's various aspects, but also reviews some of the newer books in the field. Now and then some of the more general educational journals present discussions and reviews which brush aside the veil from the educational past—notably *The Educational Forum*, the *Harvard Educational Review*, *Teachers College Record*, and a handful of others.

Beginnings

For cultural matters which apply to all the colonies, whether those in New England or the South or those sandwiched betwixt the two, there is a staggering assortment of material. For a beginning there is Herbert Levi Osgood's *American Colonies in the Seventeenth Century* (3 vols., 1904–1907) and its successor on the century following (4 vols., 1924). Moses Coit Tyler made the first important tracks in the field of literary history with his *History of American Literature, 1607–1765* (2 vols., 1878; reissued, 1949) and *The Literary History of the American Revolution* (1897). In addition the student should make acquaintance with Robert Earnest Spiller and others, *Literary History of the United States* (eds., 3 vols., 1946); Clinton Rossiter's thoroughgoing inquest of colonial political thought, *Seedtime of the Republic* (1955); and

Louis Booker Wright's brief *Cultural Life of the American Colonies* (1957). The best single study, so far, of colonial culture is Thomas Jefferson Wertenbaker's *Founding of American Civilization* (3 vols., 1938–1947). The first three volumes of *A History of American Life* by Arthur Maier Schlesinger, the elder, and Dixon Ryan Fox (eds., 1927–1948) cover the social aspects of the colonial epoch. Strung on the same strand though they are, needless to say, they are not jewels of the same worth.

There are numerous special studies of colonial culture, but the following stand out: Carl Bridenbaugh, *Cities in the Wilderness: The First Century of Urban Life, 1625–1742* (2d ed., 1955) and *The Colonial Craftsman* (1950); Arthur Wallace Calhoun, *A Social History of the American Family* (3 vols., 1917–1919); Marcus Wilson Jernegan, *Laboring and Dependent Classes in Colonial America, 1607–1783: Studies of the Economic, Educational, and Social Significance of Slaves, Servants, and Poor Folk* (1931); Michael Kraus, *Intercolonial Aspects of American Culture* (1928) and *Atlantic Civilization: Eighteenth Century Origins* (1949); Sidney Fiske Kimball, *The Domestic Architecture of the American Colonies* (1927); Abbott Emerson Smith, *Colonists in Bondage: White Servitude and Convict Labor in America, 1606–1776* (1957); Anson Phelps Stokes, *Church and State in the United States* (3 vols., 1950); and William Warren Sweet, *Religion in Colonial America* (1942).

Chapter 1 Antecedents

For the particular phases of culture the settlers conveyed from the Old World to the New, there are several excellent surveys, some short, some long. One thinks at once of Basil Wiley's *Seventeenth Century Background* (1914) and its sister volume for the hundred years following. Portrayed on a more spacious cloth is George Macaulay Trevelyan's meticulous, yet amazingly entertaining, *English Social History* (4 vols., 1949–1952). For the reigning economic system of the era, the student should apply himself to Eli Filip Heckscher's *Mercantilism* (trans., Mendel Shapiro, 2 vols., 1935). The best single volume on the state of European thought and culture at the time of colonization very likely is Paul Hazard's *The European Mind* (1953). Traversing similar ground from 1543 to 1776 is Preserved Smith's well-known *A History of Modern Culture* (2 vols., 1930–1934). It scrutinizes art, letters, science, politics, religion, superstition, manners, and a few other human engagements. Louis Wright's short, perceptive, and pertly written *Middle-class Culture in Elizabethan England* (1935), though it is now in its thirties, continues to hold up. Another excellent supplement is Arthur Stanley Thurberville's eye-fetchingly illustrated *English Men and Manners in the Eighteenth Century* (2d ed., 1929). Summing up the whole business in one grand sweep is Wallace Notestein's *The English People on the Eve of Colonization, 1603–1630* (1954).

As for education, there is the usual run of general texts of which the following are the most recent: *A Cultural History of Western Education* (2d ed., 1955) by R. Freeman Butts; *A History of Education* (2d ed., 1960) by James Mulhern; *A History of Western Education* (2d ed., 1960) by Harry G. Good; *An Educational History of the Western World* (1965) by Adolphe E. Meyer; and *A History of the Problems of Education* (2d ed., 1966) by John S.

Brubacher. For a closer accounting of English education, the student should look into Arthur Francis Leach's *English Schools at the Reformation, 1546–1548* (1895) ; and Ancel Roy Monroe Stowe's *English Grammar Schools in the Reign of Queen Elizabeth* (1908).

No matter how virile and how bursting with powerful scholarship books may be when they break their findings to the world, even the best of them are doomed, like people, to suffer from time's corrosive touch. To keep up with some of the questions and problems which occupy colonial historians today, and the newer explanations some of them are venturing to offer, the student would be well rewarded to eye the contents every once in a while of the *William and Mary Quarterly*, published jointly by the College of William and Mary and the Institute of Early American History at Williamsburg, Virginia. It is chock-full of interesting stuff on colonial life and doings, including learning, science, and education, and its critical estimates of important new writings in the field are often spacious and instructive. Similarly loaded are *The New England Quarterly*, *The Mississippi Historical Review*, and the *Southern Historical Review*. There is a mine of material, sometimes very rich, to be unearthed in the various organs of local historical associations, as, say, *The Pennsylvania Magazine of History and Biography*, *The Virginia Magazine of History and Biography*, and the *Virginia Cavalcade*. In addition there are the publications of the American Antiquarian Society, the Colonial Society, and several other alliances like them. Finally, there is the *American Heritage*, edited by the Pulitzer laureate Bruce Catton. It is full of amazing and instructive Americana, handsomely put and delightfully begauded, and now and then it gives some earnest thought to our educational past.

Chapter 2 The Bible Commonwealth

During the twenties it was high fashion among the intelligentsia to tug at the pedestal of the nation's worthies in order—as the vulgate has it—to "debunk" them. Such was the freehand way of Vernon Parrington in his *Main Currents in American Thought* (1927) and Charles Angoff in his *Literary History of the American People* (1931) and a whole herd of biographers and historians from James Truslow Adams to Harold Ordway Rugg and William E. Woodward. There is something to be said for their tactic, for obviously our Washingtons and Lincolns were scarcely the archangels which were sprung from the poetic fancy of the writers of our everyday schoolbooks. Ironically, dunking the national heroes in the debunking pool often washed away whatever virtues they actually had, so that in the end the image that remained was no more genuine than before. In the process, the New England Fathers became an easy mark, and where once they were hymned for their halos, they were now damned for their arrow-headed tails, with the latter more talked about than the former. Since then, the wheel of fashion has turned, and the likenesses which of late have issued from the scholar's bench—mostly out of the ancient Puritan fastness itself, namely Harvard—are far more ingressive and discerning, and hence somewhat closer to truth and justice.

The preeminent debunker of debunkery has been Samuel Eliot Morison, for most of his working days a promoter of learning at Harvard. A savant of the first order, he is also a master of an amusing and effervescent prose. The rare combination of the twain and a touch of irridescent wit has given us fresh and helpful insights into the Puritans, and instead of seeing them as a somber and ulcerous folk, we now behold them gurgling with human juices, with all the virtues and vices therewith in association. From Morison's pen has gushed a cataract of words, phrases, and sentences into book after book, tumbling but recently into his *Oxford History of the American People*, already referred to. The student can assign himself most advantageously to the examination of the Puritan culture and its attendant education by pondering Morison's *Builders of the Bay Colony* (1930). His briefer *Intellectual Life of Colonial New England* (1956) is a revision of his *Puritan Proanos* (1936), which embodied the substance of a batch of addresses Morison pronounced at New York University. At this point a caveat of caution should be laid down, for in his zeal to repair the damage done the Puritans by the debunking carnivora, Morison is sometimes more the prosecutor than the judge. There remain Morison's three masterful volumes on Harvard College (its founding, 1935; the seventeenth century, 2 vols., 1936), summarized and pulled together in *Three Centuries of Harvard, 1636–1936* (1936).

Those wishing to apprise themselves of the nature and meaning of Puritanism should pry into the études of Perry Miller, in particular his *New England Mind: The Seventeenth Century* (1936; reprinted, 1954); also his *New England Mind: From Colony to Province* (1953) and his *Orthodoxy in Massachusetts* (1933). Those seeking some sort of account out of the Puritans' own mouths, but who are daunted by the magnitude of such an undertaking, will find a fair sampling in *The American Puritans* (1956), judiciously put together by Perry Miller. For the more eager and ambitious ones, there is William Bradley's unmatchable *History of Plymouth Plantations* (Samuel Morison, ed., 1952); *John Winthrop's Journal*, also known as *The History of New England from 1630 to 1649* (ed., James Savage, 2 vols., 1853); and Cotton Mather's *Magnalia Christi Americana* (2 vols., 1853). At first glimpse, this looks like a grisly dish, heavily greased with Greek, Latin, and Hebraic citations. But let the reader spoon this jetsam aside. It is but the gaud of Mather's vainglory, and it has little bearing on the essence of the work, which in spots rises to the majesty of an epic.

Less amicable to the Bible Staters' cause is James Truslow Adams's *Founding of New England* (1921) and his *Revolutionary New England* (1923). Samuel Morison at times has gone after Adams with an ax—even so, for an understanding of the anti-Puritan case, Adams is required reading, and so, by the same score, is Brooks Adams's *Emancipation of New England* (1887).

Colonial New England, as is well known, is noted for its towns and their way of life. For their story, and especially their European links, the student should confide in Allan Forbes, *Towns of New England and Old England, Ireland and Scotland* (2 vols., 1921). Useful also in this connection is John Fairfield Sly, *Town Government in Massachusetts, 1620–1930* (1930); and George Lee Haskins, *Law and Authority in Early Massachusetts: A Story of Tradition* (1960).

The tale of New England's first ventures in schooling is related in Walter Herbert Small's *Early New England Schools* (1914). Although this slight volume has seen more than fifty years, it is not yet ready for the bier. In fact, in both its scope and thoroughness it has no betters. Another useful study, though not easy to get hold of, is George Emory Littlefield's *Early Schools and School-books of New England* (1914).

The best treatise on the Puritan's view of childhood is Stanford Fleming's *Children and Puritanism* (1933). Its author is a Ph.D. in theology and scarcely a man given to exaggeration. His work, which is luxuriantly documented, shows the infant damners in some of their most damning moments. Useful too, but less sophisticated and more hackneyed, is Alice Morse Earle's *Child Life in Colonial Days* (1899). The field of children's literature, especially in its earlier phases, remains largely unworked. An excellent introduction to it is William Sloane's *Children's Books in England and America in the Seventeenth Century: A History and Checklist, Together with the Young Christian's Library, the First Printed Catalogue of Books for Children* (1955). A first-rate discussion of the *New England Primer's* numerous emanations is George Parker Winship's *Notes on a Reprint of the New England Primer Improved for the Year 1777* (1922). Mr. Winship deliberated on thirteen varieties of his specialty. An excellent analysis of the famous *Primer* may be found in Paul Leicester Ford's *The New England Primer* (1897). Michael Wigglesworth's despairful *The Day of Doom* has been reprinted at least in part in most of the larger standard anthologies of American letters. The best general study of its author, though extremely hard to find, is John Ward Dean's *Memoir of the Rev. Michael Wigglesworth, Author of "The Day of Doom,"* (1871).

Other helpful and illuminating works on particular aspects of education in colonial New England may be found in George Leroy Jackson's *The Development of School Support in Colonial Massachusetts* (1909); Colyer Meriwether's *Our Colonial Curriculum* (1907); Robert Francis Seybolt's *Public Schools of Colonial Boston, 1635–1730* (1935); Henry Suzzalo's *The Rise of Local School Supervision in Massachusetts, 1635–1827* (1908); Harlan Updegraff's *The Origin of the Moving School in Massachusetts* (1908).

Chapter 3   From Puritan to Yankee

The flow of secular currents and their attendant effect on New England's life and thought is examined from various angles in works mentioned a few pages ago. Look especially at Carl Bridenbaugh's two volumes on the *Rise and Growth of Cities*, and Marcus Jernegan's *Laboring and Dependent Classes in Colonial America*. The beginnings of trade and commerce and their prospering are effectively set down in Bernard Bailyn's *The Colonial Merchants in the Seventeenth Century* (1955). More concentrated in its inspection, and in a manner something of a success story, is William Threipland Baxter's *The House of Hancock: Business in Boston* (1945). The advance of the Boston Babbitts in worldly goods and the estate and power that went with it, are put down expertly and clearly in Robert Eldon Brown's *Middle-class Democracy and the Revolution in Massachusetts, 1691–1780* (1955). The most complete, but scarcely the most exhilarating, account of this phase of culture is contained in William Babcock Weeden's *Economic and Social History of New England, 1620–1789* (2 vols., 1890).

As for education, Small's *Early New England Schools*, Meriwether's *Our Colonial Curriculum*, and Updegraff's *Origin of the Moving School in New*

England—all previously referred to—still stand ready to give a helpful hand. In addition there is Robert Seybolt's *Private Schools of Colonial Boston* (1935) and Pauline Holmes's *A Tercentenary History of the Boston Latin School (1635–1935)*. For the Harvard story during this period, the high priest is, of course, Samuel Eliot Morison. Of special interest are the thesis subjects, heaved and grunted over by Harvard students aprowl for the master's degree. The titles have been virtuously translated, arranged, and stowed for posterity in Edward James Young's leaflet, *Masters' Degrees in Harvard College, 1655–1791* (1880). Though their authors composed their works in deadly earnest, when we look at these titles in retrospect, some of them cause smiles to flicker around the lips.

The literature on Yale (Collegiate School of Connecticut), like that on Harvard, is immense and requires at least a gross of drawers to accommodate it in the files of any well-stocked library. Among the run of references, note especially the following: Franklin Baxter Dexter, *Sketch of the History of Yale University* (1887). Dexter is also the editor of a *Documentary History of Yale University under the Original Charter of the Collegiate School of Connecticut, 1701–1745* (1916) and *The Literary Diary of Ezra Stiles* (1916). See also Timothy Dwight, *Travels in New England and New York* (4 vols., 1821–1822); William Lathrop Kingsley, *Yale College: Sketch of Its History* (2 vols., 1879); Edwin Oviatt, *Beginnings of Yale (1701–1726)* (1916). Brown University (College of Rhode Island) is dealt with by Walter Cochrane Bronson in the *History of Brown University, 1764–1914*, and Dartmouth is treated by Frederick Chase in *A History of Dartmouth College* (2 vols., 1891–1913) and Leon Burr Richardson in his similarly titled study (2 vols., 1932). For a general history of the native higher learning, there is Frederick Rudolph's lively yet carefully drawn *The American College and University* (1962). The book is prodigiously documented, and its bibliography on the various academic groves in the republic leads the pack by several miles.

It was during the eighteenth century that science in the Colonies began to rustle. Its forms and manifestations have been competently put down in Brooke Hindle's *Pursuit of Science in Revolutionary America* (1956). The work bristles with bibliographic references, and anyone wishing to track down the early history of science in America will find a careful leafing through its pages a profitable investment.

Chapter 4   Southern *Laissez Faire*

The most useful introduction to life in colonial Virginia is probably Philip Alexander Bruce's *Economic History of Virginia in the Seventeenth Century* (2 vols., 1895; reprinted, 1935), which its author followed with his *Institutional History of Virginia* (2 vols., 1907). Bruce worked with an infinite industry, as witness the explanatory titles of his two works, the one, *An Inquiry into the Material Condition of the People, Based upon Original and Contemporaneous Records*, the other, *An Inquiry into the Religious, Moral, Educational, Legal, Military, and Political Condition of the People, Based on Original and Contemporaneous Records*. Though sent forth more than fifty years back, the latter book is still of a high tone and one of the best recountals of the educational past of the Virginia commonwealth—especially its say on libraries and illiteracy. For all his scholarly propensities, Bruce enjoyed a free and easy fancy which served him for good and ill. It led him into cracks and corners which otherwise he might easily have overlooked, but it also caused him to daub some of his interpretations with an inordinate admiration for the colony. Even so, Bruce's four volumes should go a long way toward satisfying all but the most ravenous searchers.

In Bruce's tracks have followed several other scholars, some with a flair for fashioning a sleek and jaunty phrase, all full of intellectual resolution, and not a few of them sharing their predecessor's sympathetic disposition toward the Old Dominion. The student might do well to set his sights by familiarizing himself with Bridenbaugh's *Myths and Realities of the Colonial South* (1952). Louis Booker Wright's *First Gentlemen of Virginia* (1940), especially its second part, offers a vivid picture, often with overtones of a sly waggery, of the intellectual concerns of the Southern ruling class.

Some of the most valuable studies have been turned in by Thomas Jefferson Wertenbaker, but lately absorbed into the cosmos. Note especially his *Patrician and Plebeian in Virginia* (1910), the *Planters of Colonial Virginia* (1922), and *Virginia under the Stuarts, 1607–1688* (1914), now all quartered in a single volume, *The Shaping of Colonial Virginia*. Wertenbaker's last work of any consequence was *Give Me Liberty: The Struggle for Self-government in Virginia* (1958). The fashioner of a spirited and absorbing narrative, Wertenbaker was nonetheless a punctilious scholar, avoiding the pitfall of writing for mere popularity. It was Wertenbaker's scrutiny of a host of court records that blew up the view, commonly esteemed, that the generality of colonial Virginians wallowed delightedly in illiteracy; and it was Wertenbaker's probing of the social antecedents of the early Virginia settlers that exploded the pretensions to a place of high social quality of so many of their latter-day heirs, assigns, and successors—the so-called "cavalier myth"—a Wertenbaker thesis which, in fairness, it must be reported, is now being quarreled over *in academia*.

For special phases of cultural history there are rafts of useful investigations, in illustration, Frederick Bowes, *The Culture of Early Charleston* (1942); Wesley Frank Craven, *The Dissolution of the Virginia Company: The Failure of a Colonial Experiment* (1932); Rutherford Goodwin, *A Brief and True Report Concerning Williamsburg in Virginia* (3d ed., 1940); Brooke Hindle, *The Pursuit of Science in Revolutionary America, 1735–1789* (1956); Marcus Jernegan, *Laboring and Dependent Classes in Colonial America, 1607–1783* (1949); Arthur Pierce Middleton, *Tobacco Coast: A Maritime History of Chesapeake Bay in the Colonial Era* (1953); Edmund Sears Morgan, *Virginians at Home: Family Life in the Eighteenth Century* (1952); Joseph Clarke Robert, *The Story of Tobacco in America* (1949); Albert Emerson Smith, *Colonists in Bondage: White Servitude and Convict Labor in America, 1607–1776* (1957); Mary Newton Stanard, *Colonial Virginia: Its People and Customs* (1917); and Lyon Gardiner Tyler, *Williamsburg: The Old Colonial Capital* (1907).

The literature on religion, as might be expected, runs to great length. For the essential facts there is George MacLaren Brydon's *Virginia's Mother Church and the Political Condition under Which It Grew* (2 vols., 1947–1952). Though its treatment is transparently slanted to redound to the glory of the

Mother Church, for the casual reader it remains the most informative in the field. Good supplements are Sadie Bell, *The Church, the State, and Education in Virginia* (1930); Arthur Lyon Cross, *The Anglican Episcopate and the American Colonies* (1902); Elizabeth Davidson, *The Establishment of the English Church in the Continental American Colonies* (1936); Edward Lewis Goodwin, *The Colonial Church in Virginia* (1927). As for non-Anglicans, it was not until 1699, under the Act of Toleration in the reign of William and Mary, that Presbyterians acquired a measure of official recognition. Though Anglicans as a rule were not gnawed, as were the Puritans, by questions of theological and moral science, and though Southern Anglicans swigged from the jug and kicked up their heels in dance, and even flirted and necked more flagrantly than the Calvinists, yet they were just as proscriptive of dissent as were the Bay Colony Puritans. See "For the Colony in Virginea Britanea. Laws Diuvine, Morall, etc.," as amended by William Strachey in 1612, in Peter Force, *Collection of Historical Tracts* (vol. 3, no. 2, 1836–1846).

Luckily for posterity the Virginians, like the New Englanders, have left some firsthand accounts of themselves and their day-to-day doings as they struggled to come to terms with the vast and forlorn wilderness. Among the most useful and interesting, though scarcely of the lofty surge of those of New England's best, are the *Travels and Works of Captain John Smith* (ed., Edward Arber, 2 vols., 1910); Robert Beverley, *The History and Present State of Virginia* (1705; ed., Louis Booker Wright, 1947); Hugh Jones, *The Present State of Virginia* (1724; ed., Richard Lee Morton, 1956); William Stith, *The History of the First Discovery and Settlement of Virginia* (1747; reprinted, 1865); and the *Writings of Colonel William Byrd of Westover in Virginia* (ed., John Spencer Bassett, 1901). In science there is the almost classic work of William Byrd, *Natural History of Virginia* (1737; ed., Richard Croom Beatty and William J. Mulloy, 1904). John Clayton's pioneer work in botany was incorporated in Johannes Fredericus Gronovius, *Flora virginica exhibens ...d. d. Johannes Claytonus*, etc. (1739; 1762). For those hungering for primary sources two compilations stand out, both of them stupendous, namely Suzan Myra Kingsbury, *The Records of the Virginia Company of London* (ed., 4 vols., 1906–1935); and William Waller Hening, *The Statutes at Large; Being a Collection of All the Laws of Virginia from the First Session of the Legislature in the Year 1619* (ed., 13 vols., 1810–1823). Some of its contents of educational consequence have been translated to the pages of Edgar Knight and Clifton Hall's *Readings in American Educational History* (1951).

The most notable summary of Southern educational history by a scholar who was privy to his science is set down in Edgar Wallace Knight's *Public Education in the South* (1922). For the sniffer in archives, Knight's *Documentary History of Education in the South before 1860* (5 vols., 1949–1953) comes close to being the actual thing itself. Some other works of interest are Elsie Worthington Clews (born Parsons), *Educational Legislation and Administration of Colonial Governments* (1899); Charles William Dabney, *Universal Education in Virginia* (1916); *Journal and Letters of Phillip Vickers Fithian, 1773–1744: A Plantation Tutor of the Old Dominion* (ed., Huntington Dickinson Farish, 1943); Guy Fred Wells, *Parish Education in Colonial Virginia* (1923).

For special topics, as, for instance, private schools, tutors, book sales, and the like the student would do well to examine Lester Jesse Cappon and Stella Duff's *Virginia Gazette Index 1736–1780* (1950). *The Gazette* itself was photographically reproduced for the Massachusetts Historical Society, Boston, in 1925.

The College of William and Mary has not been blessed with a Samuel Eliot Morison to merchant its tale—in truth, very few groves of learning have been so lucky. There is a bald summary of the College's past in Herbert Baxter Adams, *College of William and Mary: A Contribution to the History of Higher Education* (1887), and a somewhat less barren one in Lyon Gardiner Tyler, *The College of William and Mary in Virginia: Its Work and History, 1693–1907* (1907). Searching the *William and Mary Quarterly*, especially the first and second series, will snare a number of scattered but revealing articles on some of the historical aspects of the College. For an account of the man chiefly responsible for getting the school on its legs, and also its first president, there is Daniel Elsten Motley's *Life of Commissary James Blair* (1901). In some of its passages, to be sure, it dilates somewhat rhapsodically, but until something better is invented, its revelation is all we have. The story of Phi Beta Kappa, which threw out its first shoots at the College of William and Mary in 1779, is told by Oscar McMurtrie Vorhees in *The History of Phi Beta Kappa* (1945). For a sorrowful sidelight, and one, if need be, from which moral science may draw a lesson, let the reader turn to Julian Parks Boyd's *Murder of George Wythe* (1949). Appointed as the College's Professor of Law and Police in 1779, Wythe was the first to warm the juridic chair in collegiate America.

Chapter 5   Middle Colony Parochialism

New York   For the culture—the foundation stones, as it were—on which New York's schools were built, see Edmund O'Callaghan's towering works, *Laws and Ordinances of New Netherland, 1638–1674* (1915), *Documents Relative to the Colonial History of the State of New York* (1909), and *History of New Netherland* (2 vols., 1846–1848). Useful also are Irving Mark's *Agrarian Conflicts in Colonial New York, 1711–1775* (1940); Ellis Roberts's *New York: The Planting and Growth of the Empire State* (1887); Phelps Stokes's *Iconography of Manhattan Island* (6 vols., 1915) and Maude Wilder Goodwin's once-over-lightly *Dutch and English on the Hudson: A Chronicle of Colonial New York* (1920). The best reference by long odds on Columbia University (King's College) is *The Bicentennial History of Columbia University* (19 vols., 1954) of which a separate volume is reserved for each of its various seminaries of learning, from architecture, business, and engineering, to Barnard, Columbia, Teachers College, and the New York School of Social Work. An earlier work, but still good, is that of John Howard Van Amringe, and others, *A History of Columbia University, 1754–1904* (1904). Columbia's first executive-in-chief is examined by Herbert and Carol Schneider in *Samuel Johnson, President of King's College* (eds., 4 vols., 1929).

The standard authority for education in Dutch America—even after more than fifty years—is still William Heard Kilpatrick's *The Dutch Schools in New Netherland and Colonial New York* (1912). Although in his later years its author turned his back to Clio to keep an appointment with fame at

Columbia University's Teachers College for his work in pedagogy, and even more for his sterling performance as a teacher, yet, so far, fortune has refused to efface his name from the tablet of significant contributors to American educational history. Helpful and instructive, particularly when employed to supplement Kilpatrick's study, is Thomas Edward Finegan's *Free Schools: A Documentary History of the Free School Movement in New York State* (1921). Finegan's book is rich, and some of its contents reach back to the colony's infancy. Another reference of some sweep, and the lodgment of a number of reprinted primary sources, is Daniel Johnson Pratt's *Annals of Public Education in the State of New York, 1626–1746* (1872), which, among other riches, displays a variety of advertisements placed in the gazettes of their day by optimistic privateers as they scrambled for students. There remain a few studies which wrestle with special concerns, as witness William Webb Kemp, *Support of Schools in Colonial New York by the Society for the Propagation of the Gospel in Foreign Parts* (1913), and Charles Frederick Pascoe, *Two Hundred Years of the SPG, 1701–1900* (1901). For the society's founder, the most informative book, though lacking in sharp discernment, is Henry Paget Thompson's *Thomas Bray* (1954). Thompson is also responsible for *Into All Lands: A History of the Society of the Propagation of the Gospel in Foreign Parts, 1701–1950* (with an encouraging foreword from the Archbishop of Canterbury, 1951). Finally, there is Emma Van Vechten's brief *Early Schools and Schoolmasters of New Amsterdam.*

New Jersey   New Jersey's background is somewhat interlaced with that of New York. For scattered and often scarce source matter, the student can do no better than to consult the Proceedings of the New Jersey Historical Society. New Jersey's educational history during its first quarter of a millennium or so is skillfully dealt with by Nelson Rollins Burr in his *Education in New Jersey, 1630–1871* (1942). Burr has made his way through its tangled mazes with astounding success and he reveals his flushings with an easy and sometimes roguish charm. His bibliography on his specialty is the largest in Christendom and should rejoice the most exigent bibliomaniac.

Material on the Great Awakening, the first important evangelistic revival to roll over the land, is as plentiful almost as the country's beer parlors. For a start the student should head into Charles Hartshorn Maxson's *The Great Awakening in the Middle Colonies* (1920). The movement's foremost theologian and rhetorician and the remote father of all later Billy Sundays and Billy Grahams has been ably portrayed in Perry Miller's *Jonathan Edwards* (1949). This is brief, but it runs deep. The student who craves yet more should resort to Vergilius Ferm's *Puritan Sage: Collected Writings of Jonathan Edwards* (ed., 1953).

For the rise and growth of the higher learning in colonial New Jersey, the best introduction to Rutgers (Queen's College) is William Steele Demarest's *History of Rutgers College, 1776–1924* (1924). For Princeton (College of New Jersey) the literature runs to a much greater length. The most scholarly yet lively account of Old Nassau is Thomas Jefferson Wertenbaker's *Princeton, 1746–1896* (1946). An old standby, frazzled a bit by time, but still helpful, is John MacLean's *History of the College of New Jersey* (2 vols., 1877). Connoisseurs of antiquaria would do well to check the files of the *Princeton College Bulletin,* which now and then offers a jewel. See, as an example, James Ormsby Murray's "Historical Documents: The First Charter of Princeton College. A Discovery." (February, 1891) ; also "Jonathan Dickinson and the Founding of the College" (January, 1896).

Pennsylvania   In several ways, Pennsylvania was the most colorful of the Middle Colonies—in fact, for a fleeting sun-kissed second it was the most civilized place in the New World, and its capital outranked even Boston as the intellectual center of America. Though it sags with the weight of years, Thomas Francis Gordon's *History of Pennsylvania from Its Discovery by Europeans to . . . 1776* (1829) still has its moments, and consulting it for knowledge and direction is usually fruitful. As for the Quakers, the literature about them overflows. One of the most simple and adroitly treated discourses is Rufus Matthew Jones's—himself a Friend—*Quakers in the American Colonies* (1911) and his *Later Periods of Quakerism* (2 vols., 1921). Skillfully handled also is Elbert Russell's *History of Quakerism* (1942). Those wanting to delve deeper into its origins should examine Henry Cadbury's revision of William Charles Braithwaite's *The Beginnings of Quakerism* (1955). To Braithwaite also we are indebted for *The Second Period of Quakerism* (1919). There are several able recountings of the Quakers' good works and public service. Note especially the following two: Arnold Lloyd, *Quaker Social History, 1669-1738* (1950) and Auguste Jorms, *The Quakers as Pioneers in Social Work* (1931). For Penn's views in this department, the best to be had at the moment is Edward Corbyn Obert Beatty's *William Penn as a Social Philosopher* (1939).

Today's most industrious historian of American Quakerism of any standing in all likelihood is Frederic Barnes Tolles. Himself one of the Children of Light, Tolles manages to handle his material with discreet impartiality. His essays are innumerable, and they concern themselves usually with special topics, in illustration, "The Transatlantic Quaker Community in the Seventeenth Century," *Huntington Literary Quarterly* (May, 1951) and "The Culture of Early Pennsylvania," *Pennsylvania Magazine of History and Biography* (1957). Among Tolles's most noteworthy books are his *Meeting House and Counting House: The Quaker Merchants of Colonial Philadelphia* (1948); *George Logan of Philadelphia* (1953); and *James Logan and the Culture of Provincial America* (1953).

Other notables whose doings on earth have been immortalized on paper are George S. Brookes's *Friend Anthony Benezet* (1937), a very charming fellow, sometimes even in a negative sort of manner; Samuel M. Jannay's *Life of William Penn* (1852); Ethyn Kirby's *George Keith, 1638-1716* (1942); Charles Janeway Stillé's *Life and Times of John Dickinson, 1732-1808* (2 vols., 1891); Carl Van Doren's *Benjamin Franklin* (1939), a thick book with a rippling tone. For his art and diligence, Van Doren was elevated into the Pulitzer pantheon.

Though silence sat on Quakers in their sacred séances as they carried on their personal *tête-à-têtes* with Omnipotence, happily for us no such reticence befell them when it came to setting down their prized thoughts with pen and lulu. For an appetizer the student should savor John Woolman, *Journal and*

Other Writings (Everyman's Library, 1952), and George Fox, *The Journal of George Fox* (with a foreword by William Penn, 1924). An edited version of the *Journal* is also available under the title of *George Fox: An Autobiography* (ed., Rufus Matthew Jones, 1919). Most of Penn's compositions have been emptied into *A Collection of the Works of William Penn* (ed., Joseph Besse, 2 vols., 1726). Penn's *Rise and Progress of the People Called Quakers*, written more than two and a half centuries ago, is still making its rounds (1695; reprinted, 1886). Penn's views on education are scattered. Some are stated in *Fruits of Solitude and Maxims Relating to the Conduct of Human Life* (reprinted, 1906), and others are in his "Address to Protestants," in the first volume of his *Works*, mentioned a few lines back. Penn's contemplation of education as a means to scotch the scourge of war is given brief utterance in his *Peace of Europe* (undated).

The most fecund producer of the written word in colonial Pennsylvania, it scarcely need be said, was Benjamin Franklin, admired and venerated, but also suspected and denigrated, in his own day, as he still is in ours. His self-accounting, with a brief selection of some of his other literary exudations, may be found in his *Autobiography* (ed., Nathan Gerson Goodman, 1932). At present, the outstanding collection of Franklin's writings is still the one put out some sixty years ago by Albert Henry Smyth (10 vols., 1907). No doubt it will soon succumb to what has been hailed with the usual fanfare of brass bands as "the definitive edition," now in preparation at Yale under the editorial vigilance of Lyman Butterfield.

There remain a few more. An inviting selection of early Quaker writings is to be found in Ezra Michener's *A Retrospect of Early Quakerism* (1860). Students of the psyche should follow George Keith in his *Journal and Travels ...on the Continent of North America* (1706; University Microfilms, American Culture Series, No. 101, Roll 9). It serves as a splendid couch on which to analyze that mixed-up man. Finally, there is Anthony Benezet's effort to save us all—*The Mighty Destroyer Displayed in ...the Dreadful Havok Made by ... Spirituous Liquors* (1774). It should be sipped prudently, and repeated as necessary.

The writings which have been flung upon this harried world to inform it about the non-Quaker Pennsylvanians would fill several bank vaults. Henry Jones Ford's *The Scotch-Irish in America* (1944) is one of the better ones in its specialty. The writings of Julius Friedrich Sachse, though composed more than threescore years ago, are still very helpful. See especially Sachse's *The German Pietists of Provincial Pennsylvania, 1694–1708* (1895) and *The German Sectarians of Pennsylvania* (2 vols., 1899–1900). For an excellent account of the Germans, there is Jesse Leonard Rosenberger, *The Pennsylvania Germans* (1923). As might be expected, the dialect to which some of them are still addicted has hatched many hundreds of studies. An examination of some of the leading works on the subject yields not only the usual philological data, but offers also a very useful insight into the culture of the Pennsylvania Germans. See in particular Abraham Horne's *Pennsylvania German Manual* (1905). For the dark powers of the Pennsylvania air, the student should turn the pages of Edwin Muller Fogel, *Beliefs and Superstitions of the Pennsylvania Germans* (1915). It should make his hair stand up.

The first general educational history of Pennsylvania was James Pyle Wickersham's *A History of Education in Pennsylvania, Private and Public, Elementary and Higher: From the Time the Swedes Settled on the Delaware to the Present Day* (1885). Befitting the considerable proportion of its title, Wickersham's study requires an expanse of almost seven hundred pages to spread its message. A more up-to-date interpretation of the subject may be found in the *History and Organization of Education in Pennsylvania* (1930) by Louise Gilchriese Walsh and Matthew John Walsh. The most serviceable, all-around study of early Quaker schooling, short, sweet, and scholarly, is Thomas Woody's *Early Quaker Education in Pennsylvania* (1920). His colleague on the University of Pennsylvania faculty, James Mulhern, is responsible for the excellent *History of Secondary Education in Pennsylvania* (1933).

Supplementing this more or less general run, there ranges the usual array of specialized treatises, in illustration, Martin Grove Brumbaugh, *The Life and Work of Christopher Dock* (1908), which contains a translated version of Dock's *Schul-Ordnung*, the first book on pedagogy to make a stir in this country, and published originally in German as long ago as 1760. Sparse up to now, and sugared perhaps by the enchantment of distance, our knowledge of Dock has been enhanced and amended by Frank Klassen's newer investigation which at the moment is being set in type under the title of *Christopher Dock, Eighteenth Century Educator*. Another recent study is Janice Leonara Gorn's *John Locke's Educational Theory and Some Evidence Thereof in Pennsylvania: 1682–1755* (University Microfilm #64–250; 1963). It is not only one of the best-informed studies of the educational views of John Locke we have, but it also shovels away some of the myths about colonial Pennsylvania's education and culture which generations of historians have poll-parroted—without checking—down the ages. The up-and-doing Francis Daniel Pastorius, immigration agent for the colony and founder of Germantown, and upon his retirement a practicing birchman, has been competently reconstructed in Marion Dexter Learned's *Life of Francis Daniel Pastorius* (1908). The irrepressible Pastorius was also the father of several schoolbooks, most of which have long since vanished from sight. The following titles are fair samples: *Lingua Latina or Grammatical Rudiments; Collection of English Rhymes, Alphabetically Arranged; A Breviary of Arithmetick and Arithmetical Hotch-Potch;* and *Formulae Solennes or Several Forms of Such Writings as Are Vulgarly in Use, Whereunto an Epistolography Is Annexed.* What we know of Pastorius's pedagogy, save that his clouting hand was ever ready, is very little. Some inkling of it may be gathered from his *New Primer or Methodical Directions to Attain the True Spelling, Reading and Writing of English,* wherein its author let it be known, "examples prevail above precepts." A photostatic copy of a facsimile of the original work was made by the Massachusetts Historical Society in 1936.

A number of books dealing with the educational enterprise of particular sects are available, as witness: Mabel Haller, *Early Moravian Education in Pennsylvania (1740–1840)* (1953); Margaret Adair Hunter, *Education in Pennsylvania Promoted by the Presbyterian Church, 1726–1837* (1937); Charles Lewis Maurer, *Early Lutheran Education in Pennsylvania* (1932); Samuel Edwin Weber, *The Charity School Movement in Colonial Pennsylvania, 1754–1763* (1905).

Brooke Hindle's *Pursuit of Science in Revolutionary America* has already been cited. It is the product of a genuine notable, and for the cyclorama it presents of intellectual activity in Philadelphia, it is one of the best. Hindle is also the author of *David Rittenhouse* (1964), a somewhat labored study, but one whose central character makes it fascinating for all that.

The first head of what is currently celebrated as the University of Pennsylvania (College of Philadelphia), a somewhat divided soul, puffing now as an Anglican man of God, now as a devotee of Newton, and sometimes splitting his personality down the middle by trying to be both at the same time, has been examined in Albert Frank Gegenheimer's *William Smith, Educator and Churchman* (1943). Unfortunately, it is little more than a stump speech, and it never gets beyond the bare words of its title, so that in the end it fails to come to grips with the enigma of that complicated man himself. Smith, the spinner of pink visions, is best revealed in his own *A General Idea of a College of Mirania* (1753), a sort of pedagogical lotus land when it came out, but today many of its recommendations are not at all unseemly—in fact, even in Smith's own day some of them found their way into practice. For Smith, the level-headed administrator, read his *Account of the College, Academy and Charitable School of Philadelphia* (1751). In connection with the Academy, the handiwork in large measure of Benjamin Franklin, the best summary of the subject is Thomas Woody's *Educational Views of Benjamin Franklin* (1931). For a picture of Franklin's haunt—and Smith's—the following stand out: Carl and Jessica Bridenbaugh's *Rebels and Gentlemen: Philadelphia in the Age of Franklin* (1942); Maxwell Struthers Burt's *Philadelphia, Holy Experiment* (1945); and Thomas Jefferson Wertenbaker's *The Golden Age of Colonial Culture* (1942).

There are a number of general studies of the University of Pennsylvania. In order of appearance, if not in merit, the standard ones are George Bacon Wood, *Early History of the University of Pennsylvania* (3d ed., 1896); Thomas Harrison Montgomery, *A History of the University of Pennsylvania from Its Foundation to A.D. 1770* (1900); and Edward Potts Cheney, *A History of the University of Pennsylvania* (1940). Brisk and to the point is Beverly McNear's piece "College Founding in the Colonies, 1745–1775," laid out for us in the *Mississippi Valley Historical Review* (1955).

Of special interest to the scrutineers of primary sources are the American Philosophical Society's many-volumed *Transactions*, whose first official number made its bow in quarto in 1771, and which, in addition to exercising itself cerebrally on "natural things and all useful arts, manufactures, mechanic practices, engynes, and inventions by experiments," besides "trade and commerce, mechanics and architecture, husbandry and American improvements," disclosed descriptions and calculations which had issued from the observations of the transit of Venus. The first volume was bathed in eulogy everywhere. Even the mother country, by the 1770s somewhat chary in her praise of things American, saluted the work as "the first literary production with which we ever were presented by any society beyond the Atlantic Ocean"—a historical truth if ever there was one. Edward Grant Conklin, a past president of the society, wrote its history in 1946. His "Brief History of the American Philosophical Society," is available for consultation in the *American Philosophical Yearbook* (1963).

Chapter 6   After Yorktown

The general works which turned their light on the colonial era will in most cases serve usefully for the period following. To the writings of Parkman and Bancroft, those of the Beards, husband and helpmeet, and those of Morison, the reader should annex Henry Adams's massive *History of the United States during the Administration of Jefferson and Madison* (9 vols., 1889–1891). Like his predecessors, Adams performed his operations before the coming of the so-called "scientific historians," namely, the trained professionals, and his findings often run counter to those of the current surgery. Even so, because of his insight and breadth of view and, in particular, his felicity of expression, his work is not easy to mark for retirement. It will be read, doubtless, long after some of the scientific historians are suffering for their sins in Hell.

Though diaries, letters, and similar personal effects must necessarily be taken with the prescribed dose of salt, sometimes they offer us views and appraisals which otherwise might elude us. William Bentley, a parson in the Unitarian cloth, as well as a man of some knowledge and affairs, duteously kept a record of his day-by-day life in Salem, where he passed his years from 1784 until he died in 1819. Published by the Essex Institute (4 vols., 1905), the Bentley *Journal* abounds in vivid and valuable information. Connoisseurs of economics will find a commendable treatment of their specialty for the post-Revolutionary era in Henry David's weighty *Economic History of the United States* (ed., 1951–). For details of the early state constitutions, consult Benjamin Perley Poore, *The Federal and State Constitutions, Charters and Other Organic Laws of the United States* (2 vols., 1877).

Other writings, less embracing but no less helpful, are James Truslow Adams, *Revolutionary New England* (1923); Charles Arthur Beard, *Economic Origins of Jeffersonian Democracy* (1915); Claude Gernade Bowers, *Jefferson and Hamilton: The Struggle for Democracy in America* (1927); Avery Craven, *Democracy in American Life: A Historical View* (1941); Elisha Douglass, *Rebels and Democrats: The Struggle for Equal Political Rights and Majority Rule during the Revolution* (1955); Merrill Jensen, *The New Nation: A History of the United States during the Confederation* (1950); John Chester Miller, *The Federalist Era, 1789–1801* (1960); Edmund Sears Morgan, *The Birth of the Republic, 1763–1789* (1956); William Warren Sweet, *Religion in the Development of American Culture, 1765–1840* (1952); Charles Sackett Sydnor, *The Development of Southern Sectionalism, 1819–1847* (1948).

The idea of human betterment has been gravely considered historically and philosophically for over two hundred years, and the writings thereon are sufficient to fill a fleet of trailer trucks. The one who started the business on its way was Abbé de Saint-Pierre, a French metaphysician who, in 1737, put out his *Observations on the Continuous Progress of Universal Reason*, a work which looked at in the perspective of the centuries, is almost singular. It remained for another Frenchman, a mathematician this time as well as a philosopher, the Marquis de Condorcet, to become the doctrine's most voluptuous spokesman. His *Historic Sketch of the Progress of the Human Mind* (*Esquisse d'un Tableau Historique de l'Esprit Humain*), which appeared in 1795 after its composer's death, is put under the inquiring glass in Jacob Schapiro's *Condorcet and the Rise of Liberalism* (1934). Two other useful discourses on the subject are John Bagnell Bury, *The Idea of Progress: An Inquiry into Its Origin and Growth* (1955) and Arthur Alphonse Ekirch, *The Idea of Progress in America, 1815–1860* (1944).

Until lately, the only work on the views of certain early patriots who, counter to the popular mind, favored the establishment of a national system of schooling, was Allen Oscar Hansen's *Liberalism and American Education in the Eighteenth Century* (1926). The book runs numerous quotations from the essayists who shed their intellectual sweat for a prize of $100 offered by the American Philosophical Society. Though Hansen appears to have tailored his interpretations somewhat to fit his pragmatic leaning, for rare light on the advanced thinking for this period, his book needs reading. More recent and more inclusive is the collection of writings assembled by Frederick Rudolph in his *Essays on Education in the Early Republic* (ed., 1965). In addition two unpublished doctoral theses are available, one by Ashley Foster, *The Educational Views of Samuel Knox*, (1951), the other by Seymour Malcom Brostoff, *The Social and Political Views of Samuel Harrison Smith* (1952). Both dissertations were inspired at New York University where they are presently to be read and wondered over.

For various proposals for the establishment of a national university, from Washington down to his countrymen of the recent past, far and away the best study is Edgar Bruce Wesley's *Proposed: The University of the United States* (1936). Brevity is its soul—still it is far from being cursory. A newcomer is David L. Madsen's doctoral study, *History of an Idea: The University of the United States* (1961). The work was incubated at the University of Chicago. Washington's words on a national university, including those in his last will and testament, have been preserved in the *Old South Leaflets* (#76).

The few ready references on Jefferson's educational reflections as expressed by himself have already been singled out previously. For those who want to introduce themselves to Jefferson's writings but who wish merely a passing acquaintance, there is Philip Sheldon Foner, *Basic Writings of Thomas Jefferson* (ed., 1944); Adrienne Koch and William Peden, *The Life and Selected Writings of Thomas Jefferson* (eds., 1944); Saul Kussiel Padover, *Thomas Jefferson on Democracy* (ed., 1949); and Francis Coleman Rosenberger, *Jefferson Reader* (ed., 1933). For a portrait of the man see Dumas Malone's stirring *Jefferson and His Time* (1948). Jefferson's account of himself has been brought between covers in Paul Leicester Ford's *The Autobiography of Thomas Jefferson* (ed., 1914). Jefferson's thirst for Greco-Roman culture is well known. The object of his affection, it not only warmed his ardor for the ancient tongues and letters, but also showed itself in his style of living in the mode, say, of Cicero and Horace, and even Pliny. His architectural inspiration, whether expressed in the stately simplicity of his Monticello home or in the classical grace of the University of Virginia, flows from the spigot of Roman antiquity. Not so generally known is Jefferson's unsparing effort to name various parts of the newly acquired Louisiana Territory for historic Greek towns. A learned yet interesting treatment of this phase of this many-sided man may be found in Henry Close Montgomery's *Thomas Jefferson and the Classical Tradition* (1945), a doctoral dissertation executed at the University of Illinois and now available for examination and reflection in its library.

Jefferson, almost as much as Franklin, employed a good deal of his energy in the promoting of science and invention. A onetime president of the American Philosophical Society, he was on familiar terms with anatomy, botany, meteorology, physics, mechanics, and engineering. In Paris he gave thought to balloon ascensions, and presently he delivered himself of several papers on "The Aeronautic Art." His inventions run from a portable folding chair to a duplicating system of writing and a weather-monitoring device. An admirable summary, with pictures, lies in Edward Thomas Martin's *Thomas Jefferson: Scientist* (1952).

Those looking for knowledge of the early developments of higher learning in the South would do well to consult the following: Herbert Baxter Adams, *College of William and Mary* (1887); Kemp Plummer Battle, *History of the University of North Carolina* (2 vols., 1907–1912), to which Louis Round Wilson, *The University of North Carolina, 1900–1930: The Making of a Modern University* (1957) makes a fine supplement; Robert Preston Brooks, *The University of Georgia under Sixteen Administrations, 1785–1955* (1956); Philip Alexander Bruce, *History of the University of Virginia* (5 vols., 1922); Daniel Walker Hollis, *University of South Carolina* (1916).

Chapter 7 Early Practices

The best way to get to know early American schoolbooks, needless to say, is by a firsthand examination of the books themselves. But this is easier to say than to do, for several of them, in illustration, the *New England Primer*, have become almost as rare as wrought-iron spitoons. They may be viewed and fingered now and then behind the gratings of rare-book cells in the larger libraries throughout the land, both public and academic. Luckily, there are a number of auxiliary works on the subject, all full of knowledge and crammed with pictures. The first on the scene was Clifton Johnson's *Old-time Schools and School-books* (1904). Though it carries neither documentation nor an index, as an introduction it is of sufficient adequacy. More scholarly is John Alfred Nietz's *Old Textbooks* (1961). Nietz, who worked his spell at the University of Pittsburgh's Cathedral of Learning and who himself corralled one of the largest herds of schoolbooks in this republic, speaks with apostolic authority. Unhappily, he is not similarly dowered with the gift of tongues; his book, in short, is correct and decorous but also somewhat wearisome. Another to tackle the subject is Charles Carpenter, *History of American Schoolbooks* (1963). This is not only a solid work of educational history; it also affords the reader the best bibliographic commentary that can be found on the subject of American schoolbooks. There remain a few afterclaps, in example, Daniel Knowlton's "The United States Constitution in the Schoolbooks of the Past," *The Social Studies* (1938); Michael Kraus's *A History of American History* (1937); Ruth Miller's *Guardians of Tradition: American Schoolbooks of the Nineteenth Century* (1964); and Alice Winifred Spieske's *The First Textbooks in American History and Their Compiler* (1938).

The figure which dominates the early schoolbook field is, of course, Noah Webster, Jr., Esq. The daddy of all present-day dictionaries that bear his name, he was also the author of the famous blue-covered spelling book, the so-called "blue-back," the first secular best seller published in America, and even now driving a pretty fair trade. Rather curiously, old Noah still awaits a biographer who will do him honest justice. The best portrayal of him at present is Harry Redclay Warfel's *Noah Webster: Schoolmaster to America* (1936). Although Webster was not the man to keep his light under a bushel, rather strangely he left no full-sized memoir of himself. The best close-up we have of him rests in his *Letters* (ed., Harry Redcay Warfel, 1953). Webster's salient shorter writings have been incarcerated in his *Collection of Papers on Political, Literary, and Moral Subjects* (1843).

The rise and growth of free education in New York City has been successfully handled by William Oland Bourne in his *History of the Public School Society of the City of New York* (1870). The study, which is 2½ inches thick and weighs 3½ pounds, not only renders a full account of the Public School Society and its hopes and labors, but also offers a good deal of information about the city's general educational situation. Another exemplary work in this connection is Archie Emerson Palmer's *The New York Public School: Being the History of Free Education in the City of New York* (1905). Yet another is *Public Education in the City of New York: Its History, Condition, and Statistics* (as reported to the Board of Education by Thomas Boese, Clerk of the Board, 1868).

On the Sunday school movement there are any number of studies, but nearly all yield to their self-interest. The following have something to say which is more or less worth knowing: Marianna Catherine Brown, *Sunday School Movements in America* (1901); Asa Ballard, *Fifty Years in the Sabbath Schools* (1876); Henry Frederick Cope, *The Evolution of the Sunday School* (1911). A realistic history of the Sunday school, free of camp-meeting rhetoric, still awaits its author.

Plenty has been put on paper about the kindergarten, but useful material on its forerunner, the infant school, continues to be scarce. An informative commentary on the evolution of the infant school is contained in the "Report of the Boston Infant School Society" in the *American Annals of Education* (vol. 3, 1833). The life of the man who begot the infant school has been put under eye in several studies, and although none of them is wholly satisfactory, the following are helpful: George Douglas Howard Cole, *The Life of Robert Owen* (1930); Lloyd Jones, *The Life, Times, and Labours of Robert Owen* (1905); and Frank Podmore, *Robert Owen: A Biography* (2 vols., 1906).

The essence of Owen's pedagogical viewpoint and the practice which issued therefrom has been summarized in a pamphlet by his eldest son, Robert Dale Owen, *An Outline of the System of Education at New Lanark* (1824). Appraisals of Owen's work and thought vary as does the wind. The eminent Jeremy Bentham, one of his business partners, let it be known that "Robert Owen begins in vapor and ends in smoke." John Quincy Adams, after having laid eyes on the man briefly while he was in Washington, lost no time to preserve and pickle him in his diary (1844) as "a speculative, scheming, mischievous man," who in his own land practiced "dupery" on his fellow citizens. Those who want to know about Owen, "the moralist among manufacturers," would do well to peek into William Lucas Sargant's *Robert Owen and His Social Philosophy* (1906). Sargant, a contemporary of Owen and given to waspishness, nevertheless manages to strike a judicious balance.

Owen's efforts to hatch his socialist heaven at New Harmony, Indiana, and persuade other sufferers of optimism to crawl into it, are dealt with, along with other Edens, in Arthur Eugene Bestor, *Backwoods Utopias* (1950); Vernon Louis Parrington, *American Dreams: A Study of American Utopias* (1947); Alice Felt Tyler, *Freedom's Ferment: Phases of American Social History to 1860* (1944); and Margaret Young, *Angel in the Forest* (1945; reprinted, 1966). Finally, there is Arthur Bestor's piece, "Education and Reform at New Harmony," Indiana Historical Society, *Publications* (1949).

The most informed authority on the monitorial system as it sprouted and thrived in America, but certainly not the system's severest critic, is the man who planted its seed, Joseph Lancaster. See, in particular, his *Improvements in Education, Abridged: Containing a Complete Epitome of the System of Education, Invented and Practised by the Author* (1808); *Hints and Directions for Building, Fitting Up, and Arranging School Rooms on the British System of Education* (1809); and *The Lancasterian System of Education with Improvements* (1821). All these writings are short—none, in fact, gets past ninety pages. It was in New York City where the monitorial necromancy had its biggest innings, and where the Public School Society was its enraptured booster. Its opinion on the Lancasterian elixirs, and how to employ them, is explained in the *Manual of the Lancasterian System of Teaching Reading, Writing, Arithmetic, and Needle-work, as Practiced in the Schools of the Free-school Society of New York* (1820). For the story of Joseph Lancaster the only piece we have so far is David Salmon's seventy-six-page *Joseph Lancaster* (1904) which, though at times it smells suspiciously like a testimonial, presents the essential facts. Finally, bringing the whole shebang together, clinically as well as descriptively, is John Franklin Reingart's *The Lancasterian System of Instruction in the Schools of New York City* (1916).

A full and sober study of the academy movement, comparable to what has been done with the common school and the high school, has not yet materialized. In fact, until recently, possibly because its enterprise was nearly always private and hence presumably against democracy, the academy has been slighted as an object of historical investigation by the generality of diggers in our educational past. What we have, in consequence, represents little more than a scuffing of the surface, in instance, Charles Lee Coon, *North Carolina Schools and Academies, 1790–1840* (1915); Edgar Wallace Knight, *The Academy Movement in the South* (1919); Harriet Webster Marr, *New England Academies before 1826* (1959); and George Frederick Miller, *The Academy System of the State of New York*, Fifteenth Annual Report of the New York State Education Department (vol. 2, 1922).

One of the newer emissions on the subject is a small paperback, *The Age of Academies* (1964), put together by Theodore R. Sizer, a learned man and a dean at Harvard's Graduate School of Education. Besides Sizer's explanatory prelude, the work offers samplings of the pedagogical virtuosity of John Milton, Benjamin Franklin, and James Gordon Carter, of which none, however, had previously escaped being thrust into print. Instructive and elevating, and in afterlight of a somewhat sad humor, are the lesser-known "Circular of the Albany Female Academy," the "Rules for the Regulation of the Professors and Teachers of the New Braunfels Academy," and a set of ordinances for the preservation of decorum and tranquility among "students and patrons" of Braunfels.

On the history of higher learning during the early Federal period, the number of satisfactory references is still skimpy. The best for general purposes, as has already been said, is Frederick Rudolph's *The American College and University* (1962), to which should be added John Brubacher and Willis Rudy's *Higher Education in Transition* (1957). Before the appearance of these works, the common favorites were Donald George Tewksbury's *Universities before the Civil War: With Particular Reference to the Religious Influence Bearing on the College Movement* (1932), and Charles Franklin Thwing's *A History of Higher Education in America* (1906). Both are well put together with reference notes in droves and a prose which would fetch their authors a passing grade in any course in Freshman English. Absolutely necessary to the grubber in original sources is Richard Hofstadter and Wilson Smith's *Higher American Education: A Documentary History* (2 vols., 1961).

There are a number of accounts of the Dartmouth College case, most of them either too cursory or too technical to be of much help to the average journeyman in educational history. The best exposition at hand is probably Leon Burr Richardson's *History of Dartmouth College* (vol. 1, pp. 287ff., 1932) or Walter Fairleigh Dodd's *Cases and Other Authorities on Constitutional Law* (pp. 1,306ff., 1937). For Jefferson's view of the case there is Andrew Adage Lipscomb and Albert Ellery Bergh, *The Writings of Thomas Jefferson* (eds., vol. 15, p. 46, 1903). For Webster's stand look at Stephen K. Williams, *Cases Argued and Decided in the Supreme Court of the United States, 1815–1819* (lib. 4, p. 598).

The student who longs to know more about the rise and growth of our early legal education should turn to some of the following: Samuel Herbert Fisher, *The Litchfield Law School, 1774–1833: Bibliographical Catalogue of Students* (1946); Paul Hamlin, *Legal Education in Colonial New York* (1939); and Joel Parker, *The Law School of Harvard College* (1871). For medical education he should initiate himself in Joseph Carson, *History of the Medical Development of the University of Pennsylvania* (1869); Thomas Francis Harrington, *The Harvard Medical School: A History* (3 vols., 1905); and William Frederick, *Medical Education in the United States before the Civil War* (1944).

Those wishing a more general introduction should consult Elbert Vaughan Wills, *Growth of American Higher Education: Liberal, Professional, and Technical* (1936).

Growth and Evolution

Chapter 8   The Cradle of the Common School

The general studies of the American past, especially the spacious undertakings of Morison and the Beards, which reach into the twentieth century, can still be plumbed advantageously. In supplement, many more suggest themselves, but among these the two following suffice for most ends: Edward Channing's *History of the United States* (6 vols., 1905–1925), and John Bach McMaster's *History of the People of the United States, from the Revolution to the Civil War* (8 vols., 1883–1913). More confined to the era under scrutiny in this chapter are Arthur Maier Schlesinger, the younger, *The Age of Jackson* (1945); Frederick Jackson Turner, *The United States, 1830–1850: The Nation and Its Sections* (1951); Glyndon Garlock Van Deusen, *The Jacksonian Era,*

1824–1848 (1959) ; and James L. Bugg, *Jacksonian Democracy—Myth or Reality?* (ed., 1952).

The literature which addresses itself to the many particular aspects of this extraordinarily dynamic and expansive period is so voluminous as to be almost overpowering. Hence, the ensuing selection is a mere snowflake, as it were, snatched from a blizzard. Nearly all these works display extensive book lists, and the student seeking something extra would do well to scan them.

For a broad vista of the economic developments of the era, there is Louis Morton Hacker's *The Triumph of American Capitalism: The Development of Forces in American History to the End of the Nineteenth Century* (1947). For the correlative phases of the nation's economic growth, the following are fairly standard: John Chamberlain, *The Enterprising Americans: A Business History of the United States* (1963) ; Arthur Hamilton Clark, *The Clipper Ship Era* (1910) ; Victor Seldon Clark, *History of Manufactures in the United States* (3 vols., 1916–1929) ; Paul Wallace Gates, *The Farmer's Age: Agriculture 1816–1860* (1961) ; Courtney Robert Hall, *History of America's Industrial Science* (1954) ; Oscar Handlin, *Boston's Immigrants* (rev., 1951) ; Edward Chase Kirkland, *Men, Cities, and Transportation: A Study in New England History, 1820–1900* (2 vols., 1948) ; Lois Kimball Mathews, *The Expansion of New England* (1962) ; Samuel Eliot Morison, *Maritime History of Massachusetts* (1921) ; John William Oliver, *History of American Technology* (1956).

For the development of the nation's transport and transportation, note the following: Edwin P. Alexander, *Iron Horses* (1941) ; John Harrison Morrison, *History of American Steamboat Navigation* (1903) ; John C. Hunter, *Steamboats on the Western Rivers* (1949) ; John F. Stover, *American Railroads* (1961) ; George Rogers Taylor, *The Transportation Revolution, 1850–1860* (1951) ; Madeline Saddler Waggoner, *The Long Haul West: The Great Canal* (1958).

For the rise and growth of cities, there is Constance McClean's *American Cities in the Growth of the Nation* (1957) and Blake McKelvey's *Urban America* (1964). An older study, but still worth looking into, is Arthur Maier Schlesinger, the elder, *The Rise of the City* (1933).

There are several excellent studies of American labor. Henry Pelling's *American Labor* (1960) should make a good introduction. It has a fine selective bibliography. Somewhat more particularized is Norman Joseph Ware's *Industrial Worker, 1840–1860* (1924). Finally there is Walter Hugins's *Jacksonian Democracy and the Working Class: A Study of the New York Workingman's Movement, 1829–1837* (1960).

The era which saw the rise and spread of so many material things was witness also to a fevering nationalism. Its doctrine of Manifest Destiny and the part it played in American history is dealt with by Frederick Merk in *Manifest Destiny and Mission in American History: A Reinterpretation* (1963). Somewhat more conventional is Albert Katz Weinberg's treatment in his *Study of Nationalist Expansionism in American History* (1935). It comes clothed in paper.

Rather strange to say, the humanitarian, moral, and religious upsurge, with its zeal to deliver us of all the woes and worries which have roweled mankind from time long since forgotten, has not been put between the covers of a single study. Under the circumstances all the student can do is to make his way through a number of specialized works. A good start is Arthur Mann, *Yankee Reformers in the Urban Age* (1954). The following, taking one with another, should satisfy most appetites: Lewis Orlando Faulkner, *The Development of American Prisons and Prison Customs* (1936); Louis Filler, *The Crusade Against Slavery, 1830–1860* (1960); Eleanor Flexner, *Century of Struggle: The Women's Rights Movement in the United States* (1959); Charles Albert Johnson, *The Frontier Camp* (1955); Helen E. Marshall, *Dorothea Dix: Forgotten Samaritan* (1937); Blake McKelvey, *American Prisons* (1936); Josiah Quincy, *Remarks on Some of the Provisions of the Laws of Massachusetts Affecting Poverty, Vice, and Crime* (1822); Timothy Lawrence Smith, *Revivalism and Social Reform in Mid-nineteenth-century America* (1955).

Chapter 9   The Educational Awakening

The number of studies on the subject of the common school, the forces which combined to set it on its feet and those which sought to knock it off, its heroes and its knaves, male and female, rises to a skyscraping height. For a beginning the seeker should introduce himself to Sidney Louis Jackson's *America's Struggle for Free Schools* (1941) and follow it with Lawrence Arthur Cremin's *The American Common School* (1951). Both studies bear the scholar's mark and are impressively and powerfully documented.

A rough idea of the part played by the fourth estate in the combat for free schools may be gathered from Vera Minnie Butler's *Education as Revealed by the New England Newspapers Prior to 1850* (1935). What the pedagogical reviews had to say on the subject may be culled from James Mollison Milne's *History of Educational Journalism* (1893) and Sheldon Elmer Davis's *Educational Periodicals during the Nineteenth Century* (1919), a governmental bulletin. Needless to say, the student would do well to cast his line into the journalistic pool itself, especially into some of the deeper ones, as, say, Mann's *Common School Journal*, Barnard's *Connecticut School Journal*, Wiley's *North Carolina Journal of Education*, the *Annals of Education*, and the deepest of them all, the *American Journal of Education*.

For the part played by organized labor, if not by its underlings in the ranks, at least by some of their chosen superiors, the best analysis—in truth, the only one of any scope—is Richard Raphael V. Curoe's *Educational Attitudes of Organized Labor in the United States* (1936), which came into being as a doctoral thesis at Columbia's Teachers College. The workers' stand is also aired in *The New York Free Inquirer* (Nov. 7, 1829), and *The Boston Courier* (Aug. 28, 1830). A newcomer with something to say, though his words are not yet in print, is Jay Pawa in a doctoral dissertation, *Attitude of Labor Organizations in New York State on Public Education, 1829–1890* (1964).

Although the American Lyceum made a considerable rumble in its effort to augment and ameliorate the content of the American brainpan, educational historians have been sadly remiss in chronicling its superlative feats. Indeed, even its father, Josiah Holbrook, very likely the archsire of Chautauqua and adult education in America—or, as the phrase runs now, "continued learning" —is still looking for a biographer to reconstruct him and his wonders in a book that will render him his full and glorious due. Up to now the most penetrating historical account of the lyceum and its intellectual good works is Carl Bode's

The American Lyceum: Town Meeting of the Mind (1956). An older study, not so brisk, but useful even so, is Cecil Branner Hayes's pamphlet, *The American Lyceum: Its History and Contributions to Education* (1932). See also David Mead, *Yankee Eloquence in the Middle West* (1951) and John Samuel Noffsinger, *Correspondence Schools, Lyceums and Chautauquas* (1926). Finally, like a burst of Schubert after a long hard day, there is John B. Wilson, "Henry Thoreau's 'Village School,'" *Adult Education* (1964).

That America's Educational Awakening was borne upon by educational developments abroad, especially by the advanced industry of the Prussians, is today pretty well conceded, except by a few skeptical and suspicious 100-percent Americans, though precisely how deeply the European fire reached and how far its flames swept is still a matter of scholarly disputation. The various reports on European schools rendered by American overseas observers have nearly all seen publication, and except in one or two instances they are not hard to obtain. There is, to begin, Alexander Dallas Bache's *Report on Education in Europe to the Trustees of Girard College for Orphans* (1839). The student who explores it should be prepared to brave slightly fewer than seven hundred pages. The Rev. Calvin Ellis Stowe, the lesser half of the immortal Harriet Beecher Stowe, morselled out his first words on European education at the Western College for Teachers. They may be read today in the *Transactions* of the Western Literary Institute (1835). Two years later Stowe entertained the Ohio Legislature on the subject of European schools, whereupon 10,000 copies of his harangue were struck off in type and broadcast throughout the republic. For the edification of the general populace the report was subsequently planted between binders as *Elementary Instruction in Europe* (1838). Stowe's views on teacher training, which were of Germanic provenance, were preserved for the ages under the designation of *Common Schools and Teachers' Seminaries* (1839). Horace Mann barnstormed the Old World in 1843, and the pedagogical memorabilia he volunteered thereon are embedded in his annual message to the Massachusetts Board of Education in his famous *Seventh Report*, dated 1843.

The first account of any consequence of Prussian education to reach America was the work of Victor Cousin, a Frenchman in the hire of King Louis Philippe as head of France's foremost normal school. His exposition was submitted in 1831 as the *Rapport sur l'état de l'instruction dans quelques pays en Allemagne, et particulièrement en Prusse.* Translated into English by Sarah Austin, it went into general circulation in 1834 at London as the *Report on the State of Public Instruction in Prussia; Addressed to the Count de Montalivet, Peer of France, Minister of Public Instruction and Ecclesiastical Affairs.* Cousin's survey, or at any rate a large portion of it, was promptly reprinted by the American press. Its substance may be found in Barnard's *American Journal of Education.*

The man who laid down the barrage for the educational renewal of Massachusetts, the Hon. James Gordon Carter, is not known for his overflowing pen. Indeed, aside from his two historic letters on the free schools of New England, he published almost nothing. These letters saw their first publication in the *Boston Transcript* (1824). Later, somewhat enlarged and rhetorically repaired and ornamented, they appeared on the market as *Letters to the Hon. William Prescott, L.L.D., on the Free Schools of New England: With Remarks on the*

Principles of Instruction (1824) and *Essays on Popular Education: Containing a Particular Examination of the Schools of Massachusetts and an Outline of an Institution for the Education of Teachers* (1826). For his first effort, Carter consumed 120 pages; for the second, his wind gave out on page 60.

By contrast, the Mann literature, as confected both by Mann himself and others, is of a Brobdingnagian scale. The story of his days on earth was first told by Mary Tyler Peabody Mann, his relict, in *The Life and Works of Horace Mann* (5 vols., 1891). One of its volumes, *The Life of Horace Mann*, was gorgeously reborn in 1937 in the Centennial Edition. Its author is also the composer of *Christianity in the Kitchen: A Physiological Cook-book* (1858). On the heels of Mary Mann's first account of her departed spouse followed Burke Aaron Hindsdale's *Horace Mann and the Common School Revival* (1898), whereupon came Edward Irwin Franklin Williams's *Horace Mann: Educational Statesman* (1937) and Louise Hall Tharp's *Until Victory: Horace Mann and Mary Peabody* (1953). The latter is the latest, and though some of its pages gush with schoolgirlish adulation, where it stays with the facts it makes for an informative recital. Another biographic study is currently in preparation by Jonathan C. Messerli, a trained historian who professes his specialty at Columbia University. If one may judge from his article "Horace Mann's Childhood: Myth and Reality," *The Educational Forum* (January, 1966), Messerli may be counted on to perform a critical dissection of the first order.

Of Mann's own writings, his important ones, historically, are to be found in his *Annual Reports* (1837–1848). There are an even dozen of them, and besides parading the usual awesome data which gives such literature its reason for being, in addition each volume dilates on some special topic, in illustration, the *Twelfth Report*, subtitled *The Capacities of Our Present System to Improve the Pecuniary Condition and to Elevate the Intellectual and Moral Character of the Commonwealth*. Another lode of Manniana runs through the *Common School Journal*, which Mann founded in 1838 and which he adored and succored to its end some ten years following. Some years after his renunciation of office in Massachusetts, Mann published his *Lectures on Education* (1855).

For the sacerdotal war on Mann see the *Christian Witness and Church Advocate* (February, 1844); also the *Common School Controversy* (1844). Notice the fireworks set off by the Rev. Mathew Hall Smith and Mann in the former's *Ark of God on a New Cart* (1847) and the latter's *Sequel to the So-called Correspondence between the Rev. M. H. Smith and Horace Mann, Surreptitiously Published by Mr. Smith* (1847). For Mann's views on the place of religion in the public school, the likeliest starting point is Raymond Benjamin Culver, *Horace Mann and Religion in the Massachusetts Public Schools* (1939). Mann's social canon is weighed and assayed in Merle Curti's *Social Ideas of American Educators* (3d ed., 1964). An interesting study of phrenology, a science which in Mann's heyday stood almost as high in the public esteem as that of moral theology, and of Mann's confidence in its theorems, may be found in Robert McLaran Sawyer, *The Introduction and Early Influence of Phrenology in the United States* (1953), an unpublished thesis composed at the University of Illinois. There are a number of works dealing with Latin America's interest in Mann's school reforms. William Spence Robertson deals with the theme in his *Hispanic-American Relations with the United States* (1923), and so do W. S. Stewart and William Marshall French in "The Influence of Horace Mann on the Educational Ideas of Dominigo Faustino Sarmiento," *Hispanic-American Historical Review* (February, 1940). Freighted somewhat with old age, but historically still of some consequence, is a composition by Mary Tyler Peabody Mann, "Senor D. F. Sarmiento," *American Journal of Education* (1866). Finally there is the *Selective and Critical Bibliography of Horace Mann* (1937), a WPA project.

Rather curiously, the literature on Mann's magnificent contemporary, Henry Barnard, is comparatively scrawny. No biographer has succeeded in putting him satisfactorily on paper. Indeed, the accounts we have of him are nearly all confined to his educational doings, and those which essay to come to grips with the man himself diffuse all too often into a gaseous drivel. The few which follow are in their way probably the most satisfactory: Anna Lou Blair, *Henry Barnard: School Administrator*; Will Seymour Monroe, *The Educational Labors of Henry Barnard* (1893); and Armory Dwight Mayo, *Henry Barnard* (1898). There is a brief Baedeker approach to him under the guidance of Mildred Sandison Fenner and Eleanor C. Fishburn in their *Pioneer American Educators* (1944).

A digest of the man's pedagogy may be found in John Brubacher's *Henry Barnard on Education* (1931). But the book is a mere midget, with scarcely more than a little fingernail's space for a subject so tremendous its rehearsal calls for a stage of several acres. Yet until something more substantial comes along, it is the most able single volume we have. Luckily, Barnard himself brandished a prolific pen, and those who want to sit at a more ample table can help themselves by turning to his own writings. They will find food for thought in Barnard's *Reports*, rendered to his superiors whom he served in Connecticut and Rhode Island. Extra helpings may be had from Barnard's *Connecticut School Journal* (3 vols., 1838–1842) and the *Journal of the Rhode Island Institute of Instruction* (3 vols., 1845–1849). Finally, there is the *American Journal of Education* (32 vols., 1855–1882), which stands in the front rank of American educational journalism and for the range and quality of its discourse remains without challenge no matter where on earth. Anyone prospecting the gold fields of Barnard's *Journal* would do well to consult Richard Emmons Thursfield's *Barnard's American Journal of Education* (1945).

Chapter 10 The State System Comes of Age

Except for different landmarks, the territory explored in this chapter is more or less the same as that examined in the pages immediately preceding; in consequence, not a few of the references previously singled out for consultation should continue to render effective aid. In addition, the following offer some special advantages. The spooky mystery, for example, of school support is reduced to simple, understandable terms by Fletcher Harper Swift in his *Federal and State Policies in Public School Finance* (1931). Swift, who speaks with authority in his field, is also the author of *A History of the Public Common School Funds in the United States, 1795–1905* (1911). Even after more than a half century, it remains the best all-around account we have of these funds. Students of a statistical cast of mind will find Frank Wilson Blackmar's *History of Federal and State Aid to Higher Education* (1890) of interest. The year 1837, which saw the country bedamned and bedeviled by hard times, rather oddly was witness also to a $28 million surplus. Edward Gaylord Bourne has chronicled this epochal event in his *History of the Surplus Revenue of 1837* (1885). It is, its subtitle tells us, an "Account of Its Origin, Its Distribution among the States, and the Uses to which It was Applied." The enactment which established the first permanent school fund in the land is recorded in *Connecticut Acts and Laws* (p. 487, 1795).

The legislation which created Pennsylvania's pauper schools is stretched out full length in Benjamin Perley Poore, *The Federal and State Constitutions, Colonial Charters and Other Organic Laws of the United States* (1887). The man credited with unhorsing the pauper school in the Keystone state was the Hon. Thaddeus Stevens. A dazzling hero in Pennsylvania's educational annals, he is the same Stevens who, as the servant of the people of Pennsylvania, led the anti-Southern Congressional bloc in the years following Appomattox. As a result, in the late Confederacy he is recalled not as a saint but as a rogue. Half seer, half windmill, Stevens was a powerful and seductive speaker. His historic words, which made an end of the pauper school in Pennsylvania, are reproduced in Thomas Edward Finegan's *Free Schools: A Documentary History of the Free School Movement in New York State* (1912). They are also stored in Rena L. Vassar's *Social History of American Education* (2 vols., 1965). An impartial probing of the man and his life remains to be done. Taking one with another, any of the following three does a fair job—though none actually manages to get its man into focus: Samuel Walker McCall, *Thaddeus Stevens* (1899); Thomas Frederick Woodley, *Thaddeus Stevens* (1934); and Elsie Singheiser, *I Speak for Thaddeus Stevens* (1947).

A full and scholarly historical treatment of educational administration and supervision in America has yet to be achieved. Its absence should be no cause for wonder, since, as everybody knows, the administrative and supervisory gentry are men of action, immersed in the problems of the present and not given much to wasting their time on a backward look. Edward Hartman Reisner, who tilled the historical field at Columbia's Teachers College, gives the development of administration and supervision a few inquiring looks in his *Nationalism and Education since 1789* (1925). Ellwood Cubberley, who worked now as an educational historian, now as an administrator, beams some light on the origin of administrative problems in *State School Administration* (1927). Nevertheless, the work is written for administrators, real and would-be, and its historical offerings are little more than so many tallow drips. Edgar Knight, Cubberley's contemporary, sprinkled some interesting source material through the pages of his *Readings in Educational Administration* (1953). New York's singular system of state educational administration is explained by Sidney Sherwood in *The University of the State of New York* (1900), a circular of information issued by the U.S. Bureau of Education.

Rather curiously, the history of the local educational authority has been more amply searched than that of the state. On the city superintendency, the office and its labors, we have two full-length studies, one by Theodore Lee Reller, *The Development of the City Superintendency* (1935), the other by Thomas McDowell Gilland, *Origin and Development of the Powers and Duties of the City School Superintendent* (1935). Neither can claim an accolade, though the first has somewhat more to say than the second. Although the American school principal is a man of consequence in America, akin somewhat in his say and grandeur to a police lieutenant, strangely enough only one book on the history of his office, its functions and responsibilities, has so far been ventured, to wit, Paul Revere Pierce's *The Origin and Development of the Public School Principalship* (1935).

The state and church positions in the struggle to secularize public education during the nineteenth century have been variously considered by Burton Confrey, *Secularism of American Education* (1931) and Sterling Wade Brown, *Secularization of American Education* (1912). The one is of the Roman rite; the other seeks to enter Heaven as a Protestant. The best brief historical statement of this controverted question is probably Conrad Henry Moehlman's *School and Church* (1934), to which Robert Freeman Butts's *The American Tradition in Religion and Education* (1950) gives a fine supplementation. See also William Sherman Fleming, *God in Our Public School* (1944) and John Seiler Brubacher, *The Public School and Spiritual Values*, Seventh Yearbook of the John Dewey Society (ed., 1944). Several works report on the church-state campaign as it unrolled in this sector or that, notably: Sadie Bell, *The Church, the State and Education in Virginia* (1930); Sherman Merritt Smith, *The Relations of the State to Religious Education in Massachusetts* (1926); Arthur Jackson Hall, *Religious Education in the Public Schools of the State and City of New York* (1914). Horace Mann's part in the controversy is set forth in Raymond Benjamin Culver's *Horace Mann and Religion in Massachusetts Public Schools*.

Chapter 11   Books, Subjects, and Schools: The New Look

The publication of schoolbooks which would match the moods and needs of the infant American republic had its beginnings in the eighteenth century's closing decades. A trickle at the start, it picked up force and volume as the nation passed through puberty, to become a well-established industry which, of course, it has been ever since. Writing the history of the American schoolbook has been essayed in one way or another by men of learning, and their meditations, already singled out for reference for students of an earlier period, should continue to serve enlighteningly for the period under consideration in this chapter.

Most famous among American schoolbooks of the 1830s and long after that are the *Readers* of the incomparable Rev. William Holmes McGuffey. As American as flapjacks and buffaloes, they are the cause of talk even today. For Americans who cherish their national heirlooms, the McGuffey Museum at Oxford, Ohio, displays several hundred of these precious volumes, a few of them in their first edition. Some years ago the *Readers* were reprinted by the American Book Company, and for a modest ransom copies may be currently obtained.

Needless to say the McGuffey literature is expansive, especially the part which has made its appearance in the periodical press. After breaking himself in with the *Readers* themselves, the novice should make acquaintance with Alice McGuffey Ruggles's *The Story of the McGuffeys* (1950). Although its tone is a trifle laudatory, it presents the vital facts, and it does it with dispatch. More learned is Henry Hobart Vail's *A History of the McGuffey Readers* (1910). For McGuffey as a professing Christian, the most perceptive study at the moment is Richard David Mosier's *Making the American Mind: Social and Moral Ideas in the McGuffey Readers* (1947; rev., 1965). Finally there is Marjorie Grace Culbertson's *The McGuffey Readers and Their Influence on Modern Education and Readers* (1959), a thesis submitted to the faculty at Kent State University, Ohio.

Among the plethora of magazine pieces, some sedate and scholarly, some light and jocund, but all in their way instructive, the following have attained some recognition: Paul S. Anderson, "McGuffey vs. the Moderns in Character Training," *Phi Delta Kappan* (pp. 53ff., 1956) Henry Steele Commager, "McGuffey and His Readers," *Saturday Review* (pp. 50ff., 1962); John Alfred Nietz, "Why the Longevity of the McGuffey Readers?" *History of Education Quarterly* (pp. 119ff., 1964); Henry Fowles Pringle and Katherine Douglas Pringle, "He Scared the Devil out of Grandpa," *Saturday Evening Post* (pp. 112ff., 1955).

There is no satisfactory single book dealing at length with the history of the curriculum of the American lower school. Most of the available material concerns itself with particular subjects or is scattered in the general treatises on the American educational past, in illustration, Edward Hartman Reisner, *Historical Foundations of Modern Education* (1927); Stuart Nelson Noble, *A History of American Education* (1938); and Harold Ordway Rugg, *American Life and the School Curriculum* (1936). For individual subjects, the following have their points: Edward Bailey Birge, *History of Public School Music in the United States* (1937); Henry Johnson, *Introduction to the Social Sciences in School* (1932); Rollo La Verne Lyman, *English Grammar in American Schools before 1850* (1921); Will Seymour Monroe, *The Development of Arithmetic as a School Subject* (1917); Rudolph Rex Reeder, *Historical Development of School Readers and Methods of Teaching Reading;* Emmett Ainsworth Rice, *A Brief History of Physical Education* (1923).

There are several good histories of the American secondary school. One of the earliest on the scene, but still first-rate as far as the tether of time lets it go, is Elmer Ellsworth Brown's *The Making of Our Middle Schools* (1903). First to narrate the advent of the high school effectively was Alexander James Inglis in *The Rise of the High School in Massachusetts* (1911). A more up-to-date treatment of the subject is Edward August Krug's *The Shaping of the American High School* (1964). More hedged-in in scope is Emit Duncan Grizzell's *Origin and Development of the High School in New England before 1865* (1923). The most thoroughgoing study of the secondary school, in the Old World as well as the New, is doubtless Isaac Leon Kandel's *History of Seconday Education* (1930). In addition to the aforesaid the student will find a number of satisfactory accounts of the rise and growth of secondary education in particular states. Let him note especially James Mulhern's well-known study, *A History of Secondary Education in Pennsylvania* (1933). Another is Orwin Bradford Griffin's *The Evolution of the Connecticut State School System with Special Reference to the Emergence of the High School* (1928), which, as the tone of its title betrays, was disgorged as a doctoral thesis. Walter John Gifford performed a similar operation on New York with his *Historical Development of the New York State High School System* (1922), and what Gifford did for New York, Paul Everett Belting in a measure did for Illinois in his *Development of the Free Public High School in Illinois to 1860* (1919). Reaching out over wider ground, though somewhat confined in the material it deals with, is John Elbert Stout's *The Development of High School Curricula in the North Central States* (1921). For the Kalamazoo decision, see the *Michigan Reports* (1874–1875).

The rise of the state university and the advent of the higher technical learning are set forth clearly and competently in Frederick Rudolph's *The American College and University* (1962) and John Brubacher and Willis Rudy's *Higher Education in Transition* (1958). Older in years, but still reliable as history, is Elmer Ellsworth Brown's *The Origin of American State Universities* (1903). The sources of the epoch-making land-grant legislation are traced in Edmund Janes James's *Origins of the Land-grant Act of 1862* (the so-called "Morrill Act") *and Some Account of Its Author* (1910). Additional light on the subject is projected by Earle Dudley Ross in *Democracy's College: The Land-grant Movement in the Formative Stage (1944)*. Its bibliography on the subject is extensive, one of the roomiest, in fact, that we have. As might be expected, the festivities commemorating the Land-grant Act's centenary spawned a shoal of special publications, of which many were little more than sonorous trash. Among those of merit, the two following stand out: *After 100 Years: A Report by the State of Vermont Land-grant Centennial Committee* (1962) and *Illinois and the Land-grant Tradition* (1961). For Jonathan Baldwin Turner, acclaimed by his partisans as the true father of the land-grant college, the reader should contemplate Mary Turner Carriel's *The Life of Jonathan Baldwin Turner* (1911). Those wanting only a snapshot of the man should steer for Earle Dudley Ross's "The Father of the Land-Grant College," *Agricultural History* (pp. 151ff., 1938). Finally, for those panting for source materials, the act itself may be found in *House Miscellaneous Documents, Fifty-third Congress* (vol. 37, part 5, p. 543).

Far and away the most informed and comprehensive discussion of the rise and growth of higher education for women is Thomas Woody's *A History of Women's Education in the United States* (2 vols., 1929). Another first-rate account, but more concerned with the social environs out of which women's education sprouted, is Louise Schutz Boas's *Women's Education Begins: The Rise of Women's Colleges* (1935). A third study, though suffering somewhat from the infirmity of its age, is James Monroe Taylor's *Before Vassar Opened: A Contribution to the History of the Higher Education of Women in America* (1915). For an enjoyable session of an evening by the lamp, the student must reserve a few hours for Eleanor Wolf Thompson's *Education for Ladies, 1830–1860* (1947). Though displaying a vigorous scholarship, this is a piquant dish, full of odd facts and amusingly written. Somewhat heavier, both in its bulk and its utterance, is Robert Samuel Fletcher's *A History of Oberlin College from Its Foundation through the Civil War* (2 vols., 1943). Oberlin was the hatchery of American collegiate coeducation, and Fletcher is at pains to reveal all the important facts about this shattering event. Cornell, the first coed college in the East, uncovers its past in Waterman Thomas Hewett's *Cornell University: A History* (1905). The cautious instigator of Cornell's integration of the sexes, and the school's first president, is ably examined by Walter Pingrey Rogers in his *Andrew White and the Modern University* (1942). For more light on the matter, see White's *Report Submitted to the Trustees of Cornell University in Behalf of a Majority of the Committee on Mr. Sage's Proposal to Endow a College for Women* (1872).

Other instructive matter on early efforts to improve the intellect of the fair ones may be found in W. Charles Barber, *Elmira College: The First Hundred Years* (1955). Launched in 1852 as the Auburn Female University, the school, rechristened Elmira Female College, bestowed its first academic letters upon its graduating gals in 1859, the so-called *artium baccalaureata,* which is to say the bachelor of arts, feminine gender. Further useful and inspiriting information on some of the primeval groves devoted in one way or another to educating women may be tapped from James Monroe Taylor and Elizabeth Hazelton Haight's *Vassar* (1915) and Arthur Charles Cole's *A Hundred Years of Mount Holyoke College: The Evolution of an Ideal* (1940). The story of Holyoke's founder, tinted on silk in a dulcet rose, may be witnessed and appreciated in the pages of Beth Gilchrest's *Life of Mary Lyon* (1910).

Though our first lady pedagogues were nearly all dowered with an enormous energy, the most productive, in a literary sense, was the irrepressible Catharine Esther Beecher (also known as Catherine). Her written animadversions run from slavery and abolition to motherhood, the home, votes for women, and education. Among her books, the following are representative of her constructive idealism: *Suggestions Respecting Improvements in Education* (1829); *An Essay on the Education of the Female* (1835); *A Treatise on Domestic Economy* (1845); *The Evils Suffered by American Women and Children* (1847); *The American Woman's Home* (1869); *Woman's Profession as Mother and Educator* (1872). An exposition and measured judgment of Miss Beecher's work and thought may be found in Mae Elizabeth Haverson's *Catharine Esther Beecher, Pioneer Educator* (1932), an unpublished Ph.D. thesis presented at the University of Pennsylvania. For the seeker who moonlights and has to do his reading between one job and another, Willystone Goodsell's capsule *Pioneers of Women's Education in the United States* (1931) should serve to brief him on the main feats of such bearers of the torch as Emma Willard, Catharine Beecher, and Mary Lyon. For a chaser, let him befriend his librarian for Margaret Farrand Thorp's *Female Persuasion* (1949).

Chapter 12   Up from Appomattox

A first-rate introduction to the principal developments of this period is offered by Allan Nevins in his *Emergence of Modern America* (1927). For a closer glimpse at the era's social phenomena, and those of the sub-Potomac region in particular, Ellis Merton Coulter's *The South during Reconstruction* (1947) should meet all but the narrowest requirements. Later aspects of the Southern culture, and some of the correlative educational enigmas, are anatomized and held up to public view by William Edward Burghardt DuBois in *Black Reconstruction* (1935) and Virginius Dabney in *Below the Potomac* (1942). DuBois, a Negro and a son of Harvard, made history by helping to incubate the NAACP. Dabney, who mans the editorial bridge of the *Richmond Times-Dispatch* is a civilized liberal, and even more, a man of courage who, when he has found himself borne upon by the sovereign masses in what he conceived to be right and decent, has refused time and again to knuckle under. In consequence, he has been suspect, but in liberal circles the reputation of his newspaper stands high among Dixie's more enlightened dailies, of which, unhappily, the supply is far from flush.

There are no up-to-date histories of Southern education. Though it was inaugurated not quite fifty years ago, Edgar Wallace Knight's *Public Education in the South* (1922) remains the kingpin. In fact, banged though it has been by time, at the moment it still has no apparent heir, save, maybe, Charles William Dabney's *Universal Education in the South* (2 vols., 1926). Until some competent inspector of the past effects a more complete and up-to-date examination of Southern educational history, the serious student would do well to ponder Herman Glenn Richey's clinical commentaries, "Reappraisal of the State School Systems of the Pre-Civil-War Period," *Elementary School Journal* (pp. 121ff., 1940), and "The Persistence of Educational Progress during the Civil War," in print in the same review (pp. 359ff. and pp. 461ff., 1942). While the student is about it, let him also look at Paul Herman Buck's "The Poor Whites of the Ante-Bellum South," *American Historical Review* (October, 1945). Are up-to-date general histories of Southern education as rare as teeth of the fabled hen? Then, happily, there is no lack of material on individual Southern states. Note, in example, William Kenneth Boyd, "The Antecedents of the North Carolina Convention of 1835," *Southern Atlantic Quarterly* (January and April, 1910); Edgar Wallace Knight, *Public Education in North Carolina* (1916); and Frank Le Rond McVey, *The Gates Open Slowly: A History of Education in Kentucky* (1949). Finally, a search of Tewksbury's *Founding of the American Colleges*—that moss-covered standby already referred to—will bring forth a listing of "Circulars of Information," issued at various intervals by the U.S. Bureau of Education, and which cover education in the Southern states during the Reconstruction interregnum.

Good material dealing with the efforts of the more prominent organizations dedicated to salvaging the liberated slaves is pathetically hard to find. The most authoritative up to now is Julius Hall Parmelee's "Freedmen's Aid Societies, 1861–1871," *Negro Education*, a publication of the U.S. Bureau of Education (vol. 1, pp. 244ff., 1916). The story of the federally supported Bureau of Refugees, Freedmen, and Abandoned Lands, its work and policies, may be pieced together from the details set down in Walter Sherman Fleming's *Documentary History of Reconstruction* (vol. 2, pp. 165ff., 1907). George Peabody and his multimillion-dollar fund, which served so admirably to straighten out the reeling Southerners and get them started on the long road back, is narrated by Jabez Lamar Monroe Curry in his *Brief Sketch of George Peabody and a History of the George Peabody Fund through Thirty Years* (1898). Curry, who performed his onerous duties as the Fund's second administrator, is himself portrayed by Edwin Anderson Alderman and Armistead Gordon in *J. L. M. Curry: A Biography* (1911) and by Jessie Pearl Rice in *J. L. M. Curry: Southerner, Statesman, and Educator* (1949). For the essence of Peabody's and Curry's social outlook see Merle Eugene Curti's *Social Ideas of American Educators* (rev., 1964). Walter Hines Page's magniloquent "The Forgotten Man," which he let loose in 1897 in an auditorium in a Greensboro, North Carolina, normal school, rings forth again in his *Rebuilding of Old Commonwealths* (1902).

The best authority on the life and work of Booker Taliaferro Washington, though not always the most precise, is undoubtedly Old Booker himself. See especially his *Up from Slavery* (1906) and his *My Larger Education* (1911). The essentials of his pedagogy are distilled in his *Character Building* (1902) and his *Working with the Hands* (1904). A record of his more impressive vocal ascensions has been preserved in S. Davidson Washington's *Selected Speeches of Booker T. Washington* (ed., 1932). For an appraisal of the man and his accomplishments, the best at present is Samuel R. Spencer, Jr., *Booker T. Washington and the Negro's Place in American Life* (1955). Though it is plain that Spencer admires the object of his scrivening, he also knows all the hazards and pitfalls of his trade, and his narration is never fulsome.

Chief among Washington's critics stood the late W. E. B. DuBois, mentioned a few pages ago. His onslaught on Washington's strategy, which DuBois rejected as appeasement of the Southern whites and doomed to failure and futility, was launched with considerable pungency in *The Souls of Black Folk* (1929).

The student who wants to inform himself on the so-called "New South," should consult Virginius Dabney's *Liberalism in the South*. Though put into type as long ago as 1932, it remains an able piece of work. The South's educational stirring early in the century, designated by some as its "Second Revival," is treated critically but all too briefly in Edgar Knight's *Education in the United States* (3d ed., 1950). His prescription for brighter days in the South may be found in the same work (p. 49). Less watered with generalisms is William Gee's *Research Barriers in the South* (1932). Though not a few of the things considered in it have undergone alteration since the book's appearance, some on the other hand still prevail, and a reading of Gee is worth the effort.

Chapter 13   The Development of Educational Theory

The literature on the educational theory laid bare and inspected in this chapter is colossal—so colossal, indeed, that anyone who would hazard to study even half of it would require not only a Promethean perseverance, fortified with science and prayer, but also a stay on earth far beyond anything heard of since the Old Testament.

The totality of Rousseau's writings, apart from a few of his lesser literary flurries, has made its way into his "complete works," which may be found nearly always in the nation's better-stacked libraries. His *Emile* and *The Social Contract* have been reprinted many times, and they are not hard to come by. Recently (1962) *Emile*, or at least a fragment of it, became privileged to serve humanity as a paperback. Edited by William Boyd, an English savant but recently gone to his reward, it has taken its place in the "Classics in Education," a series issued under the colophon of Teachers College, Columbia University. The same house has put its stamp on the same editor's *Minor Writings of Jean Jacques Rousseau*, and it too is embodied in a paper skin (1962). An older analysis of Rousseau's pedagogy, but still full of sense, is Samuel Chester Parker's *History of Modern Elementary Education* (pp. 161ff., 1912). It abounds in appropriate and discreet quotations from *Emile*. The best American biography of the mercurial Genevan is Matthew Josephson's *Jean-Jacques Rousseau* (1931). A professional writer and a trained and accomplished reporter, Josephson has marshaled the fundamental data, and with light from psychological science has embroidered them into an absorbing tale, full of understanding and discernment. There is an excellent bibliography. A newcomer, at all events in English, is Jean Guehenno's *Jean-Jacques Rousseau* (trans., John Weightman, 2 vols., 1966).

Finally there is Rousseau on Rousseau, which is to say his *Confessions* (1st ed., 1781–1788), but lest a reader be taken in by Rousseau's frequent recourse to the poet's license, let him bear in mind Nietzsche's warning against the autobiographies of great men. The *Confessions* have passed through many printings, and the work is obtainable in most libraries in this free republic, forgetting, of course, places where the guardians of virtue and rectitude have succeeded in putting it under ban.

The Pestalozzian literature, though not so copious as that on Rousseau, is nevertheless of an imperial scale. Among Pestalozzi's own writings the important ones, for a start, are his historic *Leonard and Gertrude* (trans., Eva Channing, 1895); *How Gertrude Teaches Her Children* (trans. Lucy E. Holland and Frances C. Turner, 1894); and in cases of maternal solicitude, his *Letters on the Education of Infancy Addressed to Mothers* (1830). The first Pestalozzian in our own land to express himself in writing on the new pedagogy was Joseph Neef. His *Sketch of a Plan and Method of Education* (1808) and his *Method of Teaching Children* (1813), though scarcely causing a ripple when they came out, have since become collectors' items.

Among representative secondary accounts see Auguste Pinloche, *Pestalozzi: The Foundation of the Modern Elementary School* (1901); Lewis Flint Anderson, *Pestalozzi* (1931); Sister Mary Romana Walch, *Pestalozzi and the Pestalozzian Theory* (1952). A resume of Pestalozzi's pedagogy "Pestalozzi's Principles and Methods of Instruction," resides in the *American Journal of Education* (William Russell, ed., pp. 98ff., 1892). The accounts of Pestalozzi's life which are available in English are nearly all of an ancient brew, and the occasional newer bottlings as, for example, Käte Silber, *Pestalozzi: The Man and His Work* (1960), offer nothing new to lave the scholar's pylorus. Among the familiar older ones, in order of seniority, are Hermann Kruesi, Jr., *Pestalozzi: His Life, Work, and Influence* (1875); Baron Roger de Guimps, *Pestalozzi: His Aim and Work* (trans., J. Russell) (1890); John Alfred Green, *Life and Work of Pestalozzi* (1913). Like their titles, all these studies say more or less the same thing, and apart from the Baron, their authors write without the slightest regard for the ease and gratification of their readers. In a class by itself is *Pestalozzi and His Times: A Pictorial Record* (1928), edited by the Pestalozzianum and the Zentralbibliothek, both adorning the Swiss city of Zurich. A feast for the eyes, this Louvre between book covers should serve to make a modest retribution for any discomfort the reader may have suffered at the hands of the prosemongers just listed.

The student seeking to make acquaintance with Pestalozzianism in America would do well to ground himself in Will Seymour Monroe's *History of the Pestalozzian Movement in the United States* (1907), which describes the enterprise of Neef, Owen, Sheldon, and other leading apostles. A standard handbook for years has been Ned Harland Dearborn, *The Oswego Movement in American Education* (1925). Discharged as a doctoral dissertation at Teachers College, Columbia University, it is for all that soothing and instructive to read. To hymn the one-hundredth anniversary of what began life as the Oswego Normal School and to woo good will for its current incarnation, the Oswego College of Education of the State University of New York, Dorothy Rogers wrote *Oswego: Fountainhead of Teacher Education: A Century of Sheldon Tradition* (1961). The book is loaded with engaging observations, but unlike Dearborn's cerebration, it is more of a museum than a history.

There are scores of studies dealing with special aspects of the Pestalozzian revelation. Anyone wishing more light, for example, on oral instruction, should resort to the *Reports* of the National Teachers Association from 1860 to 1875. Papa Johann's approach to nature study is examined in the *Nature Study Review* (1905). The foremost authorities on geography are Carl Ritter and Arnold Henry Guyot, both congregants in the Pestalozzian temple. The one is the author of *Geographical Studies* (1861) and *Comparative Geography* (1865) ; the other is responsible for *Geographic Teaching* (1867). The leading American arithmetician under the Pestalozzian banner was Warren Colburn. His method and influence, if any, are discussed by Jacob W. Keller in "Warren Colburn's Mental Arithmetic," *Pedagogical Seminary* (pp. 162ff., 1923). Absolutely necessary, of course, to any serious study of Colburn is his famous book, *First Lessons in Arithmetic on the Plan of Pestalozzi* (1821; rev., 1884). The chief musicologist of the Pestalozzian clan was Lowell Mason. He practiced the tonal art mainly in Boston, in whose public schools he sponsored the teaching of music along Pestalozzian lines. His ideas are embodied in two books, *Manual of the Boston Academy of Music* (1834) and *The Pestalozzian Music Teacher* (1871). For the man and what he did see Arthur Lowndes Rich, *Lowell Mason* (1946).

The pickings in English on Pestalozzi's disciple, Phillip Emmanuel von Fellenberg, and his manual labor schools, are extremely lean. One of the earliest accounts we have is *What de Fellenberg Has Done for Education* (1839). For the movement in the United States, its rise and decline, the searcher will find the following helpful: Edgar Wallace Knight, "Manual Labor Schools in the South," *South Atlantic Quarterly* (July, 1917) ; Lewis Flint Anderson, *History of Manual and Industrial School Education* (2 vols., 1926) ; Charles Alpheus Bennett, *History of Manual and Industrial Education up to 1870* (1926). For a brief and informative discussion, though approaching its fortieth anniversary, the most serviceable is still William Paul Sears, *The Roots of Vocational Education* (1931).

As in the case of his eminent forerunners, the literature on Froebel is far from being cadaverous. All his important writings have long since been put into English, and though some of them are hard to get, the Sherlocks of the interlibrary loan exchange will unfailingly help to dog them down. The indispensable source, needless to say, is Froebel's *Education of Man* (trans., William Nicholas Hailmann, 1892). Those who cannot make head or tail of Froebel's mystical vapors should consult William Henry Hereford's *The Student's Froebel* (2 vols., 1911–1912). It states Froebel's main themes with scarcely a gaseous whiff. *Froebel's Mutter- und Koselieder*, as adapted for warbling by American kiddies, became available as *Songs and Music of Friedrich Froebel's Mother Play* (translated and arranged, Suzan Elizabeth Blow, 1895). A later version was made in 1906 by Fannie F. Dwight and Josephine Jarvice. Its title then became *Mother-play and Nursery Songs, Poetry, Music, and Pictures for the Noble Culture of Child Life.*

Froebel's sojourn on this most marvelous of all planets has been variously recorded and explained, but the most helpful work is still his *Autobiography* (trans., Emilie Michaelis and H. Keatly Moore, 1886). Though it lacks the sleek grace of Rousseau's *Confessions*, on the other hand Froebel is at pains at all times to tell the truth. Useful also are Froebel's *Letters on the Kinder-*

garten (trans., Hermann Poesche, 1906), and *Letters by Froebel* (trans., Arnold H. Heinemann, 1893). There remain the *Reminiscenses of Friedrich Froebel* as recalled by the most prodigious Amazon the pedagogical world has yet encountered, Baroness Bertha von Bülow-Wendhausen (trans., Mrs. Horace Mann, born Mary Tyler Peabody).

On the kindergarten movement in our own land, there is no end of material. Note among many the following few: Suzan Elizabeth Blow, *The Kindergarten in America* (1908); International Kindergarten Union, *Pioneers of the Kindergarten in America* (1924); and William Torrey Harris, "Early History of the Kindergarten in St. Louis," *United States Commissioner of Education Report* (vol. 1, pp. 899ff., 1896–1897). For the debits and credits charged to Froebel, though in afterlight perhaps erroneously, the outstanding audit, mistakes and all, even after fifty years, is still William Heard Kilpatrick's *Froebel's Kindergarten Principles Critically Examined* (1916).

The manual training movement, once all the rage in America's forward-looking lower schools, but nowadays scarcely ever mentioned, is dealt with in Hamilton Ross Smith's *Development of Manual Training in the United States* (1914), a doctoral thesis of some ninety pages. Some space is also granted it in Lewis Flint Anderson's *History of Manual and Industrial School Education* (2 vols., 1926); and Charles Alpheus Bennett, *A History of Manual and Industrial Education, 1870–1917* (1937). All these works offer additional bibliographic counsel.

Unhappily for the monolingual American, the best and most up-to-date writing on Herbart is in German. Of the professor's own writings, the following have been set into English, though this is not saying they are always easy to obtain: *ABC of Sense Perception* (trans., William Julius Eckoff, 1896); *The Application of Psychology to the Science of Education* (trans., Beatrice C. Mulliner, 1898); *An Introduction to Herbart's Science and Practice of Education* (trans., Henry M. and Emmie Felkin, 1893); *Outlines of Educational Doctrine* (trans., Alexis Frederick Lange, 1901); *The Science of Education: Its General Principles Deduced from Its Aim and the Aesthetic Revelation of the World* (trans., Henry M. and Emmie Felkin, 1908); *A Textbook in Psychology* (trans., Margaret K. Smith, 1891).

Amidst the swarm of secondary treatises on Herbart, the following are old familiars, and though some of their interpretations are currently under scowl, as tools of historical study they serve very helpfully: Richard Davis Chalke, *A Synthesis of Herbart and Froebel* (1905). The same year saw the completion of John Angus MacVannel's *Educational Theories of Herbart and Froebel,* a doctoral thesis offered the *fratres in facultate* of Teachers College, Columbia University. Rather oddly, two years later Richard Percival Cole was fetching water from the same pond with his *Herbart and Froebel: An Attempt at Synthesis*, another doctoral thesis compounded at Teachers College. Still another thesis from the ever-ready Teachers College is Dorothy McMurry's *The Herbartian Contribution to History Instruction in American Elementary Schools* (1947). The salient French treatise on Herbartian psychology and pedagogy is Gabriel Compayré's *Herbart and Education by Instruction* (trans., Maria Findlay, 1907). The book is brightened by a sketch of Herbart's life, and for all the author's Gallic heart, it is written with understanding for the Teuton. Among Americans who followed Herbart's trail, three rise above all others, namely, Charles de Garmo, Charles Alexander McMurry, and his brother Frank Morton McMurry. The first is remembered for his *Herbart and the Herbartians* (1895), the second for *The Elements of General Method Based on the Principles of Herbart* (1892), the third for "Concentration," *First Yearbook*, National Herbart Society (1895).

Before shutting the dossier on Herbart, the student might profit by scanning one or two of the following: Alexander Darroch, *Herbart and the Herbartian Theory of Education* (1903); John Davidson, *A New Interpretation of Herbart's Psychology and Educational Theory through the Philosophy of Leibniz* (1906); John Dewey, *Instruction as Related to Will* (1895) and *How We Think* (1910); George B. Randel, *The Doctrines of Herbart in the United States* (1909); Robert Robertson Rusk, *The Doctrines of Great Educators* (rev., 1954). Does the reader seek yet more? Then let him ponder the *Yearbooks* of the National Herbart Society, the first of which came out in 1895.

When, in July, 1859, Herbert Spencer put forth his celebrated essay "What Knowledge Is of Most Worth?" he set off a controversy which flared not only in Anglo-Saxondom, but in most of the advanced lands in western civilization as well. Yet for all the debate and wrangle they obtained in the academic hermitage, Spencer's propositions brought forth no vast and enduring literature—indeed, even when it is empty of all polemical handwringing, what remains is mainly negligible. Not so, however, with the whiskered Herbert's own effusions. Sheltered between covers, "What Knowledge Is of Most Worth?" together with three pieces that followed it in the *Westminster Review*, appeared in book form in 1861 as *Education: Intellectual, Moral, and Physical*, and over and over since then it has enjoyed one reincarnation after another. Taken with Spencer's *Social Statics* (1865; rev., 1903), it comprises the essence of his pedagogy, and for the diligent it is, of course, required reading.

Coming of Age

Chapter 14 The Rise of a Native Pedagogy

A man of action rather than of letters, Francis Wayland Parker confined his bookwriting to but three publications, all of them somewhat slight, namely: *Talks on Teaching* (1891), *Talks on Pedagogics* (1894), and *How to Study Geography* (1897). In addition he embodied his thought in a number of articles, some of which had preceded their appearance in print as platform rhetoric. Of these the following will bear reading: "The Training of Teachers," *Addresses and Proceedings* of the National Education Association (1895); "The Quincy Method," *American Journal of Sociology* (vol. 4, 1900); "Art is Everything," *Addresses and Proceedings* of the National Education Association (1900); "An Account of the Work of the Cook County and Chicago Normal School from 1883 to 1899," *The Elementary School Teacher* (1902).

The most understanding treatment of the colonel and his labor in this world of hazards is Edward Dangler's *The Educational Philosophy of Francis Parker*, a doctoral dissertation submitted in 1939 to the faculty of New York University's School of Education. Though Dangler's work never enjoyed translation into type, luckily for us its author was at pains to disclose some of his knowledge to the periodical press, as, in illustration, "Consequences of Colonel Parker's Educational Philosophy," *Education* (1942); "Francis W. Parker and Democracy in Education," *School and Society* (1948) ; and "Philosophy of a Great American Educator," *Education* (1949). A first-rate account of the man, his thought, and industry, is from the pen of Flora Juliette Cooke, his friend and coworker, "Colonel Francis W. Parker: Through the Work of the Francis W. Parker School," *The Elementary School Teacher* (1912). For a discourse on Parker's venture at Quincy, Massachusetts, saluted by many of the colonel's admirers as the cradle of American progressivism, see Nicholas Murray Butler's "The Quincy Movement," *Educational Review* (1900). Although the years have laid heavy hands upon it, employed historically, Old Nick's piece still commands some serious attention.

The material about Dewey, it need scacely be mentioned is magnitudinous —in truth, no other American educator, save possibly Horace Mann, has been treated so generously in print. Nor was Dewey himself a loafer in this respect. His lifetime printed output, it has been estimated, embraces some eighteen thousand pages of books and some five thousand more of magazines, a verbal mileage which easily puts him ahead of Plato and, if one may guess, of Aristotle as well. A work of major canon among Dewey's writings on education, and imperative reading in any attempt to come to terms with his educational philosophy, is, of course, *Democracy and Education* (1916). It not only lays down the capital of his educational theory, it also puts the critical blade on some of the pedagogical propositions which had preceded his own. There is no gainsaying that *Democracy and Education* has toiled up the steep stile of fortune to become an educational classic—the first and only one so far to ascend from this republic. In the process it has been transplanted into the world's great parlance, venerable tongues like Chinese, Japanese, Arabic, and Turkish, besides, of course, the common Western ones—a distinction which, unless memory runs astray, befell only one other educational work, namely John Amos Comenius's *Orbis Pictus* (1658), which made its way from its author's Czechish vernacular into some forty other languages.

Much briefer than its epoch-making predecessor, but pithy just the same, is *Experience and Education* (1938), delivered originally at Atlantic City as the Phi Delta Kappa Lecture. Wrestling with the problem of "traditional and progressive education," the book affords its author the chance not only to clarify his own views on the subject, but also to do execution on some of the more unseemly grotesqueries of progressive education. Though *Experience and Education* is of a small proportion, what it had to say made itself heard the world around, and it too was celebrated with numerous translations. The shortest statement of Dewey's general outlook is contained within the bounds of a thirty-six-page pamphlet, *My Pedagogic Creed* (1897), which also has been generously and frequently translated.

For an inside view of what Dewey was up to in his Chicago Laboratory School, read his *The School and Society* (1899; rev., 1915). In this connection see also Katherine Camp Mayhew and Anna Camp Edwards, *The Laboratory School of the University of Chicago, 1896–1903* (1936), which includes an explanatory amplification by John Dewey, "The Theory of the Chicago Experiment," (pp. 463ff.). A brief selection from some of the aforementioned writings is embalmed in *Dewey and Education* (ed., Martin S. Dworkin, 1959).

One of the most understandable explanations of the Dewey pedagogy to appear in type up to now is Melvin Charles Baker's *Foundations of John*

Dewey's Educational Theory (1955). The advanced searcher should confront some of the numerous effusions of Sidney Hook, as, say, *John Dewey: An Intellectual Portrait* (1939) ; *Education for Man* (1946) ; *John Dewey: Philosopher of Science and Freedom. A Symposium.* (ed., 1950). William Heard Kilpatrick, sometimes styled as Dewey's "great interpreter," confined his written elucidations mostly to short essays of which the following are typical: "The Child and the Curriculum," Progressive Education Bulletin #12, *Freedom and Education* (pp. 33ff., 1939) ; "Dewey's Philosophy of Education," *The Educational Forum* (pp. 143ff., 1953) ; "Education by Interest and Effort," *The Humanist* (pp. 265ff., 1959) ; "John Dewey and his Educational Theory," *Educational Theory* (pp. 217ff., 1959).

Among Dewey's leading critics, on both philosophical and educational grounds, the most assiduous was probably Herman Harrell Horne. His *The Democratic Philosophy of Education* (1932) upholds the idealistic viewpoint, contrasting it to its advantage with Dewey's pragmatism as laid down in the latter's *Democracy and Education.* Another educator of no little note to cry down Dewey's philosophy was Alexander Meikeljohn. See especially his *Education between Two Worlds* (1942).

The student who would probe yet more deeply should address himself to Milton Halsey Thomas's monumental *John Dewey: A Centennial Bibliography* (1962). Put together with an almost superhuman perseverance, the volume contains a complete listing of Dewey's writings from 1882 on, leading off with "The Metaphysical Assumptions of Materialism," *Journal of Speculative Philosophy* (April, 1882) and hauling up with "Correspondence with John Dewey," *The Morning Notes of Adelbert Ames, Jr.* (ed., Hadley Cantril, pp. 171ff., 1960). In addition, Thomas has cataloged a listing of books, articles, and other significant references to Dewey, storing his findings alphabetically from Nicola Abbagnano's "Dewey," *Storia della filosofia* (pp. 650ff., 1950) to Meyer E. Zinman's "John Dewey's Philosophy and the Classroom Teacher," *High Points* (pp. 31ff., 1932).

At the moment, the Cooperative Research on Dewey Publications, a project under the direction of George Edward Axtelle and Jo Ann Boydston at Southern Illinois University, is in possession of the most complete bibliographical record of Dewey's writings and writings about Dewey to be found anywhere.

As is to be expected, the material dealing with nonpragmatic philosophies as they bear on American education is less profuse. For an introduction, the student can serve himself by sampling James Donald Butler's *Four Philosophies and Their Practice in Education and Religion* (1951; rev., 1957). More recent is Harry Samuel Broudy's *Building a Philosophy of Education* (1954) ; rev., 1961). Broudy, who is currently the striking exponent of classical realism, writes a vigorous and effective prose, free of blather. For light on Broudy's realism consult his "Realism and the Philosophy of Education," in *The Return to Reason: Essays in Realistic Philosophy* (ed., John Daniel Wild, 1953). In years not so long ago the head spokesman for the idealistic philosophy in education was Herman Harrell Horne. His first book in the field, *Idealism in Education*, was written back in 1910. More substantial is his *The Philosophy of Education: Being the Foundation of Education in the Related Natural and Mental Sciences* (1927). Horne's *The Democratic Philosophy of Education* has already been mentioned.

To ground himself in Catholic scholasticism, the nontheological layman would do well to read William Joseph McGucken, "The Philosophy of Catholic Scholasticism," *Philosophies of Education,* Forty-first Yearbook, National Society for the Study of Education (pp. 260ff., 1942). One of the simplest accounts of a complicated subject, it is also thorough and authoritative. True to its title, the volume which encloses it is also host to other representative philosophies of education. For a fuller analysis there is Frans de Hovre, *Philosophy of Education* (trans., Rev. Edward B. Jordan, 1931). The outstanding Catholic philosopher among the laity is Jacques Maritain, a Thomist, only yesterday a writer of vast fecundity, but now tapering off in his eighties. Though his main reflections lie in the field of general philosophy, Maritain has devoted some of his ruminations to the theory and problems of education. See especially his *Education at the Crossroads* (1943) and *The Education of Man* (1962).

The crown for advanced thinking among Neo-Scholastics, it has been bruited about, rests on the head of Mortimer Jerome Adler. His "In Defence of a Philosophy of Education," is recorded in the Forty-first Yearbook (1942) referred to a few lines back. More recondite is his *The Idea of Freedom: A Dialectical Examination of the Conceptions of Freedom* (1958). The book spins its dialectical thread for more than seven hundred pages. The transcendental figure among Neo-Scholastics, and in his salad days also their handsomest, has been Robert Maynard Hutchins. He has been their head surgeon of the intellect, and his pronunciamentos, couched in a mellifluous prose and spiced at intervals with a lashlike wit, have enlivened, if not altered, the American educational scene. For the Hutchins viewpoint, study *The Higher Learning in America* (1936); *No Friendly Voice* (1936); *Education for Freedom* (1943); *The Conflict in Education* (1953); *The University of Utopia* (1953). A critical vivisection of the Hutchins syllogisms was undertaken by Harry David Gideonse in *The Higher Learning in a Democracy: A Reply to President Hutchins' Critique of the American University* (1953). In addition the student might brush his eyes over a number of other critical opinions, in illustration, any or all of the following: Theodore Burkhard Hart Brameld, "President Hutchins and the New Reaction," *The Educational Forum* (March, 1937); John Dewey, "Rationalism in Education," *The Social Frontier* (December, 1936) and "President Hutchins' Proposals to Remake Higher Education," *The Social Frontier* (January, 1937); James Marshall, "Plato, Buddha and President Hutchins," *Harpers* (February, 1941); Buell Gordon Gallagher, "Mr. Hutchins and Mr. Dewey," *The Christian Century* (January, 1945).

Chapter 15   The Psychological Movement in Education

Although its discourse runs only as far as the late 1920s, Edwin Garrigues Boring's *A History of Experimental Psychology* (1929) still offers the student the most satisfactory introduction to the field. A good supplement is Richard Stanley Peters, *Brett's History of Psychology* (1912; rev. 1953 and 1965). For an account of the rise and development of educational psychology, the best we have right now is Robert Irving Watson's monograph "A Brief History of Educational Psychology," *Psychological Record* (pp. 209ff., 1961). Taking a different tack is Henryk Musiak, *The Philosophical Roots of Scientific Psychology* (1961). In addition a shaft of light has been directed into some of the science's special chambers, in illustration, Howard Crosby Warren, *History* of *Association Psychology* (1921); Walter Scott Monroe, *Teacher-Learning Theory and Teacher Education, 1890–1950* (1952); Horace Bidwell English, *Historical Roots of Learning Theory* (1954); F. J. McDonald, "The Influence of Learning Theories in Education," *Theories of Learning and Instruction,* Sixty-third Yearbook of the National Society for the Study of Education (1964).

The serious writings of William Bradford Titchener are nearly all immensely technical, and for the psychologically uninitiated they are often not a little baffling. The best introduction to Titchener's structural viewpoint resides in his "The Postulates of Structural Psychology," *Philosophical Review* (September, 1898) and "Structural Psychology," *ibid.* (May, 1899). For the general range of Titchener's psychology the reader should put his mind on his *A Primer of Psychology* (1898). The student who wants yet more should consult William Silliman Foster's comprehensive bibliography of Titchener's writings, *Studies in Psychology: Titchener Commemorative Volume* (1917). For a profile of the man, there is Edwin Garrigues Boring's "Edward Bradford Titchener," *American Journal of Psychology* (October, 1927). For a very warm and appreciative picture of the man, see Grace Kinckle Adams, one of Titchener's students "Titchener of Cornell," *The American Mercury* (December, 1931).

Before tackling the psychology of William James, let the student relax a bit by scanning the pages of Charles Herrick Compton's *William James, Philosopher and Man: Quotations and References in 652 Books* (1957). For the story of the man, the standout biography is Ralph Barton Perry's *The Thought and Character of William James* (1935). It is a pretty special bundle of more than sixteen hundred pages; yet it is also an absorbing tale, expertly handled and full of knowledge. Clock watchers doubtless will be daunted by its stupendous stretch. Let them turn instead to Margaret Knight's *William James* (1950), a Penguin paperback stripped to a mere 248 pages. From the vast sea of James's own writings, the work of greatest historical consequence is, of course, his tremendous *Principles of Psychology* (2 vols., 1890). The two books—all 1,380 pages to the last jot and tittle—are to be had in paper covers (Dover Publications, 1950). Similarly bound is James's *Talks to Teachers,* first issued in 1899, but resurrected several times since. Oddly enough, James put no stock in the notion that psychology could give teachers the pedagogic guidance they longed for. Teaching, he argued, was at bottom an art, and psychology a science. Though the years have paled and shaken some of the views expressed in the *Talks,* despite such griefs, the work is still representative of what James had in his head, and in the business of getting it on paper he is, as usual, superb.

More than three hundred publications have been credited to the pen of Edward Lee Thorndike. His connectionist psychology is the subject of three thick volumes, *Educational Psychology* (1913–1914; rev., 1921). A shorter version is *Educational Psychology: A Briefer Course* (1914; rev., 1922). Some of this material was later siphoned into Thorndike's *Selected Writings from a Connectionist Psychology* (1949). Narrower in its confines, but very helpful for an understanding of the Thorndike revelation, is *The Influence of Wants, Interests, and Attitudes* (1935). Among his herd of articles, the following handful deserve scrutiny: "Contributions of Psychology to Education," *Journal of Educational Psychology* (January, 1910); "The Nature of Intelligence," *Educational Record* (January, 1925); "Learning from Six to Sixty," *Survey*

Magazine (April, 1928). There have been several attempts to assay the man and his work, some cherishing them too lovingly and a few maintaining a strictly sober tone. Note especially these: Arthur Irving Gates, "The Writings of Edward L. Thorndike," *Teachers College Record* (October, 1949); Irving Lorge, "Thorndike's Contribution to the Psychology of Learning," *Teachers College Record* (May, 1940); Walter Thomas Pax, *A Critical Study of Thorndike's Theory and Laws of Learning* (1938); William Fletcher Russell, "Edward L. Thorndike," *Teachers College Record* (October, 1949).

For an understanding of behaviorism as developed by its energetic and effervescent herald, John Broadus Watson, the learner should turn to his *Behaviorism* (1925). Put together for the consumption of the common man, it is of a facile and sometimes even racy tenor. More solid and less rotarianlike in its converse is Watson's earlier *Psychology from the Standpoint of a Behaviorist* (1924).

A good introduction to the gestaltists and their various claims and attainments may be effected by reading Robert Sessions Woodworth's *Contemporary Schools of Psychology* (1931), which, among other things, contains a first-rate summary of Wolfgang Köhler's work. For the latter's teachings see his *Gestalt Psychology: An Introduction to New Concepts in Modern Psychology* (1947). The professor's exploits with his simian undergraduates are gravely recounted in his *The Mentality of the Apes* (trans. from the 2d German edition by Ella Winter, 1931). The mentality of God's noblest creature is explored in Kurt Koffka's *The Growth of the Mind* (1924). Koffka is also the father of a textbook, *Principles of Gestalt Psychology* (1935). Among the writings of Kurt Lewin—on earth all too short a time—the following convey the essence of his thought and labor: *A Dynamic Theory of Personality* (1935); *Principles of Topological Science* (1936); and his monograph "The Conflict between Aristotelian and Gallilean Modes of Thought," *Journal of General Psychology"* (1931).

As might be expected, the effort to attach psychoanalysis to education has bred a lusty literature. A good foreword to the subject is Anna Freud's *Psychoanalysis by Teachers* (trans., Barbara Low, 1931), as well as her pamphlet *Safeguarding the Mental Health of Our Children* (1955). See also Melanie Klein, *Psychoanalysis of Children* (1932); George Fletcher Morton, *Childhood's Fears* (1925); and Willi Schohaus, *The Dark Places in Education* (1932).

The numerous divergent viewpoints compounded by psychologists in different camps are agreeably exposed in Boyd Bode's *Conflicting Psychologies of Learning* (1929). More comprehensive in its embrace is *The Psychology of Learning*, Forty-first Yearbook, the National Society for the Study of Education (1942). An excellent analysis of the diverse theories of the transfer of learning may be found in Pedro Tamensis Orata's *The Theory of Identical Elements* (1928). See also Edward Lee Thorndike, *Educational Psychology* (vol. 2, 1921); Charles Hubbard Judd, *Education as Cultivation of the Higher Mental Processes* (1936); and Robert Sessions Woodworth, *Experimental Psychology* (1938).

Chapter 16 The Scientific Movement in Education

A first cousin, as it were, of the psychological movement in education is the scientific development, and not a few of the references set down for the amplification of our knowledge and appreciation of the first can be enlisted to serve the same cause in the case of the second. Although time has moldered much of Granville Stanley Hall's scientific inquiry, and current practitioners of educational research are frequently contumacious to his conclusions, as a fugelman in both the psychological and scientific drive in education, his writings, for all their sins and errors and their arid and barbituric prose, need to be read. The best introduction to the man is his self-revelation, *The Life and Confessions of a Psychologist* (1923). It should be followed by his colleague's well-barbered words set down shortly after Hall's deliverance from earthly cares, namely, William Henry Burnham's "The Man—G. Stanley Hall," *Psychological Review* (March, 1925). The same issue carries Edwin Diller Starbuck's "G. Stanley Hall as a Psychologist." The vast longitude of Hall's searching is on show in his *Adolescence: Its Psychology and Its Relations to Physiology, Anthropology, Sociology, Sex, Crime, Religion and Education* (2 vols. 1904). See also his less garrulous *Youth: Its Education, Regime, and Hygiene* (1904) and his *Aspects of Child Life in Education* (1914). For a satisfying chaser, unwittingly humorous but earnest in its purpose, there is Hall's "What We Owe to the Tree Life of Our Ape-like Ancestors," *The Pedagogical Seminary* (March, 1916), which, but for God's will, might have been written by H. G. Wells. It should be contemplated judiciously with the smile muscles relaxed and ready.

The first shot in the measurement movement issued from the musket of James McKeen Cattell in 1890 when he published his *Mental Tests and Measurements*. The testing of mental capacity is summarized by Frank Freeman, one of its early experts, in *Mental Tests: Their History, Principles, and Applications* (1939). Though Freeman's study is brief, it is far from superficial—it is in fact the best serviceable summary to appear before the forties. An earlier summation of the subject is disclosed in a couple of articles by Edward Lee Thorndike, notably his "Intelligence and Its Measurement," *Journal of Educational Psychology* (March, 1921) and "The Nature of Intelligence," *Educational Record* (January, 1925). The first general exposition of any consequence on educational measurement, and for that reason of some historical value, was William Anderson McCall's *How to Measure in Education* (1922). Thorndike laid down his basic postulates in two articles, "The Measurement of Intelligence: The Present Status," *Psychological Review* (May, 1924) and "Quantitative Investigations in Education," *School Review Monthly* (January, 1952).

So far nobody has undertaken to compose a full and forthright history of the art and science of curriculum making. The classical sociologist's attack on the curricular mystery may be deduced from a study of Herbert Spencer's *Education: Intellectual, Moral, and Physical* (1883) and especially that part wherein he comes to grips with the question "What Knowledge Is of Most Worth?" The Herbartians expounded upon the subject at great length, but of their sizable output, the following two works should give the student a pretty good understanding of what they had in mind: Charles Alexander McMurry, *Elements of General Method* (1891) and Charles De Garmo, *Herbart and the Herbartians* (1895). At about the same time, members of the Committee of Ten on Secondary School Studies put their heads together. The result of their deliberations are stored in their historic "Report of the Committee of Ten on

Secondary School Studies," *Proceedings,* National Education Association, National Council of Education (1893). See also the "Report of the Committee on College Entrance Requirements," *Proceedings,* National Education Association (1899). What the Committee of Ten tried to do for the secondary learning, the Committee of Fifteen strove to achieve on education's lower level. Its report, published in 1895, raised some capital doubts about the elementary school curriculum, as it then was constituted.

About this time, John Dewey entered the ring with *The Child and the Curriculum* (1902). Though it runs for only forty pages, it is the best introduction to an understanding of the shifting curricular currents as they flowed into the schooling of twentieth-century Americans. The to-do over the scientific approach to curriculum making is dealt with by Harold Ordway Rugg in his *American Life and the School Curriculum* (1936). Rugg handles his theme with a fine and distinguished hand, but it must be pointed out that he loads his dice to make them roll in favor of his own predisposition. Meanwhile the Curriculum Committee of the National Society for the Study of Education put the curriculum under its glass. Its findings are conserved for posterity in the society's Twenty-sixth Yearbook, *The Foundations of Curriculum-making* (1926). But even this prodigious study did not quench the thirst of the curricular brethren, as witness the issuance in 1937 of the National Curriculum Society's *Integration: Its Meaning and Application* (1937). Its tenth to fourteenth chapters are especially pertinent.

Once curriculum making was on sturdy legs, the movement's power and momentum picked up, and presently its experts were hatching book upon book. Among the few which were more factive than fictive, the following have something worthwhile to tell us: Hollis Leland Caswell and Doak Sheridan Campbell, *Curricular Development* (1935); John Kelley Norton and Margaret Alltucker Norton, *Foundations of Curriculum Building* (1936); John Miner Gwynn, *Curriculum Principles and Social Trends* (1943); Hilda Taba, *Curriculum Development and Practice* (1962). Of some help also to the prospective curricular historian are such brochures as Virginia's *Organization for Virginia State Curriculum Program* (1932); Texas's *Handbook for Curriculum Study* (1934); and North Carolina's *Suggested Procedures for Curriculum Construction and Course of Study Building.*

The "analysis-of-the-frequency-of-use" approach to subject matter is analyzed and explained by its inventor, Leonard Porter Ayres, in *The Public Schools of Springfield* (1914). Its blood brother, the "job analysis," discovered by Werrett Wallace Charters, is dealt with by him and others in *Basic Materials for a Pharmaceutical Curriculum* (1927).

Chapter 17   The New Education

Perhaps the rise and prospering of progressive education in America and its latter-day decline and decay is a bit too close to be put effectively under the historian's cold and calculating eye. Or perhaps the business is locked too much in a bind to capture the interest of the general educational historian. However this may be, the fact is the subject has obtained little serious notice from the professional observers of significant past events. The salient study at the moment is Lawrence Arthur Cremin's *The Transformation of the School:*

Progressivism in American Education (1961). Ably put together, it is free of occult and mystifying jargon, and it flaunts an annotated bibliography which soaks up more than thirty pages of print. Though the book has been generally well regarded and its author has even been lauded by no less an authority than the *New York Times Book Review*, as is only natural in our free and brash republic, it has also frowned the visage of a number of Cremin's peers, as witness especially Joseph James Chambliss, "The View of Progress in Lawrence Cremin's *The Transformation of the School*," *History of Education Quarterly* (pp. 45ff., March, 1963).

With the professional accountants of bygone happenings so chary in their offerings, a studious youth seeking light on the course of educational progressivism in America should ponder the discourses of the progressives themselves and, needless to say, their critics and challengers as well. To be sure, these dwell almost entirely upon what happened to be in currency at the time they put their words into print; even so, looking at them over the distance of so many years gone by, what they tell us today has taken on more of a historical than a contemporary connotation.

A good start can be made by working through the thirty-four volumes of *Progressive Education*, the house organ of the lamented Progressive Education Association. Come upon America in April, 1924, it maintained itself in circulation until July, 1957, when the fates did it in. The stretch of time the magazine traverses embraces roughly the years of the Progressive movement's life. The onrush of the powerful social undertow which swept upon the PEA in the years following the Depression shows itself unmistakably at its fullest pull in the pages of *The Social Frontier*.

Of the numerous accounts of progressive schools, the first of any note is John and Evelyn Dewey's *Schools of Tomorrow* (1915). Like so many other Dewey disquisitions, it was translated into one language after another and into edition after edition until at length it fetched the supreme accolade of popular esteem by being put between paper covers. Another early venture into the progressive emprise is Harold Ordway Rugg and Ann Shumaker, *The Child-centered School: An Appraisal of the New Education* (1929). The book has become almost a register of early American progressives, renowned in their heyday, but today all too often moldering in the graveyard of the forgotten. The story of a few of these fallen pioneers is also sketched in Adolphe E. Meyer, *The Development of Education in the Twentieth Century* (rev., 1949).

Happily, not all progressives have been completely preoccupied with the onerous business of putting their ideas into actual classroom practice. Some, in fact, have been at great pains to inscribe their views on paper. Note, for example, Hughes Mearns. Journalist, novelist, lyricist, teacher, and for many years a star performer at New York University's School of Education, Mearns is credited with fathering "creative education" in America. For the flavor of the man's ideas, the student should savor his *Creative Youth* (1925) and *Creative Power* (1929), dealing with his work at the Lincoln School in New York City. His *Creative Adult* (1940) issued from his experience with grown-ups. What Hughes Mearns endeavored to do in his singular way, Satis Narrona Coleman (born Burton) essayed in hers. See her *First Steps in Playing and Composing: A Music Book for Children* (1930) and *Creative Music for Children* (1922).

It is the bellwether of a flock of similar writings. Marietta Johnson is some-times spoken of as the "American Rousseau"—for her pedagogy, that is, and not her comportment, which is as ladylike and upstanding as is humanly toler-able. Her educational credo and the school it brought forth may be found in her *Youth in a World of Men* (1929).

Three illustrious progressives, but of an organizational and administrative rather than a philosophical bent, are Helen Parkhurst, Carleton Wolsey Wash-burne, and William Wirt, the concocters, in order of the Dalton Plan the Winetka Plan and the Gary Plan. Parkhurst's scheme may be read about in her *Education on the Dalton Plan* (1922) and *An Explanation of the Dalton Laboratory Plan* (1926); Washburne's in his *Results of Practical Experiments in Fitting Schools to Individuals* (1926) and *Adjusting the School to the Child* (1932); Wirt's in his *Newer Ideas in Education: The Complete Use of the School Building* (1912).

Among the promoters of higher learning whose thinking put its mark on progressive education, the name of William Heard Kilpatrick scintillates. His writings run to a staggering number, but among them the following should give the novice a solid grounding: *The Project Method* (1918); *Foundations of Method* (1925); *Education for a Changing Civilization* (1926); and *Educa-tion and the Social Crisis* (1932). When, in 1965, Kilpatrick, then aged 94, was gathered to his forebears, the tributes which celebrated his memory resounded through the world around. Most of them as such things go, were no more than amusing glorias, noble in motive but transient in value. Among the several exceptions, the Kilpatrick memorial issue of *Educational Theory* (January, 1966) stands out. Its reflections on the departed Kilpatrick are not only edify-ing; they are also full of sense.

The misfortunes which piled upon the American people in the thirties to make a mock of some of their most prized beliefs inevitably yielded a pedagogic harvest. One can see it, as has already been observed, in the assertive but short-lived *The Social Frontier*. And one can see it again in George Sylvester Counts's historic pamphlet *Dare the School Build a New Social Order?* (1932). Maturer and less contentious, the measured thoughts of a reflective and imagi-native man, is Counts's *Education and the Promise of America* (1945). There remain the varied compositions of Harold Ordway Rugg, especially his *Ameri-can Life and the School Curriculum* (1936), already instanced, and his *Chang-ing Governments and Changing Cultures* (1932). The student wishing to make acquaintance with Rugg as a successful writer of schoolbooks should make a study of the various pamphlets, readers, and workbooks that comprise the *Rugg Social Science Course*.

Educational innovation, whether in the Periclean height of day or in the era of light we now enrich with our presence, has never been free from critical attack. The most incisive critic of progressive education, but a mild and amiable man for all that, was William Chandler Bagley. Labeled in educa-tional circles as an "essentialist," he flung down his cantos of criticism in a variety of utterance of which the following writings represent the core: "The Significance of the Essentialist Movement in Educational Theory," *Classical Journal* (March, 1939); "An Essentialist Platform for the Advancement of American Education," *Educational Administration and Supervision* (April,

1938) ; and "Just What Is the Crux of the Conflict between the Progressives and the Essentialists?" *ibid.* (October, 1940). As a force, essentialism has long since descended into emptiness, though the assumptions which gave it substance have not. A confessed and confirmed subscriber to the essential catechism is William Wolfgang Brickman, editor of *School and Society* and one of the leading footnote virtuosos in the pedagogic wonderland, both here and elsewhere. The composer of numerous compilations, he is the author of "Essentialism Ten Years After," *School and Society* (May 15, 1948). Though it is more successful as an exercise in name listing than in giving light, it needs to be read.

The critical volleys which have been directed against progressives have not always boomed from the ramparts of hostile antagonists. Indeed, some, as for example, Boyd Henry Bode, inclined on the whole to be of a progressive kidney themselves. For Bode's constructive criticism the student should refer to *Progressive Education at the Crossroads* (1938).

For some earlier onslaughts on the New Education the reader will find a searching of the lay press rewarding, particularly the issues of *The American Mercury*, during the late twenties and early thirties, as expounded in the writings of Grace Kinckle Adams, Heinrich Ewald Bucholz, and Arturo F. Ratti. More especially see T. N. Gillespie, "Masters of Pedagogy," *The American Mercury* (May, 1927). Among more recent judgments, the student might take notice of Vivian Trow Thayer, *Public Education and Its Critics* (1954) and Paul Woodring, *Let's Talk Sense about Our Schools* (1953). Both incline to be moderate and pianissimo. In contrast, the following are swollen and feverish: Albert Lynd, *Quackery in the Public Schools* (1953) and Arthur Eugene Bestor, *Educational Wastelands* (1953). An anthology of criticism, for and against, is available in Cecil Winfield Scott and Clyde Milton Hill, *Public Education under Criticism* (1954). There are also some reports based on a more or less experimental examination, in illustration, Jacob Wayne Wrightstone, *Appraisal of the Newer Elementary School Practices* (1938) ; Progressive Education Association, *New Methods versus Old in American Education* (1944) ; and John Cayce Morrison, *The Activity Program* (1941). The Eight-year Study has been anatomized in a series of reports of which the reader might find the following two of some use: Wilford Merton Aikin, *The Story of the Eight-year Study* (1942) and *Did They Succeed in College?* (1943). To lay low the possibility of any false thinking on his part, he would do himself a good turn by studying William Henry Lancelot's broadside, "A Close-up of the Eight-year Study," *School and Society* (p. 141, 1939).

Chapter 18   The Higher Learning

As has already been mentioned, several texts of recent origin are available to guide and help the searching student. For one, there is John Seiler Brubacher and Willis Rudy, *Higher Education in Transition* (1958) ; and for another, Frederick Rudolph, *The American College and University* (1962). Both works are diligently documented and both feature a prodigious list of references. Taken together, this brace of books should meet all but the most special requirements. Another standby, somewhat withered around the edges to be sure, but still full of useful information, is Robert Freeman Butts, *The College Charts Its Course* (1939) Its main weight falls on the evolution of collegiate aims and curricula. For an account of the rise and development of the Catholic higher learning, the student should turn to Edward J. Power, *A History of Catholic Higher Education in America* (1958). Although its author frequently sidetracks himself from the continuity of his narrative by his inordinately long stopovers at individual groves, his study is the best we have at present. The explorer of original sources should look into Richard Hofstadter and Wilson Smith's *American Higher Education: A Documentary History* (ed., 2 vols., 1961). In its class it has no rivals.

As is pretty well known, the place of the liberal arts in the modern higher learning is sorely controverted. In truth, even the experts, for all their knowledge and sagacity, cherish varying and even colliding views. The reader can draw a bead on the dispute by pondering the theorems of Robert Maynard Hutchins, who has been previously referred to. In addition, he ought to consult the sedate words embalmed in the Harvard report, *General Education in a Free Society* (1945) which, though once all the rage, is now scarcely ever mentioned. For still another viewpoint on the subject there is Earl James McGrath, *Toward General Education* (ed., 1948). There remain Robert Lincoln Kelly, *The American College and the Social Order* (1940) and George Paul Schmidt, *The Liberal Arts College* (1957).

Although the junior college has long since emerged from the greenery of youth, adequate historical accounts of its rise and growth remain sparse. The favorites, for all the weight of their years, are still Leonard Vincent Koos, *The Junior College* (2 vols., 1924) and Walter Crosby Eells, *The Junior College* (1946). In supplement there is John Wesley Harbeson, *The New American College* (1946), in which several chapters relate to the subject. The history of the urban higher learning has been similarly neglected—indeed, the useful available literature in this domain is limited to Roscoe H. Eckleberry's *The History of the Municipal University in the United States* (1932), a bulletin put out by the U.S. Office of Education. For the development of Academe's highest learning, the following, whether taken individually or collectively, should serve usefully: B. Berleson, *Graduate Education in the United States* (1960); Byron Joseph Horton, *The Graduate School* (1940); Will Carson Ryan, *Studies in Early Graduate Education*, Carnegie Foundation for the Advancement of Learning (Bulletin #30, 1939); Richard Storr, *The Beginnings of Graduate Education in America* (1953).

Befitting its age and magnitude and the vast diversity of its enterprise, the American higher learning has bred a host of specialized investigations. Those that follow are fair samples, though it must be said that they constitute but a drop in the proverbial bucket. To begin, there is Earle Dudley Ross's *Democracy's College* (1942). It occupies itself with the higher land-grant learning. Then there is Albea Godbold's *The Church College of the Old South* (1944). Its title explains its peculiar interest. In the same class, but on the Roman side of the wall, is Francis Patrick Cassidy's *Catholic College Foundations and Developments in the United States, 1674–1850* (1924). A study which so far remains singular is Edgar Wallace Knight's *What College Presidents Say* (1940). It seeks, among other matters, to show how weighty presidential pronunciamentos have shaped the course of college development. Finally, there is George Paul Schmidt's *The Old-time College President* (1930).

Chapter 19   Adult and Workers' Education

The literature on adult education, as might be expected, is of a considerable bulk, though only a small portion of it is of a historical nature. For a broad survey of the movement as it has evolved during the last several years, the student would do well to scan the bound volumes of *Adult Education*, which is issued jointly by the American Association for Adult Education and the Department of Adult Education, National Education Association. In addition here is Homer Kempfer's thorough compendium on the subject, *Adult Education* (1955). The results of Edward Lee Thorndike's investigation on how effectively adults can learn have been summarized by the master and some helpers in *Adult Learning* (1928). A summary of this summary is to be had in Thorndike's "Learning from Six to Sixty," *Survey Magazine* (April, 1928).

What passes as a history of adult education is presented in James Truslow Adams's *Frontiers of American Culture* (1934). One can only say sadly that it is not a work of major stature. Other accounts, short but certainly not threadbare, are to be found in Lyman Bryson, *Adult Education* (1936); Morse Adam Cartwright, *Ten Years of Adult Education* (1935); Malcolm Shepherd Knowles, *The Adult Education Movement in the United States* (1962).

On certain specialties of adult education a number of works of interest are at hand. Note especially Carl Bode, *The American Lyceum: Town Meeting of the Mind* (1956); William Henry Draper, *University Extension, 1873–1923: A Survey of Fifty Years* (1923). Walter Simon Bittner and Hervey Foster Mallory, *University Teaching by Mail* (1933). The latter is also the father of "The Status of Correspondence Courses," *Addresses and Proceedings*, National Education Association (pp. 878ff., 1930); Owen David Evans, *Educational Opportunities for Young Workers* (1926); Alfred Lawrence Hall-Quest, *The University Afield* (1926); Cecil Brunner Hayes, *The American Lyceum: Its History and Contributions to Education* (Bulletin #12, 1932), a pamphlet sponsored by the U.S. Office of Education; John Samuel Hoffsinger, *Correspondence Schools, Lyceums, Chautauquas* (1926); Robert Francis Seybolt, *The Evening Schools of Colonial New York City* (1921). For a sly and somewhat satirical examination of some of the shadier aspects of the intellectual pursuit by correspondence, see George A. Scott, "Shrines of Opportunity," *The American Mercury* (August, 1925); J. V. D. Latimer, "Putting the Psyche to Work," *ibid.* (June, 1928); and Adolphe E. Meyer, "Diploma Mills," *ibid.* (September, 1945).

Compared with the endeavor of supplying instruction and edification to the American grown-up, the somewhat similar but specialized effort of organized labor on behalf of its card carriers is more recent. Hence, as is to be expected, the literature dealing with the movement's past is still relatively slight. Probably the best general introduction to the subject lies in the pages of *Workers' Education in the United States*, Fifth Yearbook, John Dewey Society (1941). Its editor, Theodore Burghard Hart Brameld, one of the movement's most productive literati, is also the author of "Workers' Education in America," *Educational Administration and Supervision* (March, 1947). In this connection two articles from the pen of John Dewey need to be read, namely, "Freedom in Workers' Education," *American Teacher* (January, 1929) and "Labor Politics and Education," *New Republic* (January, 1929).

Both pieces deal with the American Federation of Labor's censure of the Brookwood Labor College. For the case of the AFL read its "Reply by Woll," *New Republic* (February, 1929). Some light is also shed by Samuel J. McLaughlin, *The Educational Policies and Activities of the American Federation of Labor during the Present Century* (1936), an unpublished doctoral thesis brought forth at New York University. A brief account of historic Brookwood is available in *Brookwood Labor College: Labor's Own School* (1936). For the work of the Highlander Folk School, another grove in the movement for workers' education, see Adolphe E. Meyer, *The Development of Education in the Twentieth Century* (rev., 1949). Union education below the Potomac is ably summarized in Mary Lawrence's *Education Unlimited*, published under the imprint of the Highlander Folk School. Finally there is *Labor's Library: A Bibliography for Trade Unionists, Teachers, Students, and Librarians* (1945), put together under the auspices of the Workers' Association Bureau of America.

Chapter 20 Intercultural and International Education

As in the case of the workers' educational illumination, the business of advancing a happier understanding among representatives of diverse cultures through the instrumentality of the school is still in its springtime, and the literature disgorged on the subject is all too meager. The more or less general aspects of intercultural education have been put down in several works, notably in Stewart Grant Cole and William E. Vickery, *Intercultural Education in American Schools* (1943); Theodore Burghard Hart Brameld, *Minority Problems in Public Schools* (1946); William Heard Kilpatrick and William Van Till, *Intercultural Attitudes in the Making*, Ninth Yearbook, John Dewey Society (eds., 1947). Of the three, the latter is the most comprehensive.

The groundbreaking enterprise of the Bureau for Intercultural Education can best be tracked by scanning its various bulletins and brochures and also its annual reports. For a running account of the work and progress of the College Study in Intergroup Relations, the most informative material is to be found in the bulletins issued by the directors of the study to the cooperating schools, the first number of which appeared in 1945. The epoch-making Springfield plan is described by Clarence I. Chatto, "The Springfield Program for Democratic Citizenship," *Intercultural Education News* (vol. 6 p. 1, 1946). The part played by state departments in forwarding international education has been related by Julius E. Warren in his "Intergroup Education through State Departments of Education," *Harvard Educational Review* (vol. 15, 1945).

Of a grizzly age, the idea of bringing about everlasting amity among the nations of man boasts of a fairly spacious literature. Unluckily, for those who are innocent of foreign languages, the salient historical treatment of the subject happens to be encased in French, namely, Pedro Rossello's *Les Précurseurs du Bureau International d'Education* (1943). To help those who are unable to make sense of God's favorite idiom, Marie Butts has rendered Rossello's work into an abridged English translation. Bigger and broader, but somewhat diffuse in its presentation, is David G. Scanlon, *International Education: A Documentary History* (1960). For current aspects of the subject see Christian Ottomar Arndt and S. Everett, *Education for a World Society: Promising Practices Today*, Eleventh Yearbook, John Dewey Society (eds., 1951). For the varied endeavor of the Institute of International Education during its first twenty-five years on earth there is R. Elliot, *The Institute of International Education, 1919–1944* (1944). Useful and even valuable in this connection is Stephen Duggan's Twenty-sixth Annual Report of the Director, *The Institute of International Education* (1945). The practice of combining the pursuit for knowledge aboard ship with touring alien lands purportedly to engender international understanding, a practice which at present is running at full speed ahead, has provoked some polite coughs behind the academic hand. See, for example, Isaac Leon Kandel's editorial in *School and Society* (April, 1953); likewise William Wolfgang Brickman's "Education or Tourism," in the same gazette, dated August, 1954. Favorable to the idea of the student crusade overseas for culture and good feeling among men is William Reitz, "Academic Credit and the Foreign Study Tour," also in *School and Society* (August, 1955).

Needless to say the literature on UNESCO is enormous. For a rudimentary account of its infancy see *Fundamental Education, Common Grounds for All People, Report of a Special Commission of the United Nations Educational, Scientific and Cultural Organization* (1946), which, despite its flabbergasting designation, is as clear and succinct as human heads can make it. The organization has released numerous bulls and encyclicals about its work and aspirations, some short, some long, but all of more or less worth. A list of available material and the modest fee any of it fetches if one wants to buy it may be obtained from UNESCO. Nonpartisan dissections of the organization are almost as scarce as the world peace for which it yearns and labors. The most meritorious study we have so far is Walter Laves and Charles Anthony Thompson, *UNESCO: Purpose, Progress, and Prospect* (1960).

Chapter 21   The Teacher and the Profession

A comprehensive and scholarly history of teacher education in America, befitting the majestic proportion of its enterprise, is still awaiting its author. Meanwhile there is Willard Singleton Elsbree's *The American Teacher* (1939). Its reporting of the main events is brief and pertinent, though when it comes to exercising his critical acumen, Elsbree usually wraps himself in a great silence. More limited in its chronological reach, but not without merit, is Charles Athiel Harper, *A Century of Public Teacher Education* (1939). Interesting not only for its historic substance, but also for the reminiscences of its author, an insider in the ring of teacher education, is Harold Ordway Rugg with *The Teacher of Teachers* (1952). The picture of the colonial schoolmaster is limned for us by Walter Herbert Small in a couple of chapters in *Early New England Schools* (1914). To be sure, the image is somewhat blurred by the remoteness of its subject and the lack of adequate material to summon it forth—yet Small has captured it well enough to make it recognizable and even entertaining and instructive. A summary of the principal developments in the field of teacher training during the first quarter of the present century is to be found in Isaac Leon Kandel, *Twenty-five Years of American Education* (1929). Those of the century's second quarter are treated by Edwin Samuel Evenden in "Twenty-five Years of Teacher Education," *Educational Record* (October, 1943). See also Walter Scott Monroe, *Teaching-Learning Theory and Teacher Education, 1890–1950* (1952).

For the student who wants to burrow deeper into the slim beginnings of the nation's teacher training, now so robust and colossal, several works are ready to instruct him. One of the more elderly and sometimes hard to flush from its hideaway is Samuel Penniman Bates, *Method of Teachers' Institutes and the Theory of Education* (1960). A full-blown history of the American normal school has not yet been achieved, and save for John Pancoat Gerdy's short account in the *Rise and Growth of the Normal School Idea in the United States,* a governmental circular (1891), nothing satisfactory exists. There are, however, several first-rate historical studies of normal schools in various states, as witness Vernon Lomar Magnum, *The American Normal School, Its Rise and Development in Massachusetts* (1928); Arthur Orio Norton, *The First Normal School in America: The Journals of Cyrus Peirce and Mary Swift* (ed., 1926). What Magnum undertook for the Bay State, James Lawrence Meader essayed for the Nutmeg State in his *Normal School Education in Connecticut* (1928). The Oswego movement, which was spurred onward in the chambers of what became New York's second normal school, is depicted in Ned Harland Dearborn's *The Oswego Movement in American Education* (1925), a doctoral dissertation sweated and suffered over at Columbia's Teachers College. To commemorate the first half centenary of its existence, Oswego Normal struck off a *History of the First Half Century of the Oswego State Normal and Training School, 1861–1911* (1913). Though it is more in the vein of a chronicle than of history, it is chock-full of interesting stuff, including biographical sketches of some of its major pedagogues from Edward Austin Sheldon, A.M., Ph.D., and Richard Keller Piez, Pd.D., to Lydia Ellen Phoenix, M.A., M.O., and several more. The history of the first hundred years of New York's oldest normal school (Albany), now a cog in that stupendous intellectual plant, the State University of New York, has been admirably set down by William Marshall French and Florence Smith French, *College of the Empire State* (1944). The first of the aforementioned Frenches is also the composer of "A Century of Teacher Training in New York," *Education* (December, 1935), a very useful and perspicuous summation.

The ascension of the normal school to the snow-capped heights of the teachers college has been tracked by a number of observers. Among them the following few are noteworthy: Jessie May Pangborn, *The Evolution of the American Teachers College* (1932). A doctoral study delivered at Columbia's Teachers College and hence of a somewhat cloistered caution, it nevertheless calls for reading. Covering similar ground, but more concerned with the school at Normal, Illinois, is Charles Athiel Harper's *Development of the Teachers College in America* (1935). The manner in which the training of teachers stole into the established higher learning to become in the passage of time a fixed part of the university enterprise is traced with a diligent though uninspired competence in Leigh Graham Hubbell's *The Development of University Departments of Education in Six States of the Middle West with Special Reference to their Contributions to Secondary School Progress* (1926), a doctoral thesis presented to the fathers of Catholic University of America. Dr. Hubbell is also the author of Aids to Mental Health (1942). Does the student cherish an interest in antiquaria? Then let him ask his booklender for a copy of Allen Sisson Whitney's "The First Chair of Pedagogy in an American University," *School and Society* (March, 1941). It should restore his confidence in the true, the good, and the beautiful. The history of the country's most lauded house of pedagogical learning is rehearsed by Lawrence Arthur Cremin, David A. Shannon, and Mary Evelyn Townsend in *The History of Teachers College.* The book is a charm in a bracelet spangled with eighteen others, and commissioned by Columbia University to commemorate its two-hundredth anniversary. More demure, as befits New York University's great modesty, is Elsie A. Hug's *Seventy-five Years in Education: The Role of the School of Education, New York University, 1890–1965* (1965).

The history of what aspiring Pestalozzis are put upon to learn in order to make themselves fit and able to man a teaching job has been traced by Edwin Augustus Lee in *The Development of Professional Programs of Teacher Education* (1925). More recent is Merle L. Borrowman's *Teacher Education in America* (ed., 1965), a documentary history which seeks to put its light on the old and controverted question regarding the liberal and professional training of teachers. Borrowman, who has given this angry question a long and sober study, is also the author of *The Liberal and Technical in Teacher Education* (1956). The sharpshooters who have sniped so relentlessly at the New Education have also directed their gunplay at the nation's teacher training. Their fastness, the Council for Basic Education, delivers itself of its missiles in its *Bulletin.* Its imperial wizard for years has been Arthur Eugene Bestor, whose *Educational Wastelands* (1963) has already been listed. Of a somewhat mellower frame of mind, but of a critical pungency nonetheless, is James D. Koerner, whose *The Miseducation of American Teachers* (1963) needs earnest reading, as does the carefully drawn appraisal of Koerner's theorems by Erwin Virgil Johanningmeier in the *Harvard Educational Review* (vol. 34, 1964). Less fortissimo than either Bestor or Koerner, but no less pontifical in his dicta, is James Bryant Conant's *The Education of the American Teacher,* whose advent in 1963 stirred up a hornets' nest which since then has calmed down considerably.

For an early statement on the licensing of teachers, the student should refer to John Dudley Philbrick, "Examing and Certifying Teachers" (1869). No doubt it will make him heave a sigh of envy. Some of the laments and complaints which have emanated from teachers are recorded in a booklet *Why They Teach and Quit* (1948). It is under the imprint of the Missouri Teachers Association.

The question of academic freedom, real and imaginary, is as hoary at least as Socratic Athens, and it has been aired at length in numerous effusions. Among them the following offer something more than wind: Howard Kennedy Beale, *A History of Freedom of Teaching in the American Schools* (1927); Henry Steele Commager, *Freedom, Loyalty, Dissent* (1954); Richard Hofstadter and Walter P. Metzger, *The Development of Academic Freedom in the United States* (1955); Harold Melvin Hyman, *To Try Men's Souls* (1959); Thorsten Sellin, "Freedom of Inquiry of Expression," *Annals of the American Academy of Social and Political Science* (ed., 1938).

The story of the oldest teachers' professional organization in the United States is set down in Mildred Sandison Fenner's *NEA History* (1945). More recent, and concerned as much with a scrutiny of the association's policies as with its establishment and development, is Edgar Bruce Wesley's *NEA: The*

First Hundred Years (1957). Another discourse on some of the NEA's historic activities, but one of censure rather than praise, is offered by Heinrich Ewald Bucholz, "The Pedagogues Leap to Save Us," *The American Mercury* (July, 1932). There remains Myron Lieberman's *The Future of Public Education* (1960), a comparative analysis of the National Education Association and the American Federation of Teachers. Though Lieberman is a partisan and a prophet of the latter and pumps for it with a great zeal, he manages on the whole to abstain from the indecorum of partiality.

Chapter 22   Conspectus: The Practice and the Problems

In this chapter, where the past converges on the present, the problems which are examined, though they are often enough merely old ones in modern dress, are nonetheless too hard by to lend themselves to the historian's dispassionate scrutiny. In consequence, the material selected for the reader's further instruction and illumination finds itself within the circle of the present, with the winds of controversy blowing down upon it.

A good way to set the stage is to ponder Henry Ehlers and Gordon Canfield Lee, *Issues in Education* (eds., rev., 1964), wherein the authors put their glass on loyalty, censorship, segregation, religion, soft and stiff pedagogy, and similar melancholy malaises which in one way or another have harassed and defamed our educational advance. Another useful work, already mentioned, is *The Great Debate: Our Schools in Crisis* by Cecil Winfield Scott, Clyde Milton Hill, and Hobert W. Burns (eds., 1959). For more light on the celebrated verdict of the United States Supreme Court, note the following works among a large swarm: Clark Spurlock, *Education and the Supreme Court* (1955); Truman Pierce and others, *White and Negro Schools in the South* (1955); Joseph W. Holley, *Education and the Segregation Issue* (1955); David Fellman, *The Supreme Court and Education* (ed., 1960). Literature on the various aspects of the church and state controversy in the public learning has already been cited.

To get the hang of the economic realities which bedevil the full functioning of the schools, not only in our own dear republic, but in other lands as well, the student should read Robert Hall King and Joseph Albert Lauwerys, *Education and Economics* (1956). Lest the harsh facts might still be prey to the student's soft illusion, let him riffle through the pages of Patricia Cayo Sexton's *Education and Income* (1961). For a better grip on the sociological factors which, for good or ill, beset our schools, there is Henry B. Nelson's *Social Forces Influencing Education*, Sixtieth Yearbook, National Society for the Study of Education (ed., 1961). An excellent supplement is Harold L. Hodginson, *Education in Social and Cultural Perspective* (1962).

What some schools are actually up to is unveiled by Arthur D. Morse in *Schools of Tomorrow—Today* (1960). It dwells upon team teaching, educational TV, teacher-aid plans, the Harvard program of teacher education, and similar newer wonders. In this connection see also J. Lloyd Trump, *Focus on Change: Guide to Better Schools* (1961).

Inescapably one comes upon the searching and counseling of James Bryant Conant: *The American High School Today* (1959); *Slums and Suburbs* (1960); and *The Education of American Teachers* (1963). In some of the journals of the laity they have made an impressive splash, but among the professional teachers of teachers they have been the target for lively counter-shots. See especially Archibald Wallace Anderson, Joe Ray Burnett, and Frank Klassen, "Discussion Report on J. B. Conant's *The Education of American Teachers*," *Educational Theory* (October, 1965).

For reflection and meditation and—one may hope—some earnest self-examination, consider the following: Vivian Trow Thayer, *The Role of the School in American Society* (1966) ; Robert Ulich, *Crisis and Hope in American Education* (1951); Paul Woodring, *A Fourth of the Nation* (1957).

Finally, to ring down the curtain on an agreeable note, there is Richard Armour, *Going Around in Academic Circles* (1965). It has been reviewed and recommended by no less an arbiter of the good things of life than the *Harvard Educational Review* (vol. 36, pp. 221ff., 1966).